Global Canons in an Age of Contestation

Global Canons in an Age of Contestation

Debating Foundational Texts of Constitutional Democracy and Human Rights

Edited by

SUJIT CHOUDHRY

Head of Chambers, Hāki Chambers Global, Canada

MICHAELA HAILBRONNER

Chair of International and German Public Law and Comparative Law, Law Faculty, University of Münster, Germany

MATTIAS KUMM

Inge Rennert Professor of Law, New York University School of Law, USA

OXFORD
UNIVERSITY PRESS

OXFORD
UNIVERSITY PRESS

Great Clarendon Street, Oxford, OX2 6DP,
United Kingdom

Oxford University Press is a department of the University of Oxford.
It furthers the University's objective of excellence in research, scholarship,
and education by publishing worldwide. Oxford is a registered trade mark of
Oxford University Press in the UK and in certain other countries

Published in the United States of America by Oxford University Press
198 Madison Avenue, New York, NY 10016, United States of America

British Library Cataloguing in Publication Data

Data available

Library of Congress Control Number: 2024931131

ISBN 9780192866158

DOI: 10.1093/9780191956942.001.0001

Printed and bound by
CPI Group (UK) Ltd, Croydon, CR0 4YY

MIX
Paper | Supporting
responsible forestry
FSC® C013604

Contents

List of Abbreviations

Afr Aff	African Affairs
Afr J Intl Comp L	African Journal of International Comparative Law
AJIL	American Journal of International Law
Alta L Rev	Alberta Law Review
Am J Comp L	American Journal of Comparative Law
Am J Jur	American Journal of Jurisprudence
Am Pol Sci Rev	American Political Science Review
Amer Bar Found Res J	American Bar Foundation Research Journal
Annual Rev L & Soc Sci	Annual Review of Law and Society Science
BC Int'l & Comp L Rev	Boston College International and Comparative Law Review
BYU J Pub L	Brigham Young University Journal of Public Law
BYU L Rev	Brigham Young University Law Review
Can J Law Jurisprud	Canadian Journal of Law and Jurisprudence
Case W Res L Rev	Case Western Reserve Law Review
CEDAW	Convention on the Elimination of All Forms of Discrimination Against Women
Colum J Transnat'l L	Columbia Journal of Transnational Law
Colum L Rev	Columbia Law Review
Comp Pol	Comparative Politics
Const Comment	Constitutional Commentary
CRPD	Convention on the Rights of Persons with Disabilities
CSSH	Comparative Studies in Society and History
CUP	Cambridge University Press
DSS	Department of Social Services (United States)
Duke J Const L & Pub Pol	Duke Journal of Constitutional Law & Public Policy
ECHR	European Convention on Human Rights
ECOSOC	United Nations Economic and Social Council
ECtHR	European Court of Human Rights
FCC	Federal Constitutional Court (Germany)
FIU L Rev	Florida International University Law Review

Glob Const	Global Constitutionalism
Harv Hum Rts J	Harvard Human Rights Journal
Harv Int'l LJ	Harvard International Law Journal
Harv L Rev	Harvard Law Review
Hastings Int'l & Comp L Rev	Hastings International and Comparative Law Review
Health and Hum Rts J	Health and Human Rights Journal
HRL Rev	Human Rights Law Review
Hum Rts Q	Human Rights Quarterly
HUP	Harvard University Press
IACtHR	Inter-American Court of Human Rights
ICESCR	International Covenant on Economic, Social and Cultural Rights
ICJ	International Court of Justice
ICON	International Journal of Constitutional Law
IDP	internally displaced person
IHL	international humanitarian law
IJCL	International Journal of Comparative Law
ILO	Israeli legal order (Israel)
Int'l Const'l L	International Constitutional Law
Int'l J Equity in Health	International Journal of Equity in Health
Isr L Rev	Israel Law Review
J Afr Stud	Journal of African Studies
J Democr	Journal of Democracy
J L & Soc'y	Journal of Law and Society
J Pol Philos	Journal of Political Philosophy
Jerus Rev Leg Stud	Jerusalem Review of Legal Studies
JMAS	Journal of Modern African Studies
KADU	Kenyan African Democratic Union
KANU	Kenya African National Union
L & Soc Inq	Law and Social Inquiry
L Rev/LR	Law Review
Lat Am Perspectives	Latin American Perspectives
LGBTQ+	lesbian, gay, bisexual, transgender, queer/questioning, and others
LJ	Law Journal
Md Int'l L Rev	Maryland International Law Review
Melb J Int'l L	Melbourne Journal of International Law
Minn L Rev	Minnesota Law Review

MLR	Modern Law Review
Mont L Rev	Montana Law Review
NARC	National Rainbow Coalition (Kenya)
NGO	non-governmental organization
Nordic J of Hum R	Nordic Journal of Human Rights
NUJS L Rev	National University of Juridical Sciences Law Review
NYU J Intl L & Pol	New York University Journal of International Law and Politics
NYU L. Rev.	New York University Law Review
OFAC	Office of Foreign Assets Control (United States)
Ohio St LJ	Ohio State Law Journal
OJLS	Oxford Journal of Legal Studies
OTLO	Occupied Territories legal order (Israel)
OUP	Oxford University Press
PAN	Partido Accíon Nacional (Mexico)
Phil & Pub Aff	Philosophy and Public Affairs
PRB	People's Party of Brunei (Brunei)
PRD	Partido de la Revolución Democrática (Mexico)
PRI	Partido Revolucionario Institucional
RCDA	Revista Catalana de Dret Ambienta
SAcLJ	Singapore Academy of Law Journal
SAJHR	South Africa Journal on Human Rights
SAP	structural adjustment programme
SMU L Rev	Southern Methodist University Law Review
Stan L Rev	Stanford Law Review
Sup Ct L Rev	Supreme Court Law Review
Sup Ct Rev	Supreme Court Review
TCP	Tribunal Constitucional Plurinacional (Bolivia)
Tex L Rev	Texas Law Review
Theo Inq L	Theoretical Inquiries in Law
Theory Pract Legis	Theory and Practice of Legislation
U Chi L Rev	University of Chicago Law Review
U Chi Legal F	University of Chicago Legal Forum
U of Miami Inter-Am LR	University of Miami Inter-American Law Review
U Miami L Rev	University of Miami Law Review
U Pa Asian L Rev	University of Pennsylvania Asian Law Review
U Toronto LJ	University of Toronto Law Journal
UC Davis L Rev	University of California Davis Law Review

UCLA L Rev	University of California Los Angeles Law Review
UDHR	Universal Declaration of Human Rights
UP	University Press
UTLJ	University of Toronto Law Journal
Vand L Rev	Vanderbilt Law Review
VRÜ/WCL	Verfassung and Recht in Übersee/World Comparative Law
Wash U Glob L Studs LR	Washington University Global Studies Law Review
Wis L Rev	Wisconsin Law Review
Wm & Mary L Rev	William and Mary Law Review
Yale Hum Rts & Dev LJ	Yale Human Rights and Development Law Journal
Yale JIL	Yale Journal of International Law
Yale LJ	Yale Law Journal

List of Contributors

Adrienne Stone is Melbourne Laureate Professor, Melbourne Law School, University of Melbourne, Melbourne, Australia. https://orcid.org/0000-0003-3981-8208

Alexandra Huneeus is the Evjue-Bascom Professor of Law and Director of the Global Legal Studies Center at the Law Faculty of the University of Madison- Wisconsin, United States.

Ana Micaela Alterio, PhD is Full time Professor, ITAM (Instituto Tecnológico Autónomo de México), Ciudad de México, Mexico, CONAHCYT (Consejo Nacional de Humanidades, Ciencias y Tecnologías), Ciudad de México, Mexico. https://orcid.org/0000-0001-8729-9647

Catherine O'Regan is Professor of Human Rights Law and Director, Bonavero Institute of Human Rights, University of Oxford, United Kingdom. https://orcid.org/0000-0002-2125-4972

Chien-Chih Lin is Research Professor, Institutum Iurisprudentiae, Academia Sinica, Taipei City, Taiwan, Graduate Institute of National Development, National Taiwan University, Taipei City, Taiwan. https://orcid.org/0000-0003-2427-7445

David Dyzenhaus, DPhil is University Professor of Law and Philosophy, University of Toronto, Toronto, Canada

David Schneiderman is Professor of Law and Political Science (courtesy), University of Toronto, Toronto, Canada. https://orcid.org/0000-0002-3463-3610

David Landau is Mason Ladd Professor and Associate Dean for International Programs, Florida State University College of Law, Tallahassee, United States

Francisca Pou Giménez JSD is Senior Researcher, Institute for Legal Research, National Autonomous University of Mexico (UNAM), Mexico City, Mexico

Frankenberg, Dr Dr is Professor em. of Public Law, Comparative Law and Legal Philosophy, Institute for Public Law, Goethe University Frankfurt am Main Germany, Germany. https://orcid.org/0000-0001-5550-8512

Jaclyn L. Neo is Associate Professor of Law, National University of Singapore, Singapore

James Fowkes is Professor of Foreign and International Law, University of Münster, Germany. https://orcid.org/0000-0001-8714-885 7 Gün ter

Katharine G. Young, SJD (Harv), LLB (Melb) is Professor and Associate Dean of Faculty and Global Programs, and Dean's Distinguished Scholar, Boston College Law School, Newton, United States. https://orcid.org/0000-0002-3614-4722

Kai Möller is Professor of Law, Law School, London School of Economics & Political Science, London, United Kingdom

Kevin Y. L. Tan is Adjunct Professor, Faculty of Law, National University of Singapore and Senior Fellow at the S Rajaratnam School of International Studies, Nanyang Technological University. https://orcid.org/0000-0002-7974-3952

Mark Tushnet is William Nelson Cromwell Professor of Law emeritus, Harvard Law School, Cambridge, United States. https://orcid.org/0000-0002-9316-0905

Michaela Hailbronner is Chair of International and German Public Law and Comparative Law, Law Faculty, University of Münster, Germany

Marcela Prieto Rudolphy is Associate Professor of Law and Philosophy, Gould School of Law, University of Southern California, Los Angeles, United States, Universidad Adolfo Ibáñez, Santiago, Chile. https://orcid.org/ 0009-0001-1279-8916

Mattias Kumm is Inge Rennert Professor of Law, New York University School of Law, New York, United States, WZB Social Science Research Center, Berlin, Germany

Michael Riegner, Dr, LLM (NYU) is Professor of International Law and International Administrative Law, University of Erfurt, Erfurt, Germany. https://orcid.org/0000-0003-4777-6896

Phoebe Okowa is Professor of Public International Law, Queen Mary, University of London, London, United Kingdom

Rosalind Dixon, SJD, Harvard Law is Professor, Faculty of Law and Justice, University of New South Wales, Kensington NSW, Australia. https://orcid.org/0000-0002-6613-8032

Ran Hirschl is the David R. Cameron Distinguished Professor in Law and Politics at the Faculty of Law, University of Toronto, Canada.

Renata Uitz is Professor of Law and Government, University of London, Royal Holloway, London, United Kingdom and Senior Research Fellow, Central European University, Democracy Institute, Budapest. https://orcid.org/0000-0002-3488-8488

Richard Albert is William Stamps Farish Professor in Law, Professor of Government, and Director of Constitutional Studies, The University of Texas at Austin, United States. https://orcid.org/0000-0001-5212-5292

Roberto Niembro Ortega is Professor of Constitutional Law, Postgraduate Legal Studies UNAM, Mexico City, Mexico

Sergio Verdugo is Professor of Law, IE University, Spain. https://orcid.org/0000-0002-9232-0786

Sujit Choudhry is Head of Chambers, Hāki Chambers Global, Canada. https://orcid.org/0000-0002-6543-6644

Tom Ginsburg is Leo Spitz Distinguished Service Professor of International Law, University of Chicago Law School, Chicago, United States. https://orcid.org/0000-0003-3128-3392

Victor Ferreres Comella is Professor of Constitutional Law, Pompeu Fabra University, Spain, University of Texas at Austin, Austin, United States. https://orcid.org/0000-0002-9582-7312

Vlad Perju (SJD, Harvard Law School) is Professor and Dean's Distinguished Scholar, Boston College Law School, Newton, United States

Wen-Chen Chang, JSD is Distinguished Professor, College of Law, National Taiwan University, Taipei, Taiwan. https://orcid.org/0000-0001-7221-2027

Yoon Jin Shin is Associate Professor, School of Law, Seoul National University, Republic of Korea. https://orcid.org/0000-0001-5291-3301

Yonatan T. Fessha, PhD is Professor, Faculty of Law, University of the Western Cape, Cape Town, South Africa

1

Introduction

Sujit Choudhry, Michaela Hailbronner, and Mattias Kumm

I. Introduction

Comparative constitutionalism has emerged as a central field of legal research and teaching. Articles, journals, monographs, edited volumes, and academic societies are increasingly dedicated to opening up the world of constitutionalism, drawing on diverse national experiences in ways that speak and connect to a broader global audience. Even scholarship that focuses on a single system frequently does so with reference to comparative materials and debates. Courts, too, increasingly participate in global conversations with other courts. Politicians and participants in processes of constitutional adoption and reform around the world invoke examples from elsewhere in support of their own ideas, both as models to be adapted or dangers to be avoided. This is not surprising. The language of constitutionalism, human rights, democracy, and the rule of law has become universal.

But it is also a moment of conservative backlash against global or regional norms and standards, and of the assertion of specific national histories and identities.[1] Not all critiques come from the right. International human rights, and international human rights institutions, are increasingly criticized by the left, on the basis that they are allied with neoliberalism and capitalism or because of their elitism and eurocentrism. Scholars have highlighted the close links between the origins of constitutionalism and colonialism, leading some to advance a post-colonial critique that questions the utility of shared concepts such as constitutionalism and/or their normative appeal altogether.[2]

[1] William Partlett and Dinesha Samararatne, 'Redeeming the National in Constitutional Argument' [2021] *World Constitutional Law* 461.

[2] Boaventura de Sousa Santos, Sara Araújo, and Orlando A. Andrade (eds), *Decolonizing Constitutionalism: Beyond False or Impossible Promises* (1st edn, Routledge 2023), in particular ch. 8 by Tshepo Madlingozi, 'On Settler Colonialism and Post-Conquest Constitutionness'; see also for a sympathetic overview of this literature, Lena Salaymeh and Ralf Michaels, 'Decolonial Comparative Law: A Conceptual Beginning' Beginning' [2022] 86(1) *Rabel Journal of Comparative and International Private Law* 166–188; on human rights, Makau Mutua, *Human Rights: A Political and Cultural Critique* (University of Pennsylvania Press 2002).

Sujit Choudhry, Michaela Hailbronner, and Mattias Kumm, *Introduction* In: *Global Canons in an Age of Contestation*.
Edited by: Sujit Choudhry, Michaela Hailbronner, and Mattias Kumm, Oxford University Press.
 DOI: 10.1093/9780191956942.003.0001

In this context, a global volume on canons in comparative constitutional law may seem somewhat anachronistic. It may look like a nostalgic and misplaced attempt to revive the 1990s, when comparative constitutionalism re-emerged as an academic discipline amidst the fall of the Berlin Wall and the Third Wave of democratization. As that moment has receded into the past, the global political order has given way to a fragmented and multi-polar world, which unsurprisingly is reflected in the current state of the discipline of comparative constitutionalism. These broader changes in the global context within which conversations about comparative constitutionalism occur have in turn meant that the tone of debates has changed. Critical voices have become louder[3] and more radical in recent years, even compared to 2015. That year, the United States Supreme Court by a narrow majority affirmed a constitutional right to same-sex marriage. It was, in fact, where this project started, with one of us asking if the Supreme Court's judgment in *Obergefell* should be considered canonical not just from an American but from a broader global perspective.[4] Today, *Obergefell* increasingly looks like the last liberal landmark judgment of a court once famous for its civil rights jurisprudence. The years since 2015 may seem to be marked by a sense of systems turning in upon themselves, and by the closing of minds.

We take a different view. The premise of this volume is that it is more important than ever to have an open discussion about our shared disciplinary premises and normative commitments. It is a standard trope that, in a crisis, it is often necessary to return to fundamentals. Yet, it is not wrong. This is a good time to ask if we should revisit our foundational premises and rethink them, and if we should reaffirm and rejuvenate them. This project seeks to engage with this challenge from a new perspective: the search for the canonical texts of comparative constitutional law.

For further progress on the shared project of democratic constitutionalism, both in scholarship and praxis, requires more than the use of shared terminology across different constitutional systems. Terms such as constitutionalism, human rights, democracy, and the rule of law are capable of more than one meaning. We frequently have different conceptions of these terms, which translate into different understandings of how they apply to the interpretation

[3] e.g. Martin Loughlin, *Against Constitutionalism* (Harvard University Press 2022); see also the increasingly critical literature on human rights, e.g. Samuel Moyn, *Not Enough: Human Rights in an Unequal World* (Harvard University Press 2019); Stephen Hopgood, *The Endtimes for Human Rights* (Cornell University Press 2013).

[4] *Obergefell v. Hodges*, 576 U.S. __ (2015) (US Supreme Court); Michaela Hailbronner, 'Constructing the Global Constitutional Canon: Between Authority and Criticism' [2005] 69 *University of Toronto Law Journal* 248.

and application of constitutions in specific legal disputes. These disagreements do not always occur in good faith. As the literature on 'abusive constitutional borrowing' has demonstrated, authoritarians can make cynical use of the language of constitutionalism, a practice which, if left unchecked, could corrode the credibility of the constitutional project itself whose success can no longer be taken for granted.[5]

II. Why Canons?

The idea of a canon consisting of canonical texts is familiar in a range of different fields, most prominently in literature and theology. Typically, canons represent a set of standard examples that create a grammar enabling participants in an interpretative community to speak with one another. Knowledge of the canonical texts enables us to have informed conversations based on shared knowledge. It is also a way to introduce students to a field.[6]

For example, in literature, canonical works represent the core of what it is felt should be kept alive and passed on, and what should be used to judge new works and understand the literary tradition as a whole. As such, they contribute to the creation of communities and disciplines. At certain times and in some contexts, canonical texts are also understood as authoritative in the sense of providing a set of examples to emulate. Canons play a role as sources of authority in many religions, for example.[7]

Though canons have long served as key materials in interpretation, the concept of a canon has been marginal to contemporary legal scholarship. Around the turn of the millennium, a debate on canonical texts emerged among US constitutional lawyers.[8] Scholars worried in particular that the material traditionally presented in US law schools contributed to marginalizing groups such as African Americans and women in scholarly debates. They set out not

[5] Rosalind Dixon and David E. Landau, *Abusive Constitutional Borrowing: Legal Globalization and the Subversion of Liberal Democracy* (Oxford University Press 2021).

[6] E.g. George Allan, *Higher Education in the Making: Pragmatism, Whitehead, and the Canon* (State University of New York Press 2012), at 142.

[7] Moshe Halbertal, *People of the Book: Canon, Meaning, and Authority* (Harvard University Press 2009).

[8] See in particular J. M. Balkin and Sanford Levinson (eds), *Legal Canons* (NYU Press 2000); Peter Rubin, 'Taking Its Proper Place in the Constitutional Canon: Bolling v. Sharpe, Korematsu, and the Equal Protection Component of Fifth Amendment Due Process' [2006] 92 *Virginia Law Review* 1879; Richard Hasen, 'The Democracy Canon' [2009] 62 *Stanford Law Review* 69; Samuel Brenner, '"Airbrushed out of the Constitutional Canon": The Evolving Understanding of "Giles V. Harris", 1903–1925' [2009] 107 *Michigan Law Review* 107, 853; Jamal Greene, The Anticanon' [2011] 125 *Harvard Law Review* 379.

to abandon the very idea of the canon, but rather to reform or renovate the existing canon to render it more inclusive. In German public law, questions of reception and canonical status have recently been raised in an edited volume on forgotten texts entitled *Apokryphe Schriften*, albeit focusing on scholarly works rather than judgments.[9] No doubt, similar projects exist elsewhere.

Whether canons are a useful analytical device in law, let alone comparative law, is not a straightforward question, however, and it is one that many of our authors engage with in this volume. The answer will likely depend on the functions we want a canon to fulfil. Different approaches raise different challenges to the idea of a canon itself.

If we seek to use the concept of a canon primarily as a teaching tool and a way to lower entry costs to those familiarizing themselves with the discipline, as Rosalind Dixon argues in her contribution to this volume, we will select those texts that are already widely discussed and familiar to all. This risks, of course, entrenching existing Northern and Western biases in the discipline. In other words, through a canon, students are likely to continue studying the same cases they already do—for example, *Brown v. Board of Education*, *Lüth*, and perhaps *Makwanyane* as a token African example. The same can be true for other primary sources such as constitutions and political statements of constitutional ideals (e.g. the French Declaration of Rights of Man and Citizens of 1789 or President Franklin Roosevelt's 'Four Freedoms' speech in his 1941 State of the Union Address). Students will then not encounter much work from jurisdictions outside the 'usual suspects' of comparative law—that is, the United States, Germany, Canada, the European Court of Human Rights, Israel, South Africa, India, and Colombia, to name the most obvious contenders. If the canon were expanded to institutions, it would include not only the United States (presidential) but also the United Kingdom (parliamentary) and France (semi-presidential).

David Law has recently labelled this a tourist's approach to comparative constitutional law.[10] Yet, the idea of introducing students to a discipline through standard examples is rarely only concerned with familiarity or citation counts. Rather, it is concerned with what Law has labelled *representativeness*, which he treats as a distinct (and superior) approach. We agree that representativeness is key, but we believe that it should not be understood, as Law does to a large extent, in numerical terms. Since Asia holds 60% of the world's population,

[9] Nikolas Marsch, Laura Münkler, and Thomas Wischmeyer (eds), *Apokryphe Schriften: Rezeption und Vergessen in der Wissenschaft vom Öffentlichen Recht* (Mohr Siebeck 2019).

[10] David Law (ed.), *Constitutionalism in Context: Comparative Constitutional Law and Policy* (Cambridge University Press 2022) (hereafter Law, *Constitutionalism in Context*).

60% of the chapters in David Law's volume *Constitutionalism in Context* focus on Asian examples.[11] That is decidedly not our approach here. We understand representativeness differently, selecting cases that stand for different *conceptual* approaches our authors believe to be representative of particular ways of thinking about certain key themes of constitutional democracy. This approach is consistent with that of the first casebooks introducing students to comparative constitutional law, such those by Norman Dorsen et al.,[12] and Mark Tushnet and Vicki Jackson.[13] It does mean, however, that major jurisdictions such as China are not represented in this volume.

But what makes a case or text representative? Does it matter which court or country first adopted a particular approach and thus came to be associated with it? In practice, certainly. What else counts? Clearly, the more criteria like influence and familiarity matter, the more our approach will have a bias towards jurisdictions with a long-standing jurisprudence and influence. Some courts, most notably the United States Supreme Court, have historically exercised de facto greater global influence than others, although that court's global influence has sharply declined as its doctrinal cleavages map ever more onto partisan divides. More broadly still, we might say that the institutions and lawyers of the North Atlantic world have been influencers much more than influenced, due to their economic and political power (United States), as former colonial empires (France, England), or sometimes due to their soft power, rooted in the attractiveness of their institutions and accessibility of their sources (Canada). Accordingly, systems like these have long shaped the debates on the central concepts of constitutional law. To be sure, they have been joined by other jurisdictions, such as the classic examples of post-authoritarian (Germany, South Africa) and post-colonial (India, South Africa again) rule, and rebuilding constitutional institutions in the wake of civil wars (Colombia) and the horrors of the Holocaust and the Second World War (Israel, the European Court of Human Rights). But nonetheless, the question now is how to respond to these established imbalances in the context of a project such as this one. We believe the way to confront this history and its largely Western bias is not by abandoning concepts such as constitutionalism and rights, which universalize a set of particular values, but rather to use the idea of a canon as a platform

[11] David Law, 'Introduction: Pedagogy and Conceptualization of the Field' in Law, *Constitutionalism in Context* (n 10) 19.

[12] Norman Dorsen et al. (eds), *Comparative Constitutionalism: Cases and Materials* (West Academic Publishing 2016).

[13] Vicki Jackson and Mark Tushnet, *Comparative Constitutional Law* (3rd edn, Foundation Press 2014).

for debate, to push it beyond the 'usual suspects' in terms of cases, texts, and themes, and to conceive of this canon not as a stable entity, but as one that in its very conception invites a continual process of contestation, self-criticism, and reconstruction.

In other words, we believe that the lingering colonial backdrop of Western constitutionalism and its accompanying problems of bias are bad reasons not to embark upon the project of a canon in constitutional law. Within the field, there is clearly an increased demand to revisit and sometimes re-lay the foundations of the discipline. Moreover, thinking in terms of standard examples is a natural heuristic in the face of a bewildering array of primary source materials. There will be an informal, implicit, or unstated canon, whether or not we desire it. As Stanley Fish points out, canonical texts may be contextualized or criticized, but we will still engage with them.[14] As such, they retain a hold over our imagination as paradigms in terms of which we think, even if only unconsciously. Refusing to embark upon the task of deliberating upon a canon is therefore merely to refuse an open conversation about such a canon and the stakes of relying on it. It may also have the effect of entrenching the implicit canon that already exists. Given the relatively recent rise of comparative constitutional law and human rights, the many competing hegemonies they implicate, and the political uncertainties we face today, it is better to have this conversation now rather than at an uncertain point in the future when the constitutional project itself may be under greater strain.

Thus, we are interested in this volume both in which texts currently count as canonical in our discipline and whether they should, as well as which texts should, be canonized but at the moment are not. Our authors shed new light on old and well-known texts that may or may not deserve their prominence. All of us can name certain texts that are considered foundational to understanding the birth and rise of constitutionalism, but do they still deserve that status? We have therefore encouraged our authors to explore if these texts continue to warrant their place in the canon, or whether they should perhaps be replaced or supplemented by others, including those that engage more critically with the nature of constitutional democracy. Finally, we take up the question of whether there is an anti-canon in the field and of what it might consist.

In doing so, we expect to learn about our discipline as well as its existing biases and blind spots. By combining some general reflections with a more inductive approach, we endeavour to get a better sense of what kind of criteria

[14] Stanley Fish, 'Not of an Age, But for All Time: Canons and Postmoderism' [1993] 43 *Journal of Legal Education* 11.

should be relevant to assessing whether texts should be in a canon that is both theoretically informed and rooted in constitutional practice.

All of this, of course, raises the question of whether there is any normative dimension to this project. The answer is yes and no.

This project is *not* about establishing some kind of canon of good or best approaches to particular rights or principles. Though constitutions and human rights treaties frequently overlap and address a similar set of rights, there is no one institution to define rights or anything else in an authoritative manner, and this is a good thing. Comparative law is and always has been interested in exploring differences as much as similarities. Thus, this project should not be understood to be universalizing in the sense of providing a set of best practices or best interpretations.

Rather, what we seek to establish is a shared discursive space within which constitutional actors can argue about the meaning of constitutional democracy. That meaning is inherently contestable and is currently more contested than usual. The goal of creating a discursive space is to provide a shared language within which that contestation can take place. Such a shared language allows us to identify and render intelligible grounds of disagreement; it also allows us to recognize and understand points of disagreement. Canons are positive examples of the legal embodiment of constitutional democracy.

Finally, the search for canons also enables the identification of anti-canons that represent those examples that exemplify what we all reject or should reject, independently of our cultural and political differences. While anti-canons have long been part of the very idea of a canon—that is, defining what a canon is in terms of what it is not—there is a more contemporary motivation at play as well. Authoritarians around the globe now cynically appropriate the terminology, institutions, and argumentative techniques of constitutionalism to seize and weaponize its core concepts, such as democracy, constitutionalism, and the rule of law. They do so to lay claim to the mantle of legitimacy that flows from describing their actions in constitutionalist terms. So while we accept that a canon creates a discursive space for contestation over the very meaning of constitutional democracy, it is nonetheless a bounded space. It excludes not only cynical appropriation of the language of constitutional democracy, but also constitutional texts, forms, and practices that do not even aspire to instantiate some version of constitutional democracy.

III. Methodology

We start this volume with a set of methodological reflections on the questions of canon-building in comparative law. But the bulk of the contributions in this volume are dedicated to issue-specific chapters on discrete areas of constitutional law which concern either institutional structure or rights. We have asked the authors to select representative texts that shed light on particular concepts in a useful manner and illuminate different understandings and central challenges inherent in the respective concepts. We have chosen this approach over others, such as Eleonora Bottini's recent project of identifying exemplary texts for a particular jurisdiction,[15] because our interest is in illuminating these shared concepts rather than in identifying texts characteristic for individual jurisdictions in the sense of expressing a distinct constitutional identity. While that may be an interesting project in its own right, our goal in this volume is different. We are more interested in building spaces for a shared conversation than in exploring distinct national identities.

We have, moreover, decided to focus in this volume on primary texts, i.e. either constitutional or political documents or constitutional court judgments, rather than scholarship (though there are some exceptions such as Abbé Sieyès' manifesto on the Third Estate). While this may seem like a questionable choice, we have made it deliberately because comparative constitutional law in its current iteration is a relatively young field. It would be both premature and awkward at this point to consider questions about the disciplinary importance of scholarly works.

Because the issue of canonicity is so fraught with questions of bias and hierarchy, we have endeavoured to invite a diverse range of authors, in terms of regional origins as well as gender and levels of seniority. We have succeeded better in some respects than in others. Unfortunately, this project has been long delayed and has lost several authors in response to the Covid pandemic, which has significantly affected many of our authors, in particular those working in systems with limited institutional support and/or care responsibilities. As a result, this volume still has an obvious Western bias, which we openly admit is far from ideal. We acknowledge this as a shortcoming and hope that it will nevertheless serve to contribute to a genuinely open and more balanced conversation in the field to which others are already contributing.

[15] Eleonora Bottini, 'Guest Editor's Introduction: Constitutional Landmarks in the Commonwealth' (*IACL-AIDC Blog*, 3 December 2019) https://blog-iacl-aidc.org/constitutional-landmark-judgments-in-the-commonwealth/2019/12/3/guest-editors-introduction-constitutional-landmark-judgments-in-the-commonwealth accessed 30 October 2023.

We have left the decision of what texts to explore to our authors. To provide the project with a coherent structure, we have, however, asked the authors to identify a maximum of three primary legal sources (i.e. a judicial decision or legal text), of which one must be an anti-canon, and to explain what justifies the inclusion of their chosen source in the canon or anti-canon. We have also encouraged the authors to include new texts where these seem to fit the criteria of canonicity, guided by their own approach and understanding of this context, albeit mindful of our broader goals for this volume. While most contributions grapple with specific rights or structural features, some authors also address foundational issues of constitutionalism, in a few cases even from a specific regional focus where such an approach seemed important to provide balance to a Western-dominated canon of constitutionalism. This freedom for our authors has unavoidably produced some eclecticism in the overall volume but has also contributed to what we believe is a very interesting collection of chapters.

IV. Outline

The volume is divided into four parts. The contributions in Part I offer some general reflections on the potential role and functions of a canon of comparative constitutional law, as well as a set of chapters exploring potential candidates for a canon of constitutionalism and constitutional legitimacy, with several authors exploring the idea of constituent power. Part II continues these discussions, but also addresses other broader structural principles such as the separation of powers, the idea of unamendability, and questions of secession. Part III moves on to individual rights and related concepts such as proportionality. Finally, in Part IV, we range beyond the standard focus on the nation-state and individual rights, taking up questions of transnationalism, the role of corporations, as well as of rights of nature.

A. Part I: Foundations

Rosalind Dixon ('A Global Constitutional Canon v Quasi-Canon? Towards a More Informed and Inclusive Comparative Constitutionalism') argues that one plausible role for a canon is the functional one of enabling easier access to newcomers to the field of comparative constitutional law. In line with such a functional imperative, texts to be included would need to be both widely known and influential. Dixon highlights in particular that influence will typically depend on the representativeness of the relevant text to broader trends or ideas in comparative constitutional law. Three factors in particular, Dixon argues, will be relevant to both knowledge and influence: the innovativeness of a text in its approach, its authorship, and whether it has an 'inbuilt' sphere of influence. Dixon lucidly shows how lowering barriers to entry in this way comes at the cost of diversity. This leads her to suggest the need for a second 'quasi-canon' that broadens the scope of available knowledge and is more inclusive, while acknowledging the pluralistic and provisional nature of all ideas of canonicity.

Starting from existing discussion of canonicity in American law, **Mark Tushnet** ('The Jurisprudence of Canons of Comparative Constitutional Law') analyses different potential meanings and purposes of a canon of comparative constitutional law. Tushnet outlines that such a canon might serve to set out core understandings of contemporary liberal democracies or, more broadly, as a showcase for the relationship between constitutional law and human flourishing, which would accordingly pay more attention to issues outside the traditional scope of liberal democracies such as effective government and environmental protection. Additionally, if we understand the field more in terms of comparative politics, or indeed seek to construct a canon for a 'legal realist comparative constitutional law', we would focus on other texts, e.g. examples that might demonstrate how little influence written constitutional norms may have on actual political outcomes in a given polity. Tushnet concludes by pointing to the challenges, but also potential interest, in a more eclectic approach that would combine all of the different meanings here, as we indeed understand the issue-specific chapters in this volume.

From these broader discussions, we move to considering specific texts. We start by looking at foundational questions of constitutionalism and constitutional legitimacy with two chapters that discuss very different texts. **Victor Ferreres Comella** ('Emmanuel Sieyès, "What is the Third Estate?" (1789)') opens up by discussing Abbe Sieyès' famous text as a foundational article for understanding the relationship between the sovereign people as the constituent power and constitutionalism, and in doing so foregrounds many of the later themes of this value such as constitutional review or limits on constitutional amendability. Ultimately, Ferreres Comella argues that we must discard Sieyès' approach today: 'A "natural" sovereign nation, operating in a world without legal rules, cannot exist. Positive law is everywhere.' In doing so, he also provides an implicit negative answer to the question of whether canonical texts are necessarily normatively admirable, even where they may be representative of a certain approach or a certain way of thinking.

If Sieyès' work is firmly rooted in the context of the French Revolution and thus the traditional Western canon, the first Haitian Constitution has long been ignored in standard treatises on the origins of constitutionalism, albeit that this has more recently been changing. **Günter Frankenberg** ('A Haitian Turn') takes up the Haitian story in his chapter, highlighting how the Haitians challenged the 'liberal hegemony' of the time by abolishing slavery and emphasizing equality, in stark contrast to the much more famous US Constitution's inherent betrayal of its claim of universal rights.

Next, **David Dyzenhaus** ('Exemplary but not Canonical: The South African Voters Rights Cases') offers a discussion of the foundational theme of the relationship of law and oppression and the associated question of the role of lawyers and judges in applying the law in the context of three cases from apartheid South Africa as exemplary, albeit non-canonical texts which speak to the struggle between courts and parliament over the exclusion of coloured voters from the voters' roll under the 1950s apartheid government. Through the prism of these texts, Dyzenhaus illuminates the meaning of seemingly theoretical debates on legal positivism with reference to Hart and Kelsen.

We remain outside Europe and North America in the next two chapters. Africa is routinely ignored in the classical Western canon of constitutionalism, especially if one looks beyond the South African case. **James Fowkes** ('A Constitutional Canon for Africa') considers two examples of how one might rectify this obvious gap. The first is the anti-canonical Act No. 7 of 1982 amending the Kenyan Constitution to prohibit multiparty democracy: 'There shall be in Kenya only one political party.' The second is the decree convening a national conference to draft a new constitution in Benin in 1990, which provided a template for a new wave of African constitutions drafted at the end of the Cold War. Both, Fowkes argues, are representative of distinct times and traditions of post-independence African constitutionalism. Their inclusion enriches a global canon, and not only by making it more representative.

Micaela Alterio and **Roberto Niembro** ('The Mexican Constitution of 1917: A Canon for Latin American Constitutionalism') discuss the Mexican 1917 Constitution as a central example of a very early instance of a revolutionary, post-liberal, and transformative constitution which included social rights even before Weimar two years later, albeit rooting them within a hyper-presidential constitutional context where the emancipatory character of social rights was ultimately subordinated. Alterio and Niembro see the doctrine of the 'permanent constituent power' which granted the political branches unlimited power to amend the constitution developed by Mexican jurist Tena in contrast as an anti-canonical example for its entrenchment of the power of political elites over the people.

B. Part II: Structures

Kevin K. L. Tan ('Separation of Powers') addresses the separation of powers, and selects two canons—the 1787 Constitution of the United States and the decision of the Judicial Committee of the Privy Council in *Don John Francis Douglas Liyanage & Ors v. The Queen*—and an anti-canon, the 1984 Constitution of the Kingdom of Brunei. The Constitution of the United States built on Montesquieu's initial formulation of the separation of powers, but elevated the role of the judiciary and added the notion of checks and balances between each branch. But, as shown in *Liyanage*, even in the absence of the entrenchment of the separation of powers, courts can go beyond the constitutional text and make structural arguments to find that the separation of powers inheres in a constitutional regime, even in a Westminster-style constitution such as Sri Lanka's, where the legislative and executive branches are fused through responsible government and the cabinet system. Brunei's 1984 Constitution, by contrast, creates the framework for an absolutist monarchy, that concentrates all power in the Sultan, and is an anti-model to be avoided.

Sergio Verdugo ('Global Canons, Term Limits, and the Constituent Power Theory') argues that candidates for inclusion in a canon have to meet two criteria, the advancement of core values associated with democracy or human rights, and historical impact. He considers two Latin American decisions on presidential term limits: the Constitutional Court of Colombia's 2010 decision which prevented President Álvaro Uribe from serving a third term in 2010 and the Constitutional Tribunal of Bolivia's 2017 decision which removed presidential term limits for President Evo Morales. Verdugo argues that the Colombian decision is canonical, because it strengthened the minimum core of competitive democracy and has had an impact. By contrast, the Bolivian decision is anti-canonical, because it has had an impact but undermines that same core. Both decisions advance our understanding of the relationship between international human rights law, the theory of constituent power, and the democracy protecting the role of the courts in adverse conditions. If courts deploy the idea of constituent power as a judicial doctrine, Verdugo argues, they should follow the Colombian example and avoid the Bolivian one.

Chien-Chih Lin and **Wen-Chen Chang** ('The Canon of "Constitutional Unamendability" and "Basic Structure Doctrine" in Global Constitutional

Studies') also examine the issue of unconstitutional constitutional amendments. They argue that the existing scholarship pays insufficient attention to the phenomenon of constitutional relativity on the distinction between constituent power and constituted power, which reflects divergent constitutional and legal cultures, especially in nascent democracies in Asia. What counts as a constitutional amendment (which does not trigger unamendability doctrines) and replacement (which does) is not self-defining and may be controversial, does not always mirror the magnitude of constitutional change, and may depend on contingent political logics. A 'new' constitution may substantively continue the previous one as part of a political pact between the old and new regimes, or purported constitutional amendments may in substance create a new constitutional regime while concealing the degree of the change (e.g. Japan, South Korea, Taiwan). They propose three canonical examples: Article 79(3) of the German Basic Law and the Supreme Court of India's decision in *Kesavananda v. State of Kerala* (which accept judicial review of constitutional amendments on the basis of unamendability) and the United States Supreme Court's decision in *Coleman v. Miller* (which rejects judicial review of constitutional amendments). Read in their context, Article 79(3) of the German Basic Law and the Indian basic structure doctrine were applied in a manner attentive to political context, and *Coleman* retained the Court's power to determine the boundaries of constituent power.

Yonatan Fessha ('The Secession and Constitutionalism Canon') addresses the question of secession and constitutionalism. He proposes the decision of the Supreme Court of Canada in the *Quebec Secession Reference* for inclusion in the canon, and Article 39 of the Ethiopian Constitution as anti-canonical. Fessha observes that the *Quebec Secession Reference* has had a broad global impact on constitutional adjudication and constitutional politics. It has been cited by domestic courts in Spain and Sri Lanka and has figured in debates on secession in Scotland and Montenegro. It has also been cited by the International Court of Justice in its *Kosovo Advisory Opinion* for its analysis on the international legal framework for secession. For Fessha, the *Quebec Secession Reference* has been influential because it rejected the right to unliteral secession but also crafted a legal framework for secession rooted in unwritten constitutional principles, that give weight to the interests of competing majorities within which secession could occur. It also recognized that political institutions would have to assess what constituted both a clear majority and a clear question on secession. Article 39, by contrast, is anti-canonical because it entrenches an unqualified right to secession that is not a constitutional vehicle for an orderly and peaceful secession—for example, the nature and clarity of the reference question.

C. Part III: Rights

Marcela Prieto Rudolphy ('The Questions of Dignity') observes that human dignity is fundamental to post-Second World War international and constitutional law, but that there is no consensus on what dignity is or what it demands. Dignity rarely shows up alone; rather, it is invoked by courts to interpret other rights. Moreover, dignity claims often appear on both sides, supporting opposite interpretations of rights or judicial outcomes. Nevertheless, she suggests two canonical cases: the Constitutional Court of Colombia's decision that decriminalized abortion in three limited circumstances, and the Supreme Court of Israel's decision on the legality of targeted killing. They should be canonical because they provide a comprehensive starting point for discussions about dignity. Specifically, the cases engage with the most important conceptions of dignity, are explicit about the necessity and difficulty of balancing dignity against competing values, and address the relationship between international and domestic law's treatment of dignity. They also address *who* is a bearer of dignity and *what* dignity requires. But both decisions are also flawed. The outcomes in both cases (the very limited right to abortion, and permitting targeted killing in certain circumstances) 'are far from being universally applauded'. In addition, both cases adopt a balancing approach to dignity, in contrast to the Constitutional Court of Germany's absolutist approach in its celebrated *Aerial Security Act* decision. As an anti-canonical case, she proposes the United States Supreme Court's decision in *Deck v. Missouri*, where the Court was indifferent to the dignity-related objections to shackling a convicted offender, who it seemed to assume was not a bearer of dignity.

Kai Möller ('*Lüth* and the "Objectives System of Values": From "Limited Government" Towards an Autonomy-Based Conception of Constitutional Rights') argues that the Constitutional Court of Germany's decision in *Lüth* was the birth of a now globally dominant conception of constitutional rights. Although *Lüth* claimed that the German Grundgesetz created an 'objective system of value', Möller argues that this terminology obscures the true importance of the decision. What *Lüth* did was to set out that rights are not about disabling governments but about enabling citizens to live their lives autonomously. The doctrinal implications of this theory of rights includes horizontal effect (because individual autonomy can be threatened by private actors relying on private law), and the state's positive duties to protect an individual's autonomy from other private parties, and social rights which protect the preconditions of autonomy. As an anti-canonical judgment, he proposes the United States Supreme Court's judgment in *DeShaney v. Winnebago County* *of Social Services*, which rejected the idea of a general doctrine of positive obligations, because the point of the Due Process Clause was to protect people from the state by preventing governments from abusing their powers. Even the dissenting judges shared this conception of rights, and argued that the government had acted unconstitutionally because it had entered the field of child protection. The choice between these two conceptions of rights matters: in *DeShaney*, it meant that the state had not acted unconstitutionally by failing to protect a child from being beaten into a coma by his father.

Francisca Pou Giménez ('Global Proportionality Canons from Latin America') observes that the global scholarship on proportionality has been centred on the jurisdictions that dominate comparative constitutional law (e.g. Germany, Canada, Israel). She argues that the exclusion of Latin America 'leaves in the shadow' important dimensions of the contemporary practice of proportionality. She argues that Latin American examples expand the global canon methodologically, functionally, and thematically. Methodologically, she points to: (a) the Constitutional Court of Colombia's integration of the American tiers of scrutiny into the framework of proportionality, yielding different tests for soft, intermediate, and strict scrutiny, in Decision C-091/03, and (b) the integrated retrogression test to evaluate legislative backsliding in the protection of economic, social, and cultural rights, in Decision C-038/2004 of the Constitutional Court of Colombia. Functionally, she provides the following examples: (a) the *Quisberth Castro* decision of the Supreme Court of Argentina, which applied proportionality to social rights to require the state to attend to the needs of persons in situations of extreme vulnerability; and (b) Decision C-822/05 of the Constitutional Court of Colombia, which set out the principle of conditional validity—i.e. a statute is constitutional only if applied with perfect proportionality in every case.

Adrienne Stone ('Freedom of Expression and the Constitutional Canon') proposes *Lüth*, *New York Times v. Sullivan*, and *R. v. Keegstra* as three canonical cases on freedom of expression. Each of these cases can be taken to reflect a fundamental value: for Germany, dignity; for the United States, liberty; and for Canada, equality. Liberty arguably expands the scope of freedom of expression, and dignity and equality can justify reducing its scope. However, Stone observes that dignity, equality, and liberty are inextricably linked. As a consequence, 'equality and dignity can be invoked in favour of freedom of expression as well as in support of its limits'. Equality protects the speech of political minorities from censorship; dignity underlines the individual self-fulfilment justification for freedom of expression. These values exhibit 'double-sidedness' because they can both justify more and less freedom of expression. How they operate depends on the background commitments of the constitutional order, which are reflected in both the structure and strength of rights. *Lüth* established the horizontal and positive operation of freedom of expression, in the service of transformative constitutionalism; *New York Times v. Sullivan* reflects liberal constitutionalism's commitment to negative rights to protect individuals from state power; and *Keegstra* at once reflects liberal constitutionalism's commitment to checking state power, but also gestures towards collective rights that secure the welfare of communities or peoples, and unlike American constitutional doctrine accepts as a legitimate purpose the redistribution of opportunities for expression from the powerful to the powerless.

Jaclyn L. Neo ('Freedom of Religion') observes that the right to religious freedom is among the most commonly protected in national constitutions and international instruments, but that the scope of the right is deeply contested, as one moves from 'the right to profess and practice established, communal religion to an arguably wider right to belief and conscience'. Moreover, the right to freedom of religion stands at the centre of debates surrounding secularism, democracy, and individual rights. She proposes four cases which 'have served as turning points' in shaping how scholars think about religious freedom, and how courts decide cases in this area. *West Virginia State Board of Education v. Barnette* (United States) and *Kokkinakis v. Greece* (European Court of Human Rights) are from the Global North, and *Commissioner, Hindu Religious Endowments, Madras v. Sri Lakshmindra Thirtha Swamiar of Sri Shirur Mutt* (India) and *Lina Joy v. Majlis Agama Islam Wilayah* (Malaysia) are from the Global South. *Barnette* has been conceptualized both as a religious freedom which protected the rights of a small religious minority (Jehovah's Witnesses), but also as a freedom of expression case which raises the question of whether a distinct guarantee of religious freedom is necessary. *Kokkinakis* also protected the rights of religious minorities in a pluralist democratic society but, at the same time, has been invoked to justify restrictions on freedom of religion to justify restrictions on harmless religious expression (e.g. religious clothing) in the name of religious pluralism. *Shirur Mutt* created the 'essential practices doctrine' of Indian constitutional law, which protects modes of worship essential to the religion and permits the regulation of non-essential practices. It has empowered courts to adjudicate upon questions of religious orthodoxy, raising questions about the legitimacy of a secular court imposing rationalist ideas upon religious adherents. *Lina Joy* is a potential anti-canonical decision, because of the refusal of the Malaysian courts to interpret religious freedom to guarantee the right to choose one's religion, if one accepts religious freedom as premised on individual autonomy.

David Schneiderman ('Comparative Constitutional Law of Property') argues that there are two dominant paradigms for property rights. The first is the classical version of property which emphasizes exclusivity of ownership, exchanged in a self-regulated market between buyers and sellers. The second treats property as inherently regulated from the outset, and as subject to 'other constitutional rights, limits and projects' which include social functions. Schneiderman proposes three cases for inclusion in the global property canon: *Pennsylvania Coal v. Mahon* (United States), *James v. United Kingdom* (European Court of Human Rights), and *Port Elizabeth v. Various Occupiers* (South Africa) which 'represent a movement from' from the first to the second conception of property. *Pennsylvania Coal* introduced the doctrine of regulatory takings into American constitutional law, if regulation 'goes too far'. This created a balancing test, which Schneiderman argues has contributed to the chaotic nature of US takings law. *James* turned back a challenge to leasehold enfranchisement, whereby legislation authorized the transfer of property rights to leaseholders. *Port Elizabeth* concerned a municipality's attempt to evict informal dwellers from privately owned land. The Constitutional Court conceptualized the case as raising the relationship between constitutional property rights and housing rights. It refused to order the eviction because of the lengthy period of occupation, the lack of any need to put the land to other uses, the failure to engage in dialogue with the occupiers, and the lack of suitable alternatives.

Renata Uitz ('The Shifting Canon of Constitutional Equality?') emphasizes the importance of equal recognition of persons in any liberal democracy. Yet, the meaning of equality remains contested, and more formal and more material understandings of equality are frequently in tension with each other. Thus, giving specific rights to a certain group in order to promote material rather than merely formal equality raises questions about equal treatment. Renata Uitz grounds her selection of two candidates for canonical texts—the Interamerican Court's Advisory Opinion of 2017 on a right to same-sex marriage and the UN Committee on the Rights of Persons with Disabilities, *General Comment No. 6*—in a broader comparative analysis of the case law, emphasizing the connection of equality with a Kantian reading of dignity. In this context, Uitz also puts forward a more general argument for a substantive approach to equality. Her anti-canonical example—the US Supreme Court's judgment in *Plessy v. Ferguson*—speaks to the flaws of a formalistic approach as inherent in the 'separate but equal' formula of *Plessy* that ignores social realities. Uitz highlights how gains of previous years are currently under threat in the context of the broader global wave towards what are sometimes more conservative understandings of equality, but sometimes openly racist or sexist approaches.

Yoon Jin Shin ('Gender Discrimination and Canons for Constitutional Review') observes that gender discrimination has been both historically pervasive and prohibited by most constitutions. Her chapter examines three issues: the doctrine of indirect discrimination, the relationship between tradition and gender equality, and intermediate scrutiny of distinctions based on gender. Indirect discrimination is a canonical doctrine found in a wide range of international, regional, and national jurisdictions on gender discrimination. Citing leading decisions from Germany, South Korea, and the United States, she devotes the greatest attention to *Fraser v. Canada* (Canada), which rejected 'choice'-based justifications for gender discrimination. *Fraser* centred on the structural inequality facing women—in that case, arising from childcare responsibilities—and holds that laws should not perpetuate those inequalities. The Korean Constitutional Court's decision striking down the *Hojuje* or household system, whereby a household was headed by the eldest male and made every woman citizen in South Korea belong to her father at birth, to her husband in matrimony, and to her son after her husband's death, represents her second canonical example of the relationship between tradition and gender equality. Notably, the Court harmonized the interpretation of the constitutional guarantee of gender equality within marriage and the state's constitutional duty to sustain Korea's constitutional heritage and required tradition to be reinterpreted based on the two core constitutional commitments of gender equality and individual dignity. The American jurisprudence on intermediate scrutiny for gender-based distinctions—exemplified by *United States v. Virginia* (the VMI case)—should be considered anti-canonical, because it is unclear how it fits within the global standard of proportionality, within the American system of tiered scrutiny, and adopts the same intensity of review 'regardless of the particular nature, gravity, or circumstances of an individual case'.

Katharine G. Young, ('The Canons of Social and Economic Rights') proposes three texts: *Republic of South Africa v. Grootboom*, the Universal Declaration of Human Rights, and *San Antonio School District v. Rodriguez*. *Grootboom* should be part of the canon, which Young defines as an exemplary claim of constitutional and democratic practice, based on its reasoning, pedigree, and visibility. *Grootboom* resolved the 'obstacle of justiciability' by adopting reasonableness review, but infusing it with substantive content—most importantly, the prioritization of the needs of vulnerable people in material crisis—while at the same time declining to adopt the 'minimum core' approach established by *General Comment No. 3* of the Committee on Economic, Social and Cultural Rights.

A proto-canon, on Young's conception, was at one point a canon by virtue of its reasoning, pedigree, and visibility, whose canonical status later waned. The example she provides is the Universal Declaration of Human Rights, which reflected earlier constitutional guarantees of social and economic rights and guided the core human treaties, regional human rights instruments, and dozens of constitutional instruments. Young offers *Rodriguez* as a counter-canon or anti-canon, which 'dwells on the path not followed', because it marked the 'interpretive closure' by the United States Supreme Court of constitutional arguments for socio-economic rights and the jurisdictional allocation of authority of the right to education to the states. An irony of *Rodriguez* is that education rights cases surged in US state courts under state constitutions.

David E. Landau ('The Unsettled Canon of Social Rights Enforcement in Latin America') observes that social rights are central to the modern constitutional history of Latin America, beginning with the Mexican Constitution of 1917. Over the course of the twentieth century, all of Latin America's major countries would include these rights, notwithstanding 'great diversity in constitutional ideology'. Unlike the Mexican Constitution, these rights were understood from the outset to be justiciable. Landau proposes the decision of the Colombian Constitutional Court (T-025 of 2004), on the rights of internally displaced persons (IDPs), as a canonical case, because the Court deployed a creative and aggressive remedy (by converting the individual *tutela* into a structural remedy through aggregation, and declaring an 'unconstitutional state of affairs') and careful monitoring to improve bureaucratic functioning of a complex social problem. However, its model is difficult to replicate. The Brazilian Supreme Court's decision in *Gonçalvez Cordeiro* is anti-canonical, because it 'enforces the right to health in ways that are heedless of the broader consequences or systemic impact'. The Court ordered a state government to provide experimental medical treatment that cost 20 times per capita GDP, which spurred a massive number of successful claims for public funding of particular treatments or medicines.

Tom Ginsburg ('The Due Process Canon') observes that the right to due process is inherent in any system of law, and is found broadly in national, supranational, and international law. He accordingly offers three canonical cases, one from each of these contexts: *Matthews v. Eldridge* (United States), *Kadi* (European Union), and *Neer* (US-Mexican Claims Commission). But he begins with the anti-canonical case of *Lochner v. New York* (United States), which interpreted the Due Process Clause of the Fourteenth Amendment to accord substantive protection to freedom of contract, and to prohibit the legislature from passing general legislation affecting individuals' freedom at the same time. This decision is anti-canonical because it is formalistic and ideological. *Matthews* arose under the Due Process Clause of the Fifth Amendment, and set out a famous three-part test for how much process is 'due' in any particular context being whether 'government should adopt procedures up to the point where the marginal cost is equal to the marginal benefit', which in practice often produces the same result as proportionality. *Kadi* is canonical for several reasons: for including within the right to due process the principle of legality, which requires review by a court to which an individual has access; and for the insistence by a court (the ECJ, in this context) on that right in relation to the United Nations Security Council itself, notwithstanding the lack of such a right under the United Nations Charter. *Neer* arises under international investment law, and set out the content of the 'denial of justice' standard to be accorded to foreigners, with respect to the administration of justice. At its core, it obliges the state to meet a minimal standard, which binds not only the courts but also law enforcement authorities and even the executive or legislature.

Catherine O'Regan ('Drawing Their Own Boundaries: Constitutional Interpretation and the Constitutional Role of Courts') identifies three canonical texts that concern the interpretation of constitutional provisions affecting the court's constitutional jurisdiction: *Boilermakers* (Australia), *Kesavananda* (India), and *Doctors for Life* (South Africa). *Boilermakers* established that only judicial bodies established under Chapter III of the Australian Constitution may exercise federal judicial power, and such courts may not exercise executive or legislative powers. In that case, the High Court struck down the conferral of labour arbitration powers to a court. *Kesavananda* held that the power of constitutional amendment under Article 368 of the Constitution of India did not encompass the power to amend the 'basic structure' of the Indian Constitution, even if such amendments had been adopted in accordance with constitutional procedures. It thus reconfigured the separation of powers between legislatures and courts. *Doctors for Life* determined that the Constitutional Court could consider 'whether Parliament had acted properly to facilitate public involvement in the law-making process and if it found that Parliament had failed to do so would render the relevant legislation invalid'—again, if the formal requirements of the legislative process had been met. O'Regan argues that each of these cases reshaped the separation of power within the constitutional order through an innovative interpretation that changed prevailing understandings of the ambit of judicial power.

Richard Albert ('Techniques of Judicial Avoidance') introduces 'a peculiar form of self-imposed limitation on judicial power', which he terms 'judicial avoidance', i.e. 'when judges choose to avoid certain disputes presented squarely before them despite there being no constitutional rule requiring them to decline to adjudicate these matters'. The central historical example is *Marbury v. Madison*, which asserted the power of judicial review without exercising it. He proposes two canonical cases—*Reference re Manitoba Language Rights* (Canada), the Conseil Constitutionnel's decision on the direct election of the French President (France)—and one anti-canonical case, *Bush v. Gore* (United States). *Reference re Manitoba Language Rights* is an example of 'remedial judicial avoidance', because the Supreme Court of Canada asserted the power to declare a statute invalid but delayed the coming into force of the judgment for a set period to permit the enactment of constitutionally compliant legislation, in a case where it found that virtually all of a province's laws were unconstitutional for failing to have been enacted in both English and French. The Conseil Constitutionnel's decision not to review the constitutionality of De Gaulle's constitutional amendment through a referendum—which the Constitution did not provide for—is an example of 'jurisdictional judicial avoidance', whereby the court 'determines that it lacks the jurisdictional authority to intervene even if the dispute does indeed involve a legal dispute'. *Bush v. Gore* is anti-canonical, because it refused to apply the American political questions doctrine, which is an example of 'substantive judicial avoidance', which reflects 'the court's own evaluation of what is a politically appropriate function for judges to exercise'. Albert argues that the United States Supreme Court should not have inserted itself into the election of the American president. He argues that all three techniques of judicial avoidance can be deployed strategically to preserve or increase judicial power.

D. Part IV: Beyond the State and the Individual

Ran Hirschl ('The City as an Anti-Canonical Concept in Constitutional Law (and Recent Attempts to Change That)') reflects on the peculiar fact that even though agglomeration and the emergence of mega-cities are one of the most significant demographic and geopolitical phenomena of our time, the city does not figure as a central constitutional concept in constitutional discourse. Hirschl examines the reasons for the existence of what he claims is a 'constitutional blind spot' and then discusses three notable attempts to 'insert the city … into mainstream constitutional discourse'. He first discusses the French philosopher Henry Lefebre's 'Right to the City' and the emergence of cities' human rights charters that it spurned as an innovative, but ultimately vague and legally limited, intervention. He then describes the practical effects of the constitutionalization of city status in South Africa in 1996, outlining how various legal features have worked together to allow urban centres to have become meaningful voices and decision-makers in addressing the political challenges associated with agglomeration. Finally, he analyses 'the constitutional emancipation of Mexico City': its establishment as a state in the Mexican Constitution in 2016, enabling it to give itself a constitution and exercise all the powers exercised by states in Mexico, thus invigorating citizen engagement and city-based collective identity with core values of democracy, transparency, and self-government.

Alexandra Huneeus ('The Canon of Nature Rights') describes how a growing cluster of laws, judgments, and resolutions have made nature rights 'become part of the transnational lexicon of rights'. The chapter explores three foundational texts: a US Supreme Court 1972 dissent by Justice Douglas in *Sierra Club v. Morton* arguing that a valley in the Sierra Nevada should have standing to defend itself in court; the Ecuadorian Constitution of 2008, introducing nature as a rights holder as an end in itself and not just a means for human sustenance; and the 2016 judgment in which the Colombian Constitutional Court declared the Arato River to be a rights-bearing body. These cases, she argues, challenge not only how we engage the environment at a time when climate change has made itself felt in daily life; but they are also attempts to insert into national constitutional law ideas and values advanced by indigenous peoples and other ethnically identified communities and to rewrite relations with the state, while altering how the state conceptualizes their lands.

Michael Riegner ('Canonizing the Corporation: Liberal, Social, and Transformative Varieties of Corporate Constitutionalism') argues that 'uncovering the role of the corporation as a constitutional protagonist' allows us to reflect on 'implicit assumptions about constitutional agency, economic organization, and political economy'. He analyses three constitutional cases, exhibiting what he calls 'liberal, social, and transformative' constitutionalism, respectively. The United States Supreme Court's 2010 *Citizens United* case, striking down a legislative attempt to curb the role of corporate money in elections, is analysed as part of a liberal anti-canon. The German Federal Constitutional Court's 1979 judgment on co-determination upholding a law that required parity in representation between employees and shareholders on corporate supervisory boards is analysed as part of the social democratic constitutional canon. The 2018 decision by the Constitutional Court of Ecuador in the case against Chevron is an instance of transformative constitutionalism, pitting the rights of a corporation against the rights of nature and upholding a $9.5 billion judgment against Chevron for its environmentally damaging activities in the Amazon region. It illustrates how the recognition of nature as a rights holder can have significant practical implications for assessing economic activities undertaken by powerful global corporations. Together, these cases provide ideal typical instantiations of varieties of corporate constitutionalism, that offer an analytical framework for further comparative study.

Phoebe Okowa ('Act of State and Diplomatic Protection in the Modern Constitution: Two Case Studies') describes how deeply entrenched international law concepts, that have traditionally limited the possibility for national courts to enforce citizens' rights against their respective governments for their behaviour in their conduct of foreign affairs, have come under pressure from constitutional courts interpreting the rights of citizens. In the South African case of *Kaunda*, the court recognized that whether and how South Africa exercises diplomatic protection on behalf of one of its citizen against the rights-violating behaviour of another state may well be a question of discretion under international law. But human rights ground protective obligations that guide and limit the exercise of that discretion. In *Belhaj*, the Supreme Court of the UK determined that even though the 'act of state doctrine' normally bars national courts from assessing the legality of acts of foreign sovereigns (sovereigns as equals may not sit in judgment over one another), the rule does not apply when assessing the behaviour of other governments in the context where a case is brought against a national government colluding with foreign governments to violate the rights of UK citizens. In both cases, traditional international doctrines were not simply pushed aside as irrelevant, but carefully qualified and limited to allow for the vindication of those rights. These cases exemplify in a canonical fashion how modern human rights orientations push for the reinterpretation of traditional international law doctrines imposing rights-based restrictions on the behaviour of states in foreign affairs in contexts where previously rights and courts did not impose such limits.

Vlad Perju ('The Hollow Canon of Transnational Constitutional Engagement') discusses the South African constitutional judgment of *S v, Makwanyane* and the US Supreme Court case of *Roper v. Simmons*, exemplifying two ways in which national constitutional courts have engaged foreign law, drawn from a time in which such engagement seemed to have the potential to transform constitutional reasoning. Yet 'nowhere ... has transnational engagement delivered the doctrinal transformation it had once promised.' To illustrate that point, Perju traces the disappearance of references to foreign law in the decisions following *Roper v. Simmons*. Critically discussing pragmatist justifications as well as Jeremy Waldron's 'Partly Laws Common to all Mankind' from 2012, he argues that the practice of citing foreign laws has 'more often evaded rather than met the burden of justifying the use of foreign law in constitutional interpretation' and that 'at least in part as a result of that failure, such usage has declined'. Hinting at the task of theorizing not a gap-filling *jus gentium*, but a transnational *jus civile*, he emphasizes the importance of thinking 'seriously and creatively about foreign law for the purpose of preparing the next act' on the success of which, he claims, depends 'more than just the future of comparative constitutionalism'.

V. Conclusion

As this summary shows, this volume offers a mix of more familiar texts and others that bring in new ideas and perspectives. Some, albeit not many, texts are put forward as candidates for a canon in multiple contributions. No doubt, many others might have been discussed. One perhaps surprising insight from this project has been how heavily texts from certain jurisdictions—notably the United States—feature even in work by authors from very different jurisdictions. We suspect that this is related to the fact that many scholars working on comparative constitutional law have some ties to US law schools. Another insight of this volume is the importance of global, but even more so *regional*, human rights institutions such as the European Court of Human Rights and the Interamerican Court of Human Rights. Decisions of both feature in multiple chapters, speaking to the connection between supranational human rights discourses and comparative constitutionalism. Not least, the volume also speaks to the incredible range of what we understand as questions of constitutional law today, as the chapters on the role of corporations and nature as well as the rise of cities illustrate. These chapters in particular reflect that the end times of constitutionalism are not here, yet. Rather, constitutionalism is everywhere. The question is how to address this fact—and this is where the chapters discussing the role of courts and legal interpretation come in, illustrating that the question 'how to do constitutionalism' still demands answers and that those answers will have to be rooted in specific legal and political cultures and contexts.

Through the lens of specific texts and themes, therefore, the volume offers a picture of the discipline of comparative constitutionalism, highlighting its liberal and Western bias but also its desire to change and open itself up, in particular to voices from the Global South. It speaks to the fact that most of those working in the field ultimately share a strong commitment to liberal democracy and constitutionalism. Whether the volume will still provide insights in twenty years remains to be seen. The answer to that question will depend not just on the state of comparative constitutional law as a discipline, but also on the broader global prospects of democratic constitutionalism. For now, the volume should be understood as an entry into a conversation about liberal democratic constitutionalism as a global model—at a time when the 1990s enthusiasm for the model has dampened, but in which its roots also still run deep around the world.

PART I
FOUNDATIONS

2

A Global Constitutional Canon v Quasi-Canon?

Towards a More Informed and Inclusive Comparative Constitutionalism

*Rosalind Dixon**

I. Introduction

A 'canon' means different things in different contexts.[1] And in law, as Jack Balkin and Sandy Levinson note, '[t]he canon of interest to academics may be quite different from the canon that is important to the practicing lawyer', and that of interest to students.[2]

The focus of this chapter is on the idea of a canon in comparative constitutional scholarship. And for this purpose, the chapter argues, the best way of understanding the canon is through a functionalist lens[3]—i.e. by asking how we can create a common body of knowledge that helps encourage a richer and more diverse set of contributions to the field of comparative constitutional studies ('CCS').[4] A common body of knowledge of this kind can help reduce the 'transaction costs' to new and early-career scholars entering the field of CCS, [5] and thereby both the breadth and depth of contributions to the field.

* Professor of Law, UNSW Sydney. Thanks to the editors and Mark Tushnet for helpful comments and to Melissa Vogt for outstanding research assistance.

[1] On the Western canon, see, e.g., Harold Bloom, *The Western Canon: The Books and School of the Ages* (Harcourt Brace, 1994).

[2] Jack M. Balkin and Sanford Levinson, 'The Canons of Constitutional Law' (1998) 111 *Harvard Law Review* 976–981; Michael Hailbronner, 'Constructing the Global Constitutional Canon: Between Authority and Criticism' (2019) 69 *University of Toronto Law Journal* 248, 254.

[3] Compare Balking and Levinson (n 2), 967–968, 980; Hailbronner (n 2), 257; Mark Tushnet, 'Canons Project: General Thoughts' (Working Paper, 16 June 2019). On functionalism more generally, see also, e.g., Rosalind Dixon, 'The Functional Constitution: Re-Reading the 2014 High Court Constitutional Term' (2015) 43 *Federal Law Review* 455.

[4] Ran Hirschl, *Comparative Matters: The Renaissance of Comparative Constitutional Law* (Oxford University Press, 2014).

[5] See Rosalind Dixon and David Ginsburg, 'Deciding Not to Decide: Deferral in Constitutional Design' (2011) 9 *International Journal of Constitutional Law* 636, 641–642; Rosalind Dixon and Samuel

Rosalind Dixon, *A Global Constitutional Canon v Quasi-Canon?* In: *Global Canons in an Age of Contestation.*
Edited by: Sujit Choudhry, Michaela Hailbronner, and Mattias Kumm, Oxford University Press.
DOI: 10.1093/9780191956942.003.0002

This will only occur, however, if the relevant body of knowledge is accessible and realistic in scope. Otherwise, the attempt to construct a canon risks increasing, rather than decreasing, the costs of entry into the field. This also implies a relatively stringent and narrow definition of the global constitutional canon. It suggests that the relevant constitutional text should be understood to have truly 'canonical' status if and only if two conditions are met: it is (i) well known to large numbers of constitutional lawyers and/or scholars; *and* (ii) highly influential on subsequent constitutional practice either within the relevant jurisdiction or globally, or reflective of a widespread set of norms or understandings.

Conceptually, these criteria could apply to any constitutional text, including the text of a written constitution, judicial interpretations of that text, or secondary sources including pieces of constitutional scholarship.[6] In all these contexts, the knowledge and influence of a text may also be shaped by its novelty or innovation, the skill and reputation of its author, and inbuilt communities of influence.

These criteria may apply differently over time: knowledge, for example, may rise or fall quite rapidly, whereas influence will generally require a longer time frame. Canonical status may likewise be a question of degree: a constitutional text may be canonical within a given country, or legal tradition, but not globally (i.e. part of a 'localized' canon).[7] Or it may be influential within a particular legal sub-field, but not across an entire field (a 'specialized' canon). But over the long run, no constitutional text should be understood to be part of the *global* constitutional canon unless both these conditions are met; and met on a truly global scale—i.e. across different countries, legal traditions, and subfields or communities within public law. Texts that meet some but not all these criteria, the chapter suggests, are best understood as *quasi-canonical* rather than canonical in nature.

The quasi-canon still serves a useful and important function in promoting broader and deeper forms of global public law scholarship. But it does so in a more pluralistic way, which invites varying degrees of attention from different scholars, and the construction of shared knowledge through overlapping forms

Issacharoff, 'Living to Fight Another Day: Judicial Deferral in Defense of Democracy' [2016] *Wisconsin Law Review* 683, 687–688.

[6] For the most part, the editors have chosen to restrict our focus to the former categories of constitutional text—i.e. authoritative constitutional norms and decisions, rather than secondary materials explicating or critiquing those texts.

[7] Compare David Kennedy and William Fisher, *The Canon of American Legal Though* (Princeton University Press, 2006) 14–16 (on what makes their canon 'American').

of comparative scholarship.[8] It could, in this sense, be seen as similar to an approach to the canon that is *discursive* and provisional rather than authoritative and fixed. The very fact of discussing whether to include texts in a canon is generative of knowledge, and potentially also of productive debate about what defines our notions of constitutional 'importance'.

The canons project itself, therefore, could be seen as contributing to this kind of discursive, quasi-canon product, even if we ultimately disagree with many of the texts it ultimately includes or selects as canonical or anti-canonical in status.

The remainder of the chapter is divided into three section. Section II sets out in more detail the key definitional concepts that animate the chapter, and some thoughts on the causal mechanisms that are likely to drive inclusion in the global canon and quasi-canon of constitutional thought. Section III offers a brief conclusion.

II. A Global Canon v Quasi-Canon: Definitions and Criteria

As Jack Balkin and Sandy Levinson, Michaela Hailbronner, and Mark Tushnet have all separately argued, the best way of approaching the construction of a constitutional canon is through a functionalist lens—i.e. to focus on the relevant aims or goals of the project concerned.[9]

One set of goals for a constitutional canon could be substantive or political-theoretic in nature: for example, the aim of the canon might be for us to better understand how constitutions can best promote liberal democratic goals, or stable forms of government conducive to human flourishing.[10]

A second set of goals could be more internal to law and legal methods: a 'legal realist' canon, for instance, would aim to highlight contingency and choice as part of constitutional construction.[11]

But a third plausible purpose for a global canon of constitutional *thought* could be to construct a set of shared texts that everyone in the field of CCS 'ought to know',[12] so as to encourage both broader and deeper forms of contribution to the field in the future. As Hailbronner notes, 'a collective enterprise'

[8] Compare Rosalind Dixon, 'Toward a Realistic Comparative Constitutional Studies?' (2016) 64 *American Journal of Comparative Law* 193; Tushnet (n 3).
[9] Compare Hailbronner (n 2); Tushnet (n 3).
[10] Tushnet (n 3).
[11] ibid. See also Tushnet, Chapter 3.
[12] Compare George Conyne, 'Review: The Canon of American Legal Thought by David Kennedy and William W Fisher' (2008) 42 *Journal of American Studies* 372.

such as CCS 'requires that there be some shared understandings among those participating in it, and a canon can help to furnish these'.[13]

To serve this function, a global canon of constitutional thought must achieve one key aim: it must reduce the 'transaction costs' associated with any serious scholarly attempt to contribute to the field of CCS by established scholars working in closely related fields (e.g. domestic constitutional law or international human rights law)[14] ('new' scholars) or early-career scholars at the beginning of an academic career.[15] Or in Hailbronner's less Chicago-inflected language: it must 'introduce key concepts or ideas without which other texts cannot be properly understood or which are at least particularly helpful in understanding other texts'.[16]

To achieve this, it must also be reasonably comprehensive *and* accessible. New and early-career scholars must be able to read and understand the canon relatively quickly, rather than spend months or years grappling with its basic contours. It thus cannot be large. If it is, it will tend to create new, rather than reduced, barriers to entry to the field, and thus end up defeating rather than advancing its aims.

Traditionally, one way the field has achieved this was by having a quite narrow geographic scope, or by focusing on constitutional ideas emanating from the 'Global North'.[17]

But this is both an exclusionary and misleading way in which to construct the field of comparative constitutional studies: it excludes the voices and perspectives of those living and working in the Global South and misses the important perspectives they may have as to the full range of comparative constitutional

[13] Hailbronner (n 2). There are, of course, also other sources of shared understanding that do not rely on this same idea of a canon. Research handbooks are one leading example: see, e.g., Mark Tushnet, Thomas Fleiner, and Cheryl Saunders (eds), *Routledge Handbook of Constitutional Law* (Routledge, 2013); Michael Rosenfeld and András Sajó (eds), *The Oxford Handbook of Comparative Constitutional Law* (Oxford University Press, 2012). For my own contributions to this literature, see also, e.g., Tom Ginsburg and Rosalind Dixon (eds), *Comparative Constitutional Law* (Edward Elgar, 2011); Erin F. Delaney and Rosalind Dixon (eds), *Comparative Judicial Review* (Edward Elgar, 2018).

[14] On the value of a global constitutional canon in promoting dialogue with international human rights law in particular, see, e.g., Hailbronner (n 2), 259.

[15] Hailbronner (n 2), in fact suggests that the aims should be seen as more closely related, and that we should construct our shared body of knowledge in the light of shared normative commitments, albeit with parallel attention to the idea of 'an anti-canon'. I am sympathetic to that idea, but take a thinner, more agnostic view of the substantive commitments of the field and thus do not (need to) make the same distinction.

[16] ibid 257.

[17] See Daniel Bonilla Maldonado, 'Introduction: Toward a Constitutional Review of the Global South' in Daniel Bonilla Maldonado (ed.), *Constitutionalism of the Global South: The Activist Tribunals of India, South Africa and Colombia* (Cambridge University Press, 2013) 1. Philip Dann, https://www.semanticscholar.org/paper/Southern-turn%2C-Northern-implications%3A-rethinking-of-Dann/dda89e61a5460deebdc781a91ffe625f9982bc2e

practices and experiences.[18] And it is one reason many, including myself, have reservations about any canons project, even one that is designed with a view to overcoming these kinds of bias.

Any defensible approach to a modern canon, therefore, must be explicitly based on criteria for narrowing the scope of the canon that are not premised on this kind of Anglo-American or continental heritage, but instead on *conceptual* criteria that are capable of generating a truly balanced and pluralist global constitutional canon.[19]

My suggestion, however, is that we should overlay this approach with substantive criteria for judgements about importance, which are based on: (i) whether a text is well known to large numbers of constitutional lawyers and/or scholars; and (ii) influential on global constitutional practice and/or thinking, or else reflective of broader global currents in constitutional development or thought.

These criteria are similar to those adopted by David Kennedy and Terry Fisher in *The Canon of American Legal Thought*.[20] In constructing the *American Canon*, Kennedy and Fisher aimed to identify 'important works of legal scholarship … with which every law teacher should be familiar'.[21] And they relied heavily on a process of peer review, which aimed to identify those scholarly works that were best known to legal scholars (publicity/knowledge), and that certain legal scholars regarded as 'important', 'innovative', and influential.[22] The key difference is that Kennedy and Fisher give greater priority to methodological innovation than I think is appropriate or feasible at this stage of development for the field of CCS.[23]

A. Definitions

The first criterion is one of publicity or 'knowledge'—i.e. that a work is well known to a large number of lawyers or scholars. Knowledge of this kind will depend on a range of factors, including most notably how easy it is to access it

[18] On the field, and the relevance to it of the Global South critique, see, e.g., Hirschl (n 4).

[19] On the pluralism challenge, see especially Hailbronner (n 2), 263–264 ('Asking what the canonical texts in our disciplines are represents … [an] effort to address the tension between difference and universalism').

[20] Kennedy and Fisher (n 7).

[21] ibid 13.

[22] ibid 13–14.

[23] See n 40. Note that compared to this canons project, Fisher and Kennedy also relied on a stronger norm of peer review, or the views of a larger numbers of participants in the field, as compared to asking leading scholars to identify the canon within their particular area of expertise or interest.

online or otherwise, and if it is published (either in the original version or in translation) in a language that other lawyers and scholars can read.

But it may also depend on the degree to which secondary commentary engages with these primary texts: some constitutions, and constitutional decisions, are more likely than others to feature in social media posts and discussions, field blogs, and scholarly articles. Some texts are also more likely to be included in reading lists, or casebooks, in ways that affect the knowledge of those texts among the next generation of lawyers and scholars. Case books in particular may also be especially significant in this context.[24]

When editing a casebook, scholars will often have certain ideas or dynamics in mind that they wish to highlight as important in the field, paired with an awareness of multiple different examples that could be used to illustrate those dynamics. Their choices about which examples to include will also often be influenced by a desire to include a *mix* of examples that include both well-known cases that are highly accessible to students and less well-known examples, which involve a greater investment of time to understand fully, but which are drawn from a variety of different constitutional systems and contexts. These choices, therefore, will also tend both to cement the status of existing canonical examples and help construct new ones—by privileging some 'non-usual suspects' above others for inclusion.

The second criterion for canonicity is importance, judged either by reference to a text's *influence*, or the degree to which it is representative or '*prototypical*' of broader constitutional developments or ideas.[25]

The influence of a text may be either positive or negative: it will be 'positive' where others are persuaded of the normative appeal of its central features or claims, and 'negative' where lawyers elsewhere, or at later time periods, actively consider a text, but then choose to reject it as offering potential solutions to a similar legal problem. There might also be cases in which the reception of a text is more mixed, or changes with intervening developments.

Both positive and negative influence may also vary in intensity: weak forms of influence will generally involve a form of 'dialogic' engagement, or consideration of a canonical text as a form of foil or provocation; whereas stronger forms of influence may involve either convergence or 'aversive' reactions that involve the adoption of the exact opposite approach to that suggested by a canonical text.[26] However, a key premise of the project is that if a text exerts a

[24] See Tushnet (n 10).

[25] Compare Hirschl (n 4).

[26] Vicki Jackson, *Constitutional Engagement in a Transnational Era* (Oxford University Press, 2013); Richard Primus, 'A Brooding Omnipresence: Totalitarianism in Postwar Constitutional Thought' (1996) 106 *Yale Law Journal* 423; Kim Lane Scheppele, 'Aspirational and Aversive Constitutionalism: The Case

strong and negative influence this will be sufficient to take it outside the scope of the canon, and give it what Jamal Greene has called 'anti-canonical' as opposed to canonical status.[27]

The influence of text may also be explicit or implicit in nature. Often, texts that meet the requirements for canonicity will also be highly cited in other constitutional courts, and scholarly contexts: knowledge tends to beget citation, and citation knowledge.[28] Similarly, citation tends to promote readership and influence, and influence citation. This is one reason many current measures of research 'impact' use citations as a key indicator.[29]

But citation is not synonymous with influence.[30] A text may be cited because it is the first to make a certain point, or address a question, but still lack any real causal effect or influence on subsequent thinking and practice. It may subsequently be proven wrong. Or it may provide a response to, or an explanation of, a phenomenon or question that later scholars find either unpersuasive or uninteresting.

Conversely, a text may contribute to the development of concepts that themselves become so canonical that those ideas come to replace the original work in the broader legal consciousness. This, in part, is what Jack Balkin and Sandy Levinson mean by the idea of the 'deep canon' in constitutional law—i.e. the set of arguments, problems and approaches, narratives, and examples that define our collective 'ways of thinking, talking and arguing' but that are not necessarily associated closely with any single canonical work.[31] Often, the best indication of this will be if ideas are mentioned *without* any form of direct citation to any specific scholarly work, or even not mentioned at all—because the idea has become so well known that it is no longer seen as necessary to make explicit reference to it.[32] Citation alone, therefore, is not necessarily a sufficient proxy for substantive influence.[33]

for Studying Cross-Constitutional Influence Through Negative Models' (1993) 1 *International Journal of Constitutional Law* 296.

[27] Jamal Greene, 'The Anticanon' (2011) 125 *Harvard Law Review* 379.

[28] See, e.g., Gunther Eysenbach, 'Can Tweets Predict Citations? Metrics of Social Impact Based on Twitter and Correlation with Traditional Metrics of Scientific Impact' (2011) 13 *Journal of Medical Internet Research* e123.

[29] See, e.g., Dag W. Aksnes, Liv Langfeldt, and Paul Wouters, 'Citations, Citation Indicators, and Research Quality: An Overview of Basic Concepts and Theories' (2019) *Sage Open*, https://journals.sagepub.com/doi/full/10.1177/2158244019829575#articleCitationDownloadContainer; Ludo Waltman, 'A Review of the Literature on Citation Impact Indicators' (2016) 10 *Journal of Infometrics* 364.

[30] Compare Hailbronner (n 2), 252.

[31] Balkin and Levinson (n 2), 984–994.

[32] I am indebted to Mark Tushnet for this point.

[33] Compare Kennedy and Fisher (n 7), 13 ('Although citation frequency is one useful measure of significance, we have not relied heavily on it in making our selections. Citation fashions change, and citation practices travel in packs. Most legal citation is not directed at methodological precursors').

A text may likewise be canonical because it is *representative* of a broader set of ideas or developments in comparative constitutional law.[34] Here, canonicity will also depend on a twofold judgement about the significance of a certain category of ideas or models within comparative constitutionalism, and the degree to which a specific text is a good illustration or example of those ideas or models.

In many cases, this will also imply an understanding that a specific text represents a *successful* instantiation of a broader constitutional model of set of ideas, or at least one that is not patently a sham, pretextual, or abusive in nature, or clear failure in terms of substantive constitutional implementation.[35]

Judgements about importance, therefore, are ultimately closely linked to substantive accounts of the aims of CCS as a field. As Tushnet notes, one view of the canon is underpinned by liberal democratic commitments, albeit commitments that can be understood in more or less classical, neoliberal or what I have called (with Richard Holden) 'democratic liberal' terms.[36] But another takes a more external or realist view, focused on understanding how constitutional politics shapes constitutional law, or how legal moves are made or play out in ways that support different constitutional outcomes. Which viewpoint one adopts—or whether one takes a more eclectic view of the field—will also have an important impact on the texts we judge to be significant and normatively attractive examples within the field. In some theories, a text may be viewed as canonical in status, whereas in others it may be viewed as anti-canonical simply because of the normative commitments it embodies.

There is also an interesting point here about the relationship between different accounts of the field and the idea of the 'anti-canon'. Given this variety of starting points, a text could be viewed by some within the field as canonical in status, and by others as reflecting normative underpinnings that make it anti-canonical in status. (Think of how democratic liberals, as compared to classical or neoliberal scholars, might view certain far-ranging social rights decisions such as the *IDP* case in Colombia, or *Grootboom* in South Africa, or the participatory budgeting process in Brazil.[37])

[34] See, e.g., Conrado Hubner Mendes, 'A Global Constitution of Rights: The Ethics, The Mechanics and the Geopolitics of Comparative Constitutional Law' in Oscard Vilhena, Upendra Baxi, and Frans Vilijoen (eds), *Transformative Constitutionalism: Comparing the Apex Courts of Brazil, India and South Africa* (Pretoria University Law Press, 2013) 52.

[35] Compare David Law and Mila Versteeg, 'Sham Constitutions' (2013) 101 *California Law Review* 863; Rosalind Dixon and David Landau, '1989–2019: From Democratic to Abusive Constitutional Borrowing' (2019) 17 *International Journal of Constitutional Law* 489. I am indebted to Mark Tushnet for the latter understanding, developed in conversation at the February 2021 workshop on the project.

[36] Tushnet (n 11). See also Rosalind Dixon and Richard Holden, 'Fair Markets: Liberalism After COVID' (Unpublished manuscript, 2021).

[37] See discussion in Landau, Chapter 22; Young, Chapter 21, xxx, Chapter xxx.

Another possibility, however, is that both the canon and anti-canon should be understood as more closely connected and reflecting something like an overlapping consensus among different comprehensive theories about the *significance* of certain texts—i.e. agreement among scholars of different viewpoints not about the merits of a particular text, but its significance for debates about the proper boundaries or a democratic or institutional authority. The decision of the US Supreme Court in *Roe v. Wade* might be seen as a classic example of this: there is broad disagreement within the United States and elsewhere about its 'correctness' as a decision, but agreement that it is an important reference point in debates about the boundaries of a court's role and authority in a democracy.[38]

There will also be important questions about the time-horizon for these various judgments.

The idea of a canon implies some degree of stability, or long-term importance, for certain constitutional texts. But some constitutional texts may have limited immediate impact, but significant impact on future constitutional developments;[39] whereas others may have greater short-run impact but fail to endure as sufficiently influential to remain in the contemporary constitutional canon.

There may also be important differences between the time-horizon for judging questions of knowledge and influence. Knowledge in a field may be quite dynamic: it may shift within weeks or months, and certainly over one or two years. But influence tends to have a longer lag-time.[40] True influence may also increase or decrease with time: some ideas clearly have a large influence on the ideas of a given period, but then lose direct influence as new ideas take their place.[41] The fact that these new ideas may cite the older ones ensures their continuing relevance at the level of citation, and some indirect influence, but does not mean they have the same direct influence as in earlier periods.[42]

And what about the scope or audience for these judgements? Some constitutional texts may be leading texts within a legal system, or particular region, but have limited recognition outside it (i.e. part of a 'localized' canon). This could be because of language barriers that make certain works inaccessible to a broad

[38] See Rosalind Dixon, 'Responsive Judicial Review' (Unpublished manuscript, 2021).

[39] Contemporary work on environmental constitutionalism might be a leading example: see, e.g., Huneeus, Chapter 28.

[40] In a scholarly context, e.g., see Andrew B. Watson, 'Comparing Citations and Downloads for Individual Articles' (2009) 9 *Journal of Vision* 1.

[41] Compare Balkin and Levinson (n 2), 1006–1008 (noting the temporal dimensions to a canon, including the idea that 'cases and opinions become timeless … when the time is right').

[42] Compare Kennedy and Fisher (n 7), 14.

global audience, or a substantive focus that gives a text limited relevance to constitutional debates elsewhere. The 1917 Mexican Constitution might be one candidate in Latin America,[43] and in Australia, there are several cases—such as the *Engineers* case[44]—that are seen as foundational, but for reasons that are so specific to the Australian federal and interpretive context that they are little known beyond Australia, or at least the common law constitutional world.[45] But other texts may be far better known and seen as offering useful lessons on a truly global scale.[46]

Another question of audience will be whether a work is known by a broad audience, or only a quite specialized scholarly one. Some texts are well known to those across the field of global public law—including in sub-fields outside those where they were first developed or applied, and by scholars trained and working in other disciplines (a 'generalist' canon). Other texts tend to be known, cited, and influential within a given sub-field, but not more broadly (a 'specialized' canon). Some social rights decisions (*Grootboom*, for example) are well known to all comparative constitutional scholars, whereas there are important decisions of the Colombian and Brazilian courts that are well known only among comparative social rights lawyers and scholars.[47]

It may also be that a constitutional text should only be considered part of a *global* constitutional canon, in this context, if they enjoy a broad global and general public law audience. Otherwise, their claim is to be part of a distinctive localized or specialized, but not truly global, constitutional canon.

B. Causal Factors

This concern about circularity aside, what factors predict whether a constitutional text is likely to become part of the global constitutional canon? In this section, I highlight three factors as relevant, if not exclusive determinants of canonicity: (i) the degree to which a text is novel or innovative in its substance or approach; (ii) is drafted or created by leading lawyers or political actors; and (iii) has an 'inbuilt' sphere of influence or following. Each factor has some

[43] Alterio and Niembro, Chapter 8.

[44] *Amalgamated Society of Engineers v. Adelaide Steamship Co Ltd* (1920) 28 CLR 129.

[45] On their perceived significance in Australia, see, e.g., recent *Public Law Review* (vol. 31(1), 2020) and *Australian Law Journal* (vol. 94(11), 2020) symposia on the case's 100th anniversary.

[46] This is one reason Alterio and Niembro identify the Mexican Constitution of 1917 as canonical–i.e. its status as a reference point in twentieth century Latin American constitutional debates and developments.

[47] See, e.g., discussion in Young, Chapter 21 and Landau, Chapter 22, respectively.

relevance in explaining the canonical status of a text, including written constitutions, constitutional case law, or secondary constitutional sources. But it is also useful to consider the ways in which these factors may play out differently, in each of these contexts.

1. Innovation or Novelty

One of the important determinants of constitutional canonicity will be novelty or innovation, or the degree to which a particular text is the 'first' to develop or exemplify a particular (usually promising or successful) constitutional approach.

This emphasis on novelty may raise challenges in some contexts: if something is too new, there may not have been the opportunity for it to develop the enduring influence or importance necessary for canonical status. But it may be on a clear path to long-term significance, in ways that make it proto-canonical in status. Conversely, if something is too old, it may no longer be viewed as sufficiently 'novel' to be canonical. But that, too, may be a mistake. It may have been innovative *for its time* in ways that explain its influence on later constitutional developments, or status as a 'paradigm' or prototypical case within the field.[48]

But novelty is clearly one important predictor of canonicity for a text, especially where it involves a response to what are perceived as pressing social, political, or economic challenges,[49] and some degree of lawyerly *skill* in responding to that problem.

One of the interesting things Kennedy and Fisher found in constructing the *American Canon* was that almost all the pieces they separately identified for inclusion in the *Canon* were 'excellent' in terms of legal scholarly *craft*. The authors did not have to agree with the arguments or approach of the article to see this. Indeed, they often disagreed with them. But they could recognize the stylistic and analytic appeal of the relevant works, separate from their substantive approach or contribution. Each of the works nominated for inclusion in the *American Canon*, they suggest, were 'sophisticated and nuanced', and of the highest quality, quite apart from their innovation or substantive appeal.[50]

[48] Hirschl (n 4). See also Jed Rubenfeld, 'The Paradigm-Case Method' (2005) 115 *Yale Law Journal* 1977.

[49] This is evident, e.g., in how Hirschl has recently described and developed the idea of 'imaginative constitutionalism'. See Ran Hirschl, 'Constitutional Studies for 2030' (Speech delivered at the Global Summit, University of Texas at Austin, School of Law, 12 January 2021).

[50] Kennedy and Fisher (n 7), 13.

This will also tend to be true for written constitutional provisions, constitutional case law, and scholarship. The only difference may be that, for scholarship, there will be broader scope for novelty—at the level of diagnosing as well as offering solutions to relevant problems or adding new methodological tools and approaches that others can use to help address them. Scholarly works that combine attention to novel questions with new or innovative methods or approaches are especially likely to be noticed, and influential, in this context. They provide other scholars with a new (low transaction cost) framework for analysing a wide range of scholarly questions. They thus also increase the incentives for other scholars to read, cite, and engage with their work, as part of their own scholarly agenda.[51]

In the *American Canon*, Kennedy and Fisher in fact suggest that 'methodological innovation' is necessary for a work to be included in the *Canon*: their understanding of the *Canon* is that it aims to 'collec[t] moments *of methodological innovation* that have left lasting traces in the legal reasoning practices of American lawyers and judges'.[52] In global public law, however, I would suggest that methodological innovation helps predict canonical status, but is not definitional of or necessary to it: the field is too young, and there have been too few discrete methodological interventions, for methodology alone to be defining in this way.[53]

2. Reputation and Skill

Another factor will be the reputation and skill of the author of a text. The *skill* of an author will influence their capacity for successful innovation; and their *reputation* the chances that others pay attention to that innovation. Lawyers who are both well known and respected, therefore, will be more likely to produce canonical texts than their lesser known, less well-respected peers.

Of course, legal reputation and skill are not always perfectly correlated in this way: being well known in the legal profession is in part the product of skill, but also successful marketing and a significant degree of luck, or contingency. Some lawyers may be well known without being highly skilled, and some highly skilled lawyers may work in relative obscurity.

[51] Compare ibid (suggesting that each work in the Canon 'was methodologically innovative, and the innovations of each gave rise to further productive work').

[52] ibid (emphasis added).

[53] Otherwise, one might think there are only a very small number of works that could be candidates for inclusion in the canon: see, e.g., Vicki Jackson, *Constitutional Engagement in a Transnational Era* (Oxford University Press, 2013); Hirschl (n 4). Compare Hailbronner (n 2), 265 (suggesting that a 'final and only subsidiary factor to consider would be judicial engagement with core questions of methodology that are at the heart of comparative constitutional law and/or human rights scholarship').

Reputation is also likely to be more important in some contexts than in others. For constitutional scholarship, authorship will be extremely important. In principle, all scholars should have an equal chance of producing a work that gains recognition as part of the global constitutional canon—at least if we adjust for the quality and quantity of a scholar's output. But, in practice, there are several reasons to think there may be greater path-dependence to this process: well-known authors may find it easier to publish in high-quality journals, and thus gain attention to their work. Younger scholars are likely to find it more rewarding if they engage with their work, as the basis for debate or scholarly exchange, than if they exchange with lesser-known scholars. And their reputation may affect the degree to which the field judges it 'obligatory' versus 'optional' to cite their work, when working at the margins of the same area. We might therefore expect a form of 'author spill-over effect': authors who have produced highly influential or even canonical work are more likely to be seen as candidates to produce further additions to the canon.[54]

For case law, authorship will likewise be important in many, but not all, jurisdictions. Many courts in both the common law and civilian traditions have a long tradition of signed opinions, which give prominence to particular judges as authors. Consistent with this, there are also judges in these systems who develop a reputation—as leading or even 'towering' judges[55]—that leads other judges to pay close attention to their opinions, even when they are not bound to do so. But some courts have a norm of issuing unsigned, unanimous opinions, which removes authorship as a factor driving the attention given to decisions.

For constitutional provisions, in contrast, the multi-member nature of the drafting process will often mean that individual 'authors' come to be seen as having limited significance. But that is also clearly not always true: the US framers are perhaps the leading example, but many Latin American or South Asian scholars might point to Alberdi or Ambedkar as falling into the same category of influential drafters.[56]

[54] The relationship between an author's general citation patterns and authorship of an especially high citation paper can be measured by comparing h and g indices: see 'Maximising the Impact of Academic Research', *LSW Impact Blog*, https://blogs.lse.ac.uk/impactofsocialsciences/the-handbook/chapter-3-key-measures-of-academic-influence/.

[55] See Rehan Abeyratne and Iddo Porat (eds), *Towering Judges: A Comparative Study of Constitutional Judges* (Cambridge University Press, 2021).

[56] See framer worship piece from US; Roberto Gargarella, *Latin American Constitutionalism, 1810–2010: The Engine Room of the Constitution* (Oxford University Press, 2013) 62ff (on Alberdi); Madhav Khosla, *India's Founding Moment: The Constitution of a Most Surprising Democracy* (Harvard University Press, 2020); Madhav Khosla, 'Marking Constitutional Traditions: The Law and Politics of Constitutional Implication in South Africa' in Tim Ginsburg and Aziz Z Huq (eds), *From Parchment to Practice: Implementing New Constitutions* (Cambridge University Press, 2020) 76 (on Ambedkar).

Authorship, however, will almost always be one important factor shaping the canonicity of a text, and it is a factor that introduces special concerns when it comes to the construction of a pluralist, inclusive form of constitutional canon. In some contexts, there simply will not be sufficient diversity in the authorship of constitutional norms to allow for the inclusion of texts by a diverse range of authors, including female-identifying authors. In others, there may be sufficient numbers of texts available, but unconscious biases may inflect our judgements about the significance of certain texts—based on the race or gender of the author.[57]

The best evidence suggests that there is limited gender bias in the peer review and editorial assessment of work by female as opposed to male scholars.[58] But there may still be a tendency for scholars to attribute greater *importance* to the work of male scholars. This is often described as the 'Matthew effect'—i.e. the tendency for 'men's research [to be] viewed as the most central and important in a field'.[59]

Individual reviewers may also contribute to this effect, even without suffering any form of individual conscious or unconscious bias: often, scholars may answer questions about importance by reference to what they think other leading thinkers in the field are likely to consider important.[60] Unless those constructing a canon are explicitly invited or think to correct for this, this may also mean that processes of peer review tend to increase the effects of various sources of implicit bias in our judgements about 'importance' and 'influence' in a field.

3. Inbuilt Influence or Following

A final factor will be the pre-existing community of influence for a given text. In a scholarly context, the chances of a work being judged canonical will depend in no small part on the ingoing size and power of a particular legal subfield: the field cannot be so densely populated that novelty is impossible. But,

[57] This, of course, has been one of the major sources of criticism of the canon in the liberal arts, in addition to critiques based on colonial influence: for discussion, see, e.g., Balkin and Levinson (n 2), 1015–1016.

[58] David Card et al., 'Are Referees and Editors in Economics Gender Neutral?' (NBER Working Paper No. 25967, June 2019), http://papers.nber.org/tmp/99058-w25967.pdf.

[59] Michelle L. Dion, Jane Lawrence Sumner, and Sara McLaughlin Mitchel, 'Gendered Citation Patterns across Political Science and Social Science Methodology Fields' (2018) 26 *Political Analysis* 312. Dixon and Versteeg, https://academic.oup.com/icon/article/21/2/407/7187073

[60] Compare Kennedy and Fisher (n 7), 13 ('our sense is that these are the articles legal scholars would name if asked to list the articles they imagined a majority of their colleagues would also name as canonical'); Balkin and Levinson (n 2), 979 ('Canonicity is not simply a matter of what one thinks important; it also a matter of what one thinks others think important').

equally, it cannot be too small for innovative work to attract a meaningful audience, or to exert meaningful influence.[61]

For constitutional provisions and case law, it will depend on the existence of pre-existing pathways for the 'migration' or transfer of innovative constitutional ideas.[62] Constitutional ideas 'travel' or migrate across national boundaries through a dense set of networks of political leaders, lawyers, judges, and scholars.[63] These networks are also influenced by geography, language, legal history, and regional ties and institutions, in ways that create very different pathways for influence for different ideas.

So, for example, ideas tend to travel within the former British Commonwealth based on a mix of colonial ties, shared language, and legal history—and an ongoing commitment to a common law legal system and parliamentary-based form of government.[64]

Ideas tend to 'travel' within Europe and Latin America, and even between the two, far more than in Asia—or between Asia and Latin America.[65] Many European and Latin American countries share important legal historical influences, and there is important 'traffic' between Europe and Latin America via linguistic and legal–scholarly communities within the Lusophone and Spanish-speaking world.[66] In each case, the European Union and Council of Europe, and the Organization of American States (OAS) and Inter-American Human Rights System, also serve as pathways for the influence of certain (especially rights-based) constitutional ideas beyond national boundaries.

The same is true for Africa, and the relationship between Africa and French-speaking Europe. Ideas frequently travel between France and French-speaking Africa, and among French-speaking African countries, based on a common language, legal history, and a common set of legal and political traditions—and, often, the concerted efforts of the French government. Within Africa, there is

[61] This is arguably a challenge facing all scholars working in the field of CCS, but also scholars in some sub-fields more than others.

[62] See Sujit Choudhry (ed.), *The Migration of Constitutional Ideas* (Oxford University Press, 2007).

[63] See Anne-Marie Slaughter, 'Judicial Globalization' (1999) 40 *Virginia Journal of International Law* 1103; Laurence R. Helfer and Anne-Marie Slaughter, 'Toward a Theory of Effective Supranational Adjudication' (1997) 107 *Yale Law Journal* 273.

[64] See Stephen Gardbaum, *The New Commonwealth Model of Constitutionalism: Theory and Practice* (Cambridge University Press, 2013).

[65] See, e.g., [think the cite is inrto to my and TR SA edited book – or tom and In my edited Latin America book – need to check].

[66] This, e.g., is one potential reason explaining the influence of the 1917 Mexican Constitution within Latin America, and therefore its claim to canonical status. See Ana Michaela Aletrio and Roberto Niembro, 'A Critical View of the 100-Year-Old Mexican Constitution' in Mark A. Graber, Sanford Levinson, and Mark Tushnet (eds), *Constitutional Democracy in Crisis?* (Oxford University Press, 2018). Though note there are also dangers to this kind of regional influence metric in any attempt to construct a post or non-colonial form of constitutional canon.

also an increasingly dense set of regional institutions, under the auspices of the African Union, that encourage the sharing and diffusion of constitutional ideas and norms between English- and French-speaking Africa.[67]

In Asia, in contrast, there are important differences between countries influenced by the common law versus civilian tradition, or Germany versus the United States or the UK.[68] There are also greater linguistic differences, or barriers between countries, and fewer regional institutions with a democratic constitutional mandate or focus.[69]

This is one reason we should be cautious about thinking that the canon we have produced *in English* is in fact a truly global, rather than partial and incomplete form of, transnational constitutional canon. It may be that a canon does quite well in reflecting European and Latin American, and even some South African and Asian, texts and ideas, but does less well in capturing developments in Francophone and Saharan Africa and other parts of Asia.[70]

That may change, over time, as English becomes more of a global lingua franca.[71] But, for now, it remains only one of several leading global languages, and hence a canon constructed in English may tend to privilege works written in or translated into English.

III. Conclusion

The idea of a global constitutional canon has obvious advantages: a canon of this kind could help broaden and deepen the field of comparative constitutional studies, and thereby expand the capacity of the field to answer some of the most pressing social, economic, and political challenges of our time. There are also a range of ways to define the scope of a global constitutional canon. One especially promising approach is to focus on constitutional texts that are broadly known among comparative constitutional scholars, and influential on comparative constitutional practices.

But the idea of a global constitutional canon also has equally clear dangers: like any canon, it threatens to reproduce existing hierarchies and power

[67] 'African Human Rights System', *International Justice Resource Center*, https://ijrcenter.org/regional/african/.

[68] See Po Jen Yap, *Constitutional Dialogue in Common Law Asia* (Oxford University Press, 2015).

[69] ASEAN, e.g., has been criticized for lacking such a focus. See, e.g., Jorn Dosch, 'ASEAN's Reluctant Liberal Turn and the Thorny Road to Democratic Promotion' (2008) 21 *Pacific Law Review* 527.

[70] Two important exceptions are Fessha, Chapter 12 and Neo, Chapter 17 on freedom of religion (discussing the *Linah Joy* case).

[71] Philippe Van Parijs, 'Tackling the Anglophones' Free Ride: Fair Linguistic Cooperation with a Global Lingua Franca' (2007) 20 *AILA Review* 72.

structures in global governance arrangements—by privileging the constitutional texts of the Global North, or a small subset of constitutional systems deemed sufficiently interesting and worthy of attention by scholars working in or trained in the Global North.

The most logical response to this danger is to expand and pluralize the idea of the canon.

But doing so also carries its own dangers: it risks increasing, rather than decreasing, the (transaction) costs associated with new entry to the field, and thereby deterring rather than encouraging new voices and contributions to the field. To serve its aim, of expanding the field itself, this chapter therefore argues that the idea of a global canon of constitutional thought ultimately needs to be defined quite narrowly and stringently—to include only those works that constitute truly mandatory background reading for new and early-career scholars wishing to enter the field.

At the same time, a narrow 'canon' of this kind could be complemented by a broader form of *quasi-constitutional canon*, which is more pluralistic, and includes a wider range of significant constitutional texts, and is inherently more provisional, revisable, or 'unsettled' in scope.[72]

In this two-track model, knowledge of the actual canon could be treated as close to mandatory background knowledge for any serious attempt to contribute to the field, whereas the quasi-canon would have a more optional and context-dependent character. Both its content and force (i.e. demand for attention or citation) would depend on the relevant jurisdiction, sub-field, and topic on which an author is writing.

In this sense, it would resemble the approach to the global canon suggested by Hailbronner in her early work on the topic—i.e. a canon that 'make[s] room for diversity with regard to its subject matter, the authors' ideological position and jurisdictional origin'.[73] But it would treat these as criteria that primarily inform and guide a secondary layer of widely shared, but not truly mandatory, background knowledge in the field.[74]

Scholarship that relied on a quasi-canon of this kind would clearly have dangers: it could create a distinctly non-dialogic form of constitutional scholarship, which bypassed meaningful scholarly exchange across countries,

[72] Compare O'Regan, Chapter 24 (on provisional canon); Landau, Chapter 22 (on the 'unsettled' canon).

[73] Hailbronner (n 2), 263–264.

[74] It is, is this sense, consistent with the approach adopted by Erin Delaney and myself in assembling the works included in *Comparative Judicial Review*: Delaney and Dixon (n 13). As we note in the introduction, our aims in this context were to embrace 'jurisdictional and methodological pluralism', even while providing a canon-like introduction to the field of comparative judicial review.

fields, and topics. The answer to this danger, however, cannot be to create an unwieldly global canon, which creates its own barriers to entry to and dialogue in the field. Rather, it must be to embrace a form of overlapping, provisional approach to comparative constitutional study, which acknowledges the pluralism and porousness inherent in both the idea of quasi-global canon and a truly global approach to comparative constitutional studies.[75]

This might also ultimately be one way in which to view the value of the canons project itself.

Rather than seeing the project as designed to produce a stable and authoritative list of texts, which can serve as an introduction to the field for new and emerging comparative scholars, the project could be viewed as a discursive exercise—designed to encourage debate within the field our own methodological and substantive commitments and assumptions. If that were the case, it would then matter less which texts were ultimately included in a list of canonical or anti-canonical texts, than whether we engaged in vigorous dialogue as a scholarly community in generating that list—and in discussing it with readers. And on that criteria, the project already seems well on the way to success.[76]

[75] Rosalind Dixon, 'Toward a Realistic Comparative Constitutional Studies?' (2016) 64 *American Journal of Comparative Law* 193.

[76] Chapters, e.g., were workshopped first in Santiago in June 2019, then again via intensive zoom workshops in February 2021.

3

The Jurisprudences of Canons of Comparative Constitutional Law

Mark Tushnet[*]

I. Introduction: Legal Canons and Their Jurisprudence(s)

In *The Ages of American Law*, Grant Gilmore described a casebook on credit transactions compiled by Wesley Sturges as consisting of "the most absurd cases, along with the most idiotic law review comments, which he had been able to find."[1] As Gilmore presented it, Sturges developed the materials to counter a formalist jurisprudence that arranged seemingly disparate doctrines and cases into a coherent and rationally defensible unity. On this view, Sturges's casebook was intended as a *counter*-canon, an alternative non-formalist (Legal Realist) view of the law of credit transactions.[2]

When a field has a canon, the canonical materials are what anyone who purports to be a participant in the field's intellectual life should know. Before identifying a canon, though, we have to identify the field: The canon for literature is, of course, different from the canon for the history of science, and the canon for English literature is different from the canon for world literature. We might think that we could define the field arbitrarily—what we happen to be interested in. That, though, rapidly proves unsatisfactory. Is "The Odyssey" in translation to be considered for inclusion in the field of English literature? After all, you can't fully understand James Joyce's "Ulysses" without understanding "The Odyssey." Similarly, is the Stalin Constitution of 1937 to be considered for inclusion in the field of comparative constitutional law other than as an example of something *not* within the field, as something like a component of an anticanon?

* William Nelson Cromwell Professor of Law emeritus, Harvard Law School.

1 Grant Gilmore, *The Ages of American Law* (2nd edn. Yale UP 2014), 72–73.

2 A legal counter-canon offers an alternative to an existing canon; a legal anticanon assumes the existence of a canon and provides materials from within the field that are to be rejected because they are inconsistent with the normative positions asserted in the canonical texts.

Mark Tushnet, *The Jurisprudences of Canons of Comparative Constitutional Law* In: *Global Canons in an Age of Contestation.* Edited by: Sujit Choudhry, Michaela Hailbronner, and Mattias Kumm, Oxford University Press.
 DOI: 10.1093/9780191956942.003.0003

Another example from law helps move the inquiry forward. Is the fellow-servant rule part of the canon of contract law because it involves the liability of one contracting party to another, or part of the canon of tort law because it involves liability for harms caused by a wrongful act? Of course, the fellow-servant rule could be part of both canons. When considered in the canon of contract law, though, it will be related to other rules dealing with the allocation of risks between contracting parties; when considered in the canon of tort law, it will be related to other rules such as the last-clear-chance rule asking which of the parties involved in the harmful action had the better opportunity to prevent the harm.

These examples show that defining the field of interest requires some *theoretical* commitment. For law and its subfields, the relevant theory is a theory of law—a jurisprudence of some sort. Proponents of competing jurisprudences offer competing canons until for sociological reasons one canon becomes hegemonic, leaving alternative canons in the hands of scholars who find themselves at the field's margins.

In this chapter, I explore several candidate jurisprudences that might shape a canon of comparative constitutional law. The first candidate defines the field as something akin to "contemporary liberal democratic moral and political theory as applied to basic institutions of government"—what David Landau and Rosalind Dixon call the "democratic core."[3] The second candidate defines the field somewhat more broadly as "applied political theory for achieving human flourishing."

The canons generated by these two definitions will include what Jamal Greene calls "anti-canonical" examples.[4] These are examples, like the Stalin constitution, of institutional arrangements, doctrines, and cases that are inconsistent with liberal democratic theory and human flourishing. In both, some attention is paid to the proposition that context matters—or, to put it more jurisprudentially, that liberal democratic theory accommodates different specifications of its core principles (but also rules out some possibilities as inconsistent with those principles).

A third candidate places even more emphasis on context, and specifically upon the political contexts in which constitutions are located.[5] At least so far, though, the canon of politically oriented comparative constitutional

[3] David Landau & Rosalind Dixon, 'Abusive Judicial Review' [2019] 53 UC Davis L Rev 1313.

[4] Jamal Greene, 'The Anti-Canon' [2011] 125 Harv L Rev 379.

[5] We can understand this canon as related to Ran Hirschl's call for a transformation from comparative constitutional law to comparative constitutional studies. See Ran Hirschl, 'From Comparative Constitutional Law to Comparative Constitutional Studies' [2013] 11 Int'l Const'l L 1.

law focuses mostly on variations within liberal constitutional orders, sometimes with the constitutional arrangements of authoritarian nations used as anticanonical.

The final candidate is the jurisprudence driving Sturges's casebook, American Legal Realism. Here, the normative content is less obvious, but probably should be understood as a jurisprudence aimed at deflating claims about how much law (here, constitutional law) can do to advance liberal democratic goals and human flourishing. What is included here might be understood as a *counter*-canon as distinct from an anticanon as described above.

The remainder of this chapter provides examples of how, guided by their respective jurisprudences, we can choose what to include in each of these canons. The examples follow the conventional distinction between rights and structures, but in different proportions and, sometimes, with different facets of rights and, especially, structures receiving greater emphasis. Further, I use some specific topics in more than one canon to show that the jurisprudences associated with each canon can claim to approach comprehensiveness in scope. Finally, I use topics rather than individual cases or doctrines because choices at that level of specificity depend upon the audiences for the materials: It is one thing to develop a list of one hundred things you ought to know about comparative constitutional law to be included in an academic article, and another to develop a set of teaching materials.

II. A Canon for Liberal Democratic Comparative Constitutional Law

Coursebooks and readers are traditional formats for presenting a canon. Conveniently, we already have a good example of a coursebook treating comparative constitutional law as an exercise in applied liberal democratic theory. That theory provides the organizing principle of the Dorsen et al. coursebook on "Comparative Constitutionalism" (the use of the second word signals the work's commitment to the liberal-democracy paradigm).[6] Roughly one-third of that work deals with constitutional foundations and structures, two-thirds with rights. With respect to both parts, the approach is guided by the question, How are different arrangements compatible with the premises of liberal democracy as a theory of politics?

[6] Norman Dorsen et al., *Comparative Constitutionalism* (3rd edn, West Academic Publishing 2016).

Moving beyond the particular choices made by that work's authors, we can describe the canon's components more generally. The materials in this canon would be presented in strongly normative terms. Within the canon, some arrangements and decisions are "good" because they are compatible with liberal democratic theory, others bad because they are incompatible. And, again within this canon, structured proportionality provides the best method to translate liberal democracy into legal doctrine because it takes all relevant considerations into account, whereas more categorical approaches expressly exclude from judicial attention some relevant considerations.[7]

Seen in this way, the canon is not really "about" comparative constitutional law. Rather, materials from a number of jurisdictions provide grist for the mill of liberal democratic theory.[8] A Canadian case about assisted suicide might provide better insights than a U.S. or a Colombian case into the reasons liberals have for supporting or opposing laws regulating the practice, and so the Canadian case would be included in the canon. For the purpose of exploring the idea of human dignity, the French case dealing with so-called "dwarf-tossing" might be as good as an Israeli case dealing with the infliction of degrading treatment during interrogation.

A truly comparative note can be sounded, though, within the liberal-democracy canon. We identify the principles of liberal democracy at a reasonably high level of abstraction: free expression, an independent judiciary, adherence to the rule of law. Constitutional law brings these principles to ground through more concrete specifications of their meanings in particular contexts: campaign finance regulations, for example, or methods of judicial selection and removal.[9] The canon of liberal democracy would include materials from different jurisdictions specifying the abstract principles in different ways. Some might be outside the bounds of reasonable specifications of the abstract principle, but others would show that liberal democracy accommodates a range of reasonable specifications. With respect to the latter, the canon would look for explanations of differences in the social or historical contexts of the different liberal democracies.

[7] U.S. cases about free expression and affirmative action/positive discrimination might be set against proportionality-based cases on those topics from one of several jurisdictions.

[8] Many books on the substance of liberal-democracy political and constitutional theory use examples drawn from Canadian, U.S., and U.K. cases to explicate the author's theory of liberal democracy. Authors choose the cases just as they use exemplary political practices—to illustrate their more general theses. That is basically how the canon of liberal democracy treats the materials it includes.

[9] Drawing on the canon law of the Roman Catholic Church, scholars sometimes refer to a specification as a *determinatio*.

Consider some examples from the constitutional law of free expression. Some varying forms of campaign finance regulation might be suitable vehicles for exposing the range of reasonable alternatives within liberal democracy, with the U.S. approach that provides substantial immunity from regulation testing the limits of reasonableness. Contextual matters would appear close to the surface in examining variations in the regulation of hate speech, in so-called "memory laws," and in the regulation of political parties in the service of militant democracy.

The canon of liberal democracy would include materials on the regulation of public demonstrations. Some liberal democracies regulate such demonstrations more heavily than do others, using content-neutral standards for regulation such as the size, time, and location of the demonstration. The canon could contrast relatively loose restrictions (common in the United States) with more stringent ones (as occur in many other liberal democracies) and, important as well, with facially neutral regulations gerrymandered to inhibit protests against government policies.[10]

I forgo discussion of equality within the canon of liberal democracy. The general contours of equality's treatment would be the same as those for freedom of expression and other rights: identifying a range of reasonable specifications (for example, differences in the degree to which affirmative action/positive discrimination is constitutionally acceptable or mandated), seeking explanations for choices within that range, and determining what is outside the bounds of reasonable specification.

A word about economic rights: Historically, such rights weren't part of the democratic core, as the conventional label "second-generation rights" indicates. One question would be whether such rights should be part of the canon of liberal democracy. Another might be how those rights *are* part of the canon because of their relation to other rights that are unquestionably within the democratic core. Here, one might point to the Indian cases using the justiciable right to life as the textual hook for importing into the judicially enforceable domain rights that are presented in the constitution as directive principles of public policy, or the Indian "street dwellers" case to show the connection between economic rights and human dignity.

And, finally, in the domain of rights: How would the canon of liberal democracy present environmental rights, including the rights of nonhuman animals,

[10] A relatively recent Polish law giving priority to demonstrations that had traditionally occurred at an identified time and place, over new demonstrations there and then, is such a gerrymandered regulation.

and rights to cultural preservation, including linguistic rights? Again, one way would be to ask whether they should be part of this canon, or, relatedly, whether they can't be accommodated within a political theory centered on the promotion of *individual* (and human) liberty.

Problems of conflicts among constitutional rights (or implicating constitutionally inflected interests) would be occasions for discussing balancing or proportionality as a mode of analysis but also for exploring how context matters. Liberal democratic systems strike the balance between press freedom and privacy in varying ways, some favoring the former over the latter, others doing the opposite. The explanation for the variations almost certainly lies in contextual factors, some cultural or ideological as James Whitman has developed,[11] some institutional (such as the relative prevalence of responsible versus "yellow" journalism in a nation). And there's some possibility that the extreme approach taken in the United States, strongly preferring press freedom to privacy, might be treated as raising questions about where (and how) to set the limits on reasonable specifications.

On structural issues, the canon of liberal democracy would examine the ways in which federalism and centralization can be both liberty-enhancing and liberty-restricting, perhaps focusing on cultural variations (if any) between residents of different geographic units within the nation. Similarly with the choice between parliamentarism and presidentialism: The animating question would be, Under what circumstances are each liberty-enhancing and liberty-restricting?

Within the domain of structure, the canon of liberal democracy must also include materials examining the mechanisms for ensuring that federalism and the arrangement of powers on the national level are liberty-enhancing rather than liberty-restricting. The candidates for enforcement are Madisonian competition—"ambition countering ambition"—and judicial review. With respect to the former, the materials would raise questions about the efficacy of such competition in today's world (including the role of political parties, discussed in more detail in Section IV later). With respect to the latter, the materials would ask whether courts can reliably distinguish between liberty-enhancing and liberty-restricting arrangements.[12]

[11] James Whitman, 'The Two Western Cultures of Privacy: Dignity Versus Liberty' [2004] 113 Yale LJ 1151.

[12] e.g., on federalism one might include *Shelby County v. Holder*, 570 US 529 (2013), which invoked federalism concerns to block the implementation of what proponents presented as a liberty-enhancing exercise of national power. On other structural issues, one might include some cases holding constitutional amendments unconstitutional, such as the Colombian decision on civil service reform and the Indian decision on altering the judicial appointment process.

III. A Canon for Human Flourishing Comparative Constitutional Law

A great deal in the canon of human flourishing would overlap with the canon of liberal democracy because the liberties on which the latter focus are often components of human flourishing. Often, though, but not always: A canon of human flourishing would be more attentive to the distinction between liberty and license, for example. That distinction might give a different focus to materials on sexuality and sexually explicit published materials—and, it should be obvious, would bring into the canon views conventionally labeled conservative more easily than such views can be presented in the canon of liberal democracy.

Another shift in focus might accompany the presentation of the material on economic rights, which would be founded upon ideas about human flourishing rather than as aspects of liberty. Rights to cultural preservation fit comfortably within this canon. Environmental rights and (especially) the rights of nonhuman animals fit less comfortably. There are now materials available that could be used to raise questions about whether environmental protection is desirable solely because of its benefits to humans or rather is desirable for the sake of the environment itself.[13] And the recent inclusion of rights of nonhuman animals in constitutions allows one to question the normative defensibility of taking *human* flourishing as the canon's basis.

One important feature of this canon would be explicit consideration of how effective government is in delivering on its promises. One vehicle for doing so would expand upon the treatment of the government's structure by drawing attention to differences in functional capacity among the branches. Material on emergency power, for example, could deal with arguments that the executive branch can move more quickly and rely upon information that is both fast-changing and sometimes quite technical, than can either legislatures or courts. It could also explore the possibility that these functional differences might be diminished, or even overcome, by innovations within the legislature—through specialized standing committees, for example—and the courts. As to the latter, material on contemporary forms of what Abram Chayes called "public law litigation," such as public interest litigation in India, could be contrasted with Lon Fuller's arguments about "the forms and limits of adjudication."[14]

[13] To date, the most readily accessible such materials deal with granting standing to rivers and like features of the environment.

[14] Abram Chayes, 'The Role of the Judge in Public Law Litigation' [1976] 89 Harv LR 1281; Lon L. Fuller, The Forms and Limits of Adjudication' [1978] 92 Harv LR 353.

Economic rights might be considered under the heading of judicial capacity, with older arguments about the inability of courts effectively to order large-scale expenditures juxtaposed with newer arguments about iterative and weak-form constitutional review, for which there is already a limited purpose canon consisting of *Grootboom* and *Occupiers of 51 Olivia Road* from South Africa. And the "engagement" remedy developed in the latter case can be used to discuss the way in which some courts, including the Interamerican Court of Human Rights, have dealt with rights to cultural preservation.

Fourth-branch institutions supporting constitutional democracy, as the South African Constitution describes them, could be presented as institutions designed to give citizens confidence that their government is indeed working effectively. Descriptions of electoral management bodies, and cases arising from disputed elections, might be used here: For example, contrasting the results of electoral management bodies' and court decisions dealing with disputed presidential elections in Kenya in 2013 and 2017 might be a helpful case study. Similarly with anti-corruption efforts, with the *Glenister* case (on the merits) used to examine why anti-corruption agencies should sometimes be given constitutional status.

This canon's focus on institutional capacity presents the conflict between proportionality and categorical analysis in a different light from that offered in the canon of liberal democracy. In the canon of liberal democracy, proportionality is favored over categorical analysis because, at the level of application to the problem at hand, the former takes everything relevant into account, whereas the latter disregards some relevant matters. In the canon of human flourishing, attention shifts to a different level. Here, the relevant question is, Will courts promote human flourishing by sometimes adopting a categorical approach rather than always using proportionality analysis? The canon of human flourishing allows one to examine the possibility that the answer is Yes, because courts taken in the aggregate, composed of fallible human beings who will sometimes make mistakes in reaching all-things-considered conclusions within a proportionality framework, will actually do better for the society by screening out some considerations that are sometimes but not always truly relevant to reaching a sound conclusion.

On this matter, my preferred candidate for inclusion in the canon is hate speech regulation in the United States compared to other nations: The decentralized nature of hate speech enforcement in the United States makes it difficult for the Supreme Court to supervise enforcement to ensure that it is always proportionate; this counsels in favor of a rule strongly disfavoring hate speech regulation entirely. In other systems, enforcement is more highly centralized and the number of potential enforcers of hate speech laws is smaller, making it possible for high courts to review the vast majority of enforcement efforts to determine whether the regulation is proportionate in the circumstances.

IV. A Canon for Comparative Constitutional Law as Comparative Politics

In contrast to the preceding canons, a canon that treats comparative constitutional law with a focus on politics would probably give priority to structural issues over rights ones. The question that animates the choice of materials is (in various forms), What incentives do political actors—officials and voters—have to support the inclusion or interpretation of some provision in a constitution? And, though this is less clear to me, I suspect that the materials would be presented in a way that distinguishes importantly among constitutional systems on the basis of their party-based composition—from authoritarian single-party states to competitive authoritarian states (or dominant-party states) to multiparty states (in several forms) to two- to-four party states, on the theory that this dimension captures more variation in incentives than any other.

Topically this canon would present materials illustrating the "insurance" and "counterhegemonic preservation" theories about the establishment or expansion of constitutional review.[15] It could include materials on Hans Kelsen's explanation for the need for a constitutional court to adjudicate conflicts between executive and legislature in a party-political world, and illustrate that with the provisions for constitutional review in the French Constitutional Council and—more provocatively—with an account of the retrenchment of constitutional review in Hungary from an expansive, human-rights-based system to a more purely Kelsenian one.

Materials on justiciability might illustrate how courts can develop doctrines that help them *build* institutional capital (expansive standing rules for public interest litigation in India, for example). Other materials on justiciability could illustrate how judges *preserve* their institutional capital by considering the possibility that other political actors might retaliate against them if the judges

[15] One obvious difficulty here is that these are what would conventionally be called 'external' accounts of constitutional review's origins. No constitutional framer actually adverts to these theories in defending the creation of constitutional review, and no judge does so in interpreting a constitution in place. Still, it's not that difficult to imagine a presentation of *Marbury v. Madison*, 5 US (1 Cranch) 137 (1803) in its political context to illustrate the 'insurance' theories and *United Mizrahi Bank v. Migdal Cooperative Village*, CA 6821/93, (1995) 49(4) PD 221 (Isr. 1995) to illustrate counterhegemonic preservation.

overreach (materials on limitations on standing developed by judges themselves or as with truly Kelsenian courts, built into the design of the constitutional court).

Materials dealing with legislative–executive relations would, of course, have to treat modern parliamentary systems differently from presidential systems. For the former, the materials might include constitutional rules and cases dealing with the power of opposition parties.[16] It would be helpful, too, to have materials on the constitutional rules bearing on how prime ministers manage their own parties when they have a majority and how they manage coalitions when they don't. One might use excerpts from the British Cabinet Manual, for example, and constitutional provisions and cases dealing with the regulation of "aisle crossing," when parliamentarians shift their party allegiances in ways that either strengthen or weaken a coalition. Here, though, it would also be important to emphasize that constitutional law and scholars have relatively little to say about how these systems actually operate, compared to what political scientists have to say.

The organizing principle for materials on presidential systems would be Madison's proposition that "ambition must be made to counter ambition," and its varying effectiveness depending upon the nature of the party system.[17] Focusing on the concentration of responsibility in a chief executive and its diffusion among members of the legislature (and again attentive to the differences between parliamentary and presidential systems), the canon might include material on the distribution of authority to commit armed forces in international engagements and on the phenomenon, widely observed but not universal, of power flowing to the chief executive in times of emergency.[18]

Materials on fourth-branch institutions, discussed in Section III earlier, might also be included, at least for the purpose of showing how Madisonian mechanisms might not work well in some configurations of party power. The materials would also have to point out that, from a political incentives point of view, the mere fact that something doesn't work well doesn't give politicians or even citizens strong incentives to do something about it. For citizens, the reason lies in well-known collective action problems, which the materials would develop.

[16] See, e.g., David Fontana, 'Government in Opposition' [2009] 119 Yale LJ 548.

[17] See, e.g., Daryl J. Levinson & Richard H. Pildes, 'Separation of Parties, Not Powers' [2006] 119 Harv LR 2311.

[18] I think it worth noting that this canon's emphasis on political incentives would relegate to a secondary place the functional questions of information and expedition that are more prominently addressed in what I have called the canon of human flourishing.

Those collective action problems might also be included in the framework for dealing with rights questions in this canon. Put another way: *Carolene Products*' Footnote Four, interpreted through the lens of public choice theory, would provide that framework. Economic regulation would be the natural place to start, with scores of possible examples.[19] The constitutional law of equality fits readily into this framework, with the terminology of "discrete and insular minorities" interpreted—and queried—in public choice terms.[20] Finally, some aspects of the law of free expression can be framed, as John Hart Ely did, with reference to the incentives politicians have to *dis*favor certain kinds of speech.[21]

This canon would also have materials on the political economy of constitutional litigation, particularly rights-based litigation. A case like *Treatment Action Campaign* could be the vehicle for examining the roles of "support structures" and social movements in both generating litigation and making more legally plausible claims that otherwise might seem purely political. And material on right-to-medication litigation could be used to raise questions about the distributional impact of constitutional litigation.

This canon would also have to confront one puzzle. It provides an account of why politicians might want to create independent constitutional courts. That means that judges on those courts *could* interpret the constitutional with reference to public-choice questions. It does not tell us, though, why or when they *will* do so.

V. A Canon for Legal Realist Comparative Constitutional Law

Karl Llewellyn wrote that his survey of statutory decisions by numerous state supreme courts in the United States revealed that they used a relatively small number of what I call "argument forms"—Llewellyn's term was "describable ways"—to justify the results they reached. For him, "What is important is that

[19] My personal favorite among non-U.S. examples is a German decision holding unconstitutional a ban on selling chocolate-covered rice candies, justified on consumer-protection grounds but clearly the result of interest-group lobbying by chocolate-candy manufacturers. 53 BVerfGE 135 (1980), excerpted in Donald P. Kommers, *The Constitutional Jurisprudence of the Federal Republic of Germany* (2nd edn, Duke UP 1997), 279. The French 'dwarf-tossing' case mentioned earlier is another interesting example of the imposition of a majority's views about morally appropriate behavior on freely contracting parties, one group of which might face constrained economic opportunities.

[20] The most prominent 'querying' comes from Bruce A. Ackerman, 'Beyond Carolene Products' [1985] 98 Harv LR 713.

[21] To the extent that the canon seeks comprehensiveness, other aspects of free expression might be presented in the equality materials (hate speech, sexually explicit materials) or the economic regulation ones (commercial speech).

all 26 ways (plus a dozen others ...) are correct."[22] In Llewellyn's Legal Realist jurisprudence, a judicial opinion conformed to the law when it used the argument forms available within the court's legal system.

This jurisprudence has corrosive effects on the approaches taken to judicial decisions in the liberal-democracy and human-flourishing canons. The most obvious effect is that majority opinions and dissents are equally correct when, as will almost always be the case, they use available argument forms. One can occasionally find opinions that seem a bit incongruous, and they might be included in the Legal Realist canon.[23] So, for example, one might include *Texas v. Johnson*, a decision striking down a statutory prohibition on flag-burning as a means of political protest,[24] and raise questions about the propriety of Justice Rehnquist's quotation in full of a famous poem in his dissent, or the *DeShaney* case, about the state-action doctrine to raise similar questions about Justice Blackmun's opening words, "Poor Joshua."[25] Yet, the very fact that Supreme Court justices wrote these opinions suggests that what they did actually did deploy an available argument form (and the analyst's task is to identify what that form is).

These cases aside, in the Legal Realist canon dissents show that, whatever the liberal-democracy and human-flourishing canons might say about the moral or political-theory correctness of a decision, both outcomes are *legally* correct. That in turn strongly suggests that we can't count on law to achieve outcomes that are correct according to some theory about liberal democracy or human flourishing.

The Legal Realist approach might be helpful in comparative constitutional law by bringing to the fore the questions, What counts as an available argument form in this legal system, and would some form count as such in another legal system? Here, the canon might draw upon Duncan Kennedy's account of the three globalizations of law and legal thought.[26] For each of the three periods, the canon would use cases from several jurisdiction to show how they used the same argument forms—and how the repertoire of argument forms changed from one period to the next.[27]

[22] Karl Llewellyn, 'Remarks on the Theory of Appellate Decision and the Rules or Canons About How Statutes Are to be Construed' [1950] 3 Vand L Rev 395, 396.

[23] One must be deeply conversant with a specific legal system's argument forms to be able to identify such opinions, which is why I offer examples only from the U.S. caselaw.

[24] 491 US 397 (1989).

[25] *DeShaney v. Winnebago Cty Dep't of Social Serv.*, 489 US 189 (1989).

[26] Duncan Kennedy, 'The Three Globalizations of Law and Legal Thought: 1850–2000,' in David M. Trubek & Alvaro Santos eds., *The New Law and Economic Development: A Critical Appraisal* (CUP 2006).

[27] Were I constructing this canon, I would also use materials that show that argument forms that became prominent in later periods were available, at least in nascent form, during prior periods.

In a different vein, consider cases in which argument forms available within one system are seemingly unavailable in another. The Hong Kong Court of Final Appeal's flag-burning decision more or less explicitly says that it has to reject the constitutional challenge because otherwise the People's Republic of China would come down hard on Hong Kong. Would such an overtly political argument be available in other constitutional systems? The materials might note here that concerns about preserving judicial capital, as discussed in Section IV earlier, are sometimes thought implicit in U.S. constitutional decisions and that some opinions advert expressly to such concerns.

Another example involves invocation of expressly religious arguments to support results. Here, the materials might include so-called "sharia compliant" constitutional clauses and their interpretations in different Muslim-majority legal systems, and cases relying on the fact that the nation's constitution expressly establishes a religion or relying on the nation's strong religious traditions to support some outcomes (as in *Lautsi*). Again the materials would ask whether (or when) expressly religious arguments are available within other legal systems.[28]

The Legal Realist canon on constitutional structures would be relatively simple. It would consist of materials showing how structures have no systematic effects on outcomes—more concretely, how parliamentary and presidential systems can lie anywhere on the spectrum from authoritarian to liberal democratic. Here, the materials would be similar to those used in the comparative-politics canon.

Indeed, overall the materials included in Legal Realist canon might not be that different from those included in the other canons. The lesson to be drawn from the materials would be quite different, though: Constitutional *law* can't be a reliable basis for liberal democracy or human flourishing. Or, even more strongly, no one should count on constitutional law to contribute even marginally to sustaining liberal democracy or human flourishing.[29] Studying comparative constitutional law might have some intrinsic interest, akin to the interest some people have in abstract mathematics or, perhaps more

[28] Examples from the United States might include *Church of the Holy Trinity v. United States*, 143 US 457 (1892), which relied on the fact that the United State was a Christian nation to interpret a statute to allow a church to contract with a non-U.S. citizen to provide preaching services, and *Zorach v. Clauson*, 343 US 306 (1952), where the majority opinion relied on the fact that 'we are a religious people whose institutions presuppose a Supreme Being' to uphold a program in which public school students were released from classes so that they could attend classes providing instruction in their faith traditions.

[29] Recent scholarship has suggested that the weaknesses of constitutional law as a foundation for liberal democracy can be offset by pro-constitutional norms. My personal view is that the Legal Realist critique can be deployed against this suggestion as well. See Mark Tushnet, 'The Pirate's Code: Constitutional Conventions in U.S. Constitutional Law' [2018] 45 Pepperdine L Rev 481.

pertinently, the interest some anthropologists have in showing the rest of us the bewildering diversity of human experience.

VI. Conclusion: The Attractions of Eclecticism

I have discussed several candidates for a canon of comparative constitutional law, each drawing its organizing themes from a theoretical account of the field (what I have called a jurisprudence). The first two candidates—liberal democracy and human flourishing—seem to me to have more adherents among today's scholars of comparative constitutional law than alternatives.[30] Neither, though, seems to me to have become hegemonic.

The consequence is that participants in the field won't be comfortable identifying "a" canon (and "its" anticanons), but will feel some impulse to define the field eclectically. Yet, eclecticism creates its own tensions because the jurisprudences associated with competing canons can be inconsistent when applied to specific issues. A crude example: The canon of liberal democracy might include a case upholding some free-expression claim because the claim falls within the democratic core, but the canon of political context might question why some courts do and others do not uphold that right. And, in the event that the materials in the liberal-democracy canon present alternative possibilities for rights-based rulings depending upon context, the Legal Realist canon would suggest that the alternatives are defensibly available within *any* context.

Eclecticism does have at least one advantage, though. Consider the possibility of a meta-canon: Take a specific topic—economic rights, federalism and centralization, the structure of constitutional review, or something else—and examine it from the perspectives of liberal democracy, human flourishing, political context, and Legal Realism. The meta-canon would consist of those topics thought to be best in exposing the strengths and weaknesses of all four ground-level canons.

The remaining question would then, of course, be, What is the jurisprudence associated with the meta-canon?

[30] I believe that this sentence can be supported by an examination of the most recent programs of the field's major scholarly conferences.

4

Emmanuel Sieyès, 'What is the Third Estate?' (1789)

Victor Ferreres Comella

I. Introduction

The writer and clergyman Emmanuel-Joseph Sieyès (1748–1836) published this pamphlet in January 1789, before the outbreak of the French Revolution. The piece was meant to serve the cause of the representatives of common citizens in the particular circumstances of French politics at that time. It was written in two months, while he was in the countryside.[1] Its publication was an immediate success. The text was widely read, launching the author to political fame.[2] Sieyès became the intellectual spokesman of the Revolution. He was revered and attacked on this ground throughout his life.

The piece articulated certain abstract ideas that proved to be very influential. French constitutional scholarship has traditionally converged on the themes and ideas advanced by Sieyès.[3] The impact of this work transcended French boundaries. In his book *Constitutional Theory*, for example, Carl Schmitt refers to Sieyès' text as the source of a radically new political principle.[4] Karl Marx, in turn, in emphasizing the great scientific progress achieved by Pierre-Joseph Proudhon's 'What is property?', asserted that the latter's importance for modern economy was equivalent to that of Sieyès' piece for modern politics.[5]

[1] Jean-Denis Bredin, *Sieyès. La clé de la Révolution française* (Éditions de Fallois 1988) 84.

[2] More than 3,000 copies were sold in a few weeks, and four editions were published in one year. The first three editions were anonymous, while the fourth finally stated the name of the author: Emmanuel Sieyès. See Bredin (n 1) 79.

[3] An important nineteenth-century study of Sieyès' work is Paul Bastid, *Sieyès et sa pensée* (first published in 1939, Hachette 1970). Raymond Carré de Malberg, a prominent constitutional legal scholar, made frequent references to Sieyès in his monumental *Contribution à la Théorie Générale de l'État* (first published in 1920 and 1922, Dalloz 2004), especially when discussing sovereignty and the constitution-making power.

[4] Carl Schmitt, *Constitutional Theory* (first published 1928, Duke University Press 2008) 125–135.

[5] Karl Marx and Friedrich Engels, *The Holy Family, or Critique of Critical Critique* (first published 1856, Foreign Languages Publishing House 1956) 46.

Victor Ferreres Comella, *Emmanuel Sieyès, 'What is the Third Estate?' (1789)* In: *Global Canons in an Age of Contestation*. Edited by: Sujit Choudhry, Michaela Hailbronner, and Mattias Kumm, Oxford University Press.
 DOI: 10.1093/9780191956942.003.0004

The central notion Sieyès presented in 'What is the Third Estate?' concerns the distinction between the *pouvoir constituant* and the *pouvoirs constitués*.[6] The basic idea is this: the collection of individuals that form a nation possess the 'constituent power', the power to frame a Constitution. By means of the Constitution, the people distribute distinct powers—the legislative, executive, and judicial powers—among separate governmental bodies. Such bodies are (or hold) 'constituted' powers, since their existence derives from the Constitution, and they must observe the limitations fixed in it. According to Sieyès, because the nation is the ultimate source of all laws, it cannot be subject to any law. In particular, the nation is free to enact a new Constitution whenever it wants, in whatever manner it chooses.

This is, in a nutshell, one of the most important doctrines Sieyès bequeathed to future generations of constitutional theorists. I will first offer a brief historical background of Sieyès' piece. I will then describe with some detail his ideas about the *pouvoir constituant*. I will next explore the normative consequences of the theory. As I will argue, Sieyès' conception can be used to buttress some plausible normative claims, but it exhibits serious flaws.

II. The Historical Context

In 1788, France was facing a serious financial crisis, due in part to the government's support of the American War of Independence against Great Britain. There was lots of talk of reforming the existing institutions. The king, Louis XVI, finally decided to convene in Versailles the 'Estates General', the French legislative assembly, which had not met since 1614. Under the rules of the regime (the *ancien régime*, as it was soon to be called), the assembly was divided into three branches, each representing a specific order: the clergy, the nobility, and the common people. Votes were taken by orders and not by heads. So even if the third estate was the voice of the vast majority of the population, it could be outvoted by the other two orders representing a small minority.[7]

Such were the constitutional rules in France. There was no written Constitution in the modern sense of the word, but several laws and customs structured the state in a particular fashion. The tripartite composition of the parliamentary assembly was a core feature of the arrangements in place.

[6] The distinction figures in ch. V, entitled 'What Should Have Been Done. First Principles on This Matter'. See Emmanuel Sieyès, 'What is the Third Estate?', in Sieyès, *Political Writings* (Hackett Publishing Co. 2003) 133–144.

[7] Christopher Hibbert, *The French Revolution* (Penguin 1982) 19–46.

When the representatives of the three orders met in Versailles in May 1789, a constitutional crisis broke out. The third estate claimed to speak for the French people as a whole and insisted that the representatives of the other orders should join the third estate to form a single chamber, where decisions would be made by majority rule. The move was eventually successful. On 17 June 1789, the third estate constituted itself into the National Assembly.[8]

Among other things, the Assembly undertook the task of writing a Constitution for the country. Because of the central importance of individual rights and liberties, the Assembly proclaimed the 'Declaration of the Rights of Man and of the Citizen' in 1789. It later enacted the Constitution in 1791, incorporating the Declaration of Rights. It is important to recall the tenor of article 16 of the Declaration of Rights, for it captures the prevailing beliefs at that time about the point of the constitutional enterprise: 'Any society in which no provision is made for guaranteeing rights or for the separation of powers, has no Constitution.'

Sieyès played a crucial part in this enormous political transformation. Not only did he publish the pamphlet that served as the blueprint for the political action of the representatives of common citizens, he also had the opportunity to put his ideas into practice, since he managed to be elected representative by the third estate in May 1789 (even if he was a clergyman). On the strength of his great popularity, he triggered the parliamentary chain of events that ended up with the establishment of the new constitutional assembly.[9]

Sieyès was aware, of course, that the rules of the *ancien régime* did not empower a unicameral parliament to adopt a new Constitution. It was thus necessary to legitimate the legal break with the past. Here enters his idea that the nation possesses the unlimited authority to enact a new Constitution, without being bound by existing legal rules. This idea later acquired a life of its own, when it became disconnected from the specific circumstances of French politics that had prompted Sieyès to produce his piece.

Interestingly, similar ideas had been voiced in America around that time. The framers of the United States Constitution of 1787 knew that the procedure they had followed to adopt the Constitution had not observed the rules of change stipulated by the Articles of Confederation. Among other things, the framers had deviated from the provision requiring the unanimous consent of all member states for a constitutional revision to be adopted. The ratification by nine states was held to be sufficient. By way of defence, the framers appealed

[8] ibid 49–66.
[9] Bredin (n 1) 107–112.

to the people, whose will would be registered in special constitutional conventions at the ratification stage. In Federalist No. 40, for example, James Madison acknowledged that the Articles of Confederation had been deviated from. But 'in all great changes of established governments', he argued, 'forms ought to give way to substance'.[10] A rigid adherence to forms 'would render nominal and nugatory the transcendent and precious right of the people', announced in the Declaration of Independence, 'to abolish or alter their governments as to them shall seem most likely to effect their safety and happiness'. Ultimately, what matters is the will of the people: as the new Constitution 'was to be submitted *to the people themselves*, the disapprobation of this supreme body would destroy it forever; its approbation blot out antecedent errors and irregularities'.[11]

So Sieyès was not alone in invoking the unlimited constituent power of the people. His text was particularly influential in Europe, however, because of the tremendous impact of the French Revolution. When the first Spanish Constitution was written in 1812, for example, Sieyès was widely read and referred to by political actors. The notion that the people possess an unbounded constitution-making power was later invoked by political movements challenging the constitutional orders in many countries in Europe. Spreading democracy in the world seemed to require the acceptance of this idea.

It is important to note, however, that Sieyès was not a radical democrat. He was committed to representative government, and dreaded forms of direct democracy. He thus criticized a constitutional proposal Condorcet presented in 1793 contemplating the possibility of organizing a popular referendum to veto acts of political representatives.[12] For Sieyès, the principle of representation is of fundamental importance. Political representatives alone can speak in the name of the nation. It was therefore imperative to guard representatives against popular pressures. To this effect, Sieyès advanced a legislative proposal in 1795 to protect the National Assembly against mob action in the streets.[13] As the French Revolution led to Robespierre's regime of terror, Sieyès realized the dangers of unconstrained popular will. In an important parliamentary speech delivered on 20 July 1795, he explained that popular sovereignty needs to be circumscribed. Individuals have only transferred a limited amount of power to the state, so that basic liberties can be preserved. The *Ré-public*, Sieyès points

[10] *The Federalist* (first published in 1788, Modern Library edn 2000) 253.

[11] ibid 253–254, emphasis in the original. For a commentary on Federalist No. 40, see Sanford Levinson, *An Argument Open to All. Reading* The Federalist *in the 21st Century* (Yale University Press 2015) 149–151.

[12] Bredin (n 1) 257–258.

[13] ibid 343–344.

out, should not become a *Ré-total*. The conception that, following Rousseau, assigns unlimited power to the people is a continuation of the traditional view that attributed all powers to the monarch. The French, Sieyès rather provocatively claims, still hold many royal superstitions.[14]

Sieyès, moreover, played a key role in bringing Napoleon to power in 1799 to restore political order. Sieyès helped construct a new Constitution, aimed at curbing popular sovereignty. An intricate multi-tiered electoral system was designed to make it possible for an enlightened elite to run the government with a minimal degree of popular support. Citizens were not empowered to directly elect their representatives. Various bodies at the apex of the system would appoint representatives from lists of candidates drawn up by citizens below. Sieyès' basic convictions against direct democracy were clear: 'brute democracy is absurd', he asserted in the notes dictated to his secretary in 1799, for 'the people in its political activity only exists in national representation; it is embodied there'.[15]

So what Sieyès wrote in his 1789 pamphlet about the constituent power of the nation was later seen by him as an exaggeration, as a statement that could not be taken literally. The dramatic events he had witnessed caused him to seek constitutional serenity and qualify his previous views.

Yet, constitutional theory in many quarters is still under the spell of Sieyès' original idea. The existence of a sovereign people is often postulated as the fountain of the Constitution and the rest of the law. The powers of the people are deemed to be independent from all positive law.

Let us see in more detail what Sieyès says in 'What is the Third Estate?' One of the advantages of Sieyès' style is its clarity. His claims and arguments are very straightforward, based on distinct ideas and principles. As a good rationalist, he wanted language to be simple. As a great music lover, moreover, he dreamed of a written discourse moved by the unity of melody.[16]

III. Sieyès' Theory of the Constituent Power

Sieyès devotes chapter V of 'What is the Third Estate?' to present his general doctrine about the *pouvoir constituant*. Sieyès starts with the proposition that the people who have freely consented to form a political association constitute

[14] ibid 365–366.
[15] ibid 468.
[16] ibid 82–83.

a 'nation'. This nation, he says, is 'the origin of everything'.[17] All laws ultimately derive from it. It follows that the nation is not bound by any legal rules. 'Its will is always legal.' Positive law must always yield to the will of the nation. Only natural law restricts the actions of the nation: 'Prior to the nation and above the nation there is only natural law.'[18]

Sieyès distinguishes, next, between 'constitutional laws' and 'laws in the proper sense'. The former are the laws that regulate the organization and function of the legislative and 'active' (executive) bodies. They stand in contrast to the laws properly so called, the ordinary laws issued by the legislative assembly to regulate ordinary matters in order to protect individual rights and public interests. Sieyès maintains that constitutional laws are 'fundamental', meaning that the legislative and active bodies cannot modify the laws that set them up and regulate their functions. 'No type of delegated power can modify the conditions of its delegation.'[19]

Interestingly, Sieyès observes that the rules that ultimately matter are ordinary laws. Constitutional laws are merely instrumental, in that they create the bodies charged with the task of issuing legislation. Ordinary law is the ultimate end; constitutional law is the means to that end.

Importantly, Sieyès puts both constitutional laws and ordinary laws in the same 'positive law' box. The governmental structure can only exist through the enactment of positive law. We need positive law to generate governmental institutions. The nation, in contrast, is not subject to positive law, as already noted. The nation does not need positive law for its existence. 'A nation is formed solely by *natural law*.'[20]

The upshot of all this is that the nation is not bound by the Constitution it enacts. The nation can always change its will. It is legally impossible for a nation to be limited by a Constitution. Who would be the other party the nation would be concluding an agreement with? The nation cannot enter a contract with itself, Sieyès contends. 'What is a contract with oneself?'[21]

Actually, he claims, even if it were possible for a nation to put some brakes on its future will by means of a Constitution, it would be dangerous to do so. A tyrannical regime might manage at a certain historical moment to produce a Constitution subjecting the people to certain legal norms, thus keeping the people from breaking the chains of despotism in the future.

[17] Sieyès (n 6) 136.
[18] ibid.
[19] ibid 136.
[20] ibid 136–137, emphasis in the original.
[21] ibid 137.

It bears emphasizing that Sieyès not only rejects the establishment of substantive limits on the will of the nation. He also refuses the stipulation of formal or procedural conditions, for the nation is always in the state of nature. 'There is no reason to be afraid of repeating the fact that a nation is independent of all forms and, however it may will, it is enough for its will to be made known for all positive law to fall silent in its presence, because it is the source and supreme master of all positive law.'[22]

Sieyès is nevertheless cognizant of the need to devise procedures to capture the will of the nation. Which procedures does he favour? Sieyès does not endorse direct democracy, as already noted. He advocates a representative form of government, where citizens elect representatives to a seat in parliament. In this context, he distinguishes between 'ordinary' representatives, charged with enacting legislation within the existing constitutional framework, and 'extraordinary' representatives, empowered by citizens to hammer out a new Constitution. The latter are elected in exceptional circumstances. They carry out a specific constitutional task, and are appointed for a limited period. While ordinary representatives must observe constitutional forms when they perform their legislative function, the extraordinary representatives are independent from all constitutional forms. 'It is enough for them to will as an individual would will in the state of nature.'[23]

Sieyès, moreover, rejects universal suffrage. He is in favour of conditioning the vote on the payment of an economic contribution to the state. In this connection, he introduced in his writings a distinction between 'active' and 'passive' citizens, a distinction later embodied in the Constitution of 1791. Political representatives were supposed to speak for the nation as a whole, while only active citizens were empowered to participate in public affairs.

Sieyès also touches upon procedural issues when he argues in his piece that representatives should make decisions in accordance with majority rule. He claims that it is obvious that the nation can never wish that the opinion of the minority be made to prevail. Citizens should have the same degree of influence in the decision-making process. 'The common will cannot destroy itself.' It would be 'an act of madness', he writes, for the majority to allow the minority to express the will of the nation. 'Reasoned argument is pointless if for a single

[22] ibid 138.

[23] ibid 139. It should be noted that the French National Assembly in 1789 did not respect this distinction between two types of representation. The Assembly acted both as a constitutional convention and as an ordinary parliament tasked with the legislative function. Ideally, Sieyès would have preferred to keep the two tasks separate.

moment one abandons the self-evident principle that the common will is the opinion of the majority, not the minority.'[24]

Sieyès also asks the question, who is authorized to consult the nation? The people need to be convened by someone; they cannot gather spontaneously. Sieyès gives a simple solution to this problem. It does not matter who exactly has that authority, he maintains. When the country faces an extraordinary crisis, any governmental body that can help convene the people should do so. The executive branch has the administrative capacity to organize the elections, but the king can also take the step to call for them, if a constitutional assembly needs to be instituted to confront an exceptional political situation.

This is, in a nutshell, Sieyès' picture of the constituent power of the nation. As we will see next, the theory can be used to serve some good causes, but it exhibits important flaws.

IV. The Bright Side of the Theory of the Constituent Power

Postulating the existence of a sovereign people or nation that holds an unlimited constituent power has some potential advantages. It can help reinforce the democratic case in favour of certain institutional arrangements we may have good reason to establish and maintain. Even if there are independent normative justifications for such arrangements, the theory of the constituent power may be thought to inject a degree of democratic legitimacy into such arrangements to hedge them against democratic objections.

Take the issue of judicial review of legislation, for example. Is it acceptable for courts to be given the authority to test the validity of legislation against constitutional norms? A rich debate has developed concerning the democratic deficit of judicial review, as we all know. Arguably, there are sound grounds to support this institution, which can be understood to protect certain rights and values that may be infringed by transient ordinary majorities in parliament. This instrumental justification may be deemed to be insufficient, however, to alleviate democratic qualms. We may want to secure a democratic warrant for courts to have the power to review laws.

Here enters Sieyès' theory. The Constitution, we may say, documents the will of the nation. Ordinary statutes, in contrast, are the product of the legislative body, made up of ordinary representatives. If we emphasize the connection between the Constitution and popular will, on the one hand, and de-emphasize

[24] ibid 142.

the link between ordinary statutes and popular will, on the other, judicial review appears to be democratically acceptable. Indeed, when courts strike down an ordinary statute, they can be taken to be preserving the will of the people against erosion by the legislative body. Of course, courts may make mistakes when interpreting the meaning of the constitutional text, but the important point is that judges are not expected to restrain popular will but to preserve it.

This argument figures in the *Federalist Papers*, for example. In Federalist No. 78, Alexander Hamilton defends judicial review of legislation against the charge that it implies the superiority of the judicial role to the legislative power. According to Hamilton, judicial review 'only supposes that the power of the people is superior to both; and that where the will of the legislature, declared in its statutes, stands in opposition to that of the people, declared in the Constitution, the judges ought to be governed by the latter rather than the former'.[25] Hamilton acknowledges that sometimes the law that breaches the Constitution has been 'instigated by the major voice in the community'. But courts should not defer to the legislature in such cases. The Constitution is still the supreme law, and constitutional forms matter: 'until the people have, by some solemn and authoritative act, annulled or changed the established form, it is binding upon themselves collectively, as well as individually'.[26] The Supreme Court of the United States followed in Hamilton's steps when it ruled in 1803 that the judiciary had the power to disregard unconstitutional laws.[27] The Court portrayed the Constitution as the fundamental law laid down by the people, as the source of all political power. Judges protect the will of the people when they verify the conformity of legislation to the Constitution. This democratic understanding of the institution of judicial review has been elaborated upon by constitutional scholars in recent decades. According to Bruce Ackerman, for instance, when courts strike down a law on constitutional grounds they seek to preserve the will of the people expressed in rare 'constitutional moments', against the actions of political representatives in normal times.[28]

It is worthy of note that Sieyès was one of the few voices in France to advocate the introduction of a mechanism of constitutional review of legislation. In 1795, he proposed the institution of a 'constitutional jury', a council of wise men selected by the National Assembly to check the validity of laws against constitutional precepts.[29] His proposal was rejected at that time, but it clearly

[25] *The Federalist* (n 10) 499.
[26] ibid 501.
[27] *Marbury v. Madison*, 5 U.S. (1 Cranch) 137 (1803).
[28] Bruce Ackerman, *We the People. Foundations* (Harvard University Press 1991).
[29] Bredin (n 1) 366–369.

influenced the establishment of a *Sénat conservateur* as the guardian of the Constitution later on, in 1799.[30] Sieyès was a pioneer in this regard. We must remember that it took a long historical period of time for most European countries to allow courts—whether ordinary courts or specialized constitutional tribunals—to control statutes for their constitutional validity.[31]

A related area where Sieyès' appeal to the *pouvoir constituant* can help buttress particular institutional arrangements concerns constitutional amendment. As we know, Constitutions lay down specific procedures for their amendment, which are typically more burdensome than those employed to enact and modify ordinary statutes. The adoption of a constitutional amendment may require the approval of a parliamentary supermajority, for example, or the holding of a specific constitutional assembly, or ratification by the people in a referendum.

A case can be built in favour of some measure of constitutional rigidity to guarantee political stability and safeguard rights against legislative override by bare majorities in parliament. This instrumental justification, however, may be considered insufficient to answer democratic worries. At this juncture, an argumentative strategy drawing inspiration from Sieyès can be helpful. It may insist that the amendment power is a 'constituted' governmental power. All the organs of the state, including those with the ability to alter the Constitution, are constitutional creatures of the people. They must accordingly respect the legal bounds set out by the latter. Indeed, if the people have decided that gathering the votes of a simple majority in parliament is not sufficient to modify the constitutional text, democracy requires us to respect that choice.[32]

Constitutions sometimes go further and place certain principles or institutions or rules beyond the reach of the amendment power. An explicit 'intangibility or eternity clause' may name certain things that can never be amended. Alternatively, interpreters may read into the constitutional text implicit limitations on the amendment power. A number of basic principles, for example, may be regarded to be so fundamental to the Constitution's identity that they must always be maintained.

[30] ibid 476–477, 481–482.

[31] On the reasons for the reluctance in Europe to embrace judicial review of legislation as practised in the United States, see Victor Ferreres Comella, *Constitutional Courts and Democratic Values. A European Perspective* (Yale University Press 2009).

[32] On the legally constrained nature of the amendment power, see Yaniv Roznai, *Unconstitutional Constitutional Amendments. The Limits of Amendment Powers* (Oxford University Press 2017), and Richard Albert, *Constitutional Amendments. Making, Breaking, and Changing Constitutions* (Oxford University Press 2019).

Again, there may be reasons of an instrumental kind to warrant the establishment of certain substantive restrictions on amendments. These restrictions are open to democratic challenges, however. When facing such challenges, Sieyès' theory can prove useful. We may invoke Sieyès to point out that there is nothing undemocratic in ensuring observance of the limitations laid down by the sovereign people. The body created by the people to carry out the task of amending the Constitution should abide by the norms the people have issued, including those setting out substantive limitations on the amendment power.

So Sieyès' doctrine about the *pouvoir constituant* offers normative resources we can draw on, for the purposes of building a democratic defence of particular institutional arrangements we may wish to support, even if we believe we already have independent reasons in justification of such arrangements.

Sieyès' theory, however, does not survive serious intellectual scrutiny. It exhibits important flaws.

V. The Impossibility of a Legally Unlimited Constituent Power

We should remember, first of all, that Sieyès situates the nation in the state of nature. He claims that the nation has the power to will whatever it wants and to express its will in any manner it chooses.

Of course, as an empirical matter, it is not true that the people or their representatives are totally free when discussing and enacting a Constitution. They inevitably face economic, political, military, and cultural obstacles. Ferdinand Lassalle was not off the mark when he famously asserted, in a speech delivered in Berlin in 1862, that Constitutions reflect the power structures that are dominant in a given place and time.[33] Sieyès was not politically naive, so we cannot read him to be saying that the nation is totally free, as a matter of fact, to draft any Constitution it pleases.

Nor can Sieyès be understood to contend that the constituent power of the people is morally unfettered. As we have seen, Sieyès explicitly mentions natural law and morality as a limit on the constituent power. 'Morality', he wrote, 'is what should regulate all the ties binding men to one another, both in terms of their individual interests and their common or social interest.'[34] Sieyès, after all, was a child of the Enlightenment. Liberal principles were part of the basic

[33] Ferdinand Lassalle, 'Über Verfassungswesen' (first published in 1862, English translation available at https://www.marxists.org/history/etol/newspape/fi/vol03/no01/lassalle.htm).

[34] Sieyès (n 6) 133–134.

political morality he referred to. Actually, Constitutions at that time were conceptually linked to fundamental rights and separation of powers, a link that was explicitly asserted in article 16 of the French Declaration of the Rights of Man and of the Citizen, as we have seen. A legal document on the organization of the state that disregarded such norms would not be considered an authentic Constitution.

Indeed, if we believe that certain principles of political morality require the state to behave in a certain way when exerting its authority over its citizens, those principles must do their work when Constitutions are being written. If the state ought to respect such principles, then the people ought to respect them as well when they design the constitutional rules that will govern the state. If, morally speaking, the state should not discriminate on grounds of race, for example, the people should not, morally speaking, enact a Constitution that licenses the state to discriminate on grounds of race. Morality is not silent when the constituent power is being exercised.

So the unrestricted nature of the constituent power that Sieyès describes can only refer to legal rules. But is it plausible to maintain that the constituent power is legally unbound? Not really. Positive law is everywhere, even in the space the nation occupies when it originates a Constitution.

Here are some examples to illustrate this point. To begin with, who belongs to the group of people wielding the power to draft a Constitution? Sieyès assumes that only citizens are part of it, so foreigners are excluded.[35] Obviously, we need legal rules to specify the grounds of nationality. Moral principles can constrain legislative choices in this matter, but positive law must ultimately specify the rules regarding nationality.

Furthermore, not all citizens can be entitled to participate in constitutional politics (or in ordinary politics, for that matter). Minors, for instance, should not be allowed to vote. The question, then, is who counts as a minor. We obviously need legal rules to specify this, as Sieyès acknowledges.[36]

And what happens when the population living in a particular territory within the state wishes to secede from it and form a separate state? Is secession authorized? Sieyès' theory does not have enough resources to provide an answer to this question, which has been widely debated in political theory. On the one hand, Sieyès writes that a nation 'is a body of associates living under a *common* law, represented by the same *legislature*, etc'.[37] On the other hand,

[35] ibid 107.
[36] ibid.
[37] ibid 97, emphasis in the original.

he argues that nobody can impose laws on a multitude of individuals to unite them into a nation. The association must be 'voluntary and free'.[38] Maybe secession is warranted, in the name of the right to association? This is a controversial question. In any event, constitutional law and international law have a part to play in providing an answer.

Procedures, moreover, are required for the nation to convey its will. As noted earlier, Sieyès suggests that citizens should elect extraordinary representatives, endowed with the specific mandate to frame the Constitution. After deliberating on the matter, the vote of the majority must prevail. Sieyès appeals to first principles to justify the superiority of this scheme to alternative ones. There is much to be said for the specialization of political functions, given the advantages of the division of labour. And there is certainly an argument in favour of majority rule, which relates to the principle of equality (and to status quo neutrality), although we may have good grounds to deviate from that rule at the constitutional stage: to enhance the stability of the Constitution, it may be necessary to require representatives to seek broad consensus and meet a supermajority threshold. In any event, even if we agree with Sieyès that simple majority rule is better, we must resort to positive law to translate individual votes into collective decisions according to specific electoral and parliamentary procedures.

There is another consideration that deserves emphasis in this context. The constituent power is simply one power among others. It consists in the authority to enact a Constitution. There are other powers, of course, such as the legislative, executive, and judicial powers, to follow Montesquieu's famous tripartite classification. It is important to understand that these other powers are to be kept separate from the constituent power.

Indeed, the fact that the constituent power ranks higher than the ordinary powers does not mean that the former can absorb the latter. The constituent power designs the bodies that will be trusted with the legislative, executive, and judicial functions. We can thus say that these ordinary powers 'flow' from the constituent power. But they flow from the constituent power not because they were originally part of the constituent power, but because it is the task of the constituent power to set up the organization of the state, which entails distributing those ordinary powers among various bodies.

Of course, it would be possible to envisage an assembly wielding all the powers—not only the constituent power, but all the rest. The assembly would thus be authorized to write a Constitution, enact ordinary laws, hear cases as

[38] ibid 137.

a court of justice, enforce the laws as if it were the executive branch, supply public services as the administration does, etc. Arguably, this concentration of powers in a single organ would be monstrous. It would certainly breach the liberal principle of separation of powers. The idea that it is better for the powers to be distributed among different bodies applies in all contexts, including the constitutional stage. The distinction between the constituent power and the constituted powers is itself a manifestation of the principle of separation of powers. The constituent power cannot exercise the powers it institutes. Its task is simply to institute them.[39]

It is interesting to observe in this connection that Jean-Jacques Rousseau argued that the people express the general will when they frame general and abstract laws. 'When I say that the province of the law is always general, I mean that the law considers all subjects collectively and all actions in the abstract; it does not consider any individual man or any specific action', he wrote.[40] Objectivity disappears if a particular fact or right is being dealt with, on a matter that has not been settled by an earlier general rule, he observed. This must also be true of constitutional laws ('political laws' or 'fundamental laws', as he calls them), which are a type of law, according to Rousseau. This being the case, it would be incoherent for the institution that expresses the general will to be conferred the authority to adjudicate cases at the same time.

This observation is in keeping with the spirit of Sieyès' conception. Sieyès certainly believed that the nation exerting the constituent power should not absorb all the other powers. As we have seen, he proposed that the extraordinary representatives of the nation should end their activities after writing the Constitution. They should not go on to undertake the ordinary legislative function. And when drafting the Constitution, they should not interfere with the legislative power. Sieyès was always emphatic on the need to organize political institutions in accordance with the principle of division of labour. As a great admirer of Adam Smith, he thought that specialization was the hallmark of both markets and governments.

A tension emerges in Sieyès' theory, therefore, when he asserts that the elected representatives of the nation charged with writing a Constitution are

[39] Carré de Malberg (n 3) 510. Carré de Malberg maintained that the idea that a constitutional assembly can concentrate all the powers is 'one of the biggest mistakes committed in France since 1789,' ibid 549. Interestingly, he argues that because only the nation (an abstract entity) is sovereign, no institution can claim to enjoy sovereign power. A constitutional assembly is one institution among many, in spite of the relevance of its mission. It cannot hold all the powers as if it were the nation itself. Ibid 550–551. For a discussion of this issue with examples drawn from recent constitutional assemblies, see Joel Colón-Ríos, *Constituent Power and the Law* (Oxford University Press 2020) 226–261.

[40] Jean-Jacques Rousseau, *The Social Contract* (first published in 1762, Penguin 1968) 81–82.

not constrained by any law, not even by laws that specify forms, procedures, and competences. This absence of limits runs against the principle of specialization he cherishes.[41]

Turning to another issue, we should bear in mind that the Enlightenment project meant the introduction of legal order in the relationships among states. International law should develop according to moral principles to facilitate and constrain the actions of governments when they interact on the global plane. The national Constitution can be regarded as the supreme law of the land in a given country, but it can only regulate the sphere of matters that international law puts in the hands of each individual state. The *pouvoir constituant* is not beyond the reach of international law.

We can conclude from these various remarks that there is no radical distinction between the constituent power and the amendment power, as far as the operation of legal rules is concerned: both are subject to them.

It is true, as was the case in France in 1789, or in the United States in 1787, that the legal rules that are effectively employed to govern the framing of a new Constitution may imply a break with earlier law. Indeed, a considerable number of Constitutions have not been enacted in compliance with the procedures of constitutional amendment or revision stipulated in earlier Constitutions. Sometimes this breach is justified, other times it is not. One can maintain that if the existing rules of constitutional change are clearly dysfunctional, so that the community is disabled from addressing the extraordinary political challenges it faces, deviating from them is a reasonable course of action. It is important, however, that the new Constitution rests on a certain degree of consensus in society, instead of registering the pure will of those coming into power at a particular moment.

In sum, we cannot dispense with positive law altogether. The constituent power is in the hands of the nation, but the nation is a legal construction. There is no nation inhabiting the state of nature. Only positive law brings the nation into existence for constitutional purposes.

VI. The Constituent Power and the Death of God

There is an obvious parallelism between Sieyès' doctrine of the constituent power and theological views.[42] According to traditional religious

[41] Carré de Malberg (n 3) 534–535 discusses this internal friction in Sieyès' work.
[42] Colón-Ríos (n 39) 60.

understandings, God is omnipotent. He freely decides to create the world and chooses the laws the world will be subject to. God can suspend the operation of those laws, through miracles. And he could extinguish them: he could destroy the world and make a new one governed by different laws, if he so willed.

A similar picture is offered by Sieyès in the constitutional domain, as far as legal limitations are concerned. The sovereign nation freely decides to create the governmental structure of the state. It lays down the constitutional rules the state must abide by, including the rules regulating constitutional amendment. Because of its sovereignty, the nation can always come back to the political stage and originate a new Constitution, disregarding the extant rules on constitutional amendment.

In theological thought, moreover, postulating the existence of an infinite God is important to emphasize the finite nature of the world. In addition, the idea of a morally and intellectually perfect God helps us stress the fallibility of human beings and their institutions. Similarly, in the realm of political thought, assuming the existence of an original, unlimited constituent power permits us to highlight, by way of contrast, the legally constrained nature of both the ordinary legislature and the body endowed with the constitutional amendment power.

As noted earlier, the doctrine of the constituent power of the nation can be enlisted to contribute to the defence of constitutional rigidity and judicial review of legislation. We already have independent reasons of an instrumental kind, however, to support these institutional arrangements. Such reasons, I submit, should be deemed sufficient. We do not need to postulate the existence of a legally omnipotent nation in the background, as the fountain of all laws, in order to shield those arrangements against democratic censure.

Nietzsche famously said that God is dead. Our civilization has killed God, though we are still not aware of the grave consequences of this action. Nietzsche called for the transfiguration of values. He feared we might enter a nihilist phase once we realized that the traditional source of values had been destroyed.

The theory of the constituent power offered by Sieyès in 'What is the Third Estate?' makes no sense, I have argued. A 'natural' sovereign nation, operating in a world without legal rules, cannot exist. Positive law is everywhere. We should come to terms with the fact that such a natural, extra-legal nation is dead as a constitutional concept. Fortunately, we have independent grounds to support the institutions we have. Imagining the existence of an extra-legal sovereign is not necessary for justification purposes. In the same way that we can observe the fallibility of human beings without presupposing the existence of God, we can insist on the limited character of the ordinary legislature and of the constitutional amendment power without assuming, by way of contrast, the existence of an omnipotent people who can arise at any time and make a new Constitution.

The death of the constituent power, so understood, can be liberating. We can discuss the pros and cons of various institutional schemes in light of normative principles, including democratic principles, without being obsessed with the question whether the nation ever chose to create them.

This is not to deny that there may be something special in constitutional moments, in terms of the intensity and extension of popular participation. The authority of the Constitution may derive in part from the democratic quality those moments display, as Bruce Ackerman has argued in the American context.[43] But the difference between ordinary politics and constitutional politics is one of degree, not of kind. Importantly, there are always legal rules constructing and limiting the people. A truly sovereign nation is a myth.

The death of the extra-legal constituent power as a concept should cause us to be particularly careful when designing the procedures of constitutional amendment. The level and type of rigidity we choose for the Constitution should be the right one in light of the social and political conditions of each country. We should not relativize the importance of this institutional choice by pointing out that, after all, the sovereign nation can always come down from the skies to pronounce its will, without being bound by operative constitutional rules. The constitutional enterprise cannot succeed if we assume the existence of this mysterious subject, entitled to appear at any moment to destroy the constitutional order and start things from scratch. The amendment rules may have to be disregarded when they become dysfunctional at extraordinary political moments, as I have suggested, but such a breach should count as a failure of the constitutional project, not as the way things are supposed to be in a world where such an omnipotent subject exists.

The natural and legally unlimited constituent power that Sieyès painted in his famous pamphlet is dead. But the institutions that were historically associated with it can survive that death.

[43] Ackerman (n 28).

5

A Haitian Turn

Günter Frankenberg[*]

I. The Canon and the Hidden Faces of Constitutional Modernity

Haiti's Constitutions[1] of 1801 and 1805 never traveled. At no time were they on display in the global constitutional showroom.[2] The Caribbean "subaltern" had spoken but her constitutional voice remained unheard for almost two centuries. In the spirit of authoritarian, at least hegemonic, liberalism, "the most horrific system of slavery ever seen in human history," the "contagious revolution,"[3] and its constitutional documents were assiduously overlooked. They were silenced or trivialized by enlightened philosophers and critical theories, notably the antipodes Hegel and Marx.[4] Anglo-European constitutional scholarship at large[5] did not find Haiti's constitutional revolution relevant, once again revealing the coloniality of power/knowledge based on Anglo-Eurocentric hierarchies of attention and radical schemes of classification,[6] as well as a disregard for a concept of liberty not as a license (for disposing of one's property) but as freedom

* I am indebted to Michaela Hailbronner, Klaus Günther, and, Tim Wolff for very thoughtful comments on a previous version of the text.

1 To be precise, the Constitutions of Saint-Domingue (1801) and the Empire of Hayti (1805). In the following, Haiti will be the common denomination, in a tribute to the island's precolonial inhabitants.

2 Concerning legal/constitutional transfer and the (IKEA-) showroom, see G. Frankenberg, "Legal Transfer" in M. C. Foblets et al. (eds.) *The Oxford Handbook of Law and Anthropology* (OUP 2022) and id., *Comparative Constitutional Studies—Between Magic and Deceit* (E. Elgar 2018) 111.

3 D. A. Bell, "The Contagious Revolution" *The New York Review of Books* (New York, December 19, 2019).

4 J. Ehrmann, "Haitian Revolution" (2018) 2 Krisis—Journal of Contemporary Philosophy 69; and her impressive study *Tropen der Freiheit—Die Haitianische Revolution und die Dekolonisierung des Politischen* (Suhrkamp 2024); M.-R. Trouillot, *Silencing the Past: Power and the Production of History* (Beacon 1995).

5 For references, see S. Fischer, *Modernity Disavowed: Haiti and the Culture of Slavery in the Age of Revolution* (Duke UP 2004) with further references; S. Buck-Morss, "Hegel and Haiti" (2000) 26 Critical Inquiry 821; and E. Grüner, *La oscuridad y las luces* (Edhasa 2008) ch. 6.

6 A. Quijano, "Coloniality of Power, Eurocentrism, and Latin America" (2000) 1 Nepantla: Views from the South 533.

Günter Frankenberg, *A Haitian Turn* In: *Global Canons in an Age of Contestation*. Edited by: Sujit Choudhry, Michaela Hailbronner, and Mattias Kumm, Oxford University Press. © Günter Frankenberg 2024.
DOI: 10.1093/9780191956942.003.0005

(from slavery) combined with parental and economic duties and a responsibility to preserve the general emancipation.[7]

At long last, historians, anthropologists, and philosophers—not lawyers, mind you—took the "Haitian turn" mainly in the 1990s[8] and thereafter. They discovered, at least recognized, the world's largest and first successful slave revolt of 1791–1804 that transformed colonial Saint-Domingue into independent Hayti, until the country was financially re-colonized under its debt-burden during the first decades of the nineteenth century.[9] In contrast, constitutional scholars of history, theory, and comparison remained entrenched and comfortably numb in their Anglo-European provincialism, and diligently waited on the much overplayed tradition of considering Philadelphia, Paris, and the U.S. Supreme Court to be the epicenters of constitutionalism, modernity, and humanism. Ignorance or lack of curiosity—or both—ratified the constitution as a North Atlantic universal, ruled out alternative narratives of constitutional modernity, and sanctioned the irrelevance of "other-constitutions," like Haiti's. Only in recent years have a few authors from the Global South crossed the "colorline", entered the zone of interest, and focused on the Haitian Revolution as an event of emancipation, on history and literature rather than the post-revolutionary constitutions.[10]

The project of distinguishing and exhibiting canonical texts runs the risk of, once again, confirming the terms of this debate, providing more dignity and security for the settled knowledges and ratifying the prevailing

[7] See Arts. 3 and 14 Constitution of 1801 and Arts. 9–11 Constitution of 1805. See C. Moïse, *Le Projet national de Toussaint Louverture et la Constitution de 1801* (Éditions Mémoire 2001) 5, 66–67; and C. E. Fick, "The Haitian Revolution and the Limits of Freedom: Defining Citizenship in the Revolutionary Era" (2007) 32 Social History 394, 410.

[8] e.g. M. Hector (ed.) *La révolution française et Haïti* (Editions H. Deschamps 1995); Trouillot (n 4); D. B. Gaspar and D. P. Geggus (eds.) *A Turbulent Time: The French Revolution and the Greater Caribbean* (University of Indiana Press 1997).

[9] The brutal, extended struggle against slavery in Saint-Domingue (since January 1, 1804, Haiti) and the European colonial powers began in 1791. The abolition of the slave system was declared in 1793, constitutionally confirmed in 1801, and then again in 1805. See L. Dubois, *Avengers of the New World: The Story of the Haitian Revolution* (Belknap 2004); C. L. R. James, *The Black Jacobins. Toussaint L'Ouverture and the San Domingo Revolution* (Secker & Warburg 1938); J. Gonzalez, *Maroon Nation: A History of Revolutionary Haiti* (Yale UP 2019); J. S. Scott, *The Common Wind: Afro-American Currents in the Age of the Haitian Revolution* (Verso 2018); D. P. Geggus (ed.) *The Impact of the Haitian Revolution in the Atlantic World* (Columbia 2003). Concerning the re-colonization, see the illuminating analysis of L. Obregon, "Empire, Racial Capitalism and International Law: The Case of Manumitted Haiti and the Recognition of Debt" (2018) 31 Leiden Journal of International Law 597.

[10] e.g. A. Adéèkó, *The Slave's Rebellion: Literature, History, Orature* (Indiana UP 2005); L. Dubois, *Avengers of the New World. The Story of the Haitian Revolution* (HUP 2004); M. L. Daut, *Tropics of Haiti: Race and Literary History of the Haitian Revolution in the Atlantic World, 1789–1865* (Liverpool UP 2015); E. Grüner, "Haiti: A (Forgotten) Revolution" (2009) 28 Sociedad (Buenos Aires) 1; history, political science, and a constitutional focus are combined by Moïse (n 7).

perspective in comparative constitutional studies.[11] For this project to make sense and a difference, it would therefore be crucial to overcome the ideological amnesia and topographic myopia of constitutional research and imagination by including quite different documents in the epistemic order of constitutionalism and by revealing one or the other "hidden face of modernity"[12] and rethinking modern constitutionalism from the periphery of the dominant center by confronting it with counter-narratives[13] that deconstruct its universalism as myth, and appropriate and transform it, as will be shown later. This way a "canon" could begin to vindicate its existence as an archive of the multiple narratives and readings of constitutional modernity:

> Any concept of modernity ought to have something to contribute to an analysis of how the particular varieties of radicalism articulated through the revolts of enslaved people made selective use of the ideologies of the western Age of Revolution and then flowed into social movements of an anti-colonial and anti-capitalist type.[14]

As a further step to absolve its reputation and sever its ties to the stories told and retold by mainstream comparative constitutional scholars, a (critical) canon would have to deconstruct the Western gaze and hegemony and, by the same token, encourage the development of a perspectival hermeneutic, rather than reiterating the Anglo-European view. A perspectival hermeneutic helps interpret the Haitian Revolution, and the revolutionary constitutions it brought about, not as offspring of the European Enlightenment[15] but, on their own terms, as original documents.[16] "On their own terms" means studying and teaching how the early Haitian constitutions were informed by the daily experiences of ordinary enslaved people, who participated in the revolution with interests and goals that embodied their own needs, visions, and fears, and with correlative constitutional aspirations, and how they were tied to colonial capitalism.[17] Unsilencing the past, looking at the margins, introducing

[11] Critical of the established ways of studying constitutional world-making and calling for attention to "other-constitutions" such as Haiti's: Frankenberg, *Comparative Constitutional Studies* (n 2) especially ix–x, 7–12.

[12] I borrow this expression from M.-R. Trouillot, "North Atlantic Universals: Analytical Fictions 1492–1945" (2002) 101 The South Atlantic Quarterly 839, 847.

[13] J. Ehrmann, "Konstitution der Rassismuskritik. Haiti und die Revolution der Menschenrechte" (2015) 1 Zeitschrift für Menschenrechte 35.

[14] P. Gilroy, *The Black Atlantic: Modernity and Double Consciousness* (HUP 1993) 44.

[15] James (n 9).

[16] Fick (n 7); Ehrmann (n 13).

[17] M. Drexler and E. White, "The Constitution of Toussaint: Another Origin of African American Literature" in G. A. Jarrett (ed.) *A Companion to African American Literature* (Wiley-Blackwell

perspectivity, reading constitutions into their context, and decentering the "West," this program moves the canon well ahead on its way to recognizing counter-constitutions[18] and maroon constitutions.[19]

II. Maroon Constitutions

Constitutional scholarship of the Global North treated Haiti's post-revolutionary charters as maroon constitutions, for all intents and purposes banned from normal science and research to intellectual leper stations. In contrast, I argue that they deserve to be included in the canon. While they may be eccentric, they are quite remarkable, both as *alter-natives*, which lay bare the contradictions in Enlightenment thought and liberal constitutionalism, and as documents in their own right that capture the revolutionary and anti-slavery spirit generated and executed in Haiti. Their peculiar architecture and grammar (see the appendix at the end of the chapter) confront the Western "rights of all mankind" rhetoric with its specific historical content—the scandal of slave labor and trade, not as a metaphor for oppression but as the most brutal system of exploitation in the history of capitalism,[20] based on the ownership of human beings as "movable property." The original text of the U.S. Constitution counted each enslaved "other person" as three-fifths of a person in terms of representation and prohibited Congress from banning enslavement until 1808.[21]

In contrast, Haiti's 1805 charter already challenged the hegemony of the liberal paradigm by divorcing the marriage of freedom and property (arranged for the benefit of proto-industrial capitalism that depended on the slave trade),[22] and by delegitimizing slavery as one of the core institutions of the

2010) 59; S. Beckert and S. Rockman (eds.) *Slavery's Capitalism: A New History of American Economic Development* (University of Pennsylvania Press 2016); O. U. Ince, *Colonial Capitalism and the Dilemmas of Liberalism* (OUP 2018).

[18] I discuss "other-constitutions" in Frankenberg, *Comparative Constitutional Studies* (n 2) ix.

[19] The term was borrowed from Gonzalez (n 9).

[20] P.-V. Baron de Vastey, *Le système colonial dévoilé* [1814] (Nabu Press 2014);D. B. Davis, *Inhuman Bondage: The Rise and Fall of Slavery in the New World* (OUP 2006); L. Dubois, *Avengers of the New World: The Story of the Haitian Revolution* (Belknap Press 2004); and James (n 9).

[21] F. Douglass, "The Constitution of the United States: Is It Pro-Slavery or Anti-slavery?," Speech in Glasgow, March 26, 1860, https://www.blackpast.org/global-african-history/1860-frederick-douglass-constitution-united-states-it-pro-slavery-or-anti-slavery/ (accessed November 18, 2020).

[22] e.g. S. Beckert, *Empire of Cotton. A New History of Global Capitalism* (Penguin 2015); E. Williams, *Capitalism and Slavery* (UNC Press 1994); and E. D. Genovese, *From Rebellion to Revolution: African-American Slave Revolts in the Making of the Modern World* (LSU Press 1979).

capitalist economy. Slavery inspired republics of the Americas to decree an end to the trade in humans and to abolish slavery by 1853, beginning with Mexico's Constitution of 1829.[23]

That "all men are created equal" and are "endowed by their Creator with certain inalienable Rights"[24] did not end slavery right there in the United States in 1776 (nor did it provide for gender equality). Instead, a century of struggle of abolitionists against slaveholders followed, which was punctuated by two shameful landmark decisions of judicial racism (*Dred Scott v. Sanford* (1857) and *Plessy v. Ferguson* (1896)[25]), Lincoln's much-revered Emancipation Proclamation in 1862, and the Thirteenth Amendment formally abolishing slavery and involuntary servitude in 1865. All of these constitutional moments testify to the originality and priority of the Haitian moment:

> Americans declared a new ideal of popular sovereignty but only succeeded in founding a new white man's republic, according power and honor to white slaveholders, none to enslaved African Americans, and precious little to free blacks. The French Revolution first ignored slavery, then accorded civic rights to colored proprietors. Only in 1793–94 ... did it forge an alliance with insurgent blacks and strike down what remained of slavery in the colonies it still controlled.[26]

One might say that Haiti pushed natural rights universalism to its ultimate fulfilment[27] by revealing its particularist core and extending the rhetoric of freedom, equality, and fraternity to the colonized people. Disproving Hegel's conservatism and racism, Haiti became significant for world history[28] (albeit not for Hegel's world spirit) and also for constitutionalism by completing the American and French Revolutions,[29] challenging property rights, proclaiming racial equality, and granting its citizens civic liberty.[30] The concept of popular

[23] R Blackburn "Haiti, Slavery, and the Age of Democratic Revolution" (2006) 63 The William and Mary Quarterly 643.

[24] See the thoughtful analysis by L. Hunt, "The Paradoxical Origins of Human Rights" in J Wasserstrom et al. (eds.) *Human Rights and Revolutions* (Rowman & Littlefield 2000) 3.

[25] In *Dred Scott v. Sanford*, 60 U.S. 393 (1857)—regarded as one of the catalysts of the Civil War—the U.S. Supreme Court held that the U.S. Constitution did not include American citizenship for black people, enslaved or free. *Plessy v. Ferguson*, 163 U.S. 537 (1896) upheld racial segregation in trains.

[26] Blackburn (n 23) 672. Blackburn also claims that "Haiti has saved the honor of the New World revolutions." The honor of the French Revolution was compromised, as regards slavery, when Napoleon and the counterrevolutionary forces reintroduced slavery and turned against Haiti again.

[27] Fick (n 7) 395.

[28] For Hegel's repeated, foolish, and racist statements about Africans, slaves, and slavery, see Buck-Morss (n 5) 857–863.

[29] Declared "incomplete" by Baron de Vastey (n 20).

[30] Blackburn (n 23); Trouillot (n 12); and Trouillot (n 8) 98.

sovereignty, the egalitarian spirit, the detailed regulations of citizenship, and that "no armed body can deliberate" (No. 4 of the General Dispositions) of the 1805 Constitution especially resonate with the 1793 Jacobin Constitution. Not unlike the French Constitutions of 1791 and 1793, both Haitian Constitutions were equally short-lived; they should not be misunderstood as copies of the French documents, though. In France, the National Convention operated under emergency powers and postponed the Constitution's implementation. Despite its popularity, the Jacobin Constitution set aside indefinitely by the Convention of October 10, 1793, superseded by the ensuing Reign of Terror, and eventually supplanted it with the Directory Constitution of 1795. In Haiti, Jacques Dessalines,[31] the emperor and military leader, was assassinated in 1806. Thereafter, Haiti was divided into a northern kingdom and a southern republic.[32]

A series of over twenty Haitian Constitutions followed the two post-revolutionary charters until today, many of them struggling with their military–autocratic origins: In the north, Henry Christophe[33] established himself as president for life, then king (after Toussaint Louverture), advised by a council of state staffed by military leaders (1811), while Alexandre Pétion followed Jacques Dessalines to become president for life of the southern republic. Throughout the nineteenth century, until the formal independence of the Dominican Republic in 1875, several military leaders (Jean-Baptiste Riché, Charles Rivière-Hérard, Michel Domingue, and Louis Pierrot) followed the revolutionaries of the first hour as presidents of Haiti.

Despite significant changes, the 2012 Constitution still echoes, if only faintly and filtered through the liberal vocabulary, the chorus of liberation from slavery, the anti-privilege orientation, and the social (rights and obligations) spirit of the founding period. Both documents transcended, as will be shown later, the racialized matrix of Anglo-European constitutionalism and portrayed the contours of a radically egalitarian contrast to the French

[31] Jacques Dessalines, former slave, then general, followed Louverture as military leader. He was framer and signatory of the 1805 Constitution, usurped all power, and declared himself Emperor. Regarding Haiti's relationship with France, the Commander in Chief authorized the famous proclamation of independence: "It is not enough to have expelled the barbarians who have bloodied our land for two centuries; ... We must, with one last act of national authority, forever assure the empire of liberty in the country of our birth; we must take any hope of re-enslaving us away from the inhuman government ... In the end we must live independent or die" (The Haitian Declaration of Independence, 1804). On Dessalines, J. Gaffield, *Haitian Connections in the Atlantic World: Recognition After Revolution* (University of North Carolina Press 2015).

[32] Blackburn (23).

[33] On Christophe, D. L. Garraway, "Empire of Liberty, Kingdom of Civilization: Henry Christophe, the Baron de Vastey, and the Paradoxes of Universalism in Postrevolutionary Haiti" (2012) 16 Small Axe no. 3.

Revolution; one might characterize them as examples of genuine, transformative constitutionalism rather than just an extension, "key supplement," or "translation" of 1789.[34] On February 4, 1801, seven years after the abolition of slavery by the National Convention, the *Toussaintienne*[35] of Saint-Domingue set the agenda for the liberation of the people of African descent without altogether abolishing the post-slavery plantation economy. While it tried to accommodate the colonial power by adopting French administrative structures, Catholicism was endorsed as the colony's religion to hold at bay traditional (voodoo) religious practices, likewise the colonial administrative structures and law were in part transferred. Its dualist conception of sovereignty was remarkable, combining the Haitian practicality with symbolically French supremacy.

The *Dessalinienne* of 1805 further departed from the North Atlantic constitutional consensus and its narratives of legitimation. It created a non-hereditary empire, confirmed the declaration of independence for all Haitians, and banned most "whites" (that is, foreigners) from citizenship. All in all, it combined features of authoritarian paternalism[36] with racial equality and the protection of family.

III. Layered Narratives

Constitutions are texts with purposes written for audiences.[37] Interesting constitutions come with a plurality of (often conflicting) purposes that can be read as layered s, where structural elements interact with archetypical features and purposes.[38] Haiti's instructive and fascinating post-slavery constitutions,[39] transient as they were, are no exception.

[34] e.g. M. Hardt and T. Negri, *Empire* (CUP 2007) 118; S Ẑiẑek regarded them as a key supplement, see Fischer (n 5).

[35] Named after Toussaint Louverture (1743–1803), Haitian general and charismatic leader, credited with transforming the revolt into a revolution. See James (n 9). Napoleon ordered Toussaint Louverture's deportation to France, where he died in prison in 1803.

[36] For a more elaborate discussion, see G. Frankenberg, *Authoritarianism—Constitutional Perspectives* (E. Elgar 2020).

[37] ibid., ch. 8.

[38] The concept is explained in G. Frankenberg, "Comparing Constitutions: Ideas, Ideals and Ideology. Toward a Layered Narrative" (2006) 4 International Journal of Constitutional Law 439.

[39] Fischer (n 5) 228.

A. First Layer: Audiences

As with many other constitutions of the era, Haiti's post-revolutionary charters acknowledged the imaginary presence of "the Supreme Being" and "all nature" (1805), however, they appealed to the inhabitants of Saint-Domingue as French citizens in 1801. The Constitution of 1805 invoked "the people of Hayti" as the new collective subject—not only as an ethnic, alternative self-designation for French citizens but to confront the white, male, propertied Enlightenment subject with the "radical alterity" of the indigenous origin and injustice suffered by the people of Hayti.[40]

In 1789, the people consisted of roughly 500,000 slaves of African descent (most of them illiterate), 40,000 "whites" (foreigners, most of them from Europe), and 30,000 *mulattoes*. They had survived the seemingly endless and merciless struggle against several European colonial powers (Spain, Britain, France), unlike the Island Arawak,[41] who had succumbed to colonial genocide and had virtually been forgotten. Both Constitutions were collectively drafted by the military elite and addressed themselves to any person who might be waiting for a moment to usurp power. To be on the safe side, Toussaint Louverture constitutionally secured his position as Governor and General-in-Chief (Art. 29 ff.), reserved for himself the right to nominate a successor, and proclaimed substantial law-making and executive powers—at a salary of 300,000 francs. Furthermore, the 1801 Constitution declared the armed forces to be "essentially obedient."

Whereas Haiti had severed its ties with France when declaring its independence, the earlier constitution of the Saint-Domingue colony still documented the ambiguity of the revolutionary situation and the impact of the colonial tradition in several appeals to the *ancien régime*. All classical elements of statehood were first submitted for the French Directory's blessing: The Governor, who had overthrown the former regime by revolutionary force, claimed to exercise power in the name of the French Empire and in a colony that was still "part of the French Empire" (Art. 1). In consequence, he sent the Constitution to Paris "for the approval of the French government" (Art. 77). Quite surprisingly, Louverture's Constitution introduced a dualist concept of sovereignty. Though part of the French Empire, the colony was to be "subject to particular laws" and all laws needed the prior approval of the Assembly of Saint-Domingue (Arts.

[40] Ehrmann *Tropen der Freiheit* (n 4).

[41] J. D. Hill and F. Santos-Granero, *Comparative Arawakan Histories: Rethinking Language Family and Culture Area in Amazonia* (University of Illinois Press 2006).

1 and 19). By the same token, the citizens were "born and die there"—"and French." Since it remained unclear how French authority could be exercised in the colony, one might think of a fractured sovereignty that departed from the abstract, holistic concept developed by Bodin and Hobbes or of the dualism of two bodies of sovereignty—the *natural-practical* one being revolutionary, and the other one remaining (for the time being) *symbolically* French. A different reading would interpret these clauses as an attempt to appease the colonial master, very much like the adoption of Catholicism as the colony's religion and, more importantly, the protection of the plantation economy in Title VI "On Cultivation and Commerce."[42]

B. Second Layer: Purposes of Founding

With a focus on possible purposes, notably the 1805 Constitution suggests that it was meant to unite Haiti, like a social contract, based on fantasies of founding an independent state as a national family (Arts. 1, 3, and 14). As a result, its framers tried to negotiate the tensions between different political visions. Straight away, the Preamble addressed what Western observers might have considered a fundamental contradiction between an egalitarian project and the recognition of diversity in the new polity. With a transcendental twist and a dose of constitutional realism, the Supreme Being was introduced as the authority "before whom all mankind are equal" but who had (tolerated colonialism and) scattered "so many species of creatures" and thus produced a considerable "diversity of his works," confronting humanity with the "outcast children" of Haiti. The text reiterated the tension between a society of equals on the one hand and its members (to be precise: laborers and soldiers) on the other, who had suffered past injustices and were charged with special obligations and tasks[43] to protect the newly founded state: "Law is the same to all" and "property is sacred"; "whitemen" were excluded from acquiring private property (Arts. 4 and 12).

Another purpose pursued by the authors of both documents was to keep a distance from the particularism of the colonial center that came in the guise of Philadelphia- or Paris-style universalism. While the periphery of the global center was enslaved and excluded from human rights, it could only respond constitutionally by confronting the universalist particular of a North Atlantic

[42] Especially Art. 17. See Fischer (n 5) 229–230.
[43] Fick (n 7).

world where slavery was the rule and where its own particularism was only thinly disguised by the veil of "color-blindness." In 1801, this constellation may have inspired in particular the conception of sovereignty, the clause "All men can work at all forms of employment, whatever their color" (Art. 4), and the defense of the plantation economy: "The colony, being essentially agricultural, cannot allow the least interruption in its labor and cultivation" (Art. 14 and Title VI, 1801). More dramatically and radically, Dessaline's Constitution implicitly denounced the abstract universalism as white mythology of 1776 and 1789, and the racist, taxonomic lunacy of colonialism by de-naturalizing and politicizing the meaning of race and skin-color distinctions:[44]

> All *distinction* of color among the children of one and the same family, of whom the chief magistrate is the father, being necessarily to cease, the Haytians shall hence forward be known only by the generic appellation of Blacks. (Art. 14, 1805)[45]

That all Haitians—those of African descent, white immigrants, *mulattoes*, and others—were considered *generically Black* reversed the classical delusion of "all mankind" being equal and constitutions being "color-blind," and with one stroke deconstructed the colonial officers' taxonomic gaze. The Indigenous "is transformed form a mark of a radically transnational understanding of citizenship and residence" into a concept of "national identification."[46]

"If the earlier idea was that of Haiti as liberated territory—a kind of safe haven for anyone who was escaping genocide and slavery—the new idea of Haiti is the land of those who avenged the Indians and acquired a special right of residence."[47]

At this point, the Haitian framers entered into the "difficult realm where universalist ideas of the equality of the races and identity-based claims of past injustices and future redemption" had to be negotiated in the semantic and political arena of race, color, and membership rather than class and nation.[48] And they found (or even founded) a postcolonial solution[49] that was more

[44] For a more thorough discussion of Art. 14 of the 1805 Constitution, see Buck-Morss (n 5). Fischer (n 5) 232 reports over 100 different terms for the varieties of racial mixture and color; Grüner (n 10). See also F. Fanon, *Black Skin, White Masks* (Grove Press 2008).

[45] The term "acception" in the French version of the document could be translated as distinction or meaning, importance or significance.

[46] Fischer (n 5) 244.

[47] ibid.

[48] ibid., 227–228, 236.

[49] The solution was abandoned by later constitutions. Throughout the nineteenth century, conflicts between blacks and *mulattoes* kept returning and shaping Haitian politics. See Fischer (n 5) 235.

original and more revolutionary, definitely more risky than a present-day constitution daring to declare that all Americans or Germans "shall hence forward be known only by the generic appellation of migrants."

The Haitian social contract is also noteworthy for combining the political with the social and the economic. The postcolonial framers tried to strike a balance between political–cultural freedom and economic necessity: They protected not only their political independence but were to end their economic dependence on sugar by prohibiting the import of products "of the same nature as [Haiti's] own" (Art. 18, 1801), requiring citizens to "possess a mechanic art" (Art. 11, 1805). They linked citizenship to a person's financial standing and means (Art. 8, 1805) making "cultivators and workers ... shareholder[s] in the revenues of the manufactory" (Arts. 15 and 16, 1801).

C. Third Layer: In Search of a Constitutional Voice

The postcolonial constitutions document that Haitians tried to speak with an authentic constitutional voice. Ever since Philadelphia, Virginia, and Paris, constitutional elites have referred to and habitually used the standard terminology of freedom, equality, and property. In contrast, Haiti's framers applied themselves to finding their own language which would resonate in a colony, then a state liberated from slavery, most of whose people were illiterate. According to the new grammar, they rejected racial exclusivism and abolished the traditional hierarchies informed by skin color. Denoting all Haitians as black was a political act that politicized and denaturalized the term and thus kept alive the anticolonial struggle in every repetition of the word.

The search also included the question how to characterize the new polity, a militarized plantation country. While Louverture declared Saint-Domingue a republic, Dessalines proclaimed Hayti a free state and empire that would abstain from conquest and interfering in its neighboring countries' affairs.[50] Both operated with a view to their former masters: Louverture simply adopted the denomination of the French Republic, whereas Dessalines, having heard of Napoleon's coronation plans, moved forward to remain at eye level with the dictator and to preserve what he considered the balance of power. Both advertised the new collective of the people as a family.[51] This concept may be regarded as an attempt to invoke a postcolonial collective identity, create, within

[50] Art. 36, Constitution of 1805; Art. 2, Constitution of 1806; Arts. 36–37, Constitution of 1807.
[51] Art. 15, 1801 and Art. 14, 1805.

the constitution, an anticolonial subject, and claim his/her right to determine politics. Both Constitutions reaped the symbolic connotations of paternalism, rather than tapping into the French culture of the nation and nationalism—one of the drivers of colonialism.[52]

D. Fourth Layer: Upending the Master-Slave Dialectic

Courageously, the Framers addressed their former masters. Their Constitutions echoed and radicalized the debates in the French National Assembly before the 1791 Constitution, outlawing the privileges of the master class. Adopting the semantics of the *Déclaration* of 1789, they held property to be sacred, not for whitemen, though, should they ever return, and banned slavery even though the plantation economy was retained. Thus, they taught a lesson to the members of the European intelligentsia of mercantile and proto-industrial capitalism, who deemed themselves to be enlightened. The celebrated documents of 1776 and 1789 treated slavery as a metaphor for oppression and, likewise, philosophers justified or silenced it, such as Montesquieu warning that "[s]mall minds exaggerate the injustice done to the Africans," Locke remaining a shareholder of the Royal African Company, or Hegel conceptualizing the master–slave relationship against the background of the revolution in Haiti without openly referring to the events he must have thought were world-historical.[53] The latter may not have realized that, by revolting, the Haitians upended the master–slave dialectic denying the former lords constitutional recognition.[54]

E. Fifth Layer: The Sexual Contract

Toussaint Louverture and Jacques Dessalines, their rivals, and supporters celebrated the Haitian Revolution, the declaration of independence, and the constitutions of the new state and the wartime economy within the narrative logic of a masculinist, heroic storyline. It obscures the contradictions of this revolution in the intersections of race and gender. The emancipation from

[52] D. A. Bell, *The Cult of the Nation in France: Inventing Nationalism* (HUP 2001).

[53] Though not ignorance. For references, see Buck-Morss (n 5); D. A. Duquette, "Hegel's Social and Political Thought" (2001) Internet Encyclopedia of Philosophy (accessed February 9, 2012); D. Schaub, "Montesquieu on Slavery" (2005) 34 Perspectives on Political Science 70.

[54] In return, one might say, the U.S. Government withheld recognition of Haiti until 1862, when wartime necessity compelled it to establish cordial relations with the strategically important Caribbean nation.

slavery happened outside the racialized matrix of European Enlightenment and colonialism but within a context of what might be called authoritarian patrimonialism, determining the President as the father and the citizens as "outcast children."[55] However, it came with a sexual contract at the bottom of the layered narrative. The contract recognized only laborers, soldiers, fathers, husbands, brothers, and sons.[56] Mothers are mentioned once, daughters not at all, women only as "white women who have been naturalized Haytians" (Art. 13, 1805). So, the two Constitutions do not tell us a solely heroic story but divulge a complex narrative of a military society, its territory divided into six military divisions, its ranks defined by revolutionary achievements. The family[57] functioned as the basic social unit and fountain of social virtues, but it turned into an iron cage after divorce had been outlawed and family ties "solidified."[58]

Epilog

Since their war of liberation, the Saint-Domingue and Hayti slaves had obviously come to trust the destructive force of their arms and the power of their will as soldiers more than their political freedoms. Tragically, they were soon to learn that the former colonial masters would neither accept defeat on the battlefield nor Haiti's independence. Assisted by the law of nations, France defended the logic of racial capitalism and burdened Haiti with substantial indemnity claims,[59] a ransom one might say that helped turn the liberated nation into a commercial colony and the once opulent island into one of the poorest countries of the world.

[55] See L. Dubois et al. (eds.), *Documents constitutionnels d'Haïti 1790–1860* (De Gruyter 2013) 63.
[56] See Arts. 3, 9, and 10.
[57] Regarding the family as a metaphor and social unit: Arts. 15 and 16, 1801.
[58] "Divorce will not take place in the colony" (Art. 10, 1801). See also Arts. 9 and 11, 1801.
[59] See Obregon (n 9).

APPENDIX

Excerpts from the Constitutions of 1801 and 1805

The Constitution for Saint-Domingue, still a colony of France, was completed in May 1801, signed by Toussaint Louverture in July 1801, and passed on to the French Government for approval.

The Constitution of Hayti was promulgated by the Emperor Jacques I (Dessalines) on May 20, 1805 and published in the *New York Evening Post*, July 15, 1805.

1. Constitution of Saint-Domingue (1801)

First Title
On the territory

Art 1—The entire extent of Saint-Domingue, and Samana, Tortuga, Gonave, the Cayemites, Ile-a-Vache, the Saone and other adjacent islands, form the territory of one colony, that is part of the French Empire, but is subject to particular laws.

Art 2—The territory of this colony is divided into departments, *arrondissements*, and parishes

Title II
On its inhabitants

Art 3—There can be no slaves on this territory; servitude has been forever abolished. All men are born, live and die there free and French.

Art 4—All men can work at all forms of employment, whatever their color.

Art 5—No other distinctions exist than those of virtues and talents, nor any other superiority than that granted by the law in the exercise of a public charge. The law is the same for all, whether it punishes or protects.

Title III
On religion

Art 6—The Catholic religion, Apostolic and Roman, is the only one publicly professed.

Art 7—Every parish provides for the maintenance of the religious cult and its ministers. Manufactured goods are especially destined for this expense and for presbyteries and the lodging of ministers.

Art 8—The governor of the colony assigns to each minister of the religion the scope of his spiritual administration, and these ministers can never, under any pretext, form a body within the colony

Title IV
On morals

Art 9—Since marriage, by its civil and religious institution, tends to the purity of morals, those spouses who practice the virtues demanded by their state, will always be distinguished and specially protected by the government
Art 10—Divorce will not take place in the colony
Art 11—The state of the rights of children born through marriage will be fixed by laws that will tend to spread and maintain social virtues, and to encourage and solidify family ties.

Title V
On men in society

Art 12—The Constitution guarantees individual freedom and safety. No one can be arrested except by virtue of a formally expressed order, issued by a functionary who the law gives the right to arrest and detain in a publicly designated place.
Art 13—Property is sacred and inviolable. Every person, either by himself or his representatives, has the free disposal and administration of that which is recognized as belonging to him. Whoever infringes upon this right renders himself criminal towards society and responsible as concerns the person troubled in his property.

Title VI
On cultivation and commerce

Art 14—The colony, being essentially agricultural, cannot allow the least interruption in its labor and cultivation.
Art 15—Every habitation is a manufactory that demands a gathering together of cultivators and workers; it's the tranquil asylum of an active and constant family, of which the owner of the land or his representative is necessarily the father.
Art 16—Every cultivator and worker is a member of the family and a shareholder in its revenues. …

2. Constitution of Hayti

We, H. Christophe, Clerveaux, Vernet, Gabart, Petion, Geffard, Toussaint, Brave, Raphael, Roamin, Lalondridie, Capoix, Magny, Daut, Conge, Magloire, Ambrose, Yayou, Jean Louis Franchois, Gerin, Mereau, Fervu, Bavelais, Martial Besse …

As well in our name as in that of the people of Hayti, who have legally constituted us faithfully organs and interpreters of their will, in presence of the Supreme Being, before whom all mankind are equal, and who has scattered so many species of creatures on the surface of the earth for the purpose of manifesting his glory and his power by the diversity of his works, in the presence of all nature by whom we have been so unjustly and for so long a time considered as outcast children.

Do declare that the tenor of the present constitution is the free spontaneous and invariable expression of our hearts, and the general will of our constituents, and we submit it to the sanction of H.M. the Emperor Jacques Dessalines our deliverer, to receive its speedy and entire execution.

Preliminary Declaration.

Art. 1. The people inhabiting the island formerly called St. Domingo, hereby agree to form themselves into a free state sovereign and independent of any other power in the universe, under the name of empire of Hayti.

2. Slavery is forever abolished.
3. The Citizens of Hayti are brothers at home; equality in the eyes of the law is incontestably acknowledged, and there cannot exist any titles, advantages, or privileges, other than those necessarily resulting from the consideration and reward of services rendered to liberty and independence.
4. The law is the same to all, whether it punishes, or whether it protects.
5. The law has no retroactive effect.
6. Property is sacred, its violation shall be severely prosecuted.
7. The quality of citizen of Hayti is lost by emigration and naturalization in foreign countries and condemnation to corporal or disgrace punishments. The fist case carries with it the punishment of death and confiscation of property.
8. The quality of Citizen is suspended in consequence of bankruptcies and failures.
9. No person is worth of being a Haitian who is not a good father, good son, a good husband, and especially a good soldier.
10. Fathers and mothers are not permitted to disinherit their children.
11. Every Citizen must possess a mechanic art.
12. No whiteman of whatever nation he may be, shall put his foot on this territory with the title of master or proprietor, neither shall he in future acquire any property therein.
13. The preceding article cannot in the smallest degree affect white woman who have been naturalized Haytians by Government, nor does it extend to children already born, or that may be born of the said women. The Germans and Polanders naturalized by government are also comprized [sic] in the dispositions of the present article.
14. All acception [sic] of colour among the children of one and the same family, of whom the chief magistrate is the father, being necessarily to cease, the Haytians shall hence forward be known only by the generic appellation of Blacks.

6

Exemplary but not Canonical

The South African Voters Rights Cases

David Dyzenhaus[*]

I. 'Canonical' or 'Exemplary'?

'Canonical', according to the *Oxford English Dictionary*, means 'of or belonging to the canon of scripture, or any other sacred canon'. That makes the idea that there is a 'constitutional canon' an easy target. To place certain judgments by apex courts in the realm of the sacred is to privilege an elite vision of the fundamental values of a society. Given the prevalence of such ideas in the powerful nations of the West, especially in the USA, the idea may well seem part of a neoliberal ideology that shores up the postcolonial, Western hegemon.

No wonder that discussions of the constitutional canon often become agonized debates about teaching and scholarship, or that there is a turn in comparative constitutional law to political science in a cynical mode that seeks to debunk the pretensions of the 'high priests' of constitutionalism.[1] If the choice in comparative constitutional law is between theology and cynical political science, no scope is left for a positive but also critically self-aware account of the possible virtues of constitutionalism that relies principally on the reasoning in the judgments of apex courts.

I argue here for the existence and importance of such scope which is afforded in appreciating that the judgments on which we focus are exemplary rather than canonical. There is nothing sacred about an example. It has at most persuasive force. Put differently, the exemplary compels attention, not worship. It does so mainly by bringing to light a normativity of which we were not fully

* University Professor of Law and Philosophy, Toronto. I thank Austin Ray for research assistance as well as helpful comments on drafts, Ellen Ann for editorial help, and Sujit Choudhry and Michaela Hailbronner for helpful suggestions at the workshop.

[1] My claim here is confined to a reactive mode of analysis in constitutional scholarship and has no bearing on most work in social science on constitutionalism which is perfectly compatible with—even complementary to—normative accounts.

David Dyzenhaus, *Exemplary but not Canonical* In: *Global Canons in an Age of Contestation*. Edited by: Sujit Choudhry, Michaela Hailbronner, and Mattias Kumm, Oxford University Press.
 DOI: 10.1093/9780191956942.003.0006

aware or perhaps not aware at all.[2] We understand better, say, what it is for any individual to lead an exemplary life—what the life reveals by way of a coherent narrative or identity over time.

Since the sacred is beyond criticism, to claim this quality for human judgements is to deem them beyond evaluation. In contrast, the exemplary is open to question. One can set a bad example. The 'exemplary' thus debunks the idea of the 'canonical' in that it takes the items out of the category of the sacred and renders them vulnerable. It does, however, require an engagement which the cynical political scientist refuses. Coherent narrative or identity in the context of comparative constitutionalism is most fundamentally that of a people, of 'We, the people'. That may make the cynical refusal seem justified, as engagement involves buying in provisionally to the thought that some legitimating basis for a political order is at stake.

Here, I argue on what may seem the unpromising terrain that such engagement is worth undertaking. My main focus is apartheid South Africa in the late 1950s, when the newly elected National Party government was intent on turning an already vicious form of postcolonial white domination into something even more extreme. The exemplary cases are three decisions of the Appellate Division, at that time South Africa's apex court, between 1952 and 1957 on the voting rights of one of the groups subject to the government's racist policies.

The cases exemplify the vices as well as the virtues of constitutionalism. This double-edged aspect gives rise to some important insights about constitutionalism in general, as illustrated by the afterlife of the cases both in two other legal orders, the Rhodesian and the Israeli, as well as in philosophy of law. In Section II, I will set out these cases in their context and draw attention to the significance of the role of one of the judges, Oliver Schreiner, whose lone dissent in the last case sustained the judicial attempt to understand the South African 'people' as all South Africans, not just the white minority. Section III reflects on the cases' jurisprudential implications, while Section IV sketches their impact in Rhodesia and Israel, as well as on one of the major works of the last century in philosophy of law, H. L. A. Hart's *The Concept of Law*.[3] Section V concludes by returning to the question of what these cases exemplify. That I acknowledge is a normatively loaded question. But its normative load, once

[2] Alessandro Ferrara and Amy Allen, *The Force of the Example: Explorations in the Paradigm of Judgment* (Columbia University Press 2008) 3.

[3] H. L. A. Hart, *The Concept of Law* (2nd edn, Clarendon Press 1994) (hereafter Hart, *The Concept of Law*).

rendered explicit, makes it a question of more than academic interest. It is also pertinent to practitioners of human rights law.

II. The Voters' Rights Cases

In 1948, the National Party became the majority party and formed the government that set about turning the system of racial supremacy in South Africa into the version it named 'apartheid'. A priority was to remove the 'Coloureds'—mixed-race South Africans—who still had the vote from the common electoral roll. In 1909, the British Parliament had enacted the South Africa Act which put in place the Constitution of the Union of South Africa. Section 152 of the Act required that certain of its provisions could be changed only by a two-thirds vote of both Houses of Parliament—the House of Assembly and the Senate—sitting together. One such provision was section 35, which protected the right to vote of all those entitled to vote under 'laws existing in the Colony of the Cape of Good Hope at the establishment of the Union' and precluded their disqualification from being registered as voters 'by reason of ... race or colour only' unless the special procedure were followed.

The Act had been negotiated at a National Convention by the thirty white delegates of the four South African colonies, who decided to maintain in the Constitution the franchise rules of each colony, which ranged from not permitting any non-white participation in the franchise to permitting a limited participation.[4] Section 35 was designed to protect the male[5] Coloured and African voters of the Cape Province and was, in 1948, anathema to a government intent on ensuring a more complete white domination.

Only Coloured voters were in issue at that time because in 1937 Parliament had already used the special unicameral procedure to enact the Representation of Natives Act, which removed protected black voters from the common roll and gave them separate representation. In *Ndlwana v. Hofmeyr*,[6] a challenge to this statute was dismissed by the Appellate Division. The Court relied on the Statute of Westminster, a 1931 Act of the British Parliament that removed the power of the Imperial Parliament to enact laws for the Dominions such as Australia, Canada, the Union of South Africa, and New Zealand. Since, the judges reasoned, the Statute had made the South African Parliament the

[4] Ian Loveland, *By Due Process of Law: Racial Discrimination and the Right to Vote in South Africa 1855–1960* (Hart Publishing 1999) 113–117.

[5] At that time, the franchise was limited to men.

[6] *Ndlwana v Hofmeyr* [1937] AD 229.

supreme and sovereign law-making body, it had no power to pronounce on the validity of a duly promulgated statute.[7]

In 1951, the National Party government brought about the enactment of the Separate Representation of Voters Act providing that Coloured voters who were on the common roll be represented separately from whites. The government could not muster the two-thirds majority of both Houses of Parliament required by the South Africa Act to effect this change, so it passed the statute using the bicameral procedure for ordinary legislation—a simple majority in separate sittings of the two Houses.

In *Harris v. Minister of the Interior*,[8] the Appellate Division declared the statute invalid. Centlivres CJ, giving the unanimous judgment of the Court, accepted that the Parliament had, in 1931, become the supreme and sovereign law-making body. But, he reasoned, the fact that it could validly enact certain laws only when sitting unicamerally did not affect its sovereign status. This, he claimed, was a result brought about in a completely ordinary process of statutory interpretation.

> The Court in declaring that such a Statute is invalid is exercising a duty which it owes to persons whose rights are entrenched by Statute. Its duty is simply to declare and apply the law and it would be inaccurate to say that the Court in discharging that duty is controlling the Legislature. It is hardly necessary to add that Courts of law are not concerned with the question whether an Act of Parliament is reasonable or unreasonable, politic or impolitic.[9]

Parliament responded by enacting, again by the bicameral ordinary procedure, the High Court of Parliament Act of 1952. It provided that when the Appellate Division declared a statute invalid, its decision would be subject to review by the 'High Court of Parliament' on the application of a member of the Cabinet. Every member of the two Houses would be a member of this court; one would be appointed as President by the Governor-General (the head of state); the President would select a ten-member 'judicial committee' from the members of Parliament to make a recommendation to the full body; the full

[7] In particular, Section 2 (2) provided that no law made by one of the Dominion Parliaments 'shall be void or inoperative on the ground that it is repugnant to the law of England, or to the provisions of any existing or future Act of Parliament'. On one interpretation, this removed the constitutional protections in the South African Constitution because a statute enacted bicamerally was merely repugnant to a British statute. Ndlwana's lawyers used an ingenious argument: the Statute of Westminster removed the requirement for the special procedure, and therefore the Act was invalid because it was not enacted at a separate sitting.

[8] *Harris v. Minister of the Interior* 1952 (2) SA 428 (A).

[9] ibid, 456.

body would then decide the matter by majority vote and that decision would be taken as final and binding, to be executed as if it were a decision of a division of the Supreme Court.[10]

The High Court of Parliament Act was challenged in *Minister of the Interior v. Harris*.[11] In the main judgment, Centlivres held that the Constitution envisaged that the rights protected by section 152 would be enforceable by the sanction of invalidity exercised by a 'Court of law', and that while Parliament had the power to enact laws that established courts, the bodies had to be courts in substance not just in form. Since, in substance, the High Court of Parliament was no different from a select committee of parliamentarians, it was not a 'Court of law'. Rather, it was a court only in name, which stripped the constitutional protections of any force. Hence, the statute was invalid.

It is important to note that the term 'Court of law' was not used in the Constitution. But Centlivres pointed out that section 152 entrenched a right and provided the sanction of invalidity for a statute that infringed the right unless enacted in proper form. Since it is judges who, in the course of deciding disputes, determine whether an enactment is invalid, the issue in such cases must be decided by a 'Court of law'.[12] Thus, he rejected the government's 'startling proposition' that the High Court Act affected only unentrenched 'procedural law', and not the entrenched 'substantive right'.[13]

I want to emphasize just one passage from Schreiner JA's concurring judgment, because it both prepared the way for his dissent in the next case and proved a shrewd anticipation of what was on the cards. He stated that he would not proceed on the lines that the High Court of Parliament was not a 'Court of law' because that would permit an Act passed bicamerally to nominate, for example, a magistrate's court as the final court in constitutional cases. That would be a 'Court of law' but nevertheless 'a radical departure from the judicial hierarchy set up in the Constitution and a grave impairment of the protective system implicit in sec. 152'.[14] In his view, an 'entirely sufficient and convincing reason … for holding that the High Court of Parliament Act is invalid' was that 'implicit' in the Constitution was 'a protective judicial system … with the Appellate Division set up at the apex'.[15]

[10] ibid, 496.
[11] *Minister of the Interior v. Harris* 1952 (4) SA 769 (A).
[12] ibid, 780.
[13] ibid, 780–781.
[14] ibid, 788.
[15] ibid, 788–789.

The government responded with the Senate Act of 1955, which provided for the reconstitution of the Senate in such a way that the government secured the two-thirds majority it needed in a unicameral session. The South Africa Act Amendment Act of 1956 was then passed. It disenfranchised the Coloureds and 'compensated' them with a separate roll which elected four members to the House of Assembly and one to the Senate.[16] In addition, the Appellate Division Quorum Act of 1955 enlarged the Court from six to eleven judges and provided that all eleven had to sit in cases to determine the validity of a statute. In defending the Act in Parliament, the Minister of Justice said that by it the government intended to 'reinstate the sovereignty of Parliament'.[17]

The Senate Act was challenged in *Collins v. Minister of the Interior*.[18] Centlivres held that although the purpose of the Senate Act was plain, it was irrelevant as Parliament sitting bicamerally had 'plenary power to reconstitute the Senate'.[19] He recognized that the Act rendered the rights protected by the Constitution 'nugatory' in the same way as the High Court of Parliament Act. But he responded that the Senate Act did not affect protected rights since a further legislative step was required. In addition, the reconstituted Senate was a Senate, while the High Court of Parliament was not a 'Court of law'.[20] Eight of the judges concurred with this result, including all judges from the old bench, save for Schreiner.

In his lone dissent, Schreiner focused on the 'proviso' to section 152 of the Constitution: that a statute amending the section must be 'passed by a two-thirds of the total number of members of both Houses … at [a] joint sitting'. For the purposes of the proviso, he reasoned, the Senate was the body as contemplated by the Constitution, even if Parliament could constitute the Senate in any way it liked. For instance, Parliament could not use the two-step process to set out an education requirement for the franchise and, subsequently, prohibit persons of a particular race from attaining that qualification. There are, he said, 'only two separate fields if they are really kept separate, not if they are only separate as a matter of form. Once legislation in the one field is used as a stage preparatory to legislation in the other, there ceases to be real separation and in substance they become one field'.[21] In response to the argument that purpose

[16] In 1968, this representation was abolished by the Separate Representation of Voters Amendment Act. A Coloured Persons Representative Council was set up through the Coloured Persons Representative Council Amendment Act of 1968. However, the Council was to be sabotaged from within.

[17] House of Assembly Deb. 1955, cols 4425–4427.

[18] *Collins v. Minister of the Interior* (1957) (1) SA 552 (A).

[19] ibid, 565.

[20] ibid, 568–569.

[21] ibid, 575.

was irrelevant, he reasoned that if in issue is a 'legislative plan to do indirectly what the Legislature has no power to do directly ... the purpose may be crucial to validity'.[22]

III. We, the People?

D. V. Cowen had set out the basis for the reasoning of the Court in the first two cases in a short monograph published in 1951.[23] It relied, he claimed, on 'accepted statutory cannons of interpretation' of the South African Act considered as 'being no more than an Act of the United Kingdom Parliament'. He also thought that:

> the same conclusion could be reached on the basis that the South Africa Act is a fundamental declaration of the will of the South African people. That Act was forged after much travail at a National Convention. At the request of the four self-governing Colonies, it embodied the essential terms of a contract entered into between them to unite for the purposes of government. Accordingly, it would not be a contention without force that the South Africa Act is a British Act in form only, but in substance a constitution created by the will of the South African people.[24]

But he added that such 'a contention would ... raise difficult legal problems. Jurisprudentially, the ultimate nature of what Kelsen would call the *grundnorm* of the South African legal system is involved.'[25] Cowen was right that such a contention raises complex theoretical questions. In addition, there is the question of what exactly was the will of the South African people in 1909, indeed, of who were the South African 'people'.

[22] Steyn JA delivered a separate judgment relying on the rationale of the High Court decision, which turned on there being a necessary inference from the sanction of invalidity in the proviso that only a Court of law had the authority to decide the issue of invalidity. But he reasoned that no such inference could be drawn from the use of the words 'Houses of Parliament'; ibid, 586–587. When Centlivres CJ retired, Steyn was appointed to his position, leapfrogging over the more senior judges including Schreiner JA, the most senior. He then presided over a Court that seemed anxious to provide juridical support for the legislative entrenchment of apartheid. See also Edwin Cameron, 'Legal Chauvinism, Executive-Mindedness and Justice: LC Steyn's Impact on South African Law' (1982) 99 *South African Law Journal* 38.

[23] D. V. Cowen, *Parliamentary Sovereignty and the Entrenched Provisions of the South Africa Act* (Juta 1951).

[24] ibid, 49.

[25] ibid, fn 125.

As Edward McWhinney subsequently pointed out, in 1953 the National Party had been re-elected with a greatly increased majority, albeit one not large enough to exploit the unicameral procedure. He suggested that in 'none of the crisis situations in the great English-speaking countries where courts have been involved in power conflicts with executive or legislative authority, have the courts for any considerable length of time withstood a co-ordinate authority that has a substantiality of public opinion behind it'.[26] Despite this counsel of doom, McWhinney did not endorse the Court's reasoning. Rather, he found that Centlivres and most of the judges resorted to a positivistic or formalistic mode of reasoning in the vain hope that it would help them avoid a confrontation with the government. However, as we have seen, that mode in the end made it impossible for them to find legal resources to continue their resistance. They relied on what Centlivres in a 1955 lecture called a 'strict and complete legalism'[27]—very formal modes of reasoning that left the substantive issues buried below the surface. And that put them in a position that the government could exploit by manipulating form in a way that reliance on form alone could not resist.

In this light, one can appreciate the significance of Schreiner's disagreement with Centlivres in the second case which gave him the conceptual resources required for his dissent in the third. He connected form to substance in a way that permitted him to keep substance in place as the basis for repudiating future manipulations of form. Lorraine Weinrib aptly comments that 'Schreiner's remarkable vision was to see in the South Africa Act the components of a modern constitutional instrument protecting fundamental rights and freedoms, as higher law, against encroachment by the ordinary political process'. She continues:

> in exercising the role of guardian of these entrenched rights …, Schreiner invoked the deepest values of modern constitutional ordering. He recognized the interests at stake as subjective legal entitlements, protected by courts as

[26] Edward McWhinney, *Judicial Review in the English-Speaking World* (2nd edn, University of Toronto Press 1960) 195–196 (hereafter McWhinney, *Judicial Review in the English-Speaking World*).

[27] In September 1955, Centlivres and other distinguished judges attended a conference at Harvard Law School on 'Government under Law'. In his paper, he kept carefully away from direct comment on the Voters Rights Cases of the 1950s, though he did set out the constitutional protection in section 152. He adopted from a speech of Sir Owen Dixon, the Chief Justice of Australia, who also attended the conference, the idea that there is no 'other safe guide to judicial decisions in great conflicts than a strict and complete legalism'. In a system with an omnipotent parliament, the sole question for the courts is whether 'an enactment is *intra* or *ultra vires* the Constitution', a question unrelated to 'the merits or demerits of legislation'. See also Albert van de Sandt Centlivres, 'The Constitution of the Union of South Africa and the Rule of Law' in Arthur E. Sutherland (ed.), *Government Under Law* (Harvard University Press 1956) 427.

> impartial adjudicators of disputes between the rightholders and the state. He rejected arguments that rendered these claims as fragile, formal interests. He evaluated the legitimacy of state power by the purposes and effects of its exercise. He persevered in his role as guardian of the freedom and equality of all members of the political community, especially the weakest members. He constrained the temporarily elected government to the higher law strictures of the South Africa Act, understood, to the extent possible, as the framework of a polity of free and equal citizens.[28]

Weinrib's qualification 'to the extent possible' is important. McWhinney also pointed out that an 'activist' judicial approach maintained beyond the first two cases would eventually have had to consider 'principles of political representation going beyond the 50,000 "coloured" voters affected by the Separate Representation of Voters Act of 1951'. In this regard, he said, 'both major contending European factions (English and Afrikaner) seemed to be agreed on fundamentals', which he summed up as 'the general principle of political *non*-representation of the non-European majorities in the Union of South Africa'.[29]

In sum, it may seem that at best the judges could have done more to keep alive the glimmer of an idea of the unity of the people not based on racial grounds. But they were incapable of challenging the basic fact of apartheid and the system of racial segregation that preceded it, both designed to maintain white supremacy in the political domain to ensure continued dominance in the economic and social domains. It may also seem to follow that the exemplary force of these decisions is to teach us about the futility of relying on constitutional protections and adjudication to resist a determined and powerful elite, even when (like the National Party) the elite wishes to respect, or at least to pay lip service to respecting, the rule of law.[30] As long as the elite is willing to make its actual intentions ever more public and articulate in the law, the form of law can be used to implement any content. Finally, as we will now see, these conclusions may seem further supported by the impact of the cases in Rhodesia, Israel, and philosophy of law. But as I will argue in the last section, their memory is ambiguous in a way which contains an important lesson for human rights lawyers.

[28] Lorraine E. Weinrib, 'Constitutionalism in the Age of Rights—A Prolegomenon' (2004) 121 *South African Law Journal* 278, 283.

[29] McWhinney, *Judicial Review in the English-Speaking World* (n 26) 197 (emphasis added).

[30] See the excerpts from the parliamentary debates quoted by Geoffrey Marshall in his chapter on South Africa in *Parliamentary Sovereignty and the Commonwealth* (Clarendon Press 1957) 182–248.

IV. The Impact

A. The *Grundnorm* case

In 1965, the white minority government of the British colony of Southern Rhodesia issued a Unilateral Declaration of Dependence (UDI) and purported to create a new Constitution that made it a sovereign state.[31] It constituted the sitting High Court as the High Court of Rhodesia and provided that judges who refused to accept the 1965 Constitution would automatically lose office.

In *Madzimbamuto v. Lardner-Burke*,[32] the Court was faced with a challenge to Daniel Madzimbamuto's detention under emergency power regulations. Although he had been initially detained before 1965, his continued detention was authorized under emergency regulations issued under the 1965 Constitution. Madzimbamuto's wife claimed that the declaration of the state of emergency and the detention order were invalid because the government was illegal.

The majority rejected the challenge. The case is widely known as the *Grundnorm* case because of the centrality of Hans Kelsen's legal theory to two of these judges. They relied on his argument that at the basis of any effective legal order is a basic norm or *Grundnorm* which requires that the constitution of the order be obeyed. On this basis, the judges reasoned that a successful legal revolution takes place when the legal order of the usurping government is effective. At that point, the basic norm that authorizes the constitution is simply presupposed: the government is not only an authority in fact but also legitimate and judges are under a duty to apply its law.

Only Fieldsend AJA staked out a clearly contrary position, based on his view that the old Constitution 'was not only granted by the Sovereign on the authority of the British Parliament, but accepted by the electorate of this country acting on behalf of the country as a whole'.[33] The Constitution, he reasoned, 'assured' 'both the country's connection with the United Kingdom, and the protection of the various races that make up the population against their being

[31] The Declaration was modelled after the US Declaration of Independence except that it did not assert that 'all men are created equal' nor did it claim that governmental power was derived 'from the consent of the governed'; Claire Palley, *The Constitutional History and Law of Southern Rhodesia, 1888–1965* (Clarendon Press 1966) 750 fn 4.

[32] *Madzimbamuto v. Lardner-Burke* [1968] UKPC 18; [1968] 3 All ER 561.

[33] ibid, 422.

overreached by any one racial group, whether it be a majority in the country, or whether it has a majority in the Legislative Assembly'.[34]

Moreover, relying on the first two Voters Rights decisions, in particular on Schreiner's judgment in the second, he reasoned that the courts are the 'guardians of the constitution' but also derive their authority from the 'legal supremacy' of the constitution. 'The natural corollary of this', he said, 'is that the Court cannot sit to determine whether the constitution under which it was created has disappeared. Nor can it continue to exist to enforce some other constitution.'[35] It followed that '[j]udges appointed to office under a written constitution, which provides certain fundamental laws and restricts the manner in which those laws can be altered, must not allow rights under that constitution to be violated'.[36]

Three years later, Fieldsend resigned from the bench, stating in effect that constitutionalism was dead in white-supremacist Rhodesia. He returned as Chief Justice in 1980 to serve as the first Chief Justice of Zimbabwe and for some twenty years thereafter the courts resumed a role as the guardians of constitutional order and the rule of law. But they were unable to prevent the slide into authoritarianism presided over by President Robert Mugabe and his ZANU party.[37]

B. All that Succeeds is Success?

The *Grundnorm* case provoked one of the most interesting debates in legal theory in the second half of the twentieth century. In contrast, the Voters Rights cases get no attention from philosophers of law except in the pages of a twentieth-century classic, Hart's 1961 *The Concept of Law*.

There, Hart poured scorn on Kelsen's idea that there is a *Grundnorm*—the ultimate norm of a legal order. It should, he argued, be replaced by his version of the most fundamental rule of legal order, the 'rule of recognition' to be found in the practice of judges and which contains the criteria for certifying other rules as valid. He thus claimed to have replaced Kelsen's 'redundant' idea that there is a basic norm that stipulates that all other norms are to be obeyed with a fact of the matter—a fact about judicial practice and the criteria that judges

[34] ibid, 423.
[35] ibid, 429.
[36] ibid, 430.
[37] Theunis Roux, 'The Postcolonial Adaptation of Authoritarian Legalism in Zimbabwe' in Theunis Roux (ed.), *The Politico-Legal Dynamics of Judicial Review* (Cambridge University Press 2018) 193.

happen to accept as the criteria of correct decision.[38] As he acknowledged, that left him with the problem of what to say about cases in which there is no uncontroversial fact of the matter about what the rule of recognition requires. He concluded that in such cases all that matters is a political, legally unconstrained decision that is capable of sticking: 'Here all that succeeds is success.'[39]

Hart's conclusion may seem to capture the truth about the Voters Rights cases, as the saga in fact unfolded. Never discussed by philosophers of law is that his account is haunted by that saga. At the end of his chapter 'The Foundations of a Legal System', he describes the first two cases, and said:

> Had this process not been stopped (because the Government found it unwise to pursue this means of getting its way), we should have had an endless oscillation between two views of the competence of the legislature and so of the criteria of valid law. The normal conditions of official, and especially of judicial, harmony, under which alone it is possible to identify the system's rule of recognition, would have been suspended.[40]

He returned to this topic in the next chapter, 'Formalism and Rule-Scepticism', and observed that when courts decide 'previously unenvisaged questions concerning the most fundamental constitutional rules, they *get* their authority to decide them accepted after the questions have arisen and the decision has been given'.[41] Thereafter followed the conclusion about success as a criterion of success plus the observation that the 'constitutional question at issue may divide society too fundamentally to permit of its disposition by a judicial decision'.[42]

It is somewhat strange that Hart, writing some years after the third case was decided, seemed not to be aware of it. But it seems clear that the only difference that case would have made is to his sense of who had won the political battle. More important is that a trawl through the text and his long endnotes reveals how deeply his book is marked by the era of decolonization as well as the aggressive assertion of white supremacy in South Africa. The most agonized and passionate passages in this otherwise austere work in philosophy of law are prompted by the 'pathologies' that arise when law is used as the instrument of oppression to the extent that either the consensus about

[38] Hart, *The Concept of Law* (n 3) ch. VI, 292–293.
[39] ibid, 153.
[40] ibid, 122.
[41] ibid, 153.
[42] ibid.

constitutional fundamentals needed to sustain legal order breaks down or, which may be worse, the oppressed become sheep-like and are passively led to the 'slaughterhouse'.[43]

C. The Basic Law Decision

In 1995, in *United Mizrachi Bank v. Migdal Cooperative Village*,[44] Aharon Barak, the new President of Israel's Supreme Court, greeted the Basic Law: Human Dignity and Liberty as a 'constitutional revolution',[45] as Israel's entry into the 'community of democratic countries ... with constitutional bills of rights'.[46] In support of this conclusion, he reasoned that the best interpretation of democracy requires judicial review. Central to his argument was the idea of judges as guardians of the constitution;[47] and he recognized the provenance of this view in the tradition of common law constitutionalism, notably in the Voters Rights cases.[48]

However, he and his Court never intended these rights to reach the millions of Palestinians subject to rule by the Israeli state in the Occupied Territories despite the fact that the Israeli Supreme Court is not only the apex court for both legal orders but had elevated itself to that position. On the one hand, within the Israeli legal order (ILO), the supreme legislative authority is the parliament, the Knesset, which legislates subject to the regime of constitutional law developed out of Israel's Basic Laws by the Supreme Court. On the other hand, within the legal order of the Occupied Territories (OTLO), the supreme legislature is the military which legislates subject to the regime of law developed by the same Court and the Knesset for that order. But, to a large extent, the two legal orders are sealed off from each other.[49]

[43] ibid, 117.

[44] CA 6821/93 *United Mizrahi Bank Ltd v. Migdal Cooperative Village*, 49(4) PD 221 (1995) (Isr.).

[45] ibid, 141.

[46] ibid, 139.

[47] ibid, 219.

[48] ibid, 222: 'Indeed, a long list of judicial decisions throughout the common-law world has recognized—in the absence of an express constitutional provision—judicial review of constitutionality (see, e.g., *Harris v. Minister of Interior* ...)'.

[49] I say 'to a large extent' because it appears that the Supreme Court has recently started to rely more on constitutional law than on public international law in its rulings on Palestinians in the OTLO. See also Tamar Hostovsky Brandes, 'International Law in the Decisions of the Israeli Supreme Court concerning the Occupied Territories' (2020) 18 *ICON* 767. She argues that this shift is consistent with a deliberate eradication of the distinction between Israel and the Occupied Territories by the Parliament and the government. Note that appeals can be made from the OTLO to the Israeli administrative courts.

One does not have to be a cynical political scientist to conclude that the reason for creating this 'parallel state' was to require the inhabitants of the Occupied Territories to participate in legitimating the occupation by recognizing the authority of the Israeli state while denying them the protections afforded by the ILO's most fundamental norms.[50] In that case, the lesson of the Voters Rights cases may well seem to be not only that all that succeeds is success, but also that the success is that of might covered with a thin veneer of legal right.

V. Constitutionalism and Legal Theory in Divided Societies

Overall, then, one might suppose that the lesson for constitutionalism is that its success in a society as deeply divided as Hart understood South Africa to be depends on whether one of the groups is sufficiently powerful to assert its will over the rest. However, it was not the case in South Africa that with the formal constitutional protections of Coloured voters gone, there was nothing substantive left. What Schreiner called the 'protective judicial system … with the Appellate Division set up at the apex' remained intact. There remained in place in apartheid South Africa a commitment to constitutionalism that gave to judges the resource to interpret statutes in such a way as to preserve, as we saw Weinrib put it, 'to the extent possible … the framework of a polity of free and equal citizens'.[51] The content of this commitment was no more (but also no less) than the resources of a legal tradition that had inherited from both British common law and Roman Dutch law presumptions of the liberty and equality of individual legal subjects, presumptions which were supposed to inform the judicial interpretation of statutes.

In the apartheid state, human rights lawyering was possible because the mark of such a state is that all are subject to the same law except insofar as particular enactments carve out areas in which certain groups are subject to

[50] For relevant discussion, see David Kretzmer, *The Occupation of Justice: The Supreme Court of Israel and the Occupied Territories* (State University of New York Press 2002). See also David Dyzenhaus, *The Long Arc of Legality: Hobbes, Kelsen, Hart* (Cambridge University Press 2022) ch. 5 (hereafter Dyzenhaus, *The Long Arc of Legality*).

[51] See John Dugard, *Human Rights and the South African Legal Order* (Princeton University Press 1978); A. S. Mathews, *Freedom, State Security and the Rule of Law: Dilemmas of the Apartheid Society* (Juta 1986); Richard Abel, *Politics by Other Means: Law in the Struggle Against Apartheid* (Routledge 1995); Jens Meirhenrich, *The Legacies of Law: Long-Run Consequences of Legal Development in South Africa, 1652–2000* (Cambridge University Press 2008); David Dyzenhaus, *Hard Cases in Wicked Legal Systems: Pathologies of Legality* (2nd edn, Oxford University Press 2010) (hereafter Dyzenhaus, *Hard Cases in Wicked Legal Systems*).

a discriminatory regime. Individuals in these groups were thereby relegated to the status of second-class citizenship. The idea of second-class citizenship does not here pertain to one's political standing in the sense of X is a citizen of Canada. Rather, it pertains to one's juridical standing, one's standing before the law. The second-class citizen has one foot in the space of first-class citizenship or full status before the law, with the other in a space of law-created inferior status. Such second-class status is much more *legally* problematic than the status of slavery, so long as the enslaved persons are relentlessly consigned to the status of objects or things. For if one is legally recognized as having status as a legal subject for some purposes but not for others, the parts of the law which seem to relegate one to inferior status are put into question by those parts which do not when a legal challenge is mounted to the inferior status.

It should be noted that only a minority of the judges were determined to deploy these presumptions and they were generally in the lower courts so were often overruled by the appellate courts. In addition, the legislature was astute to react by closing what the government saw as a gap in the legislation and by ensuring that new legislation did not provide similar opportunities. To achieve that end, the government had to be explicit in its legislation that certain groups of people were not to be treated as free and equal, or prohibit judicial review of the implementation of its decisions, or impede access to legal advice to the victims of the decisions. These strategies, often combined, had the effect of putting those affected beyond the reach of the rule of law. They were governed not by law but by the diktat of the officials who staffed the particular legal regimes.

To the extent that South Africans found themselves governed by legally unconstrained executive prerogative, the apartheid state at times verged on becoming a 'dual state'. This term was coined by Ernst Fraenkel to describe the Nazi state, which he said consisted of two states that existed side by side: the 'normative state', which contained whatever remained of the law and institutions of the 1919–1933 Weimar legal order, together with the statutory regimes enacted after 1933 and implemented through those institutions; and the 'prerogative state', which consisted of the apparatus of the Nazi Party wherein the leader's will was the ultimate source of decision-making authority.[52]

It is important that Fraenkel's analysis was based on his experience of legal practice in Berlin between 1933 and 1938. On this basis, he observed that the law of the normative state governed relationships between individuals, and between individuals and state institutions, only as long as an official in the

[52] Ernst Fraenkel, *The Dual State: A Contribution to the Theory of Dictatorship* (Oxford University Press 2017).

prerogative state did not consider it in the interests of the Nazi Party to override that law. He concluded that the rule of law did not obtain in Nazi Germany because the protections of the normative state were subject to the discretion of Nazi officials.

One could thus not be a human rights lawyer in Nazi Germany. As Fraenkel said, in the final phase of his legal practice in Berlin he frequently described his work to friends as that of a 'switchman'.

> That is, I regarded it an essential part of my efforts to ensure that a given case was dealt with under the auspices of the 'normative state', and not end up in the 'prerogative state'. Colleagues with whom I was on friendly terms confirmed that they, too, had repeatedly worked towards making sure that their clients were punished in a court of law ...[53]

At best, then, Fraenkel could switch the matter into the normative state and from what is known about the detail of his legal victories, they did not depend on any residual legal rights available within the normative state. Rather, they depended entirely on the effective use of legal procedures to his clients' advantage in cases in which judges were not subject to direct pressure from officials in the prerogative state or were prepared to try to resist such pressure and do their jobs.[54] This was all that was possible because the 'always cramped space' of the normative state contracted as the Nazi grip on power increased until the point when 'the normative state meant not the rule of law but the technical administration of the law'.[55] And even that technical administration could be set aside if an official in the prerogative state so decided.

In contrast, in the apartheid state, human rights lawyers could hope to get a matter switched into the space governed by the fundamental legal norms that applied in principle to all inhabitants of South Africa. And this can be contrasted again with the situation in the legal order which unifies the ILO and the OTLO. For there, human rights lawyers practising in the OTLO are denied the possibility of switching a matter into the space of the ILO and so must have recourse to the norms of international law that are supposed to govern occupation.[56] That makes human rights lawyering a particularly fraught endeavour.

[53] ibid, xix.

[54] Douglas G. Morris, 'The Dual State Reframed: Ernst Fraenkel's Political Clients and his Theory of the Nazi Legal System' (2013) 58 *Leo Baeck Institute YB* 5.

[55] ibid, 5 and 19. See also Douglas G. Morris, *Legal Sabotage: Ernst Fraenkel in Hitler's Germany* (Cambridge University Press 2020).

[56] See Aeyal Gross, *The Writing on the Wall: Rethinking the International Law of Occupation* (Cambridge University Press 2017). Gross argues that the Israeli Supreme Court navigates the parts of public international law most suitable for shoring up the legality of the occupation while avoiding those

As Michael Sfard argues in his book on practising human rights in the Occupied Territories, regime change cannot be an aim of human rights lawyers because they accept the limits the law imposes on their practice.[57] Moreover, not only do their losses in court help to shore up the legitimacy of the regime, but also their occasional victories, because the latter support the authorities' claim to be ruling in accordance with the rule of law. That fact has made Sfard and others wonder whether they should discontinue their practice, because overall the calculus is that they do more harm than good. But they find themselves unable to give up because the victims of the oppressive laws turn to them for help.

There is another reason for continuing. The experience of human rights lawyers in apartheid South Africa looms large in Sfard's understanding.[58] On the last page, he asserts that 'one day the occupation will end, like apartheid in South Africa' and, when it does, 'we'll find that we are not entirely bereft of a culture of good government, that we do have moral foundations to draw on'. That provides the reason why 'human rights lawyers must hold their heads high and know that they have a role in the appearance of cracks in the occupation'.[59]

Sfard does not note that just such a culture of good government was the basis for constitutionalism in post-apartheid South Africa and has proved of the utmost importance at a time when trust in government is low because of widespread corruption and incompetence infecting all levels during a decade of 'state capture'. The human rights lawyers of the apartheid era maintained the idea that the law embodied an ideal of the unity of the people that transcended

which do not. There is a way in which Palestinian subjects of the parallel state are virtual second-class citizens in the legal sense sketched earlier complicates my argument. The Israeli Supreme Court presides over a state—the ILO—in which there are first-class citizens, although the Palestinian citizens of Israel are in significant respects second-class citizens. See Hassan Jabareen, 'Hobbesian Citizenship: How the Palestinians Became a Minority in Israel' in Will Kymlicka and Eva Pföstl (eds), *Multiculturalism and Minority Rights in the Arab World* (Oxford University Press 2014) 189. Within the Occupied Territories, while Palestinians are all subject to the same law, they also live side by side with the Israeli settlers in the fortified enclaves which are illegal extensions of and subject to the protection of the Israeli state. Dramatic examples here are the separate systems of roads established by the Israeli Defence Force for settlers and Palestinians, the wall built to cut Palestinians off from contact with Israel and settler enclaves, as well in many cases from their means of livelihood. See John Dugard and John Reynolds, 'Apartheid, International Law, and the Occupied Palestinian Territory' (2013) 24 *European Journal of International Law* 867. See also Hassan Jabareen, 'How the Law of Return Creates One Legal Order in Palestine' (2020) 21 *Theoretical Inquiries in Law* 459. Palestinians in the Occupied Territories are, that is, virtual second-class citizens because they live under an occupation which provides full status for settlers and an inferior status for them while the Supreme Court's jurisdiction over them gives them a toehold if not a foothold in the first-class space.

[57] Michael Sfard, *The Wall and the Gate: Israel, Palestine, and the Legal Battle for Human Rights* (Metropolitan Books 2018). See especially the concluding chapter, 'Sand on the Slope'.

[58] ibid, 443–444 and 447–448.

[59] ibid, 455.

the political divisions of the day, and which was worth struggling for against the odds.

Without the example of a few cases such as the Voters Rights cases, there would have been no basis for these lawyers' practice.[60] The ideal for which they strove required them to adopt what can be termed a 'regulative assumption'. Such an assumption does not aim to reflect all the brute facts about the world. It seeks instead to shape the world by engaging in a practice that builds on some elements in it in order to make the world live up to the ideal that informs the assumption. In my view, it is this kind of idea that Kelsen was after when he argued that jurists must hypothesize a basic norm if they are to make sense of legal order as a unified order of norms.[61] There is an element of choice in the 'if', as there is in the choice to be human rights lawyer in an unjust regime. But whatever choice one makes, the idea of the exemplary in comparative constitutional law is indispensable.

[60] Dyzenhaus, *Hard Cases in Wicked Legal Systems* (n 51).
[61] For a full defence of this claim, see Dyzenhaus, *The Long Arc of Legality* (n 50) ch. 4.

7

A Constitutional Canon for Africa

James Fowkes

I. Introduction

Africa is the continent least studied by comparative constitutional lawyers. Relative neglect by the West or the North is a familiar theme. But Global South discussion, too, usually overlooks Africa apart from South Africa, and intra-African comparison remains limited to a degree that might surprise outsiders. An African lawyer today is still more likely to know or consult a source from their state's former colonizer than one from another African state.

An African constitutional canon cannot alter all the reasons for this, but there are some that it can address squarely. One is the belief that Africa is just not very constitutionally interesting: because constitutional law's hold on the continent is generally thought to be weak, or because African problems and societies are seen as too different for comparison to be relevant. This is simply false, but few constitutional scholars have the time or inclination to do the comparative work necessary to find that out. A canon of accessible, short examples can make it sufficiently easy to learn enough to challenge this common assumption.

A canon can also address the second, related problem that inattention in comparative law is a self-fulfilling prophecy. It is always easier and more respectable to study the cases that have been studied before. So the marginal cases stay marginal. Each decision not to engage African cases in comparative law provides reasons for the next decision not to do so.

This state of affairs is preventable. It is partly just a matter of overcoming the inertia. This task is also modestly realistic. Witness the fact that, for all that Eurocentrism is real, non-locals and non-specialists invariably approach 'European constitutionalism' in terms of a few notable ideas and examples from the most prominent European systems. Something similar is true for US constitutional law. It is most comparativists' second constitutional language, but most speak it only to a very limited degree. This is a level of knowledge, of

James Fowkes, *A Constitutional Canon for Africa* In: *Global Canons in an Age of Contestation*. Edited by: Sujit Choudhry, Michaela Hailbronner, and Mattias Kumm, Oxford University Press.
DOI: 10.1093/9780191956942.003.0007

awareness, of status, of presence in the discussion, to which an African canon can realistically aspire.[1]

This contribution will discuss two texts. Both are short. Neither is South African. One is from Kenya, East African and Anglophone. One is from Benin, West African and Francophone. The former happens to be the anti-canonical one, and the latter the canonical; I could easily have picked otherwise, or drawn from, say, Lusophone or Islamic Africa, or the diaspora.

But this pair will suffice to illustrate what an African canon for today might look like, and what it might be able to achieve. Too often, the continent appears on the comparative map as an undifferentiated and sometimes hostile terrain, with few navigable rivers and a reputation for barrenness. The most important aim for an African canon is to put down some basic landmarks for easier navigation. This is the best way to open up the continent for the more serious constitutional attention it merits.

II. 'There shall be in Kenya only one political party': The Anti-Canonical Act No. 7 of 1982

One approach to an African anti-canon is to make it about the things we most wish to repudiate—slavery, for example, or colonialism, or genocide, or dictatorship—and pick anti-canonical texts accordingly. If we do this, however, we will often find ourselves talking about texts with little connection to African constitutional law. We will also be talking about Africa as a place where bad things happen, rather than taking it seriously as a site of legal interest. For this reason, I focus here on an anti-canonical example that, while not of the worst in moral terms, comes squarely from within African constitutional law and its debates. Among the advantages of this approach are the links it can establish between Africa and current issues in comparative constitutional law: in this case, for example, between Kenyan history and contemporary debates about autocratic legalism and abusive constitutionalism.[2]

My chosen example is Kenya's Act No. 7 of 1982, just two pages and nine sections long. Several items of interest are hidden in those sections. But the

[1] I have discussed this approach and the issues in the preceding paragraphs in James Fowkes, '10 Boxes: Wie globale, kontextualisierte Vergleichung machbar ist' in Rolf Gröschner, Matthias Jestaedt, and Anna-Bettina Kaiser (eds), *Fundamenta Juris Publici* (Mohr Siebeck 2023); English translation in *Verfassung und Recht im Übersee/World Constitutional Law* (forthcoming).

[2] See, originally, David Landau, 'Abusive Constitutionalism' (2012) 47 UC Davis L Rev 189; Javier Corrales, 'Autocratic Legalism in Venezuela' (2015) 26 Journal of Democracy 37; Kim Scheppele, 'Autocratic Legalism' (2018) 85 U Chi L Rev 545.

most obvious point is stated openly: the Act amended the Kenyan Constitution of 1969 by inserting a new section 2A: 'There shall be in Kenya only one political party, the Kenya African National Union.'

The Kenya African National Union (KANU) is Kenya's party of national liberation. It held power continuously during the country's first thirty-nine years as an independent state. KANU was the party of Jomo Kenyatta, who became Kenya's first President in 1963. Kenyatta's successor, who ran both KANU and Kenya from 1978 until 2002, was Daniel arap Moi.

The 1982 Act came early in Moi's tenure. Two KANU members, Oginga Odinga and Paul Anyona, who had already established a reputation as party dissidents under Kenyatta, announced their intention to break away and form a new radical party, the Kenyan African Socialist Alliance. Parts of Moi's response involved tactics already established under Kenyatta. The responsible state body refused to register the new party.[3] The pair would also be subject to arrest, bans, and detention. But with the 1982 Act, Moi went further. The Act made membership of KANU a requirement for membership of the National Assembly, and loss of membership a disqualification.[4] This created a formidable tool for party discipline: giving the party a monopoly on political power gives the party leader a monopoly on access to that power. Conversely, party discipline became the discipline of all formal political activity.

The same theme can also be detected in the only parts of the 1982 Act that are not directly about a political party. Two of its sections work to centralize control over the civil service, including by installing a new 'Chief Secretary' as 'head of the public service'.[5] This is an example of a post-independence government using a colonial-era device to exercise power: the position of 'Chief Secretary' had first been introduced during colonial rule, to assist in the exercise of the broad authority held by the British governor.[6] Its 1982 revival under Moi expanded on an earlier centralizing constitutional amendment under Kenyatta, which had given the President the power to appoint and dismiss any member of the civil service.[7]

This strategy of concentrating power in the executive is logically part of the same Act that concentrated power in KANU, for the simple reason that each

[3] Gabrielle Lynch, *I Say To You: Ethnic Politics and the Kalenjin in Kenya* (Chicago UP 2011) 113–114.

[4] Act 7 of 1982 (hereafter '1982 Act'), s. 5, read with Constitution of Kenya, 1969 (hereafter '1969 Constitution'), s. 34; 1982 Act, s. 6, read with 1969 Constitution, s. 39.

[5] 1982 Act, ss. 4, 8.

[6] Githu Muigai, 'Constitutional Amendments and the Constitutional Amendment Process in Kenya (1964–1997): A Study in the Politics of the Constitution' (PhD Dissertation, University of Nairobi 2001) 154.

[7] Constitution of Kenya Amendment Act 14 of 1966.

change served to concentrate power in President Moi, as head of both. Political power in Kenya was and remains highly personalized. Though it is formally about a one-party state, the 1982 Act can be usefully understood as part of Moi's efforts to ensure that Kenya remained a one-leader state.

The word is 'remained' because it is not as if the 1982 Act destroyed a richly pluralist, competitive, multi-party democracy.[8] After independence, President Kenyatta's approach of reconciliation and harambee ('all pull together' in Swahili) brought opposition leaders and MPs into the KANU fold.[9] That included Moi, until 1964 a member of KANU's rival Kenyan African Democratic Union (KADU).[10] 'The merger of KADU with KANU made Kenya a de facto one party state and paved the way for a despotic executive.'[11] Kenyatta's KANU used its state power to skew the political playing field, including by bribery, misinformation, intimidation, arrest and detention, and blocking the registration of election candidates.[12] Political freedoms and the powers of parliament were eroded throughout the 1970s, including through the use of constitutional amendments.[13] So Moi's moves in 1982 hardly marked the closure of what had previously been an open political system.[14]

They did, however, form part of a trend towards relatively greater repression, compared to the Kenyatta era.[15] Presidential powers to detain without trial had been recognized under the Kenyatta government, but Moi's regime used them much more often. The 1980s saw unions and student groups either banned or co-opted. In 1986, state corporations were brought under direct presidential control. Interference in elections also increased significantly under Moi.[16] In the Westminster tradition, both backbench MPs and civil servants are important checks on executive power, and under Kenyatta each retained a degree of meaningful independence. That, too, changed under Moi. Parliament

[8] Charles O. Oyaya and Nana K. Poku, *The Making of the Constitution of Kenya: A Century of Struggle and the Future of Constitutionalism* (Routledge 2018) 86.

[9] Jennifer A. Widner, *The Rise of a Party-State in Kenya: From 'Harambee!' To 'Nyayo!'* (U C Press 1992) 56–57.

[10] Lynch (n 3) 91–92.

[11] B. A. Ogot, 'Transition from a Single-Party to Multiparty Political System, 1989–93' in B. A. Ogot and W. R. Ochieng (eds), *Decolonization & Independence in Kenya 1940–93* (Ohio State UP 1995) 239; Makau wa Matua, 'Human Rights and State Despotism in Kenya: Institutional Problems' (1994) 41 Afr Today 50, 50; W. R. Ochieng, 'Structural and Political Changes' in Ogot and Ochieng, 102.

[12] see also Widner (n 9) 69–70.

[13] Widner (n 9) 68–70, 98–110, 128–131.

[14] Lynch (n 3) 94–97, 106–107, Norman Miller and Rodger Yaeger, *Kenya: The Quest for Prosperity* (first published 1994; 2nd edn, Routledge 2018) 45–47.

[15] Peter Anyang' Nyong'o, 'State and Society in Kenya: The Disintegration of the Nationalist Coalitions and the Rise of Presidential Authoritarianism, 1963–78' (1989) 88 Afr Aff 225; Lynch (n 3) 114–115, 123–125.

[16] Lynch (n 3) 119–120, 125–128; Miller and Yaeger (n 14) 40–43, 59; Widner (n 9) 68, 137, 143–147, 150–154, 158–161, 165–171, 178–179.

became a rubber stamp, as we will see, and after 1985, Moi used the one-party state device to further increase his control over officials by legally requiring all civil servants to join KANU.[17]

Moi also changed the party itself. In Kenyatta's time, KANU had been both relatively inactive and quite small. Under Moi, party membership increased enormously, rising from a few hundred thousand members in the Kenyatta era to one million by 1984 and eight million by 1988. Membership became far more important as a means to gain access to jobs and patronage and to avoid intimidation and the loss of benefits. KANU never became an all-pervasive state party on the scale of, for example, Mobutu Seso Seko's Mouvement populaire de la révolution in the former Zaire.[18] But Moi nevertheless used the party far more then Kenyatta as a tool of power and an instrument of governance—and so expanding his control meant expanding the party's role. The 1982 Act symbolizes this change.[19]

A. Taking the One-Party State Seriously

The candour of the Act—openly proclaiming a *de jure* one-party state, not just slyly bringing about a de facto one—reminds us that Moi's strategy was much less provocative in 1982 than would be true in the 1990s. It was an era when (not for the last time) the one-party model was often treated as a serious alternative to 'Western' multi-party democracy. Kenyatta believed that having one party, with a mass base, was just as democratic as having two mass parties.[20] He was not alone. Here, for example, is the Commonwealth Secretary General introducing the report of a 1976 seminar on the one-party state organized by the International Commission of Jurists:

> ... a number of developing countries have turned away from ... Westminster democracy... to a one-party system. To the casual observer, these new forms may have the appearance of totalitarianism; yet, as the [conference] proceedings have shown, a one-party state can afford citizens more genuine opportunities for genuine choice than the multi-party system it has displaced....[21]

[17] Widner (n 9) 151, 169–170.

[18] ibid 204–208.

[19] Lynch (n 3) 117–118; B. A. Ogot, 'The Politics of Populism' in Ogot and Ochieng (n 11) 202–208; generally Widner (n 9).

[20] Widner (n 9) 55.

[21] Shridath Ramphal, 'Preface' in International Commission of Jurists, *Human Rights in a One-Party State* (Search Press Ltd 1978) 8, available at www.icj.org/wp-content/uploads/1978/01/human-rights-in-one-party-state-conference-report-1976-eng.pdf accessed 17 October 2022.

Among African leaders, perhaps the sincerest supporter of the idea was Julius Nyerere, in neighbouring Tanzania (where the International Commission of Jurists' conference had been held). Nyerere advocated one-party rule as the best form of government to bring about development in fragile African states with ethnically divided populations, arguing that a multi-party system would inevitably produce divisive inter-tribal competition. If this was the model, Kenya also seemed a good match for it. In a typical example, the Kenyan scholar J. B. Ojwang wrote in 1990 that 'the one party system appears as an alternative mode of political organization which accords with the economic and social conditions prevailing in Kenya'.[22]

For Moi, whose motives were more expedient than Nyerere's, such arguments offered a convenient defence of his monopoly on power. Greater pluralism had to wait until Kenyan society was more cohesive; until then, he could paint any opposition as disloyal and dangerous.[23] The 'coming together' of Kenyatta's 'Harambee' slogan stood for anti-tribalism and Kenyan nationalism but also, to those ends, for the imperative to unify under one leader. It was a populist strategy, in that Kenyatta was claiming to be the one who spoke for the people as a whole, where other leaders merely had narrow tribal constituencies. Moi's version, 'Nyayo', means 'follow in the footsteps'. It was partly a gesture of respect to Kenyatta. But it also positioned Moi as inheriting Kenyatta's one-man power, telling Kenyans to follow in the footsteps of the President: to follow where Moi led.[24] The populist claim to truly represent the people was being turned, as it so often is, into a claim on their loyalty that turned dissent into treason. The need for solidarity had become the duty to obey.

If the one-party state is taken constitutionally seriously, this concentration of power might only imply the need for greater checks and balances elsewhere. Some criticized the 1982 Act on that basis at the time. The criticism—perhaps also reflecting what was possible or prudent under the Moi regime—was that the Act was flawed because it did not create any mechanisms to compensate for its abolition of multi-party competition.[25]

Certainly, such institutional checks were not in evidence in Moi's Kenya. The position of Chief Secretary, already discussed, had only a brief life. Moi abolished it four year later, by a further constitutional amendment, when it

[22] Jackton B. Ojwang, *Constitutional Development in Kenya: Institutional Adaptation and Social Change* (Acts Press 1990) 65.

[23] Ogot, 'Transition' (n 11) 241.

[24] Lynch (n 3) 115–116, Widner (n 9) 44, 130, 161, 163, 168–169; Ogot, 'Politics of Populism' (n 19) 193–204.

[25] For an example, see Jackton B. Ojwang and Phoebe N. Okowa, 'The One-Party State and Due Process of Law: The Kenya Case in Comparative Perspective' (1989) 1 Afr J Intl Comp L 177.

threatened to become a site of independent power.[26] At the same time, he abolished the tenure protections of the Auditor General and the Attorney General, with the sycophantic incumbent of the latter position loudly praising his own neutering.[27] As another Attorney General, Amos Wako, would revealingly put it a few years later in 1991, 'a characteristic of the rule of law is that no man, save for the President, is above the law'.[28] Wako would serve as Kenya's Attorney General until 2011.

The courts, too, failed to be an effective check on the one-party power the Act had created. In the colonial era, judges had served at the pleasure of the Crown. Although the Constitution of 1966 formally protected judicial independence, both the Kenyatta and Moi regimes 'treated the courts just like any other agency within the executive'.[29] Judicial security of tenure was in fact formally removed from the Constitution in 1988, before being restored in 1990.[30] But the pattern of judicial deference was hardly confined to that brief period.

We can see this in the failure of a legal challenge brought against the 1982 Act itself. Section 80 of the 1969 Constitution protected freedom of assembly and association. The 1982 Act did not purport to amend the section, and the legal challenge tried out the argument that the 1982 Act was invalid because it was contrary to section 80. It failed. Section 80, ruled the court, did not guarantee a right to found or join political parties, and the National Assembly in any event had unfettered sovereign power to amend the Constitution.[31] If the 1982 Act was an experiment with a new constitutional form of the state, Kenya's judges undertook no general, creative, re-imagining of Kenya's constitutionalism to match.

The limited role of the judiciary in the Westminster model is doubtless part of the explanation for this. But it is not a sufficient explanation. An imposed common law tradition had not prevented India, across the ocean, from developing a doctrine of unconstitutional constitutional amendment some years earlier.[32] The difference is that the Kenyan judiciary was an altogether more subservient institution, including for local structural reasons.

[26] Muigai (n 6) 157–158.

[27] Act 14 of 1986; Oyaya and Poku (n 8) 87.

[28] Quoted by Makau Matua, 'Justice under Siege: The Rule of Law and Judicial Subservience in Kenya' (2001) 23 Hum Rts Q 96, 100.

[29] ibid 101–102.

[30] Constitution of Kenya Amendment Act 4 of 1988; Constitution of Kenya Amendment Act 1 of 1990.

[31] *Imanyara v. A-G*, unreported civil appeal No. 7 of 1991.

[32] *Golak Nath v. State of Punjab*, AIR 1967 SC 1643; *Kesavananda Bharati v. Union of India* (1973) 4 SCC 225. For a succinct summary of the emergence of the doctrine in India, see Arun K. Thiruvengadam, *The Constitution of India: A Contextual Analysis* (Hart Publishing 2017) 220–229.

The judge who wrote the judgment upholding the constitutionality of the 1982 Act was Norbury Dugdale. He was a so-called 'contract judge': one of a group of expatriate, mostly British, judges, for whom the 1969 Constitution made no provision. The Kenyatta and Moi regimes both took the position that contract judges' appointments could be rescinded at any time, and both used contract judges extensively because of the control this afforded. (This is the explanation for the otherwise odd presence of white British judges in Kenyan courts decades after independence.) Contract judges who handed down rulings unfavourable to the regime could simply be removed. Since these were usually people who would not be able to obtain such high posts in their home countries, many—like Dugdale—stuck closely to a path of ingratiating deference to the regime.[33]

Even if the judiciary had shown more resistance to the 1982 Act, however, we can be confident that the attempt would ultimately have failed. Witness what happened a few years later when Moi's government sought to make certain offences non-bailable. That statute created a much more direct constitutional problem, because it squarely contravened the right to bail, and the courts did indeed strike down the statute. But the KANU legislature promptly overruled the decision, by means of yet another constitutional amendment.[34]

This outcome further confirms the limits of common law tradition as an explanation. In the Westminster tradition, the legislature is supposed to be the most powerful institution and, under the doctrine of responsible government, the greatest check on those holding executive power. In the years immediately after independence, Kenya kept at least some meaningful connection to the tradition.[35] But now Parliament was just as ineffective a check as the judiciary. The reasons included the bluntest. Reportedly, MPs at a KANU parliamentary meeting were warned that they would be imprisoned without trial if they resisted the 1982 Act.[36] It passed with just two dissenting votes.[37] During the 1980s, state structures were successfully drained of their institutional ability to check Moi's one-party power.[38]

[33] Matua, 'Justice under Siege' (n 28) 107–116.

[34] *Ngui v. Republic*, Criminal Application No. 4 of 1985; Act 20 of 1987; Stephen Ndegwa et al. (eds), *History of Constitution Making in Kenya* (Konrad Adenauer Foundation 2012) 22; Oyaya and Poku (n 8) 88.

[35] Widner (n 9) 157.

[36] ibid 145.

[37] Oyaya and Poku (n 8) 86.

[38] Widner (n 9) 36, 162, 180, 228.

B. Constitutionalism in a Post-Colonial State

The final absent check on Moi's one-party state is more abstract: less about formal constitutional structures than about the spirit of constitutionalism surrounding their use.

Studying the 1982 Act among the other constitutional amendments under Moi, it is hard to escape the impression of an almost entirely instrumental approach to constitutional amendment, with changes driven simply by narrowly tactical political calculation. This confirms the problem of taking the one-party state seriously in constitutional terms: it is a big bet, on long odds, that the one party, and its leader, will be equally constitutionally serious.

Moi, however, did not invent this approach to the Constitution. Part of the explanation for what he did, and for how he was able to do it, was that Moi was continuing a pattern.

To begin with, constitutional instrumentalism was certainly also visible under Kenyatta. Moi himself had been a target of it. Those who opposed his succeeding Kenyatta had tried to change the Constitution to prevent Moi, as Vice-President, from automatically becoming acting President when Kenyatta died. The 'Change-the-Constitution' group did not succeed, largely since Kenyatta himself opposed the move. But earlier, a constitutional amendment had successfully been used to block Odinga automatically succeeding Kenyatta when Odinga was Vice-President.[39] A constitutional amendment was also part of Moi's response to an earlier breakaway from KANU in the 1960s.[40] In light of this history, it is not surprising that Moi treated tactical constitutional amendment as part of how the game was played.

But the historical argument goes back further still. The 1982 Act is also a fruitful site for debate about colonialism's effects on post-colonial African constitutionalism.

Independent Kenya's first, 1963, Constitution was drafted with significant involvement from the departing British, a familiar pattern in decolonizing Africa.[41] The British exerted what influence they could in favour of a parliamentary system, a decentralized federal state, and a bill of rights. Their aim was to protect minorities, notably including the small and vocal white settler

[39] ibid 112–118; Ogot, 'Politics of Populism' (n 19) 188–189; Constitution of Kenya Amendment Act 2 of 1986.

[40] Constitution of Kenya Amendment Act 17 of 1966.

[41] Charles H. O. Parkinson, *Bills of Rights and Decolonization: The Emergence of Domestic Human Rights Instruments in Britain's Overseas Territories* (OUP 2007), on Kenya in particular see 216–225, 240–244.

community, but also including smaller tribal interests. This policy meant challenging KANU—the largest party backed by the biggest ethnic groups. It also meant favouring KANU's rival KADU, which represented smaller ethnic groups and also supported decentralized federalism.[42]

Even as the 1963 Constitution was being enacted, however, it was clear that its days were numbered. The British quickly departed and, as we have seen, KADU was soon merged into KANU. When KANU won an absolute majority in the independence elections, fundamental constitutional change began almost immediately. Ten amendments in five years centralized power and created a presidential system. These shifts were then codified in a new 1969 Constitution. Within six years, the earlier British- and KADU-preferred model had been effectively reversed.[43]

How much is this history related to the 1982 Act, and to the pattern of constitutional instrumentalism it represents? One reason the 1982 Act is a useful site to debate this issue is because it is a site for *debate*: definite claims are hard to make here.

It is easy to imagine an independent state founded with less antagonism between its ruling party and its constitution than Kenya; in turn, it is easy to see why British colonialism is fundamental to the explanation for how that happened—for how majority democratic power and constitutionalism could be born so far apart. Colonial rulers, in the pre-independence constitutional instruments of 1954, 1957, and 1960, as well as in the 1963 Constitution, used constitutional engineering to stack the political game for or against certain groups.[44] Control over the constitutional rules was treated as a tactical power, to be used tactically.[45]

A similar long-run argument can be made about colonialism and tribalism. The 1982 Act includes no ethnic categories, but its tribal stakes would have been clear to all Kenyans. Under Kenyatta, KANU rule meant particular benefits for his own Kikuyu people; under Moi, it meant the turn of the Kalenjin grouping. A study in 1998 found that, after two decades of Moi's favouritism in spending and government services, the under-5 child mortality rate among the Kalenjin was *half* that of other ethnic groups, even though the Kalenjin

[42] B. A. Ogot, 'The Decisive Years: 1956–63' in Ogot and Ochieng (n 11) 70; Widner (n 9) 54; Oyaya and Poku (n 8) 56–65; Parkinson (n 41) 218–219, 241–253.

[43] Miller and Yaeger (n 14) 31–33; Ochieng, 'Structural and Political Changes' (n 11) 94. For succinct summaries of the pre-1982 amendments, see Ndegwa (n 34) 11–18; Oyaya and Poku (n 8) 80–84.

[44] Oyaya and Poku (n 8) 41–56; Parkinson (n 41) 217–218, 223.

[45] Oyaya and Poku (n 8) 33, 37–38, 60–63, 69–71, 79–80, 84–85, 89.

lived disproportionality in rural areas.[46] Tribalism can have brutally direct consequences.

It is therefore natural to wonder if the real problem was tribalism. We will be more sympathetic to colonial constitutional engineering if we see it as an attempt, clumsy and heavy-handed in its paternalism but nevertheless necessary, to manage an age-old problem of inter-tribal tensions. This is certainly how British administrators explained it at the time.[47] And if we think this way, we will naturally see the strategic, zero-sum nature of post-independence Kenyan constitutional politics, including the 1982 Act's manoeuvres, as the continuation of this enduring inter-tribal competition by modern constitutional means.

The truth, however, is that these ethnic categories are far more created and contingent than such an argument implies. Witness the fact that 'Kalenjin', as a grouping, did not exist until the second half of the twentieth century. It was a Kenyan, not a British, creation, but it was created in response to a state increasingly being organized, by the British, into tribes.[48] As John Illife put it years ago, European colonial rulers often treated tribes like the nationalities they knew in Europe, where each person belonged to one nation with its associated government and territory, rather than the more fluid identities that were usually the African reality.[49] Colonialism's effect here was to entrench tribal membership as an exclusive category—everyone has one tribal membership—and then to use those tribal categories as political and administrative units, including for the crucial issue of allocating land.

Colonial rule thus created a powerful incentive for previously rather disparate groups to organize tribally. 'Kalenjin' was created in this era in order to compete with the then-more established, powerful tribes like the Kikuyu, who had been the first to organize politically against British colonial rule. This was not a fixed, ancient identity, in other words, but a contingent, strategic political grouping. In turn, Moi enjoyed ethnic support, not because he 'was' Kalenjin, but because he used patronage to reward people for maintaining loyalty to a grouping that supported his power, for as long as they did so. He resisted benefits for the Kalenjin which did not come from him, and used repression against Kalenjin groups, too.[50]

[46] Michaela Wrong, *It's Our Turn to Eat: The Story of a Kenyan Whistleblower* (Harper Perennial 2009) 56.

[47] Oyaya and Poku (n 8) 45–70; Parkinson (n 41) 219.

[48] Lynch (n 3) 31.

[49] John Illife, *A Modern History of Tanganyika* (Cambridge UP 1979) 323.

[50] Lynch (n 3) 31–50, 78–80; Miller and Yaeger (n 14) 20–21.

We can therefore see the cynicism in arguing, as colonial rulers did, that colonial rule was necessary to keep the peace between competing ethnic groups. Throughout Africa, colonial regimes used tribal categories, including artificially, in ways that incentivized locals to think and organize themselves in that way. Colonial rule also deployed divide-and-rule tactics that pitted one group against another to reduce the chances that they would unite in resistance. When departing British administrators in the independence era used constitutional engineering to try and manage ethnic divides, they were responding (albeit in those later years often quite sincerely) to a problem they had played a large role in creating.

In turn, we can see both the long-run path dependence and the continuing cynicism of Moi's 1982 Act. It created a one-party state, defended based on the need to promote national solidarity and transcend tribalism in an ethnically divided country. But, in reality, it was the means to power of a leader who without scruples played on ethnic divides and dispensed patronage along ethnic lines in order to maintain his own power. That Moi and his enablers did this is the part that is cynical, as it was cynical of colonial rulers who acted similarly.[51]

But Moi's regime also did this in the entirely realistic expectation that political rivals would use the same tactics against them if *they* gained control of the state. Each group, fearing the ethnic favouritism that would follow someone else's victory, felt compelled to use tribalist tactics to try and secure their own. This was a self-perpetuating cycle of suspicion, always at risk of descending into viciousness. And colonial rule, far from doing its best to manage that dynamic, served to deepen and entrench it as a political logic in Kenyan society until its force became very hard for any politician to escape when constructing a following.

It is debatable just how much colonialism can be said to have *created* the tribalism of post-independence Kenya, just as the precise links between colonialism and other post-independence problems in Africa are debatable. It is not, after all, as if ethnic tensions were absent from the continent before the Europeans arrived. But the long-run history of the 1982 Act, and the constitutionalism for which it stands, are as good an example as any of why it is only the details of colonialism's causal role that stand to be debated, not the fact of it.

[51] Wanyabari O. Maloba, 'Decolonization: A Theoretical Perspective' in Ogot and Ochieng (n 11) 17, noting the extent to which the arguments of the Moi regime echoed the colonial line.

C. The End of the Act, but not of Moi

The last piece of the 1982 Act's puzzle is economic. In addition to anti-tribalist arguments, the one-party state also drew legitimacy from the need to generate economic development. It thus invoked the same tacit bargain as exists, for instance, in today's China: the regime offers the population economic growth and rising living standards in exchange for accepting restricted political freedoms. Kenyatta enjoyed more favourable economic conditions than did Moi.[52] As the 1980s progressed, Moi's regime struggled to deliver its side of the bargain, while repression intensified. With formal institutions weakened, opposition came mainly from civil society: from churches, student groups, the private bar, the business community.

In February 1991, with the 1982 Act still in force, the veteran Odinga announced the formation of another new party, the National Democratic Party. A few months later, he joined a large, loose coalition of opposition leaders to form a 'pressure group', the Forum for the Restoration of Democracy (FORD).[53] This time, Moi did not succeed in crushing the opposition to his one-party regime. In December 1991, section 2A was repealed.

But even in the manner of its death, it reminds us of what would change, and what would not. The key decision to repeal section 2A was taken at the KANU party conference, not in the National Assembly. (A formal constitutional statement that Kenya was a 'multi-party' state would not come until 1997.)[54] And Moi retained power, by the old tactics of electoral manipulation and playing on the fears of Kikuyu domination, and now also by exploiting the divisions of a fracturing opposition in the new political landscape.[55] After winning elections in 1992 and 1997, he retired in 2002, at the age of 78. A constitutional cynic to the last, one of his final decisions was to dissolve Parliament early in order to disrupt efforts to draft a new constitutional text for Kenya.[56] On his death in 2020, he received a state funeral.

This lack of official repudiation of Moi, despite his political tactics, speaks to how much those tactics have survived him. Politics in Kenya is still highly personalized. Tribalism, including corruption and patronage organized along

[52] Widner (n 9) 47.
[53] Oyaya and Poku (n 8) 96.
[54] Constitution of Kenya Amendment Act, 1997.
[55] Korwa Adar, 'The Internal and External Contexts of Human Rights Practice in Kenya: Daniel Arap Moi's Operational Code' (2000) 4 African Sociological Review 74, 84; Mutua (n 11) 50.
[56] P. L. O. Lumumba, 'A Journey though Time in Search of a New Constitution' in P. L. O. Lumumba and Kiwinda Mbondenyi (eds), *The Constitution of Kenya: Contemporary Readings* (LawAfrica Publishing 2011) 41.

ethnic lines, remains a powerful force. In 2002, a fragile coalition of opposition parties, under the name of the National Rainbow Coalition (NARC), would hold together long enough to bring an end to KANU's thirty-nine-year monopoly on Kenyan political power. But the acronym of NARC, went the cynical joke in Kenya at the time, stood for 'Nothing Actually Really Changes'.[57]

As a judgement on post-Moi Kenya, the joke is an exaggeration. Much *has* changed, including in the wake of the new 2010 Constitution. But what completes our picture of the 1982 Act is the degree to which its repeal did *not* change things, symbolized by the full decade by which Moi's rule outlasted the Act. It was merely a device, a tool of forces that could simply reach for other tools to serve the same old ends, and did so.

This is a final reason for the place of the 1982 Act in the African anti-canon. Its passage in the first place stands for cynical instrumentalism in formal constitutional engineering. But the rather limited effect of its repeal stands, too, for the limits of what more admirable, formal constitutional engineering can achieve. Reform efforts in Africa can be obsessed with finding the right forms of constitutional law: the optimal design of mechanisms, the perfect wording of the right, the design that will finally, at long last, produce constitutional success. The postscript to the 1982 Act is an important reminder of the limits of this kind of thinking.

III. '... there shall be convened a National Conference ...': The Canonical Decree No. 90-40

One of the most well-known statistics about post-Cold War Africa is that, in 1989, there were no less than twenty-nine *de jure* one-party states in Africa. More than half the states on the continent openly banned one-party democracy. A few years later, every one of those laws had been changed.[58] Section 2A in Kenya was one of those washed away. But if we want to see where this African wave first rose and crested, there is no better answer than Benin.

If canonical examples are supposed to be drawn from the larger, richer, better-known African countries, Benin would miss out. Many comparativists, in the privacy of their own heads, might acknowledge some uncertainty as to its location on the map. Benin's status as the star case of post-Cold War

[57] Wrong (n 46) 80.

[58] Michael Bratton and Nicolas van de Walle, *Democratic Experiments in Africa: Regime Transitions in Comparative Perspective* (Cambridge UP 1997) 8.

constitutionalism in Francophone Africa is also now in serious doubt. All opposition parties were excluded from the 2019 parliamentary elections. In 2020, Freedom House lowered Benin's status from 'free' to 'partly free', where it remains.[59]

Benin's place in the modern African canon is surely affected by these recent developments. But it does not rest on them. That place rests, above all, on la Conférence Nationale, the National Conference of 1990, and on its influence. As a canonical text, I use Decree No. 90-40, issued on 23 February 1990 by President Mathieu Kérékou, which formally established the conference—although, as we will see, the Decree itself in fact reflects the extent to which, even as he issued it, Kérékou had already lost control over what was happening in Benin.

By 1990, Mathieu Kérékou was in his eighteenth year of ruling over a country he had taken over by military coup and converted into a one-party state. Benin was bankrupt. Economic prospects were dismal. Kérékou had been reduced to desperate strategies, such as contracting to store foreign toxic waste.[60] Salaries and scholarships increasingly went unpaid and, as a result, 1989 saw widespread protests from students, teachers, and civil servants. Kérékou's links to the Soviet Union had never rested on any particularly strong principled commitment—his ideology was jokingly called 'laxism-Leninism'—and with the Soviet Union's collapse, those links were now valueless. It was a crisis that would produce unity. In this lies the explanation for 'the remarkably smooth transition from military dictatorship to civilian rule in Benin—a country not hitherto known for smooth transitions of any kind ...'[61]

In an effort to regain the political initiative after lesser concessions had failed, Kérékou tried a major policy shift. He announced the abandonment of Marxism–Leninism, abolished the one-party state, and formed a committee of ministers to prepare for a conference of national stakeholders. But when the National Conference met, in the last ten days of February 1990 in the Hotel PLM-Aledjo in Cotonou, it quickly became clear that Kérékou could not control it. On the first day, 19 February, the 488 delegates rejected him as chairperson, in favour of Archbishop Isidore de Souza. Kérékou's regime was then criticized in devastating terms. A few days later, the Conference declared itself

[59] Sarah Repucci, 'Freedom in the World 2020: A Leaderless Struggle for Democracy', https://freedomhouse.org/report/freedom-world/2020/leaderless-struggle-democracy accessed 17 October 2022.

[60] Samuel Decalo, 'Benin: First of the New Democracies' in John F. Clark and David E. Gardiner (eds), *Political Reform in Francophone Africa* (Routledge 1997) 50.

[61] ibid 43.

sovereign.[62] Soon, it had appointed a new interim prime minister, Nicéphore Soglo, and a cabinet of its own choosing. It dissolved both the existing legislature, l'Assemble Nationale Revolutionaire or National Revolutionary Assembly, and Kérékou's government: he would stay on only as the interim head of state. The Conference also announced the repeal of the Constitution, the Loi Fundamentale or Fundamental Law of 1977, and the creation of a new Haut Conseil de la Republique or High Council of the Republic to draft a new Constitution (which would be overwhelmingly approved in a referendum held later that year). In March 1991, Kérékou lost a presidential election to Soglo, and left office peacefully.[63]

The official date of Decree No. 90-40 is an eloquent testament, hiding in plain sight, to the grand failure of Kérékou's strategy. The text of the Decree repeatedly asserts the authority of the presidency, the government, and of his party, the Parti de la revolution Populaire du Bénin or People's Revolutionary Party of Benin. Article 1 of the Decree tries to frame the National Conference as resulting from a decision of the party's Central and Standing Committees, and the National Executive Council. But the language is exposed in its full and impotent plaintiveness by the fact that the Decree was only officially issued on 23 February 1990—issued, in other words, when the National Conference had already been meeting for four days, and had already made clear its fundamental challenge to Kérékou's authority. The Decree was written as if Kérékou were still in the saddle. But the horse had gone.

A. The Birth of a Model

At least as notable as its success at home is the wider resonance of Benin's National Conference abroad. Within a few years, depending on how you count, something like one-sixth of all African countries would hold their own National Conferences, or close equivalents.[64] Something about Benin's Conference resonated far beyond its borders.

[62] For details, see Jennifer C. Seely, *The Legacies of Transition Governments in Africa: The Cases of Benin and Togo* (Palgrave Macmillan 2009) 67–71.

[63] Decalo (n 60) 53–55; Jacques L. Koko, *National Conference as a Strategy for Conflict Transformation and Peacemaking* (Adonis & Abbey Publishers 2008) 117–118.

[64] Bratton and van de Walle (n 58) 111, list Benin and ten other countries as examples, as at 1997. Their count debatably (in my view mistakenly) includes the deliberative constitution-drafting assemblies in South Africa and Ethiopia in the first years of the 1990s. Note that the trend also did not end there: consider, e.g., the 2003 National Conference in the Central African Republic.

The wider relevance of the *goals* of Benin's National Conference is easy enough to explain. According to the Decree, it had two aims. The Conference would draw up 'une charte d'Union Nationale', a charter of national union, to serve as the basis for 'une nouvelle Constitution fondée sur les principes démocratiques', a new constitution founded on democratic principles. And it should 'définir un nouveau projet de société conforme aux principes du libéralisme économique contenus dans le programme d'Adjustement Structurel'—define a new social project for society, in accordance with the principles of economic liberalism set out in the Structural Adjustment Programme (SAP). This last item is a reference to SAP I, a package of conditional loans which Kérékou had begun negotiating with international financial institutions including the World Bank and the International Monetary Fund in 1987. The African Development Bank was also involved. SAP I ran from 1989 to 1991, and was followed by other structural adjustment programmes.[65]

These were the concerns of many African states. For angry and disappointed people whose states were bankrupt in more ways than one, the need for something new was patent. In 1990, democratic constitutionalism and neoliberal economics were the languages of the moment. Now, a state had to at least pretend to be founded on multi-party democracy. The *de jure* one-party state did not disappear in Africa because robust competitive democracies suddenly appeared, but because a government's legitimacy now depended on at least the formal ritual of competitive elections.[66] Neoliberal economic reform had similarly become the only game in town. It is no coincidence that these are the two main ideas in the Decree: Kérékou was reaching for the key available sources of international legitimacy.

The two elements of the package, of course, were not equally welcome to all. Kérékou, as the political incumbent, would have preferred the emphasis to be on economic reforms. He tried to make this the focus on the first morning of the Conference.[67] But the delegates would not accept this. For other leaders, like Soglo, economic and political reform had to work hand in hand. Soglo had spent much of Kérékou's regime working for international organizations including the World Bank and the International Monetary Fund. His position

[65] For a summary, see African Development Bank, *Benin: Structural Adjustment Programmes I, II, III: Programme Performance Evaluation Report* (2003), https://afdb.org/fileadmin/uploads/afdb/Documents/Evaluation-Reports-_Shared-With-OPEV_/00157875-EN-BENIN-PAS-I-II-III.PDF accessed 10 August 2022.

[66] This is part of a global pattern of superficially democratic post-1989 regimes: see e.g. Steven Levitsky and Lucan A. Way, *Competitive Authoritarianism: Hybrid Regimes After the Cold War* (Cambridge UP 2010).

[67] Mathurin C. Houngnikpo, *Determinants of Democratization in Africa: A Comparative Study of Benin and Togo* (UP of America 2001) 69, 93.

aligned with theirs and he enjoyed their support. International donors made further financial aid conditional on political reforms, decisively thwarting Kérékou's strategy and supporting Soglo's.[68] While the National Conference was underway, a World Bank delegation based in another Cotonou hotel was pressuring Kérékou to compromise.[69] The French government, as we will see, took a similar stance.

For yet others at the Conference and within Benin society, by contrast, political change was essential but economic reforms were feared or resented, especially as part of externally-imposed structural adjustment programmes. In a moribund economy, many depended on state salaries and stipends. The early effects of SAP I on these payments were a key cause of rising public discontent in the months leading up to the Conference. Students and unions, including those representing workers in higher education, public administration, and the postal service, were key agents of rebellion against Kérékou's regime in the lead-up to the Conference. Soglo's later pursuit of structural adjustment as President would encounter increasing opposition, and would ultimately lead to his political downfall in 1996 at the end of his first term in office.[70]

As a matter of substance, then, themes from Benin's Conference matched debates also occurring in many other countries. However, the model the Conference offered as a process is at least as important in explaining its wider resonance, and perhaps more so.

The Conference was a broad, general gathering of stakeholders. As the Decree put it, it would gather 'es Représentants de toutes les forces vives de la Nation quelles que soient leurs sensibilités politiques': it would be an assembly of all the living forces of the nation, whatever their political views.[71] Although the Conference leaders followed a strategy of soliciting public opinion on important decisions, in practice 'living forces' meant various elite groups rather than the ordinary citizens at the grassroots.[72] But the approach nevertheless recalled traditional participatory gatherings such as village assemblies—not a uniquely African phenomenon, of course, but one of deep legitimacy in many parts of the continent.

[68] ibid 90.

[69] Decalo (n 60) 54.

[70] Houngnikpo (n 67) 71, 91; Seely (n 62) 36–41; John R. Heilbrunn, 'Social Origins of National Conferences in Benin and Togo' (1993) 31 JMAS 277, 283–285, 290–293.

[71] This translation from the original French, rather freer than those I have used elsewhere, is from Anna Rotman, 'Benin's Constitutional Court: An Institutional Model for Guaranteeing Human Rights' (2004) 17 Harv Hum Rts J 283, 283; and is endorsed by the Benin-born African legal expert Horace Sègnonna A. T. Adjolohoun, 'The "Right of Reparation" as Applied Under the African Charter by Benin's Constitutional Court' (LLM thesis, University of Pretoria 2007) 3.

[72] Seely (n 62) 62, 64–65; see also 73, 77, 82–85.

The National Conference also loosely recalls the Estates General turned National Assembly of revolutionary France. The French Revolution, too, had begun with the offer of reforms as a political concession by the embattled incumbent of a bankrupt state. It, too, had led to an ostensibly limited national gathering breaking free to declare its own sovereignty. And these parallels would have been lost on no one involved in the Benin process.

The bicentennial of the start of the French Revolution was 1989, and activists and human rights organizations had sought to make the most of the auspicious date. The Fédération internationale des ligues des droits de l'Homme (International Federation of Human Rights), one of the world's oldest human rights organizations, held a conference on human rights in June 1989 in Paris which was sometimes referred to as an 'Estates General'. In November 1989, the Benin-based PanAfrican Social Prospects Centre held a conference on 'Africa and the French Revolution: Lessons for the 21st century'. The format of a national assembly, therefore, was very much in the air by the time Kérékou's Decree formally announced Benin's Conference.[73] The final section of the PanAfrican Social Prospects Conference, on human rights abuses under Kérékou's regime, was organized by the Centre's President, Albert Tevoedjre, and by Paulin Hountondji. Three months later, when Benin's Conference was held, Tevoedjre would be its rapporteur and Hountondji one of its key moving forces.[74]

As in the earlier French revolutionary case, the National Conference's successful appropriation of governing authority meant that the National Conference *model* acquired the status of a legitimate means to claim sovereign power on behalf of the nation. It was a way to embody and express sovereignty, and to exercise it for reform and rejuvenation as an authority superior to the incumbent ruler. This, too, had an obvious appeal in many African contexts after 1989, whether the desire for a reinvention process was sincere or cosmetic—a point important to explain why, despite Kérékou's failure to control his own Conference, both opposition forces and incumbents elsewhere would draw on it as a model.

But the Conference model also had a subtler attraction in a certain sort of state. It tended to be influential in states that had been politically closed but were experiencing pressures to open up: states, in other words, where democratic rituals were gaining currency but where there was little recent history

[73] See generally Pearl T. Robinson, 'The National Conference Phenomenon in Francophone Africa' (1994) 36 CSSH 575.

[74] ibid 593.

of actual political competition.[75] For incumbents in such states, a National Conference was, of course, not the first choice. If protests could be silenced with lesser concessions, or with force, established authoritarian leaders might well prefer those options. But this was not always possible, as it was not possible in Benin. Kérékou's earlier more modest undertakings did not end the protests, and he did not attempt to use crushing force.[76] Although he had begun his career as a military man, Kérékou had resigned from the army in 1987 and, by 1990, he had poor relations with the military apart from his own elite guard. In that situation, the Conference model held out to Kérékou and leaders like him the possibility of a superficially democratic ritual, to quieten the streets, subvert the protest movements, and ultimately reassert power.

For the opposition forces, meanwhile, the National Conference offered a solution to their own lack of organization. The post-1989 opponents of one-party rule in Africa faced a serious dilemma. Their goal was multi-party elections. But if an election were actually held, straight away, the incumbent regime might well be expected to win. Opposition forces were often fragmented, weakened by repression and by a simple lack of opportunity to operate and build their organizations. The regime would have the resources and infrastructural advantages that came from a long blurring of party and state, plus the advantage of a head start while everyone else tried to establish their parties as electoral machines.

In this situation, the National Conference model was particularly appealing. It might, of course, produce division amongst opposition forces that the incumbent could then exploit. But it could also provide a forum in which the loose, disorganized forces of the opposition could work together on the first steps towards the new system. It additionally offered at least some time to prepare for electoral competition before an election would actually occur.

Finally, the process might identify national leaders around whom the anti-regime forces could rally, as with Soglo in Benin. Like many such leaders, Soglo's political position was not a very strong one. Many, in fact, resented the way he used his position as prime minister to become a national political figure, including since many thought the Conference had agreed that whoever it installed as prime minister would not later run for president.[77] Soglo won

[75] Bratton and van de Walle (n 58) 173–175, on whom I also draw in the paragraphs that follow. In Benin's case, this is best refined as a claim about limited *national-level* political competition, since pre-1990 Benin was most democratic at the local level. See Thomas Bierschenk, 'The Local Appropriation of Democracy: An Analysis of the Municipal Elections in Parakou, Republic of Benin, 2002–03' (2006) 44 J Afr Stud 543, 543–545.

[76] Heilbrunn (n 70) 285–286; Seely (n 62) 36–41.

[77] Seely (n 62) 88–89.

the 1991 election convincingly, but he lost his re-election bid in 1996—to none other than Kérékou, now a born-again Christian, and still in a position to wield decisive political power. But if Kérékou's 1996 win marked a return of the old leader, it was not a return to the old regime. The National Conference provided a place, and some time, in which to find an alternative leader who could rally the opposition for long enough for a transition to hold.

Also important was the manner of Kérékou's failure—or one might rather say, the manner of Benin's success. The Benin version of the National Conference was a peaceful, civil society-driven transition to democracy, in many ways astonishingly smooth and swift. Archbishop de Souza played an important diplomatic role as chairperson.[78] Reconciliation was a key theme, as was ensuring an acceptable exit for Kérékou.[79] Reportedly, before the Conference declared itself sovereign, Kérékou received reassurance by phone that he would receive immunity from prosecution. On the last day of the Conference, in a brief address that seems to have taken many of his own supporters entirely by surprise, and which many saw as a last-minute decision on his part, Kérékou publicly accepted the Conference's decisions. He stayed on as interim President, and co-operated substantially with the transitional legislative body, the High Council of the Republic.[80] Although he did not immediately concede defeat to Soglo in the 1991 elections, he soon left office peacefully after receiving further promises of immunity from prosecution, and a lifetime pension.[81] Benin's model stood out as a way in which one-party rule could end without bloodshed.

If this explains the breadth of influence the Benin National Conference had, however, we also need to explain why that influence was not broader still. The conditions and challenges to which the Conference responded were present in far more post-Cold War African countries than the fraction, albeit a substantial fraction, that held a National Conference of their own. Why was the trend not even wider?

For one thing, the failure of Kérékou's strategy, in so time-honoured a fashion, did dissuade some incumbents elsewhere from trying it themselves. Nearby rulers including Paul Biya in Cameroon and André Kolingba in the Central African Republic (CAR) were careful to resist calls for local National Conferences in their own states.[82] (Biya remains in power today, as Africa's

[78] Houngnikpo (n 67) 94.
[79] Seely (n 62) 181.
[80] ibid 74, 78–82.
[81] ibid 90, 156.
[82] Bratton and van de Walle (n 58) 112, 172.

oldest head of state; Kolingba clung on only until 1993, and the CAR in fact held a National Conference of its own in 2003.)

The influence of the National Conference was also overwhelmingly a Francophone African phenomenon.[83] The divides of legal family can be strong in Africa, and even so significant an example as Benin is no exception. The backdrop of the bicentennial of 1789 held, of course, an especially Francophone significance. But the Conference model also arose in the particular context of shifts in France's stance towards its former African colonies.

On the one hand, while Benin's Conference was in session, Jacques Chirac (then Mayor of Paris) made his infamous comment, at a conference of Francophone mayors in Abidjan in Côte d'Ivoire, that multi-party democracy was 'a kind of luxury' and a 'political error' for developing countries.[84] In addition to its imperialist condescension, Chirac's comment was an obvious show of support for President Félix Houphouët-Boigny, the long-time French client who ruled Côte d'Ivoire under a one-party system for thirty-three years, from independence until his death in 1993. Chirac's comment, and its support for the old regime in Francophone Africa, pointed up the contrast to the broad stakeholder democracy and the commitment to local agency for which Benin's Conference was becoming a symbol.

On the other hand, a few months later, in June 1990, French President François Mitterrand announced at a Franco-African summit that French aid would henceforth be linked to democratization.[85] This created very concrete reasons for all kinds of Francophone African leaders to pursue democratic reforms, at least superficially. France was not, of course, the only source of pressure in this direction. I have already noted the stance of international financial institutions, such as the IMF and the World Bank, which mattered to Francophone and non-Francophone states alike. And France under Mitterrand would not follow through consistently on the new commitment: a year later, for example, he would dilute the message by saying that countries should find 'their own rhythm' on democratic change.[86] But, in this context, the Conference model represented by far the most obvious way for an aid-receiving Francophone African country to democratize or appear to be doing so.

At the time, the National Conference was also covered extensively in the French-language media, including Radio France International and in every

[83] See also Babacar Kante, 'Models of Constitutional Jurisdiction in Francophone West Africa' (2008) 3 Am J Comp L 158, 159.

[84] Houngnikpo (n 67) 152–153.

[85] Robinson (n 73) 589; Heilbrunn (n 70) 280.

[86] Heilbrunn (n 70) 294.

Francophone African country with a free press.[87] The impact in the English-speaking world was much smaller. There, South Africa's roughly contemporaneous but more drawn-out transfer of power, headlined by Nelson Mandela, received far more attention. Benin's and South Africa's transitions seem to have been no more than vague influences on one another while underway, and subsequent comparative legal scholarship has not brought the two cases any closer together. That divergence reflects the divide in the templates on which African countries drew, and still draw.

B. Benin's Outlier Success

The final piece of the National Conference's legacy is that nowhere else was the model as successful as the original version. The great achievement of Benin's Conference lay in the degree to which leaders came together to exercise the sovereign power they had seized and constructed a new foundation for the nation. That magic never worked quite as well elsewhere. The explanation for this is a multifaceted matter of local detail.

One part of the explanation is that Kérékou's regime had seen only limited abuses, comparatively speaking. His fear of retribution, and the public desire for it, were accordingly relatively low. That made a peaceful transfer of power, with immunity for Kérékou, easier to arrange.[88] The comparison with neighbouring Togo is instructive.[89] There, in the wake of greater abuses, the National Conference process was initiated with a more vengeful intent. This gave the Togolese incumbent, Gnassingbé Éyadéma, a stronger reason to think that safety lay in repudiating the Conference and trying to cling to power, which is what he did.

A second crucial point is the degree to which Kérékou had run out of other options, even compared to other embattled incumbents facing the winds of post-Cold War change. Kérékou had earlier alienated France by challenging its role in West Africa. Benin also lacked strategic resources, which meant that France did not have incentives to prop up an authoritarian incumbent in the name of stable supply as it did, for example, in nearby Togo or Gabon.[90] Kérékou's previous Marxist alignment, and Benin's low geostrategic importance, further contributed to his lack of attractiveness as an ally or a client.

[87] Robinson (n 73) 576.
[88] Nic Cheeseman, *Democracy in Africa* (CUP, 015) 100–101.
[89] See generally Houngnikpo (n 67); Heilbrunn (n 70); Seely (n 62).
[90] Robinson (n 73) esp. 585–590.

Outsiders, notably France, were content to let Kérékou sink, especially given that there were solid available alternatives, including Soglo.[91] The French Ambassador was openly involved in supporting the democracy movement in Benin.[92] For some observers, Kérékou deserves more credit for the peaceful transfer of power than he usually receives in English-language scholarship.[93] Others emphasize that he simply had no option left besides exit.[94]

Something similar might be said of the military. The military has often been decisive in African politics—as in many other cases when systems attempt to transition from dictatorial rule to democracy[95]—and so the army's choice to support the National Conference can be seen as decisive in Benin. Though the army and Kérékou were no longer allies by 1990, they were in similar positions. Neither could plausibly hold power in light of Benin's dire economic situation. Neither had any economic options left that did not include democratic reform. Since the regime's relatively less brutal record was also the military's, the army, too, had less reason to cling to power. Togo is again an instructive contrast. The military there had responded to protests more brutally, and had more hopes of economic relief via French assistance. Togo's military repudiated Togo's National Conference, as did Togo's leader Éyadéma; Benin's military joined Kérékou in choosing to accept Benin's.[96]

A local ethnic division also helps to explain the supportive position of Benin's military. Kérékou, coming from Benin's north, had been associated with a northernization of the army, to the dissatisfaction of southerners. For southerners, the Conference offered the possibility of a reset, while Kérékou's rapid fall from effective power left northerners struggling to organize themselves. The Conference therefore held an appeal to each faction of Benin's military.[97] The military's acquiescence is the dog that did not bark, the silent foundation of the Conference's celebrated status as a civilian coup d'etat.

A final piece of the puzzle concerns the civil society that pulled off this feat.[98] The Decree of 1990 spoke of the vital, living forces of the nation. Kérékou had tried to stack the Conference with his own party members, but had to retreat

[91] Cheeseman (n 88) 94; Seely (n 62) 71.

[92] Houngnikpo (n 67) 156.

[93] Thomas Bierschenk, 'Democratization without Development: Benin, 1989–2009' (2009) 22 International Journal of Politics, Culture & Society 337, 339.

[94] Decalo (n 60) 54; Houngnikpo (n 67) 175.

[95] See Samuel P. Huntington, *The Third Wave: Democratization in the Late Twentieth Century* (Oklahoma UP 1991) 231–252.

[96] Houngnikpo (n 67) 14, 137–138; Seely (n 62) 69.

[97] Houngnikpo (n 67) 182–183.

[98] Another important contrast to Togo: see Heilbrunn (n 70) esp. 298–299; John R. Heilbrunn, 'Commerce, Politics, and Business Associations in Benin and Togo' (1997) 29 Comp Pol 473.

after furious opposition in the so-called 'Quota War'.[99] He had also hoped that most of those invited would not turn up. But turn up they did: from all parts of civil society, from the north, from the south, from the diaspora. Long-run explanations for this vibrancy point to Benin's tradition of internal political resistance and free speech.[100] This must be coupled with the desire of present-day actors to learn from past mistakes. Before Kérékou's 1972 coup, Benin's political parties had been divided and ineffectual, to the degree that many had welcomed his seizure of power. The success of diverse stakeholders in coming together at the Conference in 1990 speaks to their determination to not again pay the price of political apathy and division.[101]

Such explanations are, of course, not unique to Benin. For example, the fear of repeating past errors was also a powerful imperative in nearby Anglophone Ghana. It overcame a coup-riddled past to carry out a successful democratic transition of its own, and today Ghana stands alone as the most resilient post-Cold War democracy in West Africa. Brave and energetic civil society forces can be found all over Africa, which is why factors such as the military and France's stance are also essential for explaining what happened in Benin. But if Benin's civil society is not sufficient as an explanation, it was surely necessary. Without it, one cannot account for the political agency, at once pragmatic and bold, that made the Conference work.

In the end, the National Conference succeeded in Benin in establishing that elusive thing, a new spirit of constitutionalism.[102] That spirit helped Benin through several rather wobbly electoral transitions in the years that followed. Though transfers of power were seldom seamless, successive leaders nevertheless declined to push the system to the brink. Election results were accepted without too much delay. Two-term limits were ultimately respected. Benin's Constitutional Court began to find its feet as an institution, and as a creative force in Francophone and African constitutionalism.[103] The Estates General

[99] Seely (n 62) 41.

[100] Houngnikpo (n 67) 166–171.

[101] On opposition unity, including joint pre-Conference preparations, see Seely (n 62) 42–43, 62, 65–66, 71, 75.

[102] ibid 91–95, 144–161; Mariana Llanos et al., 'Informal Interference in the Judiciary in New Democracies: A Comparison of Six African and Latin American Cases' in *GIGA Working Papers No. 245* (Global Institute for Global and Area Studies (GIGA) 2014), refer to Benin's 'different "spirit" of constitutionality' to explain its over-performance, given its background conditions.

[103] See e.g. Richard Banégas, 'Brief—Benin: Challenges for Democracy' (2014) 113 Afr Aff 449; Matthias Basedu and Alexander Stroh, 'Do Party Systems Make Democracy Work? A Comparative Test of Party-System Characteristics and Democratization in Francophone Africa' in Gero Erdmann and Marianne Kneuer (eds), *Regression of Democracy?* (VS Verlag 2011); Rotman (n 71); Bruce A. Magnusson, 'Democratization and Domestic Insecurity: Navigating the Transition in Benin' (2001) 22 Comp Pol 211; Christopher Fomunyoh, 'Democratization in Fits and Starts' (2001) 12 Journal of Democracy 37.

model was reused to seek broad public consultation on several key issues.[104] For Benin, the National Conference was a great moment in history, a source of pride, and a constitutional achievement in the richest and most constructive sense, with ripples felt far beyond the country's borders.

As the time since the delegates had gathered in the Hotel PLM-Aledjo lengthened, that spirit began to show signs of running out—or, perhaps, to reach the limits of what spirit alone can achieve. Post-1989 Benin has sometimes succeeded in mitigating its economic troubles, but it has never resolved them, and poverty remains an exhausting millstone around the neck of its politics. Benin's democracy has eroded significantly amidst the present global democratic reversal, although whether it will fall further, or rebound, remains to be seen.

But whatever happens, for a generation after 1990, Benin was the constitutional star of Francophone Africa. In West Africa, only Anglophone Ghana can claim comparable post-Cold War democratic success, and only a handful of states in Africa as a whole—South Africa, Namibia, perhaps Kenya—can stand with Benin as post-1989 peers. (Botswana is an older case). Indeed, Benin merits a bigger claim. Few other post-1989 democratic transitions anywhere in the world could claim Benin's degree of success, whether or not we control for the challenges of poverty, weak institutions at the time of its founding, or a difficult neighbourhood. Whatever happens in the future, Benin's story merits a degree of comparative attention that matches this achievement. The National Conference of 1990 was one of the most important and influential events in recent constitutional memory. It belongs in any constitutional canon, African or global, that is worthy of the name.

[104] Seely (n 62) 146–147, 160.

8

The Mexican Constitution of 1917

A Canon for Latin American Constitutionalism

Ana Micaela Alterio[*] *and Roberto Niembro Ortega*[**]

I. Introduction

Mexico is a case of revolutionary constitutionalism,[1] which resulted in a post-liberal[2] and transformative[3] constitution. Indeed, we can consider the Mexican Constitution of 1917 as part of the canon[4] of comparative constitutional law because of its early incorporation of social rights as a response to the popular classes' claims in the 1910 Revolution,[5] which predates the Weimar Constitution of 1919, and the influence it has had on the incorporation of social rights in other constitutions of the region. Although the influence of the Mexican Constitution in Latin America has been documented by several scholars,[6] the Mexican Constitution itself has been understudied by

* Full time Professor at ITAM (Instituto Tecnológico Autónomo de México), Level 2 of the National System of Research-CONAHCYT México.

** Posgraduate Professor at UNAM. Level 1 of the National System of Research- CONAHCYT México.

[1] Stephen Gardbaum, "Revolutionary Constitutionalism" (2017) 15 IJCL 173. For a brief introduction to the Revolution, see: Felipe Ávila and Pedro Salmerón, *Historia Breve de la Revolución Mexicana* (Instituto Nacional de Estudios Históricos de las Revoluciones de México, Siglo XXI Editores, 2015).

[2] Jorge M. Farinacci-Fernós, "Post-Liberal Constitutionalism" (2018) 54 Tulsa L Rev 1.

[3] Rainer Grote, "The Mexican Constitution of 1917. An Early Example of Radical Transformative Constitutionalism" in Armin von Bogdandy et al. (eds.), *Transformative Constitutionalism in Latin America* (OUP 2017) 150–155.

[4] Jack M. Balkin and Sanford Levinson, "The Canons of Constitutional Law" 111 Harvard L Rev 963 (1998).

[5] Javier Garciadiego "¿Por qué, cuándo, cómo y quiénes hicieron la Constitución de 1917?" (2017) 66 Revista Historia Mexicana 1994; Ávila and Salmerón (n 1) 272, 274.

[6] Roberto Gargarella, *Latin American Constitutionalism 1810–1820* (OUP 2013) 8. Gargarella considers Latin American constitutionalism a social–conservative model; see Roberto Gargarella, "Inequality and the Constitution. From Equality to Social Rights" in Philipp Dann, Michael Riegner, and Maxim Bönnemann (eds.), *The Global South and Comparative Constitutional Law* (OUP 2020) 243–246; Jaiver Couso, "The Economic Constitutions of Latin America" in Rosalind Dixon and

Ana Micaela Alterio and Roberto Niembro Ortega, *The Mexican Constitution of 1917* In: *Global Canons in an Age of Contestation*. Edited by: Sujit Choudhry, Michaela Hailbronner, and Mattias Kumm, Oxford University Press.
 DOI: 10.1093/9780191956942.003.0008

comparative constitutional legal scholars.[7] One possible explanation for this lack of study is that the Mexican Constitution's influence has been limited to Latin American, Spanish-speaking countries.

This chapter aims to address this gap in scholarship. The 1917 Mexican Constitution should form part of the canon of comparative law not only for its early incorporation of social rights (labor and peasant's rights, arts. 123 and 27 respectively), but also because it matched those social rights with hyper-presidentialism.[8] The Constitution is not a canon in the normative sense, but because of the possibilities it opens for academic debate.[9] These two identities of the Constitution—as a promoter of both social rights and hyper-presidentialism—influenced the constitutionalism of other Latin American countries. As Roberto Gargarella has argued, Latin American constitutionalism adopted a hyper-presidential system during the nineteenth century, cemented it in the twentieth century, and then reasserted it in the New Latin American constitutionalism at the beginning of the twenty-first century.[10] Considered in this context, the text of the Mexican Constitution and its development through the twentieth century has allow us to reflect on the trend in Latin America constitutionalism regarding the concentration of power in the executive branch and the inefficiency of the economic constitution.[11]

The adoption in the 1917 Constitution of a very strong executive power[12] was a response to the weakness that some critical commentators thought the 1857 liberal Constitution established: this executive power was the "necessary"

Tom Ginsburg (eds.), *Comparative Constitutional Law in Latin America* (Elgar 2017) 359. For a discussion of the foreign influence on the social question of the Mexican Constitution, see Ignacio Marván Laborde, *Cómo hicieron la Constitución de 1917* (Fondo de Cultura Económica 2017) 195, 200.

[7] Bruce Ackerman, *Revolutionary Constitutions, Charismatic Leadership and the Rule of Law* (Harvard UP 2019).

[8] Martín Díaz y Díaz, *La Constitución ambivalente. Notas para un análisis de sus polos en tensión* (1st edn., Instituto de Investigaciones Jurídicas 2019) 79. As Gargarella notes, "The new Mexican Constitution became known worldwide because of its radical openness to the 'social question' ... however, it reaffirmed the old-style hyper-presidential system of government ... The result was a 'mixed' document like the ones that would become more typical in the Latin American context during the mid-twentieth century." Gargarella (n 6) 100–101.

[9] Michaela Hailbronner, "Constructing the Global Constitutional Canon: Between Authority and Criticism" (2019) 69 U Toronto LJ 248, 255.

[10] Gargarella (n 6) 200. In his words: "Ultimately, and after many different attempts ... what remained was a 'new' constitutional model, characterized by a robust declaration of rights and a still highly concentrated organization of power."

[11] Hailbronner (n 9) 2; Couso (n 6) 353–354. For a discussion of the types of legal reform and its implications for Latin America, see: Keith Rosenn, "The Success of Constitutionalism in the United States and Its Failure in Latin America: An Explanation" (1990) 22 U of Miami Inter-Am LR 1. See also Jorge L. Esquirol, "The Failed Law of Latin America" (2008) 56 Am J Comp L 75

[12] As an authoritarian executive power. Marván (n 6) 244. See also Martín Díaz y Díaz and Antonio Azuela in Instituto de Investigaciones Jurídicas (ed.), *Rabasa y Molina Enríquez: Un diálogo*

solution between dictatorship and the Constitution's ineffectiveness.[13] That's why, for most scholars, the 1917 Constitution is the bridge between the *porfiriato* (the previous dictatorial regime (1884–1911)) and the revolution, constituting the perfect synthesis: "the revolutionary ideology through the methods of the porfiriato."[14] The 1917 Constitution also included a procedural rule that guaranteed the stability of the authoritarian political regime:[15] the president could not be reelected under any circumstance.[16] Since 1930, respect for this rule has formed the basis of peaceful relations among the Partido Revolucionario Institucional[17] (PRI) elites and remains part of the constitutional identity.

If we take a dynamic perspective and focus on an extended period,[18] the Constitution in the twentieth century lost its social identity while preserving its hyper-presidential one.[19] As Díaz y Díaz said in the 1990s, "the beginning of the Mexican twentieth century set up, barely, an unrealized modernity."[20] Presidential identity took precedence over the social one because the president, for many years, held the power for land distribution and for resolution of agrarian and labor disputes,[21] powers that were very effective political instruments.[22] From their inception and for a long period

autoritario en el origen de la Constitución (Universidad Nacional Autónoma de México and Instituto de Investigaciones Jurídicas 2019) 238; Daniel Cosío Villegas, "El sistema político mexicano" (1982) 13 Cuadernos de Joaquín Mortiz 22, 23.

[13] Emilio Rabasa, *La Constitución y la Dictadura* (2nd edn., Porrúa 2002), Daniel Cosío Villegas, *La Constitución de 1857 y sus críticos* (2nd edn., Fondo de Cultura Económica-Clío-El Colegio Nacional 2007); Garciadiego (n 5) 1189; see also Arnaldo Córdova, *La Formación del poder político en México* (38th edn., Era 2018) 17–18; Diego Valadés, "El sistema presidencial mexicano. Actualidad y perspectivas" (2011) *130 Boletín mexicano de Derecho comparado* 283; Charles A. Hale, *Emilio Rabasa y la supervivencia del liberalismo porfiriano* (Fondo de Cultura Económica-CIDE 2011) 25, 32, 50, 95, 294.

[14] Gargarella (n 6) 88; Jesús Silva Herzog, "Emilio Rabasa" in IIJ (ed.), *La constitución mexicana de 1917: ideólogos, el núcleo fundador y otros constituyentes* (IIJ-UNAM 2016) 295; Charles A. Hale, *Emilio Rabasa y la supervivencia del liberalismo porfiriano* (Fondo de Cultura Económica-CIDE 2011) 247.

[15] It is paradoxical that the rule is a democratic one. However, it also helped to stabilize the authoritarian regime. Jorge Castañeda, *La herencia. Arqueología de la suscesión presidencial en México* (1st edn., Alfaguara 1999).

[16] Constitución Política de los Estados Unidos Mexicanos (Const.) as amended, art. 83 (Diario Oficial de la Federación 1917 (Mex.)). This rule was amended in 1927 to allow for one nonconsecutive reelection. In 1933, it was amended again to reestablish the absolute prohibition.

[17] Ilene V. O.'Malley, *The Myth of Revolution: Hero Cults and the Institutionalization of the Mexican State, 1920–1940* (Greenwood Press 1986) 31; Daniel Cosío Villegas, "El sistema político mexicano" (1982) 13 Cuadernos de Joaquín Mortiz 31.

[18] Gary Jeffrey Jacobsohn and Yaniv Roznai, *Constitutional Revolution* (Yale UP 2021) 22, 33, 58, 136; Díaz y Díaz (n 8) 63.

[19] Córdova (n 13) 45, 48, 53, 57.

[20] Martín Díaz y Díaz, *La Constitución ambivalente. Notas para un análisis de sus polos en tensión* (1st edn., Instituto de Investigaciones Jurídicas 2019) 61.

[21] Juan Antonio Cruz Parcero, "Los derechos sociales en la Constitución de 1917: un balance en su centenario" in Juan A. Cruz Parcero (ed.), *Los Derechos Sociales en México Reflexiones sobre la Constitución de 1917* (Instituto de Estudios Constitucionales de Quéretaro 2020) 64.

[22] Córdova (n 13) 19, 21, 33; Díaz y Díaz (n 20) 243.

thereafter, the social rights of the 1917 Constitution were political mechanisms to control peasants and labor workers and to legitimate the regime.[23] They were not normative rights that people could claim before a court. In fact, social rights were the legal means for the Revolutionary State to establish a paternal relationship with the masses and enhance the power of the government.[24] The government oversaw protection of the weak against the powerful, the peasants against the *hacendados* (landowners), the workers against the entrepreneurs, the poor against the rich, but it did not give the popular classes rights.

This chapter is divided into the following three sections. In the first section, we explain the ideological tool[25] that the hyper-presidential regime used to subordinate the Constitution to its political agenda: Revolution idolatry. According to Revolution idolatry, the Constitution was not a supreme and binding document, and the amendment power was used to reflect the political program of the president and the majority.[26] In the second section, we discuss the anticanonical concept of the "permanent constituent power" (*poder constituyente permanente*) created by an influential constitutional law scholar and justice of the Supreme Court to justify an unlimited amendment power. In our opinion, it is anticanonical because it gives rise to a misuse of the amendment power against any degree of stability, justifies constitutionalizing the momentary ideas of the political elites, and represents the unlimited sovereign.[27] Moreover, we exemplify how the Supreme Court used the "permanent constituent power" to refuse to limit the amendment power. In the final section, we conclude by arguing for a change in the amendment process which incorporates popular participation. In our opinion, popular participation would be a means of stabilizing institutions by decreasing the number of amendments.

[23] Díaz y Díaz (n 20) 69; Parcero (n 21) 64; Ávila and Salmerón (n 1) 20, 24; Roger Bartra, *La jaula de la melancolía Identidad y metamorfosis del mexicano* (1st reimp., Penguin Random House 2015) 164; Daniel Cosío Villegas, "La crisis de México" [1947] Cuadernos americanos 194.

[24] Alan Knight, "Popular Culture and the Revolutionary State in Mexico, 1910–1940" (1994) 74:3 Hispanic American Historical Review 401; Ávila and Salmerón (n 1) 276–278.

[25] O´Malley (n 17) 289, 298; Ávila and Salmerón (n 1) 289, 298.

[26] Francisca Pou-Giménez, Andrea Pozas-Loyo, and Camilo Saavedra-Herrera, "Interpreting the Ship of Theseus: Constitutional Hyper-Reformism and Judicial Review in Mexico (1917–2019)", 32, 40 (on file with the author).

[27] Yaniv Roznai, *Unconstitutional Constitutional Amendments* (OUP 2017) 170.

II. Revolution Idolatry and Constitutional Subordination

The Mexican Constitution has evolved according to its hyper-presidential identity.[28] Therefore, the Constitution was not a normative and binding law until the end of the twentieth century, when the authoritarian system slowly collapsed, leading to the establishment of democratic life.[29] The executive power and the PRI used the Mexican Revolution idolatry as a useful ideological tool to subordinate the Constitution to its political agenda. The development of a Revolution idolatry, rather than a constitutional faith, become a reactionary ideology[30] and an obstacle for the bindingness of social rights. Moreover, Revolution idolatry was not enough to prevent a constitutional dismemberment[31] and loss of social identity[32] in the 1980s and onwards, when the political elites adopted a neoliberal ideology contrary to state interventionism.[33] Neoliberalism caused a partial destruction of the Constitution's social identity but not a reconstruction of a new one. In this sense, neoliberalism was not a new revolution.[34] Rather, it had a strong relationship with hyper-presidentialism.

Moreover, according to Revolution idolatry, the amendment power was used to reflect the political program of the president and the majority,[35] developing into an unlimited practice of constitutional amendment. Revolution idolatry, we argue, shaped an amendment culture that accelerated constitutional change.[36]

To an external observer, the fact that Mexican politicians kept amending the Constitution, even though they did not consider it as the supreme law, may be perplexing. For Revolution idolatry, however, the Constitution was important in a symbolic and political sense. Renowned politicians and intellectuals considered it variously as a modern costume for an old political lie,[37] a terrific

[28] Jacobsohn and Roznai (n 18) 35, 55, 176. (Evolution is a process of developing in detail what is implicit in an idea or principle.)

[29] ibid 34.

[30] Córdova (n 13) 32, 33. Arnaldo Córdova, "La Historia Maestra de la política" in *Historia ¿para qué?* (Siglo XXI Editores 1980) 138–140; Carlos Monsiváis, "La pasión de la historia" in *Historia ¿para qué?* (Siglo XXI Editores 1980) 180; Bartra (n 23) 214–215.

[31] Richard Albert, "Constitutional Amendment and Dismemberment" (2018) 43 Yale JIL.

[32] Gary J Jacobsohn, *Constitutional Identity* (HUP 2010), Michel Rosenfeld, "Constitutional Identity" in Michel Rosenfeld and András Sajó (eds), *The Oxford Handbook of Comparative Constitutional Law* (OUP 2012); Monika Polzin, "Constitutional Identity as a Constructed Reality and Restless *Soul*" (2017) 18 German LJ 1595.

[33] Ávila and Salmerón (n 1) 295.

[34] Jacobsohn and Roznai (n 18) 62.

[35] Pou-Giménez, Pozas-Loyo, and Saavedra-Herrera (n 26) 32, 40.

[36] Albert (n 31) 111, 112.

[37] Octavio Paz, *El laberinto de la Soledad* (22nd edn., Fondo de Cultura Económica 1950) 133–134.

instrument of power,[38] or a legal construction of a fictitious state.[39] More recently, during the centennial of the Constitution, a prestigious historian declared the Constitution to be the most important document of the Revolution, of our contemporary history, and for the present and future of the country.[40]

To understand the difference between Revolution idolatry and constitutional faith, we draw on the seminal work of Sandy Levinson. In our understanding, constitutional faith demands a critical evaluation of the requirements of the Constitution, not a veneration of it.[41] The Constitution is the central text, but constitutional faith does not exhaust the object of faith. The text is complemented by the event that gave rise to the Constitution, which in Mexico was the 1910 Revolution.[42] For the development of a constitutional faith, the Constitution needs relative stability: this means a moderate rate of amendment processes that does not alter the fundamental identity of the Constitution, which is preserved.[43] It is important that citizens share this constitutional faith, taking seriously the political conversation that the Constitution frames.[44]

In contrast, Revolution idolatry is a veneration of an ideal.[45] It requires citizens to leave aside their critical assessments and defend an ideology.[46] The main focus of idolatry is the event that gave rise to the Constitution, which, again, in Mexico is the 1910 Revolution.[47] According to Revolutionary idolatry and political discourse, the Mexican Revolution was fought for and by the people;[48] on a deeper level, however, its leaders disdained the culture of the lower classes, political discourse notwithstanding.[49] For Revolution idolatry, the Constitution remains in second place, subordinated to the revolutionary ideal, and thus Constitution stability is unnecessary and the amendment

[38] Córdova (n 13) 45–48.
[39] Guillermo Bonfil Batalla, *México Profundo. Una civilización negada* (Fondo de Cultura Económica 1987) 106–107.
[40] Garciadiego (n 5) 1183.
[41] Sanford Levinson, *Constitutional Faith* (Princeton UP 1988) 88.
[42] ibid 96, 134.
[43] ibid 121, 153.
[44] ibid 98, 168, 193.
[45] For a similar concept such as revolutionary civil religion, see Adrian A. Bantjes, "Idolatry and Inconoclasm in Revolutionary Mexico: The De-Christianization Campaigns 1929–1940" (1997) 13 Estudios Mexicanos 88, 90, 105. According to Knight, "the revolutionary radicalism certainly borrowed from religious forms and built on traditional rituals," Knight (n 24) 430. See also O´Malley (n 17) 27, 131–132.
[46] O´Malley (n 17) 125, 128.
[47] Jose Ramon Cossío, "Los derechos sociales como normas programáticas y la comprensión política de la Constitución" in Fernando Serrano (ed.), *Estudios Jurídicos en Homenaje a Felipe Tena Ramírez* (Porrúa 1999) 90.
[48] Córdova (n 13) 58. According to Knight, "the Mexican Revolution involved a mass mobilization unprecedented in Mexican or even in Latin American history," Knight (n 24) 400.
[49] Bantjes (n 45) 95; Knight (n 24) 403, 404; O´Malley (n 17) 100.

process is unlimited: what is important is that the Constitution adapts to Revolution ideology. The Constitution does not frame a deliberative process among citizens, but rather works as an instrument in the hands of the political elites. The legitimacy of the Constitution is based on its social ends, not upon establishing democratic procedures.[50] In this way, the Constitution does not accomplish "the submission of politics to law,"[51] but rather just the opposite. The Constitution is relevant as a political document but not as a binding law for politics.[52]

For a long period of the twentieth century in Mexico, Revolution idolatry prevented the Constitution from being regarded by Mexican politicians as supreme law.[53] According to Revolution idolatry, the Mexican Constitution was a succinct expression of the Revolution's promises, not a superior law that limited the government. Political elites subordinated the Constitution to the Revolution as an idea: the presidency and its political party PRI were the final interpreters of the Constitution,[54] deciding what the Constitution meant and how far it should be enforced according to the revolutionary needs of the moment.[55] In this sense, the Revolution became a powerful, vague, and malleable idea in the hands of the political elites and turned into a reactionary ideology to manipulate the masses.[56]

Take, for example, this part of President Ruiz Cortines's discourse on the XLIV anniversary of the Revolution in 1954:

> This November 20th proves, once again, that the same postulates of the revolution transformed into the "Law of Laws" are a compendium of the aspirations of Mexicans since 1810 or maybe even from before. It is because of this that the national consciousness finds more and more interpreters of its ideas and feelings and rejects any other theory that is not our Mexican Constitution, the one we should follow and uphold fervently convinced that this is the authentic path of our "mexicanness."[57]

[50] Martín Díaz y Díaz, "Rabasa y Molina Enríquez: Un diálogo autoritario en el origen de la Constitución" (1989) 13 Revista de Investigaciones Jurídicas 187, 246.

[51] Dieter Grimm, "A Political, not a Legal History of the Rise of Worldwise Constitutionalism" in Richard Albert (ed.), *Revolutionary Constitutionalism Law, Legitimacy, Power* (Hart 2020) 11.

[52] ibid.

[53] Ana Micaela Alterio, "La relación entre rigidez y supremacía constitucional: un análisis a la luz de las reformas constitucionales en México" (2017) 4 Revista del Centro de Estudios Constitucionales 209.

[54] Díaz y Díaz (n 50) 72; Cosío Villegas (n 17) 21, 61.

[55] Cossío (n 47) 95–96.

[56] Córdova (n 13) 74; Cosío Villegas (n 17) 49, 55, 70; Hale (n 14) 313; O´Malley (n 17) 4, 7, 9, 111, 117.

[57] Our translation. Presidencia de la República, *Los presidentes de México. Discursos políticos 1910–1988* (El Colegio de México 1988) 379.

Furthermore, the lack of constitutional supremacy had an unfortunate consequence: it allowed the president to use social rights—one of the distinguishing features of the Mexican Constitution—as political instruments[58] and supported one of the first experiences with populism in the region in 1934 with a welfare state.[59] This lack of constitutional supremacy meant that social rights and the inspiring promises for social justice of the 1917 Constitution fell prey to Revolution idolatry.[60] The social rights promised in the Constitution were not binding rights[61] but rather became instruments of control and negotiation in the hands of the president.[62]

This subordination of social rights was not a coincidence. Some scholars argue that since the origins of the 1917 Constitution, social transformation was envisaged through executive power.[63] The strengthening of executive power to protect social rights, particularly peasants' rights to land distribution, addressed the deep inequality that existed before the Revolution between the peasants and the *hacendados*.[64] A strong state and a strong president were "necessary" to accomplish the constitutional promises. Only after achieving material equality would democracy be possible.[65]

While the executive was strengthened to solve social problems, according to Revolution idolatry, the people were taught "to wait for a savior of saving themselves."[66] The idea of an all-powerful president as a benevolent patriarch and friend of the masses determined the subordination of social rights.[67] Social rights enforcement depended on the goodwill of the president and the party. These rights were not entitlements to public services, but rather a constitutional promise that the president would look out for you in exchange for veneration.[68]

The subordinated role of the Constitution to Revolution idolatry began to change in 1980, when the political elites adopted a neoliberal ideology that

[58] Ávila and Salmerón (n 1) 275. For a similar Ecuadorian experience, see Rosalind Dixon, "Constitutional Rights as Bribes" (2018) 50 Connecticut LR 767.

[59] Juan Antonio Cruz Parcero, "Los derechos sociales en la Constitución de 1917: un balance en su centenario" in Juan A. Cruz Parcero (ed.), *Los Derechos Sociales en México Reflexiones sobre la Constitución de 1917* (Instituto de Estudios Constitucionales de Quéretaro 2020) 67; Alicia Hernández Chávez, *La mecánica cardenista* (2nd edn., El Colegio de México 2005).

[60] Cossío (n 47) 90.

[61] Parcero (n 59) 61.

[62] Córdova (n 13) 19, 21, 73. In a similar understanding, see Zackary Elkins, Tom Ginsburg, and James Melton *The Endurance of National Constitutions* (CUP 2009) 195.

[63] Díaz y Díaz (n 50) 187.

[64] ibid 222–225. Referring to Molina Enríquez, the man whose ideas influenced art. 27 of the Constitution.

[65] ibid 233, 237, 244.

[66] O´Malley (n 17) 28.

[67] ibid 59, 60–61.

[68] ibid 132, 141.

needed the rule of law and the Constitution as instruments to further their agenda. Neoliberalism became the government ideology in 1982, with the election of President Miguel de la Madrid, and lasted for thirty-six years until 2018.[69] As is well known, neoliberal ideology needs and promotes the rule of law to guarantee economic liberties.[70] However, it does not require bottom-up constitutional change nor a more democratic system. Some examples of neoliberal constitutional reforms were: the 1992 amendment that suppressed the right to land distribution, allowed joint stock companies to buy agricultural land, and recognized the property rights of the *ejidos*; the 1994 amendment that strengthened the Supreme Court as the final arbiter of constitutional conflicts;[71] and the 2013 amendment that allowed private investment in oil and hydrocarbon, to mention but a few. All these amendments (like many others constitutional reforms) were carried out without popular participation.[72]

It is noteworthy that the binding conception of the Constitution defended by neoliberalism did not include social rights. Indeed, social rights were, until very recently, considered as programmatic or non-binding norms.[73] This explains the constitutional amendments of the 1980s which incorporated the right to shelter and the right to health. These social reforms allowed the president to stop the deterioration of the regime that began in the 1970s but without making any serious commitment to social change.[74]

Furthermore, the need for a binding Constitution and rule of law was not enough to leave behind the hyper-presidential identity. According to that tradition, the president can pursue any constitutional amendment they regard as necessary for their political agenda.[75] In this sense, the stability and the social identity of the Constitution has been strongly compromised with each six-year term. With more than 250 constitutional amendment decrees and its wide

[69] María Eugenia Romero Sotelo, *Los orígenes del neoliberalismo en México. La escuela austriaca* (Fondo de Cultura Económica 2019).

[70] Simon Springer, Kean Birch, and Julie MacLeavy (eds.), *The Handbook of Neoliberalism* (Routledge 2016), Fernando Escalante, *Historia Mínima del Neoliberalismo* (El Colegio de México 2015), Mariana Velasco Rivera, "The Political Sources of Constitutional Amendment (Non) Difficulty in Mexico" in Richard Albert, Carlos Bernal, and Juliano Zaiden Benvindo (eds.), *Constitutional Change and Transformation in Latin America* (Hart 2019) 253–254.

[71] See Arianna Sánchez, Beatriz Magaloni, and Eric Magar, "Legalist versus Interpretativist. The Supreme Court and the Democratic Transition in Mexico" in Gretchen Helmke and Julio Ríos-Figueroa (eds.), *Courts in Latin America* (CUP 2011); Andrea Castagnola and Saúl López Noriega, "Are Mexican Justices True Arbiters Among the Political Elites? An Empirical Analysis of the Court´s Rulings from 2000–2011" in Andrea Castagnola and Saúl López Noriega (eds.), *Judicial Politics in Mexico. The Supreme Court and the Transition to Democracy* (Routledge 2017).

[72] Jacobsohn and Roznai (n 18) 257.

[73] Cossío (n 47) 91.

[74] ibid 111.

[75] Velasco (n 70) 247, 249, 256.

scope, the 1917 Constitution is something very different today than it was at its inception.[76]

In other words, even though from 1980 the political elites began to consider the Constitution as normative, the hyper presidential identity remained alive and allowed a high number and ever-increasing rate of constitutional amendments.[77] This tradition explains why the amendment rate did not decline even though political pluralism progressively grew.[78] Since 1982, there have been more than 150 decrees amending the Constitution. With the high number of constitutional amendments that followed the neoliberal path, the Constitution lost its social identity.[79] In this way, neoliberalism accomplished the dismem berment of the Mexican Constitution.

In our opinion, the Mexican presidentialist experience exemplifies a belief in persons rather than in institutions.[80] According to this perspective, since the president has the answer to all the problems the Republic faces, then the Constitution should be amended according to his will.[81] In contrast, following Arendt, a successful revolution needs a Constitution[82] that is stable and to which people feel attached. The Constitution establishes the boundaries for politics, but it is not subordinated to politics. On the contrary, the Constitution binds politics even though it may be interpreted in different ways.[83] Once there is a Constitution in place, lasting institutions need to take the lead over what we have called Revolution idolatry.[84] The stability and durability of the institutions are two important values about which we should care.[85]

[76] Ana Micaela Alterio and Roberto Niembro, "Constitutional Culture and Democracy in Mexico. A Critical View of the 100-Year-Old Mexican Constitution" in Mark A. Graber, Sanford Levinson, and Mark Tushnet (eds.), *Constitutional Democracy in Crisis?* (OUP 2018).

[77] Velasco (n 70) 246.

[78] María Amparo Casar and Ignacio Marván, *Pluralismo y reformas constitucionales en México: 1997–2012* (CIDE 2012) 11. Another possible explanation is that constitutional amendments were found by the three parties (PRI, PAN, and PRD) to be the way to make credible political commitments during the transition to democracy, especially after 1988 when PRI lost the necessary deputies to amend the Constitution unilaterally. See Pou-Giménez, Pozas-Loyo, and Saavedra-Herrera (n 26) 13; Francisca Pou and Andrea Pozas-Loyo, "The Paradox of Mexico´s Constitutional Hyper Reformism: Enabling Peaceful Transition While Blocking Democratic Consolidation" in Richard Albert, Carlos Bernal, and Juliano Zaiden Benvindo (eds.), *Constitutional Change and Transformation in Latin America* (Hart 2019) 221, 231–235; Velasco (n 70) 252

[79] Díaz y Díaz (n 50) 83. In 2018, the government announced that it wanted to recover the social identity of the Constitution. Within three years, it had passed eighteen amendment decrees which reformed fifty-five articles of the Constitution. See "Presentará la 4t una 'nueva' constitución; alistan 18 reformas" (*El Universal*, July 12, 2021).

[80] Hannah Arendt, *On Revolution* (Penguin Books 1963) 65–66.

[81] There has not yet been a female president in Mexico.

[82] Arendt (n 80) 133.

[83] ibid 148.

[84] ibid 82, 114, 117, 221.

[85] ibid 214, 215, 221.

This does not mean that the spirit of the revolution disappears or is no longer important once the Constitution is enacted.[86] In the Mexican case, we think the spirit of the Revolution consisted in the idea of a new egalitarian beginning that included peasants and workers. Today, that spirit should guide constitutional amendments and interpretations, including traditionally excluded voices such as women, indigenous people, people with disabilities, etc. Of course, the difficulty lies in having at the same time stability and respect for the spirit of the Revolution. In this regard, the authority of the Constitution should be considered "as the point of reference for all subsequent politics."[87]

III. The "*Permanent* Constituent Power" and the Preservation of the Hyper-Presidential Identity

Revolution idolatry has supported a permanent and unlimited amendment power in Mexico, as the Supreme Court has ruled on several occasions.[88] In our opinion, this amendment power mirrors the hyper-presidential identity.[89] Article 135[90] of the 1917 Constitution establishes the amendment procedure, which is almost identical to article 125 of the 1857 Constitution. In the constituent assembly of 1917, there was no debate regarding article 135. However, there was an interesting debate in the constituent assembly of 1857. Before approving the final version of article 125 of the 1857 Constitution, the assembly discussed two proposals:[91] the first established the intervention of two subsequent Congresses and popular approval by the voters; the second established

[86] ibid 212, 214.

[87] Jeremy Waldron, "Arendt's Constitutional Politics" in Dana Villa (ed.), *Revolution and Constitution* (CUP 2000) 201, 212–213.

[88] The last time the Supreme Court ruled that it could not review a constitutional amendment was in 2016. See Recurso de reclamación 2/2016-AI, Segunda Sala de la Suprema Corte de Justicia de la Nación [SCJN] [Supreme Court] 2016 (Méx.).

[89] Marván (n 6) 244.

[90] Art. 135. This Constitution may be subject to additions and reforms. For additions and reforms to be incorporated into the Constitution, it is required that Congress, by a vote of two-thirds of its present members, agrees on reforms and additions and that they are approved by the majority of the state legislatures. Congress, or its permanent body if that is the case, will count the votes cast by the state legislatures and will declare which additions and reforms are approved.

[91] Art. 125. This Constitution may be subject to additions and reforms. However, for the additions and the reforms to be incorporated into the Constitution, it is necessary for Congress, through a nominal vote of two-thirds of its present members, to agree which articles are to be reformed; that such agreement is published in all the newspapers of the Republic three months before the next immediate Congress is elected; that voters, having reviewed such notice, state that they agree with such reform, in which case they will manifest it in the respective power of their congressman; that the new Congress makes such reforms; and that they are subject to a vote by the people in the next immediate election. If an absolute majority of voters decides in favor of the reforms, the executive will sign them into the Constitution.

the intervention of two subsequent Congresses but did not include popular participation. However, neither were approved. Some of the constituent deputies considered the proposed amendment procedure to be too slow and to confuse pure democracy with representative democracy. They believed that the people were represented by the deputies and *incapable of having the necessary knowledge* to approve a constitutional amendment.[92]

The hyper-presidential system needed more than an ideology: it required the construction of constitutional concepts. Permanent constituent power was a concept created by an influential constitutional law professor and justice of the Supreme Court, Felipe Tena Ramírez. His book, first published in 1944, today has more than fifty editions; as of 2009, more than 230,000 copies had been printed.[93] Many generations of lawyers have learned constitutional law from his book; among his students are renowned Supreme Court justices who have quoted him in the Court´s plenary discussions on limitations on the amendment power.[94]

Tena Ramirez asserted that the amendment power was a "permanent constituent power" with no substantive limitations, only procedural ones. He argued that the *amparo* procedure was a proceeding action to claim procedural violations. According to Tena, article 135 of the Constitution established an organ that was in a way sovereign. It provided for additions and reforms of the Constitution but did not allow for total replacement in a singular amendment. He thought that permanent constituent power could change the whole Constitution in a piecemeal way. He interpreted article 135 systematically with article 39, which establishes the popular sovereignty principle and the right of the people to change their form of government at any time. Aware of Carl Schmitt´s constitutional theory, he distinguished the amendment procedure of the Mexican Constitution from Schmitt's theory and argued that permanent constituent power could change fundamental political decisions.[95] Moreover, he argued that, according to the original intent of the founders of the 1857 Constitution, *the people were excluded from the constitutional amendment*

[92] Carlos Arellano García, "Exégesis del artículo 135 constitucional" in *Estudios Jurídicos en Homenaje a Felipe Tena Ramírez* (Porrúa 1999) 2–5.

[93] José Ramón Cossío, "Felipe Tena Ramírez y la Constitución de 1917" in José Ramón Cossío Díaz, and Jesús Silva-Herzog Márquez (eds.), *Lecturas de la Constitución* (Fondo de cultura Económica 2017) 134.

[94] See the participation of Justice Mariano Azuela in the plenary discussion of June 26, 2008. SCJN, Stenographic version of the session of the plenary of the Supreme Court of Justice of the Nation (Supreme Court of Justicce of the Nation, June 26, 2008) https://www.scjn.gob.mx/PLENO/ver_taquigraficas/jun26_2008.pdf acccesed July 20, 2021.

[95] Art. 39. National sovereignty is vested essentially and originally in the people. All public power derives from the people and is instituted for their benefit. The people have at all times the inalienable right to alter or amend their form of government.

process. Popular participation would lead to anarchy and required civic competence, and popular participation was not advisable in those days.[96]

Two reflections can be noted: On the one hand, permanent constituent power was an idea used to consolidate the endurance of the Constitution because it matched the regime´s authoritarian character.[97] Permanent constitutional amendments were an expression of and served to consolidate the authoritarian presidential identity of the Constitution. In this sense, the Mexican mania for constitutional amendments has not been a practice of destruction, but of conservation.

On the other hand, permanent constituent power is an *anticanonical concept* because it helps to justify the misuse of the amendment formula to constitutionalize the momentary ideas of the political elites.[98] Furthermore, it is anticanonical because it represents the unlimited sovereign,[99] so the Constitution does not limit the will of the political elites. According to Cossío, Tena´s constitutional theory was anchored in an unlimited sovereignty and prevented the Constitution from becoming a binding document; his theory, therefore, was necessary for the functioning of the dominant political regime in the country.[100]

Consistent with Revolution idolatry and "permanent constituent power," the Supreme Court has rejected the role of guardian of social constitutional identity by refusing to invalidate constitutional amendments and refusing on several occasions to limit the amendment power.[101] Some of the Supreme Court's rulings make use of Tena Ramirez's concept of "permanent constituent power" in their arguments. The most recent example of this judicial deference being the case against the composition of the Constituent Assembly of Mexico City in 2017.

The Mexico City Constitution was published on February 5, the same day as the 1917 Mexican Constitution. (Of course, this coincidence has symbolic importance because it represents the centenary of the development of Mexican constitutionalism). The seventh transitory article for the establishment of the Mexico City Constitution stated that 60% of the deputies would be elected by popular vote and the other 40% would be federal congresspeople or appointed

[96] Felipe Tena Ramírez, *Derecho Constitucional Mexicano* (Porrúa 2001) 58–62.
[97] Díaz y Díaz (n 50) 75.
[98] Roznai (n 27) 5; Pou and Pozas-Loyo (n 26) 229.
[99] Roznai (n 27) 120.
[100] Cossío (n 93) 145, 168, 169.
[101] Contrast the Indian Supreme Court in the Kesavanda case, Cossío (n 93) 59.

by other political elites.[102] It is important to remember that in 2012, five years before the 2017 Constituent Assembly, the PRI had won the presidential election and established a coalition with other parties to leave out the emerging political party MORENA. Mexico City, however, had long been a left-wing political city with broad support for MORENA. The electoral rules established by the seventh transitory article of the Constituent Assembly, which reduced the number of popularly elected deputies, were thus thought to favor the PRI and its allies and harm MORENA. The Movimiento Ciudadano party challenged before the Supreme Court the constitutionality of the composition of the Assembly.[103]

By a majority decision, the Court refused to hear the case. In January 2016, the Supreme Court discussed whether the "unconstitutionality action" (an abstract review process) against the seventh transitory article met the necessary legal requirements.[104] The Court ruled that the action did not meet the requirements established in article 105 of the Constitution, since the unconstitutionality action was not designed to challenge a constitutional amendment. Even though the discussion concerned standing, some justices in their discussion quoted the concept of "permanent constituent power" to justify the unlimited amendment power; and the Court used that argument in its ruling. Moreover, the Court quoted the precedent *controversia constitucional* 82/2001, which refers to the sovereign character of the amendment authority. The *ratio decidendi* of the Court was that "permanent constituent power" did not establish in the Constitution the possibility of challenging constitutional amendments, and neither did the subsequent reforms to article 105 of the Constitution permit challenges to constitutional amendments.

[102] ARTICLE SEVENTH—The Constituent Assembly of Mexico City will be composed by one hundred constituent deputies, who will be elected in accordance with the following terms:

A. Sixty will be elected under the principle of proportional representation, through a single list in/one multimember district . . .
B. Fourteen senators designated by two thirds of the votes of the members present of such chamber by proposal of its Council of Political Coordination.
C. Fourteen deputies designated by two thirds of the votes of the members present of such chamber by proposal of its Council of Political Coordination.

The federal legislators elected as constituent deputies in accordance with this and the prior section will continue to hold their seats in Congress and the Senate without being subject to article 62 of the Constitution.

D. Six designated by the President.
E. Six designated by the Major of Mexico City.

[103] Acción de inconstitucionalidad 15/2016, Pleno de la Suprema Corte de Justicia de la Nación [SCJN] [Supreme Court] 2016 (Méx.).

[104] Recurso de reclamación 8/2016-AI, Pleno de la Suprema Corte de Justicia de la Nación [SCJN] [Supreme Court] 2016 (Méx.). This challenge arose from acción de inconstitucionalidad 15/2016.

This ruling is remarkable for two reasons. It uses the concept of "permanent constituent power" and an originalist approach to interpret article 105, which establishes the unconstitutionality action. If we recall, Tena´s theory of permanent constituent power has two characteristics: it was in a way sovereign, but there were procedural limitations and *amparo* procedures to protect against procedural flaws.[105] In 2016, however, what the Court did was to maintain the idea of sovereignty but to leave aside the procedural limitations that Tena supported. The originalist approach focused on protecting sovereign "permanent constituent power." The Court did not consider either the possibility of implicit limitations[106] or the highly elitist character of the seventh transitory article being challenged. The judicial application of permanent constituent power is a good example of how "concepts should not be regarded as an intellectual exercise divorced from any real consequences."[107]

In conclusion, understanding permanent constituent power refines the assessment of constitutional amendments in Mexico. Even though it is easy to say that the Mexican Constitution has lost its identity since its text has changed substantially over 104 years, we think this is true only if we emphasize the social identity of the Constitution, but not if we focus on the presidential one. In fact, the multiple amendments of the Mexican Constitution have maintained the simulation of change by popular will in order to preserve the hyper-presidential regime.

IV. Conclusion

What can we learn from the Mexican Constitution in light of the general reflection of this volume? We argue two main points. The first is that the Mexican Constitution is *canonical* for being the first constitution to introduce social rights, within an institutional design of hyper-presidentialism. Unfortunately, but not surprisingly, the Constitution has evolved, reinforcing its hyper-presidential identity and subordinating its social one. Latin American constitutionalism has largely followed this formula, frustrating the always alleged will to advance an egalitarian path.[108]

The second point is that its permanent constituent power is *anticanonical* in a normative way. Together with Revolution idolatry, permanent constituent

[105] At the time Tena Ramírez wrote his book, an unconstitutionality action did not exist. It was established by art. 105 of the Constitution in 1995. It is worth noting that the *amparo* law changed in 2013, forbidding its use to challenge constitutional amendments [Const.] as amended, art. 61, fr. I (Diario Oficial de la Federación 1917 (Mex.)).

[106] Three justices were in the minority: Arturo Zaldivar, José Ramón Cossío, and Alfredo Gutiérrez.

[107] Roznai (n 27) 110.

[108] Roberto Gargarella "The 'New' Latin American Constitutionalism. Old Wine in New Skins" in von Bogdandy et al. (n 3) 221, 233.

power has allowed the consolidation of an authoritarian exercise of power, including the practice of amending the Constitution without any popular participation or consent. Notwithstanding the incorporation of new political subjects to the constituent power of 1917 (workers and peasants) and the political discourse that has accompanied the Constitution (linked to empowerment of the masses through social rights), Mexican constitutionalism has been dominated by the will of the political elites throughout the twentieth century.

For their own benefit, Mexico's presidents have disregarded popular participation and the limitation of power and defended the idea of social change through strong executive power. This desired social change has been pursued not by effective rights and the rule of law but rather by an all-powerful executive. More than a hundred years later, we already know that without stable institutions and strong rights, the transformative promises of the Constitution will depend on the voluntarism of the president and will be subordinated to their interests.

We have proceeded from Revolution idolatry and constitutional subordination to neoliberal ideology and the instability of the content of the Constitution. During the stage of Revolution idolatry and constitutional subordination, following the procedure of article 135 of the Constitution was not legally important. The decisions were taken by politicians not limited by the Constitution. Once Revolution idolatry was abandoned and neoliberal ideology was adopted, which needed a normative Constitution, the instability of the content of the Constitution began to increase. In other words, in Mexico a normative Constitution has not been accompanied by stability in the content of the Constitution. This is because hyper-presidentialism persists.

As we have argued in another paper,[109] if we want a truly popular Constitution (as the Revolution promised) and stable institutions, we need to limit the instrumental use of the amendment power by the president. One way of doing so is by amending article 135, which establishes the amendment process, to include deliberative participation in constitutional amendment procedures,[110] such as cooling clauses,[111] open meetings, participatory forums, public hearings, popular initiatives, referenda,[112] or deliberative polling.[113] Participatory

[109] Alterio and Niembro (n 76).

[110] See Reva Siegel, "Constitutional Culture, Social Movement Conflict and Constitutional Change: The Case of the de facto ERA" (2006) 94 California L Rev 1339.

[111] Alterio (n 53) 225.

[112] ibid 226. Gabriel Negretto, "Constitution-Making in Comparative Perspective" in *The Oxford Research Encyclopedia of Politics* online (OUP 2017) 17–19

[113] James Fishkin and Gombojav Zandanshatar, "Deliberative Polling for Constitutional Change in Mongolia: An Unprecedented Experiment" (Constitution Net, 20 September 2017), accessed July 25, 2021.

constitutional amendments would empower the citizenry, allowing them to learn and understand the content of the Constitution,[114] but more importantly, it would diminish the number of amendments, making them more difficult to achieve[115] and less manageable for the president, who would need popular support to enact them. Unfortunately, we know that amending article 135 of the Constitution asks the almost impossible: a president who is willing to limit themselves.

[114] Jürgen Habermas, *Facticidad y validez* (6th edn., Trotta 2010) 374–35, Carole Pateman, *Participation and Democratic Theory* (CUP 1970) 46.

[115] Jon Elster, *Ulises desatado. Estudios sobre racionalidad, precompromiso y restricciones* (Gedisa 2002) 124–126.

PART II
STRUCTURES

9

Separation of Powers

Kevin Y. L. Tan

I. Introduction

The doctrine of the separation of powers is central to the concept of constitutionalism, sitting as it does at the core of the idea of limited government. The concept of constitutionalism emerged as a response to absolutism and the exercise of arbitrary prerogative powers by autocratic and tyrannical rulers. The roots of the separation of powers doctrine may be traced to Aristotle's idea of 'mixed government'. In his quest for stable government, Aristotle drew upon the various constitutions of the Greek city states to develop the idea of a 'mixed government' which comprised three forms of government—monarchy, aristocracy, and democracy.[1] Though Aristotle's theory of mixed government—the combination of different forms of government in a single polity to create stable government—is quite distinct from the concept of the separation of powers, the two ideas are connected. As Maurice Vile explains:

> The theory of mixed government was based upon the belief that the major interests in society must be allowed to take part jointly in the functions of government, so preventing any one interest from being able to impose its will upon the others, whereas the theory of the separation of powers, in its pure form, divides the functions of government among the parts of the government and restricts each of them to the exercise of its appropriate function. … The theory of mixed government had as its central theme a blending of monarchy, aristocracy and democracy, and … there is a tendency to equate these, in some stages of the development of the doctrine of the separation of powers, respectively with the executive, judicial and legislative 'powers'.[2]

[1] See Carrie-Ann Biondi, 'Aristotle on the Mixed Constitution and Its Relevance for American Political Thought' (2007) 24(2) *Social Philosophy & Policy* 176–198.

[2] M. J. C. Vile, *Constitutionalism and the Separation of Powers* (Oxford: Clarendon Press, 1967) at 33.

Kevin Y. L. Tan, *Separation of Powers* In: *Global Canons in an Age of Contestation*. Edited by: Sujit Choudhry, Michaela Hailbronner, and Mattias Kumm, Oxford University Press.
DOI: 10.1093/9780191956942.003.0009

In the ensuing centuries, the idea of using a mix of governance types to prevent absolutist government by providing checks and balances on each other persisted. Both theories have the same objective and starting point: to prevent the emergence of absolutist and tyrannical government. The theory of mixed government 'opposed absolutism by the prevention of the concentration of power in one organ of the State, and the doctrine of the separation of powers starts from the same assumption'.[3] However, it was only in the seventeenth century that a key element in the separation of powers doctrine emerged—the recognition of an independent judicial branch of government which (in the case of England) would 'take its place alongside King, Lords, and Commons'.[4]

The idea of dividing state powers functionally into three branches—the legislative, the executive, and the judicial—was first set out by the French political philosopher Baron de Montesquieu in his *The Spirit of the Laws*,[5] first published in 1748. This massive comparative legal study was highly influential, especially to the drafters of the American Constitution, a subject to which we will shortly turn. In Book 11, Chapter 6, Montesquieu wrote:

> In every government there are three sorts of power: the legislative; the executive in respect to things dependent on the law of nations; and the executive in regard to matters that depend on the civil law.
>
> By virtue of the first, the prince or magistrate enacts temporary or perpetual laws, and amends or abrogates those that have been already enacted. By the second, he makes peace or war, sends or receives embassies, establishes the public security, and provides against invasions. By the third, he punishes criminals, or determines the disputes that arise between individuals. The latter we shall call the judiciary power, and the other simply the executive power of the state.[6]

Beyond separating state power by function, Montesquieu went on to argue that such a separation of powers was necessary to protect the political liberties of citizens of the state:

[3] ibid, at 36.
[4] ibid, at 37.
[5] Baron de Montesquieu, *The Spirit of the Laws* (Thomas Nugent, trans.) (New York: Hafner Press, 1949).
[6] ibid, at 151.

> When the legislative and executive powers are united in the same person, or in the same body of magistrates, there can be no liberty; because apprehensions may arise, lest the same monarch or senate should enact tyrannical laws, to execute them in a tyrannical manner.
>
> Again, there is no liberty, if the judiciary power be not separated from the legislative and executive. Were it joined with the legislative, the life and liberty of the subject would be exposed to arbitrary control; for the judge would be then the legislator. Were it joined to the executive power, the judge might behave with violence and oppression.
>
> There would be an end of everything, were the same man or the same body, whether of the nobles or of the people, to exercise those three powers, that of enacting laws, that of executing the public resolutions, and of trying the causes of individuals.[7]

Montesquieu's highly influential ideas were practically adopted and infused into the first of two of our canons—the Constitution of the United States of America, 1787. Not only has this constitution stood the test of time, it became *the* model for constitution-makers for the next two centuries. The US Constitution has thus been the quintessential canon embodying the doctrine of the separation in written and codified form. The second canonical work I have chosen[8] reinforces the concept of the separation of powers in the absence of a codified language that mandates such separation. This is the 1965 case of *Don John Francis Douglas Liyanage & Ors v. The Queen*,[9] a decision of the Judicial Council of the Privy Council in the United Kingdom, on an appeal from Ceylon. The anti-canon I have chosen is the Constitution of the Kingdom of Brunei, 1984. It is an example of the constitutions typically drafted by religious or theocratic states which rejects the separation of powers doctrine in favour of a more absolutist form of government.

[7] ibid, at 151–152.

[8] The editors of this volume have asked contributors to first select a key constitutional concept or doctrine they wish to discuss, and then identify and discuss three *primary* sources in that subject that we consider canonical. Of these, one must be anti-canonical.

[9] [1967] AC 259 (Privy Council).

II. The Constitution of the United States of America

A. Prelude to the Constitutional Convention of 1787

The Constitution of the United States of America must rank alongside Magna Carta (1215) as one of the most important and significant legal instruments in history. Both instruments are rightly famous for establishing a set of basic fundamental individual liberties and rights which are protected against state encroachment. However, the American Constitution is also important for how it created a new form of government that embedded the separation of powers through the instrument of a modern code for limited government. Two other factors add further lustre to the American Constitution—its durability and its influence in the making of newer constitutions for over 200 years.

The detailed story of the making of the American Constitution has been told in numerous important historical accounts[10] and it is not my aim to repeat them. The following historical milestones are all we need. In 1606, King James I of England issued charters to the London Company and the Plymouth Company to establish permanent settlements in the 'New World'. This led to the foundation and formation of settlements and colonies along the east coast of America. By 1732, there were thirteen colonies in America, administered by the Southern Department of the British government in London. Between 1764 and 1776, the British Parliament passed a series of tax laws for the colonies[11] which led to a revolt and a war of independence between the Americans and the British. On 4 July 1776, at the Second Continental Congress in Philadelphia, the American colonies declared their independence—through the Declaration of Independence—and drafted the Articles of Confederation as a constitution for themselves. The Articles of Confederation were approved in December

[10] See, e.g., George Ticknor Curtis, *History of the Origin, Formation, and Adoption of the Constitution of the United States with Notices of Its Principal Framers* (New York: Harper & Brothers, 1858); George Bancroft, *History of the Formation of the Constitution of the United States of America*, 2 vols (New York: D. Appleton, 1885); Max Farrand, *The Framing of the Constitution of the United States* (New Haven: Yale University Press, 1913); Catherine Drinker Bowen, *Miracle at Philadelphia: The Story of the Constitutional Convention, May–September 1787* (Boston: Little Brown, 1966); Max M. Edling, *A Revolution in Favor of Government: Origins of the US Constitution and the Making of the American State* (New York: Oxford University Press, 2003); Richard Beeman, *Plain, Honest Men: The Making of the American Constitution* (New York: Random House, 2009); and Michael J Klarman, *The Framers' Coup: The Making of the United States Constitution* (New York: Oxford University Press, 2016).

[11] These included the Sugar Act, also known as the American Revenue Act (1764); the Currency or Paper Bills of Credit Act (1751 and 1764); the Quartering Acts of 1765 and 1774; the Stamp Act (1765); the American Colonies Act 1766; the New York Restraining Act (1767); the Revenue Act (1767); The Indemnity Act (1767); the Commissioners of Custom Act (1767); the Vice Admiralty Court Act (1768); and the Tea Act (1773).

1777 and came into force—after ratification by the states—on 1 March 1781. With the end of the civil war and the conclusion of the Treaty of Paris of 1783, the American states began thinking about improving their system of government. The shortcomings of the Articles of Confederation were by this time apparent. Congress had no power to raise taxes to pay for a military or to pay off America's foreign debts. It also lacked authority to regulate foreign trade and internal commerce. Significantly, the Articles did not provide for the executive and judicial branches of government. This meant that the Confederation government had no way to enforce its own laws and treaties against non-compliant states.[12]

B. Drafting a New Constitution

A convention was organized at the Pennsylvania State House between 25 May and 17 September 1787 to revise the Articles of Confederation. While most of the state delegates believed they were there to merely revise the existing Articles, key movers of the Convention—notably James Madison of Virginia and Alexander Hamilton of New York—fully intended to create a completely new charter. The delegates elected George Washington as President of the Convention and by the end of almost four months of intense discussions and negotiations, a new charter was finalized—the Constitution of the United States of America.

As we noted earlier, Montesquieu's *The Spirit of the Laws* was extremely influential in America and was known to and read by almost all the key framers of the American Constitution, notably James Madison, Thomas Jefferson, Alexander Hamilton, George Mason, John Adams, Benjamin Franklin, and George Washington.[13] The various state constitutions that were promulgated in 1776 and 1777 also embodied the idea of the separation of powers in one form or another.[14] Indeed, by the time of the 1787 Convention, 'important sections

[12] See Klarman (n 10) at 21–23, and 47.

[13] See Paul M. Spurlin, *Montesquieu in America 1760–1801* (Louisiana: Louisiana State University Press, 1940); David J. Bederman, *The Classical Foundations of the American Constitution: Prevailing Wisdom* (New York: Cambridge University Press, 2008) at 59–85; Mathew P. Berman, 'Montesquieu's Theory of Government and the Framing of the American Constitution' (1990) 18(1) *Pepperdine Law Review* 1–42; Jacob T. Levy, 'Montesquieu's Constitutional Legacies' in Rebecca E. Kingston (ed.), *Montesquieu and His Legacy* (New York: SUNY Press, 2009) 115–138; and Ralph Ketcham, 'James Madison at Princeton' (1966) 28(1) *The Princeton University Library Chronicle* 24–54, at 44–48.

[14] Gerhard Casper, 'An Essay in Separation of Powers: Some Early Versions and Practices' (1989) 30(2) *William & Mary Law Review* 211–262; see also Jack N. Rakove, 'The Road to Philadelphia,

of opinion among its members had already accepted the two central positions of American constitutional thought'—the separation of powers and the idea of checks and balances.[15] However, the most important development—and modification—to Montesquieu's original doctrine lay in the judicial sphere. Montesquieu did not consider the judiciary to be a significant branch of government when compared to the others, arguing that it is 'in some measure next to nothing' since as it is 'no more than the mouth that pronounces the words of the law, mere passive beings, incapable of moderating either its force or rigour'.[16]

In England, Sir William Blackstone, Vinerian Professor at Oxford, took Montesquieu's doctrine and adapted it to advance the doctrine of judicial independence and, indirectly, judicial activism.[17] In some ways, Blackstone was even more influential than Montesquieu. His four-volume *Commentaries on the Laws of England*, published in November 1765, sold as many copies in America as it did in England. Indeed, Daniel Boorstin called it 'the bible of American legal institutions'[18] and went so far as to assert that in 'the history of American institution, no other book—except the Bible—has played so great a role' as Blackstone's *Commentaries*.[19]

C. Separating the Branches of Government

The US Constitution—which was based on Madison's Virginia Plan—provided explicitly for the vesting of legislative power in Congress,[20] executive power in the President,[21] and the judicial power in one Supreme Court.[22] Embedded in these various functions is a system of checks and balances, especially between the legislative and executive branches of government. So while Congress has power to pass bills, the President may veto them, but the Presidential veto may

1781–1787' in Leonard W. Levy & Dennis J. Mahoney (eds), *The Framing and Ratification of the Constitution* (New York: Macmillan, 1987) 98–111.

[15] Vile (n 2) at 153; see also Edward J. Erler, 'The Constitution and the Separation of Powers' in Levy & Mahoney (n 14) 151–166.
[16] Montesquieu (n 5) at 156 and 159.
[17] See Paul O. Carrese, *The Cloaking of Power: Montesquieu, Blackstone, and the Rise of Judicial Activism* (Chicago: University of Chicago Press, 2003).
[18] Daniel Boorstin, *The Mysterious Science of Law: An Essay on Blackstone's Commentaries* (Chicago: Chicago University Press, 1941) at iv.
[19] ibid, at iii.
[20] Art. I, section 1, US Constitution.
[21] Art. II, section 1, US Constitution.
[22] Art. III, section 1, US Constitution.

be overridden by a two-thirds vote in both houses of Congress.[23] And while the President may make appointments to the federal judiciary and executive departments, he must do so with the Senate's consent.[24] Congress has sole power of impeachment of the President and of judicial officers,[25] while the President has the power to grant 'reprieves and pardons' in all offences save for cases of impeachment.[26] Significantly, for the judicial branch, judges are given security of tenure and of remuneration, holding their offices 'on good behaviour'.[27]

Since its drafting in 1787, the American Constitution has established itself as a model for other constitution framers from around the world. George Billias pointed out that between 1776 and 1989 American constitutionalism continuously impacted constitution-drafting throughout the world, but more so in six peak periods, most of which followed a revolutionary change or transformation.[28] It is copied for a variety of reasons—its creation of the presidential system of government; its Bill of Rights; its clear separation of powers between different functional branches of government and system of checks and balances; its division of power between the states and the centre in a federal system; and the independence of the judiciary and judicial review—and thus attains its canonical status on that account alone.

III. *Liyanage v The Queen* (1965)

A. The Abortive Coup

Our second canonical source is the Privy Council decision in *Don John Francis Liyanage & Ors v. The Queen*,[29] a case which arose out of the 1962 failed Colonels' Coup in Ceylon. Word had leaked that a group of Christian officers in the military and police—disgruntled by the appointment of increasing numbers of Buddhist officers—planned to topple the Sri Lanka Freedom Party government of Prime Minister Sirimavo Bandaranaike on the evening of 27

[23] Art. I, section 7, US Constitution.
[24] Art. II, section 2, US Constitution.
[25] ibid.
[26] ibid.
[27] Art. III, section 1, US Constitution.
[28] George Athan Billias, *American Constitutionalism Heard Round the World, 1776–1989: A Global Perspective* (New York: New York University Press, 2009).
[29] [1967] AC 259 (Privy Council).

January 1962. As a result of pre-emptive action by Bandaranaike's government, the coup was never executed as its suspected organizers were pre-emptively rounded up. Don John Francis Douglas Liyanage, a senior member of the Sri Lanka Civil Service and Deputy Director of Land Development, was accused of being the mastermind behind the coup. Other co-conspirators included Colonel F. C. de Saram, Colonel Maurice De Mel, Rear Admiral Royce de Mel, CC Dissanayake (Deputy Inspector General of Police), and Sydney de Zoysa (retired Deputy Inspector General). As a result of police action, twenty-four accused were arrested. However, as no shots were fired and no troops mobilized, the government found no suitable provision in the Penal Code with which to charge them. They were then taken to Welikada Prison and placed in solitary confinement with the police hoping to extract confessions from them.

B. The Ceylon Parliament Acts

On 13 February 1962, the Ceylon government issued a White Paper giving details of the coup attempt. It named thirty alleged conspirators (including the appellants) and the parts each of them had played and concluded that it was 'essential that a deterrent punishment of a severe character' be imposed on 'all those who are guilty'.[30] About a month later, on 16 March 1962, the Ceylon Parliament passed the Criminal Law (Special Provisions) Act.[31] This law was clearly directed at the alleged coup participants since its provisions were made retrospective to 1 January 1962. Section 19 of the Act further provided that Part I of the Act 'shall be limited in its application to any offence against the State alleged to have been committed on or about January 27, 1962, or any matter, act, or thing connected therewith or incidental thereto'.

Part I of the Act legalized the *ex post facto* detention of any person suspected of having committed offences against the state for sixty days. Part II of the Act altered the mode of trial for the offences in question by making section 440A of the Criminal Procedure Code—which empowered the Minister of Justice to direct that a defendant be tried by three judges without a jury—applicable to Part VI of the Penal Code (which dealt with offences with which the accused were charged). This meant that the Minister of Justice could order the accused to be tried by a panel of three judges without a jury.

[30] ibid, at 278.
[31] Act No. 1 of 1962.

The Act amended the law to allow for arrests without a warrant for the offence of waging war against the Queen whereas a warrant was previously required. The penalty for an offence under section 114 of the Penal Code—waging war against the Queen—was amended to make the minimum punishment ten years' imprisonment and a forfeiture of all property of those convicted. Section 115 of the Penal Code was also amended to take into account the events leading up to the abortive coup. Substantial additions were made to section 115 to create new offences and enhance the penalties for them. The words in italics show where amendments were inserted:

> 115.—Whoever conspires to commit any of the offences punishable by the next preceding section, or to deprive the Queen of the sovereignty of Ceylon or of any part thereof, or of any of Her Majesty's Realms and Territories, or conspires to overawe, by means of criminal force or the show of criminal force, the Government of Ceylon, *or conspires to overthrow, or with the object or intention of overthrowing, or as a means of overthrowing, otherwise than by lawful means, the Government of Ceylon by law established, or conspires to murder, or attempts to murder, or wrongfully confines, or conspires or attempts or prepares to wrongfully confine, the Governor-General, or the Prime Minister or any other member of the Cabinet of Ministers, with the intention of inducing or compelling him to exercise or refrain from exercising in any manner any of the lawful powers of such Governor-General, Prime Minister or Cabinet Minister,* shall be punished with *death, or* imprisonment of either description which shall extend *to at least ten years but shall not extend to more than* twenty years, *and shall forfeit all his property.*

Further changes to the law included giving the Attorney-General the power to pardon any accomplice with the view of obtaining his evidence, and removing various safeguards under the law of evidence, to admit previously inadmissible evidence and confessions.

In June 1962, the twenty-four accused were charged with conspiring to: (a) wage war against the Queen; (b) overawe by means of criminal force or show of criminal force the Government of Ceylon; and (c) overthrow otherwise than by law means the Government of Ceylon by law established. Pursuant to his new powers under the new law, the Minister of Justice appointed a tribunal of three Supreme Court judges to try the accused. In October 1962, the three judges of the Ceylon Supreme Court held that because the power of their nomination had been conferred on the Minister of Justice, this was an 'interference with the exercise by the Judges of the Supreme Court of the strict judicial power of the State vested in them by virtue of their appointment' under section 52 of the Ceylon Constitution. As the power was one 'which has hitherto been invariably exercised by the Judicature as being part of the exercise of the judicial power of the State', it 'cannot be reposed in anyone outside the Judicature'.[32] As such, the Criminal Law (Special Provisions) Act (Act No. 1 of 1962) was *ultra vires* the Constitution.

Not to be thwarted, the Ceylon government passed the Criminal Law Act (Act No. 31 of 1962) in November 1962 to repeal the Minister's power of nomination under section 440A of the Criminal Procedure Code inserted a new provision empowering the Chief Justice to nominate three judges before whom the trial would be carried out.

C. The Appeal Before the Privy Council

The trial thus proceeded before a tribunal of three judges nominated by the Chief Justice. In April 1965, after 324 days of trial, the court convicted eleven of the twenty-four accused—the appellants—and they were each sentenced to ten years' rigorous imprisonment and all their property was ordered to be forfeited. On appeal to the Privy Council, the appellants made three key arguments:[33]

(a) The Ceylon Parliament could not pass legislation contrary to the fundamental principles of natural justice. The 1962 Acts offended the principles as they were not only directed against specific individuals, but also *ex post facto* created crimes and punishments and destroyed fair safeguards by which the accused could otherwise be protected;
(b) the 1962 Acts were *ultra vires* as they amounted to a direction to convict the appellants or to a legislative plan to secure the conviction and severe punishment of the appellants and were thus an unjustifiable assumption of judicial power by the legislature, or an interference with judicial power, which was outside the legislature's competence and was inconsistent with the severance of power between legislature, executive, and judiciary which the Constitution ordained; and
(c) the language of the 1962 Acts did not suffice 'in the absence of an express provision to that effect' (as required under section 6(3) of the

[32] *R. v. Liyanage* (1963) 64 New Law Reports 313, 359.
[33] *Liyanage* (n 29) at 283.

Interpretation Act) to deprive the appellants of the right to a jury which they had acquired prior to the passing of the Acts.

The appeal was heard before the Privy Council over five days at the end of October and early November 1965. At the Privy Council, the appellants were represented by some of the most distinguished lawyers then practising in Ceylon—Noel Gratiaen QC (former Attorney-General of Ceylon); Hector Wilfred Jayewardene QC (son of Justice Eugene Wilfred Jayewardene QC and younger brother of J. R. Jayewardene who later became President of Sri Lanka); Walter Jayawardena QC (who later became Solicitor-General of Ceylon); Montague Solomon, and Sam J. Kadirgamar. British lawyer, Dick Taverne QC—who had only just taken silk—appeared with the team. Appearing for the Ceylon government was Victor Tennekoon QC,[34] then Solicitor-General, R. K. Handoo, and V. S. A. Pullenayegum.

D. Separation of Powers and the Judicial Power

The Privy Council rejected the appellants' first argument on the ground that the combined effect of the Ceylon (Constitution) Order in Council 1946 and the Ceylon Independence Act 1947 gave to the Ceylon Parliament the full legislative powers of a sovereign independent state. As such, Parliament could not be constrained in the way suggested by the appellants.[35]

In response to the appellants' second argument, Tennekoon argued that the Ceylon Constitution of 1946 'did not seek to invest the judicial power of the state in a set of institutions'. Furthermore, as 'the expression "judicial powers" was not used anywhere' in the Constitution, there was 'nothing in the Constitution from which it could be inferred that the legislature was prohibited from interfering with the judge's judicial functions and judicial powers'.[36] The Privy Council rejected this argument, holding that the change in Ceylon's sovereign status did not produce any 'apparent change in the constituents or the functioning of the Judicature, and that the courts' work 'continued unaffected by the new Constitution, and the Ordinances under which they functioned remained in force'.[37]

[34] Tennekoon later became the 33rd Attorney-General of Ceylon (1970–1973), 35th Chief Justice of Sri Lanka (1973–1977), and Chancellor of the University of Peradeniya (1979–1984).

[35] *Liyanage* (n 29) at 286.

[36] ibid, at 275.

[37] ibid, at 286.

Ceylon's judicial system had been established by the 1833 Charter of Justice, and the courts established by the Charter continued to function continuously to the time in question. There was thus 'no compelling need' to 'make any specific reference to the judicial power of the courts when the legislative and executive powers changed hands'.[38] The Privy Council then launched into a structural argument by noting how the Constitution was organized and 'significantly divided' into eight parts, including a Part 6 that dealt with 'The Judicature'. Lord Pearce (on behalf of the Privy Council) said:

> And although no express mention is made of vesting in the judicature the judicial power which it already had and was wielding in its daily process under the Courts Ordinance, there is provision under Part 6 for the appointment of judges by a Judicial Service Commission which shall not contain a member of either House but shall be composed of the Chief Justice and a judge and another person who is or shall have been a judge. Any attempt to influence any decision of the Commission is made a criminal offence. There is also provision that judges shall not be removable except by the Governor-General on an address of both Houses.
>
> These provisions manifest an intention to secure in the judiciary a freedom from political, legislative and executive control. They are wholly appropriate in a Constitution which intends that judicial power shall be vested only in the judicature. They would be inappropriate in a Constitution by which it was intended that judicial power should be shared by the executive or the legislature. The Constitution's silence as to the vesting of judicial power is consistent with its remaining, where it had lain for more than a century, in the hands of the judicature. It is not consistent with any intention that henceforth it should pass to or be shared by, the executive or the legislature.[39]

Lord Pearce went further to state that while the Ceylon Parliament had power under section 29(1) to make laws for 'the peace, order and good government' of Ceylon, their Lordships could not 'read the words of section 29(1) as entitling Parliament to pass legislation which usurps the judicial power of the judicature ... if in law such usurpation would otherwise be contrary to the Constitution'.[40] The Privy Council then held that the two 1962 amendments 'constituted a grave and deliberate incursion into the judicial sphere' as 'their

[38] ibid, at 287.
[39] ibid, at 287–288.
[40] ibid, at 289.

aim was to ensure that the judges in dealing with these particular persons on these particular charges were deprived of their normal discretion as respects appropriate sentences'.[41] As the two 1962 amendments were declared unconstitutional, the Privy Council did not consider it necessary to consider the appellants' third ground of appeal.

E. Common Law Canon

The decision in *Liyanage* is justifiably canonical for two main reasons. First, it demonstrates how courts are prepared to go beyond the explicit words of a constitution to advance structural arguments to find in constitutions an inherent separation of powers between the various branches of government, even in the absence of a specific vesting of such power. Such a structural argument has even been used to elevate the doctrine to the level of a basic feature of the constitution as did the Indian Supreme Court[42] or to assert that it forms part and parcel of a constitution's basic structure and cannot thus be amended.[43] Second, this argument from structure is applicable even in Westminster-style constitutions such as that of Ceylon's, where there is essentially a fusion of powers between the legislative and executive branches of government. This is a case which, in the words of former Australian Chief Justice Sir Anthony Mason, is 'consigned to perennial distinction'.[44]

IV. The Counter Canon: Brunei's Constitution

The Constitution of Brunei of 1959 is one of the most overtly absolutist constitutions in the world.[45] Power is constitutionally reposed in the hands of the Sultan who is not only the head of state, but head of government and commander of its army. Furthermore, the Constitution does not provide for the establishment of an independent judiciary.

[41] ibid, at 290.

[42] AIR 1973 SC 1461 (India).

[43] See Chan Sek Keong, 'Basic Structure and Supremacy of the Singapore Constitution' (2017) 29 *Singapore Academy of Law Journal* 619–666. See also Kevin Y. L. Tan, 'Into the Matrix: Interpreting the Westminster Model Constitution' in Jaclyn L. Neo (ed.), *Constitutional Interpretation in Singapore: Theory and Practice* (London: Routledge, 2016) 50–74.

[44] Anthony Mason, 'Comment' (2008) 30(1) *Sydney Law Review* 95.

[45] On the making of Brunei's Constitution, see B. A. Hussainmiya, 'The Making of Brunei's 1959 Constitution' in Kevin Y. L. Tan & Bui Ngoc Son (eds), *Constitutional Foundings in Southeast Asia* (Oxford: Hart, 2019) 191–224.

The kingdom of Brunei is thought to have existed from around the tenth century BCE and at its height occupied the entire coastal areas of the island of Borneo and the Sulu Archipelago.[46] By the nineteenth century, it was a pale shadow of its former self, and to prevent his sultanate from being swallowed up by his neighbours, Sultan Hashim Jalilul Aqamaddin (1825–1906) turned to the British for help in containing the rapacious Brookes of Sarawak. This led to the signing of the Treaty of Protection in 1888 under which the Sultan was not allowed to cede or alienate any territory to any foreign powers without British consent.[47] The fate of Brunei, as noted by one scholar, 'was a matter of indifference to London, so long as its territory remained within the British sphere of influence'.[48] Over the next decade, the British Foreign Office planned to dissolve Brunei and divide it up between Sarawak and North Borneo.

At this time, Brunei was a poor and weak kingdom and the Sultan and his people were in serious financial straits. Hewett noted in 1903 that the palace 'was face-to-face with beggary'. Indeed, the people had returned to an era of hunting-gathering to eke out an existence.[49] In 1904, Britain appointed Malcolm Stewart Hannibal McArthur as its new consul to Brunei to report on the situation there. McArthur recommended that Brunei be preserved as an independent entity and that a British Resident be appointed to advise the Sultan.[50] As a result, the Sultan and the British signed a British–Brunei (Protectorate) Agreement dated 3 December 1905 on 2 January 1906, and McArthur was appointed Britain's first Resident. In consideration of acceptance of the British Resident, the Sultan was to be paid a monthly stipend of $1,000, while his two *wazirs*—the Pengiran Bendahara and Pengiran Pemancha—would each be paid $500 a month.[51] This treaty transferred effective control over Brunei's affairs to the British Resident. When oil was struck in Seria in 1929, Brunei's fortunes were reversed. No longer did the British see it as a troublesome administrative nuisance but a flourishing Protectorate.

[46] Marie-Sybille de Vienne, *Brunei: From the Age of Commerce to the 21st Century* (Singapore: NUS Press, 2015) at 32, 50–52.

[47] Art. VI, British–Brunei (Protectorate) Treaty, 17 September 1888, reproduced in B. A. Hussainmiya, *Brunei: Revival of 1906—A Popular History* (Bandar Seri Begawan: Brunei Press, 2006) at 15.

[48] ibid, at 15.

[49] ibid, at 32.

[50] B. A. Hussainmiya, 'Constitutional Practice in Brunei as Highlighted in the 1955 Memorandum of R. H. Hickling' (2006) 79(2) *Journal of the Malaysian Branch of the Royal Asiatic Society* 23, at 24–25. The McArthur report is available in printed form as M. S. H. Arthur, *Report on Brunei in 1904* (Athens, Ohio: Ohio University Center for International Studies, Center for Southeast Asian Studies, 1987), introduced and annotated by A. V. M. Horton.

[51] D. G. Campbell & M. S. H. McArthur to HH Sultan of Brunei, 'Letter of Assurances, Subsidiary to the 1905–1906 Treaty' reproduced in Hussainmiya (n 36) at 78.

Between 1905 and 1940, Britain ruled Brunei autocratically—through its Resident and in the name of the Sultan. However, the relationship began to change after the Japanese occupation and especially after Sultan Omar Ali Saifuddin III succeeded his elder brother, Sultan Ahmad Tajuddin, upon the latter's death in 1950. Sultan Omar proved to be a tough and resolute ruler who agreed to British proposals to promulgate a constitution only because he saw it as a way to renegotiate the 1905–1906 Treaty. In May 1953, Sultan Omar announced his intention to grant his people a new written constitution. However, efforts by the British to draft a constitution for a constitutional monarchy, along the lines of those it had drawn up for the rulers of the Malay states in the Federation of Malaya failed. The British planned to turn Brunei into a constitutional monarchy with the Sultan exercising largely ceremonial functions and the country being run by elected representatives and officials. It was ultimately a contest of wills and a war of attrition between the Sultan and the British High Commissioner Sir Anthony Abell, and the whole constitution-drafting process left Abell despondent.[52]

The Sultan sincerely believed that the British would help draft a constitution that would secure his position as Brunei's undisputed ruler, but was met by a High Commissioner who was more concerned with protecting Britain's economic and political interests, improving administration, and pushing through democratic reforms to bring Brunei on a par with the other British territories of Sarawak and North Borneo (Sabah) with the view to amalgamating them into the North Borneo Federation. The Sultan's position hardened considerably after 1956 when A. M. Azahari established the Partai Rakyat Brunei (PRB or People's Party of Brunei), Brunei's first political party. Sensing the threat that the mass mobilization of the electorate posed to his sovereignty, the Sultan prevaricated further and stonewalled Abell by introducing more and more amendments. The Constitution that was promulgated on 29 September 1959 was not one that the British desired,[53] but there was little they could do against a wily, intransigent Sultan whose cooperation they desperately needed to realize their plan of a North Borneo Federation.

The 1959 Constitution was promulgated alongside the signing of the Borneo–British Treaty which gave Britain control over Brunei's external relations and defence. The High Commissioner continued to have power to 'advise

[52] See Kevin Y. L. Tan, 'The Struggle to Reform Brunei's Monarchy: The Sultan and the British' in H. Kumarasingham (ed.), *Viceregalism: The Crown and Its Representatives in Political Crises in Post-War Commonwealth* (London: Palgrave-Macmillan, 2020) 311–330.

[53] On the 1959 Constitution and its operation and suspension, see Tsun Hang Tey, 'Brunei's Revamped Constitution: The Sultan as *Grundnorm*?' (2007) 9 *Australian Journal of Asian Law* 264–288.

on all matters connected with the government of the State other than those matters relating to the Muslim religion and the Custom of the Malays' which the Sultan 'agrees to accept'.[54] The Constitution provided for a two-tier electoral system. Sultan Omar, who was uncomfortable with elections and the increasing popularity of Azahari's PRB, tried to postpone elections beyond the two-year moratorium envisaged in 1959 but he could not turn the tide. In September 1962, elections for the fifty-five seats in the four District Councils were held and the PRB won fifty-four of them. The PRB was fiercely against the Greater Malaysia plan and rejected all overtures by the British and Malaya's Tunku Abdul Rahman to woo Brunei into the proposed new federation. In December 1963, an armed rebellion broke out when members of the North Kalimantan National Army (TNKU)—which was closely affiliated to the PRB, and which was supported by Indonesia—stormed the oil town of Seria, police stations, and various government facilities. Swift intervention by the British quelled the rebellion but Brunei's experiment with elections and proto-democracy was over. The Sultan proclaimed a state of emergency, banned the PRB, and arrested its leaders and suspended the 1959 Constitution. At the time of writing, Brunei is ostensibly still in a state of emergency since the 1962 Proclamation has never been retracted. Even so, the 1959 Constitution has since been amended more than ten times, with major revisions coming in 1984 (just prior to Brunei's independence from Great Britain that year), 2004, and 2006.

The current Constitution does not provide for a separation of powers between the various branches of state power. The executive authority of the state is vested in the Sultan who is also Prime Minister and Supreme Commander of the Royal Brunei Armed Forces.[55] To assist and advise the Sultan, a Privy Council made up of members appointed by the Sultan is established under Part IV of the Constitution. However, the Sultan is not bound to act on the Council's advice.[56] A Council of Ministers comprising the Prime Minister and other Ministers is established under Part V of the Constitution but all Council members hold their seats at the Sultan's pleasure.[57] And while the Sultan is required to consult with the Council of Ministers in the performance of his duties,[58] he is not bound to do so.[59] A Legislative Council is established under Part VI of the Constitution, but like members of the Council of Ministers, all members of

[54] Art. 4, Brunei–British Agreement, 1959.
[55] Art. 4, Brunei Constitution.
[56] Art. 6(5), Brunei Constitution.
[57] Art. 12, Brunei Constitution.
[58] Art. 18(1), Brunei Constitution.
[59] Art. 19(1), Brunei Constitution.

the Legislative Council hold their seats at the Sultan's pleasure.[60] The Sultan has absolute power to make 'laws for the peace, order, security and good government' of the state.[61] As mentioned earlier, there are no provisions constituting the judicial branch of government in the Constitution although the Brunei Supreme Court was established under the Supreme Court Act (Cap. 5), a piece of ordinary legislation. Under the Act, Judges and Judicial Commissioners to the Court are appointed by the Sultan provided the candidates satisfy the qualifications set out in the Act.[62] Judges have security of tenure[63] but no security of remuneration.[64] The Constitution has no bill of rights nor provisions guaranteeing any fundamental liberties.

V. Conclusion

Canons embody a set of principles that are so important that they must be studied, understood, and upheld. They are, however, not guarantees against the destruction of the very principles they encapsulate. There are many examples of how even the best-drafted constitutions—fashioned after the most canonical of models—can be torn apart by those determined to do so. One of the most well-known examples of this was how Hitler subverted the Weimar Constitution through his Enabling Act of 1933, his machinations within the Reichstag,[65] and the establishment of extra-constitutional People's Courts.[66] And even where no institutional change is made, it is still possible to overcome the system of checks and balance if political circumstances are 'right'. We saw this during the presidency of Donald Trump in the United States. In his short four-year tenure, Trump was able—with the help of a highly supportive Republican-dominated Senate—to make three Supreme Court appointments that undoubtedly transformed the political tenor of the Court.

Today, we accept that constitutionalism requires state powers to be divided between its various branches and that the doctrine of the separation of powers is necessary if the judicial branch is to be able to exercise the power of judicial

[60] Art. 31(1), Brunei Constitution.
[61] Art. 39, Brunei Constitution.
[62] Sections 7 and 11, Supreme Court Act (Brunei).
[63] Section 8(1), Supreme Court Act.
[64] Section 9, Supreme Court Act.
[65] See Karl Loewenstein, 'Dictatorship and the German Constitution: 1933–1937' (1937) 4(4) *University of Chicago Law Review* 537–574; and Gilbert Fergusson, 'A Blueprint for Dictatorship: Hitler's Enabling Law of March 1933' (1964) 40(2) *International Affairs* 245–261.
[66] See Ingo Muller, *Hitler's Justice: The Courts of the Third Reich*, Deborah Lucas Schnedider (trans) (Cambridge: Harvard University Press, 1991).

review and to interpret the constitution. The two canonical works highlighted in this chapter not only bring the doctrine to life but offer excellent lessons in how the doctrine is expected to work in states where constitutionalism is taken seriously. The US Constitution is significant in not only codifying the separation of powers as part of its structure but also by being the prime model of study and emulation in the ensuing 240 years. The case of *Liyanage* offers an excellent example of how common law judges, faced with interpreting constitutional instruments that do not explicitly codify the separation of powers doctrine, nevertheless embed its practice through a structural definition of constitutionalism. And while the case was decided back in 1965, modern courts have continued to robustly assert their judicial power to adjudicate. We saw this in the highly-publicized *Miller* case in the United Kingdom when the UK Supreme Court, against the backdrop of an unwritten constitution, asserted its judicial power to determine the legality of the Prime Minister's advice to the Queen on the prorogation of Parliament.[67] As a counter-canon, the absolutist Brunei Constitution has parallels in the constitutions of Saudi Arabia, Oman, and Eswatini (all absolute monarchies) as well as in the communist states of China, North Korea, Vietnam, Laos, and Cuba. Of course, there is nothing to stop these states from becoming constitutional democracies, as did Bhutan in 2008.

[67] *R. (Miller) v. Prime Minister (Lord Advocate & Ors Intervening) & Cherry & Ors v. Advocate-General for Scotland (Lord Advocate & Ors Intervening)* [2020] ACT 373 (Supreme Court, UK).

10
Global Canons, Term Limits, and the Constituent Power Theory

Sergio Verdugo[*]

I. Introduction

We live in a time of democratic regression and critical human rights challenges. This edited volume aims at advancing a normative goal in this context. If a *global canon* could help show how democracy and human rights can be better protected, it would thus be crucial to debate which legal or judicial texts should be considered part of that global canon. That way, those materials may get the visibility they need to become central in the study of comparative constitutional law and international human rights law. However, as Balkin and Levinson have argued commenting on the construction of the American constitutional canon, even though identifying a legal canon is partly a prescriptive exercise, we are mere "participants in building the canon that will bestow upon the next generation, and so we have as much right as duty to offer our own views, in the hope that they will influence others."[1] As such, canons are continuously in transition.

As I elaborate more in the next section, I assume that any candidate for such a global canon should meet at least two conditions: First (1), the legal text needs to advance a relevant democratic or human rights principle. Second (2), the material needs to produce a significant impact at least within its jurisdiction. If the legal material only meets (2), and deteriorates a crucial (1) value in profound ways, such as targeting what some scholars have called the minimum core of a competitive democracy, then the legal text should be considered an *anticanon*. The minimum core includes institutional arrangements, political

* Professor of Law, IE University, Spain. Email: sergio.verdugo@ie.edu. I am grateful for comments by Michaela Hailbronner, James Fowkes, David Schneiderman, Günther Frankenberg, and Mattias Kumm.

[1] J. M. Balkin and Sanford Levinson, *The Canons of Constitutional Law*, vol. 111 (Harv. L. Rev. 1998) 964.

Sergio Verdugo, *Global Canons, Term Limits, and the Constituent Power Theory* In: *Global Canons in an Age of Contestation.* Edited by: Sujit Choudhry, Michaela Hailbronner, and Mattias Kumm, Oxford University Press.
DOI: 10.1093/9780191956942.003.0010

processes, and fundamental rights crucial for maintaining a competitive democracy.[2] Assessing whether the legal material harms or strengthens the core in a significant way is a helpful—though not exclusive—way to determine how the canon or anticanon relates to (1). If neither (1) nor (2) are met, the selected material is not a good candidate for either a canon or an anticanon.

This chapter proposes incorporating two judicial decisions from Latin America into the discussion on the global canons. Both judicial decisions use the constituent power theory to evaluate rules engaging with presidential term limits in the context of presidential regimes. The discussion on presidential term limits has attracted the attention of several scholars because their maintenance or removal has been politically salient in many jurisdictions[3] and has even threatened to erode the democratic system. As Günter Frankenberg argues, autocrats (and politicians with authoritarian inclinations) tend to see these types of limits as violating their view that public office is within their property.[4]

The first ruling is the Colombian Constitutional Court's decision that declared the unconstitutionality of the constitutional amendment aimed at allowing former President Álvaro Uribe from running to serve a third term in 2010.[5] The second ruling is the Bolivian Plurinational Constitutional Tribunal's decision of 2017, which removed the term limits from the 2009 Bolivian Constitution so that former President Evo Morales and other leaders from his ruling coalition could run again, even if that meant going against the result of the 2016 plebiscite in which the citizens voted against the possibility of another reelection.[6]

I claim that the Colombian decision meets both (1) and (2) and can therefore be considered as a candidate for the global canon. The Bolivian decision should be regarded as an *anticanon* because, although it meets (2), it goes against the minimum core.

Both rulings were politically consequential for their countries, as they constrained (Colombia) or enabled (Bolivia) how an incumbent president could

[2] Rosalind Dixon and David Landau, "Competitive Democracy and the Constitutional Minimum Core" in Tom Ginsburg and Aziz Z. Huq (eds.), *Assessing Constitutional Performance* (CUP 2016) 268–292.

[3] Tom Ginsburg, James Melton, and Zachary Elkins, *On the Evasion of Executive Term Limits*, vol. 52 (Wm. & Mary L. Rev. 2011) 1807; Mila Versteeg et al., *The Law and Politics of Presidential Term Limit Evasion*, vol. 120 (Colum. L. Rev 2020) 120; Rosalind Dixon and David Landau, *Constitutional End Games: Making Presidential Term Limits Stick*, vol. 71 (Hastings L. J. 2020) 359–418.

[4] Günter Frankenberg, *Authoritarianism Constitutional Perspectives* (Edward Elgar Publishing 2020) ch. 5.

[5] Sentencia C-141 of 2010 (Corte Constitucional de Colombia).

[6] Sentencia Constitucional Plurinacional No. 0084/2017 (Tribunal Constitucional Plurinacional de Bolivia).

prolong their rule. However, although both decisions impacted the minimum core, they did it in opposite ways. While the Colombian ruling prevented a leader with authoritarian inclinations from extending his years in office, the Bolivian decision allowed the leader of a dominant-party regime to extend his rule despite the will of the majority of the voters. Although some scholars have criticized both rulings claiming that their legal arguments are inconsistent or incorrect,[7] comparative constitutional scholars tend to praise the Colombian decision[8] and criticize the Bolivian ruling.[9]

As I will show later, examining these rulings could contribute to different types of literature. The Bolivian decision engages with a (wrong) human rights argument regarding political rights,[10] and the Colombian ruling could be used to advance the literature on the politics of constitutional courts when promoting democracy in adverse conditions,[11] as well as the literature on unconstitutional constitutional amendments.[12] Furthermore, students of global canons can compare these two rulings to understand how judges can use the constituent power theory to develop legal doctrines leading to opposite

[7] Raúl Gustavo Ferreyra, *Gobierno de los jueces. La Corte Constitucional de Colombia y la "segunda reelección presidencial"*, vol. 10 (Derechos en acción 2019) 245; Laura Alessandra Nocera, *Contradicciones constitucionales: el Tribunal Constitucional Plurinacional boliviano y la reelección de morales. ¿Una práctica de abusivismo?*, vol. 23 (Anuario Iberoamericano de Justicia Constitucional 2019) 491.

[8] David Landau, *Abusive Constitutionalism*, vol. 47 (UC Davis L. Rev. 2013) 189; Samuel Issacharoff, Santiago García-Jaramillo, and Vicente F Benítez-Rojas, *Judicial Review of Presidential Re-Election Amendments in Colombia* (Max Planck Encyclopedia of Comparative Const. L. 2020) 13; Samuel Issacharoff, *Constitutional Courts and Consolidated Power*, vol. 62 (Am. J. Comp. L. 2014) 585–612; Samuel Issacharoff, *Fragile Democracies. Contested Power in the Era of Constitutional Courts* (CUP 2015).

[9] Sergio Verdugo, *The Fall of the Constitution's Political Insurance. How the Morales Regime Broke the Insurance of the 2009 Bolivian Constitution*, vol. 17 (ICON 2019) 1098–1124; David Landau and Rosalind Dixon, *Abusive Judicial Review: Courts Against Democracy*, vol. 53 (UC Davis L. Rev. 2020); Rosalind Dixon, David Landau, and Yaniv Roznai, "Term Limits and the Unconstitutional Constitutional Amendment Doctrine: Lessons from Latin America" in Alexander Baturo and Robert Elgie (eds.), *The Politics of Presidential Term Limits* (OUP 2019).

[10] See, e.g., the criticisms of the Venice Commission against the Bolivian ruling on international human rights law. European Commission for Democracy Through Law (Venice Commission), *Report on Term-Limits* (Part I, pp. 16–17) CDL-AD (2018).

[11] See, e.g., how some scholars have used the Colombian ruling in Rosalind Dixon and Samuel Issacharoff, *Living to Fight Another Day: Judicial Deferral in Defense of Democracy* (Wis. L. Rev. 2016) 691–692, 716–719.

[12] See, e.g., how scholars engaging with the unconstitutional constitutional amendment doctrine have cited the Colombian case, Yaniv Roznai, *Unconstitutional Constitutional Amendments. The Migration and Success of a Constitutional Idea*, vol. 61 (Am. J. Comp. L. 2013) 657, 682–684; Richard Albert, *Constitutional Amendments. Making, Breaking, and Changing Constitutions* (OUP 2019) 153–154; Gonzalo Ramírez Cleves, "The Unconstitutionality of Constitutional Amendment in Colombia: The Tension Between Majoritarian Democracy and Constitutional Democracy" in Thomas Bustamante and Bernardo Gonçalves Fernandes (eds.), *Democratizing Constitutional Law* (Springer 2016); Vicente Benítez-Rojas, "We the People, They the Media: Judicial Review of Constitutional Amendments and Public Opinion in Colombia" in Richard Albert, Carlos Bernal-Pulido, and Juliano Zaiden Benvindo (eds.), *Constitutional Change and Transformation in Latin America* (Hart 2019).

outcomes.[13] The relationship between this theory and the law has animated important debates among scholars,[14] the constituent power theory has been criticized by many,[15] and the scholarship exploring how judges use the theory is far from achieving an academic consensus.[16]

Despite the criticisms I have formulated elsewhere against the theory of constituent power,[17] I argue that if a constituent power theory must be developed as judicial doctrine, and in spite of its important shortcomings, it should follow the example of the Colombian—and not the Bolivian—Constitutional Court. Such constituent power theory should incorporate an examination of how the decision can impact essential democratic values, as the Colombian ruling does. This idea reinforces Rosalind Dixon and David Landau's article on how the unconstitutional constitutional amendment doctrine, promoted by scholars such as Yaniv Roznai,[18] should be used.[19] Dixon and Landau have claimed that the doctrine should be limited to prevent threats against core democratic principles.[20] By adding the Bolivian case as an anticanon to the analysis—which is a case that connects to the constituent power theory but not to the unconstitutional constitutional amendment doctrine—this chapter also contributes to expanding Landau and Dixon's argument to another use of the constituent power theory.

The following section develops some methodological remarks. Section III examines the ruling of the Colombian Constitutional Court and explains why

[13] The literature on constituent power is too extensive to cite fully. One of the most important contemporary contributions to this debate is the book edited by Martin Loughlin and Neil Walker, *The Paradox of Constitutionalism. Constituent Power and Constitutional Form* (OUP 2007).

[14] Compare David Dyzenhaus, *Constitutionalism in an Old Key: Legality and Constituent Power*, vol. 1 (Glob. Const. 2012) 229–260 and Martin Loughlin, *The Concept of Constituent Power*, vol. 13 (Eur. J. of Political Theory 2014) 218.

[15] See some prominent criticisms in the works by Zoran Oklopcic, *Beyond the People: Social Imaginary and Constituent Imagination* (OUP 2018); Zoran Oklopcic, *Three Arenas of Struggle: A Contextual Approach to the Constituent Power of "the People"*, vol. 3 (Glob. Const. 2014) 200; Andrew Arato, *Post Sovereign Constitution Making: Learning and Legitimacy* (OUP 2016); Andrew Arato, *The Adventures of the Constituent Power. Beyond Revolutions?* (CUP 2017); Richard Kay, *Constituent Authority*, vol. 59 (Am. J. Comp. L. 2011) 715.

[16] Compare David Landau, "Constituent Power and Constitution-Making in Latin America" in Hanna Lerner and David Landau (eds.), *Comparative Constitution-Making* (Edward Elgar 2019); Joel I. Colón-Ríos, *Carl Schmitt and Constituent Power in Latin American Courts: The Cases of Venezuela and Colombia*, vol. 18 (Constellations 2011) 365.

[17] Elsewhere I have formulated a criticism against the most dominant version of the constituent power theory. See Sergio Verdugo, *Is it time to abandon the theory of constituent power?*, vol. 21 (ICON) 14.

[18] Yaniv Roznai, *Unconstitutional Constitutional Amendments: The Limits of Amendment Powers* (OUP 2017). Also, Sergio Verdugo, "The Role of the Chilean Constitutional Court in Times of Change" in Richard Albert, Carlos Bernal, and Juliano Zaiden Benvindo (eds.), *Constitutional Change and Transformation in Latin America* (Hart Publishing 2019).

[19] Rosalind Dixon and David Landau, *Transnational Constitutionalism and a Limited Doctrine of Unconstitutional Constitutional Amendment*, vol. 13 (ICON 2015) 606.

[20] ibid 615–618.

the decision can be a global canon candidate. Section IV then analyzes the Bolivian Tribunal's judgment and shows how the decision fits with the idea of an anticanon. Section V offers some comparative remarks and discusses the impact of both decisions on the literature, which may be relevant for the global canon conversation.

II. Methodological Remarks

Constitutional materials like Magna Carta, the Declaration of the Rights of Man and the Citizen, the UN Declaration of Human Rights, or famous judicial decisions like *Brown v. Board of Education* are obvious canon candidates. These kinds of materials seem to fit well with Michaela Hailbronner's normative framework regarding the functions a canon is supposed to serve: they have all helped establish the foundations of a shared discourse supporting a normative agenda of democratic constitutionalism and human rights.[21] Nevertheless, the inclusion of these kinds of materials as accepted canons has been primarily driven by historical triumphs and political influences that are harder to assess regarding more modern or contemporary materials of, say, the last thirty or twenty years. Also, if a contemporary legal text has not yet helped to create a shared discourse or debate with transnational consequences, it does not mean that the legal material lacks the potential to become part of the global canon.

As this volume's goal involves *proposing* material to be discussed in the global canon conversation, those materials do not need to be part of an already established comparative or international canon. This chapter assumes that the candidate for a possible global constitutional canon, even in a weak sense—i.e. one encouraging a worldwide conversation and not a morally binding normative standard—requires, at least, two necessary conditions: (1) quality and (2) historical impact. (1) *Quality* does not mean argumentative coherence or perfect legal adherence to whatever the *Law* states (it often requires the opposite), but the advancement of core values associated with democratic political liberalism or crucial human rights norms.[22] This first condition has a normative component. (2) *Historical impact* means that the materials should have significantly

[21] Michaela Hailbronner, *Constructing the Global Constitutional Canon: Between Authority and Criticism*, vol. 69 (UTLJ 2019) 248.

[22] Also, canons such as judicial decisions do not offer a sincere reflection on the normative problems at stake. Thus, sincerity in the arguments should not be a condition. I think that (1) we will miss valuable opportunities if we exclude materials that were not released in a sincere way; and (2) it is not easy to prove or discuss how sincere the reflections were. For a diverse position, see ibid 263.

influenced the jurisdiction under which they were released. The impactful nature of the legal texts is not limited to their legal enforcement. For example, the 1789 French Declaration of the Rights of Man and the Citizen was not enforceable, but it was consequential for other reasons.

A candidate for the global canon needs to meet both conditions. Take, for example, the South African Court's ruling forbidding the death penalty,[23] the American Supreme Court decision putting an end to the *separate-but-equal* doctrine,[24] and the Chilean Constitutional Court's ruling that forced the Pinochet dictatorship to establish independent judicial supervision of the plebiscite that was going to decide on whether Pinochet would remain in power.[25] The South African and the American cases meaningfully aimed to advance human rights by strengthening principles such as due process, life, and equality. The Chilean case successfully helped the country's transition to democracy.[26] All of them initiated consequential political processes despite possible criticisms.[27]

On the contrary, anticanons need to go against the first condition (*quality*) while also fitting the second requirement (*historical impact*). The purpose of identifying legal materials as anticanons is to show what should *not* be imitated or followed. The literature has previously used the idea of "aversive constitutionalism" to show how constitutional actors reject previous models when building institutions or designing constitutional norms.[28] The aim of an anticanon, in my view, is to promote those sorts of rejections in any place that considers following the same path. This is a normative aim that differs from the explanatory way the antimodel or aversive constitutionalism has served to understand existing institutions after considering why and how other alternatives have been rejected.[29] It perhaps resembles more what Jamal Greene calls an "anticanon."[30] Though Greene is interested in the status of specific judicial decisions in American constitutional law and focuses on their *legal* status, he

[23] *S v Makwanyane*, [1995] (3) SA 391 (CC).

[24] *Brown v. Board of Education of Topeka*, 347 U.S. 483 (1954).

[25] Tribunal Constitucional de Chile 33-1985.

[26] Sergio Verdugo, *How Can Judges Challenge Incumbent Dictators and Get Away with It?*, vol. 59 (Colum. J. Transnat'l. L. 2021); Sergio Verdugo, "The Civil Law Tradition, the Pinochet Constitution and Judge Eugenio Valenzuela" in Iddo Porat and Rehan Abeyratne (eds.), *Towering Judges: A Comparative Study of Constitutional Judges* (CUP 2021).

[27] Michaela Hailbronner has argued that the South African case is widely celebrated because it succeeded in making a principled human rights stand against popular opinion and it fits well with an international human rights trend. Hailbronner (n 20) 254.

[28] See generally Kim Lane Scheppele, *Aspirational and Aversive Constitutionalism: The Case for Studying Cross-Constitutional Influence through Negative Models*, vol. 1 (ICON 2003) 296.

[29] See, e.g., D. Erdos, *Aversive Constitutionalism in the Westminster World: The Genesis of the New Zealand Bill of Rights Act (1990)*, vol. 5 (ICON 2007) 343.

[30] Jamal Greene, *The Anticanon*, vol. 125 (Harv. L. Rev. 2011) 379.

also adds a normative component. He argues that the "anticanon" is a group of judicial decisions that must be refuted by those who cite them. They are the opposite of the law, and the anticanonical status of a decision depends on how a legal community approaches the ethical propositions the decision entails. If we use this conceptualization in the context of a discussion of what constitutes a global canon, we need to be able to offer a transnational normative approach—such as crucial constitutional democratic principles and international human rights norms. An anticanon can travel. For example, Sujit Choudry has explored how the American *Lochner* jurisprudence[31] has been rejected by Canadian constitutional law in a way that helps to explain the design and jurisprudential evolution of the Canadian Charter of Rights and Freedoms.[32]

Anticanons include cases such as the infamous American case of *Dred Scott*[33] and the Chilean Supreme Court decision that outlawed the political rights of the members of the Communist Party.[34] Those decisions established legal doctrines that consolidated undesirable views on issues such as citizenship, property, and individual liberty. These cases protected the rights of slave-owners as well as unacceptable working conditions that go against a decent approach to human rights, and legislation seriously undermining political freedoms, respectively.

The canons or anticanons do not achieve their status due to the consistency of their arguments or how they respect the "law" according to the specific rule of recognition that existed in the particular jurisdiction. Indeed, anticanons can be *legal* at the time they were enacted, and canons can be *illegal*.[35] The question now is what kinds of legal materials can be considered an anticanon for a global conversation.

It is helpful to consider the legal and political issues at stake to understand how canons and anticanons can enhance or harm democratic values or human rights norms. The particular legal materials that this chapter proposes for the global canon conversation are two judicial decisions that engage with the elimination of term limits. While the Colombian ruling prevents a constitutional amendment from removing a term limit, the Bolivian judgment eliminates the

[31] *Lochner v. New York*, 198 U.S. 45 (1905).

[32] Sujit Choudhry, *The Lochner Era and Comparative Constitutionalism*, vol. 2 (Int. J. Const. L. 2004) 1–55.

[33] *Dred Scott v. Sandford*, 60 U.S. (19 How.) 393 (1857).

[34] Corte Suprema de Chile, *René Frías Ojeda*, ruling of February 3, 1949.

[35] Greene cites *Brown v. Board of Education* as a canonical case which departed from previous precedents, did not respect the Fourteenth Amendment's expected application, the text of the equal protection clause did not require the decision's doctrine, and the outcome of the decision required, using Dworkin's language, a "Herculean effort—one well beyond the Court's competence—to implement comprehensively" Greene (n 30) 382.

term limit to allow the incumbent president and other officers to run again. Both countries possess an enhanced form of presidentialism—sometimes called hyper-presidentialism. The presidents are simultaneously the higher officers of the state and the heads of the executive branch, citizens directly elect them, and a simple parliamentary majority cannot remove them. Under this system, presidents possess several legislative, administrative, and international powers that make them stronger, within their jurisdictions, than the president of the United States.

I cannot summarize the existing scholarly discussion on term limits here. Suffice it to say that, although there are arguments on both sides of the debate,[36] it is generally understood that term limits make more sense in systems where the executive branch leader is directly elected, as opposed to "assembly-confidence systems."[37] True, term limits restrict the choice of voters in electing their president. Still, they promote a more competitive political market, and they may be able to prevent a potential executive "tyranny."[38] If the constitutional system of a country gives the president too much power, so much that he or she could use it to undermine the political rights of their opponents or eliminate equitable electoral conditions, then term limits might make more sense. In such situations, term limits can help to level the playing field, secure the possibilities of rotation in power, and improve the long-term accountability of politicians at the cost of undermining the short-term accountability of the sitting president and reducing the options available to voters. Even though this is not a unanimous argument in the literature, the mainstream approach suggests that it is desirable to limit the number of terms an elected executive can serve in the context of a presidential regime.

For this reason, institutions such as the Venice Commission typically highlight the importance of presidential term limits.[39] The argument is more robust if the presidents concentrate significant powers and if the limits to their power

[36] See a summary of the arguments in Ginsburg, Melton, and Elkins (n 3) 1815–1823.

[37] I prefer to avoid the typical dichotomy of parliamentary/presidential regimes, as many hybrids exist in the literature. Instead, I follow the useful the conceptualization by ibid 1816.

[38] See a discussion in Tom Ginsburg, Zachary Elkins, and James Melton, "Do Executive Term Limits Cause Constitutional Crises?" in Tom Ginsburg (ed.), *Comparative Constitutional Design* (CUP 2012).

[39] "As a conclusion and due to the risks for the balance of powers and even for democracy as such involved in the possibility for the incumbent to be re-elected more than once, the Venice Commission has clearly expressed its critical approach towards constitutional provisions allowing for more than one re-election of the head of state in presidential or semi-presidential systems." European Commission for Democracy Through Law (Venice Commission) (n 10) 63. See another example in Markus Böckenforde, Nora Hedling, and Winluck Wahiu, *A Practical Guide to Constitution Building* (Intl. IDEA 2011) 166.

are few.[40] This might be true in the case of hyper-presidential regimes exposed to turn into a delegative democracy,[41] as has been the case of jurisdictions such as Colombia and Bolivia.

For these reasons, if a constitutional scheme includes both a strong president and presidential term limits to secure rotation in power, and there are reasons to believe that the strong president may have authoritarian inclinations, then it makes sense to claim that term limits can be part of the minimum constitutional core. It can also be argued that the minimum constitutional core can be undermined by removing those term limits solely or as part of a larger strategy to build a hegemonic ruling coalition.[42]

III. The Colombian Constitutional Court and the 2010 Uribe Ruling

According to the 1991 Colombian Constitution, presidents were supposed to last four-year fixed, non-renewable terms. Nevertheless, before President Uribe finalized his first term, he achieved the necessary majorities to amend the 1991 Constitution. A referendum was going to confirm the amendment, but the Constitutional Court was supposed to review the law calling for the referendum. The Court declared the constitutionality of the call but confirmed that it had the power to review constitutional amendments.[43] Therefore, President Uribe was able to run for reelection, which he won, and could stay in power for eight years. In 2009, as his second term was coming to an end, President Uribe tried to approve another constitutional amendment allowing him to run for a third presidential term.[44] In 2010, when reviewing the call for the new referendum, Uribe faced a Court that had renovated more than half of its members, and it was expected that the new judges would be friendly to the

[40] See, e.g., the following Venice Commission opinions: "Opinion on the Draft Amendments to the Constitution of the Republic of Azerbaijan," CDL-AD(2009)010; "Opinion on the Draft Constitution of the Kyrgyz Republic," CDL-AD(2010)015.

[41] Guillermo A. O'Donell, *Delegative Democracy*, vol. 5 (J. Democr. 1994) 55.

[42] e.g. when Rosalind Dixon and David Landau theorized on what constitutes the minimum core idea, they included the issue of term limits in the case of countries which had incumbent presidents who had both the power and the interest to undermine democratic competitiveness while extending their rule in office. Rosalind Dixon and David Landau, "Competitive Democracy and the Constitutional Minimum Core" in Tom Ginsburg and Aziz Huq (eds.), *Assessing Constitutional Performance* (CUP 2016) 280–281.

[43] Decisión C-1040 of 2005 (Corte Constitucional de Colombia). Also, see Dixon and Issacharoff (n 11); Issacharoff, García-Jaramillo, and Benítez-Rojas (n 8).

[44] The amendment—bill number 1353 of 2009—was aimed at modifying Art. 197 of the Colombian Constitution.

regime.[45] However, with a majority of seven out of nine judges, the Colombian Constitutional Court unexpectedly released a judicial decision that declared the unconstitutionality of that constitutional amendment, thus preventing Uribe from running again and staying in office for twelve years.[46]

The judicial decision justified its outcome using the "substitution doctrine." That doctrine claims that although the Constitution does not explicitly give the Court the power to review constitutional amendments on the grounds of a material or substantive infringement of the Constitution,[47] the Court does have the authority to declare the unconstitutionality of amendments when those amendments seek to "replace" the Constitution. The idea is that a constituted power like the Congress is unable to modify an inherent core, an essential part of the Constitution, a defining element, or the principles and values derived from the constitutional block, which is also composed of international treaties.[48]

The Court had created the substitution doctrine in previous cases, and it has been used to strike down other constitutional amendments.[49] Scholars typically track it to a decision from 2003[50] although some claim that the origins can be traced to the mid-twentieth century,[51] or even to the nineteenth century.[52] In each case, the Court is supposed to identify structural principles embedded in the Constitution that it aims to protect so that the Constitution is not "substituted" by the ordinary amending procedure. The core underlying idea is that if a "substitution" needs to happen, the original constituent power of the people needs to be exercised through the proper channels. If Congress seeks to replace the Constitution, it will exceed its powers, thus acting outside its competence and incurring procedural irregularity. That way, the rule allowing the Court to

[45] Mario Alberto Cajas-Sarria, *Judicial Review of Constitutional Amendments in Colombia: A Political and Historical Perspective, 1955–2016*, vol. 5 (Theory Pract. Legis. 2017) 245, 261.

[46] Decisión C-141 of 2010 (Corte Constitucional de Colombia).

[47] The Constitution only gave the Court the power to review the amending procedure and check that its formalities were fulfilled. There are no eternity clauses.

[48] Scholars use different words to conceptualize this doctrine, and that is why I have inserted words that seem to be synonyms in this context. Ramírez, e.g., uses the idea of "inherent" parts, while others use the idea of "defining elements of the essence of the Constitution", Ramírez Cleves (n 12); Santiago García-Jaramillo and Francisco Gnecco-Estrada, *La teoría de la sustitución: de la protección de la supremacía e integridad de la constitución, a la aniquilación de la titularidad del poder de reforma constitucional en el órgano legislativo*, vol. 65 (Vniversitas 2016) 59, 74.

[49] See, e.g., Decisies C-1040 of 2005, C-588 of 2009 and C-249 of 2012, C-249 of 2012, C-1056 of 2012, C-285 of 2016, and C-373 of 2016. (Corte Constitucional de Colombia).

[50] Decisión C-551 of 2003 (Corte Constitucional de Colombia).

[51] See a historical account in Cajas-Sarria (n 44). For an early explanation of the substitution doctrine, also see Gonzalo Ramírez Cleves, *Los Límites a La Reforma Constitucional y Las Garantías—Límites Del Poder Constituyente: Los Derechos Fundamentales Como Paradigma* (Universidad Externado de Colombia 2003).

[52] See García-Jaramillo and Gnecco-Estrada (n 47).

review the amendments on procedural grounds could also be used to review amendments on substantive grounds.[53]

The idea was developed in the 2003 case, where the Court argued, using a language that resembled Schmitt's theory—which was also cited—of implicit limits to constitutional amendment,[54] that the derivative constituent power—which is a constituted power—cannot replace the Constitution. Only the original constituent power can do so.[55] The way the Court characterized the constituent power of the people also followed the traditional populist notions of the unconstrained and foundational constituent power. This power remains free to exercise its political will and alter the fundamental political decisions regarding organization of the community.[56] It should come as no surprise that Colombian scholars[57] tend to relate this judicial doctrine to the constituent power theory promoted by important landmark works, such as Sieyès' "What is the Third Estate?"[58] and Schmitt's *Constitutional Theory*.[59] Constituent power theory scholars may claim that the constituent power theory should not be used because it can have an authoritarian nature,[60] among other possible criticisms. Even though I tend to agree with this type of criticism, it is important to notice that the function that the constituent power theory played in Colombian constitutional law was not authoritarian in nature. Though, one may wonder whether using that theory was necessary, as constructing alternative judicial doctrines is certainly possible, and whether the theory, as exposed by the Colombian Court, was truly consistent with Schmitt's formulation. Whatever answer we give to these questions, it is relevant to consider that canonical decisions, as explained before, do not need to have legally or logically consistent arguments.

Following the rationale of the substitution doctrine, based on the constituent power theory, when the Colombian Court reviewed the case of Uribe's second reelection, it stated that, if it had been approved, the amendment would have substituted key democratic principles: checks and balances, separation

[53] Jorge Ernesto Roa Roa, *Control de Constitucionalidad Deliberativo. El Ciudadano Ante La Justicia Constitucional, La Acción Pública de Inconstitucionalidad y La Legitimidad Democrática Del Control Judicial al Legislador* (Universidad del Externado de Colombia 2020) 505.

[54] Colón-Ríos (n 16) 365–366, 373–376.

[55] Decisión C-551 of 2003, paras. 37–39 (Corte Constitucional de Colombia).

[56] ibid paras. 29–33.

[57] Ramírez Cleves (n 12); García-Jaramillo and Gnecco-Estrada (n 47) 71.

[58] Emmanuel Joseph Sieyès, "What is the Third Estate" in Oliver W. Lembcke and Florian Weber (eds.), *The Essential Political Writings* (Brill 2014).

[59] Carl Schmitt, *Constitutional Theory* (Jeffrey Seitzer tr., Duke University Press 2008).

[60] It is, after all, an important example of abusive constitutional borrowing. See Rosalind Dixon and David Landay, *Abusive Constitutional Borrowing: Legal Globalization and the Subversion of Liberal Democracy* (OUP 2021).

of powers, pluralism, and political alternation in power. Thus, in addition to identifying constitutional irregularities in the corresponding referendum, the Court used the unconstitutional amendment doctrine to preserve structural principles of Colombian democracy. The separation of powers principle was already considered in the 2005 ruling, but in that case the Court decided that the amendment allowing for one-time reelection did not "substitute" that principle.[61] However, in 2010, the Court considered that a twelve-year presidency could restructure the institutional scheme embedded in the Constitution, producing an imbalance of power among the branches of government and undermining the limits on an executive branch that could control large parts of the institutions aimed at checking that branch. In other words, a twelve-year presidency could make the idea of checks and balances irrelevant,[62] collapsing the separation of powers. It could also solidify the ruling party and "diminish the electorate's capacity to freely choose, thus making the president increasingly difficult to dislodge from office."[63] Had the amendment been approved, Congress would have exceeded its enumerated powers by replacing the Constitution. The argument could easily fit with the minimum core rationale that I explained before. However, even though the Court did not quote Schmitt in the Uribe case, it still used the constituent power theory with a language that resembles Schmitt's rationale and cited the 2003 case—which used Schmitt's theory—while explicitly treating that case as a "precedent." It seems inconsistent and even ironic with Schmitt's overall work to use his theory to limit the ability of a president to run for reelection, because Schmitt believed that the head of the state was the true guardian of the constitution.[64]

However, despite the criticisms that can be made against the judicial decision, the way the ruling advanced democracy's minimum core by securing the competitiveness of the political system is still remarkable. Moreover, the political context in which the decision was released was challenging for the Court. Álvaro Uribe was a popular president with allies who had alleged links to paramilitary groups and significant controversies in relation to the judiciary.[65]

[61] Decisión C-1040 of 2005 (Corte Constitucional de Colombia).

[62] Roa Legislator (n 53) 370.

[63] Issacharoff, García-Jaramillo, and Benítez-Rojas (n 8).

[64] I thank Michaela Hailbronner for suggesting this criticism. Even though it is possible to counterargue that Schmitt's work on this issue was written in the specific context of a parliamentary regime where the "President" was supposed to be a sort of neutral power (*pouvoir neutre*) in the sense of Constant, there is no similar category in a presidential regime. It is the president, in any regime, who will probably decide—with few or greater differences—on the exception (paraphrasing *Political Theology*). See Lars Vinx, *The Guardian of the Constitution. Hans Kelsen and Carl Schmitt on the Limits of Constitutional Law* (CUP 2015) ch. 3.

[65] Cajas-Sarria (n 45) 260.

There was pressure from public opinion to allow Uribe to run again.[66] If he had been allowed to run, Uribe would probably have won the presidential election. But Uribe's strategy to extend his presidency, along with the serious accusations that his regime was facing, confirmed the Uribe administration's dubious commitment to democratic principles. Unable to run for another reelection, the path was open for other candidates for the presidency. Finally, Juan Manuel Santos, who would later win the Nobel Peace Prize for his peace agreement efforts, was elected. Although Santos was a former secretary of Uribe's state, and the Uribe regime originally promoted his candidacy, the result of the election marked a significant change in Colombian politics. Santos broke with the policies advanced by Uribe and Uribe became the most critical opponent of the Santos administration.[67]

IV. The Bolivian Plurinational Constitutional Tribunal and the 2017 Morales Ruling

The Bolivian Tribunal Constitucional Plurinacional (TCP) was initially created by the Constitution enacted by the Morales regime in 2009 after the previous Constitutional Court was dismantled.[68] The 2009 Constitution only allowed the president to be reelected once. However, Morales and his vice-president ran again for the 2013 elections after the Legislative Assembly enacted a law declaring that the constitutional term limits did not count the period before the approval of the 2009 Constitution—and Morales's presidency had started in 2006. The TCP reviewed the law and argued that its interpretation was constitutional[69] even though there were important legal reasons to call it into question.[70] Evo Morales was reelected in 2014 and initiated his third term. In 2015, legislators from Morales's party presented a bill allowing Morales and his vice-president to run for yet another term. The reform required a referendum, which the TCP authorized.[71] Nevertheless, Morales lost the referendum against a 51.6% majority.

[66] ibid 262.

[67] Rosalind Dixon and David Landau, *Transnational Constitutionalism and a Limited Doctrine of Unconstitutional Constitutional Amendment*, vol. 13 (ICON 2015) 617.

[68] Andrea Castagnola and Aníbal Pérez-Liñán, "Bolivia. The Rise (and Fall) of Judicial Review" in Gretchen Helmke and Julio Ríos-Figueroa (eds.), *Courts in Latin America* (CUP 2011).

[69] Declaración Constitucional Plurinacional No. 3/2013 (Tribunal Constitucional Plurinacional de Bolivia).

[70] Alan E. Vargas Lima, *La Reelección Presidencial En La Jurisprudencia Del Tribunal Constitucional Plurinacional de Bolivia*, vol. 19 (Revista Boliviana de Derecho 2015) 446.

[71] Declaración Constitucional Plurinacional No. 0194/2015 (Tribunal Constitucional Plurinacional de Bolivia).

Legislators from Morales's party presented a petition to the TCP, asking it to strike down the constitutional provisions that limited Morales's reelection and the reelection of other officers. In 2017, the TCP unanimously decided that the rules restricting the reelection were unconstitutional.[72]

The TCP's decision engaged with many themes, but two are the most important. First, the argument stating that term limits violate the political rights included in Article 23 of the American Convention on Human Rights, which recognizes the right of each citizen to vote, to participate in public affairs, and to be elected in regular elections via secret vote, as well as to access the public functions of the specific countries in equalitarian conditions. It also held that term limits violated Article 24 of the Convention, which recognizes equality and prohibits discrimination. For the TCP, term limits did not have an objective justification—such as an age limitation, as the American Convention recognizes—and they discriminated against citizens seeking reelection in a disproportionate and unnecessary way by preventing them from exercising their political rights and allowing others—those who run for the first time—to exercise those rights.[73] The TCP cited its jurisprudence and other cases of the Inter-American Court of Human Rights to claim that the Convention had a superior value, and that the TCP had the duty to enforce the Convention's rights over domestic rules, which—according to the TCP—should prevail because of the *pro homine* principle.[74]

The first argument is an incorrect interpretation of international human rights norms[75] and the inter-American human rights system.[76] Although it is common for countries in the inter-American system to establish term limits in their constitutions, as most countries in the region have presidential regimes, the Inter-American Court has never reviewed them, many countries have ratified the Convention while keeping term limits in their constitutions, and also there is no binding or persuasive international norm stating that there is a right to be reelected[77] and there are good reasons to think that limiting presidential reelection in the context of hyper-presidential regimes can actually increase

[72] Sentencia Constitucional Plurinacional No. 0084/2017 (Tribunal Constitucional Plurinacional de Bolivia).

[73] See Section III.7.3. of the Sentencia Constitucional Plurinacional No. 0084/2017 (Tribunal Constitucional Plurinacional de Bolivia).

[74] Sentencia Constitucional Plurinacional No, 0084/2017, at 15–57 (Tribunal Constitucional Plurinacional de Bolivia).

[75] Landau and Dixon (n 9) 51.

[76] I have also made this argument elsewhere. See Verdugo, *The Fall of the Constitution's Political Insurance. How the Morales Regime Broke the Insurance of the 2009 Bolivian Constitution*, vol. 17 (ICON 2019) 1121–1122.

[77] See, e.g., European Commission for Democracy Through Law (Venice Commission) (n 10) 16–17.

the competitive nature of the democratic system and help to implement the American states' regional obligation to secure effective democracy by holding authentic elections and guaranteeing rotation of power. The TCP overlooked these arguments and, instead, cherrypicked a group of references to the Inter-American Court's jurisprudence that merely showed selected and decontextualized paragraphs concerning the corresponding Articles of the Convention.

What determines the existence of term limits is the type of political regime that exists in each country. It is advisable that a system with the features of the Bolivian Constitution possesses term limits. As I explained in Section II, strong elected presidents in fragile institutional contexts with an imbalance between the different branches of governments make it advisable to limit the incumbent president's reelection.[78] Four years later, in 2021, the Inter-American Court released an advisory opinion confirming that there is no autonomous right under the Convention or under the "corpus iuris of international human rights law" to seek reelection, that limiting reelection is compatible with the Convention, and that allowing presidential reelection without term limits violates the "principles of representative democracy" and the Convention's obligations.[79]

The second argument connects to the correct way to interpret the Bolivian Constitution. The TCP cited Article 196.II of the Constitution to claim that the preferential tool of interpretation is to seek the will of the constituent power, which—according to that provision—can be found in the "documents, acts and resolutions, and also on the literal meaning of the text."[80] After citing Article 168 of the Constitution, which contains the term limits, the Court claimed that "nevertheless, to the purpose of fulfilling the constitutional mandate regarding the correct tools of interpretation ... it is mandatory to revise the documents, acts and resolutions of the constituent assembly," in particular, the debates of Committee number 7, which drafted the rule of the executive branch.[81] In attempting to connect the constituent power idea to an originalist reading of the Constitution, the TCP cited the report that the majority of the constituent assembly's corresponding committee enacted, and stated that the will of the constituent power was to allow the president and the vice-president to be reelected popularly because any president who "... has achieved optimal

[78] For a similar argument, but made in the context of the Bolivian ruling, see Sonia Eliana Roca Serrano, *La Injerencia del Órgano Ejecutivo sobre el Tribunal Constitucional: El Caso Boliviano*, vol. 37 (Academia Colombiana de Jurisprudencia 2020) 235, 250–251.

[79] Inter-American Court of Human Rights, Advisory Opinion OC-28/21, June 7, 2021, requested by the Republic of Colombia.

[80] Sentencia Constitucional Plurinacional No. 0084/2017, at 58–59 (Tribunal Constitucional Plurinacional de Bolivia).

[81] ibid 59.

results in implementing its political platform and benefits the majority of the population can have a just recognition by the sovereign, who will decide."[82] The TCP then concluded that, for the original constituent power, term limits should not have been allowed when "the continuity of the position depended on what the popular will . . ."[83]

In this way, the TCP ignored the literal meaning of the constitutional provision by invoking the opinion of some members of the constituent assembly without considering that the term limits were added later as part of the constitution-making negotiations with the opponents of the Morales regime.[84] As the TCP seems to imply, the will of the constituent power was equivalent to the choice of a small number of committee members before they succeeded in ending negotiations with the opposition. True, the constituent power idea is an abstract idea that relies on the fiction of a unified, organic, and stable political will. However, the TCP did not try to show how that fiction could be formed or argued. Instead, it merely assumed that the idea of the report that it cited was conclusive evidence of that will without taking into account all the problems that an originalist approach to the Constitution has in Bolivia.[85] Moreover, the TCP did not consider that most citizens opposed the removal of term limits in the referendum that took place in 2016, which makes the decision subject to democratic claims.[86]

The constitutional interpretation promoted by the TCP and the way the Morales regime advanced strategies to allow an extension in power helped to create the conditions for the democratic rupture that would come[87] with the accusations of electoral fraud[88] and the way Morales left Bolivia after an interim right-wing president took over. Even though Morales finally succeeded in helping his former secretary of economy to win the presidency in 2020, returned to the country, and is still considered by many to be the leading politician of his coalition, it is still unclear whether his influence will prevail.

[82] Following the same logic, the TCP added that "[t]he consecutive reelection by the will of the people is the new possibility to renew the trust deposited in a representative . . .," ibid 59–60.

[83] ibid 60.

[84] I have explained how this "insurance" was broken elsewhere. See Verdugo, *The Fall of the Constitution's Political Insurance. How the Morales Regime Broke the Insurance of the 2009 Bolivian Constitution*, vol. 27 (ICON 2019).

[85] I cannot summarize all the problems that originalism has, though they are known in the literature. In the case of Bolivia, see criticism in Horacio Andaluz Vegacenteno, *Constitución, Derechos y Jurisprudencia*, vol. 15 (Revista Boliviana de Derecho 2013) 10, 28; Vargas Lima (n 70) 668.

[86] See, e.g., Roca Serrano (n 78) 245–246.

[87] Agustín Grijalva Jiménez and José-Luis Castro-Montero, *La Reelección Presidencial Indefinida en Venezuela, Nicaragua, Ecuador y Bolivia*, vol. 18 (Estudios constitucionales 2020) 9, 41.

[88] See Organización de los Estados Americanos, "Análisis de Integridad Electoral. Elecciones Generales En El Estado Plurinacional de Bolivia."

V. On Canons and Anticanons

I have argued that while the Colombian decision fits with both conditions previously outlined and can therefore stand as a candidate for a global canon, the Bolivian judgment should be considered an anticanon. Both rulings relate to the democratic minimum core. Still, while the first enhanced the competitiveness of the political system and prevented a leader with authoritarian tendencies from serving as a president for fifteen years, the second ruling was part of a set of unfortunate decisions that helped pave the way for unlimited reelections. The Bolivian decision is a negative model for international human rights law because it developed a political rights doctrine based on the American Convention on Human Rights that has been widely rejected. I have argued that the Bolivian decision should also be considered an anticanon regarding its use of the constituent power theory. If the constituent power theory is used to build a judicial doctrine, it should enhance—and not deteriorate—the minimum core of democracy. If the ruling does the opposite, although it can be justified in a sort of *originary* constituent power theory that seeks legitimacy in the founding moment of the constitutional system, it can still harm the minimum core. Indeed, it can impair the stability of the democratic processes and the accountability of incumbent politicians while weakening political rights. On the contrary, the Colombian decision is an excellent example of how a ruling that uses the constituent power theory can not only preserve a critical norm justified in the founding moment of the constitutional system but also enhance the democratic conditions of the present system so that present and future citizens can live under a more competitive political regime.

Some may argue that a global canon and anticanon should have an impact beyond the specific jurisdiction in which the rulings were enacted. After all, the idea is to look for legal texts that can spark the interest of a *global* community. Even though there are reasons to oppose this view—e.g. the need to define what is interesting for the *global* community and to make sure that we do not focus solely on what Ran Hirschl calls the "usual suspects"[89]—it is relevant to take into account that this edited volume is a normative project. Thus, the purpose is to offer reasons why the global community *should* be interested in both decisions. At least two reasons can be provided. First, both rulings engaged with term limits in presidential regimes and were crucial for determining the continuity of a specific political regime within their jurisdiction. Term limits

[89] Ran Hirschl, *Comparative Matters. The Renaissance of Comparative Constitutional Law* (OUP 2014) 241.

are an important contemporary subject seeking to answer relevant questions for comparative constitutional studies and international human rights law. Is there a right to be reelected? What are the limits to political rights? How do term limits established in a constitution reinforce or harm the competitiveness and stability of democratic regimes? The Colombian ruling is extraordinary because, even though most presidents in consolidated democracies do not overstay and respect their term limits,[90] it is not expected that a constitutional court will declare the unconstitutionality of the removal of term limits and face an incumbent president.[91] This is particularly relevant in fragile institutional scenarios. In the case of Bolivia, the ruling is also unusual because of the way it interprets political rights. Also, it is not common for a constitutional court to declare the unconstitutionality of a specific provision included in the original text of the constitution.[92]

The second reason why analyzing these decisions can be useful for the global scholarly community is that both engage with the constituent power theory in meaningful ways. As I said in Section I, the constituent power theory has received a lot of attention from several scholars. Still, we are yet to fully understand how judges can use the theory beyond the unconstitutional constitutional amendment doctrine. The Bolivian case is a rare example in this regard for the same reasons mentioned earlier, and the Colombian substitution doctrine has become a prime example—probably along with the Indian Basic Structure Doctrine—of how judges can use a Schmittian or Sieyèsian-based theory to strike down constitutional amendments that undermine a constitutional core.

It should then come as no surprise that both the Colombian and the Bolivian rulings have already received attention in the literature beyond their respective jurisdictions. Indeed, the Colombian decision has attracted the attention of non-Latin American scholars who have used the ruling to exemplify the unconstitutional constitutional amendment doctrine,[93] to show how to prevent

[90] See a discussion of the evidence in Ginsburg, Melton, and Elkins (n 3) 1844–1850.

[91] Mila Versteeg and her coauthors have argued "that the Colombian Constitutional Court is the only court that has ever halted an evasion attempt (in Niger, the Constitutional Court tried, but failed). Perhaps more remarkably, we find that most of the time, courts act as agents of the incumbent and actually help him to serve beyond the original expiration date. ... For the most part, then, courts have actually facilitated the removal of term limits." Versteeg et al. (n 3) 179. Later, they added: "In our survey, the Colombian Constitutional Court is the only court that has successfully prevented a president from running for another term, making it the exception, not the rule," ibid 231.

[92] Also, on the exceptional cases that entail this type of decision, see generally Nicholas W. Barber and Adrian Vermeule, *The Exceptional Role of Courts in the Constitutional Order*, vol. 92 (Notre Dame L. Rev. 2016) 817.

[93] See, e.g., Rosalind Dixon and David Landau, *Transnational Constitutionalism and a Limited Doctrine of Unconstitutional Constitutional Amendment*, vol. 13 (ICON 2015) 614–620. Also, see Mark Tushnet, *Constitution-Making: An Introduction*, vol. 91 (Texas L. Rev. 2013) 1983, 2005.

constitutional abuses,[94] to exemplify how a court can assert a non-written judicial review power,[95] and to identify how courts could help to prevent authoritarian turns[96] by engaging in a successful "second-order referral"[97] or a two-step strategy that resembles the *Marbury* strategy.[98] The Colombian Court's decision has also influenced the Chilean Constitutional Court, which explicitly cited the Colombian decision when justifying its ability to review constitutional amendments in the Chilean context.[99] It is also worth noting that even some critics of the Colombian substitution doctrine have defended the decision on democratic grounds, justifying the way the decision restricted the excessive accumulation of political power in the executive branch by undermining checks on political power.[100]

Of course, acknowledging the virtues of the Colombian Constitutional Court's decision does not mean that the doctrine promoted by that ruling is free from all criticism. It is possible to criticize it on democratic grounds[101] as well as for legal reasons.[102] However, as I said in Section II, although it is desirable that canons are justified by sound legal justifications, the existence of those justifications is not a necessary condition for legal material to become a canon. Moreover, canons *can* be illegal. True, a canon may be less persuasive if the legal reasons behind it are not adequately established, and its acceptance by the legal community may be at risk. Nevertheless, many critical judicial decisions in diverse countries provide creative reasons that break mainstream understandings of how judges should apply the law and the correct tools for interpretation.[103]

The Bolivian ruling has also attracted the attention of international scholars, although in an anticanonical way. For example, Dixon and Landau claim that

[94] Landau (n 9) 202–203.

[95] Stephen Gardbaum, *What Makes for More or Less Powerful Constitutional Courts* (UCLA Public Law & Legal Theory Research Paper Series 2017).

[96] Samuel Issacharoff, *Fragile Democracies. Contested Power in the Era of Constitutional Courts* (CUP 2015) 265.

[97] Dixon and Issacharoff (n 11) 686.

[98] Sergio Verdugo, "How Can Judges Challenge Incumbent Dictators and Get Away with It?" (Towering Judges, Hong Kong, 2019).

[99] Tribunal Constitucional de Chile, 9797-2020.

[100] See, e.g., Carlos Bernal's argument: Carlos Bernal, *Unconstitutional Constitutional Amendments in the Case Study of Colombia: An Analysis of the Justification and Meaning of the Constitutional Replacement Doctrine*, vol. 11 (ICON 2013) 339.

[101] See, e.g., Ferreyra (n 7). Compare with Ramírez Cleves (n 12).

[102] See García-Jaramillo and Gnecco-Estrada (n 48); Bernal (n 100). Also, see a summary of the main criticisms in Roa (n 53) 506–509.

[103] A recent volume providing examples of *towering judges* around the world shows that it is quite common for these types of judges to use reasons that somehow change the conventional ways in which judges operate in the specific jurisdictions. See Rehan Abeyratne and Iddo Porat (eds.), *Towering Judges: A Comparative Study of Constitutional Judges* (CUP 2021).

the decision illustrates an "abusive" judicial practice.[104] Elsewhere I have asserted that the ruling helped break the democratic insurance of the 2009 Constitution,[105] and that it undermines a procedural approach to democracy.[106] Sam Issacharoff and his coauthors have used the judgment as an example of an "active promotion of the governmental interests,"[107] Mila Versteeg and her coauthors have claimed that the Bolivian ruling shows how courts can be used "to interpret away term limits in the constitution,"[108] and the Venice Commission has criticized the decision.[109] Of course, legal arguments against the decision also abound, as I have stated in Section IV.

VI. Conclusion

After explaining that this volume is part of a normative project aimed at offering a discussion on global canons and anticanons based on democratic and human rights principles, this chapter has proposed that two Latin American judicial decisions should be part of that debate: the Colombian case on the second reelection of former President Uribe and the Bolivian case on the reelection of former President Morales. Examining and comparing both decisions is helpful for advancing the field of comparative constitutional law and, though perhaps to a lesser degree, of the scholarship of international human rights law. Both rulings engage with issues that are also relevant in other jurisdictions: the way the constituent power theory can be used by judges, the removal of term limits, the right to be reelected and the right to vote, and the possibilities that constitutional courts have for preserving core democratic values in adverse conditions. Also, both rulings heavily impacted their respective political systems and have attracted the attention of comparative scholars.

While the Colombian decision on the Uribe case can be a candidate for a *canon*, as it helped to advance democracy and was politically consequential, the Bolivian decision on the Morales case might be a candidate for an *anticanon*,

[104] Landau and Dixon (n 9).
[105] Verdugo (n 9).
[106] Sergio Verdugo, *Limited Democracy and Great Distrust. John Hart Ely in Chile and Bolivia*, vol. 19 (ICON 2021).
[107] Issacharoff, García-Jaramillo, and Benítez-Rojas (n 9).
[108] Versteeg et al. (n 3) 230.
[109] European Commission for Democracy Through Law (Venice Commission) (n 10).

as it helped an incumbent regime to stay in power thus making constitutional limits to political power irrelevant. While the first decision shows one way in which judges can help to protect core democratic values, the second one provides an important example of how judges can help a leader with authoritarian inclinations while advancing an incorrect approach to human rights.

11
The Canon of "Constitutional Unamendability" and "Basic Structure Doctrine" in Global Constitutional Studies

*Chien-Chih Lin** and Wen-Chen Chang***

I. Introduction

Recent years have witnessed a global wave of judicial review of constitutional amendments on the basis of explicit or implied constitutional authorization. Supreme courts or constitutional courts in Bangladesh, Columbia, Hungary, India, Kenya, Malaysia, Pakistan, Singapore, and Taiwan, among others, have reviewed constitutional amendments and/or even invalidated them as "unconstitutional" or as violating the principles of "constitutional unamendability," "unamendable constitutions," or "basic structure doctrine." In all of these decisions on the (un) constitutionality of constitutional amendments, courts have confirmed, explicitly or implicitly, that amending constitutions must observe a legal limit because of extra-constitutional normative foundations, and, more importantly, because legal limit must be drawn by the courts, rather than by the political institutions.

These recent judicial decisions on unconstitutional constitutional amendments have confirmed—or at least seem to have confirmed—a constitutional canon developed since World War II. The canonical authorities have come from at least two key sources: one in the German Basic Law and the other in a decision of the Supreme Court of India. Specifically, Article 79(3) of the German Basic Law was the first post-WWII constitution to materialize the idea of an "unamendable constitution" or "constitutional unamendability," ensuring that amendments affecting federalism, states participation in the

* Research Professor, Institutum Iurisprudentiae, Academia Sinica, and Joint-Appointment Professor, Graduate Institute of National Development, National Taiwan University.
** Distinguished Professor, National Taiwan University College of Law, and Joint-Appointment Professor, National Yang Ming Chiao Tung University School of Law.

Chien-Chih Lin and Wen-Chen Chang, *The Canon of "Constitutional Unamendability" and "Basic Structure Doctrine" in Global Constitutional Studies* In: *Global Canons in an Age of Contestation.* Edited by: Sujit Choudhry, Michaela Hailbronner, and Mattias Kumm, Oxford University Press.
DOI: 10.1093/9780191956942.003.0011

legislative process, or the principles of inviolable human dignity and on the nature of the democratic, socialist constitutional state should not be permissible. In *Kesavananda v. State of Kerala*,[1] the Supreme Court of India confirmed that the parliament has the power to amend the Constitution but cannot alter "the basic structure" of the Constitution. The *Kesavananda* decision followed an earlier decision of a similar nature, *Golak Nath v. State of Punjab*,[2] in which the Indian Supreme Court indicated that the parliament had no power to amend fundamental rights. Later, in another case, *Minerva Mills v. Union of India*,[3] the Indian Supreme Court invalidated a constitutional amendment on the basis of destroying the basic structure of the Constitution.[4] The above two authorities have had influences on many judicial decisions in which courts have articulated *legal* limit to amending power on the basis of constitutional or extra-constitutional norms.

In the development process of "constitutional unamendability" or "basic structure doctrine," a possibly countering authority has drawn some judicial attention: a decision by the United States Supreme Court, *Coleman v. Miller*.[5] In this case, the U.S. Supreme Court—while hearing the case challenging a constitutional amendment on procedural grounds—held that the efficacy of ratification of a proposed constitutional amendment is a question for the political departments, but not the courts. It stresses that "The questions they involve are essentially political, and not justiciable. They can be decided by the Congress with the full knowledge and appreciation ascribed to the national legislature of the political, social, and economic conditions which have prevailed during the period since the submission of the amendment."[6]

This chapter is aimed at exploring particular ways in which the canon of "constitutional unamendability" and the "basic structure doctrine" have been constructed and why they have been constructed to reflect certain contextual dynamics. More importantly, in exploring the rising canon of "constitutional unamendability" and the "basic structure doctrine," this chapter also seeks to examine in what particular ways the countering canonical authority—for example, *Coleman v. Miller*—has or has not effectively competed in certain ways

[1] [1973] AIR SC 1461.
[2] 1967 AIR 1643, 1967 SCR (2) 762.
[3] AIR 1980 SC 1789.
[4] Notably, the origin and development of the basic structure doctrine in India was heavily influenced by the German scholar Dietrich Conrad. Monika Polzin, *The Basic-Structure Doctrine and Its German and French Origins: A Tale of Migration, Integration, Invention and Forgetting*, 5 INDIAN LAW REVOEW 45, 45 (2021); Aqa Raza, *Doctrine of Basic Structure: A Critique*, IX-XII INDIAN LAW REVOEW 242-313 (2020).
[5] 307 U.S. 433 (1939).
[6] ibid, at 454.

and why. The rest of this chapter proceeds as follows: Section II briefly introduces Article 79(3) of the German Basic Law, *Kesavananda v. State of Kerala*, and *Coleman v. Miller*, the three paradigmatic examples when canvassing the concept of unconstitutional constitutional amendments. Before introducing the three examples, we first analyze why they have become canons in this field. The three paradigms represent divergent constitutional and legal cultures: one legal in addressing constitutional change and the other political. Based on the analysis, Section III advances a general theory that underscores the idea of constitutional relativity. It elaborates the relativity between constituent power and constituted power, between constitutional revolution and constitutional transformation, and between a brand new constitution and constitutional amendments. This chapter suggests that current scholarship on unconstitutional constitutional amendment does not pay sufficient attention to constitutional relativity, which is particularly evident in nascent democracies in Asia. This new understanding will affect the role of courts when they tackle unconstitutional constitutional amendments, a state of affairs that may herald democratic backsliding. Section IV reinterprets the three canons, and predicated on this reinterpretation, we hope to shed new light on judicial capability in combating democratic backsliding. Section V concludes.

II. The Concept of Constitutional Unamendability

Undoubtedly, it is diabolically difficult and sometimes arbitrary to choose canons in comparative constitutional law, and any choices will certainly marginalize other important candidates.[7] When discussing constitutional unamendability, nonetheless, this problem seems relatively easy. The eternity clause in the German Basic Law and *Kesavananda* are widely if not universally regarded as the crown jewels in comparative constitutional law where constitutional unamendability is concerned. Compared with the two sources, what is often ignored and deserves more scholarly attention is *Coleman*.

Before analyzing them, it behooves us to ask what makes them canonical? To illustrate, they are canons not in the traditional religious sense that is supposed to inspire reverence and imitation;[8] Instead, they acquire their canonical status not only because their impacts have migrated across borders.

[7] *See* Jack M. Balkin & Sanford Levison, *Constitutional Canons and Constitutional Thought*, *in* LEGAL CANONS 400, 413–417 (Jack M. Balkin & Sanford Levison eds. 2000).

[8] Michaela Hailbronner, *Constructing the Global Constitutional Canon: Between Authority and Criticism* (Spring 2019) 69 UNIVERSITY OF TORONTO LAW JOURNAL 248, 249–250.

More importantly, they represent three major models of constitutional design when discussing constitutional unamendability: explicit constitutional unamendability, implicit constitutional unamendability, and non-recognition of constitutional unamendability. In fact, an increasing number of countries have adopted either one of the first two models to address unconstitutional constitutional amendments. It is against this global expansion of constitutional unamendability that *Coleman* surfaces as a contrasting canon. Although *Coleman* is less known to scholars of comparative constitutional law outside the United States, it provides a perspective through which we can rethink the necessity of constitutional unamendability. Being the paradigmatic examples, Article 79(3), *Kesavananda*, and *Coleman* have spurred much reflection and debate regarding democratic constitutionalism, which is particularly crucial in an age of democratic erosion.

A. Three Canons

The enactment of the German Basic Law in general, and Article 79(3) in particular, was driven by the collapse of the Weimar Republic and its Constitution.[9] Although the demise of the Weimar Constitution did not directly result from any (un)constitutional amendments, the weakness of the Weimar Constitution in protecting itself and constitutional democracy gave birth to the concepts of militant democracy and constitutional unamendability. Article 79(3) of the Basic Law provides that "Amendments to this Basic Law affecting the division of the Federation into Länder, their participation in principle in the legislative process, or the principles laid down in Articles 1 and 20 shall be inadmissible."[10] Being dubbed "one of the most innovative and most problematic inventions"[11] in German constitutional law, the provision is widely known as the "eternity clause." It creates a supra-constitutional criterion which all potential constitutional amendments must meet. One of the reasons for rendering these elements impervious to revision is that they form the constitutional identity of post-WWII Germany and therefore cannot be abolished unless the whole constitutional order crumbles.[12] In other words, the eternity clause restricts the

[9] Ulrich K. Preuss, *The Implications of "Eternity Clauses": The German Experience*, 44 ISRAEL LAW REVIEW 429, 439–440 (2011).

[10] https://www.gesetze-im-internet.de/englisch_gg/englisch_gg.html#p0415. To be more specific, Art. 1 refers to the inviolability of human dignity. In addition, Art. 20 entrenches the democratic and social federal political system of Germany. While this constitutional order is endangered, all Germans have the right to resist if no other remedy is available.

[11] WERNER HEUN, THE CONSTITUTION OF GERMANY: A CONTEXTUAL ANALYSIS 25 (2011).

[12] ibid at 28.

exercise of constituted power within a certain domain, but it cannot bind the constituent power of the German people.[13]

In practice, the eternity clause is not merely a parchment barrier. Since 1953, the German Federal Constitutional Court has proclaimed its authority to scrutinize the constitutionality of constitutional amendments and has repeatedly exercised that power.[14] While the eternity clause protects the core of the Basic Law from any constitutional change short of a new constitution, it inevitably grants the Constitutional Court wide discretion in demarcating the boundary of the clause. As time had passed, the scope of the eternity clause has widened as a result of the Constitutional Court's interpretation. In the Lisbon Treaty case, for example, the Constitutional Court maintained:

> In this respect, the constituent power has not granted the representatives and bodies of the people a mandate to dispose of the identity of the constitution. No constitutional body has been granted the power to amend the constitutional principles which are essential pursuant to Article 79.3 of the Basic Law. The Federal Constitutional Court monitors this. Through what is known as the eternity guarantee, the Basic Law reacts on the one hand to the historical experience of a creeping or abrupt erosion of the free substance of a democratic fundamental order. However, it makes clear on the other hand that the Constitution of the Germans, in accordance with the international development which has taken place in particular since the existence of the United Nations, has a universal foundation which cannot be amended by positive law.[15]

Unlike the German Basic Law, the Constitution of India does not plainly designate any unamendable provisions or eternity clauses. Nevertheless, the Supreme Court of India has gradually crafted the basic structure doctrine from scratch in a series of decisions involving property right. The emergence of the basic structure doctrine from property cases is hardly a coincidence, given that land redistribution was a major political agenda in post-WWII India.[16] Intriguingly, the Indian Supreme Court initially rejected the idea of

[13] JO ERIC KHUSHAL MURKENS, FROM EMPIRE TO UNION: CONCEPTIONS OF GERMAN CONSTITUTIONAL LAW SINCE 1871, 175 (2013); Helmut Goerlich, *Concept of Special Protection for Certain Elements and Principles of the Constitution Against Amendments and Article 79 (3), Basic Law of Germany*, 1 NUJS L. REV. 397 (2008).

[14] DONALD P. KOMMERS & RUSSELL A. MILLER, THE CONSTITUTIONAL JURISPRUDENCE OF THE FEDERAL REPUBLIC OF GERMANY 59 (2012).

[15] The Lisbon Treaty Case, BVerfG, Judgment of the Second Senate of 30 June 2009 [218].

[16] Madhav Khosla, *Constitutional Amendment*, *in* OXFORD HANDBOOK OF THE INDIAN CONSTITUTION 232, 235 (2016).

constitutional unamendability.[17] In a 1951 decision, *Shankari Prasad Singh Deo v. Union of India*,[18] the issue was whether fundamental rights—in this case, property rights and freedom of speech—could be curtailed by the Parliament of India under Article 368 of the Indian Constitution.[19] The Supreme Court unanimously recognized that Parliament had exclusive and absolute power to amend the Constitution, relying on the distinction between constitutional law and ordinary legislation as well as the concept of constituent power.[20] This precedent was affirmed in *Sajjan Singh v. State of Rajasthan*,[21] in which the Supreme Court revisited the question of constitutional unamendability and reached the same conclusion. However, *Sajjan Singh* was a 3–2 decision, in which two justices issued dissenting opinions questioning Parliament's untrammeled power to abrogate fundamental rights and advancing the idea of "basic features." Although they were in the minority, these two separate opinions had planted the seed for the outgrowth of the basic structure doctrine.[22]

In 1966, Indira became Prime Minister and attempted to further limit the scope of property right to facilitate land reform. At the outset, she was perceived as a weak political leader. The Supreme Court of India frustrated her efforts in the monumental 1967 decision *Golak Nath v. State of Punjab*,[23] which overruled the 1951 decision, *Shankari Prasad Singh Deo* and also *Sajjan Singh*. The Supreme Court ruled that Parliament's power to amend the Constitution was substantively limited and could not amend any provision in the chapter on fundamental rights. Moreover, the Supreme Court "found little merit in the argument based upon sovereignty or constituent power" because "amendments were similar to any other law passed by Parliament."[24] Irritated by this judicial intervention, Gandhi in 1971 retaliated by enacting the twenty-fourth constitutional amendment that overturned *Golak Nath* after her party won a landslide victory in the congressional election. Expressly stating that Parliament's power to amend the Constitution was untethered, this amendment itself, along with other constitutional amendments, was challenged in *Kesavananda v. State of Kerala*, in which the Supreme Court succumbed and overruled *Golak Nath*

[17] ibid at 236–238.

[18] AIR 1951 SC 458.

[19] Art. 368 of the Constitution of India provides: "Power of Parliament to amend the Constitution and procedure therefor (1) Notwithstanding anything in this Constitution, Parliament may in exercise of its constituent power amend by way of addition, variation or repeal any provision of this Constitution in accordance with the procedure laid down in this article (2) ..."

[20] ARUN K. THIRUVENGADAM, THE CONSTITUTION OF INDIA: A CONTEXTUAL ANALYSIS 222 (2017).

[21] 1965 AIR 845, 1965 SCR (1) 933.

[22] Khosla (n) 237; Thiruvengadam (n 19) 223.

[23] 1967 AIR 1643, 1967 SCR (2) 762.

[24] Khosla (n) 238.

by a narrow majority (7–6). The majority opinion admitted that Parliament's power to amend the Constitution extended to all parts of the Constitution so long as the exercise of such power did not undermine the Constitution's core features. Therefore, most of the impugned constitutional amendments survived judicial review except for a small part which excluded judicial review because, the Supreme Court stated, judicial review constituted part of the basic structure of the Indian Constitution. Furthermore, the majority opinion argued that "the word 'amendment' postulates that the old constitution survives without loss of its identity despite the change and continues even though it has been subjected to alterations."[25]

On the one hand, the Indian Supreme Court lost the battle and was forced to overrule its precedent by upholding the disputed constitutional amendments; on the other hand, it won the war against Parliament by conferring upon itself the power to define "basic structure" in the Constitution. This is a typical *Marbury*-like decision in the sense that the Indian Supreme Court expanded judicial power but did so in a subtle and strategic way that rendered its ruling difficult for politicians to reject. Later developments proved this point. The basic structure doctrine and its underlying reasoning have since been cited by the Indian Supreme Court time and again whenever it sees fit.[26] Although the basic structure doctrine has been accepted and has acquired canonical status not only within Indian constitutional law but also in global constitutionalism, it has encountered harsh criticism from various angles.[27] However, several Asian apex courts have borrowed from the Supreme Court of India and taken similar steps based on the basic structure doctrine.

Notwithstanding the spread of explicit or implicit constitutional unamendability around the globe, one should not see it as a lingua franca. Anything so universally applauded tends to drift into the realm of the banal. In fact, the appropriateness of constitutional unamendability has constantly encountered challenges and rejection. The United States is a case in point. In stark contrast with the previously mentioned two jurisdictions that endorse the limitations of constitutional amendments, the U.S. Supreme Court refused to recognize even the justiciability of whether a constitutional amendment had been ratified, a pure procedural issue, let alone the substantive content of constitutional amendments. The Child Labor Amendment was proposed by Congress

[25] ibid at 240.
[26] ibid.
[27] Sujit Choudhry, *How to Do Constitutional Law and Politics in South Asia*, *in* UNSTABLE CONSTITUTIONALISM: LAW AND POLITICS IN SOUTH ASIA 18, 21–23 (Mark Tushnet & Madhav Khosla eds. 2015).

in 1924 but was rejected by the Kansas legislature in the following year. In 1937, thirteen years after the amendment was first proposed, the Kansas legislature voted to ratify the proposed amendment. Several members of the Kansas legislature, including senators who had voted against the resolution, petitioned the Supreme Court of Kansas to prohibit the officers of the Kansas legislature from signing the resolution and the Secretary of State of Kansas from authenticating it and delivering it to the Governor. The Kansas Supreme Court denied the petition, and the petitioners appealed to the U.S. Supreme Court.

Although the U.S. Supreme Court agreed that the petitioners had standing in *Coleman*, it nevertheless held that the ratification of the proposed amendment was "a political question pertaining to the political departments, with the ultimate authority in the congress in the exercise of its control over the promulgation of the adoption of the amendment."[28] With regard to the lapse of time between the amendment first being proposed and the legislature's purported ratification, Chief Justice Hughes opined in the majority opinion that "we think that the Congress in controlling the promulgation of the adoption of a constitutional amendment has the final determination of the question whether by lapse of time its proposal of the amendment had lost its vitality prior to the required ratifications."[29] In fact, as Professor Ackerman suggests, the rejection of entrenchment is precisely the spirit of the American Constitution, given the negative lessons of how similar ideas have been abused (i.e. the entrenchment of the slavery system) in the U.S., at least in the domain of rights protection.[30] Perhaps because of this, the U.S. Supreme Court has never invalidated any constitutional amendment passed under Article V of the Constitution of the United States since its inauguration.[31] Instead, the Supreme Court prefers a procedural approach when reviewing the constitutionality of federal constitutional amendments, and "the very fact that the amendment had been properly proposed and ratified under Article V was enough to insulate it from unconstitutionality."[32]

[28] 307 U.S. 433, 450 (1939).

[29] ibid at 456.

[30] BRUCE ACKERMAN, WE THE PEOPLE: FOUNDATIONS 15–16 (1991).

[31] Art. V of the U.S. Constitution provides: "The Congress, whenever two thirds of both Houses shall deem it necessary, shall propose Amendments to this Constitution, or, on the Application of the Legislatures of two thirds of the several States, shall call a Convention for proposing Amendments, which, in either Case, shall be valid to all Intents and Purposes, as Part of this Constitution, when ratified by the Legislatures of three fourths of the several States, or by Conventions in three fourths thereof..."

[32] Richard Albert, *How A Court Becomes Supreme Defending the Constitution from Unconstitutional Constitutional Amendments*, 77 MARYLAND LAW REVIEW 181, 184 (2017); cf. Aharon Barak, *Unconstitutional Constitutional Amendments* 44(3) ISRAEL L. REV. 321, 330 (2011). Notably, the constitutionality of several constitutional amendments had been challenged on substantive grounds, but

B. Legal Model vs. Political Model

The three canons identified previously represent two models in terms of constitutional unamendability: the legal model and the political model. The former refers to a constitutional design which seeks to channel constitutional change that is potentially violent and destructive into an existing legal framework. The legal framework can be explicitly provided by the capital-C Constitution. Alternatively, it can be set up by top courts through their constitutional judgments, which usually constitute part of the small-c constitution. By limiting constitutional amendments within a certain scope, the purpose of this model is to domesticate the power to amend a constitution and make constitutional change more predictable and principled. Judges are usually called upon to check whether the passage of constitutional amendments follows predetermined procedures and whether the amendments touch upon provisions that cannot be altered. Both Germany and India belong to this model.

By contrast, the political model adopts a more laissez-faire attitude toward constitutional change. This model does not demarcate any boundary of constitutional change, either procedural or substantive, in advance, at least not by constitutional framers or judges. Whether or not constitutional amendments should be confined within certain areas is a political question that is not the province and duty of the judicial department. This model fully respects the will of the contemporary people by trusting the political branches with the final word on rewriting the constitution. The United States can be categorized in this group.[33]

Notwithstanding the worldwide influence of American constitutionalism,[34] the U.S. Supreme Court's prudence in this regard does not find many echoes. Instead, many countries have chosen to shield certain principles or provisions from constitutional change, either explicitly or implicitly.[35] The enormous success of constitutional unamendability should be attributed to the following

the Supreme Court has upheld them all. *See Leser v. Garnett*, 258 U.S. 130 (1922), National Prohibition Cases, 253 U.S. 350 (1920).

[33] Another example may be Vietnam, in which the concept and the scope of constitutional unamendability is politically constructed rather than constitutionally designated or judicially imposed. Notwithstanding the lack of formal constitutional barriers, the commitment to the socialist political system, including party leadership, is untouchable in Vietnam. Ngoc Son Bui, *Unconstitutional Constitution in Vietnam*, *in* THE LAW AND POLITICS OF UNCONSTITUTIONAL CONSTITUTIONAL AMENDMENTS IN ASIA 67, 80–81 (Rehan Abeyratne & Ngoc Son Bui eds. 2022).

[34] GEORGE ATHAN BILLIAS, AMERICAN CONSTITUTIONALISM HEARD ROUND THE WORLD 1776-1989: A GLOBAL PERSPECTIVE 51–356 (2009).

[35] Yaniv Roznai, *Unconstitutional Constitutional Amendments—The Migration and Success of a Constitutional Idea*, 61 AMERICAN JOURNAL OF COMPARATIVE LAW 657, 665–711 (2013).

factors, despite the contextual nuances in different jurisdictions. The horrific Holocaust certainly make many post-WWII constitutional framers feel compelled to entrench certain values in their constitutions against future authoritarian abuse. That is, constitutional unamendability often symbolizes a clear break with a sordid past and the transformation of a polity. The eternity clause in Germany, among other countries, is understood through this lens.[36] Although no constitutional entrenchment can effectively and permanently prevent revolutionary actions from overruling the constitutional order,[37] it can at least raise the political cost of attempted unconstitutional constitutional change in normal times. To be sure, there is no guarantee that locked-in values are always good ones, and this relates to the second reason why constitutional unamendability is popular, even among illiberal or authoritarian regimes.

From a rational choice perspective, constitutional entrenchment is the ultimate form of hegemonic preservation.[38] By deeply etching their preferences into the constitutions, political elites make sure that their preferred values cannot be easily altered by fickle popular attitudes. These values could sometimes be impersonal, such as a republic form of government, but, alternatively, they could also serve the interests of powerful individuals or groups, such as the monarchial system or the recognition of a state religion.

Moreover, the global expansion of judicial power also contributes to the proliferation of the basic structure doctrine. In parallel with the end of WWII and the fall of the Berlin Wall, almost every new constitution includes a bill of rights. To protect these rights, judicial review has become a backbone of modern democracies to the extent that "a democracy without some form of judicial review is considered deficient."[39] The judicialization of politics has further expanded the scope of judicial review. To properly exercise the power of judicial review, apex courts around the globe have developed a raft of interpretive methods, such as proportionality, to restrict governmental actions. The principle of the basic structure doctrine is simply another, arguably the most powerful, weapon in the judicial arsenal.

Thus far, comparative studies have suggested that constitutional unamendability, or the basic structure doctrine, may be appropriate in countries that meet certain conditions: (1) when the threshold to amend the

[36] YANIV ROZNAI, UNCONSTITUTIONAL CONSTITUTIONAL AMENDMENTS: THE LIMITS OF AMENDMENT POWERS 30–31 (2017).

[37] David Landau, *Abusive Constitutionalism*, 47 U.C. DAVIS L. REV. 189, 216–247 (2013).

[38] Ran Hirschl, TOWARDS JURISTOCRACY: THE ORIGINS AND CONSEQUENCES OF THE NEW CONSTITUTIONALISM 43–44 (2004).

[39] Doreen Lustig & J. H. H. Weiler, Judicial Review in the Contemporary World—Retrospective and Prospective, 16 INTERNATIONAL JOURNAL OF CONSTITUTIONAL LAW 315, 316 (2018).

constitution is relatively low and the process is flexible; (2) when there is one dominant party; (3) when constitutional culture has not been established; and (4) when there is no effective supranational institution that can check domestic governmental powers.[40] Different in their respective concerns, these four conditions have something in common: constitutional amendments are more likely to be misused or abused in these scenarios. Specifically, the concept of constitutional unamendability is less meaningful if it is extremely difficult to amend the constitution. Moreover, it will be difficult to justify the use of the basic structure doctrine if ratification of a constitutional amendment requires an extremely high quorum,[41] because such ratification may clearly demonstrate the willingness of the supermajority of the public. Relatedly, the more concentrated the political power in a country, the more likely it will invoke constitutional amendments to further expand and entrench its power monopoly. Thirdly, a would-be autocrat is more likely to abuse constitutional amendments to entrench his or her power. Finally, international institutions, such as international conventions or international tribunals, may contain domestic would-be autocrats and reduce the risk of abusive constitutional change. Because of these conditions, some have suggested that the concept of constitutional unamendability is most suitable in nascent democracies where respect for the rule of law and constitutionalism is fragile and unstable. Paradoxically, constitutional unamendability is more likely to be abused in such aspiring democracies than in established democracies.

To what extent this contention is true is beyond the scope of this chapter. Instead, we would like to point out that overemphasizing constitutional unamendability implies that whatever cannot be done via constitutional amendments can be done through a new constitution. That is, the concept of constitutional unamendability is based on the distinction between a new constitution and a constitutional amendment, or more theoretically, the distinction between constituent power and constituted power. Nevertheless, the distinction between a new constitution and a constitutional amendment, both in theory and in reality, has faced criticism in recent years. This is particularly

[40] Yaniv Roznai, *Why there? Explanatory theories and institutional features behind unconstitutional constitutional amendments in Asia, in* THE LAW AND POLITICS OF UNCONSTITUTIONAL CONSTITUTIONAL AMENDMENTS IN ASIA 274, 291–295 (Rehan Abeyratne & Ngoc Son Bui eds. 2022).

[41] On the difficulty of amending constitutions, see AREND LIJPHART, PATTERNS OF DEMOCRACY: GOVERNMENT FORMS AND PERFORMANCE IN THIRTY-SIX COUNTRIES 206–214 (2012); Tom Ginsburg and James Melton, *Does the Constitutional Amendment Rule Matter at All? Amendment Cultures and The Challenges of Measuring Amendment Difficulty*, 13 INTERNATIONAL JOURNAL OF CONSTITUTIONAL LAW 686 (2015).

the case in new democracies where constitutional development does not simply follow the track of established Western democracies.

III. Challenges to the Canons: Constitutional Relativity

As explained earlier, the concept of constitutional unamendability is predicated on the distinction between constituent power and constituted power.[42] Conventional wisdom has long suggested that the former refers to the "the capacity to enact a constitution, by revolutionary means or otherwise, thereby giving rise to a novel legal order."[43] This understanding of constituent power is usually attributed to Rousseau and Abbé Emmanuel Joseph Sieyès.[44] Exercised by the People, an imagined community, constituent power is external to the legal order and independent of any constitutional or legal restraints. By contrast, constituted power, which is created by constituent power, comprises the legislative, the executive, and the judicial powers. In the context of constitutional change, constituted power is the power to amend an existing constitution and is therefore subject to the rules and limitations imposed by the constitution that in turn is enacted by constituent power.[45]

The relationship between constituent power and constituted power is thus made clear: the former creates a constitution to authorize, facilitate, and regulate the exercise of the latter. That is, the former is superior to the latter in the sense that it delegates the competence of amending a constitution to the latter. It follows that constitutional unamendability "limits the delegated amendment power ... but it cannot block the primary constituent power from its ability to amend even the basic principles of the constitutional order."[46] Once exercised, constituent power usually topples an existing constitutional order and

[42] Roznai(n) at 105–120; RICHARD ALBERT, CONSTITUTIONAL AMENDMENTS: MAKING, BREAKING, AND CHANGING CONSTITUTIONS 72 (2019); JOEL COLÓN-RÍOS, CONSTITUENT POWER AND THE LAW 189–225 (2020).

[43] Hans Lindahl, *Constituent Power and the Constitution*, *in* PHILOSOPHICAL FOUNDATIONS OF CONSTITUTIONAL LAW 141, 147(David Dyzenhaus & Malcolm Thorburn eds. 2006).

[44] HANNAH ARENDT, ON REVOLUTION 154–156 (2006); HÈCTOR LÓPEZ BOFILL, LAW, VIOLENCE AND CONSTITUENT POWER: THE LAW, POLITICS AND HISTORY OF CONSTITUTION MAKING 42–46 (2021); EMILIOS CHRISTODOULIDIS, THE REDRESS OF LAW GLOBALISATION, CONSTITUTIONALISM AND MARKET CAPTURE 158 168 (2021).

[45] In the United States, nevertheless, the concept of constituent power "plays no direct role in American constitutionalism, other than through the amendment process." Stephen M. Griffin, *Constituent Power and Constitutional Change in American Constitutionalism*, *in* THE PARADOX OF CONSTITUTIONALISM: CONSTITUENT POWER AND CONSTITUTIONAL FORM 49, 65–66 (Martin Loughlin & Neil Walker eds. 2007). Hence, there is no surprise that the U.S. Supreme Court deemed the ratification of constitutional amendments to be a political question that was not justiciable.

[46] Roznai (n) at 123.

translates into constitutional revolution,[47] whereas the exercise of constituted power usually leads to incremental constitutional evolution, smaller in scale and slower in pace, which does not alter constitutional identity as it functions only within the existing constitutional framework.

A. Relativity in Constitutional Change

The clear-cut distinction between the power to enact a new constitution and the power to amend a constitution, albeit intuitively reasonable, does not stand as firm as one may think. Despite the voluminous attention the concept of constitutional unamendability has been afforded, current scholarship does not pay sufficient attention to the phenomenon that the divide between a new constitution and a constitutional amendment is capricious and increasingly blurred, a phenomenon that we call *constitutional relativity*. While we do not fundamentally reject the concepts of constituent power and constituted power, we suggest that in neither practice nor theory is there a sharp line dividing constituent power/constitutional revolution from constituted power/constitutional evolution. Rather, this chapter brings to the fore that the difference between these two forms of constitutional change—constituent power/constitutional revolution on the one hand, and constituted power/constitutional evolution on the other—is a spectrum. In other words, "constitutional change occurs over a broad band of significance"[48] in the real world.

One of us has argued that constitutional relativity has become one of the key features that characterize constitutional revisions in transitional countries that have undergone democratization and constitutional reforms since the 1980s.[49] Specifically, constitutional relativity takes places under two circumstances: First, many countries distinguish "total revision" of the constitution from "partial revision," and apply different processes and thresholds of constitutional revision. Smaller changes are understood as partial revision

[47] MARK TUSHNET, TAKING BACK THE CONSTITUTION: ACTIVIST JUDGES AND THE NEXT AGE OF AMERICAN LAW 269 (2020).

[48] Albert (n) at 69.

[49] Jiunn-Rong Yeh & Wen-Chen Chang, *The Changing Landscape of Modern Constitutionalism: Transitional Perspective*, 4 (1) NATIONAL TAIWAN UNIVERSITY LAW REVIEW 145, 166–168 (2009); Jiunn-rong Yeh & Wen-Chen Chang, *Path Dependence or Collective Institutional Choice? Modeling Constitutional Changes in the Context of Democratic Transitions*, 45(6) ISSUES & STUDIES 1, 19–21 (2006) (in Chinese). Even in the context of the U.S. Constitution, the oldest codified constitution, the distinction is "misleadingly simple as a general principle." Mark Tushnet, *Amendment Theory and Constituent Power*, *in* COMPARATIVE CONSTITUTIONAL THEORY 317, 326 (Gary Jacobsohn & Miguel Schor eds. 2018).

or amendments that apply a lower threshold while larger changes require a heightened one. In practice, however, the scale of constitutional change does not always correspond to the labels of total and partial revision, because the scale of change can be defined either qualitatively or quantitatively. As a result, what constitutes a true replacement is sometimes just nominal. Secondly, some countries have used the amendment rules to codify foundational constitutional change when there are calls for enacting new constitutions.[50] In this scenario, whether the constitution revision in question should be perceived as or called a new constitution or a constitutional amendment is controversial. The categorization of whether or not a constitutional change is a replacement may eventually depend on contingent political dynamics as much as formal legal continuity. As a corollary, it does not say much about whether a constitutional change is achieved through an amendment process or another procedure. Focusing on the process over the substance may sometimes miss the forest for the trees.[51]

Even if we focus on substance, the degree of constitutional change may still be contentious. Empirical legal studies have proved the fuzziness between a constitutional amendment and a new constitution. Employing latent semantic analysis to measure the similarity between new constitutions and constitutional amendments, scholars have attested that the labeling of constitutional "replacements" and "amendments" are often arbitrary or idiosyncratic in the sense that it does not mirror the magnitude of constitutional change. Although constitutional replacement, on average, is more likely to involve significant change than constitutional amendment, "the population of 'replacement' is, in fact heavily skewed toward minor changes ... [and] the population of formal 'amendments' is laced with some major changes that objectively deserve to be called replacements."[52] Insomuch as this takes place, the theoretical distinction between a new constitution and a constitutional amendment dissipates considerably.

The concept of constitutional relativity also implies that the gap between constitutional revolution and constitutional evolution is smaller than one might think in nascent democracies. At first glance, this sounds counter-intuitive

[50] BRUCE ACKERMAN, THE FUTURE OF LIBERAL REVOLUTION 46–68 (1999).

[51] Notably, the line between constitutional revision and constitutional adjudication is also more opaque in transitional countries, because judicial decisions are often faster than constitutional amendments in responding to socioeconomic changes. Consequently, many constitutional changes are materialized through judicial decisions.

[52] David S. Law & Ryan Whalen, *Constitutional Amendment Versus Constitutional Replacement: An Empirical Comparison, in* ROUTLEDGE HANDBOOK OF COMPARATIVE CONSTITUTIONAL CHANGE 74, 99 (Xenophon Contiades & Alkmene Fotiadou eds. 2020).

because revolution means cataclysmic change in a relatively short time, while evolution implies incremental change over time. This dichotomy is less cogent in the field of constitutional change especially for transitional democracies.[53] Constitutional revolution and constitutional evolution are two ideal types that lie at the poles of a continuum, and the precise location of any constitutional change in transitional countries largely depends on the constitutional history and politics of the country. Constitutional transformation in transitional countries cannot usually be accomplished once and for all; instead, it is usually achieved one step at a time, revising those that are most urgent and consensual first while keeping other controversial parts intact. Through this prism, constitutional revision in transitional countries is closer to the so-called "unconventional adaptation," which refers to one kind of legal change that "may reject key elements of the preexisting legal mix ... while adapting yet others into the new system of revolutionary legality they seek to establish."[54] Instead of completely repudiating the current legal framework, adaptation focuses on particular sphere(s) of social or political life.[55] In this sense, it is in harmony with Edmund Burke's incrementalism, which distinguishes reform from revolution. The former refers to slow and deliberate change that "addresses specific problems while preserving the integrity of existing institutions and traditions as much as possible."[56]

B. Examples in East Asia

What leads to constitutional relativity? We argue that power struggle, constitutional veneration, and political nostalgia all contribute to constitutional relativity in East Asia. To begin with, countries in the process of democratic transition often face a dilemma. On the one hand, the need to enact a new constitution to mark a clear break with the dark past and the birth of a nascent democracy cannot be more urgent. The old legal order and social norms have crumbled, but the new ones have not yet been established. Reforming the constitution in order to remodel the country and forge social consensus thus becomes high on the political agenda. On the other hand, the political and

[53] Yeh & Chang, *The Changing Landscape of Modern Constitutionalism: Transitional Perspective* (n 49).

[54] Bruce Ackerman, *Revolution on a Human Scale*, 108 YALE L.J. 2279, 2293 (1999).

[55] BRUCE ACKERMAN, REVOLUTIONARY CONSTITUTIONS: CHARISMATIC LEADERSHIP AND THE RULE OF LAW 28 (2019).

[56] ROBERT J. LACEY, PRAGMATIC CONSERVATISM: EDMUND BURKE AND HIS AMERICAN HEIRS 36 (2016); PETER J. STANLIS, EDMUND BURKE: THE ENLIGHTENMENT AND REVOLUTION 208 (1993).

socioeconomic conditions may not be suitable for constitution-making, an enterprise that is time-consuming and extremely costly. Time and finance are luxuries in transitional countries that endeavor to rebuild after war, economic crises, and political and social conflicts. No wonder some have lamented that "the task of constitution-making generally emerges in conditions that are likely to work against good constitution-making."[57]

In addition, in many post-authoritarian settings, transitional constitutional changes "often came as part of political deals negotiated by former regimes and current reformers. As a result, ... dark pasts were never denied completely. In order to move forward, past legacies continued and even entrenched as part of political gives and takes."[58] In fact, the coexistence of the past and the future is precisely one feature of transitional constitutionalism, which provides an alternative to a revolutionary regime change.[59] To illustrate, constitutional replacement is subject to many political and institutional constraints, such as realpolitik, constitutional tradition, super-majoritarian thresholds, and international intervention, among others. Politicians of the old regimes may oppose the enactment of a new constitution if they still possess the veto power after democratic transition. This is not rare given that political transformation in many third-wave democracies followed the so-called transplacement process, in which liberalization was achieved through negotiation between the old regime and opposition groups.[60] Consequently, transitional states may promulgate a "new" constitution in which the texts remained much the same as the previous one. In other words, it is possible that "a dramatic rupture in political continuity that produces minimal change in the constitutional experience of the polity achieves a constitutional revolution in name only."[61] The constitution remains largely intact despite the nominal change.

Alternatively, these constraints may force progressive politicians to revise the old constitution incrementally and prudentially, even if a complete

[57] Jon Elster, *Forces and Mechanisms in the Constitution-Making Process*, 45 DUKE L.J. 364, 394 (1995); *see also* Andreas Braune, *Authoritative Constitution-Making in the Name of Democracy? in* CONSTITUTIONALISM UNDER EXTREME CONDITIONS 323, 332–334 (Richard Albert & Yaniv Roznai eds. 2020).

[58] Yeh & Chang, *The Changing Landscape of Modern Constitutionalism* (n) at 147; *see also*, Catherine Turner, *Transitional Constitutionalism and the Case of the Arab Spring*, 64 INTERNATIONAL AND COMPARATIVE LAW QUARTERLY 267, 270 (2015); cf. Gábor Halmai, *Transitional Justice, Transitional Constitutionalism and Constitutional Culture, in* COMPARATIVE CONSTITUTIONAL THEORY 372 (Gary Jacobsohn & Miguel Schor eds. 2018).

[59] *See* Wojciech Sadurski, *Transitional Constitutionalism Versus the Rule of Law?* 8 HAGUE J. RULE OF LAW 337, 340 (2016).

[60] SAMUEL HUNTINGTON, THE THIRD WAVE: DEMOCRATIZATION IN THE LATE TWENTIETH CENTURY 151–163 (1991).

[61] GARY JEFFREY JACOBSOHN & YANIV ROZNAI, CONSTITUTIONAL REVOLUTION 19 (2020).

overhaul is their priority. Transitional states may adopt transitory constitutional arrangements such as an interim constitution,[62] multi-stage constitutional amendments, or even quasi-constitutional statutes in order to push for constitutional reform.[63] These constitutional amendments may even have the potential to alter the constitutional identity of a country. In other words, a new constitution may be masqueraded as constitutional amendments.[64]

This is exactly what has happened in several East Asian countries, which set up neither substantive nor procedural limits during the process of constitution-amending. As a result, many of the constitutional amendments have fundamentally changed the constitutional identity of the old constitutions, becoming new constitutions in essence. For example, the current post-WWII Constitution of Japan was adopted as an amendment to the Meiji Constitution in accordance with Article 73 of the latter. Although the Constitution of Japan was formally promulgated as a constitutional amendment, it is dramatically different from the Meiji Constitution in many important aspects, including, inter alia, sovereignty and the abolition of the feudal class structure.[65] While the Meiji Constitution was based on imperial sovereignty, the post-WWII Constitution of Japan is premised upon popular sovereignty. It is particularly noteworthy that imperial sovereignty under the Meiji Constitution was "widely considered to be unrevisable ... [and] was regarded as the very essence of the [national polity], the basic form of the state."[66] Namely, from a formally legalistic viewpoint, the Constitution of Japan itself was an unconstitutional constitutional amendment of the Meiji Constitution and thus should have been invalidated.[67] In practice, nonetheless, the post-WWII Constitution of Japan has never been amended since it took effect in 1947 and has become the most enduring, unamended constitution in the world.

Another example is South Korea. South Korea has revised its founding constitution nine times since its ratification in 1948. Whether these constitutional changes should be regarded as constitutional amendments or new constitutions has been subject to reasonable disagreements. Formally, these constitutional revisions are all constitutional amendments because they all followed

[62] Charmaine Rodrigues, *Letting off steam: Interim constitutions as a safety valve to the pressure-cooker of transitions in conflict-affected states?* 6 GLOBAL CONSTITUTIONALISM 33 (2017). ANDREW ARATO, POST SOVEREIGN CONSTITUTION MAKING 10–13 (2016).

[63] Yeh & Chang, *The Changing Landscape of Modern Constitutionalism* (n) at 147, 166–168.

[64] Richard Albert has described this kind of constitutional change as constitutional dismemberment. See Albert (n) at 84–92.

[65] Yasuo Hasebe, *The August Revolution Thesis and the Making of the Constitution of Japan*, *in* RULE OF LAW: POLITICAL AND LEGAL SYSTEMS IN TRANSITION 335, 336 (Werner Krawietz et al. eds. 1997).

[66] ibid.

[67] SHIGENORI MATSUI, THE CONSTITUTION OF JAPAN: A CONTEXTUAL ANALYSIS 18–19 (2011).

the amendment rules. Substantively, five of them are wholesale revisions that "represent substantive reorientations in the constitutional text."[68] Hence, they have been generally characterized as revolutionary, or at least transformative, because they were made to create a new republic. This resonates with the argument that all constitutional amendments are not equally significant. It also indicates that revolutionary change could happen without textual change of the capital-C Constitution.[69] Some even opine that the fundamental political identity of Korea has undergone "quiet constitutional revolution" even though the relevant constitutional text remains unchanged.[70]

Taiwan is no exception. When the Constitution of the Republic of China (ROC), which was enacted for mainland China, became unworkable in Taiwan after the ROC government was defeated by the Communists and retreated to Taiwan in 1949, the political elites decided not to write a new constitution but only to amend the Constitution for two reasons. First, the Constitution had only been promulgated in 1947 and the framers were reluctant to rewrite the original text immediately. Secondly, they wanted to bring the original Constitution back to mainland China because it served as an ideological banner.[71] Although the original text of the Constitution has remained unchanged, about one-third of its provisions have been suspended after seven rounds of constitutional amendments.[72] In parallel with the "quiet revolution" in the political arena, constitutional revolution that involves changes of statehood and political identity has been codified in the existing constitution in the name of constitutional amendments.[73] These constitutional amendments have considerably changed the central and local government structures to the extent that the constitutional identity has been changed.[74] For instance, the central government has been changed from a parliamentary system to a semi-presidential system. After the first presidential election held in 1996, the Taiwanese constitutional system took a decisive turn in the direction of full-blown presidentialism due to a combination of party politics and electoral

[68] Sung Ho Kim, *Constitutional Revolution Redux: Postwar Japan and South Korea*, 10 YONSEI L.J. 83, 92 (2020).

[69] ibid at 93–102.

[70] ibid at 99.

[71] *See* Jiunn-rong Yeh, *The Cult of* Fatung: *Representational Manipulation and Reconstruction in Taiwan*, *in* THE PEOPLE'S REPRESENTATIVES: ELECTORAL SYSTEMS IN THE ASIA-PACIFIC REGION 23, 24–26 (Graham Hassall & Cheryl Saunders eds. 1997).

[72] JIUNN-RONG YEH, THE CONSTITUTION OF TAIWAN: A CONTEXTUAL ANALYSIS 12–13, 15–16 (2016).

[73] Jiunn-rong Yeh, *Constitutional Reform and Democratization in Taiwan 1945–2000*, *in* TAIWAN'S MODERNIZATION IN GLOBAL PERSPECTIVE 47, 65 (Peter C. Y. Chow ed. 2002).

[74] Chien-Chih Lin, *We the Taiwanese People*, *in* FOUNDING MOMENTS IN CONSTITUTIONALISM (Richard Albert, Menaka Guruswamy, & Nischal Basnyat eds. 2019).

politics on the ground.[75] Also, Mongolia and Tibet are no longer regarded as local governments under the constitutional framework. More crucially, the constitutional amendments distinguish the people of the "Chinese mainland area" and the people in Taiwan,[76] implicitly recognizing the existence of the People's Republic of China.

Undoubtedly, the abovementioned constitutional amendments in East Asia have shaped new constitutional identities and replaced the (old) constitutional identities, a function that is usually shouldered by new constitutions in established democracies. This constitutional development demonstrates the prevalence of constitutional relativity. Moreover, the idea that a constitutional amendment will be regarded as unconstitutional if it breaks the constitutional identity is relatively bizarre since the new constitutional identity may not yet be established in the process of constitutional transformation, or the distinction between a constitutional amendment and a new constitution may be deemed opaque against the specific contextual backdrop. The Constitution of Japan is an illuminating example. Declaring constitutional amendments that have altered the constitutional identity as unconstitutional is close to declaring a brand new, permanent constitution unconstitutional, an issue that is theoretically debatable and rarely occurs in practice, not only in Asia but around the globe.[77] Nevertheless, constitutional relativity by no means suggests that the judiciary plays no role, a topic to which we now turn.

C. The Role of Courts

Facing constitutional relativity, courts in transitional states are more like an active player rather than an empire in a baseball game. As mentioned previously, constitutions in transitional states are unlike their counterparts in stable democracies such that they are more like transitory arrangements that are used to forge political consensus and facilitate further reform. Given this transitory nature of constitutions, courts usually have to respond to social and political needs themselves when they interpret the constitution because

[75] Jih-Wen Lin, *The Rules of Electoral Competition and the Accountability of Semi-Presidential Governments*, *in* SEMI-PRESIDENTIALISM AND DEMOCRACY 61, 76–77 (Robert Elgie, Sophia Moestrup, & Yu-Shan Wu eds. 2011).

[76] Art. 11 of the Additional Articles of the Constitution of the Republic of China provides: Rights and obligations between the people of the Chinese mainland area and those of the free area, and the disposition of other related affairs may be specified by law.

[77] Richard Albert, *The Power of Judicial Nullification in Asia and the World*, *in* THE LAW AND POLITICS OF UNCONSTITUTIONAL CONSTITUTIONAL AMENDMENTS IN ASIA 149–150 (Rehan Abeyratne & Ngoc Son Bui eds. 2022).

many constitutional issues cannot be settled before the constitutional moment elapses in the transitional period.[78]

Furthermore, courts in transitional societies are more likely to be embroiled in issues of political salience, because covetous politicians are more likely to aggrandize their power to the detriment of other branches, if not the stability of the whole country. And they often pursue self-aggrandizement through constitutional amendments. Instances abound, including prolonging their own terms, running for a third presidential election, or declaring an emergency.[79] Under these circumstances, courts may help consolidate democracies by nullifying unconstitutional constitutional amendments that are used, for instance, to abolish the term limits of presidents.[80]

However, we should not look at courts and constitutional unamendability through rose-colored glasses. Courts will not always defend democracy for three reasons. First, judicial review of legislation is in and of itself controversial, let alone judicial review of constitutional amendments, which are usually passed with a heightened threshold. As a corollary, the legitimacy of judicial review of constitutional amendments decreases along with the heightened process of constitutional amendments. Secondly, the enactment of unconstitutional constitutional amendments is sometimes tailored to the needs of charismatic political leaders. This increases the risks for courts to stand in their way. Last but not least, judicial authority and independence may not have been established in new democracies, and judicial decisions on constitutional amendment may not be implemented or may be ignored entirely. Therefore, the hope that courts can consolidate democracy by insulating certain constitutional provisions from abusive constitutional change may ring hollow in some cases. In fact, implicit constitutional unamendability imposed by courts may hinder democracy and constitutionalism when constitutions are used to exclude the minorities and entrench the majority's preference in divided contexts.[81]

[78] Yeh & Chang, *The Changing Landscape of Modern Constitutionalism* (n) at 154.

[79] *See* Aziz Huq & Tom Ginsburg, *How to Lose a Constitutional Democracy*, 65 UCLA L. REV. 78, 124–125, 139–141 (2018).

[80] Tom Ginsburg, *The Politics of Courts in Democratization*, *in* CONSEQUENTIAL COURTS 45, 50–51 (Diana Kapiszewski et al. eds. 2013).

[81] Silvia Suteu, *Eternity Clauses as Tools for Exclusionary Constitutional Projects*, *in* THE LAW AND POLITICS OF UNCONSTITUTIONAL CONSTITUTIONAL AMENDMENTS IN ASIA 257, 258 (Rehan Abeyratne & Ngoc Son Bui eds. 2022).

IV. Reinterpretations of the Canons: Mixing Legal and Political Models

In this section, we plan to engage with a powerful and popular argument that suggests that constitutional unamendability, in the form of an eternality clause or basic structure doctrine, has a beneficial effect on democratic consolidation. By contrast, the lack of such an institutional device in constitutional law is risky. This argument, we believe, is predicated on two assumptions: First, the boundary of constitutional amendments can be demarcated by either constitutional provisions or judicial rulings, such as Article 79 of the German Basic Law or *Kesavananda*. Secondly, these boundaries will be strictly obeyed. That is, in jurisdictions that are equipped with constitutional unamendability, constitutional amendments can only be carried out within these constitutional frameworks. Yet, the meaning of eternity clauses or any legal doctrines are often nebulous and subject to judicial interpretation. For example, "human dignity" is probably one of the most controversial concepts in jurisprudence. Moreover, whether constitutional amendments strictly follow these boundaries is not self-evident, even if these boundaries are clearly drawn. In short, even if the judiciary ostensibly has the final say, constitutional unamendability still invites political dialogue and even demands political action. Alternatively, courts still play a role even if they are not permitted to strike down a constitutional amendment.

To illustrate, constitutional unamendability has never been purely legal, but instead blends legal and political calculations. Take the eternity clause in Germany as an example. Germany has amended the Basic Law several times, one of which was undertaken after the unification of West and East Germany. At that time, one of the most controversial issues during the negotiations on German unification was whether the expropriations carried out by Soviet Union from 1945 through 1949 in the former East Germany should be reversed after unification.[82] The German Democratic Republic (East Germany) and the Soviet Union insisted that restitution should be excluded, and the Federal Republic of Germany (West Germany) accepted, albeit reluctantly.[83] On August 31, 1990, West Germany and East Germany signed the Unification Treaty to facilitate reunification. In this Treaty, Number 5, Section 3, Article 4 confirmed that the said expropriations would not be reversed. This provision

[82] Udo Steiner, *The Basic Law and the Process of Reunification*, 53 SMU L. REV. 461 466–469 (2000); Helmut Steinberger, *Germany Reunified: International and Constitutional Problems*, 1992 BYU L. REV. 23, 34–37 (1992).

[83] Steinberger, ibid at 35.

was transplanted and became Article 143(3) of the Basic Law. Arguably, this amendment might violate the Basic Law because the said expropriations clearly infringed on rights protection. Although the German Federal Constitutional Court held that Article 143(3) did not violate Article 79(3) of the Basic Law, its reasoning was, at least in part, highly political, stating that Article 143(3) should be upheld because it was an agreement between the two German governments and the Soviet Union during the negotiations on unification.[84] Here, political dynamics predetermined what was legal/constitutional or illegal/unconstitutional even with a legally written eternity clause already in place.

Kesavananda was no different in this regard. Although it was the Supreme Court of India, rather than the Gandhi administration, that drew the boundary of constitutional revision, the birth of the basic structure doctrine was politically motivated. At that time, the Indian Supreme Court had gutted Gandhi's plan of land reform to protect the have nots at the expense of the haves' property right. Given the landslide victory of Gandhi's party in the congressional election, it is safe to say that the Court was acting at the outset in a countermajoritarian way. Only when the democratic mandate was sufficiently glaring was the Supreme Court forced to retreat somewhat in *Kesavananda*. From this perspective, although the basic structure doctrine is highly applauded worldwide, its birth was a product more of political struggle than of legal reasoning.

On the other hand, the political model does not necessarily mean that courts play no role in shaping constitutional unamendability. In *Coleman*, invoking the doctrine of political question in this case, the U.S. Supreme Court refrained from imposing any procedural and substantive criteria regarding the limitations of constitutional amendments. Nonetheless, it is still the judiciary, and not the political branches, that define what constitutes a political question and is therefore beyond the reach of the judiciary. That is, the U.S. Supreme Court could have dismissed the case, and the result would not have been different. But it did not. Instead, the Court endeavored to legally explicate what was political in the context of constitutional amendment. From this perspective, even not recognizing constitutional unamendability, thus leaving it to the political, still needs legal backing from the judiciary.

This mixture of legal and political elements in the context of constitutional change indicates that constitutional unamendability does not necessarily function in a way that scholars usually assume. Constitutional unamendability may be under- or selectively enforced or, even worse, manipulated. Because of this nature, constitutional entrenchment is not a useful vehicle for fighting

[84] Steiner (n) at 469.

populism and democratic erosion. In the worst scenario, constitutional entrenchment without popular support may become the illiberal enclave of political power-holders.

Specifically, in parallel with its prevalence, the concept of constitutional unamendability has spurred many scholarly debates that revolve around two interrelated issues: scope and legitimacy. Some have stressed that the content of constitutional unamendability is highly contextual and varies from one country to another, notwithstanding its popularity.[85] Others have argued that courts are less legitimate for scrutinizing the constitutionality of constitutional amendments when those amendments acquire bipartisan and popular endorsement.[86] What has not been paid sufficient attention is the relationship between democratic backsliding and constitutional unamendability, either explicit or implicit, through the lens of constitutional relativity. Much ink has been spilled in the rise of democratic decay around the world in recent years. To address this problem, both politicians and academia have often invoked constitutional unamendability to deter democratic erosion. We think, nonetheless, that constitutional unamendability may be part of the problem rather than part of the solution. This does not suggest that the concept of constitutional unamendability should be discarded, but simply cautions that constitutional entrenchment or unamendability must not be seen purely through rose-tinted spectacles.

In terms of the legal model, which relies on eternity clauses or judicial interpretations, we argue that an overemphasis on constitutions as legal texts and courts as exclusive constitutional guardians has led to the domination of legal and judicial elites in the field of constitutional development. This domination has triggered the resurgence of neo-authoritarianism that has plagued many countries over the past two decades.[87] Specifically, most countries have a bill of rights and stipulate the most foundational features—including the polity, sovereignty, the separation of powers, and so on—in their constitutions. To protect democracy from erosion and to entrench fundamental rights, constitutional unamendability prohibits constitutional revision of those provisions, hoping to maintain constitutional identity and endurance. Although the prohibition

[85] Jaclyn L. Neo, A *Contextual Approach to Unconstitutional Constitutional Amendments: Judicial Power and the Basic Structure Doctrine in Malaysia*, 15 ASIAN JOURNAL OF COMPARATIVE LAW 69 (2020).

[86] Po Jen Yap, *The Conundrum of Unconstitutional Constitutional Amendments*, 4 GLOBAL CONSTITUTIONALISM 113, 136 (2015).

[87] Wen-Chen Chang, *Back into the Political? Rethinking Judicial, Legal and Transnational Constitutionalism*, 17 INTERNATIONAL JOURNAL OF CONSTITUTIONAL LAW 453 (2019).

may essentially be a parchment barrier, at least it "can be a useful red light before certain unconstitutional constitutional changes."[88]

Flexibility, however, is one critical element for a constitution to endure because it ameliorates pressures for change by allowing constitutions to adapt to new political and social progress.[89] An eternity clause is undoubtedly the most rigid form of a constitution. Reliance on constitutions in codifying and entrenching certain values may backfire when these values raise serious doubts as time elapses. That is, eternality clauses inevitably raise the concern of dead-hand control. As alluded to earlier, an eternity clause is not really eternal before a charismatic and ambitious leader who is determined to fundamentally remodel the constitutional order. When people feel compelled to reconsider an entrenchment, they will either invoke a brand new constitution or resort to a revolution that fundamentally subverts the constitutional order. From this perspective, eternity clauses can stoke the very fires they are designed to extinguish. Furthermore, constitutional unamendability may damage, rather than rescue, democratic constitutionalism when the values entrenched are not democratic. On this score, Silvia Şuteu, for example, has seriously questioned the efficacy of eternity clauses by contending that "rather than always safeguarding lofty constitutionalist goals, unamendability not infrequently serves as a tool for entrenching elite interests, majoritarian exclusion, and judicial turf protecting."[90] Her last example warns us of the danger that judges could, in fact, be self-interested politicians in robes.

Judicial review of legislation is democratically paradoxical, let alone judicial review of constitutional amendments.[91] And judicial imposition of constitutional unamendability may aggravate democratic backsliding under two circumstances. First, judges may collaborate with ambitious leaders in pursuing illiberal goals in exchange for personal promotion or institutional benefits. The Thai Constitutional Court, for example, thwarted the people's will to challenge

[88] ROZNAI, *supra* note , at 133. In this regard, Nepal is a relevant example in which the judiciary successfully invoked the concept of constitutional unamendability to enhance democracy. *See* Mara Malagodi, *Limiting constituent power? Unconstitutional constitutional amendments and time-bound constitution making in Nepal*, *in* THE LAW AND POLITICS OF UNCONSTITUTIONAL CONSTITUTIONAL AMENDMENTS IN ASIA 149–150 (Rehan Abeyratne & Ngoc Son Bui eds. 2022).

[89] ZACHARY ELKINS ET AL., THE ENDURANCE OF NATIONAL CONSTITUTIONS 81–83 (2009).

[90] SILVIA ŞUTEU, ETERNITY CLAUSES IN DEMOCRATIC CONSTITUTIONALISM 6 (2021).

[91] *But see* Jiunn-rong Yeh, *Beyond Unconstitutionality: The Public Oversight of Constitutional Revision in Taiwan*, *in* THE LAW AND POLITICS OF UNCONSTITUTIONAL CONSTITUTIONAL AMENDMENTS IN ASIA 153 (Rehan Abeyratne & Ngoc Son Bui eds. 2022) (arguing that judicial oversight over unconstitutional constitutional amendments functions as an instrument of the people's veto power against constitutional revision to make the government politically accountable). *See also* David K. C. Huang & Nigel N. T. Li, *Unconstitutional Constitutional Amendment in Taiwan: A retrospective Analysis of Judicial Yuan Interpretation No. 499 [2000]*, 15 U. PA. ASIAN L. REV. 421, 427 (2020).

the authoritarian legacy in the 2007 Thai Constitution by abusing the concept of constitutional unamendability.[92] In Latin America, too, several top courts have invoked this idea to enable or uproot the elimination of presidential term limits.[93] Therefore, granting the judiciary the power to hinder legitimate calls for constitutional change may facilitate the entrenchment of illiberal values as judges are not necessarily liberal and active. Secondly, the judicialization of politics usually results in the politicization of the judiciary, particularly when judges are disinterested. It is predictable that politicians may try to bring judges to their knees through a variety of means, such as court-packing, because the controversy of unconstitutional constitutional amendments is almost always an issue of political salience. Political attack against the judiciary unavoidably erodes the rule of law. Admittedly, the second point is not a problem of constitutional unamendability per se, but constitutional unamendability further raises the necessity of political control over the judiciary.

By contrast, the political model, which allows the political department to have the final word on the validity of constitutional amendments, may arguably be more democratically legitimate because it is the people who make the choice. Nevertheless, this model is vulnerable to populism and can be easily abused by demagogues. Recent decades have witnessed the emergence of illiberal democracies, and populist leaders often use constitutional revision as a manipulative tool for transformation.[94] Such abusive constitutional revision not only entrenches their powers but also clothes their dictatorships in a veneer of pseudo-constitutional legitimacy.

V. Conclusion

The genesis and growing popularity of constitutional unamendability is coextensive with the rise of constitutionalism and the decline of totalitarianism. Perhaps because of this, constitutional actors often invoke this concept to combat democratic decay. We believe, however, that this strategy may not be as effective as some advocates think. Theoretically, it builds on the distinction

[92] Khemthong Tonsakulrungruang, *Thailand's Unamendability: Politics of Two Democracies*, *in* THE LAW AND POLITICS OF UNCONSTITUTIONAL CONSTITUTIONAL AMENDMENTS IN ASIA 169, 170 (Rehan Abeyratne & Ngoc Son Bui eds. 2022).

[93] David Landau & Rosalind Dixon, *Abusive Judicial Review: Courts against Democracy*, 53 UC DAVIS L. REV. 1313, 1360–1363 (2020).

[94] ANDRÁS SAJÓ, RULING BY CHEATING: GOVERNANCE IN ILLIBERAL DEMOCRACY 62–66 (2021); ROSALIND DIXON & DAVID LANDAU, ABUSIVE CONSTITUTIONAL BORROWING: LEGAL GLOBALIZATION AND THE SUBVERSION OF LIBERAL DEMOCRACY 129–140 (2021).

between a new constitution and constitutional amendment, a distinction that has been blurred by what we call constitutional relativity. Practically, constitutional unamendability does not always function effectively. Sometimes, it even aggravates, rather than ameliorates, democratic deficiency. To revive democratic constitutionalism, we suggest that better civic engagement in constitutional change, which can take place with or without constitutional unamendability, may help.

12

The Secession and Constitutionalism Canon

Yonatan T. Fessha[*]

I. Introduction

Many secessionist movements are active across the world today. In Europe, uncertainties loom large on the territorial integrity of countries like Spain and the United Kingdom as they grapple with the nationalistic claims of groups and territories. These are countries that have continued to face credible and strong secessionist movements. Some are wondering whether the secessionist winds from Europe will blow on Africa's coasts.[1] The fear might be understandable given that ethnic divisions continue to characterize the political landscape of many African states. Of course, not all ethnic movements are secessionists.[2] Yet, there are also those who insist on seceding from the state.[3] Countries like Ethiopia and Sudan were forced to pay the ultimate price in the form of a political divorce and had to lose part of their territory that eventually became sovereign independent states recognized by the United Nations. Asia has had its own share of secessionist movements. In fact, globally speaking, since 1991, about thirty new states have been created. If we move the point of reference back to the turbulent times of the Second World War, the number soars to 120.[4]

* University of the Western Cape.

[1] Erk, Jan (2018) Will the North's secessionist winds blow South? The past, present, and future of self-determination and border change in Africa, *South African Journal of International Affairs*, 25(2), 153–176, DOI: 10.1080/10220461.2018.1446045.

[2] Some are demanding recognition from the state. Others want a subnational unit or a local government in which they are in a majority.

[3] They clamour for a sovereign independent state of their own. The strength of the case for secession and its capacity to serve as a strong mobilizing force has ebbed and flowed. In some states, like Ethiopia, the call for secession seems to be in a dormant phase, although it surely has not died out completely. In states like Nigeria, the call for secession that seemed to have died after the Biafra war of 1967 appear to be gaining some traction. The call for secession is, on the other hand, intensifying in countries like Cameroon. For some time now, Southern Cameroon has been engulfed in conflict that has resulted in a significant loss of life and property. Some low-intensity secessionist movements are present in several African states.

[4] Baldacchino, Godfrey and Hepburn, Eve (2012) A different appetite for sovereignty? Independence Movements in Subnational Island Jurisdictions, *Commonwealth and Comparative Politics*, 50(4), 555–568.

Yonatan T. Fessha, *The Secession and Constitutionalism Canon* In: *Global Canons in an Age of Contestation.* Edited by: Sujit Choudhry, Michaela Hailbronner, and Mattias Kumm, Oxford University Press.
DOI: 10.1093/9780191956942.003.0012

The state of secessionist sentiments and movements in Europe, Africa, and beyond calls for further scrutiny. The constitutional debate on secession involves what Michaela Hailbronner calls the 'core problems of human rights and democracy'.[5] An important element of the debate is the weight and legitimacy that should be attached to the wishes of a majority vote. But more importantly, it brings to the fore questions about 'which majority counts'—the majority of the population of a territory that is seeking for political divorce or the majority of the population of the host state. What about the interests of other communities and stakeholders? The age-old debate of individual rights versus collective interests also features strongly in the debate on secession. This is about the voice and fate of individuals that do not belong to the group that is seeking secession but happen to inhabit the same territory. This has made secession a burgeoning topic of constitutional law, which also makes it an important site for a global canon.

In this chapter, I focus on two texts that directly bear on the law of secession. The first, chosen for its status as a candidate for a global canon, is the celebrated decision of the Supreme Court of Canada that frames secession from a constitutional perspective. The second text, Article 39 of the Ethiopian Constitution, is arguably anti-canonical. This is not because it unusually constitutionalizes the right to secession but because of the scanty procedure it provides for effecting secession.

II. The *Reference* as a Global Canon

Reference Re Secession of Quebec, a landmark judgment of the Supreme Court of Canada, was delivered in the aftermath of the 1995 referendum that saw close to the majority of Quebeckers declaring their desire to leave Canada.[6] The *Reference* rejected the legality of a unilateral secession of Quebec from Canada, both under Canadian constitutional law and international law. It, however, imposed an obligation on the rest of Canada to negotiate the terms by which Quebec would accede to independence if a clear majority of the latter, faced with a clear question, voted in favour of secession. Although the Court has left the outcome of the negotiation to the political sphere, it has ruled that the secession must comply with the underlying basic principles of Canadian

[5] Hailbronner, Michaela (2019) Constructing the global constitutional canon: Between authority and criticism *University of Toronto Law Journal*, 69(2), 248–274.

[6] *Reference re Secession of Quebec*, [1998] 2 SCR 217(hereinafter *The Reference*).

constitutional law, namely the rule of law, federalism, democracy, and the protection of minorities.

It is fair to argue that the *Reference* has achieved a canonical status in Canada. This is evident from the positive reception it received, both from those that advocate and oppose the secession of Quebec from Canada. In fact, both the government of Canada and Quebec were quick to act based on the decisions of the Court. They were quick to give effect to the broadly formulated ruling of the Court, albeit based on different interpretations. This was, for example, the case with the Clarity Act[7] and Bill 99[8] that the House of Commons and the National Assembly of Quebec enacted respectively.

There is also no doubt that this is a judgment that is globally popular. A post-1995 comparative constitutional law scholarship on secession that does not refer to the *Reference* would be odd and probably hard to find. The impact of the *Reference* on other jurisdictions is clear. Many have sought to apply the Canadian solution. The Constitutional Court of Spain, albeit unconvincingly, relied upon the *Reference* when it concluded that a region in Spain 'cannot unilaterally call a referendum of self-determination to decide on its integration in Spain'.[9] It is not only the judgment that has attracted attention but also the Canadian scholarship on secession.[10] The desire to copy the Canadian solution led to the flourishing of publications on secession in Canada in the Spanish language. The *Reference* is also mentioned in a manifesto signed by more than 200 legal scholars in Spain. Sri Lanka is another country where the *Reference* has been explicitly mentioned and relied upon. The Supreme Court of that country, in *Chandrasoma v. Senathiraja*, endorsed the position that there is no unilateral right to secession.[11]

The *Reference* has also impacted the debate on the prospect of an independent Scotland joining the European Union. The *Reference* is relied upon to argue that 'an affirmative vote for Scottish independence would engage the Union law principle of democracy as a trigger for a duty to negotiate under sincere

[7] *An Act to give effect to the requirement for clarity as set out in the opinion of the Supreme Court of Canada in the Quebec Secession Reference* (SC 2000, c. 26).

[8] *Act respecting the exercise of the fundamental rights and prerogatives of the Québec people and the Québec State* (CQLR c. E-20.2).

[9] Casañas-Adam, Elisenda (2023) Constitutional Law and Secession in Spain, in Ryan D. Griffiths, Aleksandar Pavkovi, Peter Radan (eds) *The Routledge Handbook of Self-Determination and Secession*, Routledge.

[10] Romero Caro, Francisco Javier (2017) The Spanish vision of Canada's Clarity Act: From idealization to myth *Perspectives on Federalism*, 9(3), 2017.

[11] Supreme Court of Sri Lanka, *Chandrasoma v. Senathiraja and Others* (2017), SC SPL 03/2014, SC Minutes, 4 August 2017.

cooperation'.[12] The influence of the *Reference* on the opinion of the European Commission for Democracy through Law (the Venice Commission) with respect to the decision of the Montenegrin government to organize a referendum to secede from the State Union of Serbia and Montenegro was also evident.[13] This was particularly so with respect to the formulation of the referendum question and the required majority.

The influence of the *Reference* is not limited to domestic laws and pronouncements of domestic courts. It also moves to the arena of international law. The *Reference* has taken a unique position in international law. A decision by a domestic court on a matter of international law has 'become a classic of international legal literature'.[14] This is evident from the fact that the decision appears as a reference on international position on self-determination, something that 'one would expect to see a case taken from an international tribunal'.[15] The *Reference* is often invoked and relied upon by states that make submissions to the International Court of Justice (ICJ), as was the case with those that intervened in the ICJ proceedings in the Kosovo Advisory Opinion.

The fact that the *Reference* is globally popular should not be surprising. The phenomenon of part of a country breaking away from an existing state and establishing itself as an independent state is not something that is extensively regulated by law. Most constitutions are silent on secession. Although there are resolutions of the United Nations that arguably regulate the act of external self-determination that includes the possibility of secession, it is not something on which there is agreement. The *Reference* has filled an important void in this respect. It is sought as a guide in the absence of a clear legal framework governing secession.

To claim that the Canadian *Reference* has become a worldwide authoritative reference might be an exaggeration. But it is clear that the legacies of the *Reference* reverberate across the globe. That, however, does not, on its own, make it a global canon. But, it, at least, invites us to pick it as a potential candidate and examine it further to see if it also has the characteristics that make it a candidate for a global canon.

[12] Douglas-Scott, Sionaidh (2016) Scotland, secession and the EU, in Aileen McHarg et al. (eds), *The Scottish Independence Referendum: Constitutional and political implications*, Oxford University Press, 185.

[13] Choudhry, Sujit (2007) Referendum? What Referendum? *Literary Review of Canada*, 15(3), 7–9.

[14] Crema, Luigi (2019) The Reference Re Secession of Quebec, the Kosovo Advisory opinion and the question they leave open: The right to decide, the principle of stability and the duty to negotiate, in Giacomo Delledonne and Giuseppe Martinico (eds) *The Canadian Contribution to a Comparative Law of Secession: Legacies of the Quebec Secession Reference*, Palgrave Macmillan, 90.

[15] ibid.

In many respects, the *Reference* can be regarded as the pioneer in the comparative law of secession. It has directed our focus to the much-neglected comparative constitutional law of secession, inviting constitutional lawyers to grapple with how constitutional democracies should respond to secessionist claims. It has provided a valuable constitutional law perspective on a topic that is largely dominated by political science. That is not, however, the reason why it stands out. It stands out because it offers an honest and comprehensive engagement with the question of secession. It represents a major contribution towards developing a legal framework applicable to secession.

The 'sincere engagement' with the topic is evident from the fact that the Court went beyond the explicit contents of the Constitution to find a constitutional solution to the matter. 'The Constitution', the Court argued, 'is more than a written text.'[16] It made clear that the silence of a constitution on a particular issue does not mean that there are no constitutional solutions. And this is particularly important as many constitutions are silent on the question of secession. They neither permit nor prohibit secession. The approach taken by the *Reference* suggests that simply relying on the silence of the text of a constitution to deal with claims of secession is simply superficial.

In this regard, the *Reference* went beyond the text of the Constitution and inferred constitutional principles that must guide the response to claims of secession. This is about the use and impact of what the Canadian Supreme Court referred to as 'the fundamental and organizing principles of the Constitution'.[17] The Court ruled that the secession must comply with the underlying basic principles of Canadian constitutional law, namely the rule of law, federalism, democracy, and the protection of minorities.[18] Further, unlike in some cases where constitutional principles are derived from the preamble of the constitution, the *Reference* solidified the basis of the constitutional principles by referring to the preamble, the text of the Constitution, the structure and history of the Constitution, as well as historical considerations and philosophical arguments.[19]

Its sincere engagement is also evident from the fact that it has given equal attention to competing majorities and interests. An important part of the secession debate was whether the democratically expressed wishes of the majority

[16] *The Reference*, para. 148.
[17] ibid, para. 148.
[18] ibid.
[19] Gaudreault-Desbiens, Jean-Francois (2006) Underlying principles and the migration of reasoning templates: a trans-systemic reading of the Quebec Secession Reference, in Sujit Choudhry (ed.) *The migration of constitutional ideas*, Cambridge University Press.

of the population of Quebec to unilaterally secede from Canada trumped 'all other constitutional rights and duties'. The Court rejected the view that 'only the will and interests of the majority who voted in favor would prevail'.[20] According to the Court, the democratically expressed wishes of a clear majority of Quebec on a clear question of secession could only impose an obligation on the rest of Canada to negotiate the terms by which Quebec would accede to independence.[21] The Court insisted on negotiation that allows for the consideration of the interests of the federal government and linguistic and cultural minorities, including aboriginal peoples in Quebec.

The strength of the *Reference* is also that it acknowledges that the act of secession is 'as much a legal act as it was a political one'. This is evident in the many questions it left to the political sphere. For example, the *Reference* held that there must be a clear majority vote in favour of secession. It did not, however, determine the threshold that would satisfy the 'clear majority' requirement. The same with the referendum question. 'The Court was careful not to specify what would constitute a clear question or a clear majority, leaving those massively contentious criteria to a "political evaluation" given it is the political actors that have the information and expertise to make the appropriate judgment.'[22] Similarly, although the *Reference*, as mentioned earlier, rejected the legality of the unilateral secession of Quebec from Canada, it imposed on the rest of Canada the duty to negotiate. The Court has, however, left the outcome of the negotiations to the political sphere. It also stated that it has no intention to assume a 'supervisory role over the political aspects of constitutional negotiations'.[23] This has prompted the conclusion that 'the Supreme Court of Canada has adopted a much more polycentric and much less court-centered conception of constitutional law than is usual in common law jurisdictions'.[24]

The *Reference* might also be impressive in the attention it gave to the intricacies of a legal framework governing secession. Its insistence on a clear question alludes to the often controversial nature of the manner in which the secession question should be framed, a thorny issue both in Quebec and beyond. It has placed transparency at the centre of the referendum process.

[20] Mendes, Errol P. (2019) The legacy of the Quebec Secession Reference Ruling in Canada and internationally, in Giacomo Delledonne and Giuseppe Martinico (eds) *The Canadian Contribution to a Comparative Law of Secession: Legacies of the Quebec Secession Reference*, Palgrave Macmillan, 20.

[21] *The Reference*, paras 87–88.

[22] Mendes (n 20) 16.

[23] *The Reference*, para. 100.

[24] Gaudreault-Desbiens (n 19) 185.

When the Scottish Parliament demanded the organization of a referendum on Scottish independence, one of the major issues that it had to negotiate with the UK government was the wording of the referendum. The *Reference*'s emphasis on a clear majority is also another indication of a judgment that seriously engaged with the nuances and controversies surrounding the regulation of secession. The significance of its emphasis on a majority that is 'clear' became immediately evident when Quebec and the federal government disagreed over the threshold that would satisfy the 'clear majority' requirement. Thanks to the *Reference*, issues of a 'clear question' and a 'clear majority' have become a common topic of conversation in countries such as Spain and the United Kingdom that are grappling with claims of secession. Process requirements have taken centre stage.

By raising all the relevant issues and leaving room for deliberation and diversity on how to craft a legal framework applicable to secession, the *Reference* has undoubtedly made 'us think' and grapple with constitutional issues involved when dealing with secession. The open-ended nature of the *Reference* has made it possible for Spanish politicians who fall at different points on the political spectrum to use the same decision to support their conflicting positions. Interestingly, the *Reference* has been invoked by Catalan nationalists as much as by Spanish nationalists. Similar use of the *Reference* can also be noticed in the many and contradicting submissions made 'during the preliminary stage of the proceedings in the Kosovo case'. The fact that the *Reference* is invoked to buttress various positions on a secessionist crisis that a country faces, albeit in a manner that is sometimes dramatically different, shows the unique standing of the *Reference* in the comparative law of secession.

It is possible that the *Reference* has 'shape[d] existing judicial practice'. It represents a departure from the era of *Texas v. White*[25] when a constitutional avenue for secession was out of the question. The *Reference* seems to provide for a constitutional route for the possibility of a territory seceding from a state and establishing itself as an independent state after negotiations with the relevant stakeholders. It is also possible that the *Reference*'s use of underlying constitutional principles has broken new ground.[26]

[25] 74 US 700 (1869)

[26] The Constitutional Court of Italy held an attempt to organize a secessionist referendum in the region of Veneto to be 'inherently incompatible' with the 'unity and indivisibility of the Republic'. Although that court gave a radically different response to a secessionist claim, it, like the Canadian Supreme Court, relied on 'fundamental principles ... to shape the political sphere', including in the resolutions of questions pertaining to 'the unity and survival of the State'.

III. Article 39 of the Ethiopian Constitution as Anti-Global Canon

The most striking element of the Ethiopian Constitution is the right of every 'nation, nationality and people' in Ethiopia to self-determination, including the right to secession.[27] The importance attached to this specific right is evident from the fact that it cannot be suspended or limited, even in the extreme case of external invasion, a breakdown of law and order, or other calamities that warrant a proclamation of a state of emergency.[28] It is regarded as 'the ultimate extension and expression of the right to self determination'.[29]

The Constitution does not stop at simply providing a constitutional right to secession. It also provides for a procedure according to which the right to secession can be exercised. The exercise of the right to secession has to be initiated first by the approval vote of 'a two-thirds majority of the members of the legislative council of the Nation, Nationality or People concerned'.[30] If the demand for secession secures a majority vote in the referendum, the process of effecting secession should immediately follow. This happens when the federal government has transferred its powers to the newly independent state and the division of assets is effected in a manner prescribed by law.

If reception and global fame are the basis for identifying potential candidates for a global canon, the approach followed by Article 39 of the Ethiopian Constitution on matters of secession would definitely not make the cut. The Ethiopian Constitution is unparalleled in the explicit attention it gives to secession. In fact, it might be difficult to identify a comparator from its contemporaries. The idea of incorporating an explicit right to secede in one's own constitution has not received wide support. The constitution that comes the closest is the 1983 St Kitts and Nevis Constitution although, even then, the right to secession is made available only to to Nevis and not to those within Kitts. The island autonomies of Greenland, the Faroe Islands, Bougainville, the Falkland Islands, and New Caledonia have incorporated provisions that provide for a

[27] Art. 39, Constitution of Ethiopia.

[28] Art. 93(4)(c), Constitution of Ethiopia.

[29] Nahum, Fasil (1997) *Constitution for a Nation of Nations: The Ethiopian Prospect*, Red Sea Press, 53.

[30] Art. 39(4)(a), Constitution of Ethiopia. The federal government is obliged to organize a referendum within three years from the time it receives the relevant council's decision for secession. It is expected that the federal government, during the three-year cooling-off period, will engage the relevant council and the population group that wants to secede in order to try to respond to the demands of the group within the territorial framework of the state, with a view to averting secession. This is not, however, a constitutional obligation which is imposed on the federal government. If the process of accommodation fails to remove the agenda of secession from the table, then the referendum must proceed (Nahum, ibid; Habtu, Alem (2005) Multethnic Federalism in Ethiopia: A study of the secession clause in the Constitution, *Publius: The Journal of Federalism*, 35(2), 311–335).

referendum to vote on secession.[31] The Constitution of Uzbekistan also provides for secession although it is only available to a specific portion of the country (i.e. the Republic of Karakalpakstan).[32] Even countries like Canada and the United Kingdom that have countenanced the possibility of an territory seceding from the state have not dared to incorporate an explicit right to secession in their constitutions. That puts the Ethiopian Constitution in a league of its own as the only constitution that explicitly recognizes the right to secession. The past was a little kinder to those who sought a constitutional route to secession, with the likes of the 1977 Soviet Constitution and the 1946 Constitution of Yugoslavia providing an explicit right to walk away from a federation and establish an independent state.

More importantly, however, Article 39 of the Ethiopian Constitution should be a candidate for an anti-global canon because it seems to be driven by ideological commitment rather than by a serious engagement with the complexities of crafting a constitutional vehicle for an orderly and peaceful secession. The manner in which the right to secession is formulated and the procedure through which it can be exercised is dotted with controversies, many unanswered questions, and blind spots. It does not address the many intricate issues that often arise when dealing with claims of secession.

To begin with, there is some level of confusion regarding the subjects of the right to secession. The Constitution gives the right to every nation, nationality, and peoples, the term the Constitution uses to refer to ethnic groups. The right is not extended to the states—the constituent units of the Ethiopian federation. But not every ethnic group has its own state. The number of ethnic groups that inhabit the country does not match with the number of states that the Constitution has established. Although the country is home to eighty ethnic groups, only six ethnic groups are given a state of their own. The rest cannot point to a state in which they are in a majority as the remaining six states are ethnically diverse. This has brought to the fore the question whether an ethnic group first has to obtain the highest prize of internal self-determination by becoming a state before it can initiate a request for secession. In other words, the question is whether only those ethnic groups with their own state can seek secession.

Some argue that 'no people can initiate the process for secession without first becoming a state'.[33] The community that seeks to secede must first make use

[31] Ellis, Andrew (2018) Research Report 'Administration of Referendums' A Comparative Study of Independence Referendums, National Research Institute, Boroko.

[32] Art. 74, Constitution of Uzbekistan.

[33] Nahum (n 29) 159.

of the option of internal secession that is made available by the Constitution. According to Article 47 of the Constitution, ethnic groups that do not have their own states have the right to establish their own state. As convincing and as logical as this may sound, this amounts to attaching the condition of exhausting internal remedies to a right that is provided unconditionally. Unlike the Transitional Charter, which introduced the right to secession for the first time and made that right dependent on the violation, denial, or abrogation of rights,[34] the Constitution does not require seceding groups to provide reasons for their demand for secession. It simply outlines the procedure according to which the right to secession can be exercised. In other words, a group that seeks to secede is not constitutionally required to demonstrate 'the moral ground' on which it may seek secession. This makes the argument that effectively makes states the subjects of the right to secession problematic. This, of course, does not reduce the conundrum of an ethnic community that does not even have its own state exercising the right to secede.[35]

Article 39 of the Constitution also does not give sufficient attention to important process requirements. The procedure provided by the Constitution does not address some of the major issues that arise in a referendum for secession. The Constitution, for example, is silent on the nature and clarity of the referendum question. It also does not seem to appreciate the stakes involved in the outcome of a referendum on secession when it simply states that the demand for secession must only secure a simple majority vote in a referendum. It is clear that the drafters of the Constitution did not think of the need to have a clear majority in favour of secession as a requirement given that they did not bother about voter turnout. A simple majority in the context of a poor voter turnout can hardly be regarded as a clear expression of the wishes of a community.

The Constitution is not explicit on whether it provides for a unilateral or negotiated secession. The fact that it subjects secession to a procedure that includes discussion with the federal government might suggest that it does not allow for a unilateral declaration of secession. Yet, the negotiation the Constitution envisages is limited in scope. After a demand for secession has secured a majority vote in the referendum, the process of effecting the secession is complete when the federal government has transferred its powers to the newly independent state and the division of assets

[34] Transitional Charter of Ethiopia, No. 1, Negarit Gazeta, 50th Year, No. 1, Addis Ababa, 22 July 1991.

[35] At the same time, the road to secession only begins when the legislative council of the ethnic group initiates the request for secession with the support of a two-thirds majority of its members.

has been effected in a manner prescribed by law. It is not clear what the drafters of the Constitution had in mind when they referred to the transfer of powers. A newly created country would have as much power as any sovereign country would have, including the state from which it is walking away. Whatever powers it may have do not also depend on securing an agreement with the country from which it is departing. That makes the division of assets the only subject of negotiation between the seceding group and the federal government. It also means that the negotiation is only about the logistics of secession. Of course, a prudent federal government can use the negotiations over the division of assets to secure a concession on other considerations and interests.

Although the Constitution expects an orderly secession that avoids a unilateral declaration of secession, the procedure provided by the Constitution does not seem to be based on an appreciation that 'secession would give rise to many issues of great complexity and difficulty'.[36] The process ignores, or does not give enough attention to, other equally important interests and considerations. The wishes of the seceding community expressed through a simple majority trump all other considerations and interests. Save for the negotiations over the division of assets, the Constitution does not envisage negotiations that include all affected governments and stakeholders. In particular, the interests of minorities and other subnational units are not given due attention.

Clearly, the conditions for the implementation of the right to secede are not as burdensome as are often put forward. The right of secession as adopted in the Constitution is not, for example, a remedial right. Unlike the Charter of the Transitional Government, the Constitution does not require the claimant group to show a legitimate cause for secession. It only requires the claimant group to show, through the support of their legislative representatives and eventually a referendum, proven support for the secession claim in the form of a simple majority. Despite this, Ethiopia is yet to see a successful secessionist movement after the constitutionalization of the right. This is largely linked to the political practice that is opposed to the exercise of the right to secession.

Irrespective of its practical unavailability, the decision to constitutionalize the right to secession has remained the singularly most controversial element

[36] *The Reference*, para. 96.

of the Ethiopian Constitution. 'Though the right represents an unfaithful promise by the ruling coalition, it has been impeccably debated between the ruling and the opposition with considerable vehemence.'[37] This has made the constitutionalization of secession, as one author has put it, 'a federal nuisance'. The nuisances it creates is surprising given that it has largely been an empty promise.

[37] Bihonegn, Tesfa (2015) Federalization with a constitutional guarantee to secession: Controversies, paradoxes and imponderables in Ethiopia *Regional and Federal Studies*, 25(1) 45–70, 64.

PART III
RIGHTS

13
The Questions of Dignity

Marcela Prieto Rudolphy[*]

I. Introduction

Human dignity is a fundamental value in post-WWII international and domestic constitutional orders.[1] At the domestic level, "human dignity" first appeared as a central principle in the 1937 Irish Constitution,[2] later making its ways into other jurisdictions' constitutions—most prominently Germany's[3]—and constitutional jurisprudence.[4] At the international level, "human dignity" is central in human rights law[5] and international humanitarian law (IHL).[6]

Despite its importance in both international and constitutional law, the task of identifying a global canon on dignity poses some difficulties. These difficulties may first appear as reasons against constructing a canon on dignity altogether. Yet, I will argue that they can be better understood as giving us an idea of what the canon (and the anticanon) on dignity should look like—what controversies and functions of dignity it should reflect.

* Associate Professor of Law and Philosophy, University of Southern California, Gould School of Law; Profesora Adjunta Extraordinaria, Universidad Adolfo Ibáñez, Facultad de Derecho. Email: mprieto@law.usc.edu. I am indebted to Rebecca Brown, Felipe Jiménez, Nomi Stolzenberg, and the editors of this volume, Michaela Hailbronner, Mattias Kumm, and Sujit Choudhry, for their helpful comments on previous versions of this chapter.

[1] Margit Cohn and Dieter Grimm, "'Human Dignity' as a Constitutional Doctrine" in Mark Tushnet, Thomas Fleiner, and Cheryl Saunders (eds.), *Routledge Handbook of Constitutional Law* (Routledge 2013) 194–195.

[2] Samuel Moyn, "The Secret History of Constitutional Dignity" (2014) 17 Yale Hum. Rts. & Dev. L.J. 39, 96–97.

[3] Christopher McCrudden, "Human Dignity and Judicial Interpretation of Human Rights" (2008) 19 European Journal of International Law 655, 665.

[4] For a detailed treatment of dignity and its functions in constitutional jurisprudence, *see* Erin Daly, *Dignity Rights: Courts, Constitutions, and the Worth of the Human Person* (University of Pennsylvania Press 2013).

[5] Universal Declaration of Human Rights (adopted December 10, 1948 UNGA Res 217 A(III) (UDHR).

[6] *See* e.g. Geneva Convention Relative to the Treatment of Prisoners of War (adopted August 12, 1949, entered into force November 2, 1950) 75 UNTS 135 (Geneva Convention) art 3.

Marcela Prieto Rudolphy, *The Questions of Dignity* In: *Global Canons in an Age of Contestation*. Edited by: Sujit Choudhry, Michaela Hailbronner, and Mattias Kumm, Oxford University Press.
DOI: 10.1093/9780191956942.003.0013

The first difficulty is that there is no consensus on what dignity is or demands,[7] nor is there a legal definition.[8] Some jurisdictions—like Germany—have understood it as an absolute right or value[9] not subject to balancing, while most others—like Israel—take the opposite stance.[10] Second, human dignity fulfills different roles within legal orders: it can be a right, a legal principle or value,[11] and the ground or foundation of rights.[12]

These two difficulties are common to most abstract legal ideas,[13] and thus, they don't present an unsurmountable obstacle in constructing a canon on dignity. However, the third and fourth difficulties pose bigger challenges.

One of those difficulties is that dignity rarely shows up alone. When it is invoked by courts, dignity generally does some work along with other rights or values, informing the interpretation of rights[14] such as equality or non-discrimination,[15] the right to life,[16] autonomy,[17] the right to a bare minimum of conditions,[18] the prohibition on torture,[19] and so on. The fact that dignity rarely shows up alone poses a problem in constructing the canon: The obvious question is whether landmark cases, where dignity appears alongside other rights, should be understood as canonical cases regarding dignity, the accompanying rights, or both. In constructing the canon, my aim will be to distill what is distinctive about dignity.

[7] Oscar Schachter, "Human Dignity as a Normative Concept" [1983] American Journal of International Law 848; Luís Roberto Barroso, "Here, There, and Everywhere: Human Dignity in Contemporary Law and in the Transnational Discourse" (2012) 35 B.C. Int'l. & Comp. L. Rev. 331, 332.

[8] Jeremy J. Waldron, *Dignity, Rank, and Rights: The 2009 Tanner Lectures at UC Berkeley* (Oxford University Press 2009) 15; Schachter (n 7) 849.

[9] Cohn and Grimm (n 1) 202.

[10] McCrudden (n 3) 669; Georg Nolte, "5. The Bundesverfassungsgericht on the German Aerial Security Law: A Sonderweg from the Perspective of International Law?," *The Right to Life* (Brill Nijhoff 2010) 88.

[11] Conor O'Mahony, "There Is No Such Thing as a Right to Dignity" (2012) 10 International Journal of Constitutional Law 551, 559; Aharon Barak, "Human Dignity: The Constitutional Value and the Constitutional Right," *Understanding Human Dignity* (British Academy 2013) 361.

[12] O'Mahony (n 11) 559; Daly (n 4) 25; Jeremy Waldron, "Human Dignity: A Pervasive Value" (2019), available at SSRN 3463973, 1.

[13] Emily Kidd White, "There Is No Such Thing as a Right to Human Dignity: A Reply to Conor O'Mahony" (2012) 10 International Journal of Constitutional Law 575, 577.

[14] Barroso (n 7) 356.

[15] *President of the Republic of South Africa v. Hugo*, 1997 (4) SA (CC) 1; *Minister of Finance v. Van Heerden* 2004 (11) BCLR 1125; *R. v. Kapp* 2008 SCC 41 at § 22

[16] *Furman v. Georgia* 408 U.S. 238 (1972); *Kindler v. Canada* (Minister of Justice) [1991] 2 SCR 779; *State v. Makwanyane* 1994 (3) SA 868 (A).

[17] *Planned Parenthood of Southeastern Pa. v. Casey* (91-744), 505 U.S. 833 (1992).

[18] Inter-American Court of Human Rights, *Case of the Yakye Axa Indigenous Community v. Paraguay*, Judgment of June 17, 2005. *See* Jo M. Pasqualucci, "The Right to a Dignified Life (*Vida Digna*): The Integration of Economic and Social Rights with Civil and Political Rights in the Inter-American Human Rights System" (2008) 31 Hastings Int'l. & Comp. L. Rev. 1.

[19] *Public Committee Against Torture v. State of Israel* HCJ 5100/94 (1999).

The final difficulty is that dignity claims often support opposite interpretations of rights or judicial outcomes.[20] In issues such as abortion, euthanasia, pornography, and prostitution, dignity understood as privacy and autonomy—particularly understood as consent—clashes with ideas about the sacredness or worth of human life, a life lived well, and treatments worthy of humanity.[21] But a *good* life, a life with human dignity, can also function—and has functioned—as the basis for a minimum standard of material conditions.[22] In solving these tensions, it is simplistic to say that conceptions of the good life must be discarded. It is more likely that dignity contributes to enrich the arguments on both sides.[23] Canonical cases on dignity should hopefully reflect this diversity.

II. Building the Canon

Having in mind what these difficulties reveal about the canon on dignity, I will propose two cases as canonical. First, the Colombian Constitutional Court's decision that decriminalized abortion in three circumstances: rape, danger to the life or health of the mother, and fetal unviability.[24] Second, the Israeli Supreme Court's landmark decision—though its reputation is due to reasons other than its invocation of dignity[25]—on the legality of targeted killing, where the Court found that it couldn't say whether such strikes were always permissible or always forbidden.[26]

These two seemingly disparate cases can be considered canonical for several reasons. First, unlike other decisions where dignity is mentioned but not engaged with, these cases illuminate dignity's most important functions. They attempt to answer two questions distinctively associated to dignity, which Emily Kidd White identifies as "the question of the who" and "the question of the what":[27] who the bearers of human dignity are and what type of life these bearers deserve on account of their dignity. In both judgments, we will see that

[20] Christopher McCrudden and British Academy (eds.), *Understanding Human Dignity* (1st edn., published for the British Academy by Oxford University Press 2013) 1; Barroso (n 7) 332; McCrudden (n 3) 698.

[21] Stéphanie Hennette-Vauchez, "A Human Dignitas? Remnants of the Ancient Legal Concept in Contemporary Dignity Jurisprudence" (2011) 9 International Journal of Constitutional Law 32, 43–47.

[22] Daly (n 4) 55–60.

[23] Waldron (n 12) 17.

[24] Colombian Constitutional Court, Decision C-355/2006, May 10, 2006. The health of the mother includes mental health, and rape includes non-consensual insemination.

[25] Tamar Meisels and Jeremy Waldron, *Debating Targeted Killing: Counter-Terrorism or Extrajudicial Execution?* (Oxford University Press 2020).

[26] *Public Committee Against Torture in Israel v. Government of Israel.* Case No. HCJ 769/02.

[27] Kidd White (n 13) 582–584.

the second question is understood more narrowly as a question about how individuals ought to be treated by the state.[28] Because these are difficult questions to answer, I will return to them in the next section.

Perhaps precisely because of the complexity of the questions, both judgments attempt to answer them by addressing the different functions that dignity can fulfill within the legal order, as well as the surrounding controversies. The decisions reflect the prevailing disagreement around dignity rather than consolidate one conception of it. The case for their canonicity then doesn't rely on their getting the answers perfectly right, but on their providing a comprehensive starting point for discussions about dignity.[29] In other words, the difficulties I identified earlier are effectively reflected in both decisions and operate as reasons for canonicity.

First, as I said, there is no agreement about what dignity is, and the cases I am proposing as canonical address, and engage with, the most important conceptions of dignity. Second, both courts are explicit about the need for balancing competing values and about the difficulties associated with that balance when dignity (and life) are at stake, which is a theme that often arises regarding dignity. Third, these decisions engage with international and domestic law—and the relationship between them. Because dignity has become central both at the international and domestic level, their doing so provides a reason for canonicity.[30]

The Israeli decision, influenced by the nation's status as a Jewish state and humanity's creation in the image of God,[31] gives great importance to the "image of God" conception of dignity, which is also present in the Caribbean.[32] It then proceeds to the difficult task—as the Court itself acknowledges—of balancing dignity against military necessity in the context of armed conflict. In doing so, it addresses the relationship between IHL, international human rights law, and Israeli public law, and the place of dignity within these legal orders. It starts from the existence of an international armed conflict between Israel and various terrorist organizations operating in Judea, Samaria, and the Gaza Strip.[33] Given the existence of this armed conflict, the Court found that the applicable law is IHL—including the law of belligerent occupation and customary international law[34]—human rights law—when there is a gap in

[28] Daly (n 4) 7, 131.
[29] Michaela Hailbronner, "Constructing the Global Constitutional Canon: Between Authority and Criticism" (2019) 69 University of Toronto Law Journal 248, 251.
[30] *See* ibid.
[31] Daly (n 4) 29–30.
[32] ibid 29.
[33] *Public Committee* (n 26) [16], [21].
[34] ibid [19].

IHL—and fundamental principles of Israeli public law.[35] In ascertaining the permissibility of targeted killing—which requires ascertaining who is a civilian and who is a combatant—the Court resorted to customary international law provisions contained in Additional Protocol I to the Geneva Conventions,[36] as well as reports by the International Committee of the Red Cross and decisions of international courts.[37]

In the Colombian judgment, almost every conception of dignity relevant to contemporary discourse is explored. Human dignity has been understood by the Colombian Court to protect autonomy or the possibility of designing a life plan (to live as one wishes);[38] certain material concrete conditions of existence (to live well);[39] and the intangibility of non-patrimonial goods, physical integrity, and moral integrity (to live without humiliation).[40] Two of these dimensions are considered by the Court to be of particular relevance to the case of abortion: Living as one wishes and living without humiliation.[41] Both of them are explored through the Kantian idea of not treating individuals as mere means to an end. In this case, competing conceptions of dignity are central to the Court's discussion of abortion: dignity is often invoked both on behalf of the fetus and of the pregnant person.[42] Abortion is an instance, as Siegel remarks, where dignity claims have a distinct content which reflects disagreement about dignity's meaning and consequences.[43] This feature of abortion debates is of particular importance in the Colombian context: Colombia is what Siegel calls a "duty-to-protect-life-jurisdiction,"[44] that is, a jurisdiction where life is a constitutionally protected value. As a result, balancing the value of life against the woman's rights and dignity is inevitable.

The Colombian Court—as it often does[45]—engages with, and incorporates, regional and international human rights standards regarding reproductive

[35] ibid [18].
[36] ibid [32].
[37] ibid [33]–[34].
[38] Decision C-355/2006 (n 24) [258].
[39] ibid [256].
[40] ibid.
[41] ibid.
[42] Reva Siegel, "Dignity and the Duty to Protect Unborn Life" in Christopher McCrudden (ed.), *Understanding Human Dignity* (OUP 2013); Reva B. Siegel, "Dignity and Sexuality: Claims on Dignity in Transnational Debates over Abortion and Same-Sex Marriage" (2012) 10 International Journal of Constitutional Law 355, 365.
[43] Siegel, "Dignity and Sexuality" (n 42) 378–379.
[44] Siegel, "Dignity and the Duty to Protect Unborn Life" (n 42) 509.
[45] Verónica Undurraga and Rebecca J. Cook, "Constitutional Incorporation of International and Comparative Human Rights Law: The Colombian Constitutional Court Decision C-355/2006" in Susan H. Williams (ed.), *Constituting Equality: Gender Equality and Comparative Constitutional Law* (CUP 2009) 216; Camilla Reuterswärd et al., "Abortion Law Reforms in Colombia and Nicaragua: Issue Networks and Opportunity Contexts" (2011) 42(3) Development and Change 805, 816.

rights—not explicitly included in the Colombian Constitution[46]—through the doctrine of the constitutional block.[47] The Court stated that, as part of the constitutional block, these rights represent a limit to the legislator's discretion in criminalizing abortion.[48] The Court thus explicitly addresses the overlap between constitutional and international human rights law and emphasizes dignity as foundational to both.[49] The Court also cites foreign constitutional law by giving a brief overview of the most well-known decisions on abortion: *Roe v. Wade*, the 1975 and 1985 German decisions, and the 1985 Spanish decision.[50] From these decisions, the Court concludes that when constitutional courts have had to ascertain the constitutionality of abortion, they have coincided in the need to balance competing interests: on the one hand, the life of the unborn (which in the Colombian and German cases is a constitutionally protected value), and on the other hand, the rights of the pregnant person.[51] Although these three courts have decided the issue of abortion differently, the Colombian Court noted that all of them have found a total ban to be unconstitutional.[52]

There are also reasons to think about these two decisions as canonical not just considered independently from each other. Though the features discussed earlier do provide reasons for considering these decisions as part of the canon, we can also think of the judgments as canonical considered together. First, they jointly cover all the legal regimes where dignity occupies a central place (human rights law, IHL, and constitutional law). Second, the two decisions together allow us to have a wide-ranging picture of how dignity is incorporated into constitutional law: broadly or more narrowly. Colombia provides an example of a jurisdiction where the constitution incorporates dignity in various provisions, as a right and as a value, (similar to Germany and South Africa),[53] while Israel is an example of a jurisdiction where the constitutional text's incorporation of dignity is narrower[54] but has been expanded upon jurisprudentially.[55]

[46] Reproductive rights are rarely the object of explicit constitutional protection. *See* Ruth Rubio-Marín and Wen-Chen Chang, "Sites of Constitutional Struggle for Women's Equality" in Mark Tushnet, Thomas Fleiner, and Cheryl Saunders (eds.), *Routledge Handbook of Constitutional Law* (Routledge 2012) 301, 304.
[47] Decision C-355/2006 (n 24).
[48] ibid [271].
[49] ibid [248].
[50] ibid [278].
[51] ibid [282].
[52] ibid [282].
[53] Colombian Constitution, art. 1
[54] Cohn and Grimm (n 1) 201.
[55] Daly (n 4) 2; Cohn and Grimm (n 1) 201.

Finally, both decisions engage with what are among the most pressing issues in this century of backlash against democracy and human rights: abortion and targeted killing. A canon that aims to serve certain key values should be sensitive to areas where this danger is present.[56]

It may be strange to think of abortion as an issue of the twenty-first century. After all, in some countries—such as Germany and the United States—the abortion debate took place mostly in the 60s and 70s,[57] while in Latin American countries it did so in the 80s and 90s.[58] Nonetheless, this century has seen an important backlash against reproductive rights and other gender-related demands.[59] The Colombian judgment is particularly significant within this context. Moreover, given that dignity claims regarding women's autonomy, objectification, and social subordination[60] have played a fundamental and distinctive role in abortion debates—and play a fundamental part today in feminist demands—a contemporary canon on dignity that said nothing about these issues would be incomplete.

Israel's decision deals with one of the most contentious issues of our age: the limits of state power in the context of the "war against terrorism." The right to life has been often connected to dignity, especially regarding the limits of state power. Indeed, capital punishment has been treated by constitutional courts as incompatible not only with the right to life but also with dignity.[61] *Makwanyane* is perhaps the most well-known example of such a decision[62] and is certainly a candidate for the canon on dignity. Yet, the death penalty debate, though alive in the United States, has lost its contentiousness due to widespread agreement[63] about the incompatibility of that penalty with human rights and dignity. The debate of our age in this area seems to be precisely the one the Israeli Court engages with: targeted killing. The importance of targeted killing as a state policy

[56] The canon is not, then, value-neutral. *See* Hailbronner (n 29) 251.

[57] Rubio-Marín and Chang (n 46) 304; Siegel, "Dignity and Sexuality" (n 42) 357.

[58] Reuterswärd et al. (n 45) 807.

[59] *See* the U.S. Supreme Court Decision in USSC, *Dobbs v. Jackson Women's Health Organization* 142 S. Ct. 2228 (2022). Also *see* Anna Śledzińska-Simon, "Populists, Gender, and National Identity" (2020) 18 International Journal of Constitutional Law 447; Dorota Anna Gozdecka, "Backlash or Widening the Gap?: Women's Reproductive Rights in the Twenty-First Century" (2020) 9 Laws 8; Amanda Taub, *In Poland, Protests Over Abortion Ban Could Revolutionize Politics*, 7 December 2020, https://www.nytimes.com/2020/12/07/world/europe/poland-abortion-protests.html.

[60] Siegel, "Dignity and the Duty to Protect Unborn Life" (n 42) 511–512; McCrudden (n 3) 663.

[61] Meisels and Waldron (n 25) 171; Giovanni Bognetti, "The Concept of Human Dignity in European and US Constitutionalism" in Georg Nolte (ed.), *European and US Constitutionalism* (1st edn., Cambridge University Press 2005) 90–91; *Furman v. Georgia* 408 U.S. 238 (1972); *Kindler v. Canada* (Minister of Justice) [1991] 2 SCR 779; *State v. Makwanyane* 1994 (3) SA 868 (A).

[62] *State v. Makwanyane* 1994 (3) SA 868 (A).

[63] Around 170 U.N. members (of a total of 193) have abolished the death penalty or no longer apply it. *See* https://www.ohchr.org/EN/Issues/DeathPenalty/Pages/DPIndex.aspx.

in fighting terrorism; its potential to erode the boundaries between peace and war, law enforcement and armed conflict;[64] the central place of dignity both in IHL and human rights law; and the dignity considerations that arise regarding *the question of the what* provide weighty reasons for incorporating the Israeli decision into a canon of dignity for the twenty-first century.

Despite the reasons just mentioned, the case for the decisions' canonicity has—perhaps inevitably—some flaws. The first problem is that the outcomes are far from being universally applauded.

In the Colombian case, the result and reasoning can be criticized from a feminist perspective.[65] Although the dimensions of dignity the Court focuses on are consistent with the framework feminists have used to challenge the criminalization of abortion—which relies on claims about women's dignity and objectification[66]—the case resulted in the decriminalization of abortion only in three circumstances, and its enforcement has faced some challenges.[67] A 2011 study found that, in spite of the ruling, only 0.08% of abortions undertaken in 2008 in Colombia were legal and performed in a health facility.[68] Thus, this judgment may not be canonical from a feminist perspective, and it has certainly not solved the issue of access to safe abortion in Colombia.

In the Israeli case, the outcome—that targeted killing is permitted in certain circumstances—is somewhat contentious,[69] even if its treatment of targeted killing within the framework of IHL and its analysis of the concept of "civilians" and "direct participation in the hostilities" has had significant influence.[70] The contentiousness of the outcome is, perhaps, not a flaw, as the judgment discusses what is one of the most debated issues of this century.

[64] Claire O. Finkelstein, "The Equality of Combatants in Asymmetric War" in Jens David Ohlin, Larry May, and Claire Finkelstein (eds.), *Weighing Lives in War* (Oxford University Press 2017) 241–242; Gabriella Blum, "The Individualization of War: From War to Policing in the Regulation of Armed Conflicts" in Austin Sarat, Lawrence Douglas, and Martha M. Umphrey (eds.), *Law and War* (Stanford University Press 2014) 75; Rosa Ehrenreich Brooks, "War Everywhere: Rights, National Security Law, and the Law of Armed Conflict in the Age of Terror" (2004) 153 University of Pennsylvania Law Review 675, 725–728.

[65] *See* Undurraga and Cook (n 45) 236.

[66] Siegel, "Dignity and the Duty to Protect Unborn Life" (n 42) 511–512; McCrudden (n 3) 663.

[67] *See* Cecilia Barraza Morelle and Claudia Gómez López, *Un Derecho Para Las Mujeres: La Despenalización Parcial Del Aborto En Colombia* (La Mesa por la Vida y la Salud de las Mujeres 2009). In 2022, the Constitutional Court ruled that the criminalization of abortion before twenty-four weeks is unconstitutional. In that judgment, the Court relied heavily on its previous judgment, discussed in this chapter as canonical. *See* Colombian Constitutional Court, Decision C-055/22, February 21, 2022.

[68] Elena Prada et al., "Unintended Pregnancy and Induced Abortion in Colombia" (2011) 72 Causes and Consequences. Guttmacher Institute, ed. (Guttmacher Institute) 4–5.

[69] *See* Meisels and Waldron (n 25).

[70] Michelle Lesh, "The Public Committee Against Torture in Israel v the Government of Israel—The Israeli High Court of Justice Targeted Killings Decisions" (2007) 8 Melb. J. Int'l. L. 373, 378.

These issues, however, don't necessarily detract from the decisions' canonical status on dignity (though they may act as reasons against their canonical status in other areas). The reasons for canonicity I have proposed don't require the decisions to be perfect in every way, but to ask the right questions, address different conceptions of dignity, and showcase the distinctive role that dignity can play in judicial settings.

The second flaw is that both cases adopt a balancing approach to dignity. Thus, in selecting these two cases the absolutist stance towards dignity, as it exists in Germany (and in Hungary when associated to the right to life[71]), is excluded. This approach is famously reflected in the German judgment on the Aerial Security Act, whereby the Court declared that a law permitting German armed forces to shoot down a hijacked airplane carrying passengers in order to prevent a terrorist attack was a violation of the passengers' dignity.[72]

Given the place of dignity in, and the influence of, the German Constitutional Court's jurisprudence,[73] its complete omission from a canon on dignity is not ideal. In favor of its omission is the fact that the absolutist stance towards dignity is less common (and perhaps an outlier[74]) in comparison to the balancing approach present in the cases I have proposed. Making up for Germany's omission is the fact that its influence is explicitly present in the Colombian judgment.

The reasons mentioned so far explain why both decisions—even if imperfect—are canonical on dignity. Now that we have an idea of what the canon looks like, the case for anticanonicity can be made more easily. The anticanon I will propose is the canonical judgments' opposite: the United States Supreme Court's decision in *Deck v. Missouri*,[75] where the Court had to consider whether shackling a convicted offender during the penalty phase of a capital case violated the Constitution.[76] Faced with a petitioner who had been shackled with leg irons, handcuffs, and a belly chain during the sentencing procedure,[77] the Court was almost completely oblivious to dignity-related considerations as applied to the petitioner himself. Instead, it chose to emphasize

[71] McCrudden (n 3) 699.

[72] BVerfG, Judgment of the First Senate of February 15, 2006–1 BvR 357/05. A similar approach was followed in 2008 by the Polish Constitutional Court. *See* Nolte (n 10) 83.

[73] Barroso (n 7) 337–338; O'Mahony (n 11) 555.

[74] McCrudden (n 3) 711. Nevertheless, dignity has been narrowly delineated by the German Court. *See* Ariel L. Bendor and Michael Sachs, "The Constitutional Status of Human Dignity in Germany and Israel" (2011) 44 Isr. L. Rev. 25.

[75] This case is discussed by Daly in her analysis of the U.S. Supreme Court's treatment of dignity. Daly (n 4) 81. *See* USSC *Deck v. Missouri* 125 S. Ct. 2007 (2005).

[76] *Deck v. Missouri* (n 75).

[77] ibid [624]–[625].

the dignity of the court and the importance of due process (without linking the latter to dignity).[78] That, in the twenty-first century, the apex court of a democratic regime, faced with an individual shackled in such an extreme way, saw no dignity claims worth addressing seems astounding.

III. The Canon: The Who and the What

There are many reasons, as explained, why Israel's and Colombia's judgments can be considered canonical on dignity. One reason deserves especial attention: in both decisions, human dignity plays a distinctive role—different from the role of other values or rights that may also be present—in their arguments. These decisions deal, as I said, with the most complex and important questions that arise pertaining to dignity: who the bearers of dignity are and what treatment they deserve on account of their dignity.

A. The Bearers of Human Dignity

Human dignity is traditionally associated with humanity[79] and has served to distinguish the human species from others.[80] Although some constitutions speak of the dignity of living beings,[81] and in a recent decision, an Argentinean court granted a habeas corpus claim in favor of a chimpanzee that was kept in a Mendoza zoo,[82] the species-based (or speciesist)[83] approach to dignity is widely shared across legal systems. The use of dignity regarding nonhuman animals is not in any way canonical—not yet. It does, however, stand in dialogue—and perhaps in tension—with decisions on human dignity.

Within human-focused conceptions of dignity, one of the greatest difficulties about *the question of the who* is precisely the question of whether the human embryo has dignity.[84] That the embryo belongs to the human species cannot be denied,[85] but whether it is a bearer of human dignity is more contentious.

[78] ibid.

[79] Barak (n 11) 363; Michael Rosen, *Dignity: Its History and Meaning* (Harvard University Press 2012) 31.

[80] Charles R. Beitz, "Human Dignity in the Theory of Human Rights: Nothing but a Phrase?" (2013) 41 Philosophy & Public Affairs 259, 267; Daly (n 4) 13–14.

[81] Like Switzerland's. *See* Jessica Eisen, "Animals in the Constitutional State" (2017) 15 International Journal of Constitutional Law 909, 914.

[82] Expte. No. P-72.254/15, November 3, 2016, Tercer Juzgado de Garantías, Mendoza, Argentina.

[83] *See* Peter Singer, *Animal Liberation* (Random House 1995).

[84] McCrudden (n 3) 708.

[85] George Kateb, *Human Dignity* (Harvard University Press 2011) x.

This is precisely the area where the Colombian decision dwells. Dignity has been explicitly accorded to the fetus in Germany and Hungary,[86] but the Colombian Court took a different path. Within the Colombian constitutional order, human life is a constitutionally protected value[87] and a right.[88] Although the Court acknowledged the difficulties in answering the question of when human life begins,[89] it concluded that the fetus is not explicitly considered a person under international or constitutional law.[90] However, though the right to life is restricted to the human person, the Court found that the protection of life (as a value) applies to the fetus.[91] This approach—reading the fetus as deserving constitutional protection—reproduces the prevalent approach in Europe, and it has some constraining effects on the outcome of the decision.[92] Because life is a constitutionally protected value, the Court concluded that the legislator may adopt measures to protect the fetus—including prohibiting abortion.[93] And by the end of the judgment, the Court stated that the protection of women's rights cannot imply that the entirety of the provision that criminalizes abortion is unconstitutional because such a declaration would leave life unprotected,[94] notwithstanding that the legislator could decriminalize abortion in other circumstances.[95]

The Court thus partially provided an answer to one of the most important questions related to dignity—*the question of the who*—by determining the constitutional status of the fetus: the fetus is not a bearer of rights; it is not a person. This answer seemingly leaves the question of dignity open. But if we read this part of the judgment with the Court's explicit reaffirmation of the dignity of women and the fact that the Court only refers to women as "full bearers of human dignity,"[96] we can conclude that the fetus—which is not a person and has no right to life—is not a bearer of dignity, at least understood as a right. Whether dignity as a value is embodied in the fetus is left unanswered, but life and dignity, either as rights or as values, are not absolute in the Colombian order. They are subject to balancing:[97] in this case, with the rights and dignity of the woman.[98] Therefore, it may be that even if the Court had explicitly

[86] Daly (n 4) 29.
[87] Decision C-355/2006 (n 24) [228], [230]. Colombian Constitution, preamble and art. 2.
[88] Decision C-355/2006 (n 24) [228]; Colombian Constitution, art. 11.
[89] Decision C-355/2006 (n 24) [234].
[90] ibid [236]–[238].
[91] ibid [233].
[92] Rubio-Marín and Chang (n 46) 306.
[93] Decision C-355/2006 (n 24) [233]–[234].
[94] ibid [293].
[95] ibid [300].
[96] ibid [259].
[97] ibid [230]–[231].
[98] ibid [240]–[241].

recognized the fetus as embodying dignity, the outcome would have been similar.

The Israeli decision also addresses *the question of the who*, but it does so with a different goal. The Colombian Court must answer a difficult question about the limits of personhood. In contrast, the Israeli case poses no serious legal question that everyone—combatants and civilians—is a bearer of dignity (as the Court itself acknowledges). It is true that the Israeli Court is called upon to discern a difficult legal issue: what status to accord, under IHL, to members of terrorist organizations who participate in the hostilities.[99] The Court concluded that they are not combatants nor privileged combatants: they are civilians who participate in the hostilities or civilians who constitute unlawful combatants.[100] It is at this point that the Court emphatically stated:

> Needless to say, unlawful combatants are not beyond the law. They are not "outlaws." God created them as well in his image; their human dignity as well is to be honored ...[101]

This use of dignity is reiterated in the concurrent opinion of Vice President E. Rivlin. He stressed that although IHL intends to honor the lives and dignity of civilians, the dignity of unlawful combatants cannot be negated.[102] Dignity is a principle that applies to everyone, even during combat.[103]

Israel's foray into *the question of the who* does not fulfill the same role as Colombia's. It is not trying to provide an answer to a difficult legal and moral question about the limits of dignity—everyone would agree that persons, whatever they do, are bearers of dignity. The Court used the language of dignity symbolically:[104] it emphatically resisted the conceptualization of certain people as outside humanity or as having forfeited their dignity (implicitly criticizing the Bush administration's arguments in the context of the war on terror[105]). This usage of dignity plays a distinctive and fundamental role regarding *the question of the who* and is not uncommon in courts: both Makwanyane and Justice Brennan's concurrence in *Furman v. Georgia* categorically opposed the idea that individuals lose their dignity due to their actions, no matter how

[99] *Public Committee* (n 26) [24].
[100] ibid [26].
[101] ibid [25].
[102] ibid [5].
[103] ibid (Vice President Rivlin, concurrent opinion) [5].
[104] Khaitan has argued that the expressive dimension of dignity is its special contribution to human rights law. Tarunabh Khaitan, "Dignity as an Expressive Norm: Neither Vacuous nor a Panacea" (2012) 32 Oxford Journal of Legal Studies 1, 5.
[105] Lesh (n 70) 382.

atrocious the crime,[106] and the *Yamashita* dissent insisted that even "enemies of humanity" have dignity and must be treated accordingly.[107]

B. The Treatment They Deserve

Human dignity has distinctively developed as related to *the question of the what*: how should individuals be treated, what life do they deserve on account of their dignity?[108] This dimension of dignity is widely shared among domestic and international courts and can take many forms. It is tightly linked to the prohibition on torture and humiliating and degrading treatment;[109] to the Kantian view whereby treating humans as means is prohibited;[110] to the respect of autonomy and privacy,[111] rights of personal and mental integrity,[112] minimal material conditions of life,[113] equality,[114] and non-discrimination. Most of these ideas are related to questions about the limits of state power in treating individuals.

Within this area, both the Colombian and Israeli Courts use dignity to set limits on what the state can demand and do, even under pressing circumstances such as armed conflict, and even with the goal of guaranteeing constitutionally protected values.[115]

The Colombian decision, following the Kantian understanding of dignity,[116] linked dignity to the prohibition against treating individuals as mere means to an end.[117] This is a common theme throughout the decision, as the Court discussed the ways in which dignity can answer *the question of the what* as it pertains to abortion.

In considering dignity in its "living as one wishes" dimension, the Court emphasized that dignity guarantees a sphere of autonomy, which in the case of

106 *Makwanyane* (n 62) [136]; *Furman v. Georgia* 408 U.S. 238, 273.
107 Daly (n 4) 85.
108 Jacob Weinrib, *Dimensions of Dignity: The Theory and Practice of Modern Constitutional Law*, vol. 15 (Cambridge University Press 2016) 5–6; White (n 13).
109 Waldron (n 8) 18; Jean-Paul Costa, "Human Dignity in the Jurisprudence of the European Court of Human Rights," *Understanding Human Dignity* (British Academy 2013) 401.
110 *See* Beitz (n 80) 262; Rosen (n 79).
111 Connor M. Ewing, "With Dignity and Justice for All: The Jurisprudence of Equal Dignity and the Partial Convergence of Liberty and Equality in American Constitutional Law" (2018) 16 International Journal of Constitutional Law 753, 757.
112 Daly (n 4) 55–60.
113 ibid.
114 Kateb (n 85) 6.
115 Decision C-355/2006 (n 24) [263].
116 *See* Beitz (n 80) 262; Rosen (n 79).
117 Decision C-355/2006 (n 24) [260].

women includes reproductive and health rights as well as decisions concerning motherhood.[118] The Court stressed that to decide on behalf of the person is to brutally deprive her of her ethical condition, to reduce her to a mere object, reify her—to turn her into a means towards ends that are exogenously chosen.[119] In the case of abortion, the Court emphasized that when the legislator adopts criminal measures, it cannot fail to acknowledge women as human beings with full dignity.[120] It must treat them as such, rather than considering and turning them, against their will, into mere instruments of reproduction of the human species.[121]

In considering dignity in its "living without humiliation" dimension,[122] the Court connected it to the right to health (which is related to the right to life) and the right to reproductive health.[123] When analyzing pregnancies where the health of the woman is in danger, the Court concluded that it is not prima facie proportionate or reasonable for the Colombian state to impose on a person the obligation of sacrificing her own life to protect the interests of third parties, even if those interests are constitutionally relevant.[124]

These arguments about dignity as autonomy, dignity as non-humiliation, and dignity as a prohibition against objectification are typical of dignity in its different conceptions. They also drove the Court to find that the criminalization of abortion in cases of rape, danger to the mother, and fetal unviability is manifestly unconstitutional:[125] it implies a complete preeminence of one of the legal values at stake (the life of the unborn), thus entailing the absolute sacrifice of the rights of the pregnant woman.[126] The Court reiterated that this fails to acknowledge women's dignity and nature as autonomous subjects,[127] reduces them to mere receptables or tools,[128] forces them to adopt heroic behaviors,[129] and in the case of fetal unviability, submits them to cruel, inhuman, and degrading treatment.[130]

The question of the what also plays an important role in the Israeli case which, as I suggested earlier, can be understood as a revisitation of the question

[118] ibid [258].
[119] ibid [260].
[120] ibid [259].
[121] ibid [259].
[122] ibid [256].
[123] ibid [265]–[266].
[124] ibid [267].
[125] ibid [284].
[126] ibid [284], [292].
[127] ibid [285]–[287].
[128] ibid [284]–[286].
[129] ibid [286].
[130] ibid [290]–[291].

about the state's power to kill individuals,[131] no longer focused on the death penalty but on targeted killing. In addressing this question, and in contrast to the Colombian Court, the Israeli Court did not speak about the prohibition on treating individuals as means. The Israeli Court emphasized the importance of dignity, the value of the human person, and the sanctity of life, dignity, and freedom in the regulation of armed conflict.[132] Having emphasized that unlawful combatants are bearers of dignity, the Court immediately noted that their dignity doesn't entail that they cannot be harmed: just as it is permissible to harm soldiers in war, so it is with members of terrorist organizations that participate in hostilities.[133]

In doing this, the Court brought to the fore the deep tensions between human rights law and IHL: on the one hand, the Court affirmed the dignity of unlawful combatants; on the other hand, it detached their dignity from a prohibition against harming them. That is, it answered *the question of the what* as permitting targeted killing in the context of armed conflict and under certain circumstances, even though this answer is likely in contradiction with the prohibition against treating individuals as means: killing combatants in armed conflict can effectively be the means to victory. As the Court acknowledged, IHL must strike a balance between two contradictory considerations: humanitarian ones—based upon individual rights and dignity—and military necessity.[134] This tension can also be understood philosophically: IHL's rationale resembles the Benthamite or utilitarian desire to reduce suffering, while human rights law seems more directly connected to a Kantian or deontological notion of respect of the individual.[135] Both rationales can provide different answers to *the question of the what*: respect for the individual will often be in tension with a general command to reduce suffering (the latter, in fact, says little about how to treat individuals *qua* individuals).

Another recurrent theme in the Israeli case pertains to the limits of what the state can do within the context of an armed conflict against terrorist organizations. This is also a dignitary theme that provides an answer to *the question of the what*. The Court noted repeatedly that the means available to a democratic state are not unlimited, no matter how worthy the ends,[136] and it made a point to cite its previous decision on torture's inconsistency with dignity.[137]

[131] Waldron uses similar language in discussing the death penalty and targeted killing. *See* Meisels and Waldron (n 25) 166–169.
[132] *Public Committee* (n 26) [22]–[23].
[133] ibid [25].
[134] ibid [22].
[135] David Luban, "Human Rights Pragmatism and Human Dignity" in Massimo Renzo, Rowan Cruft, and Matthew Liao (eds.), *Philosophical Foundations of Human Rights* (OUP 2013) 270.
[136] *Public Committee* (n 26) [46].
[137] ibid [64].

IV. The Anticanon: *Deck v. Missouri*

In *Deck v. Missouri*, the U.S. Supreme Court had to consider whether shackling a convicted offender during the penalty phase of a capital case violated the Constitution.[138] The petitioner had been shackled with leg irons, handcuffs, and a belly chain during the sentencing procedure.[139] There was no indication that the petitioner presented any danger to the lower court. The Court held that the Constitution forbids the use of visible shackles during the penalty phase, unless their use is justified by an essential state interest specific to the defendant on trial.[140] Visible shackles may indicate to the jury that the defendant is guilty or particularly dangerous, and so they may impinge upon due process.[141]

While the outcome may have been positive for the defendant—the judgment was reversed, and the case remanded[142]—this case is anticanonical in its treatment (or lack thereof) of dignity.

As is common for the U.S. Supreme Court,[143] the decision didn't engage with comparative or international law. But the most obvious reason for anticanonicity is the Court's puzzling indifference to dignity considerations that shackling—particularly in such an extreme way—poses. Indeed, the only mention of dignity is related to the need to maintain a "judicial process that is a dignified process."[144] The Court mentioned in passing that the court's formal dignity includes the respectful treatment of the defendant,[145] but it did not consider whether shackling itself—in this case, with leg irons, handcuffs, and a belly chain—was disrespectful to the defendant, humiliating, or violated his dignity.

This case might not be anticanonical within the United States; descriptively, it is not part of the anticanon as understood by U.S. scholars.[146] It is also not entirely clear whether the outcome, in terms of dignity, is inconsistent with the U.S. legal order. One might attribute it to the fact that "dignity" does not appear in the U.S. Constitution,[147] and though the Supreme Court has invoked

[138] *Deck v. Missouri* (n 75).
[139] ibid [624]–[625].
[140] ibid.
[141] ibid [626]–[633].
[142] ibid [635].
[143] *See* Kim Lane Scheppele, "Aspirational and Aversive Constitutionalism: The Case for Studying Cross-Constitutional Influence through Negative Models" (2003) 1 International Journal of Constitutional Law 296, 301.
[144] *Deck v. Missouri* (n 75) [630]–[632].
[145] ibid [630]–[632].
[146] Jamal Greene, "The Anticanon" (2011) 125 Harv. L. Rev. 379; Jack M. Balkin and Sanford Levinson, "The Canons of Constitutional Law" (1998) Harv. L. Rev. 963. The anticanon in the U.S. is *Dred Scott*, *Plessy*, *Lochner*, and *Korematsu*.
[147] Daly (n 4) 2.

dignity in various decisions, it hasn't embraced it as other courts around the world have.[148] Indeed, several cases where questions of dignity were obviously at stake make no reference to it,[149] and the Court often invokes dignity to refer to the dignity of things.[150] As a result, this decision can be seen as in line with the Court's approach to dignity.

However, the Court's jurisprudence has evolved to focus on the dignity of persons in relation to several rights.[151] This approach is particularly prevalent in the Court's jurisprudence regarding the Eighth Amendment, which prohibits cruel and unusual punishment.[152] One might have expected to see such analysis here, rather than an insistence on the dignity of the court. And, indeed, this issue was present in the proceedings: the petition for Writ of Certiorari included the Eighth Amendment as one of the constitutional guarantees potentially violated,[153] and during oral arguments two Justices and the petitioner's attorney raised general concerns about dignity, dehumanization, and cruel or unusual punishment.[154]

Considering the above, the Court's focus in the judgment is all the more puzzling. This is not a case where the Court's jurisprudence was devoid of the necessary tools to illuminate the dignity-related dimensions at stake, or an instance where the issue was not brought up in the proceedings.

Regardless of the decision's evaluation from a perspective internal to the U.S. legal order, this judgment is decidedly anticanonical in a global context: it is not the law on human dignity[155] and should not be relied upon, except as a useful negative model.[156] The United States stands here as a "negative model" for current democracies, at least—but not only—as it pertains to the functioning of its criminal institutions. As Whitman notes, this is an area where American practices are considered not only harsh but barbarous,[157] and on the

[148] Cohn and Grimm (n 1) 197.

[149] Daly (n 4) 96; James Q. Whitman, "'Human Dignity' in Europe and the United States: The Social Foundations" in Georg Nolte (ed.), *European and US Constitutionalism* (CUP 2005) 108–109.

[150] Greene (n 146) 382; Judith Resnik and Julie Chi-hye Suk, "Adding Insult to Injury: Questioning the Role of Dignity in Conceptions of Sovereignty" (2003) Stan. L. Rev. 1921, 1933–1934.

[151] Resnik and Suk (n 150) 1933–1935; Vicki C. Jackson, "Constitutional Dialogue and Human Dignity: States and Transnational Constitutional Discourse" (2004) 65 Mont. L. Rev. 15, 16; Daly (n 4) 99; Ewing (n 111) 757.

[152] Carter Snead, "Human Dignity in US Law" in Marcus Düwell et al. (eds.), *The Cambridge Handbook of Human Dignity—Interdisciplinary Perspectives* (CUP 2014) 386; Resnik and Suk (n 150) 1935.

[153] Writ of certiorari.

[154] *Deck v. Missouri*, 2005 WL 589325 (U.S.), 13, 27–28, 46–49 (U.S. Oral. Arg., 2005).

[155] *See* e.g. the ECHR decision on *Affaire Gorodnitchev v. Russia* (2007) ECHR 24, paras. 103–108, where the Court found handcuffing during court proceedings to be inconsistent with the prohibition on degrading treatment.

[156] On the functions of the anticanon, *see* Greene (n 146) 382. On negative models and aversive constitutionalism, *see* Scheppele (n 143) 300.

[157] Whitman (n 149) 108–109.

deepest level, U.S. criminal justice "displays a resistance to considering the very personhood of offenders."[158]

Indeed, going back to the questions of *the who* and *the what*, we can see how the U.S. Supreme Court answered in the opposite direction of the cases I have proposed as canonical on dignity. Regarding *the question of the who*, it stressed the court's dignity and failed to expand upon the dignity of the petitioner. Neither did it take Israel's route of reaffirming the dignity of vulnerable individuals, who find themselves in the custody of the state. And regarding *the question of the what*, the Court found no dignity-related issue in shackling someone with leg irons, handcuffs, and a belly chain; it simply did not see it as a question of what kind of treatment those under the custody of the state deserve on account of their dignity. It was only a problem of whether the shackles were visible to the jury (thus violating due process), necessary due to security concerns, and a potential affront to the court's dignity.

V. Conclusion

I have argued that the canon on human dignity should reflect the most important discussions around this fundamental value of the post-WWII order and that the Israeli and Colombian decisions fulfill precisely these roles by, among other things, providing a broad view of the most distinctive questions regarding dignity: who the bearers of human dignity are and what treatment they are entitled to. In many ways, these decisions leave the door open for further discussion. For one thing, the debate on abortion continues, with both setbacks and progress: the Supreme Court of the United States overruled *Roe v. Wade* in 2023, while Colombia and Mexico further decriminalized abortion through their Constitutional and Supreme Courts respectively.[159] And the issue of targeted killing will continue to be debated well into the twenty-first century.

We were asked, after all, to think of global canons for an age of uncertainty.

158 James Q. Whitman, *Harsh Justice: Criminal Punishment and the Widening Divide between America and Europe* (OUP 2003) 9.

159 *See* USSC, *Dobbs v. Jackson Women's Health Organization* 142 S. Ct. 2228 (2022); Corte Constitucional de Colombia, Decision C-055/22 (n 67); Suprema Corte de Justicia de la Nación de México, *El sistema jurídico que regula el delito de aborto en el Código Penal Federal es inconstitucional por ser contrario al derecho a decidir de las mujeres y de las personas con capacidad de gestar,* Comunicado de Prensa No. 314, September 6, 2023. (https://www.internet2.scjn.gob.mx/red2/comunicados/noticia.asp?id=7504).

14

Lüth and the 'Objective System of Values'

From 'Limited Government' Towards an Autonomy-Based Conception of Constitutional Rights

Kai Möller[*]

I. Introduction

The German Federal Constitutional Court's *Lüth* judgment[1] of 1958 is famous for its claim that the basic rights of the Basic Law erect an 'objective system of values' (*objektive Wertordnung*) and for its acknowledgement of the horizontal effect of constitutional rights. In this chapter, I show that *Lüth* was the birth hour of the now globally dominant conception of constitutional rights, according to which rights are not primarily concerned with the limitation of the power of the state (or 'limited government') but rather with the adequate protection of the right-holder's personal autonomy, that is, the control a person has over his or her life (Section II). As an anti-canonical judgment, I introduce the US Supreme Court's judgment in *DeShaney v. Winnebago County of Social Services*, which places US rights jurisprudence in a stark contrast to that of large parts of the liberal democratic world (Section III). The final section (Section IV) spells out some of the implications of the commitment to an autonomy-based conception of rights and outlines how these have been addressed in the theoretical literature in the decades since *Lüth* was decided, including in the theories of rights as principles (Robert Alexy), judicial review as Socratic contestation and as giving effect to the fundamental right to justification (Mattias Kumm), the culture of justification (Moshe Cohen-Eliya and Iddo Porat, among others), and the global model of constitutional rights (in my own work).

* Professor of Law, Law School, London School of Economics and Political Science (LSE). Email: k.moller@lse.ac.uk.

[1] BVerfGE 7, 198 (*Lüth*). An English translation of the most significant parts of the judgment is available at https://germanlawarchive.iuscomp.org/?p = 51. The quotes from *Lüth* in this chapter are from this translation; references to paragraphs of the judgment refer to the German original.

Kai Möller, Lüth *and the 'Objective System of Values'* In: *Global Canons in an Age of Contestation.* Edited by: Sujit Choudhry, Michaela Hailbronner, and Mattias Kumm, Oxford University Press.
DOI: 10.1093/9780191956942.003.0014

II. *Lüth*

In 1950, Erich Lüth called for a boycott of the movie *Unsterbliche Geliebte* (*Immortal Beloved*) by director Veit Harlan, on the ground of the latter's involvement with the Nazi regime (Harlan was the author and director of the 1940 movie *Jud Süß* (*Süß the Jew*), an antisemitic propaganda movie commissioned by the Nazi government). The companies that produced and distributed the new movie applied for and were granted an injunction against Lüth, based on §826 of the German Civil Code (Bürgerliches Gesetzbuch), which prohibited him from repeating his call for a boycott. Lüth challenged this judgment before, ultimately, the German Federal Constitutional Court (FCC), arguing that it violated his constitutional right to freedom of expression (or 'freedom of opinion' in the language of the Basic Law). The main legal questions were whether Lüth's right to freedom of expression was applicable in the context of a private law dispute and, if so, whether it had been violated by the lower court's judgment.

The FCC's judgment of 1958 is significant in three regards. First, it held that the Basic Law set up an 'objective system of values'. Second, it specified the implications of this in the context of the applicability of the basic rights in a private law context, the so-called 'Drittwirkung' or horizontal effect of rights. Third, it set out certain basic doctrines regarding the right to freedom of expression. What made the judgment a rightful part of a *global* canon on human rights are the claims about the objective system of values and horizontal effect.

A. The Basic Law as 'erect[ing] an objective system of values'

The FCC began the judgment with some general reflections on the Basic Law. It first repeated the conventional idea that constitutional rights protect the individual from the state:

> There is no doubt that the main purpose of the basic rights is to protect the individual's sphere of freedom against encroachment by public power: they are the citizens' bulwark against the state.[2]

This statement is followed, in the next paragraph, by a qualification, and this is the best known passage from the judgment:

[2] Para. 24.

> But far from being a value-free system, the Constitution erects an objective system of values in its section on basic rights. This system of values, centring on the freedom of the human being to develop in society, must apply as a constitutional axiom throughout the whole legal system: it must direct and inform legislation, administration, and judicial decision. It naturally influences private law as well; no rule of private law may conflict with it, and all such rules must be construed in accordance with its spirit.[3]

As I will explain in the next section, the terminology that the Court uses here is confusing and unfortunate. But even a cursory glance tells us that the Court takes the view that constitutional rights do more than protect people against the state, and that the analytical move which makes this possible is to regard them as being part of a 'system of values'.

B. Horizontal Effect

The Court goes on to explain how the impact of the constitution on private law comes about. It cites the 'extreme'[4] views on this issue proposed in the scholarly literature, according to which rights either have no, or alternatively full and direct, applicability in private law, and then chooses what presents itself as a middle route (although it produces the same results as direct applicability), an approach that has become known as 'indirect horizontal effect' ('mittelbare Drittwirkung'): there is no direct applicability of constitutional rights in private law, but private law has to be interpreted or construed in the spirit of the constitution.[5] In particular, German private law contains many so-called 'general clauses' (*Generalklauseln*) which guide the interpretation of private law. These general clauses, the FCC claims, should be regarded as 'points of entry'[6] (*Einbruchstellen*) for basic rights into private law. Note that the Court does not simply say that rights must be 'taken into account', implying that if in a given case private law cannot adequately be interpreted in line with the requirements of the constitution, then so be it. On the contrary, the Court is clear in the

[3] Para. 25.

[4] Para. 23.

[5] While this approach presents itself as a middle route, the significance between direct and indirect horizontal effect is much smaller than commonly assumed; see Mattias Kumm and Victor Ferreres Comella, 'What is so Special about Constitutional Rights in Private Litigation? A Comparative Analysis of the Function of State Action Requirements and Indirect Effect', in András Sajó and RenátaUitz (eds), *The Constitution in Private Relations: Expanding Constitutionalism* (Eleven, 2005).

[6] Para. 27.

quote above that 'no rule of private law may conflict with [the objective order of values erected by the Constitution]'.[7] Correspondingly, a judgment which fails to observe the 'modifications of the private law'[8] which result from rights violates the constitution and can be challenged by way of a constitutional complaint (*Verfassungsbeschwerde*).[9]

III. The 'objective system of values'

Lüth is well-known for being the first judgment that acknowledges the existence of horizontal effect and for its claim that the constitution 'erects an objective system of values'. What this 'objective system of values' means is far from clear, though, and the terminology is unfortunate. Let us consider a few possibilities.

A. Values

The FCC contrasts the 'objective system of values' with 'a value-free system'. From the context, it is clear that this 'value-free system' would be one which regards rights as protecting 'the individual's sphere of freedom against the encroachment of public power' and therefore as 'the citizen's bulwark against the state'. But this contrast between value-free and value-bound does not work, for two reasons. First, given that constitutional rights are essentially human rights turned into positive law, they are of course a matter of values, and as such creatures of morality. Thus, there cannot be a conception of constitutional rights that is 'value free'. Second, the idea that the FCC mentions as an example of a 'value free system', namely the protection of the individual from the government, too, is clearly value-bound in that it claims that it is morally important to give people some protection from their governments. So we cannot make sense of the FCC's claim by contrasting a 'value-free' and a 'value-based' conception of rights. Rather, the 'objective system of values' approach pursues *different* values than the 'citizens' bulwark against the state' approach. So the question is not whether this model is value-bound but what its values are.

[7] Para. 25.
[8] Para. 28.
[9] Para. 28.

B. Subjective and Objective

The 'system of values' that the Basic Law erects is, in the view of the FCC, 'objective'. German commentators often insist on the significance of a distinction between 'subjective' rights and 'objective' law (possibly because in German, the term 'Recht' refers to both 'law' and 'right').[10] Now, obviously 'rights' and 'law' are two different things. However, in the view of the FCC, the 'objective' system of values is not only 'objective' law but creates 'subjective' rights as well. The Court makes it perfectly clear in *Lüth* that a private law judgment which fails to give effect to basic rights is not only 'objectively' wrong but also, 'subjectively', violates basic rights and can accordingly be challenged by way of constitutional complaint. Thus, the distinction between subjective and objective is a doctrinal technicality without corresponding substantive relevance and in any case cannot explain why the *Lüth* judgment should be part of a global canon.

C. The Turn From Limited Government to an Autonomy-Based Conception of Rights

The real significance of the idea of the objective system of values lies in its rejection of the once uncontroversial idea that the point of rights is to protect us from our governments, and its corresponding endorsement of the idea that the point of rights is to protect personal autonomy. Thus, rights are not about *disabling* (the government) but about *enabling* citizens to live their lives autonomously.[11]

The distinction between negative and positive freedom helps illuminate this idea. Negative freedom, or 'freedom from', regards freedom as a matter of being 'left alone': a person is free if nobody interferes with her. Positive freedom, or 'freedom to', is about being in control of one's life: a person is free to the extent that she is able to give her life meaning and direction. Positive freedom is often referred to as personal autonomy.[12]

The conventional conception of rights that the FCC rejects in *Lüth* is about negative freedom from the government, or 'limited government'. Under this

[10] See, e.g., Oliver Lepsius, 'The Standard-Setting Power', in Matthias Jestaedt et al., *The German Federal Constitutional Court: The Court Without Limits*, translated by Jeff Seitzer (Oxford University Press, 2020), ch. 3, 84–89.

[11] Kai Möller, 'Two Conceptions of Positive Liberty: Towards an Autonomy-Based Theory of Constitutional Rights', 29 (2009) *Oxford Journal of Legal Studies* 757, 758.

[12] Kai Möller, *The Global Model of Constitutional Rights* (Oxford University Press, 2012), 29–30.

conception, rights entitle an individual to be 'left alone' by the government in certain areas. For example, the government must not, or not unjustifiably, interfere with the individual's life, liberty, physical integrity, expression, religious practice, and so on. The underlying moral concern of this approach to rights appears to be the view that the government is the greatest threat to freedom and that therefore its power has to be limited. Note that the limited government conception can*not* be based on the view that the areas of freedom that it recognizes as worthy of protection are valuable for the individual. If the value of these areas for individuals was the primary reason for protecting them, then these important values would have to be protected not only against state interference but also against private interference, and in fact they would have to be protected not only against interference, but individuals' ability to enjoy them would have to be actively promoted. This, however, is precisely what the limited government conception cannot achieve and why the FCC is so keen to abandon or at least supplement it with its theory of rights as creating a system of values.

The 'objective system of values' embraces the state's duty to protect people not only from the state but also from other private individuals, as well as the state's duty to actively promote the values underlying rights. Now we can make sense of the claim that the basic rights erect a system of 'values'. What is valuable is 'the freedom of the individual to develop in society'.[13] The focus is not on limiting the government, but on creating the conditions of individual development. This is a commitment to personal autonomy, which has a number of doctrinal implications.

First, if the constitution is at its core about a commitment to creating the conditions of individual development or personal autonomy, then it follows naturally that horizontal effect of rights must be acknowledged: the areas of autonomy that are important for individual development can be threatened not only by the state but also by private actors relying on private law.[14] *Lüth* is a good example: Lüth's freedom to develop in society was threatened not only by a government potentially censoring his speech, but also by a private company that relied on private law to stop him from expressing himself.

Second, a commitment to the idea of rights as based on personal autonomy necessitates not only horizontal effect but also *positive obligations* (as they are called, for example, in the jurisprudence of the European Court of Human Rights (ECtHR)) or protective duties (as they are called in German

[13] Para. 25.
[14] Möller (n 12), 35–37.

constitutional law).[15] The idea is that the state is under an obligation to take active steps to protect people from threats to the sphere of autonomy protected by constitutional rights. Thus, states are under an obligation to protect people from the criminal acts of others that threaten, for example, their life or physical integrity.[16] They have to protect a person's picture against abuse by others[17] and demonstrations from counter-demonstrations.[18] It is interesting to note in this context that the ECtHR often does not even distinguish whether a case involves negative or positive obligations. Take, for example, the case of *Hatton v. United Kingdom*,[19] which was about night flights at Heathrow airport which created noise pollution and affected some residents' sleep. The case could be construed as being about negative obligations (the UK government had given permission to conduct night flights to the private company that operated the airport) or as being about positive obligations (the UK had failed to prevent the private company that operated the airport from allowing night flights). The ECtHR simply remarked that '[w]hether the case is analysed in terms of a positive duty on the State to take reasonable and appropriate measures to secure the applicants' rights under para. 1 of Art. 8 or in terms of an interference by a public authority to be justified in accordance with para. 2, the applicable principles are broadly similar'.[20] This indicates that the view that rights protect personal autonomy (as opposed to limiting the government) is firmly entrenched in European, indeed global, legal thought today: if rights are about autonomy, then indeed, the distinction between positive and negative obligations is a mere technicality without substantive implications for the outcome of the case.

Finally, regarding rights as based on personal autonomy also create the necessity for the acknowledgement of *social rights*: these rights protect the *preconditions* of autonomy.[21] Obviously, a person who has no access to food, drink, housing, healthcare, or education cannot, or only with much more difficulty and less likelihood of success, live his or her life autonomously. Thus, the increasing acknowledgement of social rights over the last decades is not an isolated occurrence but is indeed required by the turn from negative to positive freedom that *Lüth* initiated.

To conclude this section: the 'objective system of values' is best understood as pointing to a conception of fundamental rights that regards them as based

[15] ibid, 37–38.
[16] See, e.g., *Osman v. United Kingdom*, (2009) 29 EHRR 245.
[17] *Von Hannover v. Germany*, (2005) 40 EHRR 1, para. 115.
[18] *Plattform 'Ärzte für das Leben' v. Austria*, (1991) 13 EHRR 204, para. 31.
[19] *Hatton v. United Kingdom*, (2003) 37 EHRR 28.
[20] ibid, para. 119.
[21] Möller (n 12), 38.

on personal autonomy—the 'freedom of the human being to develop in society', as opposed to the limitation of the power of the state. This starting point inevitably leads to the acknowledgement of horizontal effect (because private people relying on private law can also affect the right-holder's autonomy), positive obligations (because autonomy can also be threatened by private people or even by natural occurrences such as pandemics), and social rights (which protect preconditions of autonomy). In order to assess the appeal of this idea, this chapter will now turn to the discussion of an anti-core case, the US Supreme Court case of *DeShaney v. Winnebago County of Social Services*, before returning to the idea of the objective order of values in Section IV, where the implications of the shift initiated by *Lüth* will be considered.

IV. An Anti-Canonical Case: *DeShaney v. Winnebago County Department of Social Services*

Joshua DeShaney was a little boy who was being physically abused by his father, Randy DeShaney. The Winnebago Department of Social Services (DSS) was involved with the family at several stages over a period of roughly two years, when Joshua was between 2 and 4 years old. The case worker did not take action when she was informed on several occasions that Joshua was treated for suspicious injuries at the emergency room, or when she made monthly visits to the family home and noticed suspicious injuries and other worrying facts, such as that Joshua had not been enrolled in school. She merely 'dutifully recorded these incidents in her files, along with her continuing suspicions that someone in the DeShaney household was physically abusing Joshua, but she did nothing more'.[22] Eventually, his father beat Joshua so badly that he fell into a coma, and while his life was saved at the time, he suffered permanent brain damage and it was predicted that he would spend the rest of his life in an institution 'for the profoundly retarded'[23] (in fact, he was later adopted and died in 2015 at the age of 36).

Joshua and his mother sued Winnebago County, the DSS, and various individual employees, arguing that their failure to protect Joshua from his father's violence had violated his constitutional right under the Due Process Clause of the Fourteenth Amendment of the US Constitution, which states that '[n]o

[22] *DeShaney v. Winnebago County Department of Social Services*, (1989) 489 US 189, 193 (Rehnquist CJ).
[23] ibid, 193.

State shall ... deprive any person of life, liberty, or property, without due process of law'. According to the precedents, it was clear that this clause protected not only a procedural right but also included a substantive guarantee of life, liberty, and property. The question before the Court was whether the Due Process Clause could be violated by a failure on the part of the state to protect people. The Court answered in the negative. Rehnquist CJ provided two reasons, one textual and one historical. Regarding the text of the Fourteenth Amendment, he stated that '[t]he Clause is phrased as a limitation on the State's power to act, not as a guarantee of certain minimal levels of safety and security'.[24] And regarding history, he argued:

> Like its counterpart in the Fifth Amendment, the Due Process Clause of the Fourteenth Amendment was intended to prevent government 'from abusing [its] power, or employing it as an instrument of oppression,' [citation omitted] ... Its purpose was to protect the people from the State, not to ensure that the State protected them from each other. The Framers were content to leave the extent of governmental obligation in the latter area to the democratic political processes.[25]

So, in this case, the US Supreme Court rejects the idea of a general doctrine of positive obligations, and its main reason is that the point of the Due Process Clause is to prevent government from abusing its power and to protect people from the state. This contrasts with the German FCC's view in *Lüth*, where the Court first pointed out, similar to the spirit of the US Supreme Court, that the purpose of the constitution was 'to protect the individual's sphere of freedom against encroachment by public power: they are the citizens' bulwark against the state', but then went on to stress that, in addition, the constitution erected an objective system of values. Such a 'system' or, as I would say, autonomy-based conception of rights, is absent in US constitutional law, which relies instead on the idea of limited government.

It should be noted that this point was uncontroversial among the justices deciding *DeShaney*. While there were three dissenting justices who would have ruled in Joshua's favour, none of them proposed a general duty of positive obligations. Rather, they claimed that the existence of Wisconsin's child protection programme constituted an active intervention by the state because it relieved other citizens of their obligation to do anything further about

[24] ibid, 195.
[25] ibid, 196.

suspected child abuse than report it to the DSS.[26] This is an interesting argument; however, it stops short of embracing anything resembling an 'objective order of values' and construes the case as being about state activity, not state passivity. Furthermore, it would, if it had prevailed, set a questionable incentive for states to discontinue their respective child protection programmes in order to avoid liability: precisely by virtue of not creating a positive obligation as such, it would have remained possible for states to move out of the area of child protection altogether, whereas a general positive obligation would have required states to take active steps to protect children from abuse.

DeShaney illustrates in stark terms that the conception of rights and freedom that we choose *matters*. Whether rights are primarily or exclusively concerned with the limitation of the power of the state or whether, alternatively, they should be understood as being based on the value of personal autonomy is not merely an interesting but ultimately practically irrelevant question to be discussed over drinks in the pub or as a theoretical puzzle in academic ivory towers. Rather, it has consequences. The challenge that proponents of the US model or substantive critics of the 'objective order of values' will have to overcome is to provide a convincing or at least plausible answer to the following question: given that human and constitutional rights include a promise of freedom to every person, how can it be consistent with this promise of freedom for a child to be beaten into a coma by his father while the state knows what is going on but does not intervene? I do not mean this primarily as an appeal to sympathy and compassion that Blackmun J demanded in his well-known dissent ('Poor Joshua!').[27] Rather, I am stating an analytical and moral question about the constitutional promise of freedom.

There are a number of potential answers to this question, although none of them are fully convincing. First, one could turn to history and claim that as a matter of history, the constitutional conception of freedom protects only negative freedom from the government. But leaving aside the fact that in the last six decades, the constitutional history of much of the Western world has by and large followed the path set out by *Lüth*, history alone cannot determine moral truth, and it is possible that this particular aspect of history turns out to be morally indefensible. Second, one might argue that governments remain the greatest threat to freedom and that any threats that emanate from non-governmental actors exist and occasionally materialize (as they did for Joshua DeShaney) can be ignored from a constitutional perspective in order to

[26] ibid, 209–210 (Brennan J, dissenting).
[27] ibid, 213 (Blackmun J, dissenting).

focus on the bigger and more important problem of the governmental abuse of power. However, one problem with this view is that constitutional protection is not a scarce resource in this regard. There is no reason why it should not be possible to effectively protect people from their governments *and also* to 'protect them from each other' (in Rehnquist's terminology[28]). Third, it could be argued that regarding rights as based on autonomy interests inevitably leads to a great expansion of the scope of judicial review and thus will have ripple effects. Perhaps the effect that would be most at odds with how US constitutional law is currently conceptualized is that taking seriously the idea that rights are about personal autonomy is the first step on a path that leads to the acknowledgement of social rights. Another change that would be necessitated by the adoption of an autonomy-based conception of rights might be that the use of balancing and proportionality, endorsed by much of the liberal democratic world but resisted by the US, would become inevitable. All these considerations ought to be taken seriously; however, they offer no principled argument against the autonomy-based conception which, as history has shown, is not only dominant in liberal democracies around the world but also clearly workable in practice.

V. Further Developments

A. *Elfes*: A General Right to Freedom of Action

My claim is that *Lüth* is the birth hour of the approach to constitutional rights that has been widely endorsed until today. In order to demonstrate this point, I have to add a further 'ingredient' to my story: rights inflation. In Germany, this was brought about by the FCC's *Elfes* judgment in 1957,[29] just one year before *Lüth* was decided. That case is well known for the FCC's claim that Article 2(1) of the Basic Law, which protects every person's right to freely develop his or her personality, should be interpreted broadly, as a general right to freedom of action. Thus, even activities such as feeding pigeons in a public park[30] or horse-riding in a forest[31] are protected by constitutional rights, meaning that they can be restricted only if the restriction is proportionate.

[28] ibid, 196 (Rehnquist CJ).
[29] BVerfGE 6, 32 (*Elfes*).
[30] BVerfGE 54, 143 (*Pigeon Feeding*).
[31] BVerfGE 80, 137 (*Riding in the Woods*).

Elfes is a renowned judgment but perhaps not part of a *global* canon; it has received less attention internationally than *Lüth*. But while other courts have not engaged with or adopted *Elfes*'s reasoning, in substance the move towards a broad scope of rights is a global phenomenon. Courts have often struggled with the task of delineating those interests that ought to be protected by constitutional rights from those which ought not, and frequently they have erred on the side of including them as protected.[32] For example, the ECtHR takes an expansive approach to the scope of Article 8 (the right to respect for private life) and has stated that the right not to be 'directly and seriously affected by noise and other pollution' is protected by it.[33] The consequence of being generous with regard to the scope of rights does not imply, of course, that applicants will win their cases more often. Rather, it means that any interference with the prima facie right will trigger the *duty of justification*. The broad scope of rights is therefore an indicator of the shift towards a 'culture of justification',[34] which claims that *all* acts of the state which place a burden on a person—and not just those interfering with one of a number of narrowly defined rights—ought to be substantively justifiable and that it is ultimately the role of the highest court applying the bill of rights to assess their justifiability.

B. *Lüth* and Contemporary Rights Theory

Taking *Lüth* and *Elfes* together, we can see more clearly the implications of this new approach for rights adjudication. Both cases led to an expansion of the scope of judicial review: *Elfes* held that freedom has to be understood in the broadest possible sense (as being about the freedom to do as one pleases) and *Lüth*'s implications are that this freedom operates against the state and affects the relationship between private persons, and that additionally it creates positive obligations on the state to protect it. Constitutional rights are therefore in play and the duty of justification is triggered whenever an act (or omission) by the state has implications for an individual's ability to live his life autonomously. Consequently, almost all acts (and omissions) by the state will affect someone's constitutional rights, trigger the duty of justification, and be reviewable by the constitutional or supreme court applying the bill of rights.

[32] Möller (n 12), 3–5.

[33] *Hatton v. United Kingdom* (n 19), para. 96.

[34] On the culture of justification, see Moshe Cohen-Eliya and Iddo Porat, *Proportionality and Constitutional Culture* (Cambridge University Press, 2013), ch. 6; Kai Möller, 'Justifying the Culture of Justification', 17 (2019) *International Journal of Constitutional Law* 1078.

This raises the risk of juristocracy: if more or less all policies and acts are reviewable, what's left for the democratic (majoritarian) institutions to decide? The answer to this question has to do with the intensity of review and more specifically the distinction between reasonableness and correctness. Under the culture of justification, an act by the state which requires justification need not be 'correct' (the 'one right answer', the 'best possible policy') to survive judicial scrutiny. Rather, it must merely be one of a range of reasonable answers.[35] The proportionality test that is used around the world to determine whether the act in question is justifiable is now widely conceptualized as a test of reasonableness.[36] Accordingly, constitutional rights entitle every person to be treated in a way that is reasonably justifiable.[37]

The conception of rights that results has been given different names in the literature: Robert Alexy's theory of rights is known under the label of 'rights as principles';[38] Mattias Kumm has proposed his theory of judicial review as 'Socratic contestation' and also referred to it as institutionalizing a 'right to justification'.[39] Others, including Moshe Cohen-Eliya and Iddo Porat, have referred to it as the 'culture of justification'.[40] In my work, I have used the term 'the global model of constitutional rights'.[41] These theorists and theories share largely the same moral commitments with regard to rights but highlight different facets. Alexy's theory of rights as principles stresses their non-conclusive nature and the centrality of proportionality analysis which has to be employed when rights/principles clash. The terms 'the right to justification' and 'the culture of justification' emphasize that there is one foundational right underlying the enumerated rights in a constitution, namely the 'right to justification', and the centrality of providing justifications for all state action that affects the right-holder in a relevant way (but perhaps underemphasize *Lüth*'s lesson that not only actions but also omissions need to be justified). The term 'Socratic contestation' highlights that courts adjudicating rights questions do not pursue a substantive agenda but rather focus on asking questions and assessing the plausibility (reasonableness) of answers that they are provided with by the state. My term of the 'global model' of constitutional rights points to the fact that this conception of rights has global appeal as opposed to being of relevance

[35] Mattias Kumm, 'The Idea of Socratic Contestation and the Right to Justification: The Point of Rights-Based Proportionality Review', (2010) 4 *Law & Ethics of Human Rights* 141, 168–170; Möller (n 12), 117–123.

[36] Kumm, ibid.

[37] Kumm, ibid; Möller (n 12).

[38] Robert Alexy, *A Theory of Constitutional Rights* (Oxford University Press, 2002).

[39] Kumm (n 35).

[40] Cohen-Eliya and Porat (n 34); see also Möller (n 12).

[41] Möller (n 12).

only in a particular jurisdiction or region (such as Europe). But despite the different facets highlighted by the various labels, the underlying substantive views are similar and belong to the same school of thought. Their central *elements* are, first, to regard rights as 'values' or, as I would prefer to say, based on personal autonomy interests; second, to view their scope as expansive; and, third, to endorse proportionality and to conceptualize it as a reasonableness test. The *moral point* of this practice is to give effect to each person's foundational right to justification: a right to be treated by the state in ways that are reasonably justifiable to him or her.

VI. Conclusion

Lüth's central claim is that the constitution sets up an 'objective system of values'. We should not dwell for too long on the unfortunate terminology: the real significance lies in the substantive idea proposed, which this chapter has interpreted as the move from a conception of constitutional rights that centres on limited government towards one that places the autonomy of the individual at its heart. I have suggested that this move is not only significant but also correct: regarding the freedom that constitutional rights grant to every person as being exclusively about negative freedom from the government leads to results that strike me as unjust and unjustifiable, as seen, for example, in the *DeShaney* case. By contrast, regarding freedom as being about personal autonomy avoids these problems and sets out an attractive constitutional conception of freedom centring on 'the freedom of the individual to develop in society'. *Lüth* and, to a lesser extent, *Elfes* laid the foundation for the conception of rights that is widely endorsed today not only in Germany but around the globe and that theorists capture with labels and concepts such as rights as principles, the global model of constitutional rights, the right to justification and the culture of justification, and judicial review as Socratic contestation.

15
Global Proportionality Canons from Latin America

Francisca Pou Giménez[*]

I. Introduction

As has been often remarked, proportionality analysis is a central component of contemporary global constitutionalism.[1] The constitutions passed after World War II include generous catalogues of rights, in pursuit of a model of constitutional democracy where political majorities are meant to observe and realize an ambitious substantive program. Because this program is usually framed in terms of principles which require optimization and mutual harmonization in specific cases, its enforcement has propitiated generalized resort to proportionality analysis.

Rights-centered constitutionalism acquired further centrality in the decade of the 90s, with the restoration of democracy in Central and Eastern Europe, and Latin America. Constitutions in these countries were conceived as documents with direct normative force, and constitutional courts were given ample rights-enforcing responsibilities—in Latin America, with the help of specific complaints channels for the guarantee of rights.[2] Another transition that occurred roughly at the same time was the one in South Africa (whose constitution includes a limitations clause framed in terms of proportionality),[3] while in

* Senior Researcher, Institute for Legal Research, National Autonomous University of Mexico (UNAM, Mexico). I am grateful for the feedback received from the editors and other participants in the associated workshop, especially to Mattias Kumm, whose comments on an earlier draft led to a substantial reorientation of the chapter.

[1] David Law, "Generic Constitutional Law" (2005) 89 Minn. L. Rev. 652; Kai Möller, *The Global Model of Constitutional Rights* (OUP 2012); Vicki C. Jackson and Mark Tushnet (eds.), *Proportionality. New Frontiers and Challenges* (CUP 2017).

[2] Rodrigo Uprimny, "The Recent Transformation of Constitutional Law in Latin America: Trends and Challenges" in César Rodriguez Garavito (ed.), *Law and Society in Latin America. A New Map* (Routledge 2015); Francisca Pou Giménez, "Supreme and Constitutional Courts: Directions in Constitutional Justice" in Rachel Sieder, Karina Ansolabehere, and Tatiana Alfonso Sierra (eds.), *Handbook of Law and Society in Latin America* (Routledge 2019).

[3] Richard Stacey, "Proportionality Analysis by the South African Constitutional Court" in Mordechai Kremnitzer, Talya Steiner, and Andrej Lang (eds.), *Proportionality in Action* (CUP 2020).

Francisca Pou Giménez, *Global Proportionality Canons from Latin America* In: *Global Canons in an Age of Contestation*. Edited by: Sujit Choudhry, Michaela Hailbronner, and Mattias Kumm, Oxford University Press.
 DOI: 10.1093/9780191956942.003.0015

Israel, a process of constitutionalization boosted by the Barak Supreme Court firmly established sophisticated versions of proportionality analysis at the center of constitutional practice.[4] As rights constitutionalism appeared, in different variants, in new places—Taiwan, Hong Kong, or South Korea, to name a few—a parallel use of proportionality analysis may be detected.[5]

These same past decades witnessed a process of constitutional "opening" that changed the position of international law in national systems and generated scenarios of multi-level protection of rights, giving centrality to rights adjudication in international human rights courts, where proportionality has also been used. In the context of the European Convention on Human Rights, some rights are codified under explicit limitations clauses, making resort to proportionality analysis by the Strasbourg Court a natural move.[6] In the context of the Inter-American System of Human Rights, the Court in San José made at the beginning limited use of proportionality methodology because the sort of cases it confronted at that time, involving mass atrocities and arbitrariness, called for a resolution on the basis of categorical rules. Over time, however, the Court has moved to different topic areas and come to address cases that require balancing or optimization to solve conflicts of rights, or enforce mandates of non-discrimination, non-retrogression, and maximum use of available resources—thus developing a relevant body of proportionality-based case law.[7]

The theorization of proportionality by the German professor Robert Alexy has been influential worldwide. This has also contributed to spread the methodology, which in many occasions has interacted with pre-existing traditions of reasonability and proportionality scrutiny. There has been scholarship developed by his students outside Europe, frequently exploring or pushing

[4] Aharon Barak, *Proportionality. Constitutional Rights and their Limitation* (CUP 2012).

[5] Kelley Loper, "Protecting Human Rights in a Mixed Constitution Context: The Case of Hong Kong" (Conference paper, The 16th International Human Rights Researchers' Workshop: Mixed Constitutions and Human Rights, Virtual Conference, College of Law and Business, Tel Aviv, Israel, 2-4 May 2021, unpublished manuscript, on file with the author). Alex Stone Sweet and Jud Mathews, "Proportionality and Rights Protection in Asia. Hong Kong, Malaysia, South Korea, Taiwan—Whither Singapore?" (2017) 29 SAcLJ 774.

[6] Articles 8–11 of the European Convention on Human Rights are enshrined with reference to the limits "prescribed by law and are necessary in a democratic society in the interests of public safety, for the protection of public order, health or morals, or for the protection of the rights and freedoms of others" (or similar formulae).

[7] Silvia Serrano Guzmán, "Proportionality in the Adjudication of Equality and Non-discrimination Cases in the Inter-American System" in Francisca Pou Giménez, Laura Clérico, and Esteban Restrepo Saldarriaga (eds.), *Proportionality and Transformation: Theory and Practice from Latin America* (CUP 2022); Julieta Rossi, "Obligation of Progressivity, Non-Retrogression and Maximum of Available Resources: Agreements and Disagreements between the Inter-American Court of Human Rights and the United Nations Committee on Economic, Social and Cultural Rights," ibid.

the methodology in new directions, in dialogue with developments in non-European courts.

Despite the global tide I have described so far, the global descriptions of proportionality as a methodology, and the rulings that are flagged up to illustrate and critically analyze how it operates, are extracted from a handful of countries not representative enough of proportionality theory and practice worldwide.[8] Proportionality scholarship in English portraying its global expansion focus mainly on Germany, the European Court of Human Rights, and the jurisdictions whose rulings are available in English—South Africa, Israel, India, and Canada.[9]

This leaves in the shadow important dimensions of the practice, and supports contentions about global traits that are not always sufficiently comprehensive. It has been suggested, for instance, that proportionality is difficult to use in the domain of social rights, when in Latin America it is ordinarily used—and theorized—in relation to the enforcement of this sort of rights, as well as in relation to mandates of progressivity and non-retrogression.[10] It is also sometimes suggested that proportionality has little to say about questions of federalism and the division of powers, but in Latin America there is an important tradition of reviewing under proportionality emergency measures adopted by the executive.[11] It has been further suggested that there is a contrast between "reasonability" deferential traditions, as exemplified by the one in the UK, and "proportionality" non-deferential, Alexian-inspired traditions, where courts examine necessity and proportionality in the narrow sense, subjecting public action to far stricter controls.[12] Yet in Latin America, there are traditions of reasonability review that include an exam of necessity, and traditions of review that do not follow the three stages canonical in the European tradition,

[8] Virgilio Afonso da Silva, "How Global is Global Constitutionalism? Comments on Kai Möller's The Global Model of Constitutional Rights" (2014) 10 Jerus. Rev. Leg. Stud. 175; Vanessa MacDonnell, "The Reductionism of Global Models of Constitutional Rights" (2018) 12 Law Ethics Hum. Rights 73.

[9] See, e.g., Niels Petersen, *Proportionality and Judicial Activism: Fundamental Rights Adjudication in Canada, Germany and South Africa* (CUP 2017); Aharon Barak (n 4); Jackson and Tushnet (n 1); Möller (n 1); Víctor Ferreres, "Beyond Proportionality" in Gary Jacobsohn and Miguel Schor (eds.), *Comparative Constitutional Theory* (Edward Elgar 2018).

[10] Stephen Gardbaum, "Positive and Horizontal Rights: Proportionality's Next Frontier or a Bridge Too Far?" in Jackson and Tushnet (n 1). See Federico De Fazio, *Teoría principialista de los derechos sociales* (Marcial Pons 2019), Laura Clérico, *Derechos y proporcionalidad: violaciones por acción, por insuficiencia y por regresión* (IECEQ 2018).

[11] See Antonio Barreto and Jorge González Jácome, "Between Exception and Transition: Proportionality and Necessity in the Colombian Quest for Peace" in Pou Giménez, Clérico, and Restrepo Saldarriaga (n 7).

[12] Katharine Young, "Proportionality, Reasonableness and Economic and Social Rights" in Jackson and Tushnet (n 1).

or are applied by courts in an unstructured way, but include strict balancing or evaluation of alternatives.[13]

In this chapter, I begin by briefly discussing questions to be considered when thinking about enriching the global canon on proportionality with contributions from Latin America, versus the slightly different enterprise of building a regional, Latin American canon. I will also comment on the distinctive status of the Colombian Court in the region, and justify the need to include an illustration of paradigms that are minoritarian but representative of alternative traditions and trends—like those we find in Argentina. Afterwards, I identify a few rulings that should join the global canon on different grounds: methodologic expansion, functional expansion, and thematic expansion.

First, *methodological expansion*. Several rulings of the Colombian Court construct a methodology in dialogue with both the German Alexian-inspired test, and the U.S. tradition of differentiated scrutiny: the integrated proportionality test. The Court expounds the fundamentals of this approach in C-093/01, and provides an interesting complement in the more recent C-345/19. Methodologically, attention must also be drawn to what some scholars have called, as we will momentarily see, the "integrated retrogression test", whose second dimension is a strict proportionality test, used by the Colombian Court to ascertain whether the mandate of non-regressivity in the enjoyment of social rights has been violated.

Second, *functional expansion*. While in the North proportionality has mainly been used to assess public or private *excessive* action, Latin American adjudication illustrates how it applies to public or private action denounced as *insufficient*. Whether an action is sufficient may be assessed under proportionality analysis alone, or in combination with the notion of a minimum core or other notions. In Latin America, proportionality has been further used to assess the constitutionality of an intermediate category: *regressive* action (a positive action which suppresses previously acquired levels of rights enjoyment or fulfillment, but functionally susceptible to be described as insufficient action, if it fails to reach the appropriate/optimum level, in view of intervening empirical and normative circumstances). We will finally see how proportionality has been used to make the validity of a statute conditional on it being applied with perfect proportionality at the administrative stage, guaranteeing integral rights optimization. To illustrate these three instances of functional expansion, we will focus on the Quisberth Castro case, where the Supreme Court of Argentina

[13] Laura Clérico and Federico De Fazio, "The Standard Reasonableness Test and Proportionality in Argentina: A Matter of Interactions" in Pou Giménez, Clérico, and Restrepo Saldarriaga (n 7).

concluded that Buenos Aires's housing policy violated the right to adequate housing; the Labor Law Reform case (C-038/04), where the Colombian Court used proportionality to evaluate statutory retrogression in the socioeconomic domain; and the Bodily Interventions case (C-822/2005), also from Colombia, on body intrusions during criminal investigations.

Third, *thematic expansion*. Latin American adjudication offers to global practice instances of the application of proportionality analysis in areas, or in connection with topics and provisions that have not been central in global portraits. We will first focus on the iconic Justice and Peace ruling (C-370/06), which illustrates how proportionality plays out in "big" politics, in connection with a rigorously contemporary legal field (transitional justice), raising questions that have generated intense political and scholarly debate (the punishment of serious human rights violations), and involving a right that many would be tempted to consider non-justiciable (the right to peace). A second big area of thematic expansion occurs, of course, in the domain of social and economic rights. The bulk of proportionality-based adjudication in the North is in the area of civil and political rights, something that makes examples of its application in connection with social and economic rights most valuable.

While I analytically distinguish the three dimensions (methodological, functional and thematic) to identify various potential sources of value and canonical status, they are cumulatively present in some rulings. Thus, the Colombian cases that enforce social and economic rights using the integrated retrogression test to make sure there are no unconstitutional setbacks in rights enjoyment exemplify simultaneously and cumulatively the methodological, functional, and thematic expansion I have in mind. Most of the time, however, reference to more than one ruling is necessary when documenting innovation. In contrast with the U.S. Supreme Court, Latin American courts issue thousands of judgments every year; the expectation of finding big canonical rulings, selected from among a limited collection of icons of case law, is difficult in that context. Cases are, moreover, usually registered by number, not name, something that makes them, formally, less memorable.

The survey ends by focusing on a largely anticanonical ruling: the Salamina ruling, also by the Constitutional Court of Colombia (T-091/18). This ruling innovates on the methodology of proportionality and reasonability, but in ways that enter into conflict with the point of the practice,[14] since in its context proportionality analysis is used not to control state action/inaction, but to

[14] Mattias Kumm, "The Idea of Socratic Contestation and the Right to Justification: The Point of Rights-Based Proportionality Review" (2010) 4 Law Ethics Hum. Rights 142.

restrain the claims that citizens can elevate in the name of the constitution. The judgment apparently forgets that methodological innovation is not an end in itself, generating results that put under menace the rights and the special protection mandates for children and people in situation of disadvantage.

II. Latin America in the Global and the Regional Canon

It is important to clarify which rationales and assumptions are behind the selection of cases I present in what follows. As Michaela Hailbronner has underlined, under a "functional" understanding, a global constitutional canon is a selection of texts and materials that contributes to create "a platform for shared conversation" and helps define a discipline that intends to be "both self-consciously normative and critical."[15]

Yet within the broad margins of this appropriate demarcation, several shared conversations may be sustained. One of these conversations can be grounded on specific Latin American concerns, such as the desire to recover the roots of proportionality in the region, identify turning points in its use in different countries, signal important landmarks in the context of certain political or legal debates, or illustrate points of convergence with constitutional practices abroad. Another conversation can, by contrast, focus on exercises of proportionality-based adjudication that enlarge the confines of the global. In this latter case, Latin American rulings are not meant to illustrate the "translation" or contextual adaptation of the "global" to the "local," or to emphasize convergence—beyond the fact that the use of proportionality marks an obvious point of convergence—but rather to help construct a new global, more faithful to the name. These rulings stand for areas of theory and practice that must be included for a portrayal of global practices to be accurate and representative. They represent instantiations of the global that diminish the asymmetric dichotomies that have pervaded comparative law from its inception, and still weight in today—implicitly or explicitly transforming developments in certain countries into definitional archetypes, and evaluative yardsticks for the rest.[16]

The selection of rulings for a regional Latin American canon and for a global canon is therefore set to be very different. In the context of a Latin American canon, it might be interesting to include, for instance, the frequently low-profile

[15] Michaela Hailbronner, "Constructing the Global Constitutional Canon: Between Authority and Criticism" (2019) 69 UTLJ 248, 262.

[16] Daniel Bonilla Maldonado, *Legal Barbarians. Identity, Modern Comparative Law and the Global South* (CUP 2021).

cases that, in countries like Perú, Chile, or Mexico, along a slow, gradual path of constitutional evolution, mark the recovery of substantive judicial scrutiny after decades of judicial deference under authoritarian rule. While crucial for the reconstruction of regional trajectories and enriching for a variety of comparative projects—such as those interested in the evolution of interpretive methods, for example—they would not be, however, of particular interest as additions to the global canon of proportionality analysis.[17]

A Latin American canon could also appropriately include the landmark rulings representing the stabilization or consolidation of proportionality in each country, or judgments that paradigmatically illustrate how proportionality has helped channel crucial social and political debates in the region, like those around sexual and reproductive rights. Thus, in this latter area, one could surely select the Colombian 2006 abortion ruling, which carefully deploys a paradigm proportionality-based analysis to sustain that total prohibition of abortion is unconstitutional, or the Inter-American *Artavia Murillo* ruling, which evaluates under proportionality analysis the rights damage done by a total ban on assisted reproduction.[18] In the area of same-sex marriage, one could focus on the Mexican saga on Oaxaca legislation, which uses proportionality to expose legislation based on prejudice and constitutionally defective reasons,[19] or on the 2019 Ecuadorian ruling, which contends that a restrictive interpretation of Article 67 of the Constitution (defining marriage as between man and woman) not allowing the operation of Inter-American law as a *complement* to the Constitution would not pass "reasonability" or "proportionality" muster.[20]

In the context of the construction of an enlarged or amended global canon, by contrast, it makes sense to prioritize exploration of how proportionality operates in the context of constitutions that are in important ways different from those that have been more influential in its portrayal and theorization. These contexts are often not minoritarian,[21] and developments in their context are

[17] Pedro Grández Castro, "Proportionality and the Construction of Democracy: Notes from the Peruvian Jurisprudence" in Pou, Clérico, and Restrepo (n 7); Verónica Undurraga and Pascual Cortés, "Proportionality in the Case Law of the Chilean Constitutional Court," ibid; Arturo Bárcena Zubieta, "Proportionality and Human Rights in México," ibid.

[18] Corte Constitutional de Colombia, C-355/06 (May 10, 2006); Corte IDH, Caso Artavia Murillo y otros (Fecundación "in vitro") v. Costa Rica. Sentencia de 28 de noviembre de 2012, Serie C, No. 257.

[19] Francisca Pou Giménez, "El matrimonio igualitario en México: protección de derechos en una corte no activista" in Marie-Christine Fuchs and Monia Larissa Hennig Leal (eds.) *Activismo judicial: Cómo deciden los tribunales constitucionales en América Latina. Un análisis a partir del matrimonio civil igualitario* (KAS 2022).

[20] Corte Constitucional de Ecuador, Sentencia N. 11-18-CN, 12 de junio de 2019. Corte IDH, OC-24/17 (guaranteeing marriage to same-sex couples).

[21] See, e.g., Courtney Jung, Ran Hirschl, and Evan Rosevear, "Economic and Social Rights in National Constitutions" (2015) 62 Am. J. Comp. L. 1043 (documenting the widespread inclusion of economic, social, and cultural rights in contemporary constitutions).

of significant objective interest to constitutionalism on a global scale. Three features in Latin American constitutions are in my view distinctive: (i) as others in the Global South, they are long and detailed documents, in order not to leave the normative project they embrace excessively undetermined;[22] (ii) they declare the judicial enforceability of economic, social, cultural, and environmental rights;[23] and (iii) they contain asymmetric mandates directing public authorities to assure the protection of the most disadvantaged.[24] As the next sections illustrate, these contexts have given rise to uses of proportionality that: (i) do not rely on abstract clauses but on the coherent integration of specific textual messages; (ii) are not deferential to public authorities in the domain of social rights; and (iii) combine horizontal harmonization of rights with minimum core guarantees and mandates of special protection for groups marked by disadvantage or absence of recognition. As I have said, this comes accompanied with a methodological, functional, and thematic expansion of proportionality analysis that portrays it in a new light.

The court that offers the widest and more sophisticated spectrum of proportionality adjudication in the region is the Constitutional Court of Colombia. Its prestige and special status stem from many factors. It is the author of widely influential doctrinal creations, such as the "unconstitutional state of affairs,"[25] the right to a vital minimum,[26] or the proportionality tests we will mention, among others. Moreover, it is a permanent reference because it decided leading-edge social topics earlier than other courts,[27] in part because it has promoted

[22] Madhav Khosla, *India's Founding Moment* (HUP 2020) (developing the substantive rationales behind the Indian founders crafting of a long and detailed document).

[23] The classic reference, which was immensely influential and has permeated mainstream legal practice, is Victor Abramovich and Christian Courtis, *Los derechos sociales como derechos exigibles* (Trotta 2002). Analyzing early regional practice, Paola Bergallo, "Justicia y experimentalismo: la función remedial del poder judicial en el litigio de derecho público en Argentina" (2005) *SELA (Seminario en Latinoamérica de Teoría Constitucional y Política) Papers* 45, https://digitalcommons.law.yale.edu/yls_sela/45; Víctor Abramovich, M. José Añón, and Christian Courtis (eds.), *Derechos sociales: instrucciones de uso* (Fontamara 2003); Víctor Abramovich and Laura Pautassi (eds.), *La revisión judicial de las políticas sociales. Estudio de casos* (Del Puerto 2009).

[24] For a useful overview, with citations to many sources, see Óscar Parra Vera, "Socioeconomic Rights" in Juan F. González Bertomeu and Roberto Gargarella (eds.), *The Latin American Casebook: Courts, Constitutions and Rights* (Routledge 2018).

[25] This notion identifies situations of multiple, interlocking violations of rights traceable to the actions and omissions of an extensive array of public and private actors, sustained over time, and calling for the adoption of structural reform (the Court has applied it to areas such as prisons, social security, and the situation of displaced people).

[26] This right refers to the basic entitlements that assure a dignified life to individuals and families, not only for food and clothing, but also for health, education, housing, social security, and the environment, all of them dimensions necessary to enjoy a dignified level of life quality. See Colombian Constitutional Court, T-011/98 (January 29, 1998), among many others.

[27] e.g. as early as in the 1990s, the Colombian Court had already addressed topics such as euthanasia (C-239/97) or personal drug consumption (C-221/94). It has delivered path-breaking rulings on the rights of non-sentient beings, such as rivers (T-622/16), and has often ruled on leading-edge topics

procedural innovations that foster access to justice, and because it often engages the legislator in the context of dialogical decisions aimed at structural reform. Finally, its rulings are theoretically informed, methodologically explicit, and didactic. For all these reasons, focusing on Colombian rulings for prospective canonical status seems to be a natural course of action.

In some Latin American countries, proportionality is less central, since courts rely on minimum core or categorical approaches, or proceed under atypical parameters. The case law of the Argentinian Court, for instance, mixes traits analogous to general regional developments with *sui generis* ones. Although this Court has been said to prefer categorical solutions based on the progressive delimitation of rights, there is actually proportionality scrutiny in many of its rulings, but it is largely unstructured, sometimes implicit, or labelled as "reasonability," despite including necessity or strict proportionality assessments. I believe that focusing on at least one ruling illustrative of these features is enriching for the global conversation, since it cautions against invisibilization of minoritarian tendencies, and against the risk of essentialism, nominalism, and the corresponding privileging of "the name" over "the thing."

III. Methodological Expansion

Proportionality methodology has been developed and refined by an important group of Latin American scholars—many of them students of Robert Alexy who later developed their views in dialogue with new contexts and debates. Carlos Bernal Pulido published two books that were important to "mainstream" the methodology in legal education and practice.[28] An important group of scholars, including the Argentinian group clustered around Laura Clérico in Buenos Aires and scholars such as Rodolfo Arango in Colombia, developed the methodology in view of the enforcement of social rights and substantive equality guarantees.[29] Another strand of proportionality-related

(from "pink taxes" (C-383/19) to the health rights of migrants (T-210/18, T-197/19, T-452/19) before the controversies reach mainstream debates.

[28] See Carlos Bernal Pulido, *El derecho de los derechos* (Externado 2004); *El principio de proporcionalidad y los derechos fundamentales* (CEPC 2005).

[29] Laura Clérico, *El examen de proporcionalidad en el derecho constitucional* (Eudeba 2009) (in German, *Die Struktur der Verhältnismässigkeit* (Nomos 2001)); Federico De Fazio, "Examen de proporcionalidad y adjudicación judicial de derechos sociales constitucionales" (2019) 51 Isonomía 95; Gustavo Beade and Laura Clérico (eds.), *Desafíos a la ponderación* (Exernado 2011); Rodolfo Arango, *El concepto de derechos sociales fundamentales* (Legis 2015) (in German, *Der Begriff der sozialen Grundrechte* (Nomos 2001)); Laura Clérico, "Hacia la reconstrucción de un modelo integrado de proporcionalidad a la luz de la jurispurdencia de la Corte Interamericana de Derechos Humanos"

scholarship has nurtured legal theory debates. Clérico's work on the webs of "balancing-derived-rules", for instance, has weighted upon debates on the relation between proportionality, legal predictability, and the authoritative character of the law, and regional proportionality scholars have been active in analytic philosophy debates on principles and rules, specificationism vs. balancing, or universalism vs. particularism.[30] Francisco Urbina, on his part, has developed a comprehensive critique of the methodology also engaging several legal theory debates.[31]

Yet all this must be complemented by methodological developments in the courts. The core reference is the Colombian Court, known for carefully setting down its methodology of analysis at the beginning of its rulings. I will underline here two constructions. The first is the integrated proportionality test, coupled with detailed orientation about when the different intensities apply. The second one is the integrated regression test, used to assess violations of the principle of non-retrogression in the enjoyment of social and economic rights.

A. The Integrated Proportionality Test

The integrated proportionality test was developed in C-091/03, where a provision stating the requirements for adopting children, including the need to be 25 years old, was examined.[32] A citizen denounced the requirement as discriminatory: the law placed no minimum age conditions on biological parents, and the relationship between being a certain age and being a mature and good parent was poor. The fact that the Court acknowledged from the beginning this imperfect relationship made the intensity of the scrutiny determinative: under

in Griselda Capaldo, Jan Sieckmann, and Laura Clerico (eds.), *Internacionalización del derecho constitucional, constitucionalización del derecho internacional* (Eudeba 2011).

[30] Laura Clérico, "Sobre 'casos' y ponderación: los modelos de Alexy y Moreso ¿más similitudes que diferencias?" (2012) 37 Isonomía 113, in dialogue with José Juan Moreso, "Ways of Solving Conflicts of Constitutional Rights: Proportionalism and Specificationism" (2012) 25 Ratio Juris 31; and with David Martínez Zorrilla, *Conflictos constitucionales, ponderación e indeterminación normativa* (Marcial Pons 2007). See also Federico De Fazio, "Sistemas nomativos y conficto constitucionales ¿Es posible aplicar derechos fundamentales sin ponderar?" (2014) 40 Isonomía 197; Carlos Bernal Pulido, "Precedents and Balancing" in Carlos Bernal Pulido and Thomas Bustamante (eds.), *On the Philosophy of Precedent* (Franz Steiner Verlag 2012); Virgilio Afonso da Silva, "Comparing the Incommensurable: Constitutional Principles, Balancing and Rational Decision" (2011) 31 OJLS 273.

[31] Francisco J. Urbina, *A Critique of Proportionality and Balancing* (CUP 2017).

[32] C-091/03 (January 31, 2001). "C" rulings derive from public actions of unconstitutionality, an abstract review channel. Public actions allow ordinary citizens to challenge general legislation in the abstract, and obtain its invalidation with *erga omnes* effects. "T" *tutela* rulings are individual or group complaints and its effects are only for the parties concerned, although the Colombian Court has devised innovative remedies and a range of intermediate effects.

strict scrutiny, the statute would fail, given its apparent degree of under- and over-inclusion; under soft scrutiny, it would survive.

This led the Court to immerse itself in a comparative exploration of theoretical and doctrinal developments on proportionality, until coming up with a four-step "integrated proportionality test" combining, the Court remarks, the superior analytical clarity of the European Alexian tradition with the American differentiated scrutiny tradition designed to be sensitive to the variable space that the Constitution grants to the political branches.[33] The *soft* integrated test requires: a non-prohibited goal; means potentially apt; and means not grossly unnecessary. The *intermediate* integrated test requires: a constitutionally important goal; means effectively apt; and means not evidently disproportionate. The intense or *strict* integrated test requires: a compelling goal; effectively apt means; and necessary means, which may not be replaced by other less detrimental rights, so that the benefits of adopting the measure exceed the restriction it poses on other values or constitutional principles.[34]

The Court discussed the criteria to be considered to determine the level of scrutiny applicable in each case and identified three hypotheses for stronger scrutiny: when a fundamental right of a person or group of persons is limited; when a statute relies on a prohibited or suspect ground; and when the constitution contains specific equality mandates, as with the mandate to equalize all religious confessions, or the regulation affects groups in a manifestly weak situation.[35] The Court also showed how this determination requires a most careful analysis of social patterns, illustrating the potential of the methodology for incorporating relevant empirical grounding. In the case at hand, the Court noted that structural exclusion was far deeper with regard to older people than with regard to younger ones, and that age thresholds imply only a temporary exclusion while age ceilings become permanent and unchangeable. These factors, together with the fact that the Court recognized no "fundamental right to adopt," made appropriate the application of only intermediate scrutiny to the challenged norm—which was passed.[36]

In deciding C-345/19—a relatively technical case on the regulation of intellectual property rights—the Court made two important additions.[37] First, it clarified again the structure of the integrated test and held that proportionality in the narrow sense does not apply when the scrutiny is soft.[38] And, second,

[33] ibid paras. 4–7.
[34] ibid paras. 6–9.
[35] ibid paras. 10–16.
[36] ibid paras. 27–38, 39.
[37] C-345/19 (July 31, 2019).
[38] ibid paras. 15, 17–19.

it systematized its case law with regard to the hypothesis in which each level of intensity applies. The Court indicated that weak or soft scrutiny applies to economic and tax policy, international policy, areas of jurisdiction specifically conferred by the constitution on an institution of constitutional status, pre-constitutional provisions, and cases when a preliminary impingement on the right is not apparent.[39] Intermediate scrutiny applies when the measures impinge on rights of a non-fundamental status, to arbitrary acts seriously affecting free market concurrence, and to measures based on suspect grounds with the goal of benefitting historically discriminated groups.[40] Strong or strict scrutiny applies when specific equality mandates are at stake (a suspect category is involved, the measure affects people in manifestly weak positions, or discriminated or marginalized groups), a fundamental right is severely impaired, or the norm creates a privilege.[41] This reconstruction is important because it shows how consistent, general standards are progressively built, bottom up, in the context of a fairly detailed constitution. It illustrates how the Court takes responsibility for its long strands of historic case law, and habilitates an exercise of reflective equilibrium or mutual adjustment between its general frameworks of adjudication and its energetic, daily exercises of decision making.

B. The Integrated Retrogression Test

The Constitutional Court of Colombia has addressed the guarantee of economic, social, and cultural rights through different techniques, among them the application of a text of non-retrogression. The Court applies what Magdalena Correa Henao and Alejandra Osorio Alvis call an *integrated retrogression test* to evaluate normative retrogression—i.e. retrogression in the enjoyment of rights due to changes in legislation, not due to administrative action or other kinds of public or private conduct.[42]

The goal of the test is to make operative the assumption that legal retrogression is prima facie unconstitutional. Correa and Osorio call it "integrated" because it embraces two types of analysis: an objective analysis that asks whether normative retrogression actually exists, and an argumentative one that asks

[39] ibid para. 18
[40] ibid para. 19.
[41] ibid para. 20.
[42] Magdalena Correa Henao and Alejandra Osorio Alvis, "Socio-Economic Rights in the Colombian Constitutional Jurisprudence: The Use of the Proportionality Test and the Prohibition of Regressive Measures" in Pou Giménez, Clérico, and Restrepo Saldarriaga (n 7).

whether such retrogression can be considered proportional.[43] The Court may detect no normative retrogression if the two norms are not really comparable at the outset, if there is no detectable backsliding in terms of enjoyment and scope of the right, or if the amended norm does not damage the objective and subjective constitutional content of the social or economic right.[44] This last step implies assessing whether the provision reduces the scope of the right within tolerable constitutional limits, both from an objective and subjective point of view.[45] To determine this, the Court resorts to the notions of acquired rights, minimum core, or "achieved content," and only finds a regressive measure prima facie tolerable when it falls within the space of progressive rights enjoyment.[46] Yet the Court may also consider the situation of the rights-holders, where problems of equality may become determinant: the impact on the conditions of subsistence of disadvantaged or specially protected groups may justify a finding of retrogression.[47]

If the existence of retrogression is confirmed, the Court then assesses whether the corresponding rights restriction is proportional.[48] The insertion of a proportionality test into the analysis of regressive measures was consolidated in a leading case on labor rights, C-038 of 2004.[49] I will describe it in more detail in the next subsection. For now it suffices to underline that, in contrast with prevailing practice in comparative social rights adjudication, in this case as in others, the Colombian Court applied strict scrutiny and used all subprinciples in a reinforced fashion that inquired whether lawmakers had ensured that the statutory measures pursued an imperative goal, and established means that were adequate, necessary, and proportional in the narrow sense.[50] Once retrogression is determined to exist, what we see is an openly non-deferential attitude, channeled through a relatively structured, four-prong strict proportionality test. While international human rights committees have established that the principle of progressivity and non-retrogression generally places a strong burden of justification on state's shoulders when adopting regressive measures in all rights-related domains,[51] the Colombian retrogression

[43] ibid 6.
[44] ibid 7.
[45] ibid 8.
[46] ibid 8–10.
[47] ibid 11.
[48] ibid 11–13.
[49] C-038/04 (January 27, 2004).
[50] Exceptionally, the scrutiny applied by the Court is intermediate, as in C-372/2011 (May 12, 2011).
[51] Committee on Economic, Social and Cultural Rights, General Comment 3, para. 9 (stating that the adoption of deliberate retrogressive measures "would require the most careful consideration and would need to be fully justified by reference to the totality of the rights provided for in the Covenant and in the context of the full use of maximum available resources").

test shows how this general standard can be technically translated into a strict proportionality test that forces a careful and demanding evaluation of social policy.

IV. Functional Expansion

Courts do not innovate methodologically in a void, but with the goal of guaranteeing certain standards of rights' satisfaction. In what follows, I identify three rulings that illustrate how courts have declared disproportional public policies that failed to cover the needs of the most disadvantaged, eliminated degrees of rights enjoyment without justification, or suggested how certain patterns of law enforcement must optimize "in concrete" the rights at stake in order to pass constitutional muster—all of them cases that go beyond the control of state excess that has classically been at the center of the use of proportionality in North-Atlantic democracies.

A. Insufficient State Action

In the Quisberth Castro case, the Supreme Court of Argentina addressed the situation of a woman from Bolivia and her son, living in desperate condition. The boy had a non-evolutionary encephalopathy that had caused him severe disabilities,[52] turning the mother into a full-time caregiver in no position to find employment.[53] They had been living in a variety of shelters, hostels, and dwellings.[54] The City of Buenos Aires had at one time granted them a subsidy but, in the application of the existing regulations, it had been terminated after ten months.[55]

The Court concluded that the City's housing policies violated the petitioners' right to housing. It observed that the fulfillment of the rights that impose positive obligations on state authorities must be subject to a "reasonability review," oriented, in Rawlsian spirit, by two principles: "democratic equality" and "difference with a mandate to protect the excluded."[56] For the Court, reasonability

[52] Corte Suprema de Argentina, Q. C., S. Y. v. Gobierno de la Ciudad de Buenos Aires s/amparo, recurso de hecho (April 24, 2012), 1.
[53] ibid 24–25.
[54] ibid 2.
[55] ibid 25–26.
[56] ibid 16–17.

meant that although the political branches enjoyed a margin of discretion in making public policy, they nonetheless had to observe the minimal guarantees indispensable for individuals to be treated like human beings in situations of extreme vulnerability.[57] The Court examined the three existing programs under these standards and found them all to be insufficient.

The first one—a housing credit program—required a minimum income and was therefore outside the petitioners' possibilities.[58] The second one—entering one of the City's shelters—provided only an impermanent nocturnal space and offered no privacy, no conditions for cooking, and inadequate sanitary conditions. The third option—a housing subsidy program—offered a small sum of money and could be awarded for up to ten months.[59] The Court addressed the City's arguments by pointing to budgetary restrictions and the principle of progressivity, but considered it "evident that the state effort realized to guarantee the social, economic and cultural rights [of the petitioners] is not sufficient nor adequate, since it does not even cover the minimum needs derived of the situation of the family group."[60] In his separate vote, Justice Petracchi noted, for instance, that whenever a social program leaves the minimum needs of the most disfavored unmet, a presumption of rights violation is apparent and it is the state authorities which must demonstrate that they have made all possible efforts to meet their obligations—not the petitioners.[61] The Court concluded that the burden was not met and ordered the City to provide to the petitioners immediate, provisional housing and social services assistance, together with inscribing them "on a current or future housing program for the permanent solution of their needs."[62]

This ruling interestingly illustrates the use of proportionality to denounce state action that violates rights by *defect*. It provides useful elements to visit several theoretical debates on the methodology of proportionality, such as that which discusses at what level of abstraction the analysis must proceed—the ruling nullifies the lower court ruling applying a precedent (the Alba Quintana case) where the Court had sustained that the reasonability of a social rights policy was to be assessed at a quite general level, not from the point of view of a particular group of rights-bearers.[63] The ruling offers yet another take on the debate of the relation between minimum core approaches and those of

[57] ibid 17, 29.
[58] ibid 19–20.
[59] ibid 20–21.
[60] ibid 19–21.
[61] ibid 21.
[62] ibid 29–30.
[63] ibid 38–39 (Petracchi's Opinion).

proportionality or reasonability, in holding public policy to be under a duty to meet a threshold; not the sort of universal, transversal threshold implied in the minimum core paradigm, but one defined by the basic needs of a particular segment: people in situations of extreme vulnerability.[64] More generally, the ruling provides an instance of proportionality-based adjudication that enforces simultaneously the right to housing, the mandate of special protection of the most disadvantaged, and the principle of progressivity, which is interesting to dissect in conceptual and methodological terms.

While the ruling speaks of "reasonability" and is best reconstructed as enforcing a "suitability" (sufficiency, under-inclusiveness) standard, it cannot be declared to apply a deferential ends–means test. The ruling suggests that something very close to a "necessity" assessment is needed when over- or under-inclusiveness is taken seriously in examining "suitability." When coupled with the shifting of the burden of argumentation attached to the principle of progressivity and the assessment of suitability from the viewpoint of people in extreme vulnerability, the analysis embodies the sort of non-deferential scrutiny we associate with proportionality analysis. The ruling, in short, illustrates that what the labels contain—"proportionality," "reasonability"—in different traditions is not always the same, and invites us to rethink what we have traditionally understood each of these modalities to imply.

B. Regressive State Action

In C-038 of 2004, the Colombian Court evaluated the constitutionality of a statute that, in times of crisis, modified labor rights along several important dimensions, including social security benefits, ordinary and nocturnal work schedules, work on Sundays and holidays, compensation for unilateral unjustified job termination, compensation for non-payment, training contracts, and flexible times schedules.[65] While in a number of other cases the Court did nullify areas of regressive public policy, in C-038/04 the reforms were found to be constitutional—something that could count against selecting it in the context of this chapter. Yet, because the issues at stake, the methodology, and the substantive reasoning are straightforward and easy to capture, I believe this judgment provides very appropriate grounds to develop comparative conversations about justified or unjustified regressive action.

[64] ibid 29.
[65] C-038/04 (January 27, 2004).

In the case, even the defenders of the law acknowledged that it was less favorable than previous regulation,[66] therefore it was unnecessary for the Court to spend time on that aspect of the retrogression test. The question was only whether the retrogression was unconstitutional. The Court highlighted that proportionality analysis in the case had to be in certain respects flexible and deferent because economic policy is a terrain where legislative freedom is wide; that suitability and necessity analysis cannot be very strict in a terrain fraught with empirical uncertainty and disagreements between economic schools; and that the more insecure or contended the empiric assumptions underlying the legislation, the less intense its review by the courts must be.[67] But in other respects, the Court added, review must be stricter, since the measures diminish the protection of a fundamental social right: the right to work. The legislative must not only respect acquired rights and the constitutional principles that regulate labor, but also proportionality: the Court must verify with more rigor that measures are proportional in view of the goals pursued, the care taken in the democratic deliberation of the issue, and the sacrifices it imposes on workers.[68]

The Court finally determined that promoting employment is a goal of sufficient constitutional importance to justify a labor reform that reduces certain protection for workers.[69] It also considered that: (i) the regressive measures were not adopted without reflection but were based on a careful study; (ii) Congress had analyzed alternative options, but considered that there were no equally effective measures that were less damaging for the protection of labor rights; and (iii) the measures were not disproportionate in the narrow sense: regression in the protection of the right to labor was not excessive compared to the gains in terms of promoting employment.[70] The Court justified this separately with respect to all the measures in question.[71] With regard to the enlargement of regular work schedules, for instance, the Court considered it critical that the resulting regulation respects the minimums set forth in international treaties; with regard to flexible time schedules, it underlined that they

[66] e.g. the law increased ordinary working hours from 6 p.m. until 10 p.m., eliminating the right to be compensated for the extra four hours (Art. 25). It reduced from 100% to 75% extra pay for weekend and holiday work, and modified the definition of occasional and habitual work for the purposes of pay (Art. 26) and reduced the pay applicable to long-term contracts, making termination less costly (Art. 28). It also conferred a special, but not strictly labor, status for training contracts, allowing payment below the minimum salary (Art. 30).

[67] C-038/04 (January 27, 2004), paras. 26–27.

[68] ibid.

[69] ibid paras. 28–30.

[70] ibid para. 31.

[71] ibid paras. 39–48.

could not be unilaterally imposed by an employer and had to respect constitutional minimums; with regard to compensation for unjustified termination, it observed that the enhanced job stability of pregnant women and unionized workers was respected by the new legislation, and that the employer was punished for incurring in the conduct.[72] In every case—convincingly or not—the Court made sure that the implied sacrifices were proportional to the gains.

C. Rights Optimization on the Ground

In C-822/05, the Colombian Court applied proportionality to an important liberty and privacy case so as to assure perfect and uninterrupted rights optimization both at the level of legislation and adjudication.[73] At issue were the provisions of the Colombian Code of Criminal Procedure dealing with corporal registers, bodily inspections, and the taking of bodily samples (blood, semen, saliva) in the course of criminal investigations. While the statute made clear that prosecutors had to secure a judicial warrant to take bodily samples, it could be interpreted to suggest that the warrant was not necessary for registers and inspections. A Colombian citizen alleged that the whole system condoned the treatment of people as objects and damaged human dignity, the right to personal integrity, the right not to self-incriminate, and the presumption of innocence.

The ruling is a small jewel in terms of reasoning and argumentation, which developed a basic argument of conditional validity: it declared the statute constitutional only if applied with perfect proportionality in every particular case. It clarified that a warrant is mandatory in all cases (registers, inspections, samples),[74] and that in considering whether to grant one, judges must conduct a most careful, strict proportionality analysis, sensitive to all the specificities of the case, and oriented by criteria that the Court sets down concerning the intensity of the scrutiny and the elements to be weighted.[75] The taking of bodily samples, for instance, which has a very serious preliminary impact on dignity, privacy, guarantees against self-incrimination, and prohibition of degrading treatment, is only proportional if practiced under an exacting set of conditions set forth by the Court.[76]

[72] ibid paras. 40, 43, 44.
[73] C-822/05 (August 10, 2005).
[74] ibid § 5.1.
[75] ibid §§ 5.2–5.5.
[76] ibid § 5.4.

The ruling paradigmatically vindicates proportionality as the core constitutional defense against the state's neglectful action in terms of rights, and the core tool that guarantees, at any moment, the optimization of the normative force of rights. It succeeds in portraying proportionality as a vector of normativity which operates as a perfect Fibonacci spiral: activating the force of rights at every incremental stage of legal operation.

V. Thematic Expansion

Constitutional practice worldwide has given visibility to proportionality-based litigation in the domain of civil and political rights. The most well-known proportionality icons, such as *Regina v. Oakes*,[77] *Makwanyane*,[78] or *Beit Sourik*,[79] all deal with civil rights, as do most cases in the historic docket of the Strasbourg Court, even if its use in the context of equality and non-discrimination cases has opened the door to new topics. The same occurs in the Inter-American context, where proportionality was initially used to resolve conflicts of rights between freedom of speech and personality rights, even if it has expanded to other terrains through its use in non-discrimination cases and, more recently, social rights ones.[80] The recent practice of the Committee on Economic, Social and Cultural Rights when addressing individual communications operates an incursion into new thematic arenas.[81] In any event, Latin American constitutional adjudication definitely brings about the opportunity of seeing proportionality applied to other domains—for instance, transitional justice and socioeconomic regulation.

A. Transitional Justice

Violence has been a protracted problem in Colombia. For many years, armed conflict between state and non-state actors, including a variety of paramilitary groups and guerrillas, has left a wretched scenario with thousands of killed, disappeared, tortured, and forcibly displaced people. The approval of the 1991

[77] Supreme Court of Canada, *Regina v. Oakes* [1986] 1 SCR 103.
[78] Constitutional Court of South Africa, *S v. Makwanyane and Another* (CCT3/94) [1995] SACR 1 (6 June 1995).
[79] Supreme Court of Israel, *Beit Sourik Village Council v. The Government of Israel et. al.*, HCJ 2056/04, Supreme Court, June 20, 2004.
[80] Serrano Guzmán (n 7), Rossi (n 7).
[81] Rossi (n 7).

Constitution was an important step in including demobilized guerrilla members in the constitutional assembly and declaring peace to be both a right and an obligation. Two political processes were later attempted, with important legal dimensions. The first, involving paramilitary groups, followed the parameters of the Law of Justice and Peace (Ley 975 of 2005). The second, involving the guerillas, was longer and more encompassing. After years of negotiation, it culminated in the Havana Agreements of November 2016, which led to the passing of an important legislative package and the creation of a dedicated tribunal—the Special Jurisdiction for Peace.

On both occasions, the Constitutional Court reviewed the constitutionality of the legislation. In reviewing the Law of Justice and Peace, the Court produced an iconic ruling entirely based on proportionality analysis: C-370/06.[82] The core matter was the validity of the regime of "alternativity" that the Law offered to paramilitary members willing to demobilize. In exchange for their cooperation with the courts, partial confession of crimes, abandonment of armed conflict, and compliance with reparations, they were offered considerably lower penalties.

The Court identified three main constitutional elements—peace, justice, and the rights of victims—which clash with one another in different circumstances.[83] It observed that it is within the jurisdiction of the legislative branch to define formulas appropriate for overcoming that tension, but said that the responsibility for policing that task remained within certain limits, through the use of proportionality.[84] The Court observed specifically that the attainment of a stable and durable peace thanks to the demobilization of armed groups may justify certain restrictions to the value of justice and the correlative right of the victims to access justice (otherwise peace would be unattainable), yet peace has no absolute scope either and cannot justify everything, limits being found on the essential content of the value of justice and the rights of the victims to justice, truth, reparation, and non-repetition.[85]

Under this paradigm, different charges are addressed. The petitioners argued, for instance, that criminal benefits amounted to a system of impunity, failing strict proportionality scrutiny in excessively sacrificing the rights of the victims to truth, justice, reparation, and non-repetition. The Court disagreed, observing that the original penalty was imposed at trial and was to be served if the person broke the conditions on which the suspension depended.[86] By

[82] C-370/06 (May 18, 2006).
[83] ibid 288.
[84] ibid 288.
[85] ibid 289.
[86] ibid 308.

contrast, disproportionate damage to the value of justice and the rights of victims was found, associated to the fact alternativity required only non-repetition of the offenses covered by Law 975 (new offenses were not relevant to the effect of denying the benefit),[87] to the fact the members of armed groups had no obligation to confess all crimes committed (they could confess only those charged by the state, in violation of the victims' right to truth, which generates a state duty to investigate the most serious offenses),[88] and to the fact benefits were not conditional on the perpetrators' confessing where forcibly disappeared people could be found.[89]

These examples suffice to illustrate how the Court proceeds. Two main features guide its analysis. First, the determination to optimize each of the rights involved: the Court does explicitly require that the provisions be brought at levels where they initially satisfy more than the rights at stake without damaging the others (seeking Pareto-superiority), or where they restore proportionality in the narrow sense. Second, the determination to ensure respect for the essential content of rights. While "proportionality" and "minimum core" approaches have been portrayed as being in opposition, here the Colombian Court again combines the two paradigms, in assuming that where the minimum core is no longer recognizable, proportionality no longer obtains. The ruling is also remarkable from the viewpoint of transitional justice, in certifying the viability of a model that strikes midway between two controversial extremes: one that defends no violations going unpunished, and the other that defends amnesty laws as necessary for reconciliation.[90] Moreover, it nicely illustrates how proportionality helps register thousands of normative and empirical considerations, and makes more transparent and manageable public debate and policymaking around thorny social problems.

[87] ibid 310.

[88] ibid 317–318.

[89] ibid 322–324.

[90] For an overview of transitional justice developments in the region, see Leonardo Filippini and Agustín Cavana, "Transitional Justice" in Juan F. González Bertomeu and Roberto Gargarella (eds.), *The Latin American Casebook* (Routledge 2018), 126–147. For a critical analysis of the ruling, Rodrigo Uprimny and María Paula Saffon Sanín, "Derecho a la verdad: alcances y límites de la verdad judicial" in Rodrigo Uprimny et al., *¿Justicia Transicional sin transición? Verdad, justicia y reparación para Colombia* (Dejusticia 2006). For a view on the debate between those who accompany the Inter-American Court in believing that the most serious crimes may never go unpunished and those who believe that, when they are product of a broad democratic deliberation, amnesty laws may be acceptable, Roberto Gargarella, "Democracy and Rights?" and the other contributions to the symposium coordinated by Alexandra Hunneus in AJIL Unbound 109 (2015).

B. Social and Economic Rights

The thematic richness in the domain of social and economic rights adjudication is, again, particularly high in Colombia. Even during the period when social rights were not recognized to be technically fundamental, half of total number of *tutelas* already dealt with social rights.[91] Social rights cases are resolved on a variety of grounds and using several argumentative strategies, not only proportionality. Yet again, there is something paradigmatic in the way it is used in Colombia to evaluate state regressive action. For this reason, in harmony with our previous emphasis, and again following the study by Correa Henao and Osorio Alvis mentioned earlier, I will now reference some of the topics that have been discussed in this area.

Correa Henao and Osorio Alvis focus on representative cases addressing controversies related to health, social security, labor rights, education, housing, and the labor and land rights of peasants. While in some of them the challenged legislation was not found to be regressive,[92] in others it was so, and its ultimate validity was assessed on the basis of proportionality analysis. We have already seen how in C-038/04 the Court used proportionality to decide on the validity of a relatively comprehensive labor reform covering working hours and days, compensation for termination, social security protections, and contract modalities. Other addressed subjects and areas that were no less impressive, given the traditional wariness of constitutional courts in the socioeconomic domain.

In C-931/04, for instance, the Court scrutinized the national budget.[93] At issue was the freezing of financial transfers to universities and their impact on the right of public servants to maintain the purchasing power of their salaries and on the right to education. The Court considered that the regulation should be placed under intense scrutiny because of its potential impact on the constitutional rights to an adjustable salary, the vital minimum, and dignity.[94] In its opinion, while the goal of permanently decreasing public expenditure to reduce a long-term deficit was constitutionally compelling and relevant, the explanations provided by the government did not satisfy a minimal argumentative

[91] On the first stage, see M. Paula Saffon and Mauricio García Villegas, "Derechos sociales y activismo judicial" (2011) 13 Rev. Estudios Socio-Jurídicos 75. Until 2008, social rights enforcement was based on the doctrine of connexity, not direct enforceability. After T-760/08, the right to health (and later others) was recognized as an independent fundamental right. Everaldo Lamprea, "Colombia's Right to Health Litigation in a Context of Health Care Reform" in Coleen Flood and Aeyal Gross (eds.), *The Right to Health at the Public/Private Divide* (CUP 2014); see also Parra Vera (n 24).

[92] C-228/11 (right to pension); C-536/12 (right to housing); C-077/17 and C-028/18 (right to land property); C-257/08 and C-135/18 (labor rights).

[93] C-931/04 (September 29, 2004).

[94] ibid paras. 5.4.2, 5.4.4, 5.4.5.

burden in terms of constitutional—not only economic—reasons.[95] The legislative had given no clear reasons why the measure was not excessive, why it was necessary because the public deficit could not be addressed through less burdensome alternatives, or why educational coverage and higher education would not be unduly restricted. As regards the implied impact on the salaries of university personnel, the Court did not find any precise reasoning indicating that the limitations on the right to maintain the purchasing power of one's salary respected: (i) the intangible nature of the right of public servants with low salaries to see the latter's value preserved; (ii) the limitable but not removable nature of the right of public servants with middle and high salaries to have the latter's value preserved; and (iii) the principles of temporality, proportionality, and progressivity that must control such a limitation.[96] The ultimate reasonability and proportionality of the limitation could not be established.

C-444/09, for its part, concerned retrogression in the quality of housing standards.[97] The new regulation spared the vendors of new housing from their previous obligation to buy insurance for stability and quality to provide compensation for potential damage to their homes. The Court considered that the measure had already failed the first subprinciple: the need to find an imperative constitutional end or goal potentially justifying the elimination of a guarantee of a home's habitability.[98] It was regressive, and it left unprotected the minimal conditions of adequate housing for specially protected people.[99] The Court crafted a ruling of conditional validity that maintained the norm in the legal system, provided it was interpreted as obliging vendors of social interest housing to provide the stability and quality insurance policy.[100]

In C-372/11, the provision under analysis substantially increased the economic stake necessary to file an extraordinary cassation appeal in cases involving labor disagreements, something that, for the Court, preliminarily impinged on equality, access to justice, the right to work, social security, and other guarantees.[101] Because of this, and notwithstanding the ordinary legislative leeway for regulating procedures, weak scrutiny was inappropriate.[102] Under an intermediate level of scrutiny, the regulation failed. The Court believed decongestion of the judicial system to be a legitimate and important

95 ibid para. 5.5.1.
96 ibid para. 5.2.
97 C-444/09 (June 8, 2009).
98 ibid para. 2.5.9.1.
99 ibid para. 2.5.9.2.
100 ibid para. 2.5.10.
101 C-372/11 (May 12, 2011), para. 2.3.1.10.
102 ibid para. 3.3.3.

goal,[103] but found no grounds for believing that restricting cassation to economically prominent cases would satisfy it with a sufficient degree of probability. The measure was not suitable because it did not address delay in the lower judicial levels and did not decrease the flow of cases that entered the judicial process.[104] It was not necessary either since there were measures less damaging for fundamental rights, and more effective for curbing congestion—the Court pointed to studies that indicated that delay is correlated to the number of cases but also to structural failures associated with insufficient operative and human capital, the structure of processes, and inadequate training of personnel, among others. The legislative authorities should have addressed these structural determinants while not disproportionally affecting access to the administration of justice.[105] The reform was not proportional in the narrow sense either because it sacrificed other constitutional principles and values of the highest importance, such as equality, access to justice, the right to work, and other workers' rights.[106]

In C-644/2012, the Court analyzed several provisions of the National Development Plan 2010–2014, which allowed peasants to sell land which they had acquired by state subsidies or by the transfer of vacant land, to participate in certain kinds of agro-industrial projects the government sought to promote.[107] In a long judgment that reconstructed the historic rationales behind land distribution and inalienability guarantees, the Court applied retrogression and sufficiency tests, carefully searching for the kind of strong justification that would eventually save measures that undermined core protections for peasants (a specially protected group), violated guarantees against land concentration, and placed food security at risk. No justification was found, and the challenged provisions were nullified.

VI. Proportionality and Social Rights Upside Down

To close, we will pause on a judgment that goes against the current and enriches the debate about the different features that lie behind what one might be inclined to consider an "anticanonical" ruling. The dense and forceful

[103] ibid para. 3.3.4.
[104] ibid para. 3.3.5.
[105] ibid para. 3.3.6.
[106] ibid para. 3.3.7.
[107] C-644/12 (August 23, 2012).

Colombian constitutional jurisprudence on socioeconomic rights is not followed on this occasion.

In T-091/18, the Court addressed the demands of eleven children of Salamina (Caquetá), whose rural school offered education only up to 9th grade.[108] The Education Department said that regulations required twenty-two of the children to study 10th and 11th grades and directed them to attend two other schools situated more than two hours away on foot (on roads not practicable in the rainy season) and between three and four hours in a collective canoe along the Yurayaco river, paid out of their own pockets.[109]

The *tutela* was denied by the lower courts, and the Constitutional Court undertook its revision.[110] Proportionality was central to its core reasoning and the Court took time to elaborate on the methodology. In the opinion of the Court, balancing should not be conceived of as dealing simply with a collision of rights, but also with different reasonable levels of satisfaction of those rights.[111] Although the Constitution does not define how rights must be guaranteed or at what level (minimal, maximal, or intermediate),[112] indetermination "can be overcome by applying a two-step balancing reasoning: (i) an interpretive analysis about the content of the right and, therefore, its reasonable level of satisfaction—reasonability analysis; and (ii) an empirical analysis on the rights mode of satisfaction—proportionality analysis."[113] Under a reasonability analysis, the Court observes, the judge must analyze the content given to the right by the legislator or the administration, which has prima facie jurisdiction to develop public policy and define the content of rights.[114] The judge must subsequently analyze whether the petition (the desired level of satisfaction) is reasonable because it can be ascribed to the content of the right, as defined by the legislator or the administration.[115] Four hypotheses may result. In any of them, a second step of proportionality analysis (suitability, necessity, and strict proportionality) follows.[116] For instance, if a petition is considered to be reasonable and therefore judicially enforceable, in matching the content of the right as legislatively or administratively defined, then it must be assessed whether the

[108] T-091/18 (March 9, 2018).
[109] ibid paras. 1–16.
[110] ibid paras. 26.5, 26.6.
[111] ibid para. 83.
[112] ibid para. 84.
[113] ibid para. 89.
[114] ibid paras. 90, 91.
[115] ibid para. 91.
[116] ibid para. 92.

satisfaction of the rights-holder is greater than the disruption caused to the authority obliged to provide such reasonable level of satisfaction.[117]

In the case at hand, the Court concluded that the petition was not reasonable, in going beyond the content of the right as set forth in Decree 1075.[118] The Court observed, however, that when this occurs but there are elements on file suggesting the existence of alternatives, judges must determine if those alternatives are empirically apt to guarantee the right and provide an appropriate judicial remedy.[119] If they are, they must subsequently be subjected to a proportionality analysis. Having concluded that the provision of free public transport to attend off-village schools was empirically apt to satisfy the right, the Court assessed its impact on the constitutionally legitimate goal that could justify its limitation: the autonomy of the Education Department to administer the economic resources within its jurisdiction.[120] The scrutiny was passed: the obligations did not fatally damage the autonomy of the Education Department in not exceeding the legislative definitions,[121] and were strictly proportional, because they satisfied the petitioners' right to education to a greater extent than the disruption caused to the Education Department.[122] The Court nonetheless refrained from issuing a specific remedial order and prompted the parties to engage in meaningful dialogue (*diálogo significativo*) about how to comply with the determination.[123]

Despite the analytical sophistication it displays, the ruling is full of anticanonical turns. It not only breaks with precedent but, as Justice Diana Fajardo remarked in her dissent, "it reformulates the meaning and constitutional function of both reasonability and proportionality" making them operate "not to safeguard the people's rights before power, but as barriers in their access to justice."[124] As Fajardo observes, the ruling terms "unreasonable" what people demand on the basis of their constitutional rights wherever it does not fit the content that the legislator or the administration has given to them[125] and contends that interpretation of the content of rights must be "wide but reasonable," while the fact is that it should be simply wide, as constitutionally

[117] ibid para. 98.

[118] ibid para. 103: "The criteria of equity, quality, and efficiency that must orientate the organization of the pool of teaching personnel are disregarded, as well as the fact the creation of these job posts is subject to budget availability, and to the margin of autonomy in resource management constitutionally granted to territorial entities."

[119] ibid para. 110.

[120] ibid para. 111.

[121] ibid para. 117.

[122] ibid paras. 118–120.

[123] ibid paras. 121–126.

[124] ibid paras. 9, 34.

[125] ibid. paras. 12, 35.

mandated.[126] Moreover, Fajardo continues, the ruling formally invocates proportionality terminology—suitability, necessity, strict proportionality—while using it not to evaluate the acceptability of rights limitations, but the acceptability of the petition, and to justify authorities not meeting their obligations.[127] The analysis assessed the damage suffered by the authorities in meeting their rights-related obligations, as if they had a "right not to fulfill" them.[128] Reasoning about proportionality in the narrow sense, Fajardo further remarked, was not used to ponder all relevant aspects of the situation, but as a pretense for a scientific method leading to an irrefutable answer, resulting in the fallacy of false precision, damaging the logic of deliberation in search of maximum rights efficacy, and presenting a structure of reasons to deny constitutional protection as if it were a scientific necessity.[129]

Fajardo identifies two final problems: first, in assuming that the "reasonable content" of rights is the one contained in statutes and regulations, the methodology leaves no place for the principle of progressivity.[130] And, second, the remedy adopted by the Court appears to be unjustified: it is not clear how meaningful engagement will work in the specific situation, or why that solution is any better than the original petition, not to mention the fact it ignores that transporting the children is risky and costly and that a boarding option may be disruptive for their family bonds.[131]

There is an ongoing debate in Latin America about the transformative impact of judicialization, the potential abuse of complaint channels, and the risks of excessively shutting down political deliberation. The Salamina ruling must surely be placed in that context. The ruling, however, did not simply apply a more deferent proportionality scrutiny, giving more leeway to the executive and legislative branches, but sidestepped the mandate of special action in favor of the disadvantaged, gave new meaning to reasonability and proportionality, and applied them to restrict citizens' claims and to protect the public authorities—all of them deeply anticanonical moves. Trying to specify with more precision what looks awkward in this ruling may certainly be enriching for the field.

[126] ibid para. 18.
[127] ibid para. 24.
[128] ibid para. 38.
[129] ibid para. 33.
[130] ibid para. 37.
[131] ibid paras. 40–41.

VII. Conclusion

Rulings are not born, but become, canonical—we might say, in Beauvoirian parlance. And it does not happen often when their authors are non-English-speaking courts of the Global South. In this chapter, I have identified several rulings that are, in my view, good candidates for providing rich, interesting anchors for our global constitutional conversations. What emerges is not a local, contextual "adaptation" of the global proportionality script, but a remarkable transformation and supplementation of that global script in methodological, functional, and thematic terms.

Perhaps the most central finding of the exercise has been to find a consolidated use of strict scrutiny in the socioeconomic realm, at least when the situation of people living in disadvantage and minimum levels of rights enjoyment are at stake, or state authorities engage in retrogressive action. This immediately obliges amendment of the widespread "global" contention that courts, while not denying the enforceability of social rights, have been generally deferential to the political branches in this domain—leaving little space for the use of proportionality for the benefit of more flexible modalities of reasonability review.

It is worth noting, however, that my suggested choices come from two "big" countries—Colombia being constitutionally big, despite its modest territorial size—and leave aside surely interesting developments from less central locations. We should therefore conceive these rulings as first-round additions to be followed by others in the future. We should take inspiration from the musical meaning of the word "canon" and embrace its diachronic nature based on the idea of repeated iterations. Yet for this canon to be a composition of the twenty-first century, each repetition must be different from earlier ones, and supersede classical polyphony for the benefit of giving space to an ever more enthralling combination of worldwide sounds.

16
Freedom of Expression and the Constitutional Canon

Adrienne Stone

I. Introduction

The canonical texts of the global law of freedom of expression are, I suggest, three decisions of apex courts: *Lüth*,[1] *New York Times v. Sullivan*,[2] and *R v. Keegstra*.[3]

The selection will immediately raise concerns among those who are critical of the tendency of Western and especially North American texts to dominate the emergent field of comparative constitutional law, at the expense of the rest of the world and the Global South in particular. There is an obvious risk that in nominating these as canonical I am simply playing in to an at best unthinking and at worst pernicious set of biases that will hinder rather than expand the field. Indeed, the risks of proposing a canonical series of free speech cases maybe more pronounced than in other aspects of constitutionalism. It is an area in which the United States Constitution has loomed especially large, and even within that system, there is a criticism that standard approaches to the First Amendment excessively prioritize freedom of speech within the constitutional order.[4] The complaint overall is that First Amendment conceptions of freedom of speech are exceptional and may even be a form of free speech fundamentalism that is normatively undesirable and, in any event, exceptional in world terms.

Finally, given the fundamental nature of contemporary challenges to freedom of expression, there are real questions as to the desirability of nominating a canon of twentieth-first century texts. In the modern digital

[1] *Lüth* [1958] BVerfGE 7: see also Donald P. Kommers and Russell A. Miller, *The Constitutional Jurisprudence of the Federal Republic of Germany* (3rd edn, Duke UP 2012) ch. 8.
[2] 376 US 254 (1964).
[3] [1990] 3 SCR 697.
[4] Mary Ann Franks, *The Cult of the Constitution* (Stanford UP 2019) ch. 3, 105.

Adrienne Stone, *Freedom of Expression and the Constitutional Canon* In: *Global Canons in an Age of Contestation*.
Edited by: Sujit Choudhry, Michaela Hailbronner, and Mattias Kumm, Oxford University Press.
DOI: 10.1093/9780191956942.003.0016

economy, norms of freedom of expression face entirely different challenges. The threat to freedom of speech now arises from the problem of 'speech clutter'; the increasing power of private actors to control the means of speech and the resulting splintering of public discourse and political polarization. A canon is naturally backward-looking but in the case of freedom of speech the question as to how much it will assist with the difficult challenges of the twenty-first century is very real.

For all these reasons, it is especially important to de-emphasize the sense of a canon as an appeal to authority. On the contrary, this canon may stand as an instance of what needs to be challenged and reformed to adapt to the increasingly globalized nature of the new digital economy. I also wish to de-emphasize the sense that this canon has a normative appeal, except to the extent that these decisions signal that freedom of expression in some form is a canonical aspect of modern constitutionalism. Rather, my principal focus is on the educational promise of a canon and especially its capacity to provoke responses and provide a framework against which new ideas can be assessed. Indeed, in freedom of speech (as elsewhere) the most important consequence of nominating a canon may be encouraging challenges to it. These three cases serve to identify important lines of thought about the protection of freedom of expression and laying them bare so as to encourage engagement and critique.

II. The Canon: A Brief Summary

Of the three decisions, *Lüth* is the first in time. It arose in 1958 in the context of postwar social struggles over addressing Germany's Nazi past.[5] The plaintiff, Erich Lüth, called for the boycott of a movie—*Immortal Beloved*—directed by Veit Harlan. Harlan was well known for writing a viciously antisemitic propaganda movie during the Third Reich. The call for a boycott was held by a civil court to have intentionally caused injury in breach of the Civil Code, a finding which led to Lüth's claim before the Constitutional Court pursuant to Article 5 of the German Basic Law.[6] The Court found, in favour of Lüth, that the action against him offended his right of freedom of opinion.

The second in time is *New York Times v. Sullivan*. The case arose in 1964 from the struggles of the civil rights era. The claim against the *New York Times*

[5] Hugh Ridley, *Law in West German Democracy: Seventy Years of History as Seen Through German Courts* (Brill 2019).

[6] *Basic Law for the Republic of Germany*, 1949 (Christian Tomuschat et al. tr., 2020) https://www.btg-bestellservice.de/pdf/80201000.pdf accessed 8 August 2021 ('Basic Law').

related to an advertisement placed in the paper by supporters of Dr Martin Luther King that was critical of the actions of the Alabama authorities during student civil rights protests when the students' dining hall at the Alabama State College was 'padlocked in an attempt to starve them into submission' and the police subsequently 'ringed' the campus.[7] In fact, the dining hall was never locked and the police presence near the campus was much less significant. In response, Sullivan (an elected official in the city of Montgomery with supervisory responsibilities for the police) sued in defamation. The *New York Times* lost the case in the Alabama courts and was subject to a verdict of record proportions before the case was heard by the United States Supreme Court.

In upholding the newspaper's appeal in the *New York Times* case, the Court established its now well-known 'public figure' defence, sharply limiting the capacity of public figures to bring actions for defamation. More precisely, the Court held that the First Amendment's protection of freedom of speech required a 'federal rule that prohibits a public official from recovering damages for a defamatory falsehood relating to his official conduct unless he proves that the statement was made with "actual malice" ... or with reckless disregard of whether it was false or not'.[8]

The third case—*R v. Keegstra*—occurred in 1992, some ten years after the adoption of the Canadian Charter of Rights and Freedoms ('Charter').[9] James Keegstra, a high school teacher, was prosecuted under the Criminal Code provision prohibiting the wilful promotion of hatred against any identifiable group for antisemitic statements made while teaching. The Canadian Supreme Court upheld the provision under section 1 of the Charter as a reasonable limit on freedom of expression. In doing so, the Canadian Supreme Court accepted that these forms of speech cause harm to their victims that goes beyond hurt feelings or offended sensibilities. In *Keegstra*, it was accepted that racist hate speech undermines the victim's social equality and 'sense of human dignity and belonging to the community at large'[10] and increases discrimination and violence against them.[11] The Canadian Supreme Court has maintained this

[7] *Sullivan* (n 2) 259.

[8] ibid 279–80. See also Adrienne Stone, '*New York Times v Sullivan* Case (US)' in Rainer Grote, Frauke Lachenmann, and Rüdiger Wolfrum (eds), *Max Planck Encyclopedia of Comparative Constitutional Law* (OUP 2017).

[9] Canadian Charter of Rights and Freedoms, pt 1 of the Constitution Act, 1982, being Sch. B to the Canada Act 1982 (UK), 1982, c. 11.

[10] *Keegstra* (n 3) 746.

[11] ibid 747.

position despite strong challenge, at least as it relates to the harm caused by sexually explicit expression.[12]

III. Canonical Significance: Liberty, Equality, Dignity

Each of these three cases stand as landmark, even iconic, decision within their own legal system. *New York Times v. Sullivan* is celebrated as a triumph of the civil rights era[13] and acclaimed for its articulation of fundamental precepts of First Amendment law that are significant beyond the particulars of the case. As US scholars immediately recognized, it put to bed a 'nagging question' about the constitutionality of the Sedition Act 1798. In doing so, it has been taken to settle the 'central meaning of the First Amendment': that defamation of government is 'an impossible notion' for a democracy.[14]

For this reason, *New York Times* is taken to have defined important national commitments in the United States. For Harry Kalven, Jr, 'the presence or absence in law of the concept of seditious libel defines the society'.[15] Others have developed the idea that the central commitments to 'uninhibited, robust and wide-open' public debate shapes American society by instilling qualities in its citizens such as tolerance, or 'good character' in the form of characteristics such as 'inquisitiveness, independence of judgment, distrust of authority, willingness to take the initiative, perseverance, and the courage to confront evil'.[16] Although not often discussed in precisely these terms, *New York Times v. Sullivan* signals the centrality of First Amendment commitments to US constitutional identity.

R v. Keegstra can also be taken as evidence of core constitutional commitments. *Keegstra* did not address a past national wrong in the way that *Lüth* did. Nor did it address a long-running controversy of the kind that underscored *New York Times*. But, it does signal a distinctive Canadian conception of freedom of expression and of constitutionalism. The Court's finding that the hate speech law survived constitutional scrutiny was grounded in section 1 of the Charter, the well-known limitation clause allowing 'reasonable limits

[12] See Richard Moon, '*R. v. Butler*: The Limits of the Supreme Court's Feminist Re-Interpretation of Section 163' (1993) 25 *Ottawa L Rev* 361; Leslie Green, 'Pornographies' (2000) 8 *J Pol Philos* 27.

[13] Anthony Lewis, *Make No Law: The Sullivan Case and the First Amendment* (Random House 1991).

[14] Harry Kalven, Jr, 'The *New York Times* Case: A Note on "The Central Meaning of the First Amendment"' [1964] *Sup Ct Rev* 191.

[15] ibid 205.

[16] Vincent Blasi, 'Free Speech and Good Character: From Milton to Brandeis to the Present' in Lee C. Bollinger and Geoffrey R. Stone (eds), *Eternally Vigilant: Free Speech in the Modern Era* (University of Chicago Press 2002) 61.

prescribed by law as can be demonstrably justified in a free and democratic society'. In *Keegstra*, the Court constructed a 'uniquely Canadian vision of a free and democratic society'[17] characterized by respect for equality and multiculturalism that justifies limitations on hateful expression.

Though overtly Canadian, this idea is deliberately formed in opposition to the First Amendment. Some aspects of the Court's reasoning do so by offering a reinterpretation of First Amendment law. Chief Justice Dixon holds out the prospect of a rehabilitation of *Beauharnais*, an old First Amendment case recognizing the possibility of group libel but one which is widely regarded as effectively overruled by *New York Times* and *Brandenburg v. Ohio*.[18] But *Keegstra* also involves a direct rejection of core First Amendment precepts. The Court's negative comparativism is explicit:[19]

> we must not hesitate to depart from the path taken in the United States. Far from requiring a less solicitous protection of *Charter* rights and freedoms, such independence of vision protects these rights and freedoms in a different way. As will be seen below, in my view the international commitment to eradicate hate propaganda and, most importantly, the special role given equality and multiculturalism in the Canadian Constitution necessitate a departure from the view, reasonably prevalent in America at present, that the suppression of hate propaganda is incompatible with the guarantee of free expression.

The rejection of First Amendment precepts is consistent with *Keegstra*'s intellectual origins. It represents the triumph of a feminist critique of freedom of speech to which Canadian feminists made important contributions, but the most prominent voices were the Americans Catharine MacKinnon and Andrea Dworkin. who developed their ideas in a campaign to unsettle First Amendment law.[20] Their claims that speech can harm equality by promoting discrimination and violence and undermine democratic participation were fully adopted by the Canadian Supreme Court which accepted the even stronger

[17] *Keegstra* (n 3) 743.

[18] See Geoffrey R. Stone, 'Group Defamation' (1978) University of Chicago Law School Occasional Paper 15/1978 https://chicagounbound.uchicago.edu/occasional_papers/12/, 9, where he says that '*Beauharnais* was "untenable at the time it was decided and, in any event is no longer controlling authority today"'.

[19] *Keegstra* (n 3) 743.

[20] Andrea Dworkin and Catharine A. MacKinnon, *Pornography and Civil Rights: A New Day for Women's Equality* (Organizing Against Pornography 1988).

claim that certain speech—specifically hate speech and pornography—may 'silence' its targets and thus undermine their free speech rights as well.[21]

Keegstra thus exhibits a complex relationship to First Amendment law. The reasoning is replete with references to First Amendment law and detailed consideration of First Amendment scholarship. It thus acknowledges the intellectual prominence of First Amendment law as a source of a canonical understanding of freedom of speech. But, at the same time, it deliberately challenges central First Amendment ideas. In doing so, *Keegstra* makes the case both for diversifying the free speech canon and for its own admission to it.

New York Times and *Keegstra* thus provide fascinating insights into core constitutional values of their respective nations. In some ways, *Lüth* provides a neat counterpart. Like *New York Times* in particular, its significance lies in part in placing a past era to rest. In vindicating Eric Lüth's right to call for a boycott of the films of Veit Harlan, *Lüth* acknowledges the 'crucial interest' of Germany in demonstrating that its people have come to understand the evils of Nazism.

Further, like both other members of the canon, *Lüth* marks a clear statement of central values of the constitutional system in the context of freedom of speech. On this question, the Court was emphatic that the Basic Law centres upon the dignity of the human person protected in Article 1 of the Basic Law[22] which in turn means that dignity in the German constitutional order is an absolute right and not submitted to the balancing process that attends most rights analysis. Consequently, as Dieter Grimm explains:

> If dignity enters into a conflict with another fundamental right, dignity always prevails. Freedom of speech is no exception. It is but relatively protected. A right that is subject to balancing cannot maintain its absolute status.[23]

The effect of the primacy of dignity in the German constitutional order can be seen in the context of freedom of speech in the careful attention given to the dignitarian harms of speech and in the close links drawn between dignity (protected by Art. 1) and the free development of personality protected by

[21] Catharine MacKinnon, *Feminism Unmodified: Discourses on Life and Law* (HUP 1987) 146–162.

[22] See Dieter Grimm, 'Freedom of Speech and Human Dignity' in Adrienne Stone and Frederick Schauer (eds), *The Oxford Handbook of Freedom of Speech* (OUP 2021) 112. He says that 'according to the provision, human dignity is "*unantastbar*", literally "untouchable" but usually translated as "inviolable", the German equivalent being "*unverletzlich*". "*Unantastbar*" is used only in connection with dignity, whereas "*unverletzlich*" is used several times in connection with other fundamental rights. This difference is levelled by translating both words as "inviolable". German jurisprudence assumes that the choice of different terms indicates that there must be a difference in substance and concludes that "*unantastbar*" has to be understood as absolute.'

[23] ibid.

Article 2. In consequence, the Constitutional Court has been comparatively willing to uphold laws protecting personal honour and reputation,[24] to vindicate privacy.[25] It also places high priority on the development of 'personality' through freedom of speech.[26]

A. The Troubling Relationship between Liberty, Equality, and Dignity

One way to understand these cases is as instances of three conceptions of freedom of expression that each appeal to different fundamental values: a conception that strongly values the liberty of expression in an unconstrained public discourse; a conception that strongly values equality; and a conception that strong values dignity. They form a 'canon' in the sense that they identify three possibilities and while they are, no doubt, not the only possible conceptions of freedom of speech, they form a shared understanding against which free speech jurisprudence in other places can be measured.

Something more must be said, however, about these values because—it hardly bears repeating—invoked at a high level of generality, ideas like liberty, equality, and dignity are insufficiently distinct to reveal distinct differences of approach. On the contrary, several complications arise if we rely on these values as indicative of the overriding character of freedom of speech in any given system.

There is first a tendency for these concepts to merge. That is especially evident in relation to dignity and equality. All three values are understood as foundational to the modern human rights order[27] and have some obvious links. Dignity may be thought to require, or be an inherent aspect of, equality. By the same token, equality may be thought to require, or be an inherent aspect of, respect for dignity. Further, equality and dignity can be seen as aspects of liberty in the sense that they are preconditions for, or constitutive of, at least some conceptions of liberty. Of this relationship, Susanne Baer has written that the three values form a 'triangle':

[24] This may be seen, e.g., in the *Strauss* case in which the Constitutional Court affirmed the civil sentence imposed on a journalist for insults levelled against a deceased former politician: *Strauss* [1990] 82 BVerfGE 272. But the point should not be overstated. The Constitutional Court is increasingly closely scrutinizing such cases: see, e.g., *Tucholsky II* (*'Soldiers are Murderers' Case*) [1995] 93 BVerfGE 266.

[25] *Lebach* [1973] 35 BVerfGE 202.

[26] *Böll* [1980] 54 BVerfGE 208.

[27] The preamble to the Universal Declaration of Human Rights (UDHR) refers to the 'the inherent dignity and ... the equal and inalienable rights of all members of the human family' as the foundation of 'justice and peace in the world': UDHR (adopted 10 December 1948) UNGA Res. 217 A(III).

> [W]e need to ask for equality in conjunction with both dignity and liberty, just as we need to understand dignity in light of liberty and equality, and liberty in light of equality and dignity. To put it differently, and again, we need to better understand what equality, dignity, and liberty mean in light of each other, in a triangle, in order to achieve what human and fundamental rights seem to be about—namely, equal conditions of freedom based on the recognition of diverse ways in which one can choose to live one's own life.[28]

These connections are rendered especially clearly in Canadian constitutional law including in its contribution to the canon in *Keegstra*. As a general matter, Canadian constitutional law is committed to a substantive conception of equality that focuses on addressing the perpetuation of arbitrary disadvantage because that perpetuation of disadvantage itself denies dignity.[29] It is hardly surprising, therefore, that the Canadian Supreme Court has also recognized that dignity (not directly mentioned in the text of the Charter) 'find expression in' and is 'inextricably bound to' the rights protected by the Charter[30] and this connection between equality and dignity is found in its understanding of freedom of expression as well. The harm in racist hate speech, according to *Keegstra*, lay in its capacity to destroy the 'sense of human dignity and belonging to the community at large'.[31] That is, a sense of dignity is a crucial element of equality conceived substantively. The same line of reasoning also demonstrates the connections between liberty on the one hand and dignity and equality on the other. The invocation of equality and dignity in the context of freedom of speech occurs as the court gives meaning to the limitation clause of section 1. That it, equality and dignity-based limitations are justified as necessary in a '*free* and democratic society'.

The problem, then, with understanding freedom of speech by reference to this triumvirate of values is that it reproduces, in the context of freedom of speech, the complex and entwined relationship among these values more generally.[32] At least part of the answer to this quandary lies, no doubt, in a more

[28] Susanne Baer, 'Dignity, Liberty, Equality: A Fundamental Rights Triangle of Constitutionalism' (2009) 59 *U Toronto LJ* 417, 430.

[29] *R v. Kapp* [2008] 2 SCR 483, 504 [21] (McLachlin CJ and Abella J), citing *R v. Oakes* [1986] 1 SCR 103, 136 (Dickson CJ).

[30] *R v. Morgentaler* [1988] 1 SCR 30; *Blencoe v. British Columbia (Human Rights Commission)* [2000] 2 SCR 307. See, generally, Emily Kidd White, 'A Role for Human Dignity under the Canadian Charter of Rights and Freedoms' in Richard Albert, Paul Daly, and Vanessa MacDonnell (eds), *The Canadian Constitution in Transition* (University of Toronto Press 2019) 310.

[31] *Keegstra* (n 3) 746.

[32] Susanne Baer (n 28) 471; Laurence H. Tribe 'Equal Dignity: Speaking its Name' (2015) 129 *Harv L Rev* 16, 22.

fine-grained analysis of these values. That is, we need to move from a concept—defined at only a high level of generality—to a particular conception of those values. There is considerable scholarship on this question. For instance, the German conception of the dignity of the person has been explained by some scholars to depend upon a conception of honour with deep roots in German culture. It has an association of equality but, as James Whitman has memorably shown, an association of a particular kind. That is, it pursues equality in the realm of insult and defamation law by 'levelling up' and extending to all the honour that was once the preserve of the elite.[33] This conception of dignity is not necessarily inconsistent with the emphasis on belonging within a multicultural community that motivates the connection between equality, dignity, and freedom of expression in Canada. But the two cases show how the particular conception of these values varies in and responds to particular histories and contexts.

B. Liberty, Equality, Dignity, and Double-Sidedness

The complex relationship between these values is revealed in a different way when the idea of freedom of expression as 'liberty' (revealed by *New York Times*) is compared with freedom of expression as 'equality' or 'dignity'. One apparent difference is that the central ideas of the liberty conception of freedom of expression (robust self-reliance in the context of a vigorous competition of ideas) are employed to *expand* the scope of freedom of speech whereas equality and dignity operate in the opposite way, identifying the limits on or boundaries of freedom of expression. Liberty is therefore often put as a value that *conflicts* with both equality and dignity.

However, equality and dignity can be invoked in favour of freedom of expression as well as in support of its limits. One common argument in favour of the traditional stance of First Amendment law with respect to hate speech (which favours liberty of expression in almost all cases) is that *equality* requires strong limitations on governmental powers of censorship to protect those least likely to dominate majoritarian processes.[34] On this account, freedom of expression has been a powerful tool for minority groups and women to challenge

[33] James Q. Whitman, 'Enforcing Civility and Respect: Three Societies' (2001) 109 *Yale LJ* 1279.
[34] Nadine Strossen, 'Hate Speech and Pornography: Do We Have to Choose between Freedom of Speech and Equality?' (1996) 46 *Case W Res L Rev* 449.

prevailing social ideas[35] and, in an inversion of the Canadian position, the Fourteenth Amendment's guarantee of equality is understood as integral to a conception of freedom of expression that bolsters, rather than weakens, the case for protecting racist hate speech.

Once again, part of the answer to this apparent contradiction lies in more fine-grained conceptions of these ideas and attention to the contexts in which they arise. One way to understand the distinctiveness of US law lies in the relative importance of the individual and communities. *New York Times* invokes the spirit of a robust and determined individual who is fearless in the face of criticism and up to the task of engaging with her critics whereas, in *Keegstra*, the invocation of equality is placed in a context that is more attuned to the significance to the individual of membership of a community and which understands that groups—and not just individuals—need protection both through free speech and against harmful speech. The Charter conception of rights is therefore open to the possibility that individual freedoms can be limited to protect groups' identities and communal practices. The Canadian law of freedom of expression in turn is especially sensitive to the individual's need to take part in the communal life of cultural groups to which they belong.

Turning thirdly to the frequently opposed ideas of liberty and dignity, something of the same dynamic can be seen again. Insofar as dignity requires the autonomous development of the self, it can pursue a liberty-driven conception of freedom of expression. The liberty to speak respects the individual as autonomous and morally capable. In this conception lies an account of human dignity that respects human agency.[36] Thus ideas of dignity are identifiable within First Amendment thought and are found especially clearly in the First Amendment vision of Justice Brandeis. He envisioned a citizenry inspired by their First Amendment freedoms to engage courageously in a vigorous public debate, to be resilient and self-reliant, and to develop good character and courage. The propensity of a liberty to speak to promote these values is summed up vividly by Justice Harlan in *Cohen v. California*:

> The constitutional right of free expression is powerful medicine in a society as diverse and populous as ours. It is designed and intended to remove governmental restraints from the arena of public discussion, putting the decision as to what views shall be voiced largely into the hands of each of us, in the hope

[35] Akhil R. Amar, 'The Case of the Missing Amendments: *R.A.V. v. City of St Paul*' (1992) 106 *Harv L Rev* 124; Timothy Zick, 'The Dynamic Relationship between Free Speech and Equality' (2017) 12 *Duke J Const L & Pub Pol* 13.

[36] Neomi Rao, 'Three Concepts of Dignity in Constitutional Law' (2011) 86 *Notre Dame L Rev* 183.

> that use of such freedom will ultimately produce a more capable citizenry and more perfect polity and in the belief that no other approach would comport with the premise of *individual dignity* and choice upon which our political system rests.[37]

Thus, in addition to the potential for merger, this comparative analysis of canonical texts of freedom of speech reveals the problem of 'double-sidedness'. That is, the values that are commonly advanced in favour of freedom of speech—including liberty, equality, dignity—can be advanced in favour of its limits as well. It leaves us with the question of why these values sometimes count in favour of more freedom of speech and sometimes against it. To understand this, we need to turn to a further dimension of freedom of speech that is revealed by these canonical texts.

IV. Canonical Significance: Background Commitments of the Constitutional Order

At least part of the answer to this double-sidedness lies in more explicit attention to less visible aspects of the constitutional system that nonetheless have a profound effect on the shape of freedom of expression. These are the 'background commitments' of the constitutional order. By this, I mean that a constitution is grounded on understandings of how it operates, at whom it is directed, and, more broadly, the purpose or remit of constitutionalism in each constitutional order. These features of a constitution are often implicit, but they are revealed in what can be termed the *structure* and *strength* of rights.

A. *Lüth* and Transformative Freedom of Expression

To see how the background commitments of the constitutional order reveals themselves, we return to *Lüth*. Perhaps the most important aspect of *Lüth* is found not in its treatment of freedom of speech, but in its articulation of fundamental features of the Basic Law and its core values. To understand this aspect of the decision, two further points of background are necessary. First, the *Lüth* case arose from an action taken by a film-distribution company against Lüth on the basis that his conduct was actionable under the Civil Code. The case

[37] 403 US 15, 24 (1971) (emphasis added).

therefore arose within the context of litigation between private individuals rather than a more typical constitutional challenge directly against the exercise of legislative or executive power by the state.

In light of that fact, the question arose whether the free speech provision (Art. 5) of the Basic Law applied at all. Article 5 contains a limitation clause that provides:

> These rights shall find their limits in the provisions of general laws, in provisions for the protection of young persons, and in the right to personal honour.

A central issue in the case therefore was whether the provision of the Civil Code that formed the basis of the action to restrain *Lüth* was a 'general law' and therefore not subject to the requirements of (and so constituted a permissible limit on) freedom of expression.

The Court accepted that the relevant provision of the Civil Code—section 826—was a 'general law' within the meaning of Article 5's limitation clause but nonetheless found a violation of Article 5. This was because this provision of the Civil Code—which provided for a tortious action for intentional actions that were an offence against good morals[38]—must be read in light of the Basic Law and specifically the fundamental importance of freedom of speech in the public sphere. The fact that Lüth's call for a boycott was grounded in a matter of high public importance and in the context of his own efforts for peace with the Jewish people and to address the Nazi persecution of the past, meant that the call for a boycott did not meet the Civil Code requirement that the act be against good morals. The fundamental right 'radiates' to private law and allows its interpretation in its light.[39] In this case, the private law concept of 'good morals' is reinterpreted in light of Article 5's commitment to freedom of expression.

It is this finding that marks the most revolutionary aspect of *Lüth*. The Court announced that the Basic Law establishes 'an objective order of values' that is capable of affecting all legislation, public administration and adjudication. This idea of an 'objective order of values' can be easily misunderstood. It is not (though it might seem so to some ears) a claim in the debate about whether moral values correspond to something in the world.[40] Rather, the idea of an

[38] The German word is *sittenwidrig* which Dieter Grimm translates as 'against public policy/immoral': Dieter Grimm, 'The Role of Fundamental Rights after Sixty-Five Years of Constitutional Jurisprudence in Germany' (2015) 13 *ICON* 9, 22.

[39] ibid.

[40] Andrei Marmor, *Positive Law and Objectivity* (OUP 2001) ch. 6.

objective order of values illuminates the meaning and purpose of constitutionalism and the relationship of the constitution to the rest of the legal order. In establishing an objective order of values, the Basic Law establishes values to which the Constitution gives effect through the whole legal order.

In doing so, *Lüth* creates a distinctive understanding of freedom of expression with important doctrinal consequences. Freedom of expression is classically conceived of as a 'first generation' right[41] that operates (a) vertically against government (and not horizontally against private parties) and (b) negatively to constrain interference rather than to confer positive entitlements. In *Lüth*, by virtue of the radiating effect of the right, freedom of expression has an 'indirect horizontal operation'. While the right does not directly bind individuals, it nonetheless guides the interpretation of the law in private disputes with the consequence that private law disputes do not escape constitutional scrutiny.[42]

This feature of *Lüth* presages further important development. As emerges later, the most distinctive aspect of the German law of freedom of expression lies in the recognition of a positive duty on the part of the state to protect the conditions in which freedom of speech is effective. This, of course, is the most powerful mechanism. It is the foundation of the very well-known German approach to public broadcasting. Drawing on a foundational understanding of the connection between public discourse and democratic government, the Court has imposed quite detailed conditions on public broadcasting as a *comprehensive* service, available to the *entire population*, containing *substantial diversity* of opinion. It must also be protected by sufficient and non-politically determined funding.[43]

Lüth thus establishes fundamental features of the *structure* of the right to freedom of expression,[44] in its horizontal and positive operation. These aspects of the structure of rights are, in turn, tightly linked to the transformative nature of German constitutionalism. In the words of Michaela Hailbronner, the German Constitution is understood as 'a comprehensive order for a more just and equal society and a tool to prompt state action to that purpose. It is this

[41] The distinction between 'first', 'second', and 'third generation' rights can be traced to Karel Vasak, 'Human Rights: A Thirty-Year Struggle' (1997) 30 UNESCO Courier 11. See, more generally, Philip Alston, 'A Third Generation of Solidarity Rights: Progressive Development or Obfuscation of International Human Rights Law' (1982) 29 *Netherlands Intl L Rev* 307.

[42] On 'indirect horizontal effect', see Adrienne Stone, 'The Comparative Constitutional Law of Freedom of Expression' in Rosalind Dixon and Tom Ginsburg (eds), *Research Handbook on Comparative Constitutional Law* (Edward Elgar 2011) 412–413.

[43] *Rundfunkentscheidung (Television I)* (28 February 1961) BVerfGE 12, 205 (Ger.). Dieter Grimm, 'Freedom of the Media in Adrienne Stone and Frederick Schauer (eds), *The Oxford Handbook of Freedom of Speech* (OUP 2021) 542, 550–551.

[44] On the structure of free speech rights, see Stephen Gardbaum, 'The Structure of a Free Speech Right' in Stone and Schauer, ibid 213.

commitment to transformation'[45]—akin to a 'second generation' social and economic right—that is perhaps the key determinant and most distinctive aspect of the shape of freedom of expression under the Basic Law.

B. *New York Times* and Liberal Freedom of Expression

Neither section 2(b) of the Canadian Charter nor the First Amendment conform to the transformative model of freedom of expression. The contrast with the German position is strongest with the First Amendment, which cleaves most closely to the traditional conception of a first-generation right and is firmly vertical and negative in its operation.

That much is made clear in *New York Times v. Sullivan* itself. That case involved a defamation action that (much like *Lüth*) was between private parties. The application of the First Amendment depended on the Court's finding that 'state action' was involved even though the law to be applied in this question was the common law applied in private litigation. The Supreme Court found:

> Although this is a civil lawsuit between private parties, the Alabama courts have applied a state rule of law which petitioners claim to impose invalid restrictions on their constitutional freedoms of speech and press. It matters not that that law has been applied in a civil action and that it is common law only, though supplemented by statute. The test is not the form in which state power has been applied but, whatever the form, whether such power has, in fact, been exercised.[46]

In addition, the First Amendment operates negatively to prevent interference with expressive freedom rather than to confer any right or entitlement that the government must act to satisfy. [47] In this respect, the First Amendment reflects the orthodox understanding of the US Constitution as 'a charter of negative liberties; [that] tells the state to let people alone; [and] does not require the federal government or the state to provide services'.[48]

This comparison can be too tightly drawn: doctrinal developments have blurred both distinctions as the canon itself reveals. *New York Times* itself shows that the First Amendment can affect the development of the private law, even

[45] Michaela Hailbronner, 'Transformative Constitutionalism' (2017) 65 *Am J Comp L* 527, 527.
[46] *Sullivan* (n 2) 265 (citations omitted).
[47] Kathleen M. Sullivan, 'Two Concepts of Freedom of Speech' (2010) 124 *Harv L Rev* 143.
[48] *Bowers v. DeVito*, 686 F 2d 616, 618 (7th Cir., 1982) (Posner J).

though the relationship between the First Amendment and private law is conceptualized quite differently than in German law. In addition, as many scholars have pointed out, there are well-known ways in which the First Amendment can be understood to have a positive aspect. Indeed, it is a standard response to the characterization of civil and political rights as 'negative' to point to the ways in which they might oblige the state to act either through the provision of public funding or other intervention.[49] In the context of First Amendment law, the 'public forum doctrine'—which in effect requires that public forums be available for the exercise of the right of freedom of speech—is arguably one such instance.[50]

All that can be conceded. But still the point remains that the structure offreedom of expression (and indeed of constitutional rights in general) revealed in *Lüth* is fundamentally different from that evident in *New York Times*. Though a positive *aspect* may occasionally be evident in First Amendment law, there is nothing remotely approaching the open embrace of positive application evident in the law of Article 5. The difference points in turn to the matter of background commitments. Although it is a mistake to characterize liberal constitutionalism as concerned *only* with limitation of government,[51] liberal rights' firm focus on protecting the people from the state marks an important difference between liberal constitutional orders and the kind of activist state with a deliberate agenda to pursue equality and justice envisaged by transformative constitutionalism.

C. The Complex Case of the Canadian Charter

At first sight, the remaining member of the canon, *Keegstra*, largely serves as an additional instance of liberal constitutionalism firmly placing Canada with the United States as a liberal constitutional order. On the question of horizontal application, a few complications arise. Although not evident in *Keegstra*, viewing section 2(b) case law more broadly, Canada is a complex case standing somewhere between the United States and Germany. As is evident from the

[49] Jeremy Waldron, *Liberal Rights: Collected Papers, 1981–1991* (CUP 1997) 1; Stephen Holmes and Cass R. Sunstein, *The Cost of Rights: Why Liberty Depends on Taxes* (WW Norton 1999).

[50] Louis M. Seidman, 'Can Free Speech be Progressive?' (2018) 118 *Colum L Rev* 2219, 223; Ronald J. Krotoszynski, Jr, 'Our Shrinking First Amendment: On the Growing Problem of Reduced Access to Public Property for Speech Activity and Some Suggestions for a Better Way Forward' (2017) 78 *Ohio St LJ* 779, 804, 817.

[51] Even in liberal orders, what constitutions enable is as important as what they prevent: see Adrienne Stone and Lael K. Weis, 'Positive and Negative Constitutionalism and the Limits of Universalism' (2021) 41 *OJLS* 1249.

Canadian counterparts (*Grant v. Torstar Corp.*[52] and *Cusson v. Quan*[53]), the operation of Charter rights on the private law is understood in terms that are closer to the German account. That is, Charter rights—or rather Charter *values*—are understood to have an 'indirect' horizontal application, affecting the development of the private law.[54]

But critically, as in the United States, constitutional law in Canada is dominated by a conception of constitutional rights that adheres largely to the traditional liberal model of negative rather than positive rights. There are some rights in the Canadian constitutional order that fall squarely within the concept of a positive right—for instance, the right to education found in section 93 of the Constitution Act 1967. In addition, the Supreme Court of Canada has generally resisted attempts to interpret constitutional rights in a manner that confers positive rights. In the context of freedom of expression, the Court has repeatedly affirmed that section 2(b) 'generally imposes a negative obligation on government rather than a positive obligation of protection or assistance'.[55]

In some respects, therefore, *Keegstra* confirms rather than extends the insights gained from *New York Times*. There are other ways, however, in which *Keegstra* points to a quite distinctive understanding of freedom of expression.

First, *Keegstra* gestures towards a third group of rights that form part of the standard understanding of rights—'third generation' or 'collective' rights that are designed to seek to secure the welfare of communities or peoples rather than individuals. As usually understood, these rights are explicitly directed to the protection of a specific group and held collectively by the group as a whole (even if an individual member has the standing to invoke them). Section 2(b) does not take this form, but in its attentiveness to the harm to communal life that expression can cause, *Keegstra* invokes the kind of reasoning that ultimately grounds these rights. *Keegstra* contain hints therefore of one of the distinctive features of the Canadian Charter (at least when compared with its closest constitutional cousins in the Commonwealth and the German Basic

[52] [2009] 3 SCR 640. See generally, Adrienne Stone, '*New York Times v Sullivan*' (n 8).

[53] [2009] 3 SCR 712.

[54] The foundational case, protecting protesters on a picket line from the private law of trespass is *RWDSU v. Dolphin Delivery Ltd* [1986] 2 SCR 573.

[55] *Baier v. Alberta* [2007] 2 SCR 673, 686 [19]. See also *Haig v. Canada* [1993] 2 SCR 995, 1035; *Delisle v. Canada (Deputy Attorney General)* [1999] 2 SCR 989, 1015 [26]; *R v. Prosper* [1994] 3 SCR 236, 267. See, generally, Robert E. Charney, 'The Shaky Foundation of "Statutory Platforms": A Comment on *Baier v. Alberta*' (2008) 42 *Sup Ct L Rev* 115. A limited exception arises in cases of underinclusive legislation: see *Dunmore v. Ontario (Attorney General)* [2001] 3 SCR 1016; *Baier v. Alberta* [2007] 2 SCR 673. But such claims are 'positive' in only a rather limited sense. There is no general obligation on the state to provide a platform for expression, it is only that governmental power to do so *selectively* is limited.

Law), its inclusion of a catalogue of collective rights including language education rights and certain rights for indigenous people.[56]

Second, the Canadian case, when examined in comparative context with the other members of the canon, help us identify variations within the liberal tradition as to the strength of rights of freedom of expression. A much-noted feature of First Amendment law is the *strength* of its negative orientation. Overall, the First Amendment confers much stronger protection in freedom of expression than most other rights of freedom of expression. That is, as a general matter, stronger justifications are required in order to justify regulations of speech. Among the most highly distinctive aspects of First Amendment law that contributes to its unique strength is a core non-distributive principle that categorically denies the relevance of some kinds of justifications for limitations on speech. Specifically, under the First Amendment, it is not open to challengers to argue that a law regulating speech can be justified on grounds of 'enhancement'. On the contrary, the US Supreme Court has famously declared that 'the concept that government may restrict the speech of some elements of our society in order to enhance the relative voice of others is wholly foreign to the First Amendment'.[57]

Keegstra stands in direct opposition to this idea. At the core of the reasoning is an acceptance of the idea of 'enhancement', by restricting forms of speech that undermine equal democratic participation.[58] In *Keegstra*, the Supreme Court concluded:

> [E]xpression can work to undermine our commitment to democracy where employed to propagate ideas anathemic to democratic values. Hate propaganda works in just such a way, arguing as it does for a society in which the democratic process is subverted and individuals are denied respect and dignity simply because of racial or religious characteristics ... Indeed one may quite plausibly contend that it is through rejecting hate propaganda that the state can best encourage the protection of values central to freedom of expression.[59]

[56] Canadian Charter of Rights and Freedoms, ss. 16–23; Constitution Act, 1982, s. 35. See, generally, Ran Hirschl, '"Negative" Rights vs. "Positive" Entitlements: A Comparative Study of Judicial Interpretations of Rights in an Emerging Neo-Liberal Economic Order' (2000) 22 *Hum Rts Q* 1060

[57] *Buckley v. Valeo*, 424 US 1, 48–49 (1976).

[58] Frederick Schauer, *Free Speech: A Philosophical Enquiry* (CUP 1982) 40–41. See also Lorraine E. Weinrib, 'Hate Promotion in a Free and Democratic Society: *R v. Keegstra*' (1991) 36 *McGill LJ* 1416, 1429–1430; Vicki C. Jackson, 'Holistic Interpretation, Comparative Constitutionalism and Fissian Freedoms' (2003) 58 *U Miami L Rev* 265, 284–288; J. Skelly Wright, 'Money and the Pollution of Politics: Is the First Amendment an Obstacle to Political Equality?' (1982) 82 *Colum L Rev* 609, 625–626.

[59] *Keegstra* (n 3) 764.

The roots of the difference on this score are exactly in those 'background commitments' that so illuminate other aspects of freedom of expression.[60] The refusal of American courts is grounded in the very well-known spirit of mistrust that animates First Amendment law. A measure of distrust of government is central to the idea of liberal rights themselves and to classical arguments for freedom of speech. But it is especially well developed in First Amendment thought, encompassing both the idea that officials will use their power to regulate speech illegally, dishonestly, or self-servingly[61] and a scepticism that government can make reliable judgements about speech, even when government is acting in good faith. There are also fears arising from the large and complex nature of modern government.[62] These are compounded by the majoritarian nature of democratic government and the natural human tendency towards intolerance, which are likely to lead government to censor ideas because they are unconventional or unpopular.[63]

In Canada, by contrast, the explicit acknowledgement in section 1—the 'central organizing principle' of the Charter—that rights are subject to limitation seems to signal that the Canadian Supreme Court should be sympathetic towards arguments for limitation on speech and defer more readily to legislative judgement.[64] The state may sometimes be acting in good faith in support of the vulnerable and, where it does so, the Court should be deferential to the legislature and mindful of its representative function.[65] At the same time, it may be that the Canadian position is sensitive to *judicial* fallibility with respect to freedom of expression (and other rights). As Peter Russell has put it: '[b]y providing a legislative counter-weight to judicial power the Canadian *Charter* establishes a prudent system of checks and balances which recognizes *the fallibility of both courts and legislatures* and gives closure to the decisions of neither'.[66]

[60] The following two paragraphs draw upon Adrienne Stone, 'The Canadian Constitutional Law of Freedom of Expression' in Richard Albert and David R. Cameron (eds), *Canada in the World: Comparative Perspectives on the Canadian Constitution* (CUP 2018).

[61] Vincent Blasi, 'The Checking Value in First Amendment Theory' (1977) 2 *Amer Bar Found Res J* 521.

[62] ibid 543.

[63] *Abrams v. United States*, 250 US 616, 630 (1919) (Holmes J): 'Persecution for the expression of opinions seems to me perfectly logical. If you have no doubt of your premises or your power and want a certain result with all your heart you naturally express your wishes in law and sweep away all opposition.' John Hart Ely, *Democracy and Distrust: A Theory of Judicial Review* (HUP 1981) 103.

[64] Jamie Cameron, 'The Original Conception of Section 1 and its Demise: A Comment on *Irwin Toy Ltd v. Attorney-General of Quebec*' (1989) 35 *McGill LJ* 253, 261. see also *R v. Edwards Books and Art Ltd* [1986] 2 SCR 713.

[65] *Irwin Toy Ltd v. Quebec* (AG) [1989] 1 SCR 927, 993.

[66] Peter H. Russell, 'Standing Up for Notwithstanding' (1991) 29 *Alta L Rev* 293, 301.

V. Conclusion and Anticanon

The canon of freedom of expression nominated here offers insights along three dimensions. First, all three cases mark defining moments in the development of constitutional law and illuminate core constitutional ideals and perhaps even national identities. In *Lüth*, we see the Federal Constitutional Court addressing Germany's Nazi past, and establishing the objective order of values that remains basal to German constitutionalism. In *New York Times*, we see the United States, in the context of the great struggles of the civil rights era, settle a long-standing question about the place of sedition in American law and articulate the profound national commitment to robust public discourse. In *Keegstra*, the Canadian Supreme Court takes a deliberately independent course, acknowledging the First Amendment tradition developed to its south but forging its own conception of freedom of expression and a distinctively Canadian conception of a 'free and democratic society'.

Second, each of these canonical decisions reveals a connection between rights of freedom of expression and the foundational values of constitutionalism: dignity, liberty, equality. In *Lüth*, dignity appears to be the dominant value, in *New York Times* there is a strong exhortation of the value of liberty or freedom, and, in *Keegstra*, equality comes to the fore. But, as we have seen, those values bear a complex relationship to each other and to the law of freedom of expression. Those complexities are appreciable only in an appropriately fine-grained and context-sensitive analysis.

Lastly, these decisions direct our attention to the background commitments of the constitutional order in which they sit. That is, they assist in identifying fundamental features of the *kind* of constitutional system in which they sit. The objective order of values established in *Lüth* identifies the transformative nature of German constitutionalism, whereas *New York Times* with its strongly negative and vertical orientation is emblematic of the strongly liberal nature of US constitutionalism. *Keegstra* complexifies the picture, while still placing Canada firmly within the realm of liberal constitutionalism—albeit a form of liberal constitutionalism that is more attentive to the significance of communal life and more permissive of governmental intervention.

Together, then, these cases form a canon that is highly illuminating of the global context for constitutionalism as well as of freedom of expression. In closing, it is worth considering whether there is a freedom of expression 'anti-canon'. That is, drawing on Jamal Greene's conception of the anti-canon, are there cases or texts the central propositions of which are now so widely reviled that their rejection is itself a prerequisite for legitimacy?[67] There certainly are cases which are now wildly out of favour. In the United States, *Dennis v, United States*,[68] almost universally criticized for upholding the conviction of leaders of the United States Communist Party, is the obvious candidate. But criticism of that case is usually levelled at the relative flexibility of the 'clear and present danger' test which was unable to insulate the Court from the political pressure to censor communists.[69] The subsequent development of relatively rigid categorical rules that now dominate First Amendment law is seen as a direct response to *Dennis* but viewed globally, however, this suspicion of flexible standards of review is not shared. On the contrary, this doctrinal rigidity is tightly linked to the distinctively strong culture of mistrust that dominates First Amendment law. In the rest of the world, proportionality, which allows for case-specific balancing, is by far the dominant approach to determining the validity of laws.[70]

Outside the United States, a plausible candidate for an 'anti-canon' might be found in *Buckley v. Valeo*[71] for its articulation of the First Amendment's core non-redistributive principle or perhaps *Citizens United v. Federal Election Commission*,[72] which extends to corporations the unlimited rights of political expenditure that follow from *Buckley*. The idea that laws regulating expressive activity in the interests of balancing public discourse or providing equal access to the political process is *necessarily* an invalid interference with freedom of expression is not shared by countries that, like Canada, are liberal but more permissive of government intervention. In countries like Germany, in which freedom of expression has a transformative character, the idea might be—to borrow a phrase from *Buckley*—'wholly foreign'.[73]

The search for an anti-canon is worthy of further consideration but this brief reflection calls the task into some doubt. First Amendment law is so unusual in world terms that its anti-canon is not shared by the rest of the world. Equally, texts foundational to modern First Amendment law might in fact be anti-canonical elsewhere. To that end, this search might simply reveal a deep cleavage in the understandings of freedom of expression globally that in turn precludes identification of an anti-canon.

[67] Jamal Greene, 'The Anticanon' (2011) 125 *Harv L Rev* 379.
[68] 341 US 494 (1951).
[69] Harry Kalven, Jr, *Worthy Tradition: Freedom of Speech in America* (Harper Collins 1982) 196–198.
[70] Grégoire Webber, 'Proportionality and Limitations on Freedom of Speech' in Adrienne Stone and Frederick Schauer (eds), *The Oxford Handbook on Freedom of Speech* (OUP 2021) 173.
[71] *Buckley* (n 57) 48–49.
[72] 558 US 310 (2010).
[73] See n 52 and accompanying text.

17

Freedom of Religion

Jaclyn L. Neo

I. Introduction

As one of the early antecedents of modern human rights, one might imagine some degree of intellectual consensus surrounding freedom of religion that could ground the search for a canon in the field. After all, the right to religious freedom is today among the most commonly found guarantees in not only modern constitutional documents, but also international and regional human rights documents.[1] The truth, however, is that the nature and scope of freedom of religion remains highly contested, standing as it does at 'a triangulation point where the individual, the faith community and the State converge'[2] and diverge. Early conceptions of *libertas religionis*, which dates back to the early third century,[3] were critically shaped by church–state relations and conflicts over political authority, rather than about individual freedom.[4] It was only after several centuries of Enlightenment that religious freedom evolved into an individual right as it started appearing in written charters of right, most notably the 1791 First Amendment to the Constitution of the United States,[5] which guaranteed that 'Congress shall make no law respecting an establishment of religion or prohibiting the free exercise thereof'.[6] Comparable provisions were written into the constitutional texts of other European nations and subsequently into modern international human rights instruments, including

[1] Nathan Lerner, *Religion, Belief, and International Human Rights* (Orbis Books 2000).

[2] Mark Hill QC, 'Locating the Right to Freedom of Religion or Belief Across Time and Territory', in Silvio Ferrari et al. (eds), *Routledge Handbook of Freedom of Religion or Belief* (Routledge 2021).

[3] For a history of religious freedom, see John Witte, Jr, 'The Right to Freedom of Religion: An Historical Perspective from the West', in ibid 11.

[4] See generally András Sajó & Renáta Uitz, 'Freedom of Religion', in Michel Rosenfeld & András Sajó (eds.), *The Oxford Handbook of Comparative Constitutional Law* (OUP 2012).

[5] Christian Walter, 'Religion or Belief, Freedom of, International Protection', *Max Planck Encyclopedia of Public International Law* (May 2021), <https://opil.ouplaw.com/view/10.1093/law:epil/9780199231690/law-9780199231690-e867> (accessed 7 April 2024).

[6] John Witte, Jr & Joel A. Nichols, *Religion and the American Constitutional Experiment* (OUP 2016) 64–116.

Jaclyn L. Neo, *Freedom of Religion* In: *Global Canons in an Age of Contestation.* Edited by: Sujit Choudhry, Michaela Hailbronner, and Mattias Kumm, Oxford University Press. © Jaclyn L. Neo 2024. DOI: 10.1093/9780191956942.003.0017

the 1948 Universal Declaration of Human Rights (UDHR) and later the 1966 International Convention on Civil and Political Rights (ICCPR).

Today, slightly different formulations are used to refer to freedom of religion. International human rights documents tend to use a broader term of *freedom of thought, conscience, and belief*, while others employ the term *freedom of religion or belief*. These formulations presumably aim to expand the scope of the protection of religious freedom to encompass more than theistic religions, but also, as the Human Rights Commission's General Comment No. 22[7] notes, 'non-theistic and atheistic beliefs, as well as the right not to profess any religion or belief'.[8] Today, texts guaranteeing the right to religious freedom typically comprise of three parts —guarantees for the freedom of belief (the *forum internum*), guarantees for the freedom of actions relating to that belief (e.g. worship, teaching, practice, observance, propagation, etc., i.e. the *forum externum*), and a set of permissible limits on those freedoms. Exactly what is to be protected under this right is subject to debate, especially as one moves from the right to profess and practise established, communal religion to an arguably wider right to belief and conscience. This raises seemingly intractable problems with definition—what constitutes 'religion' that could be the subject of constitutional protection? Is freedom of religion only a matter of choice to believe whatever one wishes and, if so, how is it different from freedom of expression? Or is freedom of religion to be understood in terms of communal association and, if so, how is it different from freedom of association? Is freedom of religion a matter of beliefs and to what extent is the protection of beliefs tantamount to the protection of religious orthodoxy? Questions have been asked why a practice should be protected simply because it is religious, and not otherwise? Some contestations exist not only at the margins of the scope of the right, but also at its core. Critics from different ends of the political and intellectual spectrum have questioned whether religious freedom should even exist as a separate right.[9] What exactly is so distinctive and special about religion that it should warrant an entire right and thereby an entire field of enquiry?[10]

The right to freedom of religion stands at the centre of a highly contentious debate about the nature of rights, democracy, constitutionalism, and secularism, and the status of religion in relation to all of these. Even contestations

[7] 'General Comment No. 22: The right to freedom of thought, conscience and religion (Art. 18)', CCPR/C/21/Rev.1/Add.4 (1993).

[8] ibid para. 2.

[9] See, e.g., Winnifred Sullivan, *The Impossibility of Religion* (1st edn, Princeton University Press 2018); Brian Leiter, *Why Tolerate Religion?* (Princeton University Press 2013).

[10] For a defence, see e.g. Arif Jamal, 'Considering Freedom of Religion in a Post-Secular Context: Hapless or Hopeful?' (2017) 6 Oxford J. of Law & Religion 433.

about the scope of religious freedom, including the most basic questions such as the right to leave one's religion (and choose another religion or no religion), whether freedom of thought and conscience is truly inviolable, and whether and to what extent religious practices are protected, are, to some extent, proxies for ideological struggles concerning the normativity of constitutionalism, between liberal and non-liberal constitutionalism, between secular constitutionalism and religious (even theocratic) constitutionalism, and between separationist secularism and non-separationist secularism. Under such conditions, one might be said to be venturing into a minefield of ideological and culture wars in trying to identify 'global canons' in the field of freedom of religion. From Saudi Arabia's first objection to the inclusion in the UDHR of the right to change one's religion, to the continuing resistance and rejection of such a right despite guarantees for freedom of religion in the constitution of some countries, one might indeed question if there is a sufficient shared consensus to speak of a shared conversation, much less one that allows for common self-reflection and building of connections. For if the purpose of a canon is to provide 'a platform for a shared conversation on the basis of certain foundational texts',[11] then the exercise will be significantly undermined by a lack of theoretical commitment,[12] even ideological commitment, within the field.

Accordingly, a discussion of global canons in religious freedom jurisprudence requires us to squarely confront the fact that canonization is very much a normative exercise, even though some of these 'canons' may be presented within their own jurisdiction as uncontroversial and settled law. If an exercise in global canons is to be productive, therefore, there is a need to recognize that in the global arena what is canonical in one jurisdiction could be seen as non-canonical, or even, anti-canonical in another, and the field of freedom of religion shows this perhaps even more starkly. Criticism of and debate about what one considers anti-canonical therefore should be underpinned by a contextual understanding of different legal traditions and social norms in each jurisdiction. This means that the claimed normative superiority reflected in the language of canons should be accompanied by the modesty of conscious self-reflection that one's claimed canons are often very much a product of historical and ideological encounters. The dominance of Global North thought and jurisprudence in what scholars and policymakers consider to be 'canons' is not simply a matter of 'superior' intellectual rationality, but a product of

[11] Michaela Hailbronner, 'Constructing the Global Constitutional Canon: Between Authority and Criticism' (2019) 69 Uni. Of Toronto LJ 248.

[12] See Mark Tushnet, 'The Jurisprudence of Canons of Comparative Constitutional Law', Chapter 3 in this volume.

history, including the history of colonial/imperialist encounters.[13] An exercise in identifying global canons, including for religious freedom, is as much a political exercise as it is a legal one.

Because religious freedom situates itself within a range of different state–religion constitutional arrangements, to identify a canon characterized by its centrality to an academic discipline, and its indispensability,[14] is fraught with difficulties. This chapter therefore embarks on the exercise of identifying canons in the field of religious freedom within constitutional law and human rights law with a critical lens. In the following sections, I will examine evidence of the canonical (and anti-canonical) status of four cases, their legacy, and criticism. Different authors have offered variations on the definition of canons; canons have been defined by their centrality to 'the legal culture's self-understanding',[15] a measure of 'competence in [an academic] discipline',[16] and as 'the hard core which gives a discipline coherence and continuity'.[17] In selecting these four cases, I applied the criteria of 'paradigmatic shifts'. In my view, these cases should be canonized because they have served as turning points within the field and in shaping how we think about religious freedom as well as how courts go about deciding religious freedom cases. The first two cases are both from the Global North: *West Virginia State Board of Education v. Barnette*[18] (hereafter '*Barnette*') and *Kokkinakis v. Greece*[19] (hereafter '*Kokkinakis*') are landmarks in establishing what today seems banal—that religious freedom protects religious minorities, thus serving to advance social/religious plurality and secularism. The next two cases are from the Global South: *Commissioner, Hindu Religious Endowments, Madras v. Sri Lakshmindra Thirtha Swamiar of Sri Shirur Mutt*[20] and *Lina Joy v. Majlis Agama Islam Wilayah*[21] both challenge a separationist perspective of religious freedom, reflecting a judicial approach that is far more interventionist in state–religion relations. *Lina Joy*, in particular, challenges a foundational claim within international human rights that the right to freedom of religion includes the right to choose one's religion without restrictions. Its inclusion

[13] This point is well noted in Hailbronner (n 11).
[14] Jamal Greene, 'The Anticanon' (2011) 125 Harv. L. Rev. 379, 385.
[15] Bruce Ackerman, 'Living Constitution' (2007) 120 Harv L. Rev. 173.
[16] Jamal Greene, 'The Anticanon' (2011) 125 Harv. L. Rev. 379, 385.
[17] Matthias Reimann, 'The Progress and Failure of Comparative Law in the Second Half of the Twentieth Century' (2002) 5 Am. J. Comp L. 671, 695.
[18] 319 US 624 (1943).
[19] App. No. 14307/88 (EctHR, 25 May 1993).
[20] [1954] AIR 282.
[21] [2007] 4 MLJ 585 (Federal Court, Malaysia). For context, see also the lower court decisions: *Lina Joy v Majlis Agama Islam Wilayah Persekutuan & Ors* [2005] 6 MLJ 193 (Court of Appeal, Malaysia); *Lina Joy v. Majlis Agama Islam Wilayah* [2004] 2 MLJ 119 (High Court, Malaysia).

points to a foundational disagreement within the field of religious freedom. A discussion of this case is also crucial as it has become part of the West's orientalist imaginary of religious freedom in the 'East' and therefore could be said to have attained the status of an anti-canon in the field of comparative constitutional law and religion.

Notably, the four cases discussed credibly form part of what Balkin and Levinson would call 'the pedagogical canon' for a distinct field of comparative constitutional law and religion, i.e. as a set of materials for educating law students. They may also form part of what Balkin and Levinson call the academic theory canon as 'benchmarks for testing academic theories about the law'.[22] The identification of these 'canonical' cases in this chapter is also an exercise in critique, as the analysis will show that such cases often create broad principles which do not always illuminate subsequent developments in the jurisprudence. Accordingly, reference to these canonical cases can, at times, obscure the more radical changes that courts are engaging in when adopting certain positions.

II. Canons of Religious Freedom

A. The Right to Freedom of Religious Thought and Conscience: *Barnette*

Barnette is one of the US Supreme Court's most well-known 'constitutional law landmark' cases.[23] In the case, the Court upheld the constitutional rights of a religious minority not to be compelled to participate in a majoritarian ritual, affirming the right to freedom of religious thought and religious conscience. The applicants had challenged the constitutionality of laws passed by the West Virginia legislature to require all schools to conduct courses of instruction in history, civics, and in the Constitutions of the United States and of the state 'for the purpose of teaching, fostering and perpetuating the ideals, principles and spirit of Americanism, and increasing the knowledge of the organization and machinery of the government'.[24] Following this, the Board of Education adopted a resolution ordering that the salute to the flag become 'a regular part

[22] Jack M. Balkin & Sanford Levinson, 'The Canons of Constitutional Law' (1998) 111 Harv. L. Rev. 963.

[23] Gregory L. Peterson et al., 'Recollections of *West Virginia State Board of Education v. Barnette*' (2007) 81 St. John's L. Rev. 755.

[24] §134, West Virginia Code (1941 Supp.), reproduced in *Barnette*.

of the program of activities in the public schools', and that all teachers and pupils 'shall be required to participate in the salute honoring the Nation represented by the Flag' and recite the pledge of allegiance. The resolution further provided that a refusal to salute the flag would be regarded as an 'act of insubordination', which could result in expulsion.

In *Barnette*, the Court held that the action of the local authorities in compelling the flag salute and pledge violated the appellants' First Amendment rights. Its momentous nature also lies in the fact that the Supreme Court decisively overruled its decision in *Minersville School District v. Gobitis*, delivered just three years earlier.[25] In *Gobitis*, the Court ruled that public schools could compel students to salute the American flag and recite the Pledge of Allegiance, despite the students' religious objections to the practices. Justice Felix Frankfurter, delivering the decision of the majority, held that the school district's interest in creating national unity was a legitimate goal and sufficient to allow it to require students to salute the flag. He placed the state's interest in 'national cohesion' at the top of the 'hierarchy of legal values', writing that:

'National unity is the basis of national security. To deny the legislature the right to select appropriate means for its attainment presents a totally different order of problem from that of the propriety of subordinating the possible ugliness of littered streets to the free expression opinion through handbills.'[26]

In upholding the state's interests over the individual liberty claims of the Jehovah's Witness applicants, he emphasized that '[c]onscientious scruples have not, in the course of the long struggle for religious toleration, relieved the individual from obedience to a general law not aimed at the promotion or restriction of religious beliefs.'[27]

The opinion of the Court in *Barnette* delivered by Justice Jackson reversed the balance between state interest and individual freedom. Instead, the Supreme Court emphasized the freedom of conscience and the right to dissent. As Justice Jackson put it in these now-famous words: 'Compulsory unification of opinion achieves only the unanimity of the graveyard.'[28] Further, he wrote: 'If there is any fixed star in our constitutional constellation, it is that no official, high or petty, can prescribe what shall be orthodox in politics, nationalism, religion, or other matters of opinion or force citizens to confess by word or act their faith therein.'[29] Justice Black and Justice Douglas, both of

[25] *Minersville School District v. Gobitis*, 310 US 586 (1940) (hereafter '*Gobitis*').
[26] ibid 596.
[27] ibid 594.
[28] *Barnette* (n 23) 641.
[29] ibid 642.

whom originally joined with the Court in the *Gobitis* case, felt the need to issue a concurring opinion. They emphasized that the First Amendment does not grant individuals an absolute right to make final decisions on everything they will or will not do, and that the courts must determine the constitutionality of particular laws that strike at the substance of religious tenets and practices. They thus concluded that the applicant Jehovah's Witnesses were conscientious objectors and that enforcing ceremonial adherence among little children 'is a handy implement for disguised religious persecution'. Similarly, Justice Murphy, in his concurring opinion, emphasized the freedom to believe and the freedom to worship. He reasoned that '[o]fficial compulsion to affirm what is contrary to one's religious beliefs is the antithesis of freedom of worship.'

Barnette was not a unanimous decision. The majority held 6–3 in dissent. Justice Frankfurter, the author of the court opinion in *Gobitis*, wrote a long and involved dissent raising alarm over what he saw as an attempt to subordinate the general civil authority of the state to what he called 'sectarian scruples'. He argued that the constitution protects the free exercise of faith whereby the individual may profess their faith according to their conscience and choice, but that faith cannot be the basis for restricting state action as long as the action is not asserted in a discriminatory way. He was vehemently against what he saw as the Court exceeding the scope of its judicial role and appropriating the legislative function in striking down the law.

To be sure, while one may agree that *Barnette* deserves canonical status in American and even global jurisprudence, one may question whether religious freedom is the correct field. Within academic scholarship and court jurisprudence, *Barnette* has frequently been invoked for its free speech principle. State and federal courts routinely invoke the case for the proposition that freedom of speech guarantees a right not to speak as well as a right to speak. In an authoritative text on religion and state, Gey suggests that *Barnette* is 'actually a free speech decision, not a free exercise decision..[30] Indeed, Justice Jackson's opinion emphasizes free speech, rather than free exercise.[31] While he acknowledged that the appellants' objections were religiously motivated, his opinion suggested that the constitutional objections do not turn on one's religious views or the sincerity with which they are held. This contrasts with the concurring opinions of Justices Black, Douglas, and Murphy, which greatly emphasized the religious nature of the objections.

[30] Steven G. Gey, *Religion and the State* (2nd edn, Carolina Academic Press 2006) 737.

[31] Note, however, that even the status of *Barnette* in free speech jurisprudence has been challenged: see Genevieve Lakier, 'Not Such a Fixed Star After All: *West Virginia State Board of Education v Barnette*, and the Changing Meaning of the First Amendment Right Not to Speak' (2019) 13 FIU L. Rev. 741.

That said, a number of academic books that examine the freedom of religious exercise, both as a stand-alone title or as part of a text on constitutional law in the United States, and this includes Gey's, identify and examine *Barnette* as a religious freedom case.[32] Moreover, a study of *Barnette* for its religious exercise doctrine is important as allows us to see it as the root of the current existential debate as to whether constitutional protection of religious freedom or free exercise is even necessary as the lines between freedom of religious exercise and freedom of expression are increasingly blurred. Some question whether we still need to have constitutional protection of religious freedom when protecting freedom of expression should be sufficient. Others argue that First Amendment protection for religious individuals is so denuded that we might as well do away with protection of religious freedom. A more trenchant critique asks why religious believers should be prioritized over others, simply because of the claimed religious nature of their practice.[33]

A contextual examination of *Barnette* further illuminates its canonical status within religious freedom jurisprudence. The case stands for the vindication of the rights of a religious minority against majoritarian imposition, reversing the negative impact of a court's prior decision. The period after *Gobitis* has been described as 'an unparalleled period of persecution of Jehovah's Witnesses'.[34] During this time, at least thirty-one states took legal steps to expel children who refused to salute the flag in schools and there were numerous reported instances of vigilantism and attacks on houses of worship.[35] *Gobitis* was strongly criticized by many sectors, with critics arguing that the Court had denuded First Amendment protection entirely and had subordinated the civil liberties of minorities to the will of the majority.[36]

The *Barnette* case was a turning point in a long line of Supreme Court cases involving Jehovah's Witnesses. It sits alongside other seminal cases such as *Cantwell v. Connecticut*,[37] in which the Supreme Court declared

[32] See, e.g., Gey (n 30) 729–737; Jesse H. Choper et al., *Constitutional Rights and Liberties: Cases, Comments, Questions* (9th edn, West Pub. Co 2001) 1019–1020 (under the chapter on freedom of religion); John T. Noonan, Jr & Edward McGlynn Gaffney, Jr, *Religious Freedom: History, Cases, and Other Materials on the Interaction of Religion and Government* (Foundation Press 2001) xi (where the introduction refers to *Barnette*, alongside *Cantwell* and *Ballard*, as 'the great trio of the early 1940s' and as 'controlling precedents').

[33] See e.g. Christopher L. Eisgruber & Lawrence G. Sager, *Religious Freedom and the Constitution* (Harvard University Press 2009) 11; Leiter (n 9).

[34] Peterson (n 23) 785.

[35] See David R. Manwaring, *Render Unto Caesar: The Flag Salute Controversy* 163 (University of Chicago Press 1962); Brett G. Scharffs, 'Echoes from the Past: What We can Learn About Unity, Belonging and Respecting Differences from the Flag Salute Cases' (2011) 25 BYU J. Pub. L. 361.

[36] See Manwaring, ibid 149–157.

[37] 310 US 296 (1940).

unconstitutional a Connecticut statute that required individuals making door-to-door religious solicitations to obtain a state licence. The Court unanimously held that the Fourteenth Amendment's due process clause served to extend the free exercise clause of the First Amendment to the states. The plaintiffs were Jehovah's Witnesses who had been going door to door in a predominately Roman Catholic neighbourhood in New Haven, Connecticut, to proselytize. In *Cantwell*, the Court held that the First Amendment's free exercise clause 'embraces two concepts—freedom to believe and freedom to act. The first is absolute but, in the nature of things, the second cannot be'.[38] This was further affirmed in *Barnette*. Besides *Cantwell* and *Barnette*, the Supreme Court handed down more than twenty opinions dealing with Jehovah's Witnesses in the period between 1938 and 1946.[39] During this period, Jehovah's Witnesses were also involved in hundreds of cases in the lower courts.[40] It has even been suggested that *Barnette*, alongside the many Jehovah's Witnesses challenges against state laws restricting their religious freedom, were foundational for the rights revolution in the 1960s.[41]

B. Religious Freedom, Democracy, and Pluralism: *Kokkinakis v. Greece*

Across the Atlantic, it might be hard to imagine today that for the first quarter of a century following its establishment in 1959, the European Court of Human Rights (ECtHR) decided no cases under Article 9 of the European Convention of Human Rights (ECHR).[42] *Kokkinakis* is the first case in which the Court squarely addressed a freedom of religion or belief challenge under Article 9.[43]

[38] ibid 303–304.

[39] Peterson (n 23) 758.

[40] See also Shawn Francis Peters, *Judging Jehovah's Witnesses: Religious Persecution and the Dawn of the Rights Revolution* (University Press of Kansas 2000).

[41] ibid.

[42] T. Jeremy Gunn, et. al, 'Introduction' in Jeroen Temperman, et. al. (eds), *The European Court of Human Rights and the Freedom of Religion or Belief: The 25 Years since* Kokkinakis (Brill Nijhoff 2019). There were several cases involving religion that came before the now-defunct European Commission of Human Rights: Carolyn Evans, 'Pre-*Kokkinakis* Case-Law of the ECHR: Foreshadowing the Future' in Temperman, ibid.

[43] An earlier case, *Johnston v. Ireland*, App. No. 9697/82 (1986), challenged Ireland's laws against dissolution of marriage, which was challenged, inter alia, on the grounds of violation of Art. 9. The Court, however, took the view that 'the freedom to have and manifest [the applicant's] convictions is not in issue'. In a separate opinion, partly dissenting and partly concurring, Judge De Meyer disagreed, holding that the applicants' religious freedom was implicated. He stated that 'complete exclusion of any possibility of seeking the civil dissolution of a marriage is not compatible with the right to respect for private and family life, with the right to freedom of conscience and religion and with the right to marry and to found a family'.

Evans calls *Kokkinakis* an 'important turning point in the history of Article 9 cases under the European Convention of Human Rights'.[44] Since *Kokkinakis*, cases challenging state restrictions on religious expression and activities under Article 9, which often also implicate other parts of the ECHR, have proliferated.[45] Within this growing jurisprudence, *Kokkinakis* is an essential cornerstone of ECtHR jurisprudence on freedom of religion and is the most widely cited judgment of the Court on this right.[46] The case features prominently in key textbooks on the ECHR. In fact, a 2019 book on the ECtHR's jurisprudence on freedom of religion or belief specifically takes *Kokkinakis* as its starting point.[47] Citation (or perhaps recitation) to this now well-known passage in *Kokkinakis* has become unavoidable and indeed, expected:

> As enshrined in Article 9 (art. 9), freedom of thought, consciences and religion is one of the foundations of a 'democratic society' within the meaning of the Convention. It is, in its religious dimension, one of the most vital elements that go to make up the identity of believers and their conception of life, but it is also a precious asset for atheists, agnostics, sceptics and the unconcerned. The pluralism indissociable from a democratic society, which has been dearly won over the centuries, depends on it.[48]

In terms of substantive principles, *Kokkinakis* is significant for having drawn out the need to protect religious freedom in a democratic society marked by pluralism. *Kokkinakis*, like in *Barnette*, involved a challenge to state regulation of the religious activities of Jehovah's Witnesses. The applicant and his wife, both Jehovah's Witnesses, were prosecuted and convicted in Greece under a law that made proselytism an offence. They were accused of 'attempting to proselytise and, directly or indirectly, to intrude on the religious beliefs of Orthodox Christians, with the intention of undermining those beliefs, by taking advantage of their inexperience, their low intellect and their naivety'.[49] The wife's conviction was quashed by a higher court but not the husband's. The challenge was directed at Kokkinakis's charge as well as Greek law criminalizing proselytization.

[44] Evans (n 42) 13.
[45] Gunn, et. al (n 42).
[46] Malcolm Evans, 'The Freedom of Religion or Belief in the ECHR since *Kokkinakis*. Or "Quoting *Kokkinakis*"' (2017) 12(2–3) *Religion & Human Rights* 83,
[47] Temperman, et. al. (n 42).
[48] *Kokkinakis* (n 19) para. 31.
[49] Judgment of the Lasithi Criminal Court convicting the Kokkinakises, as recounted in the EctHR's judgment, ibid para. 9.

For the first time, in this case, the ECtHR declared that a member state had breached Article 9 of the ECHR. To be sure, the finding of a violation in *Kokkinakis* is really more procedural than substantive, premised upon a failure of the Greek courts to give adequate reasons for the conviction for proselytization, rather than a clear disapproval of laws restricting proselytization per se.[50] In fact, in its judgment, the Court drew a distinction between 'bearing Christian witness' and 'improper proselytism'. The former is characterized as 'true evangelism', whereas the latter as 'a corruption or deformation of it'.[51] As such, *Kokkinakis* did not entirely rule out that state restriction of proselytization could be compatible with Article 9 of the ECHR. In fact, in his dissenting opinion, Judge Valticos argued that restricting proselytism that rises to the form of a 'systematic attempt at conversion' and 'an attack on the religious beliefs of others' had 'nothing to do with Article 9 ... which is designed solely to protect the religion of individuals and not their right to attack that of others'.[52] Judge Valticos further disagreed with the majority that proselytization should be allowed as long as they are not "improper", questioning whether a convention on human rights really can authorise an intrusion on people's beliefs, even if it is not a forceful intrusion.[53]

There is no doubt that *Kokkinakis* is a canonical decision for religious freedom claims under Article 9 of the ECHR by virtue of its pioneering status and its reach. If cases had an impact factor, it would surely rank among, if not at, the top. However, critics argue that its 'noble sentiments'[54] are so malleable that they have been used to justify both state restrictions on religious activity and thought, as well as to justify against them. We see, for instance, in *SAS v. France*, how the Grand Chamber cited *Kokkinakis* to emphasize both the importance of freedom of thought, conscience, and religion under Article 9 and the need for limitations of this freedom :

> As enshrined in Article 9, freedom of thought, conscience and religion is one of the foundations of a 'democratic society' within the meaning of the Convention. This freedom is, in its religious dimension, one of the most vital elements that go to make up the identity of believers and their conception of life, but it is also a precious asset for atheists, agnostics, sceptics and the unconcerned. The pluralism indissociable from a democratic society, which has

[50] Evans (n 46) 87.
[51] *Kokkinakis* (n 19) para. 48.
[52] ibid 27.
[53] ibid 29.
[54] Evans (n 46) 84.

> been dearly won over the centuries, depends on it. That freedom entails, inter alia, freedom to hold or not to hold religious beliefs and to practise or not to practise a religion (see, among other authorities, *Kokkinakis v. Greece* …).[55]

Two paragraphs down, the Grand Chamber also cited *Kokkinakis* for the following proposition justifying state restrictions:

> In democratic societies, in which several religions coexist within one and the same population, it may be necessary to place limitations on freedom to manifest one's religion or beliefs in order to reconcile the interests of the various groups and ensure that everyone's beliefs are respected (see *Kokkinakis*).[56]

Indeed, reference to *Kokkinakis* often gives the appearance that the Court has continued a consistent and authoritative line of reasoning, even while it has departed from the core of the jurisprudence. By claiming that all things lead to *Kokkinakis*, jurisprudential changes and distinctions over time may be obscured. This could lead to a failure to critically assess how subsequent cases have effectively reappraised or even reinterpreted Article 9.[57] Evans is particularly critical of what he says that 'somehow, in 25 years of jurisprudence built upon the recognition of the vital importance of religious pluralism to democratic life, we have arrived at a position in which banning religious believers from merely wearing their religiously inspired clothing in public appears capable of being necessary in a democratic society'.[58]

This criticism of *Kokkinakis* can be expanded into a broader critique of canonical texts. It is precisely its eloquence and malleability that contributes to the longevity (and hence canonical status) of cases like *Kokkinakis*. By being all things to all men, decisions like these ensure its foundational status as the reference point for all subsequent litigation. All sides of the debate can find something in these cases to support their preferred position. One sees the same phenomenon with *Barnette*, which has been invoked by the majority and in the dissent, and used to justify positions on all sides. *Barnette* featured in many seminal cases including *Masterpiece Cakeshop, Ltd v. Colorado Civil Rights Commission*[59] (majority), *Mozert v. Hawkins County Board of Education*[60]

[55] *S.A.S. v. France*, App. No. 43835/11 (EctHR, 1 July 2014), para. 124.
[56] ibid para. 126.
[57] Evans (n 46).
[58] ibid 95. Evans refers in particular to *Ahmet Arslan and Others v. Turkey*, App. no. 41135/98 (23 February 2010); *S.A.S. v. France*, App. no. 43835/11 (July 2014).
[59] 138 S. Ct 1719 (2018).
[60] 827 F. 2d 105 (1987).

(majority), *Wisconsin v. Yoder*[61] (dissent), and *Lee v. Weisman*[62] (dissent). This is perhaps the strength (and weakness) of canonical cases—their ability to be *the* point of reference for all sides of the debate.

C. Essential Practice Test: The Commissioner, Hindu Religious Endowments, *Madras v. Sri Lakshmindra Thirtha Swamiar of Sri Shirur Mutt*

The Supreme Court of India's judgment in *Shirur Mutt*[63] is another influential case that has created a significant doctrine defining the field. *Shirur Mutt* is the intellectual origin of the essentials practices doctrine, which extended constitutional protection to rituals, observances, ceremonies, and other modes of worship, which would include 'matters of food and dress' where essential to the religion. The Court held that under the Indian Constitution, 'religious denomination or organization enjoys complete autonomy in the matter of deciding as to what rites and ceremonies are essential according to the tenets of the religion they hold and no outside authority has any jurisdiction to interfere with their decision in such matters'. The essential practice test is the controlling test in India on religious freedom adjudication. Recent cases that have applied this doctrine include the triple talak case[64] and the Sabarimala temple case.[65] Its transnational influence among former British colonies in Asia[66] is an outcome of their shared constitutional and legal genealogy, testifying to the importance of historicizing in the exercise of canonization.

The essential practice doctrine draws a distinction between practices that are 'essential', and therefore protected, and those that are not and therefore can be regulated. While *Shirur Mutt* initially suggested that this determination is to be based on the religious adherents' internal determination, the judgment's ambivalence has allowed subsequent courts to take a more externalist interventionist approach to determining whether a practice is essential and deserving of protection. Accordingly, critics argue that it has developed from what appeared to be a rights-enhancing doctrine to a rights-restrictive doctrine.[67] For

[61] 406 US 205 (1972).
[62] 505 US 577 (1992).
[63] [1954] AIR 282.
[64] *Shayara Bano v. Union of India* [2017] AIR 4609.
[65] *Indian Young Lawyers' Association v. State of Kerala* [2018] AIRONLINE SC 243.
[66] See, e.g., *Fatimah bte Sihi & Ors v. Meor Atiqulrahman bin Ishak & Ors* [2005] 2 MLJ 25 in Malaysia.
[67] See Ronojoy Sen, *Articles of Faith: Religion, Secularism, and the Indian Supreme Court* (OUP 2010) 40–72.

instance, in the case of *Commissioner of Police v. Acharya Jagdishwarananda Advadhuta*,[68] the Supreme Court employed the essential practice test to decide that the performance of the Tandava dance was not an essential practice for the Ananda Margie order even though it is a ritual that has been performed publicly for a long time, and can even be traced to some religious texts. Thus, instead of leaving the determination of whether a particular practice is religious and deserving of constitutional protection, the essential practice test empowers the court to sit in determination of whether a particular practice is not only religious but whether it is integral to that particular religion. Inevitably, this means that the court becomes entangled in deciding the content of religious orthodoxy and religious orthopraxy. The doctrine also raises questions about the legitimacy of a 'secular' court making determinations about what practices are essential to a religion, which inevitably draws on theological expositions.[69] Critics argue that the test essentially empowers judges to impose 'religious fiat' and has at times been used to impose rationalist ideas upon religious adherents.[70] Dhavan and Nariman have argued forcefully against the use of the essential practice test along the following lines:

> With a power greater than that of a high priest, maulvi or dharmashastri, judges [in India] have virtually assumed the theological authority to determine which tenets of a faith are 'essential' to any faith and emphatically underscored their constitutional power to strike down those essential tenets of a faith that conflict with the dispensation of the Constitution. Few religious pontiffs possess this kind of power and authority.[71]

The essential practice test can be seen as non-canonical from a liberal–secular constitutionalist perspective insofar as it allows for an interventionist approach by the courts. This might be one reason why the essential practice doctrine, however, has yet to achieve global influence, unlike the Supreme Court of India's other more well-known doctrine—the basic structure doctrine. While the basic structure doctrine conforms to the valorization of judicial supremacy and activism within the Global North, the essential practice

[68] [1984] AIR 512.

[69] Jaclyn L. Neo, 'Definitional Imbroglios: A Critique of the Definition of Religion and Essential Practice Tests in Religious Freedom Adjudication' (2018) 16(2) Int'l J. of Constitutional Law 574,

[70] Sen (n 67) 41.

[71] Rajeev Dhavan & Fali Nariman, 'The Supreme Court and Group Life: Religious Freedom, Minority Groups, and Disadvantaged Communities' in B. N Kirpal et al. (eds), *Supreme But Not Infallible: Essays in Honour of the Supreme Court of India* (OUP 2000), 259.

doctrine seems to be at odds with the Global North's preference for state neutrality towards matters of religious orthodoxy.[72]

D. *Lina Joy v. Majlis Agama Islam Wilayah* as an Anti-Canon: Right to Religious Freedom and the Right to Choose One's Religion

The highly politicized case of *Lina Joy*[73] demonstrate the persistent resistance to a conception of religious freedom as encompassing the freedom to choose one's religion. In this case, the applicant, who was born into a Malay-Muslim family and brought up as a Muslim, had applied to the Malaysia National Registration Department to change her name on the basis that she had renounced Islam for Christianity and intended to marry a Christian. A name change is socially and legally salient in Malaysian society where one's name makes one easily distinguishable by ethnicity. For Malays, having a Malay name is also an indicator of their religious identity due to the close association of the Malay ethnicity with the Muslim religion. This social fact is reinforced by the legal definition in the Federal Constitution of Malaysia, which defines a Malay in Article 160 as one who 'professes to be a Muslim, habitually speaks the Malay language, and adheres to Malay customs'.

Lina Joy's application was initially rejected. She later succeeded on her second application for a name change but it was a pyrrhic victory because, in the interim period, the Regulations governing the content of identity cards were changed such that the religion of all Muslims would be printed on the cards. This meant that even with the name change, she would continue to be identified as a Muslim, despite her self-declaration that she was no longer one. Her application challenging the Department's decision not to remove Islam from her identity card raised administrative and constitutional law issues, chief of which was that it violated her constitutionally guaranteed 'right to profess and practise [her] religion'. She further sought invalidation of parts of the Administration of Islamic Law (Federal Territories) Act 1993, other related state enactments, and all other state or federal legislation which forbade or imposed restrictions on conversion out of Islam for being inconsistent with the Constitution's guarantee of freedom to profess and practise one's religion.[74]

[72] For e.g. in the United States, judges tend to take a more deferential approach towards religious beliefs and instead place emphasis on sincerity of belief (*United States v. Seeger*, 380 US 163 (1965).

[73] The discussion here focuses on the Federal Court judgment: *Lina Joy* (n 21).

[74] She also applied for declarations that the Syariah Criminal Offences (Federal Territories) Act 1997 and other related state enactments were not applicable to her as she was no longer a Muslim.

Under Malaysia's federalist arrangement, Islam was a matter that fell within the state's powers.

The Federal Court essentially skirted around the constitutional question of the scope of religious freedom and focused on the administrative law question, affirming as reasonable the National Registration Department's policy that the applicant produce documentary evidence from the Syariah courts showing that she was no longer a Muslim (i.e. had converted out of Islam). The majority adopted a narrow, formalistic conception of religious freedom in these terms:

> The freedom of religion under Article 11 of the Federal Constitution requires the Appellant to comply with the practices or law of the Islamic religion in particular with regards to converting out of the religion. Upon complying with the requirements of the religion and the religious authorities confirming her as an apostate only then can the Appellant profess Christianity. In other words, one cannot at one's whim and fancy renounce or embrace a religion. When professing a religion, common sense requires one to comply with the laws and practices of the religion.[75]

While the Federal Court did not explicitly state that religious freedom does not guarantee the right to choose one's religion, it effectively did so by subjecting the freedom of Muslims to leave their religion to the authority of the Syariah court. This would have been less objectionable if there was a viable procedure for Muslims to renounce Islam but states in Malaysia have either removed the procedure for renunciation from their state statutes or imposed penalties for attempted renunciation.[76]

The Malaysian courts' refusal in *Lina Joy* to vindicate religious freedom as fundamentally guaranteeing the right to choose one's religion makes it a prime candidate as an anti-canon in religious freedom jurisprudence *if* one accepts the normativity of a freedom of religion premised upon individual autonomy. International human rights law tends to present this view as a fait accompli, obscuring the fact that this is a persistent fault line within human rights law that has a long historical progeny. Whether the right to change one's religion should be included in the UDHR was one of the key disagreements among states at the point of its drafting. The voting record shows that almost half the Drafting Committee did not expressly endorse its inclusion. Predominantly, Muslim

[75] *Lina Joy* (n 21) para. 14, unofficial translation by author.

[76] Long I Lih, 'Malaysia' in *Keeping the Faith: A Study of Freedom of Thought, Conscience, and Religion in ASEAN* (Human Rights Resource Centre 2015).

countries objected to the right to change one's religion. Notably, the 1990 Cairo Declaration on Human Rights in Islam, which serves as the counterpart to the UDHR for Muslim countries, does not include the right to change one's religion. Instead, the Convention states:

> Islam is the religion of true unspoiled nature. It is prohibited to exercise any form of pressure on man or to exploit his poverty or ignorance in order to force him to change his religion to another religion or to atheism.

On the face of it, the divide between the canon and anti-canon could also be said to point to a religious divide. A strong commitment to religious conscience, and the widest protection to the right to believe and the right to choose, is commonly associated with a Lockean conception of the Christian religion which sees religious societies as voluntary organizations and where true religion is characterised by a genuine inward persuasion of the mind. The *forum internum–externum* distinction would therefore seem incongruent for religions, including traditional religions, that prioritize orthopraxy alongside or even over orthodoxy. Another manifestation of this relates to claims for legal protection of religious practice, such as the wearing of religious dress, which are granted less weight than the right against any state coercion of one's religion or belief. One may therefore see the recent controversies arising from attempts by European countries to ban the hijab or burqa as a symptom of the supposedly canonical (or anti-canonical) focus on beliefs, while seemingly undervaluing the outward manifestations of religion.

Notably, *Lina Joy* is not the only case in Malaysia or elsewhere where the freedom to choose one's religion has been denied by the state and in court. It is, however, arguably the most well-known case decided in a constitutional democracy (however flawed the democracy) with a constitution guaranteeing freedom of religion.[77] The sustained international attention stems partly from the collaboration of the local lawyers and human rights activists with their counterparts overseas. Lawyers for Lina Joy made extensive reference to international law and to the Malaysian government's international human rights obligations. The *New York Times* reported on the case multiple times.[78] The Washington DC-based Becket Fund for Religious Liberty wrote

[77] Scholarly attention has been vast, see e.g. this exchange: Thio Li-ann, 'Apostasy and Religious Freedom: Constitutional Issues Arising from the *Lina Joy* Litigation' [2006] 2 Malayan Law Journal Articles 1; Shamrahayu Abd Aziz, 'Apostasy and Religious Freedom: A Response to Thio Li-ann' [2007] 2 Malayan Law Journal i .

[78] See, e.g., Jane Perlez, 'Once Muslim, Now Christian and Caught in the Courts', *New York Times* (24 August 2006). <https://www.nytimes.com/2006/08/24/world/asia/24malaysia.html> (accessed 7 April

a legal opinion and sent its international director to observe the Federal Court hearing.[79] Its international director also wrote an opinion piece on the case in *The Wall Street Journal*[80] and testified before the United States Congressional Human Rights Caucus about the threat to individual rights in Malaysia. The case has been repeatedly referred to by the United States Department of State in its International Religious Freedom Reports.[81] Other human rights organizations, such as the United Nations Commission on Human Rights and the United Nations Human Rights Council, also repeatedly drew attention to the case. This coverage ensured that *Lina Joy* became embedded within the international human rights imaginary such that subsequent reports on religious freedom issues in Malaysia would be analysed through the lens of the tragic case of *Lina Joy*.[82]

As Tamir Moustafa has observed, international pressure surrounding the *Lina Joy* case only served to galvanize Muslim activists who saw the intervention as a Western, if not American, attack on Islam.[83] Thus, the contestation also arises as a result of historical power relations. The issue of changing one's religion is tied to the chequered history of imperialistic evangelical missionary activity.[84] The emergence of a canonical understanding of freedom of religion as encompassing the right to choose one's religion also has to be seen as an outcome of the power dynamics between states and their associated intellectual traditions. The historical context explains, to some extent, the

2024); Thomas Fuller, 'Malaysian Court Refuses to Recognize Woman's Conversion to Christianity', *New York Times* (30 May 2007), <https://www.nytimes.com/2007/05/30/world/asia/30cnd-malaysia.html> (accessed 7 April 2024).

[79] 'Malaysia—State Imposed Religious Designations—*Lina Joy*', The Becket Fund for Religious Liberty (30 May 2007), <https://web.archive.org/web/20090831190113/http://becketfund.org/index.php/case/107.html> (accessed 7 April 2024).

[80] Angela C. Wu, 'Lina Joy', *The Wall Street Journal* (7 September 2006), < https://www.wsj.com/articles/SB115757444080555464> (accessed 7 April 2024).

[81] For e.g. in 2009, 'U.S. State Department rights report give Asia mixed reviews', *New York Times* (26 February 2009), <https://www.nytimes.com/2009/02/26/news/26iht-27RIGHTS.20452424.html> (accessed 7 April 2024).

[82] See, e.g., Liz Gooch, 'Malaysian Custody Dispute Lost Between Courts', *New York Times* (1 April 2010), <https://www.nytimes.com/2010/04/02/world/asia/02malay.html> (accessed 7 April 2024).

[83] Tamir Moustafa, *Constituting Religion: Islam, Liberal Rights, and the Malaysian State* (CUP 2018); see reference to 'Kes Lina Joy Usaha Terancang Hapuskan Islam' ('Lina Joy's Case is a Planned Effort to Undermine Islam') *Harakahdaily* (15 July 2006), < https://dppwp.wordpress.com/2006/07/17/kes-lina-joy-usaha-terancang-hapuskan-islam/> (accessed 7 April 2024); 'Agensi Amerika didakwa beri sokongan sepenuhnya kepada Lina Joy' ('American Agency Accused of Giving Full Support to Lina Joy') *Harakahdaily* (15 August 2006), < https://www.mail-archive.com/harakahdaily@yahoogroups.com/msg05585.html> (accessed 7 April 2024).

[84] Linde Lindkvist, 'The Politics of Article 18: Religious Liberty in the Universal Declaration of Human Rights', *Humanity Journal* (12 June 2014), <http://humanityjournal.org/issue4-3/the-politics-of-article-18-religious-liberty-in-the-universal-declaration-of-human-rights/> (accessed 7 April 2024).

persistent contestations within freedom of religion, highlighting why canonical approaches have emerged, even while anti-canonical approaches continue to challenge them.[85] In constitutional law and human rights, anti-canons can serve to remind us of the need for positions established by canons. They can be the exception that proves the need for the norm. Indeed, *Lina Joy* points to the continuing salience of religious freedom dialogue, and the need to emphasize the protection of individual liberties, including the right to choose one's religion, as a core feature of religious freedom.[86] Some scholars have strongly criticized religious freedom as futile, Eurocentric, and even redundant, even arguing for its abolishment. [87] However, for human rights advocates on the ground, the terms of religious freedom allow them to connect to the intellectual traditions of human rights globally. The strategy is therefore to contextualize religious freedom advocacy, while employing international norms to push for change.

III. Concluding Reflections

To be sure, there are many religious freedom-related cases that could probably have been identified as canons in religious freedom. The Indian case of *Mohd Ahmed Khan v. Shah Bano Begum*[88] (on codification of religious laws), the Australian case of *Church of the New Faith v. Commissioner of Pay-Roll* (on the definition of religion),[89] the Canadian case of *Syndicat Northcrest v. Amselem*[90] (on manifestation of religion), and the English case of *R (Begum) v. Headteacher and Governors of Denbigh High School*[91] (on wearing the headscarf in public schools) are just a few well-known cases that could credibly be analysed as canons of religious freedom jurisprudence. Further, some meritorious and much-needed doctrinal articulations of freedom of religion would probably not reach the status of global canons because they originate from less well-known courts, or because they are not written in

[85] For a discussion on ASEAN, see Jaclyn L. Neo, 'Realizing the Right to Freedom of Thought, Conscience and Religion: The Limited Normative Force of the ASEAN Human Rights Declaration' (2017) 17(4) Human Rights L. Rev. 729.

[86] Jaclyn L. Neo & Brett G. Scharffs, 'Religious Nationalism and Religious Freedom in Asia: Mapping Regional Trends in a Global Phenomenon' (2021) 8 Asian Journal of Law and Society 1.

[87] Sullivan (n 9); Leiter (n 9); Elizabeth Hurd et al. (eds), *The Politics of Religious Freedom* (University of Chicago Press 2015).

[88] [1985] AIR 945.

[89] *Church of the New Faith v. Commissioner of Pay-Roll* [1983] HCA 40, [8].

[90] [2004] 2 SCR 551.

[91] [2006] UKHL 15.

the English language, or have not received publicity in the English media. Canons still tend to originate from the Western Anglo-European world, where linguistic capabilities allow for more rapid sharing of knowledge. The world of global constitutionalism remains a deeply Anglo-European world, with a few occasional forays to non-Anglo-European courts. On freedom of religion, some scholars argue that the historiography of the right to religious freedom makes it unsuitable for contexts outside the Anglo-European world. Some further question if religion is distinctly an Anglo-European concept that tends to obscure rather than illuminate studies of religion in law outside that context.[92] This is not to say that freedom of religion is necessarily an alien concept outside of the Anglo-European world. Within Asia, for instance, the first written constitutional guarantee of freedom of religion can be traced back to the nineteenth century, to article 28 of the 1889 Meiji Constitution which provided that all Japanese subjects 'shall, within limits not prejudicial to peace and order, and not antagonistic to their duties as subjects, enjoy freedom of religions belief'.[93] Further, in the African context, Garba argues that even though African countries were not directly involved in the genealogical formation of the right to religious freedom as it now stands in international law, there is a conception of religious freedom that could be said to be influenced by African traditional religions, which 'exists in the form of live and let live without any condition'.[94] What is needed, therefore, is a contextualized understanding of human rights, which engages, rather than dismisses, and which critically examines, rather than fetishizes, international human rights norms. Whether this be Ignatieff's exhortation for human rights to go global by going local,[95] or Onuma's proposal for an inter-civilizational approach,[96] it bears asking how human rights can better serve people on the ground.[97] Thus, in this

[92] See, e.g., Prakash Shah, *Law and Ethnic Plurality: Socio-Legal Perspectives* (Brill 2007).

[93] Kevin Y. L. Tan, 'The Right to Freedom of Religion: An Historical Perspective from Asia' in Ferrari (n 2) 39.

[94] Ahmed Salisu Garba, 'The Right to Freedom of Religion: An Historical Perspective from Africa' in Ferrari (n 2) 45.

[95] Michael Ignatieff, *Human Rights as Politics & Idolatry* (Princeton University Press 1999).

[96] Onuma Yasuaki, 'Towards an Intercivilizational Approach to Human Rights: For Universalization of Human Rights Through Overcoming of a Westcentric Notion of Human Right' (1997) 7 Asian Yearbook of International Law 21.

[97] David Kennedy, 'The International Human Rights Movement: Part of the Problem?' (2002) 15 Harvard Human Rights Journal 101,

productive exercise of identifying canons and anti-canons, it nonetheless bears recalling Foucault's observation that the production of knowledge is ultimately a function of power: 'In fact, power produces; it produces reality; it produces domains of objects and rituals of truth. The individual and the knowledge that may be gained of him belong to this production.'[98]

[98] Michel Foucault, *Discipline and Punish: The Birth of the Prison* (Alan Sheridan tr, 2nd edn, Vintage Books 1995) 194.

18

Comparative Constitutional Law of Property

*David Schneiderman**

I. Introduction

The Constitutional Court of South Africa, after having undertaken a survey of constitutional property clauses in various bills of rights, concluded that "no universally recognised formulation of the right to property exists."[1] Observing surface appearances that tended towards convergence, Alexander similarly discerns "several important areas of difference, both doctrinal and theoretical" amongst constitutional property clauses.[2] Klug adds that there are a "wide variety of [constitutional] formulations adopted to protect the right to property."[3] These observations are consonant with early twentieth century reflections that, despite claims to universal standards for the protection of property associated with civilized justice,[4] there were no uniform constitutional standards with regard to the protection of

* Professor of Law and Political Science (courtesy), University of Toronto (david.schneiderman@utoronto.ca). I am grateful both to participants at the Global Canons workshop and to the editors of this volume for their comments and insights.

[1] *Re Certification of the Constitution of the RSA 1996*, 1996 (4) SA 744, 798 (CC). The Court, in this passage, was determining whether the new 1996 Constitution's property clause was in conformity with constitutional principles laid out in the 1993 Interim Constitution, in particular, Principle II: "Everyone shall enjoy all universally accepted fundamental rights, freedoms and civil liberties, which shall be provided for and protected by entrenched and justiciable provisions in the Constitution, which shall be drafted after having given due consideration to inter alia the fundamental rights contained in Chapter 3 of this Constitution."

[2] Gregory S. Alexander, *The Global Debate Over Constitutional Property: Lessons for American Takings Jurisprudence* (University of Chicago Press 2006) 20.

[3] Heinz Klug, "Decolonisation, Compensation, and Constitutionalism: Land, Wealth and the Sustainability of Constitutionalism in Post-Apartheid South Africa" (2018) *South Journal on Human Rights* 34: 469, 487.

[4] International Law Association, "Report of the Protection of Private Property Committee" in *Some Opinions and Reports Bearing Upon the Treaty of Trianon and the Claims of Hungarian Nationals with Regard to their Lands in Transylvania*, vol. 1 (W. P. Griffith & Sons Ltd. 1929) 13–26, 16 ("it can fairly be stated that the principle that private property is inviolable is generally recognised and observed throughout the civilised world"); Edwin Borchard, "The Minimum Standard of Treatment of Aliens" (1939) 33 *ASIL Proceedings* 51.

David Schneiderman, *Comparative Constitutional Law of Property* In: *Global Canons in an Age of Contestation*. Edited by: Sujit Choudhry, Michaela Hailbronner, and Mattias Kumm, Oxford University Press.
DOI: 10.1093/9780191956942.003.0018

property.[5] If it is the case that property clauses are invariably the product of bargaining amongst framers operating within national constitutional spaces, it should come as little surprise that property rights will be qualified in differing ways.[6] The product of their efforts will, in short, be embedded within a larger set of constitutional commitments.

There remain, nonetheless, two dominant paradigms within the liberal legal tradition that are reflected in the canons taken up for discussion in this chapter.[7] The first is a classical legal version of property, under the influence of the private law tradition, that emphasizes exclusivity of ownership, exchanged between willing buyers and sellers via transactions occurring within self-regulated markets.[8] This conventional property rights paradigm, that took flight in the nineteenth century,[9] mandates that state laws and policies trespassing on property rights and resulting in a diminution in value, require the payment of just compensation.[10] From this angle, property is primordial in the Lockean sense—it precedes state formation and shields individual rights from societal encroachments.[11] It is a view associated with Underkuffler's "common" conception of property where collective forces are treated as "external" to the protection of property.[12]

A second paradigm treats constitutionally protected property not as a body of stand-alone rights but as internally limited from the outset. Rather than being portrayed as opposites, property and regulation go hand in hand—they

[5] Karl Strupp, "The Roumano-Hungarian Dispute Concerning the Hungarian Optants in Roumania Territory" in *Agrarian Reform in Roumania and the Case of the Hungarian Optants in Transylvania Before the League of Nations* (Impremerie du Palais 1927) 289–303, 289–299.

[6] On the idea of constitutional framers as strategic bargainers, see Jon Elster, *Political Psychology* (CUP 1993) 24 (bargaining as uttering threats and promises "with a claim to credibility"); Ran Hirschl, *Towards Juristocracy: The Origins and Consequences of the New Constitutionalism* (Harvard UP 2004) 43 (on elites seeking to preserve, through judicialization, their hegemonic preservation).

[7] See the discussion of ideal types of constitutional property in Bruce A. Ackerman, *Private Property and the Constitution* (Yale University Press 1977), 4 (describing the ideal types of "Scientific Policymaker" and "Ordinary Observer") and Laura S. Underkuffler, *The Idea of Property: Its Meaning and Power* (OUP 2003) (distinguishing between "operative" and "common" conceptions of property).

[8] For a definition of constitutional property, see David A. Dana and Thomas W. Merrill, *Takings* (Foundation Press 2002) 68–81. Rights are considered "absolute" and "not conditional on the owner's performance of any social functions" in C. B. Macpherson, "A Political Theory of Property" in *Democratic Theory: Essays in Retrieval* (OUP 1973) 120–146, 126. On the place of the buyer–seller model in U.S. constitutional law, see Gerald Garvey, *Constitutional Bricolage* (Princeton UP 1971) 20, 110 and in Canadian constitutional law, see David Schneiderman, "Exchanging Constitutions: Constitutional Bricolage in Canada" (2002) 40 *Osgoode Hall LJ* 401–424.

[9] See Karl Polanyi, *The Great Transformation: The Political and Economic Origins of Our Time* (Beacon Press 1944)

[10] Richard A. Epstein, *Takings: Private Property and the Power of Eminent Domain* (Harvard UP 1985) 95 ("*All* regulations, *all* taxes, *all* modification of liability rules are takings of private property prima facie compensable by the state").

[11] ibid 334; on the Lockean state of nature, see Jeremy Waldron, *The Right to Private Property* (OUP 1990) ch. 2.

[12] Underkuffler (n 7) 40.

are, in a sense, co-original.[13] For this reason, the classical legal version of ownership rights is described as a "mirage," offering "misty illusions."[14] Van der Walt and Piennar reject the "the idea that property rights are unlimited unless ... specifically limited by regulation." This is a proposition that "is no longer generally accepted."[15] The focus turns away from the lone "rights holder" and towards a shared understanding where measures for societal self-protection qualify constitutionally protected property rights. The approach roughly corresponds to Underkuffler's "operative" conception of property in which change is considered a part of the very idea of property.[16] The expectation is that owners will already be on notice that constitutional property undergoes shifts in emphasis and priority and that, should diminution in value occur, this may not always attract full or any amount of compensation.[17] It is a view of constitutionally protected property as "always embedded" within, and already hedged in by, a larger set of constitutional commitments.[18]

This second version portrays constitutional property rights as already crowded in by other constitutional rights, limits, and projects. It turns out to have been a well-accepted formulation of liberal legal thought in the early twentieth century. Axiomatic understandings of property must be rejected, wrote Hobhouse in 1911.[19] "The basis of property is social" in two respects, he argued. First, the benefits of an organized society—characterized as "ordered tranquility"—secures property rights for the propertied.[20] Second, there is the "social factor" in wealth, both inherited and acquired. A liberal individualism that ignores the social factor, Hobhouse wrote, will "deplete national resources,

[13] Not precisely in the sense described in Jürgen Habermas, *Between Facts and Norms: Contributions to a Discourse Theory of Law and Democracy*, William Rehg (tr.) (The MIT Press 1998) 457 (Habermas describes co-originality as a "two-stage reconstruction" where unsaturated rights are filled out and given meaning through law).

[14] Joseph William Singer, *Edges of the Field: Lessons on the Obligation of Ownership* (Beacon Press 2000) 35; Morris Raphael Cohen, *American Thought: A Critical Sketch* (Collier Books 1962) 143. In Polanyian terms, treating property rights as self-regulating and autonomous of society is "utopian" in Polanyi (n 9) 3

[15] Speaking of the 1993 Interim Constitution of South Africa in A. J. Van der Walt and G. J. Piennar (eds.), *Introduction to the Law of Real Property* (Juta & Co. 1996) 422.

[16] Underkuffler (n 7) 50.

[17] Joseph L. Sax, "Some Thoughts on the Decline of Private Property" [1983] *Washington Law Review* 481, 494.

[18] It is Polanyi's insight that "the human economy ... is embedded and enmeshed in institutions, economic and non-economic" in Karl Polanyi, "The Economy as Instituted Process" in Karl Polanyi, Conrad N. Arensberg, and Harry W. Pearson (eds.), *Trade and Market in Early Empires: Economics in History and Theory* (Free Press 1957) 243–270, 250; Polanyi (n 9) 71, 218. See discussion in Fred Block and Margaret R. Somers, *The Power of Market Fundamentalism: Karl Polanyi's Critique* (Harvard UP 2014) 10 on the "always-embedded" economy (Polanyi's embeddedness is a "placeholder term for politics, social relations and institutions"). On the uses to which Polanyian embeddedness has been put, see Gareth Dale, *Karl Polanyi* (Polity 2010) 195–206.

[19] L. T. Hobhouse, *Liberalism* (Williams & Norgate 1911) 100.

[20] ibid 189–190.

deprive the community of its just share in the fruits of industry and so result in a one-sided and inequitable distribution of wealth."[21] That very same year, Bordeaux law professor Léon Duguit delivered a course of lectures at the University of Buenos Aires that had profound influence on the writing of constitutional texts throughout the region.[22] Resisting "dogmatic" formulations of property law, Duguit articulated a version of property that serves "social functions."[23] This would require, for instance, penalties for non-cultivation of land or the taxing of unoccupied housing.[24] While individual property rights are indispensable to the "prosperity and greatness of society," owners must fulfill their social obligations, Duguit maintained. Otherwise, "the intervention of the State is justifiable to oblige him to perform his social function as a property holder. Such intervention consists of procuring at the hands of the owner the employment of his wealth, according to its nature."[25]

The three cases chosen for discussion in this chapter represent a movement from the classical version of constitutional property rights to one where property is inherently crowded in by other constitutional commitments. These might be rights to housing, land reform, Indigenous property, or ecological protection. The cases are drawn from three familiar jurisdictions (the United States, Europe, and South Africa) and so do not offer many surprises.[26] Each of the disputes, however, concerns one of the most private of property rights—the home.[27] They each offer compelling accounts where constitutional property

[21] ibid 191–192.

[22] The English translation appears in Léon Duguit, "Changes of Principle in the Field of Liberty, Contract, Liability, and Property" in Layton Bartol Register and Ernest Bruncken (eds.), *The Progress of Continental Law in The Nineteenth Century: The Continental Legal History Series*, vol. 11 (Harvard UP 1918). A newer translation by Jessica Vivien-Wilksch can be found in Paul Babie and Jessica Vivien-Wilksch (eds.), *Léon Duguit and the Social Obligation Norm of Property* (Springer 2019) 35–61. On its influence, see Thomas T. Anderson and Thomas Ruppert, "Tierra y Libertad: The Social Function Doctrine and Land Reform in Latin America" in Paul Babie and Jessica Vivien-Wilksch (eds.), *Léon Duguit and the Social Obligation Norm of Property* (Springer 2019) 207–252; Helena Alviar García, "Leon Duguit's Influence in Colombia: The Lost Opportunity of a Potentially Progressive Reform" in Günter Frankenburg (ed.), *Order From Transfer: Comparative Constitutional Design and Legal Culture* (Edward Elgar 2013) 306–321.

[23] Duguit (2018) (n 22) 129. On the origins of Duguit's formulation, see M. C. Mirow, "The Social Obligation Norm of Property: Duguit, Hayem and Others" (2010) 22 *Florida Journal of International Law* 191–226.

[24] Duguit (2018) (n 22) 135.

[25] ibid 74.

[26] Benedict Anderson, *A Life Beyond Boundaries* (Verso 2016) 130 ("the most instructive comparisons [whether of difference or similarity] are those that surprise"). The worry is also that, by confining oneself to familiar jurisdictions available in the English language, there is further entrenchment of existing hierarchies. On this worry, see Michaela Hailbronner, "Constructing the Global Constitutional Canon: Between Authority and Criticism" (2019) 69 *University of Toronto Law Journal* 248, 258.

[27] It is considered the "cornerstone justification for the existence of private property" in Margaret Jane Radin, *Reinterpreting Property* (University of Chicago Press 1993) 28, 81. The "established" home, Radin observes, is bound up with "personhood" and is distinguishable from fungible or commodified property.

clauses ordained that the rhetorically superior interests of property owners either prevail or yield to vulnerable owners of property or those with no property at all. In each case, there are degrees of precarity experienced by the weaker parties—their lives are "in some sense in the hands of the other."[28] The cases illustrate how constitutional property, even within the liberal rights tradition, is capable of being transformed in ways that resemble Polanyi's double movement: into solidaristic rights that aim to serve some societal needs.[29] The cases represent, in part, how this movement is the unfinished business of the twentieth century.[30] Increasing awareness of an old fact is finally having an influence on contemporary constitutional thought.[31]

While both ideal types continue to be available to apex courts, there remains the strong rhetorical pull of the discourse of vested legal rights which continues to have a firm hold on legal imaginations.[32] The ascendence of neoliberal legal policy throughout the world, treating markets and individual autonomy as superior to collective commitments, serves as an impediment to the rise of inherently qualified constitutional property rights. These restraints are channeled not only via national legal interpretation but through international legal commitments, such as international investment law, intended to restrain state capacity to interfere with the property and contract rights of foreign investors.[33] Some of the ways in which investment law reinforces the classical

[28] Judith Butler, *Frames of War: When is Life Grievable?* (Verso 2010) 14. "The precarity of life imposes an obligation upon us," writes Butler, 2.

[29] Polanyi describes the "double movement" as one where "powerful institutions" were devised to serve as checks on economic liberalism in order "to resist the pernicious effects of a market-controlled economy" in Polanyi (n 9) 76. On solidarity as the "bride between different modes of social and systemic integration of society," see Hauke Brunkhorst, *Solidarity: From Civic Friendship to a Global Legal Community*, Jeffrey Flynn, tr. (MIT Press 2005) at 5.

[30] Block and Somers (n 18) 18 ("The world is, in effect, struggling with the unfinished business of the 1920s and 1930s"). On the Progressive movement's influence in the U.S. on constitutional property, see Gregory S. Alexander, *Commodity and Propriety: Competing Visions of Property in American Legal Thought 1776–1970* (University of Chicago Press 1997) ch. 11.

[31] With the caveat that this is a feature of Latin American constitutional thought as well as that of German constitutional law. On Colombia, see Helena Alviar Garciá and Catalina Villegas del Castillo, *La Función Social de le Propriedad en las Constituciones Colombianas* (Universidad de los Andes 2012). On Germany, see Donald Kommers, *The Constitutional Jurisprudence of the Federal Republic of Germany*, 2nd edn. (Duke University Press 1997) 252–255. Alexander (n 2) ch. 3 attributes the German instance to the influence of ordoliberal thought. I take issue with Alexander's characterization of ordoliberalism in David Schneiderman, "Constitutional Property Rights and Elision of the Transnational: Foucauldian Misgivings" (2015) 24 *Social and Legal Studies* 65.

[32] Radin (n 27) 28. Maitland observes that the whole of English constitutional law "seems at times to be but an appendix to the law of real property," in F. W. Maitland, *The Constitutional History of England* (Cambridge UP 1919) 538.

[33] See David Schneiderman, "Investment Arbitration as Constitutional Law: Constitutional Analogies, Linkages and Absences" in Thomas Schultz and Frederico Ortino (eds.), *The Oxford Handbook of International Arbitration* (OUP 2020) 421–447; David Schneiderman, "A New Global Constitutional Order?" in Rosalind Dixon and Tom Ginsburg (eds.), *Research Handbook on Comparative Constitutional Law* (Edward Elgar 2010) 189–207.

legal paradigm of the autonomous and heroic wealth creator are discussed intermittently in the chapter. These constraints, compounded by constitutional history and practice, prompt the question of whether, in the service of transitioning to a more pliant conception of property, it would be preferable to abandon constitutional property rights altogether. This question is taken up by way of conclusion.

II. Going Too Far?

The first candidate for inclusion in the global property canon is *Pennsylvania Coal v. Mahon*, a 1922 opinion for the majority of the U.S. Supreme Court penned by Justice Oliver Wendell Holmes. It is considered a "minor classic" of U.S. Fourteenth Amendment doctrine.[34] Holmes is one of the giants in the English-language common law tradition and ordinarily is viewed as aligned in opposition to Justices who sought to use the Constitution to limit state intervention in markets. Holmes's famous dissent in *Lochner v. New York* is oft cited as representing the progressive wing of the Court for having deferred to the exercise of state police power jurisdiction.[35] Justice Holmes's reasoning in *Mahon*, if tenuously connected to his record of dissents, is distinctly different.[36] This is why *Mahon* serves as an antimodel in the global canon. More precisely, it is the common understanding of Justice Holmes's opinion in *Mahon* that serves as an antimodel.[37]

Holmes was typically cryptic about his judicial thinking. "[P]ractical men generally prefer to leave their major premises inarticulate," Holmes declared.[38] In *Mahon*, an opinion joined in by a number of the Justices who signed onto Peckham's majority opinion in *Lochner*, Holmes is understood to have introduced "regulatory takings" doctrine in U.S. constitutional law. At issue was a law requiring coal producers in the state of Pennsylvania to ensure that they did not cause the "caving-in, collapse, or subsidence" of any public buildings

[34] *Pennsylvania Coal v. Mahon*, 260 U.S. 393 (1922). It is so described in Lawrence Friedman, "A Search for Seizure: *Pennsylvania Coal Co. v. Mahon* in Context" (1986) 4 *Law and History Review* 1–22, 5 and William A. Fischel, *Regulatory Takings: Law, Economics, and Politics* (Harvard UP 1995) 14.

[35] *Lochner v. New York*, 198 U.S. 45 at 76 (1905) ("the Fourteenth Amendment is perverted when it is held to prevent the natural outcome of a dominant opinion").

[36] It is described as "almost exactly the reverse" of Holmes's due process dissents in G. Edward White, *Justice Oliver Wendell Holmes: Law and the Inner Self* (OUP 1993) 402.

[37] This is a narrower formulation of the anticanon described by Hailbronner (n 26) 261–262 ("anticanonical decisions are globally rejected and reviled" as they stand opposed to "our globally shared principles of democratic constitutionalism and human rights").

[38] Oliver Wendell Holmes, "The Theory of Legal Interpretation" in Harold J. Laski (ed.), *Collected Legal Papers* (Harcourt, Brace and Co. 1921) 203–209, 209.

or private homes as a consequence of coal mining activities (the Kohler Act).[39] The Pennsylvania Coal Company had sold surface rights to property owners, including the Mahon family, while reserving subsurface mining rights to the company. Purchasers waived any claim to damages caused by coal extraction—they would only be entitled to notice if the Coal Company took steps, such as removing coal pillars that served to support surface structures, causing subsidence.[40] Ms. Mahon sought to enjoin the company from removing coal pillars underneath her home in the City of Scranton, a municipality which was most at peril from subsidence.

Holmes insisted that the state could not require the company to cease its activities without paying for it under the law of eminent domain (the takings rule). It otherwise was an unconstitutional measure. "The general rule," Holmes declared, "at least is, that while property may be regulated to a certain extent, if regulation goes too far it will be recognized as a taking" requiring the provision of just compensation. This was a "question of degree—and therefore cannot be disposed of by general propositions."[41]

The particular facts mattered, however.[42] This was a case concerning a "single private house." Though there is a "public interest" in "every purchase and sale," typically the state refrains from interfering "in ordinary private affairs." The damage being suffered by Mahon, Holmes surmised, "is not common or public."[43] Moreover, the case concerned a right, Holmes wrote in correspondence to Felix Frankfurter, that had not been not paid for.[44] Having purchased only surface rights, owners sought to own what they had "renounced."[45] So "extensive a destruction" of constitutionally protected property rights could not be justified, particularly in light of the fact that "what makes the right to mine coal valuable is that it can be exercised with profit." Requiring measures to prevent subsidence made it "commercially impracticable" to continue mining. It amounted to the appropriation, even the destruction, of profit.[46]

[39] *Mahon* (n 34) 393–394.

[40] ibid 412.

[41] ibid 415–416; Also see Holmes's dissent in *Lochner* (n 35) 198 ("General propositions do not decide concrete cases").

[42] *Mahon* (n 34) 413.

[43] ibid 413.

[44] Letter from Holmes to Frankfurter (February 14, 1923) in Robert M. Mennell and Christine L. Compston (eds.), *Holmes and Frankfurter: Their Correspondence, 1912–1934* (University Press of New England 1996) 150.

[45] Letter from Holmes to Pollock (December 31, 1922) in Mark DeWolfe Howe (ed.), *Holmes–Pollock Letters: The Correspondence of Mr. Justice Holmes and Sir Frederick Pollock 1874–1932* (Harvard UP 1946) 108–109, 109.

[46] *Mahon* (n 34) 414. But see *Erie Railroad Co. v. Board of Public Utility Commissioners*, 254 U.S. 394, 410 (1921) (Holmes treats as constitutionally irrelevant that "States might be so foolish as to kill the goose that lays the golden egg").

Justice Holmes, on the other hand, acknowledged that government "could hardly go on" if it was required to compensate every time it diminished the value of property without paying for it. Such interests are "enjoyed under an implied limitation and must yield to the police power."[47] Holmes thereby acknowledged what was decisive for Justice Louis Brandeis in dissent—that the state law was a constitutionally defensible exercise of state police power jurisdiction to protect public health and safety by preventing the noxious use of property.[48] Though Holmes and Brandeis would "generally agree" on such matters, this was not the case on this occasion.[49] Police powers must have some limits and one factor to consider is diminution in value. Even if the "greatest weight" is to be given to the judgment of the state legislature, Holmes opined, when "it reaches a certain magnitude" compensation must be provided.[50] The worry was that, if exercises of police power are "seemingly absolute," its reach will extend "more and more until at last private property disappears." Such a goal "cannot be accomplished in this way under the Constitution of the United States," declared Holmes.[51]

When contrasted with Holmes's famous dissent in *Lochner*, the ruling in *Mahon* emerges in sharper relief. In *Lochner*, concerning a New York state law that limited maximum hours of work (both weekly and daily) for bakery workers, Holmes insisted that the Constitution did not embody any particular "economic theory." Instead, the Constitution enabled the "majority to embody their opinions in law."[52] Nothing in the Constitution should "prevent the natural outcome of a dominant opinion unless it can be said that a rational and fair man necessarily would admit that the statute proposed would infringe fundamental principles as they have been understood by the traditions of our people and our law."[53] Though the Constitution was made for "people of

[47] *Mahon* (n 34) 413.

[48] ibid 417 (Brandeis J dissenting).

[49] Letter from Holmes to Pollock (22 November 1920) in Holmes–Pollock (n 45) 58. Holmes complained to Pollock that Brandeis read his opinion as resting upon the ground that there must be "an average reciprocity of advantage" in order to avoid the obligation to compensate in ibid at 109. See Brandeis in *Mahon* (n 34) 422. But Brandeis was prompted by Holmes's reference to reciprocity of advantage as having "been recognized as a justification of various laws" promoting the safety of miners in Mahon at 415. Holmes mentions this "formula" which "neatly expressed the rationale of certain cases" in *Jackman v. Rosenbaum Co.*, 260 U.S. 22 at 30 (1922) and in his correspondence with Laski (December 22, 1922) in Mark DeWolfe Howe (ed.), *Holmes–Laski Letters: The Correspondence of Mr. Justice Holmes and Harold J. Laski 1916–1935* (OUP 1953) 465–466, 466 (Holmes–Laski)

[50] *Mahon* (n 34) 413.

[51] ibid 415.

[52] *Lochner* (n 35) 75. Whether "wise or not, the proximate test of good government," for Holmes, "is that the dominant power has its way" in Oliver Wendell Holmes "Montesquieu" in *Collected Legal Papers* (n 38) 250–265, 258.

[53] *Lochner* (n 35) 76 (Holmes J dissenting).

fundamentally differing views," Holmes declared, it had its limits. According to Hurst, vital to Holmes's idea of constitutionalism was the warrant that centers of private or public power be "subject to some check from outside [themselves] … according to criteria not finally determined by the power holders."[54] These limits were exceeded in *Mahon*.

The problem with *Mahon* is that Holmes articulated no criteria other than expressing a concern for measures going "too far." Holmes laid down a path without any signposts, absent any real guidance—he provided a map with no detail other than that the case arose out of the state of Pennsylvania in the United States of America. If constitutionalism insists upon "criteria outside" of power holders themselves, Justice Holmes offered no method for evaluating constitutionality, only something vaguely associated with fundamental principles—what he elsewhere labeled the "established consensus of civilized opinion."[55] The opinion, instead, gave expression to Holmes's skepticism about exercises of public authority on behalf of the masses.[56] Mahon thereby channeled Holmes's "anti-redistributive" streak.[57] The tendency to allow every opinion to become law, ordinarily not barred to states, was a problem that could be curbed by the Constitution's property clauses that takings be accompanied by just compensation.[58] "[D]ifferent rights are of different extent," Holmes declared in an 1899 address, and "stand on different grounds of policy and have different histories." It "does not follow," Holmes continued, that "because one right is absolute, another is." There were few rights, however, as absolute as the "right to sell property."[59]

If the fear was that much of the City of Scranton would be swallowed up by subsidence,[60] Holmes seemed indifferent to the damage to surface structures,

[54] James Willard Hurst, *Justice Holmes on Legal History* (Macmillan 1964) 6.

[55] *Laurel Hill v. San Francisco*, 216 U.S. 365 (1910) 366. "It was a question of degree," Holmes wrote to Laski, "upon which people naturally differ but the lads were with me, except B[randeis]" in Letter from Holmes to Laski (December 14, 1922) in Holmes–Laski (n 49) 462–463, 462. He adds in later correspondence with Laski (January 13, 1923) that Felix Frankurter (then Harvard Law professor) had been silent, "probably feeling an unnecessary delicacy about saying that he disagrees." Holmes, of course, understands "the possibility of thinking otherwise—I could not fail to even if Brandeis had agreed. But nevertheless when the premises are a little more emphasized, as they should have been by me, I confess to feeling as much confidence as I often do," in Holmes–Laski ibid at 473–474, 473.

[56] E. F. Roberts, "Mining with Mr. Justice Holmes" (1986) 39 *Vanderbilt Law Review* 287–304, 293.

[57] Carol M. Rose, "*Mahon* Reconstructed: Why the Takings Issue is Still a Muddle" (1983–84) 57 *Southern California Law Review* 561–599, 581.

[58] Though it was a takings case, rather than a conventional due process case, observes White (n 36) 402, the Fifth Amendment, binding on Congress, had yet to be incorporated into the Fourteenth Amendment which would bind the states.

[59] Oliver Wendell Holmes, "Law in Science—Science in Law" in *Collected Legal Papers* (n 38) 210–243, 241.

[60] Fischel (n 34) 29, 38 indicates that coal companies voluntarily took it upon themselves to ensure that subsidence would not destroy homes in which their own workers resided ("if the company caused subsidence to any surface structure, it sent a crew up to fix the damage, at company expense").

public or private. Holmes was preoccupied with the fact that standing before the Court was only a sole private dweller, whose father was not clever enough—"so short sighted as to acquire only surface rights," complained Holmes—not to waive the right to sue.[61] Cumulatively, however, there were many such sole individuals, small businesses, and public buildings that warranted enacting the Kohler law. Holmes also appeared indifferent to the cost of purchasing subsurface rights from the coal companies. The tax base was "tiny," observes Friedman. "The states were not prepared, or politically able, to raise money to buy off companies hurt economically by regulation."[62] Even if, as Justice William O. Douglas later declared, a state "may adopt a socialist economy," if were "to do so it must pay for the private property which it converts to public use."[63] Similarly, for Holmes, socialism was not beyond the realm of legal possibility but nearly impossible from a fiscal point of view. Few democratic states in the contemporary world have the resources to convert private property to public use. Certainly, Pennsylvania in 1922 did not.[64] The constitutional property clause could conveniently slow down public opinion, requiring states to find the resources with which to pay or abandon their policy prescriptions.

For a number of U.S. Supreme Court Justices, observes Treanor, Holmes's approach would later provide an "attractive basis for a reassertion of judicial authority in the economic realm."[65] It helps to explain, writes DiMento, the multifactor analysis that has come to dominate U.S. takings law.[66] Nevertheless, Holmes's anti-redistributive opinion, remains "exceptional," running counter to the "wide latitude" granted to states in takings jurisprudence.[67] That jurisprudence, however, has not moved much beyond the balancing exercise inaugurated by Justice Holmes. His disinclination for a more precise formulation, instead invoking a vague formulation about "going too far" but without any more guidance, proves to have had the most staying power.[68] The rationale

[61] *Mahon* (n 34) 415.

[62] Friedman (n 34) 18.

[63] William O. Douglas, *Anatomy of Liberty: The Rights of Man without Force* (Simon & Shuster 1963) 87.

[64] The loss of property, Carol Rose (n 55) 567 explains, "may have been negligible, but the record is silent on this point." Justice Brandeis, in dissent, surmises that it "appears that the value of the coal kept in place by the restriction may be negligible as compared with the value of the whole property, or even as compared with that part of it which is represented by the coal remaining in place and which may be extracted despite the statute" in *Mahon* (n 34) 419.

[65] William Michael Treanor, "Jam for Justice Holmes: Reassessing the Significance of *Mahon*" (1998) 86 *Georgetown Law Journal* 813–874, 866. Treanor insists, however, that Holmes's balancing test, was always "weighted in favour of government." He insisted on compensation "only when the public benefit was trivial or nonexistent" (at 868).

[66] Joseph F. DiMento, "Mining the Archives of Pennsylvania Coal: Heaps of Constitutional Mischief" (1990) 11 *The Journal of Legal History* 396, 420.

[67] Rose (n 57) 595, 597.

[68] Ackerman (n 7) 165, 236, fn. 9

for that balancing has improved somewhat thanks to Michelman's agenda-setting contribution.[69] By justifying compensation on utilitarian grounds,[70] Michelman helped to limit *Mahon*'s reach by speaking of demoralization costs. The question to be asked is "whether or not the measure in question can easily be seen to have practically deprived the claimant of some distinctly perceived, sharply crystallized, investment-backed expectation."[71] The requirement of compensation, Michelman argues, is premised on the assumption that property consisted of "several discrete 'things'"[72] and that deprivation of one of these things can be "attended by a pain of a specially acute or demoralizing kind."[73] Compensation is due, Michelman argued, "whenever demoralization costs exceed settlement costs, and not otherwise."[74] Michelman's discussion came to be incorporated, but without attribution,[75] in the multifactor analysis outlined by Justice Brennan in *Penn Central*.[76] *Mahon* was singled out as the "leading case for the proposition that a state statute that substantially furthers important public policies may so frustrate distinct investment-backed expectations as to amount to a 'taking.'"[77] The Court in *Penn Central* described the Pennsylvania statute in *Mahon* as having made it "commercially impracticable to mine the coal and thus had nearly the same effect as the complete destruction of rights claimant had reserved from the owners of the surface land." Passing reference is then made by Brennan to Michelman's law review article,[78] though no such claim of "complete destruction" was ever proven in *Mahon*.

It must be said that Holmes's decision, we can conclude, has undoubtedly contributed to the "chaotic quality" of contemporary U.S. takings doctrine.[79] It also well reflects trendlines within international law. Expropriations and nationalizations that are not accompanied by the payment of compensation representing fair market value will ordinarily attract liability under international investment treaties. In addition to criteria developed by investment

[69] Frank Michelman, "Property, Utility, and Fairness: Comments on the Ethical Foundations of "Just Compensation" Law" (1967) 80 *Harvard Law Review* 1165.

[70] Treanor (n 65) 872.

[71] Michelman (n 69) 1233.

[72] This is the proverbial understanding of property as a bundle of rights. See discussion in Joseph William Singer, *Entitlement: The Paradoxes of Property* (Yale University Press 2000) 9–13.

[73] Michelman (n 69) 1234.

[74] ibid 1215.

[75] Michael Allan Wolf, "The Brooding Omnipresence of Regulatory Takings: Urban Origins and Effects" (2013) 40 *Fordham Urban Law Journal* 1835, 1846.

[76] *Penn Central Transportation Co. v. New York City*, 438 U.S. 104, 124 (1977).

[77] ibid 127–128.

[78] ibid.

[79] Carol M. Rose, "Property and Expropriation: Themes and Variations in American Law" (2000) *Utah Law Review* 1–38, 20.

tribunals,[80] states have incorporated a version of *Penn Central*'s multifactor analysis into their treaties.[81] Having successfully elevated U.S. constitutional property law to the plane of international law, America will continue, thereby, to influence legal developments elsewhere.

III. Eliminating Social Injustice

The second candidate for the comparative constitutional property canon, more representative of dominant trendlines, is *James v. UK*, a 1986 decision of the European Court of Human Rights (ECtHR).[82] At issue in this instance was an allegation that private property had been taken without proper compensation for the purposes of securing property ownership for long-lease tenants. The estate of the Second Duke of Westminster, holding lands in central London, was forced to transfer property rights to lease holders pursuant to a 1967 Act of Parliament,[83] the culmination of a movement for leasehold enfranchisement that started in the 1880s.[84] The plan sought to secure rights to both land and buildings that were originally leased for a term of years and which would, afterward, revert to the landlord. From the tenants' perspective, this amounted to a "wasting asset."[85] The Act detailed how the market value of the properties would be calculated and, in the absence of agreement, ascertained by a leasehold tribunal with a right of appeal to the Lands Tribunal, a division of the High Court.[86] Landlords and tenants could also seek review of valuations before the County Court. Trustees of the Duke's estate claimed that property rights, guaranteed by section 1 of First Protocol to the European Convention on Human Rights, had been violated in the case of eighty leasehold properties in the high-class borough of Mayfair, adjacent to Buckingham Palace.[87]

[80] See, e.g., *Pope & Talbot Inc. v. Canada* (2000), Interim Award, Ad hoc—UNCITRAL Arbitration Rules (June 26) which had recourse to the American Law Institute's *Restatement of the Law Third, The Foreign Relations of the United States*, vol. 2 (American Law Institute 1987) at para. 712, comment (g), to fill in the meaning of the takings rule in the North American Free Trade Agreement. The ALI comment mirrors U.S. constitutional practice.

[81] See discussion in David Schneiderman, " 'Writing the Rules of the Global Economy': How America Defines the Contours of International Investment Law" (2018) *London Review of International Law* 255.

[82] App. no. 8793/79 (February 21, 1986) (*James* 1986), appeal from the European Commission of Human Rights, Report of the Commission (adopted May 11, 1984) (*James* 1984).

[83] The Leasehold Reform Act 1967 as amended.

[84] *James* 1986 (n 82) 6.

[85] ibid ("As the lease progresses, the value of the tenant's interest in the property diminishes").

[86] ibid 11. Under the Act, property could be purchased from the estate upon payment, for less valuable property, of the fair market value of houses premised on fifty-year leases and, for more valuable property, upon payment of a sum calculated on the assumption that the property was tenanted.

[87] On the origins of this development under the auspices of the Duke of Westminster see F. H. W. Sheppard (ed.), *Survey of London: Vol. 39, the Grosvenor Estate in Mayfair, Part 1 (General History)*

Property rights initially were omitted from the European Convention of Human Rights due to disagreement amongst party states. The UK government, alongside France, resisted any obligation to compensate private parties in situations where the state sought to redistribute property.[88] The Labour government, then in power, was reluctant to reward, by the payment of compensation, those who had accrued "unearned wealth" that was contemplated to be taken pursuant to the planning provisions of the Town and Country Act 1947.[89] Negotiations continued and the ensuing compromise, found in Article 1 of Protocol No. 1 to the Convention,[90] is comprised of three distinct rules, according to the Court's ruling in *Sporrong and Lönnroth*.[91] The first rule guarantees the "peaceful enjoyment of property." According to Simpson's account of the UK delegation's intentions, this first rule is meant to serve as a prophylactic to totalitarianism. The second rule addresses deprivations, which are required to be "in the public interest" and carried out pursuant to law, and in compliance with the general principles of international law. There is no mention made of the requirement of compensation. Third, is the recognition that states can "control" the uses of property in accordance with the "general interest." The whole of Article 1 of the First Protocol was described, at its inception, as "exceedingly obscure" and "quite uncertain."[92] Opinions since then have not changed much.[93] Some degree of certainty has been provided by rulings of the ECtHR which requires, among other things, the payment of some compensation, even though this is generally inconsistent with the express wishes of the framers in 1953.

(Athlone Press 1977), http://www.british-history.ac.uk/survey-london/vol39/pt1/pp6-9, accessed January 20, 2021.

[88] A. W. Brian Simpson, *Human Rights and the End of Empire* (OUP 2001) 792.

[89] IBID 782, 785. On the origins of the Act, see Philip Booth, "Nationalising Development Rights: The Feudal Origins of the British Planning System" (2002) 29 *Environment and Planning* 129.

[90] P1-1 provides:

> Every natural or legal person is entitled to the peaceful enjoyment of his possessions. No one shall be deprived of his possessions except in the public interest and subject to the conditions provided for by law and by the general principles of international law.
>
> The preceding provisions shall not, however, in any way impair the right of a State to enforce such laws as it deems necessary to control the use of property in accordance with the general interest or to secure the payment of taxes or other contributions or penalties.

[91] *Sporrong and Lönnroth v. Sweden*, App. no. 7151/75 (A/52) (ECtHR 1982),para. 61.

[92] Simpson (n 88) 798.

[93] See Tom Allen, "Compensation for Property Under the European Convention on Human Rights" (2007) 28 *Michigan Journal of International Law* 287, 292; Helen Mountfield, "Regulatory Expropriations in Europe: The Approach of the European Court of Human Rights" (2002) 11 *NYU Environmental Law Journal* 136, 137.

The trustees' complaint focused on the second rule—that the estate was deprived of property not in the public interest but "for no other reason than to confer a private benefit on a private party."[94] That is, they argued that a forced transfer could not be for the public benefit unless it was for public use. The Court rejected this interpretation of Protocol No. 1. So long as the measure was in the pursuit of "social justice"—in this instance, ensuring "fairness" in the rules governing property and contractual relations—deprivations of property can legitimately promote the public interest within the terms of the Protocol. A taking of property, the Court concluded on this point, "effected in the pursuance of legitimate social, economic or other policies may be 'in the public interest,' even if the community at large has no direct use or enjoyment of the property taken."[95] Contributing to this measure of deference was the "wide" margin of appreciation due to European states who are better placed to make determinations about what is in the public interest. Unless that judgment is "manifestly" unreasonable, the Court was disinclined to second guess.[96]

The object of the 1967 scheme, according to the 1966 White Paper in support of the parliamentary enactment, was to correct inequities—to give effect to the tenant's "moral entitlement" to ownership.[97] "Eliminating what are judged to be social injustices is an example of the functions of a democratic legislature," the Court declared.[98] It is at this point in the ruling that the judicial orientation exhibited by the ECtHR in *James*, contrasts starkly with that of the U.S. Supreme Court in *Mahon*:[99]

More especially, modern societies consider housing of the population to be a prime social need, the regulation of which cannot entirely be left to the play of market forces. The margin of appreciation is wide enough to cover legislation aimed at securing greater social justice in the sphere of people's homes, even where such legislation interferes with existing contractual relations between private parties and confers no direct benefit on the state or the community at large. In principle, therefore, the aim pursued by the leasehold reform legislation is a legitimate one.

Invoking the themes of democracy and political processes that Holmes, in other rulings, insisted would attract judicial deference, the ECtHR emphasized that leasehold enfranchisement had been a matter of public concern for more

[94] *James* 1986 (n 82) 18.
[95] ibid 19.
[96] ibid 20.
[97] ibid 20.
[98] ibid 20.
[99] ibid 20.

than a century. Housing reform had been endorsed by all major political parties, and its merits and demerits had been fully debated in Parliament.

The Court also was obliged to evaluate whether the measures adopted bore a "reasonable relationship of proportionality" to the legitimate objective sought.[100] As declared in the *Sporrong and Lönnroth* ruling, the Court would evaluate whether a "fair balance" was achieved in which an individual would not be expected to bear "an excessive burden."[101] The assessment resembles, roughly, what Michelman had in mind when he maintained that just compensation was owed if there is an especially acute demoralization cost associated with a measure—where the few are unfairly sacrificed "at the hands of the many."[102] If the "instinctive unease" (Michelman's words) of Holmes in *Mahon* pressed in the direction of compensation, the European Court was prepared to push back in the other direction.[103]

The question was not whether this was the only way to achieve the objective—the Court rejected the Trustees' proposed test of "strict necessity"—rather, it was whether the measures were "reasonably suited" to achieving the legislative end.[104] In light of the margin appreciation due to European states, it undoubtedly was. Nor was the required standard of compensation the strictest imaginable—the "just compensation" requirement of "prompt, adequate and effective compensation" that is demanded, for instance, by international investment law. Instead, compensation could be something less than full, approximating the standard of appropriate compensation demanded by states in the Global South and captured in international instruments associated with the New International Economic Order.[105]

One last matter of interest was whether the applicants could lay claim to the standard of compensation available to foreign nationals under international law because of the reference, in Protocol No. 1, to deprivations being "subject to … the general principles of international law." It was assumed by the Court that, if applicable, this would require payment on terms associated with "just," and not "appropriate," compensation, exceeding substantially the

[100] Other complaints concerned the windfall profits accruing to tenants, the alleged absence of judicial review, and the claim that the scheme gave rise to discrimination, all of which were rejected.

[101] *Sporrong and Lönnroth* (n 91) 73.

[102] Michelman (n 69) 1234, 1211.

[103] ibid 1210.

[104] James 1986 (n 82) at 22.

[105] See U.N. General Assembly, Permanent Sovereignty Over Natural Resources, s. 4, December 17, 1973, A/RES/3171, https://www.refworld.org/docid/3b00f1c64.html, accessed on August 23, 2021. For discussion, see M. Sornarajah, *Resistance and Change in the International Law of Foreign Investment* (CUP 2015) 35–42 and Nicolás M. Perrone, *Investment Treaties and the Legal Imagination: How Foreign Investors Play by their Own Rules* (OUP 2021) 92–94.

default compensation rule mandated by the Court.[106] General principles of international law, the Court surmised, were intended to favor non-nationals who were deprived of an ability to participate in political processes giving rise to the deprivation. Aliens, the Court surmised, "are more vulnerable to domestic legislation" because "they will generally have played no part in the election or designation of its authors nor have been consulted on its adoption." This may well provide a "legitimate reason for requiring nationals to bear a greater burden in the public interest than non-nationals."[107] The Court's interpretation, that general principles would only be available to non-nationals, was underscored by examination of the travaux préparatoires which revealed that the obligation to pay compensation in the case of expropriation would only be available to non-nationals.[108] This prompts the question, raised in the concurring opinion of Judge Vilhjálmmson, whether there is any right at all to compensation for European nationals for deprivations of their property.[109] The concurring opinions of Judges Bindschedler-Robert, Gölcüklü, Matscher, Pettiti, Russo, and Spielmann, by contrast, expressed skepticism about the majority ruling—why wouldn't the general principles of international law also be available to European nationals, they asked?[110]

There is some reason to doubt the political process rationale offered by the Court to justify the distinction: that aliens do not participate in the political process giving rise to a deprivation and so are deserving of heightened solicitude by way of greater compensation. Foreign firms have a variety of means to make their preferences known to local political actors, short of exercising the franchise (denied to business firms, in any event).[111] Indeed, recent empirical studies suggest evidence in the opposite direction: that foreign firms wield undue influence over host states.[112] Additionally, aliens benefit from state

[106] e.g. Tom Allen, *Property and the Human Rights Act 1988* (Hart 2005) 116 and Mountfield (n 93) 142. The assumption that they are equivalent, however, is embraced in Hélene Ruiz Fabri, "The Approach Taken by the European Court of Human Rights to the Assessment of Compensation for 'Regulatory Expropriations' of the Property of Foreign Investors" (2002) 11 *NYU Environmental Law Journal* 148–173, 172.

[107] *James* 1986 (n 82) 27 para. 63.

[108] ibid 27–28 para. 64. This is disputed by Egon Schwelb, "The Protection of the Right to Property of Nationals Under the First Protocol to the European Convention on Human Rights" (1964) 13 *American Journal of Comparative Law* 518, 540.

[109] James 1986 (n 82) 38; this is what appears to have been intended as delegates "rejected every proposal that contained a reference to compensation" in Allen (n 93) 291.

[110] James 1986 (n 82) 39. This is also the view of Ruiz Fabri (n 106) 171.

[111] See discussion in David Schneiderman, "Investing in Democracy? Political Process and International Investment Law" (2010) 60 *University of Toronto Law Journal* 909–940; David Schneiderman, *Resisting Economic Globalization: Critical Theory and International Investment Law* (Palgrave 2013) 132–133.

[112] Emma Aisbett "Powerful Multinational or Persecuted Foreigners: 'Foreignness' and Influence Over Government", Australian National University (2010) Centre for Economic Policy Research Discussion Paper No. 638 19 (April): Emma Aisbett and Lauge Skovgaard Poulsen, "Relative Treatment

protection and services typically available to every citizen (e.g. public utilities, policing, fire prevention) even though they may not "belong" to the political community in which they are housed. These "services" include protection of property and contract rights within European national legal systems.[113] That they should be required to contribute to the maintenance of those societies, of which they form a part, is not an entirely unforeseeable or unreasonable expectation, one could say.

James's discussion about heightened concern for deprivations of the property of non-nationals continues to resonate, however, in the domains of international investment law.[114] *James* has been favorably referred to as justifying greater protections for foreign investors than is available under national constitutional law. This, despite evidence, in many locales, of foreign investors' disproportionate influence over local political decision making and, moreover, the ECtHR's reluctance to rely upon general principles of international law in its own jurisprudence.[115]

IV. Land, Hunger, and Homelessness

The third case that comprises part of comparative constitutional property canon and that serves as a model for moving forward is *Port Elizabeth v. Various Occupiers*, a "groundbreaking" 2004 ruling of the South African Constitutional Court though not "globally famous."[116] The dispute concerned an application

of Aliens: Firm-Level Evidence from Developing Countries" (2016) GEG Working Paper, No. 122, University of Oxford, Global Economic Governance Programme (GEG).

[113] Hanoch Dagan, "Takings and Distributive Justice" (1999) 85 *Virginia Law Review* 741–804; see, e.g., *Fredin v. Sweden*, 192 Eur. Ct. H.R. (Ser. A) (1991) 17–18.

[114] See, e.g., Ursula Kriebaum, "Nationality and the Protection of Property Under the European Convention on Human Rights" in Isabelle Buffard et al. (eds.), *International Law Between Universalism and Fragmentation: Festschrift in Honour of Gerhard Hafner* (Brill/Nijhoff 2008) 649–666, 665. Its origins can be found in earlier international law writings, e.g. M. A. de Lapradelle, "Opinion" in *Some Opinions and Reports Bearing Upon the Treaty of Trianon and the Claims of Hungarian Nationals with Regard to their Lands in Transylvania*, vol. 1 (W. P. Griffith & Sons Ltd. 1929) 143, 154 (when the majority exercise their political rights, "foreigners do not co-operate … It is not *their action* … it is between [nationals] that the benefits are distributed to the exclusion of foreigners") (italics in original).

[115] Ursula Kriebaum, "Is the European Court of Human Rights an Alternative to Investor–State Arbitration?" in Pierre-Marie Dupuy, Ernst-Ulrich Petersmann, and Francesco Francioni (eds.), *Human Rights in International Investment Law and Arbitration* (OUP 2009) 242; Kriebaum (n 114) 660.

[116] *Port Elizabeth Municipality v. Various Occupiers* 2005 (1) SA 217 (CC) (October 1, 2004). An abridged version of the case is included in Justice Albie Sachs, *The Strange Alchemy of Life and Law* (OUP 2009) 105–109. It is described as "groundbreaking" in A. J. Van der Walt, *Property in the Margins* (Hart 2009) 153 and not so "globally famous" in James Fowkes, *Building the Constitution: The Practice of Constitutional Interpretation in Post-Apartheid South Africa* (CUP 2016) 246. It is less famous than an earlier socioeconomic rights case: *Government of the Republic of South Africa v. Grootboom* 2001 (1) SA 46 (CC), of which Port Elizabeth is considered its progeny.

by the Port Elizabeth Municipality to evict informal dwellers from lands in an area known as Lorraine. Family members of nine households and three single persons (comprised of sixty-eight persons, including twenty-three children) occupied vacant privately-owned lands adjacent to wealthy suburbs. Most had previously been evicted, anywhere from eight to two years before, from land in nearby Glenroy.[117] Informal encampments on vacant land are widespread in post-apartheid South Africa, a product of the previous era's policy of requiring black and colored South Africans to live in remote segregated "homelands."[118] From 1960 to 1982, some 3.5 million people were forcibly removed from their homes.[119] Of these, 700,000 persons were removed from areas deemed as "white."[120] With the new constitutional settlement in place (an interim Constitution was promulgated in 1993 and a final Constitution in 1996), the free movement of persons was embraced by those previously required to commute vast distances merely to survive.[121]

Their shacks were erected, the occupiers believed, with the permission of owners—a fact the owners denied.[122] Access to water, denied by the municipality, was obtained from a "gentleman at the nearby Riding Club."[123] Prompted by a petition signed by 1,600 members of the public, including "upmarket" suburban neighbors,[124] the municipality sought an eviction order pursuant to the Prevention of Illegal Eviction From and Unlawful Occupation of Land Act 19 of 1998.[125] The municipality succeeded in its initial application to the High Court, but that order was stayed on appeal to the Supreme Court of Appeal. An

[117] *Port Elizabeth* ibid [49].

[118] The legal history of forced evictions under apartheid in Gustav Muller, "The Legal-Historical Context of Urban Forced Evictions in South Africa" (2013) 19 *Fundamina* 367–396.

[119] Albie Sachs, *Advancing Human Rights in South Africa* (OUP 1992) 68 ("all transactions in relation to land were based on a species of robbery").

[120] Hein Marais, *South Africa Limits to Change: The Political Economy of Transformation* (Zed Books 1998) 22; on eviction and forced relocation of "squatters," see Catherine O'Regan, "The Prevention of Illegal Squatting Act" in Christina Murray and Catherine O'Regan, *No Place to Rest: Forced Removals and the Law in South Africa* (OUP 1990) 162–179. On the common law foundations of South Africa's "rights paradigm," see Van der Walt (n 116).

[121] Mark Hunter and Dorrit Posel, "Here to Work: The Socioeconomic Characteristics of Informal Dwellers in Post-Apartheid South Africa" (2012) 24 *Employment and Urbanization* 285 ("informal dwellers may be willing to trade off upgraded housing facilities for proximity to employment opportunities").

[122] *Port Elizabeth* (n 116) para. 50.

[123] ibid para. 52.

[124] Albie Sachs, "Judge Not, Lest Ye Be Judged" in Albie Sachs, *We, The People: Insights of an Activist Judge* (Wits University Press 2016) 201, 210.

[125] On the origins of the Act, see Juanita Pienaar and Anneke Muller, "The Impact of the Prevention of Illegal Eviction from and Unlawful Occupation of Land Act 19 of 1998 on Homelessness and Unlawful Occupation within the Present Statutory Framework" (1999) 10 *Stellenbosch Law Review* 370. For a discussion of cases decided under the Act, see Gustav Muller, "The Impact of Section 26 of the Constitution on the Eviction of Squatters in South African Law" (Ph.D. Faculty of Law, Stellenbosch University, December 2011).

order to set aside the Appeal Court's order was sought by Port Elizabeth before the Constitutional Court of South Africa. The municipality insisted that the application did not concern constitutional matters, an argument that Justice Albie Sachs unequivocally resisted. Much of the case turned, instead, on the relationship between constitutional property rights (s. 25) and constitutional housing rights (s. 26).

The constitutional property clause channels many of the presuppositions associated with the social function of property rights.[126] The Constitution incorporates no positive declaration of property rights, rather, the right is implicit in the limitations the Constitution places on state activity. The section distinguishes between "deprivations" of property which can be accomplished only through non-arbitrary laws of general application, and expropriations of property that can be accomplished only for "public purposes or in the public interest" (Art. 25[1][2]). Expropriations require the provision of compensation, but this is based on a number of factors, including the history of the property, the amount of direct state investment and subsidy in the acquisition and improvement of the property, and the property's market value (Art. 25[3]). Compensation is required to be "just and equitable, reflecting an equitable balance between the public interest and the interests of those affected" (s. 25[3]). For the purposes of the property clause, the "public interest" is defined to include "the nation's commitment to land reform, and to reforms to bring about equitable access to all South Africa's natural resources" (s. 25[4][a]). An amount less than fair market value, then, may be deemed appropriate.[127] Lastly, the Constitution expressly curtails the scope of review available under the property clause for those legislative and other measures "to achieve land, water and related reform to redress the results of past racial discrimination." The clause requires only that these measures satisfy the strictures of the limitation clause laid down in section 36 (s. 25[8]). While there was an expectation that the judiciary would help to fill in the blank spots in the final Constitution,[128] it is

[126] This paragraph draws upon David Schneiderman, *Constitutionalizing Economic Globalization: Investment Rules and Democracy's Promise* (CUP 2008) 139–140. On the constitutional property clause serving social functions, see Hanri Mostert with Cheri-Leigh Young, "Between Custom and Colony: Social Norm-Based Property Law in South Africa's Post-Constitutional 'No-Man's Land'" in Paul Babie and Jessica Vivien-Wilksch (eds.), *Léon Duguit and the Social Obligation Norm of Property* (Springer 2019) 371–402.

[127] A majority of the Constitutional Court indicated that, in the context of calculating compensation under the Expropriation Act, fair market value will form the baseline for any such assessment, after which other considerations outlined in the Constitution may apply to lessen that value. See discussion in A. J. Van der Walt, "The State's Duty to Pay 'Just and Equitable' Compensation for Expropriation: Reflections on the *Du Toit* Case" (2005) 122 *The South African Law Journal* 765.

[128] e.g. the constitutionality of the death penalty, a question resolved by the Constitutional Court in the globally notorious *S. v. Makwanyane* 1995 (3) SA 391 (CC). See discussion in Heinz Klug, "Striking

reported that, as regards constitutional property, the drafters were confident that the Constitutional Court would adopt a generous approach to state authority, following trends in other Commonwealth jurisdictions.[129]

Returning to the problem in Port Elizabeth, Justice Sachs emphasized the relationship between property rights, land reform, and socioeconomic rights. The Constitution, together with the relevant statute, sought to achieve a just and equitable balance between "land hunger, homelessness, and respect for property rights."[130] This prompts judges to play a "new role," declared Sachs. The object was to rescue "courts from their invidious role as instruments directed by statute to effect callous removals" (under the apartheid-era Prevention of Illegal Squatting Act 52 of 1951) and guide the judiciary in fulfilling "their new complex and constitutionally ordained function ... to ensure that justice and equity prevailed in relation to all concerned."[131] Courts were obliged, Justice Sachs emphasized, "to break away from a purely legalistic approach and have regard to extraneous factors such as morality, fairness, [and] social values."[132] While expressing respect for property rights, the statute, like the new Constitution, sought to reverse blatantly racist abuses by the "orderly opening up or restoration of secure property rights for those denied access to or deprived" of access to lands.[133] The 1998 Act therefore directed the Court to consider a number of factors, dependent on whether the applicant was an owner (s. 4) or a state entity (s. 6).

In circumstances where public authorities sought an eviction order under the Act, the judiciary is called upon to consider the public interest in granting

Down Death—*S v Makwanyane and Another*" (1996) 12 *South African Journal on Human Rights* 61, 65. On the ruling's global renown, see Hailbronner (n 26) 254.

[129] John Murphy, "Property Rights and Judicial Restraint: A Reply to Chaskalson" (1994) 10 *South African Journal on Human Rights* 385–398; Geoff Budlender, "The Constitutional Protection of Property Rights: Overview and Commentary" in Geoff Budlender, Johan Latsky, and Theunis Roux (eds.), *Juta's New Land Law* (Juta 1998). The Court in *First National Bank* (2002) organized property clause analysis in the final constitution around the idea of "arbitrariness." Arbitrary deprivations occur when the law "does not provide sufficient reason for the particular deprivation or is procedurally unfair." Sufficient reason will be determined by considering a "complexity of relations" (*FNB* 2002, para. 100) that includes criteria resembling, in some measure, the multifactor analysis developed by the U.S. Supreme Court in *Penn Central* (n 76), the defining case of regulatory takings jurisprudence in the U.S. (Alexander (n 2) 168).

[130] *Port Elizabeth* (n 116) para. 20.

[131] ibid para. 13. Roux describes the judgment as "philosophically ambitious" in Theunis Roux, *The Politics of Principle: The First South African Constitutional Court, 1995–2005* (CUP 2013) 325.

[132] *Port Elizabeth* (n 116) para. 33. Also see paras. 36–37 (calling for "grace and compassion" and drawing upon the Zulu tradition of *ubuntu*). Roux (n 131) 327 describes this as a "strategy" to "indigenise the Constitution."

[133] *Port Elizabeth* (n 116) para. 15. Roux (n 131) 326 describes the statute as the "logical development of the ANC's hybrid human rights tradition and therefore of the 1996 Constitution's approach to property rights."

the order, including health and safety concerns, having regard to the circumstances in which the land is occupied, the period of time it has been occupied, and the availability of "suitable alternative accommodation or land" (s. 6[3][a]–[c]). The availability of a suitable alternative preoccupied the Court in the *Port Elizabeth* case. The municipality offered, by way of a suitable alternative, housing in Walmer township. This the occupiers rejected as unsuitable. Security of tenure there was untenable (dwellings were erected without the consent of owners), and the township was described as "crime-ridden," "unsavoury," and "overcrowded."[134] The second alternative site, Greenbushes, was too far a distance from school and work.

There were no discussions with occupiers, the municipality claiming that it was "under no duty to make suitable alternative land available" to the occupiers.[135] All that was required was to make available to them participation in the municipality's housing program. This, however, would take some time to realize as the occupiers would have to join others in a very long queue. Doing anything more, the municipality complained, would amount to "squatters" queue jumping. Justice Sachs resisted this nomenclature. They are not queue jumpers, he insisted, but a community of homeless persons who had been evicted at least once before.[136]

A circumstance of central concern in determining whether an order would be just and equitable was whether mediation had been attempted.[137] "Where the need to evict people arises," the Court unanimously declared, "some attempts to resolve the problem before seeking a court order will ordinarily be required."[138] No effort at mediation was made here and, as Sachs observed, it probably was too late for that to occur—much water had passed under the bridge.[139] Summing up the Court's reasons, Justice Sachs concluded:[140]

> in the light of the lengthy period during which the occupiers have lived on the land in question, the fact that there is no evidence that either the Municipality or the owners of the land need to evict the occupiers in order to put the land

[134] *Port Elizabeth* (n 116) para. 2.
[135] ibid para. 54.
[136] ibid para. 55.
[137] ibid para. 45; this part of the ruling is excerpted in Sachs (n 119). It presumably is an aspect of his decision that Justice Sachs considers to be of significance. Roux (n 131) 327 agrees, insofar as this is the only part of the ruling in which a "hard rule of law" is laid down. On the importance of the decision in laying down the rule of meaningful engagement doctrine in the realization of socioeconomic rights, see Sandra Liebenberg, "Participatory Approaches to Socio-Economic Rights Adjudication: Tentative Lessons from South African Evictions Law" (2014) 32 *Nordic Journal of Human Rights* 312, 321–322.
[138] *Port Elizabeth* (n 116) para. 56.
[139] ibid para. 47.
[140] ibid para. 59.

> to some other productive use, the absence of any significant attempts by the Municipality to listen to and consider the problems of this particular group of occupiers, and the fact that this is a relatively small group of people who appear to be genuinely homeless and in need, I am not persuaded that it is just and equitable to order the eviction of the occupiers.

The occupiers were permitted to stay until suitable alternative housing could be arranged. Justice Sachs later admitted that the case was agonizing for him—it precipitated a "personal crisis."[141] Having fought all of his life "against unjust dispossession and inequality, [I] could not imagine myself signing an order compelling people rendered homeless by apartheid statutes, to give up their modest homes on vacant land owned by people who already had comfortable houses of their own." Sachs believed that, in the face of this contradiction, he could not uphold his oath of office: "the only course open to me ... [was] to resign" he believed. Instead, Justice Sachs could find the means, both constitutionally and statutorily mandated, by which to avoid "casting people out on the street."[142]

V. Conclusion

Even as *Port Elizabeth* pushes property rights in a solidaristic direction, the classical liberal view—that property rights are self-regulating and autonomous of politics—remains the dominant heuristic. The classical legal account, Van der Walt warns, continues to be the one that "courts often fall back on."[143] So long as individual property rights continue to dominate legal imaginations, it will be very hard to displace constitutional property as an interest of utmost concern.[144] If adjusting economic relations is the stuff of everyday politics, and change the engine of democratic life, might it not be preferable to let politics play itself out within representative institutions of democracy instead of presumptively freezing those relations in favor of the status quo? Could a universe in which constitutionalized property rights did not tilt the balance in the service of already economically powerful interests be preferable? Nedelsky's

[141] The following quotes are drawn from Albie Sachs, "Judge Not, Lest Ye Be Judged" in Albie Sachs, *We, The People: Insights of an Activist Judge* (Wits University Press 2016) 201–212, 210–211. He also discusses the dilemma posed by *Port Elizabeth* in Albert Dzur, "A Talk with Albie Sachs" (2018) 1 *International Journal of Restorative Justice* 314–326, 316.

[142] Fowkes (n 116) 248.

[143] Van der Walt (n 116) 161.

[144] Michelman (n 69) 218.

proposal that constitutional framers abandon entrenched property rights has some appeal, for this reason.

Property, Nedelsky declares, "implicates the very core issues of politics: distributive justice and the allocation of power."[145] The regulation of economic subjects such as property are, therefore, "at the heart of democratic debate." Not only do judges control the meaning of those rights, debates about the proper scope of property regulation becomes the exclusive purview of lawyers.[146] Even Michelman in 1967 preferred to de-emphasize "reliance on judicial action" to answer questions about whether compensation was due.[147] What might be preferred, instead, is that such debates return to political fora so that citizens are not deprived of an ability to address power relations fortified by constitutional property rights. Otherwise, it is argued, the separation between economics and politics will persist, fixing economic subjects as beyond the purview of political debate for fear that deviations will give rise to a decline in rates of national productivity.

Professor Nedelsky offered this advice in the context of debates about whether to entrench property in the new South African Bill of Rights. If, as widely predicted, entrenchment of property rights was to occur in South Africa, then it would be best, she surmised, to communicate to the judiciary that property is a relational right.[148] Only deprivations arising from arbitrary or discriminatory actions warranted judicial intervention, she advised. South African judges should otherwise defer to legislative determinations about the just distribution of property in radically unequal post-apartheid society. This was only a "second best option," however. It would be best not to constitutionalize property rights altogether.[149]

Given the rhetorical power of the classical liberal approach to constitutional property, it is not surprising that the new South African constitutional order turned out to be less transformative than anticipated. Disappointing outcomes in economic redistribution and land reform precipitated calls for further constitutional reform (e.g. expropriation without compensation) and even the abolition of property rights in the Bill of Rights.[150] The Constitution, it was

[145] Jennifer Nedelsky, "Should Property Be Constitutionalized? A Relational and Comparative Approach" in G. E. van Maanen and A. J. van der Walt (eds.), *Property Law on the Threshold of the 21st Century* (Maklu/Blackstone/Nomos 1996) 417–432, 427; also Jennifer Nedelsky, *Law's Relations: A Relational Theory of Self, Autonomy and Law* (OUP 2011) 252–256.

[146] Nedelsky, ibid 427.

[147] Michelman (n 69) 1167.

[148] See also Joseph William Singer and Jack M. Beerman, "The Social Origins of Property" (1993) 6 *Canadian Journal of Law and Jurisprudence* 217–248.

[149] Nedelsky (n 145) 432. This is the case in Canada, but for Aboriginal property and treaty rights recognized in s. 35 of the Constitution Act, 1982.

[150] Klug (n 3) 473.

claimed, stood in the way of government action to achieve effective redistribution.[151] However impactful the protection of property rights in the South African Constitution may be, it is hard to explain, Klug notes, why the state insists upon land reform measures only where there is a willing buyer and seller. The straitjacket of undertaking land reform absent forced transactions that deviate from the consensual model appears to be standing in the way of more aggressive redistribution efforts. Governmental inhibition, Klug maintains, is the consequence of the enduring influence of the Expropriation Act 63 of 1975. This apartheid-era law mandates that a consensual model of exchange frame discussions around the taking of property. It is a model at variance with the aspirational quality of the Constitution's provisions for land reform. Klug concludes that the explanation for the timid approach in South Africa is the absence of political courage to replace the old Expropriation Act with a new one, and not the Constitution.[152]

The South African case indicates that it is not necessarily what the Constitution expressly says that is determinative of legal outcomes but what dominant practices, traditions, and understandings say is legally required. It is, in short, constitutional culture that helps to determine the degree to which property rights either smooth or subvert transitions to economic equality.[153] Property and contract, and the economic system of which they form a constituent part, have long "laid down the law," subordinating other values to their systemic effects.[154] If it is the case that property clauses serve as the paradigmatic negative right, other rights can also be expected to operate in the service of the buyer–seller model.[155] So long as this classical version of constitutional property continues to dominate constitutional cultures in many parts of the world, serving primarily the interests of the already economically powerful, securing more solidaristic understandings of constitutional property rights will remain unrealized and continually under threat of being set back, if not reversed.

151 ibid 471.
152 ibid 477.
153 On constitutional culture, see David Schneiderman, *Red, White and Kind of Blue: The Conservatives and Canadian Constitutional Culture* (University of Toronto Press 2015) and David Schneiderman, "Banging Constitutional Bibles: Observing Constitutional Culture in Transition" (2005) 55 *University of Toronto Law Journal* 833.
154 Polanyi (n 9) 251.
155 This was the point of Garvey's intervention (n 8), describing "constitutional bricolage" as the seeking out of ready-to-hand solutions to constitutional questions by having recourse to a buyer-seller model. See discussion in Schneiderman (n 8).

19

The Shifting Canon of Constitutional Equality

Renata Uitz[*]

I. Introduction

Equality as an ideal, a principle, a value, and a right[1] permeates the canons of contemporary constitutionalism. Equality before the law forms part of a basic concept of legality that is associated with the rule of law. The recognition of individuals as persons of equal worth and liberty (moral equality) is the working premise of a liberal constitutional democracy.[2]

At its core, constitutional equality law follows a basic Aristotelian formula of treating like cases alike: 'In other words, it holds that justice involves two factors—things, and those to whom things are assigned—and it considers that those who are equal should have assigned to them equal things.'[3] Lord Hoffmann on the Privy Council described this approach as 'a general axiom of rational behaviour'.[4] It follows that constitutional equality law will have to account for differences that are relevant for the purposes of being treated alike. Indeed, the classic quote of Aristotle continues with a caveat: 'But here there arises a question which must not be overlooked. Equals and unequals—yes; but equals and unequals in what? This is a question which raises difficulties, and involves us in philosophical speculation on politics.'[5]

The exploration of the constitutional canon on equality concerns what Martha Minow called the dilemma of difference, revolving around two interrelated questions: 'when does treating people the same become insensitive

* Professor, law and government, Royal Holloway, University of London.

1 Sandra Fredman, *Discrimination Law* (2nd edn, Clarendon 2017) ch. 1.

2 Tanurabh Khaitan, *A Theory of Discrimination Law* (OUP 2017) 2–3.

3 Aristotle, *Politics*, III.1282b14, in Aristotle, *Politics*, Ernest Barker, trans. (OUP 1995).

4 *Matadeen and Others v. M. G. C. Pointu and Others (Mauritius)* [1998] UKPC 9 (18 February, 1998), § 8.

5 Aristotle (n 3).

Renata Uitz, *The Shifting Canon of Constitutional Equality* In: *Global Canons in an Age of Contestation*. Edited by: Sujit Choudhry, Michaela Hailbronner, and Mattias Kumm, Oxford University Press. © Renata Uitz 2024.
DOI: 10.1093/9780191956942.003.0019

to their difference and likely to stigmatize or hinder them on that basis?' and 'when does treating people differently emphasize their differences and stigmatize or hinder them on that basis?'[6] The cases at the heart of the constitutional canon on equality ultimately turn on whether courts are willing to recognize the adverse effects of particular differences in the legal architecture and political practices of constitutional democracies. Aligning the formal, the substantive (including redistributive), and the transformative dimensions of equality in a manner that is 'responsive to those who are disadvantaged, demeaned, excluded, or ignored' remains a fundamental challenge for constitution-makers, courts, and scholars alike.[7]

The constitutional canon of equality has long been shaped by its inherent tensions: constitutional mandates to advance or promote the conditions of particular disadvantaged social groups (or individuals belonging to them) violate the principle of equal treatment. The search for a canon of constitutional equality is part of the search for 'common normative foundations in global constitutional law'.[8] The new global wave of autocratization that lends this intellectual exercise particular urgency has brought restrictions on the rights of women and sexual and religious minorities, highlighting the continuing relevance of debates that are often older than written constitutions. The canon (as well as the anti-canon[9]) of constitutional equality is being shaped by multiple constitutional actors, including participants in political processes, courts, social movements, and their counter-movements.[10] Therefore, any engagement with the shifting canon of equality requires a departure from a court-centred approach[11] in teaching and especially in comparative scholarship.

II. Tracing the Shifting Canon of Constitutional Equality

The constitutional canon of equality offers an excellent lens for studying the (trans)formation of constitutional canons. As posited by Michaela Hailbronner, a constitutional canon is a 'platform for a shared conversation on the basis of

[6] Martha Minow, *Making All the Difference: Inclusion, Exclusion, and American Law* (Cornell UP 1990) 20.

[7] Sandra Fredman, 'Substantive Equality Revisited' (2016) 14 ICON 712, 713.

[8] Michaela Hailbronner, 'Constructing the Global Constitutional Canon: Between Authority and Criticism' (2019) 69 UTLJ 248, 274, also 249.

[9] Jamal Greene, 'The Anticanon' (2011) 125 Harv L Rev 379.

[10] Cf. Carroll Seron, Susan Bibler Coutin, and Pauline White Meeusen, 'Is There a Canon of Law and Society?' (2014) 9 Annual Rev L & Soc Sci 287 (on ways to identifying a canon empirically).

[11] Mark Graber, 'Hollow Hopes and Exaggerated Fears: The Canon/Anticanon in Context' (2011) 125 Harv L Rev 33.

certain foundational texts, encouraging self-reflection and a stronger connection between human rights and comparative constitutional law'.[12] The search for a constitutional canon seeks to capture a political community's ethical values, or *nomos*:[13] according to Jamal Greene, the canonical status of a judgment 'depends on the attitude the constitutional interpretive community takes toward the ethical positions that the decision has come to represent'.[14]

Firstly, equality law is an especially promising terrain for studying the constitutional canon as a tool of exclusion and of embedding hierarchies, as suggested by Hailbronner.[15] This is hardly surprising as scholars of equality tend to see equality law as a means of seeking recognition for difference, and even more so, if one approaches equality as a tool for contesting wilful exclusion, dominance, and subordination.[16] Collections of essays[17] and area-specific casebooks on 'race and law', 'gender and constitutional law', or 'sexual orientation and constitutional law' routinely challenge traditional canonization efforts.[18] Indeed, the search for the canon of constitutional equality requires literacy across many themes and issues in constitutional law. For instance, for the intellectual project of 'gendering constitutional law', structures of government matter as much as the anatomy of particular rights (reproductive rights, equal pay, or the prohibition of discrimination).[19]

The search for a canon of constitutional equality highlights that prominent themes and issues vary across regions and constitutional systems:[20] access to education for girls and the prohibition of forced, underage marriage are universal human rights concerns, yet, adverse practices and conditions make them a prominent issue for advocacy, litigation, and constitution-building locally.[21] At the same time, a similar focus on local contexts will permit retrogression to be addressed in key areas of equality law that have recently been detected in the Global North (e.g. in the US)—a clear departure from international

[12] Hailbronner (n 8) 250.

[13] Greene (n 9) 382.

[14] ibid 382, 381, also referred to as nomos or moral imperative at 382.

[15] Hailbronner (n 8) 256.

[16] See Susanne Baer, 'Equality' in Michel Rosenfeld and András Sajó (eds) *The Oxford Handbook of Comparative Constitutional Law* (OUP 2012) 983, esp. 986–988.

[17] Recently, e.g., Catherine MacKinnon (ed.) *Gender in Constitutional Law* (Edward Elgar 2018) and Helen Irving (ed.) *Constitutions and Gender* (Edward Elgar 2018).

[18] e.g. Katherine T. Bartlett, 'Feminist Canon' in Jack M. Balkin and Sanford Levinson (eds) *Legal Canons* (New York UP 2000) 266.

[19] See Catharine MacKinnon, 'Gender in Constitutions' in Michel Rosenfeld and András Sajó (eds) (n 16) 398.

[20] See, e.g., Beverly Baines and Ruth Rubio-Marin (eds) *The Gender of Constitutional Jurisprudence* (OUP 2005).

[21] For a quantitative study, see e.g. Siobhan Austen and Astghik Mavisakalyan, 'Constitutions and the Political Agency of Women: A Cross-Country Study' (2016) 22 Feminist Economics 183.

norms and developments traced in the Global South. Thus, close attention to shifts in the global canon of constitutional equality calls for further engagement with criteria of canonicity, especially the dilemmas posed by local lack of sincerity, practices of window dressing, and outright cynicism outlined by Hailbronner.[22] Furthermore, as illiberal actors seek to shift canons of equality, comparative constitutional scholarship will continue to face challenges questioning its normative commitment to democratic constitutionalism and to defending individual liberty as the equal moral worth of human beings.

III. Tracing Equality in Constitutions and Constitutional Jurisprudence

Provisions on equality and non-discrimination are ubiquitous in constitutions around the world.[23] The clauses themselves have revolutionary precursors that expressed high ideals from the start, even when the most abhorrent forms of legal, political, and social inequalities (such as slavery) were part of daily life. The 1776 US Declaration of Independence opens with the self-evident truth that 'all men are created equal', and a few years later the 1789 French Declaration of the Rights of Man proclaimed that 'Men are born and remain free and equal in rights.' This sentiment was echoed in Article 1 of the Universal Declaration (1948), stating that 'All human beings are born free and equal in dignity and rights.' In international law, the normative framework on equality spans from the prohibition of racial discrimination and apartheid as a peremptory norm of international law (*ius cogens*), to the 'recognition of the inherent dignity and of the equal and inalienable rights of all members of the human family' in the preamble to the International Covenant on Civil and Political Rights[24] and specialized conventions prohibiting discrimination on the basis of race[25] or gender.[26]

On the regional level, in the Inter-American system the American Convention on Human Rights (1978) drew a distinction between the duty to respect rights without discrimination (Art. 1(1)) and the right to equal protection

[22] Hailbronner (n 8) 263.
[23] Tarunabh Khaitan, 'Discrimination' in *Max Planck Encyclopedia of Constitutional Law* (2017) https://oxcon.ouplaw.com/view/10.1093/law-mpeccol/law-mpeccol-e102, accessed 20 August 2023.
[24] International Covenant on Civil and Political Rights (adopted 16 December 1966, entered into force 23 March 1976) 999 UNTS 171 (ICCPR).
[25] International Convention on the Elimination of All Forms of Racial Discrimination (adopted 21 December 1965, entered into force 4 January 1969) 660 UNTS 195 (CERD).
[26] Convention on the Elimination of All Forms of Discrimination against Women (adopted 18 December 1979, entered into force 3 September 1981) 1249 UNTS 13 (CEDAW).

and the prohibition of discrimination (Art. 24) from the start. The 2013 Inter-American Convention against All Forms of Discrimination and Intolerance addresses the individual and collective dimensions of the right to equality (Art. 3), in public and in private (Art. 2).[27] In 2006, the African Commission on Human and Peoples' Rights held that '[t]ogether with equality before the law and equal protection of the law, the principle of non-discrimination provided under Article 2 of the [African Charter on Human and Peoples' Rights] provides *the foundation for the enjoyment of all human rights*' (emphasis added).[28] In 2017, the Inter-American Court of Human Rights reiterated in an advisory opinion that:

> 61. … the notion of equality emanates directly from the oneness of the nature of humankind and is indissociable of the essential dignity of the individual. … [A]t the current stage of evolution of international law, the fundamental principle of equality and non-discrimination has entered the domain of *ius cogens*. The whole legal structure of national and international public order rests on this premise and it permeates every legal system.[29]

In contrast, the constitutional canon on equality is more modest. In theory—at least since Antiquity—the potential scope of equality spans from formal equality before the law (as a prohibition of arbitrary application of the law) to substantive economic and social equality (unjust distribution of resources). The contemporary canon differs from the classic in one crucial respect: the disconnect between legal and political notions of equality.[30] For those who see equality law as a tool of challenging social exclusion and subordination (maldistribution of power), equality is closely connected to personal autonomy and to terms of citizenship in a constitutional democracy. In the words of Susanne Baer:

> A starting point of constitutionalism is that people are fundamentally equal in that they are human beings (based on metaphysics, or on politics), but the whole point about being human is the *ability to differ*, by choosing to lead

[27] Inter-American Convention Against All Forms of Discrimination and Intolerance (adopted 6 June 2013, entered into force 20 February 2020) A-69.

[28] *Zimbabwe NGO Human Rights Forum v. Zimbabwe*, communication no. 245/2002, decision of 15 May 2006, para. 169.

[29] *Advisory Opinion* OC-24/17 requested by Costa Rica, gender identity, and equality and non-discrimination of same-sex couples, 24 November 2017.

[30] See, e.g., Vincent Azoulay, Rethinking the Political in Ancient Greece' (July–September 2014) 69:3 *Annales. Histoire, Sciences Sociales* 387, 401–402.

> one's own life, in situations that differ tremendously, around the globe, but also within a region, a city, a social entity. (Emphasis added)[31]

The South African Constitutional Court in *Fourie* (per Justice Sachs) went as far as recognizing the *right to be different*, as the ultimate expression of respect for human rights, an affirmation that 'that difference should not be the basis for exclusion, marginalisation and stigma'.[32]

Despite its potentially broad conceptual range, in practice, constitutional equality has played a relatively modest role in addressing misrecognition or maldistribution. This is due in part to a professional practice wherein 'discrimination continues to be conceived of and adjudicated along a single categorial axis of racism, sexism, casteism, homophobia, ageism, ableism, etc. at a time'.[33] As a result, in practice, judicially enforceable socio-economic rights appear to be better suited for addressing maldistribution. Recognizing the limits of a technical approach to discrimination, scholars have for decades urged litigators and courts to recognize overlaps between protected traits (intersectionality)[34] in order to capture the real-life stakes of equality claims made by the most vulnerable members of society (e.g. women who also belong to racial and/or religious minorities).

Drawing on an analysis that covers twenty-three member states, the OAS rapporteur on the rights of women noted that:

> [a]rbitrary or disproportionate distinctions can be made in the application of laws, measures, practices or policies that at first glance appear to be neutral but that in fact have an impact that is prejudicial to groups in vulnerable situations. ... Occasionally, the special measures of protection and measures to promote equality—including affirmative action—are measures to provide the guarantees necessary to ensure that certain sectors that are victims of structural equality or long-standing exclusion have access to and are able exercise certain rights.[35]

[31] Baer (n 16) 986–987.

[32] *Minister of Home Affairs and Another v. Fourie and Another; Lesbian and Gay Equality Project and Others v. Minister of Home Affairs and Others* [2005] ZACC 19, para. 60.

[33] Shreya Atrey, *Intersectional Discrimination* (OUP 2019) 1.

[34] Kimberlé Crenshaw, 'Demarginalizing the Intersection of Race and Sex: A Black Feminist Critique of Antidiscrimination Doctrine, Feminist Theory and Antiracist Politics' (1989) 1989 U Chi Legal F 139.

[35] e.g. Access to Justice for Women Victims of Violence in the Americas, OEA/Ser.L/V/II. Doc. 68, 20 January 2007, paras 89, 100. To the same effect, see e.g. Supreme Court of India: *Jeeja Ghosh & Anr v. Union of India & Ors* (2016) 7 SCC 761, 793 (para. 40) (A. Sikri, J).

The Indian Supreme Court also recognizes the impact of the vocabulary used by courts in cases on gender equality. As Chief Justice Chandrachoud notes in his foreword to the *Handbook on Combating Gender Stereotypes* published by the Court in 2023:

> Even when the use of stereotypes does not alter the outcome of a case, stereotypical language may reinforce ideas contrary to our constitutional ethos. ... [T]he language a judge uses reflects not only their interpretation of the law, but their perception of society as well. Where the language of judicial discourse reflects antiquated or incorrect ideas about women, it inhibits the transformative project of the law and the Constitution of India, which seek to secure equal rights to all persons, irrespective of gender.[36]

IV. Text No. 1 on Gender Equality and Citizenship

A. Advisory Opinion of the Inter-American Court on Gender Identity, and Equality and Non-Discrimination of Same-Sex Couples (OP 24-2017)

When the US Supreme Court overturned its long-standing precedent on access to abortion in 2022,[37] the judgment directed attention to the deep connection between gender equality, individual autonomy, and citizenship. This connection was pointed out by Justice Ginsburg of the US Supreme Court in 2007, when she recalled (in dissent) that 'legal challenges to undue restrictions on abortion procedures ... center on a woman's autonomy to determine her life's course, and thus to enjoy *equal citizenship stature*' (emphasis added).[38] According to Justice Ginsburg's dissent, with accepting restrictions on access to abortion, the 'Court deprives women of the right to make an autonomous choice, even at the expense of their safety. This way of thinking reflects ancient notions about *women's place in the family and under the Constitution*—ideas that have long since been discredited' (emphasis added).[39]

[36] Dhananjaya Y. Chandrachud, 'Foreword' in Supreme Court of India, *Handbook on Combating Gender Stereotypes* (2023) 4, https://main.sci.gov.in/pdf/LU/04092023_070741.pdf, accessed 20 August 2023.

[37] *Dobbs v. Jackson Women's Health Organization*, 597 US __ (2022).

[38] *Gonzales v. Carhart*, 550 US 124, 171 (2007).

[39] ibid 184.

Women gained the right to vote in the twentieth century as a result of persistent (and sometimes violent) social mobilization that questioned the 'male image' of citizenship and reset the terms of belonging to political community.[40] In a landmark case originating from Canada, the Privy Council (per Lord Sankey) found that women were to be considered 'persons' for the purposes of eligibility for a seat in the Canadian Senate.[41] This conclusion was reached on the premise that the constitutional text (as a living tree) was 'capable of growth and expansion within its natural limits'.[42] Contemporary contestation on gender equality and gender identity seeks to reset the constitutional terms of personhood yet again. While women's social mobilization challenges traditional gender norms, conservative (often illiberal) forces defend such traditional gender norms through exploiting tensions within the human rights regime across a wide range of issues related to gender, sexuality, family, and reproduction.[43] Consequently, constitutional contestation on gender equality is intricately intertwined with issues of individual autonomy and gender identity, including gender recognition.[44]

In recent years, social movements have made remarkable advances towards legalizing access to non-therapeutic abortion in the Americas.[45] In Argentina, in the course of heated political and legal contestation, the women's movement helped translate (vernacularize) access to abortion, shifting it from a taboo to a question of women's health and ultimately into an issue of democracy and equality.[46] The National Congress legalized the voluntary interruption of pregnancy until the fourteenth week of pregnancy, also providing for conscientious objection (leaving open the possibility for opponents to create obstacles).[47]

In Mexico, the Supreme Court recognized women's right to make decisions about reproductive autonomy under the Constitution and ended the complete

[40] Surya Monro and Diane Richardson, 'Citizenship, Gender and Sexuality' in Hein-Anton van der Heijden (ed.) *Handbook of Political Citizenship and Social Movements* (Edward Elgar 2014) 60.

[41] *Edwards v. Canada (AG)* 1929 CanLII 438 (UK JCPC), [1930] AC 124, 1 DLR 98.

[42] ibid 1 DLR 98, 106–107.

[43] Susanna Mancini and Nausica Palazzo, 'The Body of the Nation: Illiberalism and Gender' in András Sajó, Renáta Uitz, and Stephen Holmes (eds) *The Routledge Handbook of Illiberalism* (Routledge 2022) 403.

[44] Stefano Osella and Ruth Rubio Marin, 'Gender Recognition at the Crossroads: Four Models and a Compass of Comparative Law' (2024) 21 ICON 574.

[45] Agustina Ramón Michel, 'Abortion: More than Criminalization, Not Yet Constitutional Right' in Conrado Hübner Mendes, Roberto Gargarella, and Sebastián Guidi (eds) *The Oxford Handbook of Constitutional Law in Latin America* (OUP 2022) 799.

[46] Alicia Ely Yamin and Agustina Ramón Michel, 'Using Rights to Deepen Democracy: Making Sense of the Road to Legal Abortion in Argentina' (2023) 46 Fordham Int'l LJ 377.

[47] Barbara Sutton and Nayla Luz Vacarezza, 'Abortion Rights and Democracy, An Introduction' in Barbara Sutton and Nayla Luz Vacarezza (eds) *Abortion and Democracy: Contentious Body Politics in Argentina, Chile, and Uruguay* (Routledge 2021) 1, 4.

criminalization of abortion in 2021 in a unanimous judgment[48] amidst a robust nationwide campaign by women's rights organizations at the state level (where access to abortion is regulated). In 2022, in a case initiated by the Causa Justa (Just Cause) movement, the Constitutional Court of Colombia (by 5–4 votes) decriminalized abortion up to twenty-four weeks of gestation.[49] The Constitutional Court confirmed its 2001 ruling that the 'exercise of women's sexual autonomy cannot be reduced to becoming an instrument or means to achieve family formation or procreation'[50] and also reiterated its 2006 position that 'the choice of a life plan' limits the use of criminal law, recalling that criminalizing voluntary abortion 'may lead to tolerating and perpetuating discriminatory conducts against women and girls'.[51] These interrelated themes of individual autonomy and gender equality are also prominent in the opinion of Minister Luís Roberto Barroso of the Brazilian Supreme Federal Tribunal's 2016 judgment that found (3–2) the criminalization of abortion in the first trimester to be unconstitutional.[52] Although this judgment is not a binding precedent, it fits into a line of cases that thematize access to abortion in terms of women's 'full exercise of citizenship'.[53]

For a global study of the constitutional canon on equality, it is especially important to point out that the Colombian Constitutional Court's 2022 abortion judgment accorded a similarly strong protection to personal autonomy in another case in 2022 where it recognized a third gender classification for a nonbinary person,[54] holding that gender identity was a matter of self-perception and, as such, a fundamental right that the state and society are required to treat in a manner that is consistent and respectful of one's own vision of oneself.[55] This position echoed the 2017 advisory opinion of the Inter-American Court on gender identity,[56] emphasizing that the principle of personal autonomy:

[48] AI 148/2017, Press release no. 298/2021 (1 October 2021), https://www.internet2.scjn.gob.mx/red2/comunicados/comunicado.asp?id=6606, accessed 20 August 2023.

[49] Ruling C-055 of 2022 (21 February 2022), available in English at https://reproductiverights.org/colombia-<constitutional-court-ruling-c-055-2022-english/, accessed 20 August 2023.

[50] ibid 508.

[51] ibid 510.

[52] Writ of habeas corpus 124.306/RJ (29 November 2016), unofficial English translation at https://www.globalhealthrights.org/wp-content/uploads/2018/06/Brazilian-Abortion-Ruling-Translation.pdf, accessed 20 August 2023. The Supreme Federal Tribunal ordered the release of five healthcare workers who provided illegal abortion services.

[53] Marta Rodriguez de Assis Machado and Rebecca J. Cook, 'Constitutionalizing Abortion in Brazil' (2018) 5 Revista de Investigações Constitucionais, Curitiba 185, 217.

[54] Sentencia T-033/22 (4 February 2022).

[55] ibid para. 28.

[56] *Advisory Opinion* OC-24/17 (n 29).

> 88. … prohibits any action by the State that tries to exploit or utilize the individual; in other words, any action that converts the individual in means to an end which is alien to the choices about their own life, body and the full development of their personality, within the limits imposed by the Convention.

The Inter-American Court gave more concrete shape to these abstract considerations about personal autonomy in 2021 in a case that concerned the death of a woman in state custody who was sentenced to thirty years' imprisonment for aggravated homicide after suffering an obstetric emergency that resulted in the loss of her pregnancy (*Manuela v. El Salvador*).[57] Although in the case the Court did not address issues of access and reproductive health directly, it said that:

> 52. … the liberty and autonomy of women in the area of sexual and reproductive health has historically been limited, restricted or annulled based on negative and prejudicial gender stereotypes. This was because, socially and cultural, men have been assigned a dominant role in the adoption of decisions concerning a woman's body and women are seen, quintessentially, as a reproductive being. Nevertheless, women have the 'right to receive dignified and respectful reproductive health care services and obstetric care, free from discrimination and any violence.'

The Inter-American Court's emphasis on a familiar Kantian premise invokes memories of the dehumanizing experiences of dictatorship that also fuelled the women's rights movement. The 2017 advisory opinion of the Inter-American Court on the recognition of gender identity is a key contribution to the global debate on gender equality and individual autonomy, thus, ultimately, on the terms of citizenship.

Reva Siegel pointed out the formative power of social movements and counter-movements for gender equality in the US context decades ago.[58] As the canon of constitutional equality is reshaped by a similar global contestation, it is worth recalling that the legal advances on access to abortion in the Americas were supported by the efforts of social movements to destigmatize (or socially decriminalize) the practice.[59] In a global context, conservative social

[57] *Manuela and Others v. El Salvador*, Judgment of 2 November 2021.

[58] Reva B. Siegel, 'Constitutional Culture, Social Movement Conflict and Constitutional Change: The Case of the de facto ERA' (2006) 94 California LR 1323.

[59] Barbara Sutton and Nayla Luz Vacarezza, 'Introduction: Abortion Rights Strategies in Argentina, Colombia, and Mexico' (2024) 122:2 Against the Day: South Atlantic Q 378, 381.

movements and illiberal political actors seek to reset the canon of equality to reflect traditional family values and the natural 'complementarity' of women and men,[60] and thus reinstate a heteronormative conception of citizenship. Such efforts are prevalent in Europe, where political mobilization against the first European treaty against gender-based violence, the Convention on Preventing and Combating Violence Against Women and Domestic Violence (known as the Istanbul Convention),[61] re-politicized gender (and gender identity) in a pernicious manner.[62]

On the national level, in 2021 the Constitutional Court of Bulgaria went as far as stating that the concept of gender was incompatible with the rule of law under the Bulgarian Constitution, and found the ratification of the Istanbul Convention to be unconstitutional.[63] The Court relied on a traditional, binary division of (biological) sexes as the basis of human reproduction, and also recalled traditional Bulgarian values rooted in Orthodox Christianity, enshrined in Article 13(3) of the Constitution. Following this logic, in early 2023 the Bulgarian Court of Cassation barred the legal gender reassignment of transgender persons.[64]

On the supranational level, Turkey's unilateral withdrawal from the Istanbul Convention signals the fragility of the international human rights regime,[65] which is propped up by the principle of equality and non-discrimination as one of its peremptory norms. The key terms of the human rights vocabulary (including gender equality) have been tested by supporters of the Geneva Consensus Declaration on Promoting Women's Health and Strengthening the Family, a global alliance launched by the Trump administration in 2020 in order to curb access to abortion in the name of protecting women's health and dignity, and safeguarding traditional family values.[66]

Counter-movements are making unquestionable advances, and the hyper-legalized contestation on abortion ('abortion lawfare'[67]) has become the

[60] Mancini and Palazzo (n 43).

[61] Council of Europe Convention *on* Preventing *and* Combating Violence Against Women *and* Domestic Violence (adopted 11 May 2011, entered into force 1 August 2014) CETS 210.

[62] Andrea Krizsán and Conny Roggeband, *Politicizing Gender and Democracy in the Context of the Istanbul Convention* (Springer 2021).

[63] Case 6/2021 (16 March 2021).

[64] Decision 2/2020 (20 February 2023), analysed in Teodora Petrova, 'Barring Legal Gender Reassignment in Bulgaria' (*Verfassungsblog*, 2 March 2023), https://verfassungsblog.de/barring-legal-gender-reassignment-in-bulgaria/, accessed 20 August 2023.

[65] Basak Cali and Laurence Helfer, 'The Gender of Treaty Withdrawal: Lessons from the Istanbul Convention' (*EJIL: Talk!*, 28 November 2022), https://www.ejiltalk.org/the-gender-of-treaty-withdrawal-lessons-from-the-istanbul-convention/, accessed 20 August 2023.

[66] Alliance Defending Freedom, 'Global Coalition of 36 Governments Recommits to Pro-Life Women's Health Policy' (*Alliance Defending Freedom*, 17 November 2022), https://adfinternational.org/37-governments-recommit-to-pro-life-womens-health-policy/, accessed 20 August 2023.

[67] Siri Gloppen, 'Conceptualizing Abortion Lawfare' (2021) 17(3) Revista Direito GV 1.

primary site of recasting the canon of constitutional equality, even if naked equality arguments are not always prominent on the surface of these cases.[68] Domestic courts in illiberal regimes take advantage of the gaps in international human rights law[69] and are able to restrict women's rights in feigning compliance with international standards (e.g. in the name of protecting foetal rights or traditional familiar values).[70] The next step on the illiberal agenda is the adoption of an international convention on the rights of the family,[71] as a counter-convention to women's rights.

V. Text No. 2 on Disability

A. General Comment No. 6 (2018) on Equality and Non-Discrimination (26 April 2018)

The UN Convention on the Rights of Persons with Disabilities (CRPD)[72] addresses disability-based discrimination in a comprehensive manner,[73] in connection with other personal traits (intersectionality) and across specific contexts ranging from education to political participation. This was a major advance, as before the CRPD the 'mainstream legal vocabulary of human rights struggle[d] to cope with the articulation of disability right claims'.[74]

[68] See Reva B. Siegel, 'Abortion as a Sex Equality Right: Its Basis in Feminist Theory' in Martha Albertson Fineman and Isabel Karpin (eds) *Mothers in Law: Feminist Theory and the Legal Regulation of Motherhood* (Columbia UP 1995) 43; Cary Franklin and Reva B. Siegel, 'Equality Emerges as a Ground for Abortion Rights in and After *Dobbs*' in Lee Bollinger and Geoffrey R. Stone (eds) Roe v Dobbs: *The Past, Present and Future of a Constitutional Rights to Abortion* (OUP 2024).

[69] Magdalena Furgalska and Fiona de Londras, 'Rights, Lawfare and Reproduction: Reflections on the Polish Constitutional Tribunal's Abortion Decision' (2022) 55 Isr L Rev 285.

[70] Marta Bucholc, 'Abortion Law and Human Rights in Poland: The Closing of the Jurisprudential Horizon' (2022) 14 Hague J Rule of Law 73.

[71] 'The Convention on the Rights of the Family—International Guarantee in Defence of Families' (1 October 2018), https://en.ordoiuris.pl/family-and-marriage/convention-rights-family-international-guarantee-defence-families, accessed 20 August 2023.

[72] Convention on the Rights of Persons with Disabilities (adopted 13 December 2006, entered into force 3 May 2008) 49 UNTS 2 (CRPD).

[73] Committee on the Rights of Persons with Disabilities, General Comment No. 6 on Equality and Non-Discrimination (26 April 2018) para. 11.

[74] Colm O'Cinneide, 'Extracting Protection for the Rights of Persons with Disabilities from Human Rights Frameworks: Established Limits and New Possibilities' in Oddný Mjöll Arnardóttir and Gerard Quinn (eds) *The UN Convention on the Rights of Persons with Disabilities: European and Scandinavian Perspectives* (Martinus Nijhoff 2009) 164, 171.

The CRPD is often presented as a new type of international human rights instrument, developed in close cooperation with the global disability rights movement. Drawing on disability studies, the CRPD confronts the dilemma of difference by moving away from a medical model of disability and adopting a social model that recognizes disability as a social construct, and seeks to counter the adverse effects of disabling environments, whether those be physical, social, or legal.[75] The resulting human rights-based approach to disability[76]—that seeks to capture both the complexity of difference and the complexity of injustice—has been linked to the capabilities approach to protecting freedom (developed by Amartya Sen and Martha Nussbaum) and the concept of transformative equality (developed by Sandra Fredman).[77]

A similar, multifaceted approach was followed more recently in the Inter-American Convention on Protecting the Human Rights of Older Persons (2017). Article 5 on the prohibition of 'discrimination based on the age of older persons' requires state parties to take into account that older persons are:

> victims of *multiple discrimination*, including women, persons with disabilities, persons of different sexual orientations and gender identities, migrants, persons living in poverty or social exclusion, people of African descent, and persons pertaining to indigenous peoples, the homeless, people deprived of their liberty, persons pertaining to traditional peoples, and persons who belong to ethnic, racial, national, linguistic, religious, and rural groups, among others. (Emphasis added)

Human dignity is woven deeply into the fabric of the CRPD, a connection that was seen to be critical for achieving substantive and transformative equality from the time of its drafting.[78] The comprehensive approach of the CRPD reset core concepts of human rights law, and—consequently—of equality law, starting with personhood and legal capacity. 'The right to make decisions for oneself—to chart one's own life path—without interference from third parties or the state … flows from one's recognition as a person before the

[75] Rannveig Traustadóttir, 'Disability Studies, the Social Model and Legal Developments' in ibid 3.

[76] Theresia Degener, 'A Human Rights Model of Disability' in Valentina Della Fina, Rachele Cera, and Guiseppe Palmisano (eds) *The United Nations Convention on the Rights of Persons with Disabilities: A Commentary* (Springer 2017) 41–59.

[77] See, e.g., Jenny Goldschmidt, 'New Perspectives on Equality: Towards Transformative Justice through the Disability Convention?' (2016) 35 Nordic J of Hum R 1.

[78] Jessica Lynn Corsi, 'Article 5: Equality and Non-Discrimination' in Ilias Bantekas, Michael Ashley Stein, and Dimitris Anastasiou (eds) *The UN Convention on the Rights of Persons with Disabilities: A Commentary* (OUP 2018) 140, 156.

law.'[79] According to General Comment No. 6, the 'right to legal capacity is a threshold right, that is, it is required for the enjoyment of almost all other rights in the Convention, including the right to equality and non-discrimination' (para. 47).

The CRPD Committee's General Comment No. 6 on equality and non-discrimination exposes the core conceptions that are meant to inform the interpretation and application of the Convention. In particular, it seeks to address 'attitudinal barriers to disability' such as:

> enduring and humiliating stereotypes, and stigma of and prejudices against persons with disabilities as being a burden on society. ... The Committee is concerned that the laws and policies of States parties still approach disability through charity and/or medical models, despite the incompatibility of those models with the Convention. The persistent use of such paradigms fails to acknowledge persons with disabilities as full subjects of rights and as rights holders. (Paras 2–3)

The CRPD's conception of personhood also fundamentally repositions reasonable accommodation from an exception or exemption from the general requirement of equal treatment, to an element of the duty of equal treatment (Art. 5(3)).[80] This change is the consequence of a shift 'away from a "deficits-oriented" perspective on disability and towards one that views fragility as a universal aspect of the human condition and remediable with sufficient supports.'[81]

In contrast, the Canadian Charter of Rights and Freedoms uses a more careful, negative frame to highlight that the Charter's equality clause 'does not preclude any law, program or activity that has as its object the amelioration of conditions of disadvantaged individuals' (s. 15(2)). The Canadian Supreme Court emphasized that the two building blocks 'work together to promote the vision of substantive equality that underlies s.15 as a whole';[82] saying that '[t]he promotion of equality entails the promotion of a society in which all are secure in the knowledge that they are recognized at law as human beings equally deserving of concern, respect and consideration.'[83]

[79] Gerard Quinn and Anna Arstein-Kerslake, 'Restoring the "Human" in "Human Rights": Personhood and Doctrinal Innovation in the UN Disability Convention' in Conor Gearty and Costas Douzias (eds) *The Cambridge Companion to Human Rights* (CUP 2012) 36, 41.

[80] Corsi (n 78) 141–142.

[81] Quinn and Arstein-Kerslake (n 79) 40.

[82] *R v Kapp* [2008] 2 SCR 483, para. 16.

[83] ibid para. 15.

The constitutionality of reasonable accommodation and positive measures hinges on the political process (i.e. the support of the democratically elected majority) and, ultimately, on judicial discretion. This was illustrated more recently when the Supreme Court of India confirmed that Article 16(4) of the Indian Constitution does not contain a fundamental right to affirmative action, as it merely enables (but does not mandate (require)) states to make reservations for civil service positions favouring citizens in scheduled castes and tribes. When a state government decides to use its discretionary powers to that effect, it has to do so on the basis of adequate research and data.[84] The significance of such underlying conceptions for constitutional interpretation is especially profound, when the constitutional text is prima facie inconclusive on a particular measure.

In Brazil, race-based affirmative action has been controversial since it runs counter to the idea of (colour-blind) racial democracy.[85] Yet, the Brazilian Supreme Federal Tribunal's judgments on affirmative action in higher education are the ultimate counterpoint of recent US case law.[86] In 2012, a political party challenged the racial quotas used by the University of Brasília as a violation of the Constitution's equality clause (Art. 5). In the Supreme Federal Tribunal, Minister Ricardo Lewandowski's opinion (that was unanimously followed)[87] drew heavily on the Brazilian Constitution's programmatic preamble ('to institute a democratic state destined to ensure the exercise of social and individual rights, liberty, security, well-being, development, equality and justice as supreme values of a fraternal, pluralist and unprejudiced society, founded on social harmony'). The landmark opinion in the racial quotas case starts from the premise that Article 5 (XLII) of the Constitution—making racism a non-bailable offence—signals the intent of the drafters not only to reject racism, but also to support positive discrimination for the social inclusion of traditionally excluded groups.[88] The reasoning recognizes the role of university education in creating society's future leaders, acknowledging the profound effect of university education on the formation of the elites.[89] In addition, the opinion expressly marks the formative impact of an academic environment that provides an opportunity to live with others.[90]

[84] *Mukesh Kumar and another v. State of Uttarkhand*, Civil Appeal no. 1226 of 2020, para. 11.

[85] Sales Augusto dos Santos, 'Who Is Black in Brazil? A Timely or a False Question in Brazilian Race Relations in the Era of Affirmative Action' (2006) 33 Lat Am Perspectives 30.

[86] See the *Racial Quotas Case*—ADPF 186 (in public universities) and the *ProUni Case*—ADI 3330 (fellowships for students in private universities), also Keith Rosenn, 'Recent Important Decisions by the Brazilian Supreme Court' (2014) 45 Univ of Miami Inter-Am LR 297.

[87] *Racial Quotas Case*—ADPF 186 (n 86).

[88] ibid 19–20.

[89] ibid 30.

[90] ibid 31.

VI. Text No. 3

A. *Plessy v. Ferguson* and the Anti-Canon of 'Separate, but Equal'

When tracing the canons of constitutional equality through the casebooks, the US Supreme Court's landmark judgment of *Brown v. Board of Education*[91] is invariably accompanied by its nemesis, *Plessy v. Ferguson*[92]—the prime exhibit of the anti-canon in constitutional equality law. *Plessy* provides an intellectual map of the key dilemmas that continue to haunt constitutional equality jurisprudence to this day:

- the open texture of constitutional provisions;
- the process of identifying the relevant comparators in a given context;
- the extent to which legal rules recognize or exacerbate differences; and
- the lasting consequences of the judicial framing of particular issues.

Plessy is the result of a strategic litigation effort by the Comité des Citoyens, an activist group formed in New Orleans around the *Crusader* magazine, intent on challenging the constitutionality of state legislation that required racial segregation on trains (Separate Car Act of 1890).[93] Louisiana law required 'equal but separate accommodations for the white and colored races'. Racial segregation was meant to be enforced by the personnel of the railway companies. Passengers violating the rule faced a fine or up to twenty days' imprisonment. The Comité des Citoyens arranged travel for Homer Plessy (who was seven-eighths Caucasian, i.e. not 'completely white') in the train compartment reserved for white passengers and also arranged for his arrest: they retained a private detective to ensure that Mr Plessy was found to be in violation of the segregation requirement (and not some other misconduct). The railroad companies were in favour of the constitutional challenge, as the segregation requirement increased their operating costs.

The Separate Car Act was passed after the 1879 Louisiana Constitution removed the guarantees of equal rights and free access to public places guaranteed previously in the 1868 Louisiana Constitution. These constitutional

[91] *Brown v. Board of Education of Topeka*, 347 US 483 (1954).
[92] *Plessy v. Ferguson*, 163 US 537 (1896).
[93] For an account, see Steve Luxenberg, *Separate: The Story of Plessy v. Ferguson, and America's Journey from Slavery to Segregation* (W. W. Norton 2019).

changes followed in the footsteps of federal troops withdrawing from the South following the Civil War. By this time, the Supreme Court was also reading narrowly the Fourteenth Amendment to the US Constitution, and its Equal Protection Clause.[94] Thus, Plessy's constitutional challenge against 'separate but equal' public accommodation tackled what has become the standard interpretation of the Equal Protection Clause in practice. The Supreme Court rejected the challenge (with one dissenting vote) and its judgment consolidated the status quo.

The Supreme Court (per Justice Brown) carefully separated the issue of slavery and its legacy from the equal protection challenge, finding that *legal equality* of the races was a separate question from their *social or political relations*. Consequently, legal segregation did not impose a 'badge of inferiority' on its targets,[95] but merely constituted a reasonable instance of exercising the regulatory ('police') powers of the states.[96] In one of the key passages, the Court stated that:

> [l]egislation is powerless to eradicate racial instincts or to abolish distinctions based upon physical differences, and the attempt to do so can only result in accentuating the difficulties of the present situation. If the civil and political rights of both races be equal, one cannot be inferior to the other civilly or politically. If one race be inferior to the other socially, the Constitution of the United States cannot put them upon the same plane.[97]

In contrast, Justice Harlan's dissent started from the premise that the race of passengers was irrelevant for the regulation of modes of transportation. In a powerful passage, he asserted that:

> in view of the Constitution, in the eye of the law, there is in this country no superior, dominant, ruling class of citizens. There is no caste here. Our Constitution is color-blind, and neither knows nor tolerates classes among citizens. In respect of civil rights, all citizens are equal before the law. … The law regards man as man, and takes no account of his surroundings or of his

[94] See *Slaughterhouse Cases*, 83 US (16 Wall.) 36 (1873)) and *Civil Rights Cases*, 109 US 3 (1883) holding that the Thirteenth and Fourteenth Amendments do not rule out racial discrimination by private individuals.

[95] *Plessy* (n 92) 551 and 544.

[96] ibid 549 and 550.

[97] ibid 552.

color when his civil rights as guaranteed by the supreme law of the land are involved.[98]

Justice Harlan's dissent in *Plessy* raises crucial and interrelated questions about the canonization of dissent and the construction of the anti-canon. Regarding the canonization of dissents, the interesting question to ask is 'not what it is about certain dissents that makes them redeemable but *what it is that redeeming courts do* when they make dissenting opinions into canonical authority' (emphasis added).[99] There is no question that the majority's stance in *Plessy* fits with the relevant line of Supreme Court jurisprudence as well as with the prevailing understanding of the original intent behind the Equal Protection Clause; admittedly, even Justice Harlan's well-known dissent was prefaced by a paean to white supremacy.[100] According to Jamal Greene, the majority's mistake in *Plessy* was 'willfully remaining blind to the social meaning of segregation, that blacks are and should remain a permanent underclass'.[101] Yet, this wilful blindness was in line with the prevailing political compromise (status quo) on which racial segregation measures were based.

Plessy was de facto overturned by the Supreme Court, in *Brown v. Board of Education* in 1954, almost a decade after the Second World War. The road to *Brown* was charted by a carefully devised, iterative litigation strategy pursued mostly by the National Association for the Advancement of Colored People's (NAACP) Legal Defense Fund through decades of strategic litigation. Justice Harlan's thesis of the colour-blind Constitution served as an important tool for getting the Supreme Court to acknowledge its fundamental mistake about the permissibility of racial segregation under the Equal Protection Clause. Yet, the ideal of a colour-blind Constitution has also become an obstacle to defending benign racial classifications under the US Constitution, making it extremely difficult to justify such positive measures that seek to address the consequences of historically embedded racial discrimination in the US. And, in the course of a few decades, the ambiguity of the constitutionality of benign racial classifications (affirmative action) grew into intense constitutional contestation at the hands of the counter-movements.

The US Constitution is silent on affirmative action; there is no obligation on public or private actors to adopt such measures, however, when they decide to do so the measures have to pass constitutional scrutiny. The Supreme

[98] ibid 559.
[99] Richard Primus, 'Canon, Anti-Canon, and Judicial Dissent' (1998) 48 Duke LJ 243, 248.
[100] Greene (n 9) 413–414.
[101] ibid 414.

Court has been divided about the applicable constitutional standards. In 1978, in a plurality opinion, Justice Powell argued that diversity in the classroom met the highest level of scrutiny, i.e. the same test that the Court applies for both harmful and benign racial discrimination.[102] After three decades of legal experimentation and constitutional contestation, in 2007 Chief Justice Roberts expressed rather strong judicial aversion towards race-conscious affirmative action policies when he wrote in a plurality opinion that '[t]he way to stop discrimination on the basis of race is to stop discriminating on the basis of race'.[103] In the same case, Justice Kennedy's concurring opinion suggested that—in the spirit of a colour-blind reading of the Constitution—race-conscious selection criteria are acceptable as a last-resort solution. Some find this approach bizarre, if not self-defeating, as race-conscious admissions criteria are ultimately meant to address the harmful consequences of historic, structurally entrenched racial discrimination. As Justice Sotomayor put it in a dissent a few years later: 'The way to stop discrimination on the basis of race is to speak openly and candidly on the subject of race, and to apply the Constitution with eyes open to the unfortunate effects of centuries of racial discrimination.'[104]

In 2023, the majority of a divided US Supreme Court (per Chief Justice Roberts) found that the universities that sought to create a racially diverse student body through affirmative action had failed to offer a sufficiently coherent justification for their race-conscious admission practices to meet the strict scrutiny standard applied by the Court under the Constitution's Equal Protection Clause.[105] In doing so, the majority abandoned the jurisprudential path followed in similar cases since 1978.[106] According to the dissenting opinion of Justice Sotomayor, the majority's superficial colour-blindness 'subverts the constitutional guarantee of equal protection by further entrenching racial inequality in education, the very foundation of our democratic government and pluralistic society'.[107] This critique echoes the reasoning that placed *Plessy* in the anti-canon of constitutional equality.

Decisions that constitute the anti-canon of constitutional equality have long been part of the curriculum: Jamal Greene has pointed out that it would amount to professional malpractice to ignore that corpus.[108] The affirmative

[102] *Regents of the University of California v. Bakke*, 438 US 265 (1978), affirmed in *Grutter v. Bollinger*, 539 US 306 (2003) and *Gratz v. Bollinger*, 539 US 244 (2003).

[103] *Parents Involved v. Seattle School District no. 1*, 51 US 701 (2007).

[104] *Schuette v. Coalition to Defend Affirmative Action*, 134 S. Ct 1623, 1676 (2014) (dissent).

[105] *Students for Fair Admissions v Harvard*, 600 US __, 23 (2023) (Roberts, Ch. J, slip opinion).

[106] *Regents of the University of California v. Bakke*, 438 US 265 (1978).

[107] *Students for Fair Admissions v. Harvard* (n 105) 2 (Sotomayor, J, slip opinion).

[108] Greene (n 9) 382.

action cases in the US and the global success of counter-movements ushering in a retrogression of reproductive rights and LGBTQ+ rights confirm the proximity of the constitutional equality canon to its anti-canon. This proximity poses pressing questions for constitutional scholars about how much room there is for critiquing a constitutional canon before it turns into its own anti-canon.

20

Gender Discrimination and Canons for Constitutional Review

Yoon Jin Shin[*]

I. Introduction

Gender discrimination, especially discrimination against women, is among the most prevalent and enduring forms of discrimination in human history. Gender-based discrimination practices and the underlying mindset are deeply imbedded in the culture, tradition, social order, and norms of most societies, frequently having been codified into law. Yet another feature common to human societies is the fact that they have generally prohibited gender-specific discrimination, as they have adopted a modern constitutional framework. Most states' constitutional provisions on equality list sex or gender as one of the prohibited grounds of discrimination. The ability to subject gender-based discrimination to constitutional review is a remarkable development for human rights, one that brings the elements of traditional, cultural, and social prejudices against women and gender and sexual minorities under scrutiny according to constitutional principles, which themselves are constantly subjected to processes of concretization and improvement.

This chapter sheds light on important doctrinal developments in gender equality jurisprudence that possess global significance and implications. It first examines the doctrine of *indirect discrimination*, a canonical doctrine that is well established in a wide range of international, regional, and national jurisdictions in adjudicating on gender discrimination cases. Then a notable mode of constitutional interpretation from a less commonly cited jurisdiction—the Constitutional Court of Korea—is discussed as a possible candidate for a canonical interpretive approach to normative relations between *tradition and gender equality*. Lastly, a globally-known review standard

* Seoul National University.

Yoon Jin Shin, *Gender Discrimination and Canons for Constitutional Review* In: *Global Canons in an Age of Contestation*. Edited by: Sujit Choudhry, Michaela Hailbronner, and Mattias Kumm, Oxford University Press. © Yoon Jin Shin 2024.
DOI: 10.1093/9780191956942.003.0020

for gender discrimination—*intermediate scrutiny* of the Supreme Court of the United States—is examined, and the discussion reveals the standard's inadequacy in serving as a global canon in gender equality jurisprudence. While the court decisions and doctrines examined in this chapter were mainly and historically developed in the context of discrimination against women, they also have strong implications for the rights of gender and sexual minorities and other historically disadvantaged groups and individuals.

II. The Doctrine of Indirect Discrimination

A. The Concept and Legislative Adoptions

As outright discrimination against women has become less common in modern constitutional states, the concept of indirect discrimination has attained growing importance in realizing substantive equality for women and other social minorities.[1] Its doctrine has been concretized through legislative and adjudicative practices in diverse jurisdictions and has played a crucial role in bringing real-world discrimination under constitutional scrutiny. Underlying the idea of prohibiting indirect discrimination, also termed 'adverse effect' (as in Canada), 'disparate impact' (in the United States)[2], or de facto discrimination, is the recognition that a rule or practice that is apparently neutral on the surface may amount to discrimination against certain groups of persons. Such situations arise when the rule or practice causes a disparate negative impact on a group with protected characteristics (such as race or gender) and the measure does not satisfy the conditions for justification.

At the international level, the Convention on the Elimination of All Forms of Discrimination Against Women (CEDAW) incorporates the concept of indirect discrimination in the definition clause of 'discrimination against women': 'any distinction, exclusion or restriction made on the basis of sex which has the effect or purpose of impairing or nullifying the recognition,

[1] See Tarunabh Khaitan, *A Theory of Discrimination Law* (OUP 2015) 1–2. See also Denise G. Réaume, 'Harm and Fault in Discrimination Law: The Transition from Intentional to Adverse Effect Discrimination' (2001) 2 Theo Inq L 349, 350.

[2] *Griggs v. Duke Power Co.* 401 US 424 (1971) is the first known case, decided by the Supreme Court of the United States, to have adopted the concept of indirect ('disparate impact') discrimination while adjudicating on discrimination under Title VII of the Civil Rights Act of 1964. The Court held that Title VII prohibits 'not only overt discrimination, but also practices that are fair in form but discriminatory in operation'. 401 US 424, 431.

enjoyment or exercise by women, … of human rights and fundamental freedoms in the political, economic, social, cultural, civil or any other field'.[3] The CEDAW Committee underscores the need to address indirect discrimination against women in order to achieve substantive equality between women and men:

> States parties are under an obligation to respect, protect and fulfil the right to non-discrimination of women and to ensure the development and advancement of women in order to improve their position and implement their right of de jure and *de facto or substantive equality* with men. States parties shall ensure that there is neither direct, nor *indirect discrimination* against women. … Indirect discrimination against women occurs when a law, policy, programme or practice appears to be neutral as it relates to men and women, but has a *discriminatory effect in practice* on women, because pre-existing inequalities are not addressed by the apparently neutral measure. Moreover, indirect discrimination *can exacerbate existing inequalities* owing to a failure to recognize *structural and historical patterns of discrimination* and *unequal power relationships* between women and men.[4]

At the regional level, EU anti-discrimination law, through a series of Directives, explicitly prohibits indirect discrimination. With regard to gender discrimination, the relevant Directive provides: 'indirect discrimination shall exist where an apparently neutral provision, criterion or practice disadvantages a substantially higher proportion of the members of one sex unless that provision, criterion or practice is appropriate and necessary and can be justified by objective factors unrelated to sex'.[5]

[3] Convention on the Elimination of All Forms of Discrimination Against Women (CEDAW), 18 December 1979, 1249 UNTS 13, Art. 1.

[4] Committee on the Elimination of Discrimination against Women, General Recommendation No. 28 on the Core Obligations of States Parties under Article 2 of the Convention on the Elimination of All Forms of Discrimination against Women, CEDAW/C/2010/47/GC.2, para. 16 (emphasis added). See also paras 9, 13, 35.

[5] Council Directive 97/80/EC of 15 December 1997 on the burden of proof in cases of discrimination based on sex [1998] OJ L014/6, Art. 2, para. 2. See also para. 1 ('For the purposes of this Directive, the principle of equal treatment shall mean that there shall be no discrimination whatsoever based on sex, either directly or indirectly'). This definition has been succeeded to Directive 2000/78/EC of 27 November 2000 (on equal employment treatment) and Directive 2000/43/EC of 29 June 2000 (on discrimination on the basis of race or ethnic origin). See also Susanne Burri, *EU Gender Equality Law: Update 2018* (European Commission 2018); Olivier De Schutter, 'Three Models of Equality and European Anti-Discrimination Law' (2006) 57 Northern Ireland LQ 1.

The concept of indirect discrimination has been adopted by many domestic jurisdictions that have enacted anti-discrimination legislation.[6] Among them, the Equality Act 2010 in the UK provides a detailed definition of indirect discrimination.[7] The Sex Discrimination Act 1984 in Australia also embraces the concept by taking the 'effect' of disadvantaging a certain sex as an element of discrimination, and 'a characteristic that generally appertains or is imputed to persons of the sex of the aggrieved person' as one of the prohibited grounds of discrimination.[8] The Canadian Human Rights Act prohibits indirect discrimination in the same way that it prohibits direct discrimination,[9] as does South Africa's Promotion of Equality and Prevention of Unfair Discrimination Act.[10] Hong Kong enacted the Sex Discrimination Ordinance in 1996 and explicitly included indirect discrimination in the definition clause of discrimination against women.[11] In South Korea, while it has yet to adopt a general anti-discrimination act, the Equal Employment Opportunity and Work-Family

[6] See, e.g., Sandra Fredman, *Comparative Study of Anti-Discrimination and Equality Laws of the US, Canada, South Africa and India* (European Commission 2012).

[7] Equality Act 2010, s. 19:

(1) A person (A) discriminates against another (B) if A applies to B a provision, criterion or practice which is discriminatory in relation to a relevant protected characteristic of B's.
(2) For the purposes of subsection (1), a provision, criterion or practice is discriminatory in relation to a relevant protected characteristic of B's if—
  (a) A applies, or would apply, it to persons with whom B does not share the characteristic,
  (b) it puts, or would put, persons with whom B shares the characteristic at a particular disadvantage when compared with persons with whom B does not share it,
  (c) it puts, or would put, B at that disadvantage, and
  (d) A cannot show it to be a proportionate means of achieving a legitimate aim.
(3) The relevant protected characteristics are—age; disability; gender reassignment; marriage and civil partnership; race; religion or belief; sex; sexual orientation.

[8] Sex Discrimination Act 1984, s. 5(1) and (2).

[9] Canadian Human Rights Act, RSC 1985, c. H-6, s. 15(8): 'This section applies in respect of a practice regardless of whether it results in direct discrimination or adverse effect discrimination.'; s. 7 (Employment): 'It is a discriminatory practice, directly or indirectly, (a) to refuse to employ or continue to employ any individual, or (b) in the course of employment, to differentiate adversely in relation to an employee, on a prohibited ground of discrimination.'

[10] Promotion of Equality and Prevention of Unfair Discrimination Act 4 of 2000, s. 1(1): 'discrimination means any act or omission, including a policy, law, rule, practice, condition or situation which directly or indirectly—(a) imposes burdens, obligations or disadvantage on; or (b) withholds benefits, opportunities or advantages from, any person on one or more of the prohibited grounds'. Prohibited grounds related to gender discrimination include: gender, sex, pregnancy, marital status, sexual orientation, and birth. See also s. 4(2): 'In the application of this Act the following should be recognised and taken into account: (a) The existence of systemic discrimination and inequalities, particularly in respect of race, gender and disability in all spheres of life as a result of past and present unfair discrimination, brought about by colonialism, the apartheid system and patriarchy.'

[11] Sex Discrimination Ordinance, s. 5(1):
A person discriminates against a woman in any circumstances relevant for the purposes of any provision of this Ordinance if—

(a) on the ground of her sex he treats her less favourably than he treats or would treat a man; or
(b) he applies to her a requirement or condition which he applies or would apply equally to a man but—
  (i) which is such that the proportion of women who can comply with it is considerably smaller than the proportion of men who can comply with it; (ii) which he cannot show to

Balance Assistance Act explicitly includes indirect discrimination in the definition of 'gender discrimination at employment'.[12]

In many of these jurisdictions, indirect discrimination practices are prohibited as unlawful unless such practices are justified under the prescribed conditions. For example, the EU Directives stipulate the conditions as: 'unless that provision, criterion or practice is appropriate and necessary and can be justified by objective factors unrelated to sex'[13] or 'unless that provision, criterion or practice is objectively justified by a legitimate aim and the means of achieving that aim are appropriate and necessary', the conditions mainly derived from the proportionality principle.[14] The Australian Sex Discrimination Act lists several factors to consider in a 'reasonableness test', which is not inherently different from the proportionality test.[15]

With regard to the burden of proof, many of these laws have eased the load for an individual who challenges the practice of indirect discrimination. The EU Directive provides that member states should ensure that when the affected individual establishes facts from which direct or indirect discrimination may be presumed, the respondent should prove that there has been no breach of the principle of equal treatment.[16] The Australian Sex Discrimination Act assigns to the person who committed the act the burden of proving that the act does not constitute discrimination.[17] This procedural rule reflects an awareness that

be justifiable irrespective of the sex of the person to whom it is applied; and (iii) which is to her detriment because she cannot comply with it.

[12] Equal Employment Opportunity and Work-Family Balance Assistance Act (adopted 4 December 1987, last amended 18 May 2021), Art. 2, para. 1: 'an employer discriminates against an employee in employment or working conditions, or takes any other disadvantageous measures without any rational reason, on grounds of gender, marriage, status within family, pregnancy or childbirth, etc. (including where, even if the employer equally applies employment or working conditions, the number of men or women capable of satisfying such conditions is remarkably fewer in comparison with the opposite gender, thus putting the opposite gender at a disadvantage, and the said conditions may not be attested to be justifiable)'.

[13] Council Directive 97/80/EC (n 5), Art. 2, para. 2.

[14] Council Directive 2000/78/EC (n 5), Art. 2, para. 2(b)(i). In a similar manner, the UK Equality Act 2010, s. 19(2)(d) stipulates the condition as 'A cannot show it to be a proportionate means of achieving a legitimate aim.' See also Case 170/84 *Bilka-Kaufhaus GmbH v. Weber von Hartz* [1986] ECR 1607 (an EU labour law decision by the European Court of Justice that set out justificatory factors in reviewing indirect discrimination); *Griggs* (n 2), stating 'The touchstone is business necessity. If an employer's practice which operates to exclude [black applicants], cannot be shown to be related to job performance, the practice is prohibited', 401 US 424, 431.

[15] Sex Discrimination Act 1984, s. 7B(2). The provided factors include the nature and extent of the disadvantage that resulted from the measure accused, the feasibility of overcoming or mitigating the disadvantage, and whether the disadvantage is proportionate to the result sought by the person who imposed the measure.

[16] Council Directive 97/80/EC (n 5) Art. 4.

[17] Sex Discrimination Act 1984, s. 7C.

an asymmetry in power, information, and resources commonly exists between the respondents, such as the government or employers, and the plaintiffs, who are often individuals belonging to historically disadvantaged groups.[18]

B. Application in Constitutional Review

This section examines several important court decisions to illuminate how the doctrine of indirect discrimination is actually applied in constitutional review of gender discrimination cases.

Fraser v. Canada, decided by the Supreme Court of Canada in October 2020, is one of the latest landmark decisions where the highest national court explicitly applied the doctrine of indirect discrimination in constitutional review and struck down a rule for its violation of women's equal rights.[19] In this case, the Supreme Court of Canada, reversing the Federal Court of Appeal decision, held that the pension plan of the Royal Canadian Mounted Police (RCMP) violated women's equality under the Canadian Charter of Rights and Freedoms.[20] The pension plan classified workers who joined the RCMP's job-sharing programme (which provided for the option of sharing the work hours of one full-time job among multiple workers) as part-time workers and denied them the opportunity to obtain full-time pension credit for their service during the job-sharing period, unlike other full-time members who were suspended or took unpaid leave. Most of the workers who enrolled in the job-sharing programme were women who chose the option mainly due to child-care responsibilities. In a 6–3 decision, the Supreme Court of Canada held that the pension scheme violated the Charter right to equality of the claimants (three female workers who joined the programme) as it 'has a disproportionate impact on women and perpetuates their historical disadvantage'.[21]

[18] See *D. H. and Others v. Czech Republic* ECHR 2007-IV 241, para. 195 ('In these circumstances, the evidence submitted by the applicants can be regarded as sufficiently reliable and significant to give rise to a strong presumption of indirect discrimination. The burden of proof must therefore shift to the Government, which must show that the difference in the impact of the legislation was the result of objective factors unrelated to ethnic origin'); Tarunabh Khaitan and Sandy Steel, 'Wrongs, Group Disadvantage and the Legitimacy of Indirect Discrimination Law' in Hugh Collins and Tarunabh Khaitan (eds), *Foundations of Indirect Discrimination Law* (Hart Publishing 2018) ('*Foundations*') 203.

[19] *Fraser v. Canada (Attorney General)* 2020 SCC 28.

[20] The Constitution Act 1982, Part I Canadian Charter of Rights and Freedoms, s. 15(1): 'Every individual is equal before and under the law and has the right to the equal protection and equal benefit of the law without discrimination and, in particular, without discrimination based on race, national or ethnic origin, colour, religion, sex, age or mental or physical disability.'

[21] *Fraser* (n 19) para. 5.

In the reasoning, the Court elaborated on its understanding of indirect discrimination: '[T]he application of "neutral" rules may not produce equality in substance for disadvantaged groups. Membership in such groups often brings with it a unique constellation of physical, economic and social barriers. Laws which distribute benefits or burdens without accounting for those differences ... are the prime targets of indirect discrimination claims.'[22] It noted that indirect forms of discrimination are more prevalent than openly direct discrimination and can pose a greater threat to disadvantaged groups because they are not plainly visible, operating within the biased social structure.[23] It stressed that the Court's equality jurisprudence thus far 'left no doubt that substantive equality is the "animating norm" of the s.15 framework ... and that substantive equality requires attention to the "full context of the claimant group's situation", to the "actual impact of the law on that situation", and to the "persistent systemic disadvantages" ... to that group's members.'[24]

Justice Rosalie Silberman Abella, writing for the majority opinion, cited as an important point of reference empirical evidence that demonstrated that the workers who enrolled in the job-sharing programme were predominantly women with young children, due to child-care responsibilities being historically and predominantly imposed on women.[25] Multiple research reports on the disproportionate gender ratio of people working in part-time jobs in Canada and its relation to women's child-care burdens, and academic literature on systemic and adverse-effect discrimination were widely referenced throughout the decision. This approach contrasts with that of the Federal Court of Appeal, which regarded the claimants' joining the job-sharing programme as their 'choice'.[26] The majority opinion pointed out that pension plans, having historically been designed 'for middle and upper-income full-time employees with long service, typically male', have treated women unequally, since the latter often do not follow 'male pattern employment'.[27] It noted that 'the structural inequality within pension plans has tangible impacts for women upon retirement' and that the 'feminization of poverty' is an 'entrenched social phenomenon' in Canada,[28] and found that 'the negative pension consequences of job-sharing

[22] ibid para. 34.
[23] ibid para. 35.
[24] ibid para. 42.
[25] ibid paras 97–98. The Court noted that during the years 2010–2014, 100% of those who took advantage of job-sharing were women, and most of them cited child-care as a reason.
[26] ibid paras 85–86. See also para. 92, citing one of the claimants' affidavit: 'In my experience, this policy is particularly harmful to women who work in rural or isolated communities. The RCMP regularly posts women members in such communities where there is simply no around-the-clock child care available. As such, job-sharing is often the only child care solution for members with children.'
[27] ibid paras 108, 110.
[28] ibid para. 112.

perpetuate a long-standing source of disadvantage to women'.[29] The Court thus held that the RCMP pension plan's treatment of job-sharing workers had an adverse impact on women and that this adverse impact reinforced, exacerbated, or perpetuated their disadvantage—the two elements of the Court's inquiry under the Section 15(1) of the Charter.[30] The Court viewed that the Canadian government did not show 'a pressing and substantial objective' to justify the adverse impact on women limiting their equality right under the Charter, especially when considering that the job-sharing programme was introduced as a substitute for 'leave without pay' for members who could not take such an option due to personal or family situations.[31] Applying the indirect discrimination doctrine in a rich and comprehensive manner, the Court made it clear that Section 15 of the Charter upholds substantive equality over a formalistic approach.[32] As a remedy, the government was ordered to develop a methodology, with retroactive effect, for facilitating the option to buy back full pension credit for RCMP members who joined the job-sharing programme.[33]

The German Constitutional Court ruled on a comparable case in 2005, where it also applied the doctrine of indirect discrimination.[34] A female lawyer challenged the provisions of a professional pension plan for lawyers in Baden-Württemberg, which charged high monthly contributions during periods of parental leave without income and required the member to resign from legal practice in order to be exempted from such payments. The Constitutional

[29] ibid paras 108–111. The Court cited the International Labour Organization's commentary stating, 'Throughout their life cycles, women accumulate disadvantages that pile up at older ages. Double or triple discrimination is often amplified as women advance in age. Women are especially vulnerable owing to their high numbers in unpaid, low-paid, part-time, frequently interrupted, or informal economy work. As a result they are less often entitled to any contributory pension benefits in their own right', ibid para. 111.

[30] ibid para. 27.

[31] ibid paras 125, 128.

[32] ibid para. 134.

[33] ibid para. 138. The European Court of Human Rights took a similar approach in *Trizio v. Switzerland* App no. 7186/09 (2 February 2016). This case concerned the decision of the Swiss Disability Insurance Office to discontinue disability allowance for the applicant (who used to work full time before she developed back problems) once she became a parent of twins. The decision of the Insurance Office was based on the presumption that even without her disability, she would not have worked full time in order to take care of her children. The European Court of Human Rights held this to constitute indirect gender discrimination prohibited under Art. 14 of the ECHR, taking seriously the fact that 98% of the insured persons who were negatively affected by such a method of decision were women. Other cases where the European Court of Human Rights applied the concept of indirect discrimination include *D. H. and Others* (n 18), *Opuz v. Turkey* ECHR 2009-III 107 and *Taddeucci and McCall v. Italy* App no. 51362/09 (30 June 2016).

[34] BVerfG, 5 April 2005, 1 BvR 774/02. See also Sandra Fredman, *Discrimination Law* (2nd edn, OUP 2011) 181 (discussing judicial decisions applying the doctrine of indirect discrimination with regard to women's child-care burden); *Fraser* (n 19) para. 105 (providing a list of decisions by the European Court of Justice on indirect discrimination against women concerning the discriminatory treatment of workers based on their working hours).

Court ruled that this regulation amounted to de facto discrimination against women, prohibited under Article 3 paragraph 2 of the German Basic Law.[35] The Court viewed the regulation as disproportionately affecting women, in the social reality where women are still generally responsible for child care.[36] In the Court's view, there were no reasonable grounds for justifying this discriminatory effect as the pension fund's stability could be sustained even when granting fee exemptions during its members' parental leave, and the alternative option offered by the regulation, renouncing the legal profession altogether, was a considerable disadvantage for a parent lawyer.[37]

Much earlier than the above decisions, in *Dothard v. Rawlinson*, the Supreme Court of the United States held the minimum height (5 feet 2 inches) and weight (120 pounds) requirement imposed by the Alabama Department of Corrections for the position of prison guard to be sex discrimination, as prohibited under Title VII of the Civil Rights Act of 1964.[38] The Court clarified that to establish a prima facie case of employment discrimination based on sex, a plaintiff only needed to show that the apparently neutral standards in question in fact selected applicants in a significantly discriminatory pattern, and that national statistics showing the disproportionate impact of the height and weight standards on women were sufficient.[39] The Alabama Department was not able to show that the requirement had a relationship to the amount of strength essential for effective job performance as a correctional counsellor.[40]

[35] Basic Law, Art. 3(2): 'Men and women shall have equal rights. The state shall promote the actual implementation of equal rights for women and men and take steps to eliminate disadvantages that now exist.'

[36] 1 BvR 774/02 (n 34) paras 53, 64.

[37] ibid paras 58, 71. In 2010, the German Constitutional Court delivered another decision applying the concept of indirect discrimination in a gender discrimination case concerning the privatization of state hospitals in Hamburg that led to the deprivation of the right to continued employment of the cleaning staff, among whom 93.5% were women. The Court held the relevant regulation to be in breach of Art. 3(2) of the Basic Law as it predominantly affected women and thus amounted to gender-specific discrimination. BVerfGE, 14 April 2010, 1 BvL 8/08. See also BVerfGE, 16 November 1993, 1 BvR 258/86 (applying the concept of indirect discrimination in an employment discrimination case against a female applicant); BVerfGE, 30 January 2002, 1 BvL 23/96 (reviewing whether the legal exclusion of a double family name for a child constituted de facto discrimination against women, and holding in the negative).

[38] *Dothard v. Rawlinson* 433 US 321 (1977).

[39] ibid 328–332. A disparate impact on women was found where 41% of the female population and less than 1% of male population in the country were excluded by such a requirement.

[40] ibid 331. This case is comparable to another landmark decision by the Supreme Court of Canada that applied the doctrine of indirect discrimination, *British Columbia (Public Service Employee Relations Commission) v. British Columbia Government Service Employees' Union* ('*Meiorin*') 1999 SCC 48. In this case, a female firefighter challenged a mandatory aerobic standard for forest firefighters, which more women found hard to meet than men. The Court stated that a unified approach should be applied to both direct and indirect discrimination under Section 15 of the Charter, and that the employer must show that such a standard is a bona fide occupational requirement. The Court held that the government did not demonstrate that the aerobic standard was reasonably necessary to identify those persons who were able to perform the tasks of a forest firefighter safely and efficiently.

The concept of indirect discrimination was applied by the Constitutional Court of Korea when it delivered a landmark decision striking down the national public servant exam system, which gave extra points to applicants who had completed their military duty.[41] Since South Korea conscripts only male citizens into mandatory military service, this extra point system made it extremely hard, if not impossible, for women to pass the exam and become public employees.[42] In 1999, the Constitutional Court held that this exam system constituted a violation of the equality rights of women and those with disabilities and of their right to public service.[43] The Court pronounced that the Constitution ensures substantive, as opposed to formal, equality, and that it amounts to gender discrimination if a certain measure results in predominantly negative consequences for a particular gender.[44] Applying the proportionality test, the Court viewed that no legitimate purpose could justify the significant imbalance between the affected interests.[45] Following the decision, the extra point system was abolished and the rates of women who have passed the public servant exams have since dramatically increased.

C. Merits and Implications

As examined in the previous sections, the concept and doctrine of indirect discrimination are widely accepted in gender equality legislation across international, regional, and national levels and have played significant roles in constitutional adjudications in many jurisdictions. Not only its wide acceptance but also its substantive merits as a critical standard in gender equality jurisprudence may count towards the doctrine's canonical features. This section appraises the strength and implications of the indirect discrimination doctrine in both normative and practical aspects.

The doctrine enables adjudicative bodies to address widespread, harmful, but often invisible forms of discrimination against individuals who belong to historically and socially disadvantaged groups. It contributes to the achievement of their substantive, rather than formalistic, equality, especially in the

[41] Constitutional Court of Korea 98Hun-Ma363, 11-2 KCCR 770 (23 December 1999).

[42] Male applicants who had served in the military automatically received three to five additional points out of 100, when the qualification score was at times as high as 95.5. In a certain year, out of ninety-nine persons who were selected as public officers, only three passed the exam without receiving the extra points.

[43] 98Hun-Ma363 (n 41) 799.

[44] ibid 785, 790, 793.

[45] ibid 788–794.

context of social and economic rights.[46] Furthermore, the doctrine concretizes the principle of equality in a way that helps the individual overcome the problem of proving elements of direct discrimination or of establishing the discriminatory purpose or intention of the actor.[47] Concerns over the accountability of an 'innocent' actor can be mitigated by the fact that in most cases of indirect discrimination, the discriminatory impact of the measure at issue is reasonably foreseeable. The concerns can also be alleviated with social justice considerations for the disadvantaged population in society.[48]

A major hurdle in challenging discrimination in gendered societies is to bring to the light of constitutional scrutiny long-standing social injustices, structural inequality, and the patriarchal culture embedded in the law and practices that have disadvantaged women. A standard of constitutional review that incorporates indirect discrimination enables the court to take seriously these social, structural, and cultural factors in equality adjudication. Examining social realities (e.g. the burden of child care and housework labour largely and conventionally falling on women) in the process of constitutional rights review has significant implications for individuals and groups who have long suffered from socially and culturally structured oppression and biases, as women have in patriarchal societies.[49] The doctrine of indirect discrimination recognizes the socially structured nature of discrimination and aims not to perpetuate the injustice resulting from it.[50] With regard to its application, the

[46] See Hugh Collins, 'Discrimination, Equality and Social Inclusion' (2003) 66 MLR 16; *Meiorin* (n 40) para. 41 (noting that the indirect discrimination doctrine enables the court to 'go to the heart of the equality question, to the goal of transformation, to an examination of the way institutions and relations must be changed in order to make them available, accessible, meaningful and rewarding for the many diverse groups of which our society is composed'); Fredman (n 34) 14–19.

[47] e.g. *D. H. and Others* (n 18) para. 188; *Griggs* (n 2) 431–432 ('good intent or absence of discriminatory intent does not redeem employment procedures or testing mechanisms that operate as "built-in headwinds" for minority groups and are unrelated to measuring job capability').

[48] See Hugh Collins and Tarunabh Khaitan, 'Indirect Discrimination Law: Controversies and Critical Questions' in *Foundations* (n 18) 26, 28; Sophia Moreau, 'The Moral Seriousness of Indirect Discrimination' in ibid 128.

[49] See Barbara Havelková, 'Judicial Scepticism of Discrimination at the ECtHR' in ibid 85–86: ('Anti-discrimination law, and indirect discrimination especially ... depends on several acknowledgments about social reality. One is an awareness that discrimination is enabled by sociocultural and socio-economic structures, which hierarchically organise society to the disadvantage of certain groups and their members. ... an acknowledgment that it is legitimate that certain institutions be prohibited from replicating and thus exacerbating these structures'); ibid 94 ('the recognition of relevance of context is at the core of the doctrine of indirect discrimination, since it is the knowledge of the real situation people find themselves in which allows us to assess whether and how an apparently neutral rule will impact them more than others. Finding indirect discrimination is not a formal, abstract exercise, but a substantive, concrete one.').

[50] *Fraser* (n 19) para. 77 ('The root of s. 15 is our awareness that certain groups have been historically discriminated against, and that the perpetuation of such discrimination should be curtailed.'); Deborah Hellman, 'Indirect Discrimination and the Duty to Avoid Compounding Injustice' in *Foundations* (n 18) 105–121; Sophia Moreau, 'What is Discrimination?' (2010) 38 Phil & Pub Aff 143.

doctrine can work effectively within the framework of proportionality review. An adjudicative body may conduct an in-depth, multifaceted examination of the relevant social, historical, and empirical factors as it scrutinizes the legitimacy of the purpose, the appropriateness of the measure taken, whether the measure is necessary for the purpose and is the least disadvantageous among equally effective means, and whether the interests achieved by the means outweigh the discriminatory impact.

In addition, the possibility of constitutional scrutiny over indirect discrimination can have a preventive effect on decision-makers' attempts to design and impose measures that have foreseeable social consequences and an asymmetric impact on certain groups with protected traits.[51] Since the absence of discriminatory intent is irrelevant to determining whether an act or measure constitutes indirect discrimination, decision-makers need to be cautious about their actions' potential impact and justifiability, being mindful of the social context in which their decisions are implemented.[52] The doctrine can contribute to general awareness-raising of socially structured discrimination and encourage both the government and private actors in decision-making positions to be self-reflective with regard to the principles of substantive equality and concerns for social justice, which would lead to the enhancement of real-life situations of historically and socially disadvantaged groups and individuals.[53]

III. *Household Head System* (*Hojuje*): Canonizable Principles on Tradition and Gender Equality

The Constitutional Court of Korea was created by the 1987 Amendment of the Constitution of the Republic of Korea (the South Korean Constitution), highlighting a historic constitutional moment for the country that ended three decades of military dictatorship. Since its creation, the Constitutional Court of Korea, holding the power of strong, *ex post facto* concrete constitutional review that enables direct individual complaints, has been one of the most actively functioning constitutional courts in Asia and around the globe.[54] The Court's

[51] *Fraser* (n 19) para. 31 ('Accompanying this shift was the recognition that discrimination is "frequently a product of continuing to do things the way they have always been done", and that governments must be "particularly vigilant about the effects of their own policies" on members of disadvantaged groups ...').

[52] Collins and Khaitan (n 48) 27; Moreau (n 48) 145.

[53] Moreau (n 48) 144; Khaitan and Steel (n 18) 217–218.

[54] For the history of the Court and its major decisions in English, see Constitutional Court of Korea, *Thirty Years of the Constitutional Court of Korea* (The Constitutional Court of Korea 2018).

vibrancy has been facilitated by a highly energetic civil society in South Korea, which saw the constitutional review system as an effective venue for pursuing their rights projects, especially in the areas for which they had little input in the initial law-making process.[55]

Some of the most vibrant constitutional challenges put before the Constitutional Court during the thirty-five years of its operation have been in the areas of women's rights and gender equality.[56] Despite the country's democratization and rapid economic growth in the past decades, many sectors of domestic law in South Korea have remained significantly conservative in terms of gender equality. Many provisions reflected long-standing patriarchal culture and norms in society, and the male-dominant legislature had been passive about amending them.[57] In particular, family law in South Korea (adopted in 1958 after the Korean War) had openly codified a patriarchal ideology that was heavily influenced by Confucianism, which had been introduced to Korea several centuries previously. The Household Head System, *Hojuje* in Korean, was a paradigmatic example that was sustained until 2005 when the Constitutional Court held the entire system to be unconstitutional.[58] Under this system, a household was a basic family unit to which every South Korean citizen was registered automatically at birth. A household was comprised of a 'household head', *Hoju*, the eldest male in a family, and his subordinated family members, including his grandmother, mother, elder sisters, sons, and daughters. This system legally made every woman citizen in South Korea belong to her father at birth, to her husband in matrimony, and to her son after her husband's death, in a straightforward embodiment of the 'Virtue of Threefold Obedience', a traditional Confucian norm that had been imposed on women.[59]

After decades of family law reform movements, led by a national alliance of women's rights and human rights groups and lawyers, went unanswered by the legislature, the civil society alliance initiated strategic litigation in the early 2000s.[60] Several women claimants submitted applications to local government offices to appoint themselves as their household head or to change their household status as having no head. When their applications were rejected as

[55] Yoon Jin Shin, 'Cosmopolitanising Rights Practice: The Case of South Korea' in Takao Suami et al. (eds), *Global Constitutionalism from European and East Asian Perspectives* (CUP 2018) 269–271.

[56] See Yoon Jin Shin, 'Gender Equality, Individual Empowerment, and Constitutional Rights Review: South Korea's Dynamic Development' in Wen-Chen Chang et al. (eds), *Gender, Sexuality and Constitutionalism in Asia* (Hart Publishing 2023).

[57] ibid 122, 129.

[58] Constitutional Court of Korea 2001Hun-Ka9 etc., 17-1 KCCR 1 (3 February 2005).

[59] See Keith Knapp, 'Sancong Side 三从四德 (Threefold Obedience and Four Virtues)' in Xinzhong Yao (ed.), *Encyclopedia of Confucianism* (Routledge 2015).

[60] For a more detailed history and background of this movement, see Shin (n 56) 137.

anticipated, the women brought their cases to the family courts, arguing for the unconstitutionality of *Hojuje*. Many of these courts suspended the proceedings and sent the cases to the Constitutional Court of Korea. The Constitutional Court combined all these cases for a unified review and delivered a historic decision in 2005 after holding a series of open hearings.

In the 7–2 decision, the Court held *Hojuje* to be unconstitutional as it violated gender equality and individual dignity in the family. Notably, the South Korean Constitution makes specific mention of tradition and the relevant state obligation in Article 9, providing that 'The State shall strive to sustain and develop the cultural heritage and to enhance national culture.' Groups and individuals who opposed the abolition of *Hojuje* relied on this provision, arguing that preserving *Hojuje* and the traditional family order sustained by it was the constitutional duty of the state. On the other hand, the civil society alliance, demanding its abolition, invoked a different constitutional provision, Article 36, paragraph 1: 'Marriage and family life shall be entered into and sustained on the basis of individual dignity and equality of the sexes, and the State shall do everything in its power to achieve that goal.' In the main part of its reasoning, the Constitutional Court included a section titled 'Constitution and Tradition'. While the Court acknowledged that a family system possesses a cultural and historical nature, it underscored that family law is no exception in its subjection to constitutional principles: 'It is true that the institution of family bears traits as a historical and social product, but such features do not give the family system or family law a privilege to be exempted from the priority of the constitution. Otherwise, the value order of family relations would be able to be separated from the constitutional order, which is unacceptable in constitutional democracy.'[61] The Court clarified that Article 36, paragraph 1 pronounces the constitutional principle that family life must be based on gender equality and individual dignity.[62] It was emphasized that family law should not merely reflect social reality or public sentiment, but must defend and disseminate constitutional norms and values in the real-life world.[63]

Then the Court proceeded to elaborate on the normative relations between Article 9 and Article 36, paragraph 1 of the Constitution, and on how in cases of seeming conflict the two provisions ought to be interpreted. It first pointed out that the tradition and traditional culture stipulated in Article 9 retain both historical and contemporary natures and that not every traditional convention

[61] 2001Hun-Ka9 (n 58) 16.
[62] ibid.
[63] ibid 17.

receives constitutional protection for the mere fact that it existed in the past and continues to exist today.[64] The Court stated, 'The tradition that has to be succeeded and promoted under Article 9 is a moral standpoint or ethics which has suitability for contemporary social and economic environment and which holds universal validity according to today's standards.'[65] Tradition, according to the Court, should be reinterpreted based on present-day moral understandings, which should draw on 'not only constitutional values and principles, but also universal values of humanity, justice, and humanitarian spirit'.[66] A lasting custom that is still being practised today that runs counter to contemporary constitutional principles, according to the Court, may well be an 'evil custom of society' that ought to be abolished according to the preamble to the Constitution,[67] rather than a tradition deserving of protection under Article 9; and a tradition or culture that is related to the institution of family is subject to clear limitations, according to which it must not run counter to gender equality and individual dignity, the two core principles that the Constitution prescribes to family systems and relations.[68] The Court articulated that 'if a family institution succeeded from the past goes against gender equality and individual dignity under Article 36, paragraph 1, such a system cannot assert its constitutional validity by invoking Article 9'.[69]

After providing the above interpretation of the general relationship between tradition and constitutional rights and principles, the Court proceeded to review whether *Hojuje* was in violation of gender equality. The seven justices made it clear that 'discrimination which relies on a fact or a conception that traditional life relations between men and women used to be constructed in certain ways, or discrimination based on the stereotypical idea of gender roles, is not allowed'.[70] The opinion pointed out that *Hojuje* reproduced gender discrimination that was deeply rooted in traditional perceptions of male superiority and of women's passive and subordinated status in family.[71] The Court also emphasized the social and psychological impact of *Hojuje* on women and

[64] ibid 17–18.
[65] ibid 18. This view was first expressed in an earlier decision of the Court, 95Hun-Ka6, 9-2 KCCR 1, 19 (16 July 1997).
[66] 2001Hun-Ka9 (n 58) 18.
[67] The Constitution of the Republic of Korea (amended 29 October 1987), preamble: 'We, the people of Korea, ... having assumed the mission of democratic reform and peaceful unification of our homeland and having determined to consolidate national unity with justice, humanitarianism and brotherly love, and [t]o *destroy all social vices and injustice*, and [t]o afford equal opportunities to every person and provide for the fullest development of individual capabilities in all fields ...' (emphasis added).
[68] 2001Hun-Ka9 (n 58) 18.
[69] ibid.
[70] ibid 19.
[71] ibid.

girls, including the effect of developing an unstable sense of self-identity, a feeling of disconnection with their original family after marriage, and a sense of subordination to their family in laws, and fortifying the social culture of degrading women and preferring and prioritizing boys over girls.[72] The Court concluded that *Hojuje*, a system which establishes and sustains a patrilineal household, did not have any legitimate reasons for discriminating against women, and the system constituted a violation of Article 36, paragraph 1 of the Constitution.[73] The Court also held that *Hojuje* infringed on individual dignity in the family, prescribed in the same provision, since it discriminated against family members by classifying them either as a household head or as the head's subordinated members, and treating individuals as a means of succession in a patrilineal family order, and not as an equal, dignified, independent, and holistic person.[74] Following this historic decision, *Hojuje* was entirely abolished and a completely new citizen registration system was adopted in South Korea in 2007. Under this digitalized and individualized system, every South Korean citizen is registered as an independent individual on equal terms, neither as a household head nor as a subordinated family member.

Among the notable aspects of the *Hojuje* decision is the way the Court applied the proportionality test. The Constitutional Court of Korea, like many other constitutional adjudication bodies around the globe, adopts the proportionality principle as a standard of constitutional review in a wide range of constitutional rights cases (with a few exceptions, as in the case of the right to social security).[75] In equality cases, the Constitutional Court adopts a two-pronged standard. While a rationality test is taken as a basic standard, a four-step proportionality review is applied in areas where the Constitution mandates equality in concrete terms, as in Article 36, paragraph 1, and when differential treatment is regarded as causing a significant burden on relevant constitutional rights.[76] Since *Hojuje* concerned an area where equality is specifically mandated by the Constitution, the case was subject to the four-step proportionality review.[77] In the reasoning, the Constitutional Court observed that sustaining

[72] ibid 20.

[73] ibid 25.

[74] ibid 23–24.

[75] See Yoon Jin Shin, 'Proportionality in South Korea: Contextualizing the Cosmopolitan Rights Grammar' in Po Jen Yap (ed.), *Proportionality in Asia* (CUP 2020).

[76] ibid 91–93.

[77] The four-step proportionality test applied by the Constitutional Court consists of the following criteria: (1) the legitimacy of a legislative purpose; (2) the appropriateness of the means; (3) the least restrictiveness (whether the means taken for the legislative purpose is the least restrictive one among all equally effective options); and (4) the balance of interests (whether the public interest achieved outweighs the degree of rights restrictions), ibid 83–84.

a patriarchal family order does not constitute or otherwise have a legitimate purpose justifying discrimination against women, and made it clear that the mere fact that a certain practice was passed down and has continued to exist for a long time does not provide a legitimate reason for restricting constitutional rights, including the right to gender equality.[78] In other words, preserving a tradition for tradition's sake cannot serve as a valid reason for discrimination or a rights restriction. The Household Head System therefore could not even pass the first step of the proportionality review—a legitimate purpose for differential treatment. It was thus not necessary for the Court to go through the next three steps of the test to reach the decision of unconstitutionality.[79]

The *Hojuje* decision has several merits as a potential candidate for a canon of constitutional jurisprudence in the areas of gender and human rights, especially in cases where the equal rights and dignity of women and other minorities have long been denied in the name of social culture and tradition—a continuous reality in many societies. First, the decision made clear that preserving tradition for tradition's sake does not constitute justifiable grounds for restricting individuals' constitutional rights and equality. An independent, legitimate reason for the state to sustain such a tradition must be provided. In other words, the constitutional rights contestation process 'deconsecrates traditions and requires them to be justified in constitutional terms'.[80] A tradition-based law or practice that restricts individuals' rights and equality is subject to the same constitutional scrutiny as any other law or practice. The principles pronounced in the decision can have wide applicability in other jurisdictions across the globe, not only for women's rights and equality, but for any group or individual whose equal dignity has been rejected on grounds of social convention. Second, the *Hojuje* decision conducted proportionality review in a specific way that delivered a strong normative message to the government and society. It is one of the rare decisions in which the Constitutional Court of Korea held the law to be unconstitutional because it failed to satisfy the first step of a proportionality review. The decision demonstrated that the law being challenged, whose legitimacy is asserted on the basis of long-standing tradition and culture in society, cannot even pass the first step of review, and the conclusion is the same despite the constitutional provision on the state obligation to preserve

[78] 2001Hun-Ka9 (n 58) 18, 19, 24.

[79] This method of reasoning contrasts with the dissenting opinion of two justices, which applied all four steps of the proportionality review after noting that preserving *Hojuje* has a legitimate reason as it is a unique traditional family system that possesses a rationality of its own, and opined that the system satisfies the proportionality test, ibid 32–38.

[80] Shin (n 55) 267–268.

national culture and tradition. The mode of *Hojuje* reasoning provides an example of a constitutional court's principled engagement with tradition and signals to society that equality and human rights set the conditions on tradition, and not vice versa.

The *Hojuje* reasoning can thus provide a rights-based constitutional framework that empowers historically disadvantaged groups and individuals in society. Discrimination against women, a practice that has long existed in almost every society, is a paradigmatic case where a system of constitutional rights review can prove a particular strength, since the legislative body tends to be more susceptible to the preferences of dominant groups in society that have benefited from the prejudiced traditional order. In a practical aspect, the *Hojuje* reasoning can be easily applied in other jurisdictions, as it demands that any tradition in society be justified in light of the proportionality principle, the globalized structure of constitutional rights review. The point of renewed attention would be to treat the first step of review as normatively significant and make it function effectively when scrutinizing a law or practice rooted in tradition or social convention. The constitutional review mechanism enables an interpretation that integrates the universality of human rights with the particularity of local contexts in a manner that serves the equal rights of historically marginalized groups and individuals.[81] This can be achieved by reinterpreting the tradition in light of contemporary moral standards through the dynamics of rights contestation and deliberation.[82] Subjecting tradition to constitutional scrutiny empowers the voices of those who have long been oppressed by tradition and encourages them to participate in self-emancipatory projects that transform that very culture and tradition.[83] The interpretive principles and modes of reasoning provided by the *Hojuje* decision can play a canonical role in deliberating on such constitutional challenges, and provide a platform for bottom-up transformation and the development of a tradition-entrenched society into a rights-based one.

[81] See Seyla Benhabib, 'Another Universalism: On the Unity and Diversity of Human Rights' (2007) 81(2) Proceedings & Addresses Am Phil Assoc 7.

[82] See Charles R. Beitz, *The Idea of Human Rights* (OUP 2009) 88–95 (on the meaning and methods of 'progressive convergence'). See also *Obergefell v. Hodges* 576 US 644, 664 (2015) (the majority opinion stating, 'History and tradition guide and discipline this inquiry [of the identification and protection of fundamental rights] but do not set its outer boundaries ... That method respects our history and learns from it without allowing the past alone to rule the present').

[83] See also a landmark decision by the Supreme Court of India, *Navtej Singh Johar & Ors v. Union of India*, WP (Crl) No. 76 of 2016 (6 September 2018) (holding unconstitutional the Indian Penal Code that criminalized consensual sexual conduct between adults of the same sex, with Chief Justice Dipak Misra discussing critically the relationship between 'social morality' and 'constitutional morality', paras 120–123, 253).

IV. Intermediate Scrutiny: A Well-Known but Inadequate Standard as a Global Canon

As is well known, the Supreme Court of the United States has developed three levels of scrutiny for equality jurisprudence under the Fourteenth Amendment of the US Constitution. According to this formula, strict scrutiny, the most stringent standard, has been applied to cases involving 'suspect classifications' such as race, national origin, religion, and alienage.[84] For such classifications to be justified, the government must prove that the difference in treatment concerned is 'necessary' for a 'compelling' state interest. Intermediate scrutiny, a middle-level review standard, has been applied to classifications based on gender or illegitimacy. To be justified, the government must show that the classification is 'substantially related' to the achievement of an 'important' state interest. For other grounds of classifications, the rational basis test, the lowest level of scrutiny, is applied, where the government only has to show that the classification concerned is rationally related to a legitimate state interest.

In the area of gender discrimination, *Craig v. Boren* is the first decision in which the US Supreme Court ruled based on intermediate scrutiny.[85] In this case, the Court held that an Oklahoma statute prohibiting sales of beer to males under the age of 21 and to females under the age of 18 violated the Equal Protection Clause of the Fourteenth Amendment. The Court found that the state government did not show a substantial relationship between the gender-based differentiation and important governmental objectives, which here concerned the maintenance of traffic safety. Before this decision, the Court had applied the rational basis test in gender discrimination cases, as in *Reed v. Reed*.[86] In *Mississippi University for Women v. Hogan*, the substance of the intermediate scrutiny standard was applied in the case of gender-based classification, with the newly introduced phrasing, 'exceedingly persuasive justification'.[87]

[84] e.g. *United States v. Carolene Products Co.* 304 US 144 (1938); *Korematsu v. United States* 323 US 214 (1944); *Loving v. Virginia*, 388 US 1 (1967).

[85] *Craig v. Boren* 429 US 190 (1976).

[86] *Reed v. Reed* 404 US 71 (1971). In this case, the Court ruled for the first time that discrimination based on sex is prohibited under the Equal Protection Clause and held unconstitutional the Idaho Code that specified the mandatory preference for males over females in appointing administrators of estates. It applied the rational basis test, examining 'whether a difference in the sex of competing applicants for letters of administration bears a rational relationship to a state objective', 404 US 71, 76.

[87] *Mississippi Univ. for Women v. Hogan* 458 US 718 (1982). The Court stated, 'The party seeking to uphold a statute that classifies individuals on the basis of their gender must carry the burden of showing an "exceedingly persuasive justification" for the classification … The burden is met only by showing at least that the classification serves "important governmental objectives and that the discriminatory means employed" are "substantially related to the achievement of those objectives"', 458 US 718, 724.

In *United States v. Virginia*, the Supreme Court struck down the male-only admission policy of the Virginia Military Institute (VMI), as its gender-based admission policy violated the Equal Protection Clause.[88] The Court opinion, delivered by Justice Ruth Bader Ginsburg, found that the VMI did not meet the government's burden of 'exceedingly persuasive justification', while still stating the formula of intermediate scrutiny: 'the reviewing court must determine whether the proffered justification is "exceedingly persuasive" ... The State must show at least that the [challenged] classification serves important governmental objectives and that the discriminatory means employed are substantially related to the achievement of those objectives.'[89] The Court also used the terms 'skeptical scrutiny' and 'exacting standard', while underscoring the need for exceedingly persuasive justification when reviewing the persuasiveness of assertions made by the VMI regarding the merits of a male-only military education.[90] The reasoning added that 'all gender-based classifications today warrant heightened scrutiny', finding the Fourth Circuit's 'substantive comparability' test, which compared the VMI and the Virginia Women's Institute for Leadership, was an incorrect invention that displaced the 'exacting standard' developed by the Supreme Court. [91] Some critics regard the review standard adopted in this decision as a departure from the conventional intermediate scrutiny towards a stricter standard,[92] though others hold differently.[93]

Although the tripartite framework of the US Supreme Court equality jurisprudence is widely known to law students in the world as a textbook-like formula, the standard of intermediate scrutiny possesses quite a few weaknesses that would prevent it from serving as a global canon in gender discrimination adjudication. In the formal aspect, as the name of the standard indicates, intermediate scrutiny does not stand independently, but is located in the middle of the two other standards. The intermediate standard makes sense only in a jurisdiction, such as the United States, that adopts a three-tier criteria system in equality jurisprudence. In addition, it is unclear how intermediate scrutiny can be accommodated within a globally adopted constitutional review

[88] *United States v. Virginia* 518 US 515 (1996).
[89] ibid 533.
[90] ibid 531.
[91] ibid 555.
[92] Justice Scalia noted in his dissent in this case that the standard adopted by the Court opinion substantively applied a 'least-restrictive-means analysis', a higher standard than the 'substantial relation' test, and was much closer to the strict scrutiny analysis, ibid 573. See also Kevin N. Rolando, 'A Decade Later: *United States v. Virginia* and the Rise and Fall of "Skeptical Scrutiny"' (2006) 12 Roger Williams U L Rev 182; Candace S. Kovacic-Fleischer, '*United States v. Virginia*'s New Gender Equal Protection Analysis with Ramifications for Pregnancy, Parenting, and Title VII' (1997) 50 Vand L Rev 845.
[93] e.g. David K. Bowsher, 'Cracking the Code of *United States v. Virginia*' (1998) 48(2) Duke LJ 305.

structure—the proportionality test. With respect to the substantive aspect, the core elements of the intermediate scrutiny standard—an 'important' government interest, and a 'substantial relation' between the end and the means—are overly vague and too abstract to stand alone and serve as a canonical standard in gender equality review. The US Supreme Court has not elaborated on a criteria to distinguish between 'compelling', 'important', and 'legitimate' government objectives, or between the terms 'necessary', 'substantially related', and 'rationally related'.[94] The interpretation of each element of intermediate scrutiny is thus subject to the wide discretion of individual adjudicators and is likely to produce incoherency and unpredictability in its application, as demonstrated by divisions among lower courts and disagreement among scholars in understanding *United States v. Virginia*.[95]

Another major problem is that the tier system of the US Supreme Court fixes 'gender' as a basis of classification that is always subject to 'intermediate' scrutiny, regardless of the particular nature, gravity, or circumstances of an individual case. It may not persuade many courts in the world why every gender discrimination case invites medium-level review, and not a stricter or lower level standard depending on the context. The above problems of intermediate scrutiny, including its uncertain substance while being affixed to a categorical tier system, would explain why the standard is well known to other jurisdictions but has not actually been adopted by them. A more appealing approach for many courts in the world would be to review gender discrimination cases in light of the proportionality principle and to scrutinize their constitutional justifiability at each step of the test, taking into account the relevant factors

[94] See Note, 'Let the End Be Legitimate: Questioning The Value Of Heightened Scrutiny's Compelling and Important-Interest Inquiries' (2016) 129 Harv L Rev 1406, 1408–1409, 1411–1412, 1423 (noting, 'no watershed opinion has set out a clear method for determining whether any given interest is compelling, important, or merely legitimate'; 'Under intermediate scrutiny, the Court has upheld a variety of interests virtually without comment, whether in the sex-based equal protection context or in the free speech context'; 'the gradations between legitimate, important, and compelling interests are essentially rhetorical').

[95] Uncertainty increased as the Court opinion in *United States v. Virginia* emphasized the requirement of 'exceedingly persuasive justification', while not clarifying whether it is an independent, additional criteria or simply a restatement of intermediate scrutiny. Chief Justice Rehnquist in his concurring opinion stated, 'It is unfortunate that the Court thereby introduces an element of uncertainty respecting the appropriate test. While terms like "important governmental objective" and "substantially related" are hardly models of precision, they have more content and specificity than does the phrase "exceedingly persuasive justification"', *Virginia* (n 88) 599. See also Rolando (n 92) 218–227; Heather L. Stobaugh, 'The Aftermath of *United States v. Virginia*: Why Five Justices Are Pulling in the Reins on the "Exceedingly Persuasive Justification"' (2002) 55 SMU L Rev 1755. *Tuan Anh Nguyen v. INS* 533 US 53 (2001) is considered to have returned to traditional intermediate scrutiny. For diversified lower court practices of applying intermediate scrutiny, see e.g. *Cohen v. Brown University* 101 F 3d 155 (1st Cir. 1996); *Buzzetti v. City of New York* 140 F 3d 134 (2d Cir. 1998); *Tagami v. City of Chicago* 875 F 3d 375 (7th Cir. 2017); *Free the Nipple-Fort Collins v. City of Fort Collins* 916 F 3d 792 (10th Cir. 2019).

in a comprehensive, contextualized, and systemized manner.[96] There may be cases where courts are expected to accord a certain amount of deference to other branches of the government, or where a supranational human rights court, such as the European Court of Human Rights, grants a 'margin of appreciation' to a member state with respect to the interpretation of rights in a specific context and the striking of a balance between individual rights and the public interest concerned. In such cases, a proportionality review tends to be conducted in a somewhat relaxed or even formalistic manner, or is not applied at all.[97] However, this posture of deference needs to be adopted with caution in gender discrimination cases, where the affected individuals are predominantly members of socially and historically disadvantaged groups. As demonstrated by a series of decisions of the European Court of Human Rights on headscarf regulations,[98] the Court's deference to the legislative or political bodies of the national government in support of local democracies may easily result in an endorsement of the majority's preference, disadvantaging those in minority groups whose equal rights should be effectively guaranteed by an independent adjudicative body.[99]

V. Conclusion

The research on canons in gender discrimination jurisprudence illuminates important constitutional developments in various jurisdictions that hold global significance. Constitutional review brings to light for re-examination instances of 'conventionally normalized' wrongfulness that have been imposed on women and other historically disadvantaged groups. It provides a venue where cosmopolitan moral principles meet local particularities on constitutional terms and requires justification for law and practices that have been

[96] For critiques of the tiered approach to constitutional rights cases and arguing for the adoption of proportionality review in the United States, see Jud Mathews and Alec Stone Sweet, 'All Things in Proportion? American Rights Review and the Problem of Balancing' (2010) 60 Emory LJ 797; Donald L. Beschle, 'No More Tiers? Proportionality as an Alternative to Multiple Levels of Scrutiny in Individual Rights Cases' (2018) 38 Pace L Rev 384.

[97] See Yutaka Arai-Takahashi, *The Margin of Appreciation Doctrine and the Principle of Proportionality in the Jurisprudence of the ECHR* (Intersentia 2002); George Letsas, 'Two Concepts of the Margin of Appreciation' (2006) 26 OJLS 705.

[98] *S.A.S. v. France* App no. 43835/11 (1 July 2014); *Belcacemi and Oussar v. Belgium* App no. 37798/13 (11 July 2017); *Dakir v. Belgium* App no. 4619/12 (11 July 2017).

[99] See Eyal Benvenisti, 'Margin of Appreciation, Consensus and Universal Standards' (1999) 31 NYU J Intl L & Pol 843; Letsas (n 97) 729; Shu-Perng Hwang, 'Margin of Appreciation in Pursuit of Pluralism? Critical Remarks on the Judgments of the European Court of Human Rights on the "Burqa Bans"' (2020) 20 HRL Rev 361.

prejudiced against under-represented voices. The doctrine of indirect discrimination enables adjudicators to see beyond the formality of law and deliberate on socially structured inequalities and the real-life conditions of women and other minorities in the process of constitutional reasoning. The principles and the reasoning method provided by the *Hojuje* decision can serve as a model of constitutional interpretation subjecting an oppressive culture and tradition in society to the constitutional demands of human rights and equality. Both the indirect discrimination doctrine and the *Hojuje* reasoning can support the self-emancipatory project of a society to rectify its enduring wrongs and injustices and to pursue substantive equality through constitutional mechanisms. The cases discussed in this chapter also demonstrate the effectiveness of proportionality review, as opposed to tier-based intermediate scrutiny, in conducting comprehensive and principled review of conventional norms and practices accused of discrimination. A global canon for gender equality jurisprudence requires transnational applicability, not only on account of its substantive merits but also for its workability within a common grammar that enables sound contextualization.

21
The Canons of Social and Economic Rights

Katharine G. Young

I. Introduction

Social and economic rights belong to the subset of rights that require a government to use its resources and effective organization to secure adequate material resources or opportunities for its citizens and others in its territory or control. Such rights, which also attract the terminology of economic and social rights, socioeconomic rights, or social welfare rights, are integral to constitutional democracy and human rights, just as they are incorporated within concepts of human dignity, freedom, equality and even life in any modern state. The obligations they define—such as the requirement that the state avoids undermining, or must promote, or directly provide, social security, decent work, healthcare, education, housing, food, water, sanitation, land, and other goods, services, and opportunities—are imperfect in character. These obligations thus correspond to a range of possible interactions between the state (negatively to refrain from infringing rights, and positively to work to protect and provide for them), the economy, the family, and other institutions and actors. Social and economic rights attract controversy and disagreement, in many theories of the state and the international order, and the nomination of global canons is therefore cramped by misunderstandings and misgivings about law and political economy, liberal rights and imperfect obligations, the separation of powers, the role of judges and the rule of law. This chapter thus explores the idea, not only of "canons", but also of "proto-canons" and "counter-canons," to capture the consensus and dissensus around social and economic rights.

Social and economic rights attracted a significant degree of international consensus in the Universal Declaration of Human Rights of 1948, which pointed to a range of obligations on the state, private parties and in the international order, and which deemphasized the role of enforcement for its ambitious vision for human rights.[1] This moment of consensus was shortlived, and the Cold War oversaw

[1] Universal Declaration of Human Rights, arts. 22–26.

Katharine G. Young, *The Canons of Social and Economic Rights* In: *Global Canons in an Age of Contestation.* Edited by: Sujit Choudhry, Michaela Hailbronner, and Mattias Kumm, Oxford University Press. © Katharine G. Young 2024.
DOI: 10.1093/9780191956942.003.0021

markedly different ideas about legal, fiscal and social arrangements, in state planning, investments, and markets. Many of the disagreements of political economy accompanied the legal realist idea that "rights" were only those "interests" or legal relations that were enforceable by courts, and that courts could judicially manage only the "perfect" obligations that accompanied civil and political rights, and the private relations of property and contract. Hence, a great obstacle to the recognition of social and economic rights has been the challenge of justiciability. If courts could not reliably interpret, adjudicate, and enforce them, so this argument went, these "rights" could not gain the determinacy required of constitutional rights or might impair the government's efforts at realizing broader goals of aggregate, or collective, social welfare.

These disagreements have led to the irony that the "canon" of social and economic rights points merely to the case that best resolves the puzzle of justiciability, rather than to the texts or instruments that address the broader questions of law and political economy that such rights raise. This question of justiciability was prominently resolved in the 2000 South African case of *Republic of South Africa v. Grootboom.*[2] For three reasons—which I explore in Section II of this chapter as *Grootboom*'s reasoning, provenance, and visibility—the case forms an almost singular canonical reference. While other jurisdictions, notably from civil law systems, have also resolved this question, at times with great ingenuity, I suggest that the appeal of the South African Constitutional Court's apparent resolution of a judicially manageable standard for such rights, the case's proximity to the post-apartheid Constitution of South Africa, and the order's ambivalent legacy for housing rights, have combined to give *Grootboom* this canonical status.

Yet *Grootboom* is not a singular source for establishing and renewing the boundaries of the global canon for economic and social rights, and its legacy is not completely secure. Moreover, social and economic rights continue to do work outside the court-centric paradigm (and, it should be acknowledged, continue to remain marginal within it, in many places). This chapter therefore introduces the idea of "proto-canons" and "conter-canons" for social and economic rights. These concepts add to what should be a worldwide debate about foundational texts, for constitutional democracy and human rights. Indeed, proto- and counter-canons are especially useful categories for charting both

[2] *Gov't. of the Republic of South Africa v. Grootboom* [2000] ZACC 19; 2001 (1) SA 46 (CC). For the resolution reached in Latin America, see David Landau, "The Unsettled Canon of Social Rights Enforcement in Latin America," Chapter 22 this volume (comparing historical assumptions against justiciability to vibrant new examples from Columbia, Brazil, and elsewhere).

the ambitions and marginality of social and economic rights, as well as the hegemony of distinctive visions of constitutional democracy.

The chapter therefore nominates the Universal Declaration as a proto-canon for social and economic rights, as crystallizing incipient ideas of freedom from want and an institutionally broad (and non-court centric) vision of realization. Section III explores the pathways of influence of the Universal Declaration, in numerous international human rights instruments and constitutional texts. The chapter also nominates, as a counter-canon, the 1973 U.S. case of *San Antonia School District v. Rodriguez*,[3] which reversed the promise of justiciable social and economic rights in that influential jurisdiction. Section IV explores how that case marked the interpretive closure, by the U.S. Supreme Court, of available arguments for constitutional social and economic rights, and devolved the right to education to the uneven enforcement of the U.S. states.

These proto- and counter-canons help us reflect on the highly unsettled constitutional and democratic norms of the present. The trajectories of these canons have been clearly shaped by concerns about judicial power, but also by the free market ideology that views the government's role as secondary to markets in promoting access to the basic goods and services that help secure such rights. No canonical text (or at least, the meaning that the text signifies) can be expected to enjoy that status forever: I end with a note about how the very traits that have made *Grootboom* canonical may diminish it over time. It is, of course, difficult to predict, but as the human rights and constitutionalist values of global public law are threatened, in part by the lack of government support for ensuring access to the material security and forms of equality that are demanded by social and economic rights,[4] other canons may emerge.

II. *Grootboom* as Canon

The South African Constitutional Court's 2000 decision in *Grootboom* has emerged as the undisputed canon of the constitutional democratic guarantee of social and economic rights.[5] *Grootboom* is particularly advantaged by being published in English, at a time of growing engagement with comparative case law and prestige for post-Cold War, post-apartheid constitutionalism in South Africa, and for its apparent resolution of a number of

[3] 411 U.S. 1 (1973).

[4] See, e.g., Mark Graber, Sanford Levinson, and Mark Tushnet (eds.), *Constitutional Democracy in Crisis?* (OUP 2018). The law and analysis of this chapter is current as of April 2021.

[5] *Grootboom* [2000] ZACC 19; 2001 (1) SA 46.

preoccupations about justiciable social and economic rights. Alongside other key judgments from South Africa,[6] as well as those from the public interest tradition of India[7] and the *tutela* jurisprudence of Colombia,[8] *Grootboom* enjoys a kind of "proxy" hegemonic role: emanating from the Global South, but relevant to long-standing debates in the Global North. Unlike these other contenders, *Grootboom* is particularly responsive to two U.S. cases in which the debates about justiciability have been framed.[9] Yet this "proxy" role is a complex one: the judgment's connection with supposedly universal "rights" provides interesting counter-hegemonic implications;[10] but its connection with the powerful field of U.S. constitutional scholarship links its omissions to problematic blind spots for social and economic rights.

As a superficial pointer to a canon, *Grootboom* has been described as "seminal," "landmark," "watershed," and "arguably the farthest reaching of the Court's socio-economic rights decisions."[11] I claim that, beyond the evident approval of its interpretive community, *Grootboom* is propelled to the canon on grounds of reasoning, provenance, and visibility. These grounds bear a family resemblance to other hierarchical sortings of authority in public law and in public international law, including debates for conferring small-c constitutional status on landmark statutes or particular government practices,[12] and formal tests for establishing customary or general principles status on cases

[6] e.g. *Soobramoney v. Minister of Health, Kwazulu-Natal* 1998 (1) SA 765 (CC); *Minister of Health v. Treatment Action Campaign (No. 2)* 2002 (5) SA 721 (CC).

[7] e.g. *Olga Tellis v. Bombay Municipal Corp.* 1985 SCC (3) 545 (Indian Supreme Court confirming the right to life includes the right to livelihood for pavement dwellers subject to eviction).

[8] e.g. *Sala Segunda de Revisión, Sentencia T-760*, 31 July 2008; Magistrado Ponente; Manuel José Cepeda (Constitutional Court of Colombia ordering a restructuring of the health system based on constitutional right to health).

[9] The two cases that define the dangers and misdirected ambitions of "judicial supremacy" are *Lochner v. New York*, 198 U.S. 45 (1905) and *Brown v. Board of Education*, 349 U.S. 294 (1955). See further Section IV.

[10] Alan Hunt, "Rights and Social Movements: Counter-Hegemonic Strategies" (1990) 17 J. L. & Soc'y. 309; Boaventura De Sousa Santos and Cesar A. Rodriguez-Garavito (eds.), *Law and Globalization from Below: Towards a Cosmopolitan Legality* (CUP 2005).

[11] Stuart Wilson and Jackie Dugard, "Constitutional Jurisprudence: The First and Second Waves" in Malcolm Langford et al. (eds.), *Socio-Economic Rights in South Africa: Symbols or Substance?* (CUP 2014) 35, 41; see also *Constitutional Court Oral History Project* (Edwin Cameron) Interview 2: January 16, 2012, at 30 (available at http://www.historicalpapers.wits.ac.za/inventories/inv_pdfo/AG3368/AG3368-C13-001-jpeg.pdf) ("among the most meritorious achievements of this Court"). For similar assessments, outside South Africa, see e.g. Mark S. Kende, "The South African Constitutional Court's Embrace of Socio-Economic Rights: A Comparative Perspective," 6 Chapman L. Rev. 137 (2003) (comparing the "seminal" *Grootboom* with U.S. approaches); Ben Saul et al., *The International Covenant on Economic, Social and Cultural Rights: Commentary, Cases and Materials* 957 (OUP 2014) ("watershed").

[12] These aspects of constituted authority are developed further in Katharine G. Young, *Constituting Economic and Social Rights* (OUP 2012). For other relevant hierarchical sortings, see e.g. Yaniv Roznai, *Unconstitutional Constitutional Amendments* (OUP 2017); Jeremy Waldron, *"Partly Laws Common to All Mankind": Foreign Law in American Courts* (Yale UP 2012).

and laws as binding international law, even *jus cogens*.[13] While a fuller exploration is beyond the scope of this chapter, it is worth noting that what separates a global "canonical case" from these tests may be its responsiveness to the institutional concern of judicial review (which indeed *Grootboom* purports to solve).

Grootboom grew out of a complaint by a homeless community, living in crisis conditions on a community sports field, that their constitutional right to housing had been infringed.[14] Among other social and economic (and civil, political, and cultural rights), the South African Constitution guarantees:

> Everyone has the right to have access to adequate housing
>
> The state must take reasonable legislative and other measures, within its available resources, to achieve the progressive realisation of this right
>
> No one may be evicted from their home, or have their home demolished, without an order of court made after considering all of the relevant circumstances. No legislation may permit arbitrary evictions.[15]

The community had been waiting, some as long as seven years, for subsidized low-cost housing; they had moved to private land, earmarked for public housing, before their forcible eviction and the destruction of their shacks and possessions; from there, they resided on community land, under plastic sheets as winter closed in.[16] The Constitutional Court accepted that their rights had been infringed, and ordered that the state was required to devise and implement a comprehensive housing program and to make "reasonable" provision for "relief for people who have no access to land, no roof over their heads, and who are living in intolerable conditions or crisis situations."[17]

[13] Statute of the International Court of Justice, art. 38(1) (setting out sources of international law, including (b) international custom, as evidence of a general practice accepted as law; and (c) the general principles of law recognized by civilized nations). For points of crossover, see Gerald L. Neuman, "Human Rights and Constitutional Rights: Harmony and Dissonance," 55 Stan. L. Rev. 1863 (2003).

[14] The respondents, of whom Irene Grootboom was first named, included 510 children and 390 adults. *Grootboom*, paras. 7, 8.

[15] Constitution of the Republic of South Africa, 1996, Sec. 26.

[16] The conditions of the Wallacedene informal settlement consisted of shacks with no water, sewage, or refuse removal, and extremely limited (only 5% had) electricity. The conditions of the initial settlement, the eviction from the New Rust property, and the temporary structures on the sports field, were also described in the judgment. *Grootboom*, [7]–[11], [59]–[61].

[17] *Grootboom*, [99].

B. *Grootboom's* Reasoning

In declaring that the right to housing had been infringed, the Court's reasoning followed a conventional formula of judicial consideration, heavily attentive to the above-cited text and alert to separation of powers concerns. First, the Constitutional Court set out criteria for the review of social and economic rights, which inquires into the "reasonableness" of the government's action. This test injects consequentialist and contextual considerations into social and economic rights enforcement, and rejects more categorical, court-led interpretations. The test of "reasonableness" had made an appearance in social and economic rights cases before,[18] but *Grootboom* was the first in which the Constitutional Court held that a statute or policy was unreasonable, giving credence to a constitutional rationale for the right to access housing. This, the Court stated, should be understood as more than mere shelter, due in part to the connection between housing and human dignity.[19] The reasoning was deferential to the statutory and policy framework of housing provision, but nevertheless examined its features with a rights-oriented perspective.[20] *Grootboom* thus supplied the long-established administrative law "reasonableness" standard with a more substantive content.[21] Thus, while the Court was generally approving of the government's resourcing and planning for housing development, it held that it had omitted consideration of a key constituency: a vulnerable group in crisis conditions. This understanding of reasonableness was to become central to the reviewability of social and economic rights in a series of other South African cases, and was to become the express standard of review for the new complaints mechanism for social and economic rights that became operational in 2013 under international human rights law.[22]

Secondly, the attention to one omitted group—vulnerable people in material crisis—was an important addition to a named category of concern for

[18] *Soobramoney v. Minister of Health, Kwazulu-Natal* 1998 (1) SA 765 (CC).

[19] e.g. *Grootboom*, [83].

[20] For careful explication, see Sandra Liebenberg, *Socio-Economic Rights: Adjudication under a Transformative Constitution* (Juta 2010) 152–153.

[21] Murray Wesson, "*Grootboom* and Beyond: Reassessing the Socioeconomic Jurisprudence of the South African Constitutional Court" (2004) 20 SAJHR 284.

[22] i.e. the Optional Protocol to the ICESCR adopted "reasonableness" as its test for the newly articulated complaints mechanism under that treaty: art. 8(4): Bruce Porter, "Reasonableness and Article 8(4)" in Malcolm Langford et al. (eds.), *The Optional Protocol to the International Covenant on Economic, Social and Cultural Rights: A Commentary* (Pretoria University Law Press 2014). For the terms of opposition, see Michael J. Dennis and David P. Stewart, "Justiciability of Economic, Social, and Cultural Rights: Should There Be an International Complaints Mechanism to Adjudicate the Rights to Food, Water, Housing, and Health," 98 AJIL 462 (2004).

comparative and international human rights,[23] and would become significant in reviewing governmental responses to subsequent crises, including for the poor and the middle class, during the 2007–2009 global financial crisis. For example, the austerity policies that were piloted for the economic recovery in 2010 drew criticism on the grounds of both the proportionality and reasonableness of governments' responses.[24] The *Grootboom* decision cited the right to adequate housing in the International Covenant on Economic, Social and Cultural Rights (at that time, signed but not ratified by South Africa) following the domestic constitutional requirement to consider international law "as a tool to interpretation of the Bill of Rights,"[25] but declined to adopt UN doctrine in the case. And indeed, this independence from international human rights law is nowhere more pronounced that in the Constitutional Court's refusal to adopt a "minimum core" approach, established in the Committee on Economic, Social and Cultural Rights' influential General Comment No. 3 of 1990.[26] Despite careful referencing of this standard, the Court in *Grootboom* ultimately held that it lacked the information and experience to entrench a minimum threshold of social and economic rights, and elected to leave the question open for revision in the future.[27] In other respects, the Court's substantive constitutional tests—for children's rights, for evictions, for the immediate burdens of "progressive realization"—engaged fluently, but did not adopt

[23] David Bilchitz, "Socio-Economic Rights, Economic Crisis, and Legal Doctrine" (2014) 12 ICON 710. Compare with, e.g., David Weissbrot and Mary Rumsey (eds.), *Vulnerable and Marginalised Groups and Human Rights* (Edward Elgar 2011) (entirely omitting class, or market exclusion, from categories of the vulnerable).

[24] e.g. note also *I. D. G. v. Spain* (Communication 2/2014), U.N. Committee on Economic, Social and Cultural Rights (June 17, 2015) (early decision of ICESCR C'tee., under new complaints mechanisms, considering South African housing jurisprudence when querying Spain's limited procedural protections against foreclosures); Ariranga G. Pillay, Chairperson, United Nations Committee on Economic, Social and Cultural Rights, *Letter to States Parties* (CESCR/48th/SP/MAB/SW, May 16, 2012) (signaling need for proportionality); see further Aoife Nolan (ed.), *Economic and Social Rights after the Global Financial Crisis* (CUP 2014) (including discussion of austerity precursors in Latin America, as well as Europe); Eibe Riedel et al. (eds.), *Economic, Social and Cultural Rights in International Law* (OUP 2014).

[25] South African Constitution, s. 39(1)(b); see further Sandra Liebenberg, "South Africa and the International Covenant on Economic, Social and Cultural Rights: Deepening the Synergies" (2020) 3 South African Judicial Education Journal 19. See also *Grootboom* reference to *S v. Makwaynane* [1995] ZACC; 1993 (3) SA 391 (CC), noting the relevance of the United Nations, Inter-American, and European human rights tribunals and instruments.

[26] U.N. Econ. & Soc. Council (ECOSOC), Comm. on Econ., Soc. & Cultural Rights, *General Comment No. 3: The Nature of States Parties' Obligations*, U.N. Doc. E/1991/23 (1990). The General Comment is analyzed at *Grootboom*, [29]–[33]. See further Katharine G. Young, "The Minimum Core of Economic and Social Rights: A Concept in Search of Content," 33 Yale JIL 113 (2008).

[27] The Court continues to decline to recognize a minimum core as giving rise to an independent cause of action or independent content: see *Minister of Health v. Treatment Action Campaign (no. 2)* 2002 (5) SA 721 (CC), paras. 26–39; *Mazibuko v. City of Johannesburg* 2010 (4) SA 1 (CC) paras. 46–68; although the concept is arguably left open as relevant to the test of reasonableness.

or incorporate, other rights-relevant U.N. treaties and treaty body sources.[28] The Constitutional Court also noted myriad issues that also impact access to housing—access to finance, basic services, electricity, and roads, as well as enumerated rights to access land, healthcare, food, water, and social security—that may be open to review, particularly under the conditions prevailing in a country like South Africa. This decision to reject any compartmentalization of housing from other socioeconomic rights, as well as the Constitution's civil and political rights, has been influential.[29]

Thirdly, the Court dealt candidly with the issue of resources. In perhaps the most heavily-cited passage (a canonical passage of a canonical case?), the Court declared that "A court considering reasonableness will not enquire whether other more desirable or favourable measures could have been adopted, or whether public money could have been better spent."[30] At the same time, the Court opined that "It is essential that a reasonable part of the national housing budget be devoted to [those in desperate need], but the precise allocation is for national government to decide in the first instance."[31] It clarified that all three levels of government—national, provincial, and local—had obligations to realize the right to housing. The Court therefore asserted grounds for engaging expressly and yet deferentially with budgetary matters and federal divisions: both long-standing challenges for the justiciability of social and economic rights.[32] These clarifications have been extended in subsequent housing decisions, with a detectable increase in the Court's readiness to scrutinize public budgets.[33]

Finally, the Court's remedy—a declaration, alongside the approval of a negotiated settlement between the parties—attempted to resolve the remedial challenges of social and economic rights. By issuing a declaratory order, the

[28] ECOSOC, Comm. on Econ., Soc. & Cultural Rights, *General Comment No. 4: The Right to Adequate Housing*, U.N. Doc. E/1992/23 (1991); ECOSOC, Comm. on Econ., Soc. & Cultural Rights, *General Comment No. 7: The Right to Adequate Housing: Forced Evictions*, U.N. Doc. E/1998/22 (1997). It is noteworthy that at this point, "the Committee [had] dedicated more attention to the right to housing than any other right": Matthew Craven, *The International Covenant on Economic, Social and Cultural Rights: A Perspective on Its Development* (OUP 1995) 329.

[29] See, e.g., Katharine G. Young, "The Right-Remedy Gap in Economic and Social Rights: Holism and Separability," 69 UTLJ 194 (2020); see also Ben Saul et al., *The International Covenant on Economic, Social and Cultural Rights*, 957–959 (noting also its influence on cases decided under the African Charter).

[30] *Grootboom* 2000 (1) SA 46 (CC) [41].

[31] ibid [66].

[32] See Section IV.

[33] e.g. *City of Johannesburg Metropolitan Municipality v. Blue Moonlight Properties Blue Moonlight* 2011 (37) SA 11 (CC). For an argument that the judicial assessment of budgets in *Grootboom* grounds a new pathway for economic policy evaluation, see Radhika Balakrishnan et al., *Rethinking Economic Policy for Social Justice: The Radical Potential of Human Rights* (Routledge 2016) 4–5.

Court deflected the potentially usurping and politicizing managerialism of the structural injunction. Instead, the declaration implied a respect and trust of its own authority and conveyed the expectation that compliance by government would not be an issue. It engaged the Human Rights Commission as a monitor, and marked out clear reasons (queue jumping[34]) not to privilege the complainants themselves with individual compensation or substitutional relief. The Constitutional Court also noted the participatory aspects of housing decisions, setting out a framework later utilized and adapted in the "meaningful engagement" jurisprudence.[35] This contrasts with the more individualized approaches common in the Latin American jurisprudence on social and economic rights cases.[36]

These aspects of the reasons ignited influential debates about the benefits of "weak" courts and dialogic review;[37] in this way, the Court's reasons are very much related, and circular, to the provenance and visibility aspects discussed below. But as a matter of authoritative law, I suggest that it remains important to mark out the quality and normative content of its reasoning as a separate matter.

B. *Grootboom's* Provenance

I use a case's provenance to delineate its association with such rule-of-law values as past precedents, authority, and liberal legitimacy.[38] Here, it is worth noting that *Grootboom* is a unanimous decision of the "first-generation" post-apartheid Constitutional Court of South Africa. This Court was composed of a robust and illustrious bench, appointed in a process during which Nelson

[34] This concern foreshadowed issues for the future: Kent Roach, "Polycentricity and Queue Jumping in Public Law Remedies: A Two-Track Response" (2016) 66 UTLJ 3; Katharine G. Young, "Rights and Queues: On Distributive Contests in the Modern State" (2016) 55 Colum. J. Transnat'l. L. 65.

[35] i.e. *Occupiers of 51 Olivia Road v. City of Johannesburg* 2008 (3) SA 208 (CC) (S. Afr.); Brian Ray, *Engaging with Social Rights: Procedure, Participation and Democracy in South Africa's Second Wave* (CUP 2016).

[36] David Landau, "South African Social Rights Jurisprudence and the Global Canon: A Revisionist View" in David Landau and Rosalind Dixon, *Constitutional Triumphs, Constitutional Disappointments: A Critical Assessment of the 1996 South African Constitution's Local and International Influence* (CUP 2018) 406.

[37] e.g. Mark Tushnet, *Weak Courts, Strong Rights: Judicial Review and Social Welfare Rights in Comparative Constitutional Law* (Princeton UP 2008); Jeff King, *Judging Social Rights* (CUP 2012); Katharine G. Young, *Constituting Economic and Social Rights* (OUP 2012); Stephen Gardbaum, "The New Commonwealth Model of Constitutionalism" (2001) 49 Am. J. Comp. L. 707; Rosalind Dixon, "Creating Dialogue about Socioeconomic Rights: Strong-Form versus Weak-Form Judicial Review Revisited" (2007) 5 ICON 391.

[38] For an overview, see Larry Alexander, *Constitutionalism: Philosophical Foundations* (CUP 1998).

Mandela was still President and thus was very much linked to the prestige of that constitutional moment. Many of the justices of this newly established court had been anti-apartheid activist lawyers, and some had been involved in the Constitution's drafting; the Court itself was appointed to "certify" the Constitution (and had returned the draft for amendments[39]). Yacoob J, who authored the *Grootboom* opinion, had rather extraordinary credentials as a judge sensitive to the importance of human rights, having lived with disability (blindness since infancy) and racial discrimination, and had amassed an impressive biography as a lawyer in Durban, representing victims of unfair evictions and protestors of apartheid alongside a commercial practice.[40] The prestige of this first bench will probably not be replicable for South African courts in the future.[41]

The South African Constitution itself inherited similar prestige:[42] a text of fraught compromise, produced in Kempton Park under conditions of high national tensions and recently unbanned political party representatives, expert and informed negotiators including the later (fifth and current, since 2018) President Cyril Ramaphosa. The drafters borrowed from international human rights treaties and an anti-discrimination framework, and made the collective decision to include the Freedom Charter's social and economic rights,[43] alongside civil and political rights and a framework of liberal-plus (transformative) constitutionalism.[44] The ambition of this moment—and the sincere gestures toward a new "culture of justification" in South Africa—are reflected in both the Constitution's Bill of Rights and preamble.[45] The 1994 Interim Constitution was reworked and certified by 1996, and *Grootboom*, in 2000, remains proximate to, and expressive about, this moment.[46] It is notable, in this sense, that the judgment fails to mention significant socioeconomic

[39] *Certification of the Constitution of the Republic of South Africa* 1996 (4) SA 744 (CC) (S. Afr.).

[40] Justice Zak Yacoob, https://www.concourt.org.za/index.php/11-former-judges/67-justice-zak-yacoob.

[41] Theunis Roux, *The Politics of Principle: The First South African Constitutional Court, 1995–2005* (CUP 2013); Heinz Klug, *Constituting Democracy: Law, Globalism and South Africa's Political Reconstruction* (CUP 2002).

[42] Even those offering a postcolonial critique of human rights predicted that "the dramatic rebirth of the South African state ... is arguably the most historic event in the human rights movement since its emergence some fifty years ago": Makau Mutua, *Human Rights: A Political and Cultural Critique* 126 (University of Penn. Press 2002).

[43] Albie Sachs, *The Strange Alchemy of Life and Law* (OUP 2011); Hassen Ebrahim, *The Soul of a Nation: Constitution-Making in South Africa* (OUP 1998).

[44] Karl Klare, "Legal Culture and Transformative Constitutionalism" (1998) 14 SAJHR 146 (canonical article on South Africa's constitutional ambitions).

[45] Constitution of South Africa, Preamble, Sec. 7-39; See further Etienne Mureinik, "Beyond a Charter of Luxuries: Economic Rights in the Constitution" (1992) 8 SAJHR 464.

[46] e.g. citations to the prominent literature at *Grootboom*, fn. 19.

policy reversals between 1994 and 1996 that arguably already indicated a break with the redistributive ambitions and constitutional moment of 1994.[47]

Those who argued the case are also worth mentioning. Irene Grootboom's community was represented by a local lawyer who a magistrate had sought out (as pro bono) after their initial eviction,[48] and who was unapprised of the theories of structural impact litigation that would guide later community representation in social and economic rights litigation.[49] Nonetheless, the highly respected lawyer and activist Geoff Budlender of the Legal Resources Center represented the *amici* of the case, and thus the case was decided with the benefit of highly strategic, forward-thinking briefs.[50] The Constitutional Court thanked the quality of the LRC's brief while declining to follow the sophisticated theory of international human rights law that it offered. Moreover, the High Court, at first instance, had decided *Grootboom* in large part on grounds of children's rights to shelter and had ordered a structural remedy for certain services to be provided for children and the parents of children[51] (which was reversed on appeal.) This earlier case has been heard by Judge Dennis Davis, himself an influential member of the South African legal community and the author of the most heavily cited refutation of justiciable social and economic rights (which presented a familiar leftist critique).[52] For that decision to be reversed, and substituted with a far more deferential, directive-principles-like status that was closer to Dennis Davis's original academic argument, could only heighten the influence—as well as the visibility—of the case.

[47] President Mandela's 1994 Reconstruction and Development Program (RDP) was replaced with the 1996 Growth, Employment and Redistribution strategy (GEAR), a neoliberal strategy of growth stimulus that failed to deliver on poverty reduction (see COSATU). *Grootboom* does not mention macroeconomic policy nor does it delve deeply into issues of land or resource allocation; hence, while its reasons could be read as tacit criticism of neoliberal economic development with limited social protections, it avails itself of pro-neoliberal readings. See, e.g., John J. Williams, "The *Grootboom* Case and the Constitutional Right to Housing: The Politics of Planning in Post-Apartheid South Africa" in Naila Kabeer (ed.), *Inclusive Citizenship* (Zed Books 2005) 219, 225.

[48] Ibid, 225 (2003 interview with pro bono lawyer Julian Appolos).

[49] Cf. *Minister of Health v. Treatment Action Campaign (no. 2)* 2002 (5) SA 721 (CC); see further Mark Heywood, "The Transformative Power of Civil Society in South Africa: An Activist's Perspective on Innovative Forms of Organizing and Rights-Based Practices" (2020) 17 Globalizations 294 (noting both the role of TAC, as well as incorporation of AIDS Law Project into SECTION 27); Tshepo Madlingozi, "Social Movements and the Constitutional Court of South Africa" in Oscar Vilhena et al. (eds.), *Transformative Constitutionalism: Comparing the Apex Courts of Brazil, India and South Africa* (Pretoria University Law Press 2013) 537.

[50] For further background, see Jason Brickhill (ed.), *Public Interest Litigation in South Africa* (Juta & Co. Ltd. 2018), see also 2008 Legal Resources Centre Oral History Project.

[51] *Grootboom v. Oostenberg Municipality*, 2000 (3) BCLR 277 (Cape of Good Hope High Court) (Order "to provide the respondents who were children and their parents with shelter," consisting at a minimum of tents, portable latrines, and water).

[52] Dennis M. Davis, "The Case Against the Inclusion of Socio-economic Demands in a Bill of Rights Except as Directive Principles" (1992) 8 SAJHR 475.

C. *Grootboom's* Visibility

This last aspect of constructing the canon is perhaps the most contentious: how *Grootboom* has become so visible for deliberating and contesting social and economic rights. By visibility, I mean a combination of citations in prestigious and well-read forums; an accessibility to a wide and global audience; and the instigation of a highly generative debate with an array of reasonable positions. But visibility is helped by hegemony; the power and prestige of Anglo-American materials has long been subjected to general, and to particular Global South/Third World, critique.[53] Human rights, and especially social and economic rights, has also long been a flashpoint in this area, and it is ironic that a case which mainly answers U.S. sceptics has gained status by addressing this particular baseline or audience.

First, *Grootboom* is most easily measured by its republications and citations. For example, *Grootboom* is excerpted in many teaching and research texts and in materials for judicial dissemination,[54] as representative of social and economic rights jurisprudence in at least one casebook on comparative constitutional law;[55] and in the international human rights law casebook that deals most thoroughly with social and economic rights.[56] A casenote was published in the *American Journal of International Law*, amongst other places.[57] In addition to the monographs cited, the case is examined in countless law review articles, chapters, and books about housing rights;[58] as well as in articles and

[53] See generally Antony Anghie, "Third World Approaches to International Law" (2003) 2 Chinese JIL 77; Daniel Bonilla Maldonando (ed.), *Constitutionalism of the Global South: The Activist Tribunals of India, South Africa and Colombia* (CUP 2013).

[54] e.g. Judith Resnik et al. (eds.), *The Reach of Rights*, Gruber Program for Global Justice and Women's Rights II-48 (2015), https://documents.law.yale.edu/sites/default/files/global-constitutionalism-2015.pdf, accessed November 8, 2020 (Yale Global Constitutionalism Seminar).

[55] Vicki Jackson and Mark Tushnet, *Comparative Constitutional Law* (2nd edn, Foundation Press 2006); see also Norman Dorsen et al. (eds.), *Comparative Constitutionalism: Cases and Materials* (West Academic Publishing 2002) (which *describes Grootboom's* meaning as hard to determine); Stephen Ross, Helen Irving, and Heinz Klug, *Comparative Constitutional Law: A Contextual Approach* (LexisNexis 2014) (in survey of U.S., Australian, Canadian, and South African constitutional law, providing excerpt). But see Michaela Hailbronner, "Constructing the Global Constitutional Canon: Between Authority and Criticism" (2019) 69 UTLJ 248, 253 (discussing the non-representativeness of these texts).

[56] Philip Alston and Ryan Goodman, *International Human Rights* (OUP 2012); see also Ben Saul et al., *The International Covenant on Economic, Social and Cultural Rights: Commentary, Cases, and Materials* (OUP 2014) 957–958; Olivier De Schutter (ed.), *Economic, Social and Cultural Rights as Human Rights* (Routledge 2013).

[57] David D. Caron et al., "*Republic of South Africa v. Grootboom*. Case No. CCT 11/00. 2000 (11) BCLR 1169 and *Minister of Health v. Treatment Action Campaign*. Case No. CCT 8/02," 97 AJIL 669 (2003).

[58] Marius Pieterse, *Rights-Based Litigation, Urban Governance and Social Justice in South Africa: The Right to Joburg* (Routledge 2017) at 45.

collections dealing with constitutional rights, or international human rights, to healthcare, education, social security, and basic services more generally.[59]

Secondly, *Grootboom* helped seed a specialized and heavily international and comparative discourse of "reasonableness review."[60] The case is used to describe a before and after in South African jurisprudence ("post-*Grootboom*")[61] and has grounded a neologism: "the *Grootboom*-proofing of social policy."[62] This type of discourse analysis is perhaps more durable, if more contestable, than a citation or excerpt count. But this analysis is complicated by the fact that the visibility of the participants of this discourse is itself significant.[63] Cass Sunstein, a liberal/centrist U.S. constitutional scholar who penned a well-cited refutation of constitutional social and economic rights for post-communist Eastern Europe,[64] reversed this position, with a long discussion of the merits of *Grootboom* and the puzzles that it appeared to solve:[65] he went on to extol the virtues of a resurrection of F. D. Roosevelt's second bill of rights for the U.S., again citing *Grootboom*.[66] Frank Michelman, the most comprehensive of U.S. legal thinkers about social and economic rights, also responded early with discussion of *Grootboom*, in a founding issue of the *International Journal of Constitutional Law*.[67] Funding from the

[59] e.g. Helena Alviar García, Karl Klare, and Lucy A. Williams (eds.), *Social and Economic Rights in Theory and Practice* (Routledge 2015); see also, for a broader interdisciplinary effort, Malcolm Langford and Katharine G. Young (eds.), *The Oxford Handbook of Economic and Social Rights* (OUP 2022).

[60] Liebenberg, *Adjudication under a Transformative Constitution*. See sources cited, especially at n 37 earlier.

[61] e.g. Clarence Itumeleng Tshoose, "A Closer Look at the Right to Have Access to Adequate Housing for Inhabitants of Informal Settlements Post Grootboom" (2015) 30(1) Public Law 94–111.

[62] Malcolm Langford and Steven Kahanovitz, "South Africa: Rethinking Enforcement Narratives" in Malcolm Langford, César Rodríguez-Garavito, and Julieta Rossi (eds.), *Social Rights Judgments and the Politics of Compliance: Making It Stick* (CUP 2017) at 331 (noting effects on water and social security policymaking); see also Gilbert Marcus and Stephen Budlender, *A Strategic Evaluation of Public Interest Litigation in South Africa* (The Atlantic Philanthropies 2008) 66 ("the government has begun factoring these issues into its budget-making processes").

[63] Pierre Bourdieu's *Homo Academicus* is perhaps relevant in outline: (Paul Collier tr., Polity Press 1998): Bourdieu's analysis of the social origins and current positions of the French academy, as well as how they publish, how much, their institutional and media connections, and political involvements, is also worth mapping for the social field of comparatively engaged constitutional scholars, given that more subtle reputational influences may transform intellectual culture in ways that go beyond simple dialogue and debate. For the incorporation of aspects of this framework to map the international college of lawyers, see Anthea Roberts, *Is International Law International?* (OUP 2017).

[64] Cass R. Sunstein, "Against Positive Rights" in András Sajó (ed.), *Western Rights? Post-Communist Application* (Kluwer Law International 1996).

[65] Cass R. Sunstein, *Designing Democracy: What Constitutions Do* (OUP 2001).

[66] Cass R. Sunstein, *The Second Bill of Rights: FDR's Unfinished Revolution and Why We Need it More Than Ever* (Basic Books 2004). FDR's New Deal is still emblematic of a series of political positions held by the Democratic Party in the U.S.; the influence of his "four freedoms" on the UDHR is also noteworthy.

[67] Frank I. Michelman, "The Constitution, Social rights, and Liberal Political Justification" (2003) 1 ICON 13. Note that *Minister of Public Works v Kyalami Ridge Environmental Association* [2001] ZACC

Ford Foundation and other supported research projects contributed to this discourse.[68]

It is thus somewhat misleading, as Philip Alston would write, that "Rarely have the developments in the field of comparative constitutional law been so dominated by the jurisprudence not only of a single country but in this case of a single court."[69] *Grootboom*'s visibility comes not from the singular influence of South Africa and its court but rather the preoccupations of another country (the U.S.) and its powerful Supreme Court. Its visibility thus comes as a stand-in for addressing U.S. concerns, within the (hegemonic) parameters of U.S. debates about social and economic rights. Indeed, while some U.S. cases appear in the same comparative casebooks described earlier, they often do so anachronistically.[70] *Grootboom* instead stands as proxy for "what might have been," if not (audaciously) "what might become" for the U.S., as the counter-canon discussion in Section IV later highlights.

Thirdly, visibility is helped by accessibility. *Grootboom* is accessible for the clarity of its reasons, described earlier, but it is also assisted by the ease of general access to the SAFLII website,[71] a not-for profit publisher of African statutes and case law with no direct equivalent in the highly profitable U.S. legal publishing market.[72] An analysis of this and other non-U.S. websites must one day be written (see also the effect of similar platforms, such as Austlii[73]) for the somewhat immeasurable service they provide for securing a more responsive global canon.

Finally, the symbolic and material impact of *Grootboom* is itself a question that has spawned a cottage industry. Here, visibility is helped, in part, by the contestability of much of *Grootboom*'s legacy. There are radical swings in opinion. As one recent book opens its pages:

19; 2001 (3) SA 1151 (CC), a sequel to *Grootboom*, forms the main body of Michelman's analysis, which is also comparative (with the Massachusetts Supreme Judicial Court).

[68] e.g. Ford Foundation Annual Report 2001, available at https://www.issuelab.org/resources/7927/7927.pdf.

[69] Philip Alston, "Foreword" in Malcolm Langford (ed.), *Social Rights Jurisprudence: Emerging Trends in International and Comparative Law* (CUP 2008).

[70] e.g. Warren Court decisions such as *Brown v. Board of Education* have been heavily excerpted and cited in comparative settings, particularly in the second wave of constitutionalism of the 2000s.

[71] South African Legal Information Institute: http://www.saflii.org.

[72] In the U.S., access is often restricted through paid membership to Westlaw/Lexis; although open access platforms do exist, such as the Legal Information Institute of the Cornell Law School: https://www.law.cornell.edu/lii/about/about_lii.

[73] http://www.worldlii.org; see also Free Access to Law Movement (FALM) members.

> The kernel of the idea [for this book] was born in a discussion in 2009 about the impact of the South African Constitutional Court's landmark *Grootboom* judgment. Was it an illustration of everything positive or everything negative about the uptake of socio-economic rights in post-apartheid South Africa? ... was it Exhibit A of the danger that relying on socio-economic rights might narrow the frame of political struggle and leave communities and individuals without any remedies of substance?[74]

This book's opening paragraph is, in short, a rewrite of the main left–liberal preoccupations of social and economic rights, as well as liberal constitutionalism and judicial review in general: missing is the center-right, right, and far-right critiques, of course, that nevertheless exert significant pressure on the legitimacy of social and economic rights (e.g. perceptions of dependency, perversity, big government, infeasibility, and inefficiency).[75] Moreover, the ambivalence of the narrative of Irene Grootboom helps sustain canonicity. Is her story a cautionary tale (she died, penniless and without her waited-for house, eight years after the judgment[76]) or, as is now more commonly asserted, is it a motivational one (she helped to mobilize a community that ushered in a significant change in national housing policy, with some slow but incremental gains for the community, derived from a negotiated settlement[77]). Those seeking to end the ambivalence have themselves generated a range of new methodologies for serious assessment.

III. Proto-Canon: The Universal Declaration of Human Rights

The preoccupation with justiciability that has elevated *Grootboom* to canonical status is both understandable and predictable. Yet it distracts from the landmark instrument in which the rights to an adequate standard of living and to work were first enumerated as a "common standard of achievement," in

[74] "Preface" in Malcolm Langford et al. (eds.), *Socio-Economic Rights in South Africa: Symbols or Substance* (CUP 2014) xiii.

[75] e.g. Eric A. Posner, *The Twilight of Human Rights Law* (OUP 2014) (welfarist concerns). *Grootboom* marks out some of this controversy with the court's caution about rewarding a self-help strategy (land invasions and vigilantism). For a reflective engagement with utilitarianism objections and those of feasibility, see Amartya Sen, "Elements of a Theory of Human Rights," 32 Philosophy & Public Affairs 315 (2004).

[76] Pearlie Joubert, "Grootboom dies homeless and penniless" *Mail & Guardian* (August 8, 2008), https://web.archive.org/web/20190728164204/https://mg.co.za/article/2008-08-08-grootboom-dies-homeless-and-penniless, accessed November 8, 2020.

[77] Langford and Kahanovitz, earlier.

universal terms. The Universal Declaration of Human Rights, which sets out the equality of all people, in dignity and rights, also calls for an international order in which social and economic rights, alongside civil, political, and cultural rights, can be fully realized.[78] To this end, the Universal Declaration serves as a second—labeled here proto-canonical—source for social and economic rights, although the status of its own provenance and visibility was to ebb during the geopolitical hostilities of the Cold War and the attempts of later governments, including those of the Global North, to distance their human rights commitments from the social and economic guarantees to which they had earlier subscribed. Admittedly a wide category, with many contenders for social and economic rights, a "proto-canon" in this sense is a text or instrument or case that originally met the criteria I offer above (enjoying noteworthy reasoning, provenance, and visibility), but whose canonical status has been arguably interrupted by a competing set of ideas or even "common sense" about rights, law and political economy.

Forged at the highpoint of global consensus directly after World War II, and elucidating the commitment to human rights under the United Nations Charter of 1945, the Universal Declaration reflected earlier constitutional guarantees of social and economic rights and the contributions of socialist constitutionalism, social Catholicism, and the prescriptions of a social or welfare state, and the very proximate experience of a Great Depression and two World Wars.[79] The expression of commitment within the Universal Declaration, far more fulsome and generative for social and economic rights than the pragmatic resolution of justiciability represented by *Grootboom*, guided the core human rights treaties that followed, numerous resolutions of the U.N. General Assembly, the work of the U.N. special procedures, including in relation to international trade, investment, and the financial institutions, regional human rights instruments, and the text of dozens of subsequent constitutional instruments which

[78] The Universal Declaration of Human Rights, Preamble, arts. 22–26, 28. For attention to the latter requirement, see Thomas Pogge (ed.), *Freedom from Poverty as a Human Right: Who Owes What to the Very Poor?* (OUP 2007).

[79] See, e.g., Mary Ann Glendon, *A World Made New: Eleanor Roosevelt and the Universal Declaration of Human Rights* (Random House 2001); see also Daniel Ricardo Quiroga-Villamarín, "'An Atmosphere of Genuine Solidarity and Brotherhood': Hernán Santa-Cruz and a Forgotten Latin American Contribution to Social Rights," 21 Journal of the History of International Law 71 (2019) (Latin American contribution, and see also David Landau, Chapter 22 in this volume); see also Samuel Moyn, *Not Enough: Human Rights in an Unequal World* (HUP 2018) 52–57 (noting the influence of ideas of Gunnar Myrdal, T. H. Marshall, Karl Polanyi, and Georges Gurvitch). A social rights historiography dates the origins of such rights at least to the eighteenth century: Steven L. B. Jensen and Charles Walton (eds.), *Not Second Generation Rights. The Long History of Social and Economic Rights* (CUP 2022); Malgorzata Mazurek and Paul Betts, "Preface: When Rights Were Social" (2012) 3(3) Humanity 291–295; Katharine G. Young, "Freedom, Want and Economic and Social Rights," 24 Md. Int'l. L. Rev. 182 (2009).

guarantee social and economic rights. The inclusion of rights in the Universal Declaration also vastly increased the probability of their appearance in subsequent constitutions, although it remains unsettled as to whether the instrument itself, or the emergent ideas it codified, should be credited.[80] By whatever measure, social and economic rights are now vastly more likely to be constitutionalized than not, particularly in civil law systems and within Latin America and Eastern Europe.[81]

To be sure, the status of the Universal Declaration as canonical has been complicated by the colonial, gendered, and racial orthodoxies of 1948. Like the New Deal vision of Franklin D. Roosevelt's second bill of rights, set out during his State of the Union address of 1941, and itself a high water-mark for enumerating a list of social and economic rights guarantees (and informing the provisions in the Universal Declaration and the vision of international peace and security that would be gained by the guarantee of "freedom from want"),[82] the Universal Declaration has been tainted by these, and by other work-centric ideologies that formed deep grooves in American capitalist democracy. When efforts to create a codified treaty of the Universal Declaration stalled due to Cold War communist/capitalist divisions and other disagreements, the social, economic, and cultural rights were famously split from civil and political rights, drawing different adherents, with the U.S. remaining a prominent non-party to the International Covenant on Economic, Social and Cultural Rights (ICESCR). Commentators who attempt to ground human rights in the core human rights conventions, beyond the Universal Declaration,[83] must grapple with the absence of this support.

[80] See, e.g., Zachary Elkins, Tom Ginsburg, and James Melton, "Imagining a World without the UDHR" (2017), http://www.law.nyu.edu/sites/default/files/upload_documents/Zachary%20Elkins%20Paper%20September%202017%20v.2.0%20%282%29.pdf; Zachary Elkins, Tom Ginsburg, and Beth Simmons, "Getting to Rights: Treaty Ratification, Constitutional Convergence, and Human Rights Practice," 54(1) Harvard International L.J. 61–95 (2013).

[81] See findings, Evan Rosevear et al., "Justiciable and Aspirational Economic and Social Rights in National Constitutions" in Katharine G. Young (ed.), *The Future of Economic and Social Rights* (CUP 2012); Daniel M. Brinks et al., "Social Rights Constitutionalism: Negotiating the Tension Between the Universal and the Particular" (2015) 11 Annual Rev. of L. and Social Science 289.

[82] State of the Union address of 1941 (January 6, 1941); see Katharine G. Young, "Freedom, Want and Economic and Social Rights," 24 Md. Int'l. L. Rev. 182 (2009). The early input of the U.S. to the UDHR, as well as the hitherto overlooked contributions of the Global South to its follow-up instruments, is canvased in a burgeoning literature, e.g., Sally Ann Way, "The 'Myth' and Mystery of US History on Economic, Social, and Cultural Rights: The 1947 'United States Suggestions for Articles to be Incorporated in an International Bill of Rights'" (2014) 36(4) Hum. Rts. Q. 869 897; Roland Burke, *Decolonization and the Evolution of International Human Rights* (U. Penn. Press 2013); Steven L. B. Jensen, "Twentieth Century Economic and Social Rights: Decolonization and the Global South" in Malcolm Langford and Katharine G. Young (eds.), *The Oxford Handbook of Economic and Social Rights* (OUP 2022).

[83] e.g. Sandra Fredman, *Comparative Human Rights Law* (OUP 2018); Sakiko Fukuda-Parr, Terra Lawson-Remer, and Susan Randolph, *Fulfilling Social and Economic Rights* (OUP 2015). The U.S. has signed but not ratified the ICESCR.

At the very least, the ambitious social and economic rights of the Universal Declaration and its companion instruments[84] lost out—after a well-orchestrated effort—to the free market ideology that reigned, particularly since the administrations of Reagan and Thatcher in the 1980s, which retrenched various welfare state capitalisms and dislodged the broader moral and economic case for social and economic rights.[85] The powerful "Washington Consensus," established between the International Monetary Fund, the World Bank, and the U.S. Treasury, directly contradicted the premise that governments should provide a "freedom from want" when setting development aid, crisis management, or transitioning to capitalism. Instead, programs of fiscal austerity, user fees, privatization, market liberalization, and deregulation were themselves orthodoxy in a sphere occupied by financial ministers and central banks, and which set the policies that would impact on access to social security, healthcare, education, food, water, and sanitation, in the goal of greater efficiency and growth. Such programs are difficult (although not impossible) to square with economic and social rights, and yet a government uncommitted to these ideas was deemed "off track."[86] This deflected the status of the social and economic rights of the Universal Declaration, although the civil and political rights were to remain as central to fundamental rights understandings.

IV. Counter-Canon: *San Antonia School District v. Rodriguez*

So far, I have argued that *Grootboom* represents the canon, and the Universal Declaration of Human Rights represents the proto-canon, of social and economic rights. Yet to fully account for the contested status of such rights in constitutional and democratic argument, it is worth introducing a different status altogether: that of counter-canon. A counter-canon is, I argue, distinctive from, but related to, the prominent conceptualization of the "anti-canon," which is an attribute of caselaw, coined in the U.S., which represents a case or series of

[84] Both antecedent and successor international instruments were informed by the contributions cited earlier in nn. 79 and 82, as well as by John Maynard Keynes' critique of laissez-faire and embrace of globalization. These include the original Bretton Woods Agreement (1944), and the proposed Havana Charter for an International Trade Organization (1948) as antecedents; and the International Covenant on Economic, Social and Cultural Rights (entered into force January 4, 1976), and other core human rights treaties as successors.

[85] For a history of this orchestration, see Angus Burgin, *The Great Persuasion: Reinventing Free Markets since the Depression* (HUP Press, 2012).

[86] See Joseph E. Stiglitz, *Globalization and its Discontents* (Norton 2002), 42, citing an IMF phrase that signaled dissenters, which would send a negative signal to the markets. For an evaluation of two country's attempts to move outside this consensus, through constitutional social and economic rights, see Kim Lane Scheppele, "A Realpolitik Defense of Social Rights," 82 Tex. L. Rev. 1921 (2004).

cases whose central propositions all legitimate decisions of law must refute.[87] In many ways, in that jurisdiction, the enforcement of constitutional economic and social rights has been so discredited that it is itself outside the legitimate canon. This is because the majority of commentators in the U.S. have viewed constitutional economic and social rights as an "off-the-wall" proposition, implausible against the background assumptions of its constitutional culture (and the ascendent understanding of neoliberal political economy).[88]

What had discredited the idea of constitutional social and economic rights in the U.S., and following that, in other globalized settings? Undoubtedly, concerns about the risks of judicial supremacy (now commonly referred to as "juristocracy") played a large part, particularly in a large, federal jurisdiction with an aged, difficult-to-amend Constitution, and a history of juridical obstacles to progressive reforms. So, too, did broader political pressures—white backlash, taxpayer revolts, and the manipulated distinction between the worthy and the "undeserving" poor. [89] The fears that equated enforceable social and economic rights with the judicial usurpation of economic policymaking reflect the legacy of two important cases.[90] On the one hand was the *Lochner* Court's entrenchment of economic policy (ironically to overrule social rights-protective legislation through classical economic rights). On the other was *Brown v. Board of Education*, and its complicated legacy of backlash, which came to represent the bad of judicial overreach alongside the good of racial justice. These two very different cases are not really "anti-canonical" to social and economic rights, but nevertheless helped to discredit them.

The concept of a counter-canon, rather than an anti-canon, is an apt description of how texts or cases stand in for this diminishment. This concept, I suggest, dwells on the path not followed, and shows clearly why *Grootboom* serves as a canon, insofar as the marginal jurisprudence of social and economic rights is concerned. I argue that the best candidate for a counter-canon for such rights is the 1973 U.S. case of *San Antonia School District v. Rodriguez*,[91] described as "effectively the death knell for social and economic rights in the United

[87] Jamal Greene, "The Anticanon" 125 Harv. L. Rev. 379 (2011).
[88] J. M. Balkin, "Agreements with Hell and Other Objects of Our Faith," 65 Fordham L. Rev. 1703, 1734 (1997) ("off-the-wall"); Lawrence Lessig, "Colloquy, Fidelity as Translation," 65 Fordham L. Rev. 1507, 1509–1510 (1997); cf. Frank I. Michelman, "The Supreme Court 1968 Term-Foreword: On Protecting the Poor Through the Fourteenth Amendment," 83 Harv. L. Rev. 7 (1969).
[89] William E. Forbath, "Constitutional Welfare Rights: A History, Critique and Reconstruction," 69 Fordham L. Rev. 1821, 1824–1827 (2001).
[90] *Lochner v. New York*, 198 U.S. 45 (1905); For commentary, see Sujit Choudhry, "The Lochner Era and Comparative Constitutionalism" (2004) 2 ICON 1; see also Cass R. Sunstein, "Lochner's Legacy," 87 Colum. L. Rev. 873 (1987); Martha Minow, *In Brown's Wake: Legacies of America's Educational Landmark* (OUP 2010).
[91] 411 U.S. 1 (1973).

States."[92] There, in a 5–4 decision, the U.S. Supreme Court considered that the complexities of local taxation, fiscal planning, educational policy, and federalism, all counted against the judicial review of substantial educational disparities within the U.S. *Rodriguez* involved a class action challenge on behalf of schoolchildren in Texas who, as members of poor and often minority families living in school districts with a low tax base, received substantially less educational funding than others. The District Court below had held that the school financing scheme, heavily reliant on local property values, was unconstitutional, first, because dividing citizens on a wealth basis was highly suspect and, secondly, because this division directly affected the "fundamental interest" of education. Similarly, the minority of the Supreme Court emphasized the nexus between education and specific constitutional guarantees—the civil and political rights of the First Amendment, for example, which demanded a closer degree of judicial scrutiny when infringed on a discriminatory basis.[93] The majority, however, refused to take this step, albeit recognizing that education remained one of the most important services performed by the state. This meant cabining the Court's previous cases to their narrowest reasoning, as related only to absolute deprivations of constitutionally protected interests.

This counter-canon is beset by contingency. The 1960s and 1970s had involved a number of U.S. Supreme Court decisions supporting social and economic guarantees, and the *Harvard Law Review*'s 1969 Foreword—a prominent source of academic commentary—had provided an extensive grounding, in both jurisprudential and philosophical terms.[94] Indeed, the Warren Court's tentative grasp on social and economic rights had progressed from finding duties of affirmative provision for poor people when fundamental interests were at stake (rights to vote and the protections of criminal justice),[95] to the striking down of a six-month waiting period on welfare benefits for new arrivals between states,[96] and to procedural protections for welfare benefits,

[92] Cass R. Sunstein, "Why Does the American Constitution Lack Social and Economic Guarantees?" in Michael Ignatieff (ed.), *American Exceptionalism and Human Rights* (Princeton UP 2005) 90, 108.

[93] For the implications of the decision for racial equality and other goals, see Charles J. Ogletree and Kimberly Jenkins Robinson (eds.), *The Enduring Legacy of Rodriguez: Creating New Pathways to Equal Educational Opportunity* (Harvard Education Press 2015); see also Justin Driver, *The Schoolhouse Gate: Public Education, The Supreme Court, and the Battle for the American Mind* (Penguin Random House 2019).

[94] Frank I. Michelman, "Foreword: On Protecting the Poor through the Fourteenth Amendment," 83 Harv. L. Rev. 7 (1969).

[95] This line of cases included the striking down of the poll tax, *Harper v. Virginia Bd. Of Elections*, 383 U.S. 663 (1966) (striking down poll tax); to others *Griffin v. Illinois*, 351 U.S. 12 (1956) (trial transcripts to poor people appealing criminal conviction); *Douglas v. California* 372 U.S. 353 (1963) (provision of counsel on first appeal).

[96] *Shapiro v. Thompson*, 394 U.S. 618 (1969).

counting the "basic demands of subsistence" as a part of the Constitution's own guarantees.[97] Yet the election of President Nixon in 1968—a notably close one—was to change that course. As the legal realist account underlines, Nixon's four appointments to the Court, between 1970 and 1973, abruptly terminated this emerging development.[98]

Ironically, the education rights cases that surged in U.S. state courts after *Rodriguez* have proved significant, fueling a detailed comparative, as well as U.S., commentary.[99] Moreover, education rights, alongside health and social security, are more commonly represented in contemporary constitutional texts around the world—and are more often made expressly justiciable—than *Grootboom*'s rights to housing, for example, or the more recently advanced human rights to water, sanitation or a healthy environment.[100]

And yet the *Rodriguez* foreclosure of federal constitutional possibility remains salutary. Within it lies a complex amalgamation of ideas of what the U.S. constitution prohibits, permits, and requires, in terms of material security and the equality of citizens and others—as first endorsing a conception of equality that ignores material deprivation and focuses only on intent, to next invalidating policies that sought to mitigate structural inequality, and to endorsing the faith in markets and skepticism of the state described earlier.[101] In especially these latter terms, the canonical status of *Grootboom*, the proto-canonical status of the Universal Declaration, and the counter-canonical status of *Rodriguez* are all impugned by ideas and ideologies marked by those prevailing outside the juridical paradigm.

V. Conclusion

Grootboom remains canonical for its apparent resolution of judicial supremacy and social and economic rights. Its status is also helped by the ambivalence

[97] *Goldberg v. Kelly*, 397 U.S. 254 (1970).

[98] Cass R. Sunstein, "Why Does the American Constitution Lack Social and Economic Guarantees?" earlier.

[99] e.g. Jeff King, "American Exceptionalism over Social Rights" in Liora Lazarus, Christopher McCrudden, and Nigel Bowles (eds.), *Reasoning Rights: Comparative Judicial Engagement* (Hart Publishing 2014); see also Goodwin Liu, "Education, Equality, and National Citizenship," 116 Yale L.J. 330, 332 (2006). For the prominence of social and economic rights in state (subnational) constitutions in the U.S., see Emily Zackin, *Looking for Rights in All the Wrong Places* (Princeton UP 2013).

[100] See collection in Katharine G. Young (ed.), *The Future of Economic and Social Rights* (CUP 2019).

[101] See, e.g., Jedediah Britton-Purdy et al., "Building a Law-and-Political-Economy Framework: Beyond the Twentieth-Century Synthesis," 129 Yale L.J. 1784, 1808 (2020); cf. David S. Law and Mila Versteeg, "The Declining Influence of the United States Constitution," 87 NYU L. Rev. 762–858 (2012).

of its legacy, its ducking and weaving of neoliberal trends and separation-of-powers concerns, and its connection with South Africa's post-apartheid constitutional moment. Its longevity as canonical is not, however, assured. "Canon" implies authoritative norms, and the qualities of reasoning, provenance, and visibility are not impervious to the norm-busting of the current global political moment. A social and economic rights landmark produced at the close of the 1990s may be of doubtful use for the more unsettled constitutionalist pathways of the 2020s and beyond. As the challenges of weak, ineffective, captured, or otherwise corrupt governments increase, and the prestige and authority of South African and U.S. constitutionalist models decrease, new expressions of social and economic rights, especially from the Global South, may become authoritative. *Grootboom* and its progeny may become less cited and read in the legal systems inheriting civil law traditions and in particular regions outside Anglo-American common law, where social and economic rights are more prominent in constitutional text. The further health, economic, and humanitarian crises that will occur post-pandemic, as well as predictably through climate change, and further extremes of inequality and poverty, may pressure the creation of different canonical sources, with more coordinated or concrete obligations, particularly in relation to powerful private actors privileged by the system of states in the present global order. Whether the proto-canon of the Universal Declaration takes this form, or is unseated by older manifestos or newer institutions or platforms, remains to be seen.

22

The Unsettled Canon of Social Rights Enforcement in Latin America

David Landau

I. Introduction: The Rich History of Social Rights in Latin America

Social rights are central to the modern constitutional history of Latin America. Beginning in the early twentieth century, constitutional texts have sought to contend with a legacy of pervasive economic and social inequality. Mexico's 1917 Constitution, which was written in the aftermath of that country's tumultuous and complex revolution, is sometimes asserted to be the first constitution in the world to include them. Indeed, the Mexican Constitution is itself a canonical document in the region and around the world. It established a variety of important labor rights, including the right to an eight-hour workday and a minimum wage, as well as rights of collective bargaining and the right to strike.[1] It also set out the right to free public education.[2] Finally, it established the social function of property and gave the state broad powers to carry out programs of land redistribution, which had been an important objective of the revolution.

The Mexican Constitution was at the leading edge of a regional trend: all of Latin America's major countries would include these rights over the course of the twentieth century. In some constitutions, such as those of Guatemala (1945), Costa Rica (1949), and Colombia (1936 amendments to the 1886 constitution), the inclusion of socioeconomic rights was based on liberal reformist movements.[3] In others, such as Brazil (1934) and Argentina (1949),

[1] Const. Mexico, art. 123 (1917). Note though that several U.S. state constitutions included a right to education from the nineteenth century. Emily Zackin, *Looking for Rights in all the Wrong Places: Why State Constitutions Contain America's Positive Rights* (Princeton UP 2013).

[2] Const. Mexico, art. 3.

[3] Roberto Gargarella, *Latin American Constitutionalism, 1810–2010: The Engine Room of the Constitution* (OUP 2013) 111–115.

David Landau, *The Unsettled Canon of Social Rights Enforcement in Latin America* In: *Global Canons in an Age of Contestation*. Edited by: Sujit Choudhry, Michaela Hailbronner, and Mattias Kumm, Oxford University Press.
 DOI: 10.1093/9780191956942.003.0022

social rights formed a key part of constitutional projects pushed by populist presidents.[4]

Consider, too, the variety of modern constitutional projects in Latin America, all of which have included social rights in some significant form. Chile's 1980 Constitution was written under the influence conservative Catholic thought by a closed process controlled by a military dictatorship.[5] The Brazilian Constitution of 1988, in contrast, was drafted by a pluralistic constituent process during a transition away from dictatorship.[6] The Colombian Constitution of 1991 was written by an equally pluralist assembly as an escape from a deep political crisis and combined an extensive list of socioeconomic rights with neoliberal reforms.[7] Finally, the recent neo-Bolivarian constitutions found in Venezuela (1999), Ecuador (2008), and Bolivia (2009) pair continued recognition of socioeconomic rights with the inclusion of other new rights (such as environmental and indigenous rights) and institutional changes reflecting a skepticism of neoliberal economics and liberal constitutional design.[8] In short, Latin America continues to reflect great diversity in constitutional ideology, but overwhelming consensus that socioeconomic rights are central to that design. This, in turn, reflects the durable importance of economic and social inequality within Latin America. It seems that no serious modern constitution can fail to grapple with this legacy.

The 1917 Mexican Constitution, for all of its historical importance, sharply limited the scope of the new rights it included—social rights have long been viewed as non-justiciable there, via a number of different devices. Instead, the default assumption was that their achievement would be entrusted to the political branches of the government, and particularly the Institutionalized Revolutionary Party (PRI), the party that would rule Mexico as a one-party state from the 1930s until the 1990s.[9] Even after Mexico democratized, it has remained a regional laggard in finding social rights justiciable. Elsewhere in Latin America, in contrast, courts have moved firmly in the direction of justiciability, marking a clear regional trend. Contemporary debates in Latin

[4] ibid 115–121.

[5] Const. Chile (1980), art. 19 (containing rights to health, a clean environment, education, to work, to social security, and to unionize).

[6] Keith Rosenn, "Brazil's New Constitution: An Exercise in Transient Constitutionalism for a Transitional Society" (1990) 38 Am. J. Comp. L. 773, 791–793.

[7] Javier Couso, "The 'Economic Constitutions' of Latin America: Between Free Markets and Socioeconomic Rights" in Rosalind Dixon and Tom Ginsburg (eds.), *Comparative Constitutional Law in Latin America* (Edward Elgar 2017) 343.

[8] Phoebe King, "Neo-Bolivarian Constitutional Design" in Denis J. Galligan and Phoebe King (eds.), *Social and Political Foundations of Constitutions* (CUP 2013) 366.

[9] Jose Ramon Cossio Diaz, *Cambio social y cambio juridico* (Porrúa 2001).

America, as in many other regions around the world, have moved away from *whether* to include socioeconomic rights in constitutions, and towards *how* to enforce them.

The fact that socioeconomic rights are enforceable, however, says little about how they can best be enforced. Latin America may be most interesting to those working on social rights for the rich record of justiciability that its courts have developed, with a variety of interpretive approaches and remedial strategies. It serves as an underappreciated counterpart to the well-studied South African cases, which are perhaps best read as the particular response of a highly creative, but also highly constrained, judiciary.[10]

The rest of this brief chapter seeks to elaborate on the emerging canon of Latin American social rights jurisprudence. It identifies the famous Colombian case T-025 of 2004, which dealt with the rights of the country's massive population of internally displaced persons (IDPs), as a canonical case. T-025 shows how a judiciary can successfully deploy a creative and aggressive remedy, alongside careful monitoring, as a way to improve bureaucratic functioning of a complex social problem. Like other major social rights cases such as the South African *Grootboom* case,[11] it is canonical not so much for the details of the individual remedy at hand, but as an invitation to a particular kind of judicial experimentation in enforcing social rights.

Identifying a Latin American anticanon is a more difficult task. However, drawing from recent critical literature, the chapter identifies the Brazilian *Gonçalvez Cordeiro* case as an example that is emblematic of a national and regional approach that enforces the individual right to health mechanically, while ignoring fiscal and scientific considerations. It reflects a common Latin American approach to health—while refusing to stand aside as in (also anticanonical?) cases like the South African *Soobramoney* decision,[12] it enforces the right to health in ways that are heedless of the broader consequences or systemic impact.

What emerges from the discussion—both of T-025 and of cases like *Gonçalvez Cordeiro*—is how unsettled the Latin American (and global?) canon of social rights enforcement remains. T-025 is rightly an academically and practically influential case, but its model is difficult to replicate. Cases like

[10] David Landau, "South African Social Rights Jurisprudence and the Global Canon: A Revisionist View" in Rosalind Dixon and Theunis Roux (eds.), *Constitutional Triumphs, Constitutional Disappointments: A Critical Assessment of the 1996 South African Constitution's Local and International Influence* (CUP 2018) 406.

[11] *Government of the Republic of South Africa and Others v Grootboom and Others*, 2001 (1) SA 46 (CC).

[12] *Soobramoney v Minister of Health, KwaZulu-Natal*, 1998 (1) SA 765 (CC).

Gonçalvez Cordeiro are easy to caricature for a thoughtless approach to adjudication, but recent research suggests that, over time, the Brazilian approach to the right to health has become more careful and has had a notable impact on bureaucratic behavior. Perhaps above all, this counsels humility in even defining a canon of social rights—the cases explored here are best seen as invitations to experiment and perhaps as lessons to avoid wrong turns.

II. T-025 of 2004 (Colombia) and the Possibilities of Structural Enforcement

For its important jurisprudence on social rights and on many other issues, such as indigenous rights, the rights of victims of armed conflict, equality, and control of constitutional amendments, the Colombian Constitutional Court is now considered one of the canonical courts of the "Global South."[13] Indeed, the Court has become one of the world's most aggressive and creative courts in enforcing socioeconomic rights.[14] Perhaps particularly interesting is the variety of interpretive and remedial models employed by the court. Indeed, it has wrestled seriously with nearly all of the major socioeconomic rights, including rights to healthcare, housing, social security, education, and water; has employed most of the methods of interpretation recognized in international law and transnational practice, including the minimum core, non-retrogression, and proportionality; and has used a variety of remedies for violations, including both individual and stronger and weaker complex or structural remedies.[15]

There is no single case that encapsulates all of the Colombian Constitutional Court's rich jurisprudence and rhetoric on social rights, which has developed over many years. Perhaps the central constitutional concept on which it has relied is the "social state of law," encapsulated in Article 1 of the 1991 Constitution.[16]

Key to its approach has been a recognition of the centrality of dealing with poverty to the constitutional project. The famous early case T-426 of 1992, for

[13] Daniel Bonilla Maldonado, "Introduction: The Activist Tribunals of the Global South" in Daniel Bonilla Maldonado (ed.), *Constitutionalism of the Global South: The Activist Tribunals of India, South Africa, and Colombia* (CUP 2013) 1.

[14] Manuel Jose Cepeda Espinosa, "Judicial Activism in a Violent Context: The Origin, Role, and Impact of the Colombian Constitutional Court" (2004) 3 Wash. U. Glob. L. Studs. L.R. 529.

[15] David Landau, "The Reality of Social Rights Enforcement" (2012) 53 Harv. Int'l. L.J. 189.

[16] Const. Colombia, art. 1 (1991) ("Colombia is a social state of law, organized in the form of a unitary republic, decentralized, with autonomy of its territorial units, democratic, participatory, and pluralistic, based on the respect of human dignity, the work and solidarity of the individuals who belong to it, and the prevalence of the general interest").

example, deduced a right to a vital minimum, or minimum level of subsistence, from a variety of rights and principles found in the constitutional texts, including rights to life, health, and social security, as well as human dignity. It did so in the course of a decision that ordered the state to recognize and immediately pay an indigent elderly petitioner the pension that he was owed under the law. The Court noted that "[s]ocial reality nourishes constitutional law" and emphasized:

> The social state of law demands the construction of the indispensable conditions needed to ensure all inhabitants of the country a dignified life within achievable economic conditions. The goal of empowering human capacity requires that the authorities act effectively to maintain or improve living standards, including food, housing, social security, and those scarce monetary resources needed to get along in society.[17]

A second important piece of the Court's jurisprudence on social rights is a flexible, instrumental conception of the separation of powers. This was most famously articulated in another early case, T-406 of 1992, which ordered the state to complete public work on a sewage system in a timely manner, since those works were impacting the rights of those in the neighborhood to health, life, and human dignity. The Court swept aside objections to its ability to adjudicate the socioeconomic rights at the core of the case. It identified the social state principle as "the normative key that irradiates the entire constitutional text," and held that while many social rights were in the first instance dependent on political will, courts must retain the ability to enforce fundamental rights in cases where the political branches have manifestly failed in their responsibilities:

> [M]aintaining that social, economic and cultural rights are merely a link of political responsibility between citizens and the legislator is not only naïve with respect to the existence of such a bond, but also a flagrant distortion of the meaning and coherence which the Constitution must keep. If the responsibility for the effective realization of these rights were exclusively in the hands of the legislator, constitutional provisions would have no value and the validity of the will expressed by the constituent assembly would be subordinated to the legislator's volition.[18]

[17] Decision T-426 of 1992 (Eduardo Cifuentes Munoz, J.), translated in Manuel Jose Cepeda Espinosa and David Landau, *Colombian Constitutional Law: Leading Cases* (OUP 2017) 150.
[18] Decision T-406 of 1992 (Ciro Angarita Baron, J.), translated in ibid 27.

The Court's most studied and influential social rights decision is T-025 of 2004, which issued a large-scale structural remedy for IDPs who were victims of Colombia's long-running internal armed conflict. IDPs are essentially refugees—forced from their homes because of the conflict—who have not crossed international borders. A recent analysis by the U.N. High Commissioner on Refugees found that Colombia had the highest number of IDPs in the world with nearly eight million people.[19] The background to T-025 is that a number of individual plaintiffs, aided by civil society organizations, brought a constitutional complaint mechanism called a *tutela* against the state. They alleged a variety of violations of their rights, including socioeconomic rights to food, housing, healthcare, and emergency assistance, as well as rights to restitution and restoration of land. They also noted that existing legislation gave a number of rights to IDPs, but those rights were not being effectively enforced by the state because of lack of bureaucratic organization, capacity, and will.

The *tutela* was one of the most striking innovations and success stories of the 1991 Constitution, along with the creation of a specialized Constitutional Court itself. It is an informal instrument, expressly stating that petitioners need not have the assistance of a lawyer, and a rapid one, with a decision at each level required within ten days.[20] But it is also an *individual* instrument: petitioners sue alone and the direct impact of a decision only extends to the litigants. What the Court did in T-025 was convert the *tutela* into a structural remedy. First, it did so by aggregating together a number of pending claims. Second, it declared a "state of unconstitutional affairs," holding that the problems at issue reached well beyond the litigants, and thus necessitated bold structural orders.

T-025 did not invent the concept of a state of unconstitutional affairs. But it gave clearer criteria for its use, and more importantly developed an effective monitoring scheme that made compliance more likely over time. On the first issue of when a state of unconstitutional affairs should be declared, the Court constructed the following list of factors:

> When treating the repeated and constant infringement of fundamental rights, which affect many people, and whose solution requires the intervention of distinct entities to attend to structural problems, this Court has declared the existence of a state of unconstitutional affairs and has ordered remedies that

[19] United Nations High Commissioner for Refugees (UNHCR), *Global Trends: Forced Displacement in 2019*, at 72 tbl. 1, available at https://www.unhcr.org/be/wp-content/uploads/sites/46/2020/07/Global-Trends-Report-2019.pdf.

[20] Const. Colombia, art. 86 (1991).

> reach not only those who have filed a *tutela* to protect their rights, but also others found in the same situation but who have not filed a *tutela*.
>
> . . .
>
> Among the factors evaluated by the Court in order to determine whether a state of unconstitutional affairs exists, it is worth mentioning the following: (i) the massive and generalized violation of various constitutional rights affecting a significant number of people; (ii) the prolonged omission of the authorities in compliance with their obligations to guarantee rights; (iii) the adoption of unconstitutional practices, like the incorporation of the *tutela* as part of the procedure to guarantee the right at issue; (iv) the failure to issue legislative, administrative, or budgetary measures needed to avoid the infringement of rights; (v) the existence of a social problem whose solution requires the intervention of various entities, requires the adoption of a complex and coordinated set of actions and demands a level of resources that demands an important additional budgetary effort; (vi) if all of the people affected by the same problem were to utilize the *tutela* to protect their rights, greater judicial congestion would be produced. . . .[21]

The Court went over the record of the state's compliance with the constitutional, international, and statutory rights of IDPs in great detail, finding that statistical performance on every dimension (where even measurable) was abysmal. In developing the content of the rights of IDPs, the Court relied heavily on the "Guiding Principles on Internal Displacement" adopted by the United Nations High Commissioner on Refugees, and also elaborated the international law concept of the minimum core, explaining how certain rights of IDPs must be given the highest priority because their non-compliance threatened to throw many IDPs (who tended to live in extraordinary poverty on the edges of major cities) below the minimum level of subsistence.

The Court also found that the record of non-compliance was rooted in structural factors, including the disorganization of the bureaucracy and lack of budgetary resources. Finally, it noted the large and growing volume of *tutelas* brought by IDPs, which the Court interpreted as a signal of a largescale problem that was not getting resolved by ordinary administrative or judicial means. Thus, the Court declared a "state of unconstitutional affairs" with respect to state policy respecting IDPs. It emphasized that: "The State's constitutional obligation to guarantee adequate protection to citizens that are facing

[21] Decision T-025 of 2004 (Manuel Jose Cepeda Espinosa, J.), translated in Cepeda Espinosa and Landau, *Colombian Constitutional Law* (n 17) 178.

shameful life conditions due to internal forced displacement cannot be postponed indefinitely."[22]

Moreover, the Court gave a vigorous defense of its power to issue such a structural order. It noted that a 1997 law already gave a set of rights to IDPs; the main problem was that those rights were not being enforced effectively by the state. Thus:

> [T]he Court, taking into account the legal instruments [already] established to develop policies of assistance for displaced persons, as well as the design and engagements taken on by different state entities, is invoking the constitutional principle of harmonic collaboration among the branches of government in order to ensure compliance with the obligation to offer effective protection to the rights to which all residents in our national territory are entitled. This falls within the province of constitutional judges in a social state of law whenever rights that have a clear welfare dimension are being violated.[23]

The Court thus stressed the flexible and collaborative conception of the separation of powers that has become its trademark reading of the "social state" principle. It argued that its powers were limited, but that "[w]hen the state declines without a constitutionally acceptable justification to take measures before the marginalization suffered by some members of society, and that refusal violates a fundamental constitutional right, the function of the judge is not to replace the organs of public power, but to order them to comply with their duties."[24]

The result of the declaration of a state of unconstitutional affairs was that the Court issued two sets of orders. The first were individual orders, typical of *tutela* cases, where the Court sought to resolve the situations of the individual petitioners. But the second were a set of structural orders that sought to deal with the broader problems. These orders were initially relatively open-ended; they mainly ordered relevant state entities to develop a plan (including budgetary resources) within a fixed period of time to overcome different aspects of the problem.

What was unique and effective about T-025 was not the granting of structural orders, which had been done in other cases in the region (e.g. in Argentina) and in prior cases in Colombia. Indeed, the "state of unconstitutional affairs"

[22] ibid.
[23] ibid.
[24] ibid.

doctrine was invented not in T-025, but in a 1997 case involving the pension system in one part of the country.[25] It had then been reiterated in a number of subsequent cases involving retirement benefits, the system of selection of notaries, and most famously in cases involving overcrowding in the prison system.[26] The trouble with many of these prior declarations is that the Court issued structural orders, but did not effectively monitor compliance.

Much of the genius in T-025 lay in the Court's creation of an effective monitoring scheme alongside its structural remedy.[27] First, the Court maintained jurisdiction over the case, and put a standing panel of three justices in charge of issuing follow-up orders. The Court would also create a substantial bureaucracy of clerks and lower-level staff who were entirely or primarily tasked with the monitoring process. Second, it ordered the relevant state agencies, as well as independent accountability institutions, to issue periodic reports on compliance. Third, it created a special "Monitoring Commission" composed of civil society actors, academics, former justices, and others, which would become a key part of the compliance process, both by formulating policy ideas and by holding the state accountable for lack of progress. Finally, it held periodic public audiences, some of which were televised—these events served as a focal point for public and media attention on the issue, where state officials were forced to appear and representatives of IDPs often made dramatic presentations pointing out limitations or failures in their response.

The result of all this, as Rodríguez Garavito and Rodríguez Franco have shown, was an iterative or dialogic process that achieved significant (although highly imperfect) progress on enjoyment of rights by IDPs over time.[28] With the help of the Monitoring Commission and accountability institutions, the Court issued a huge number of follow-up orders, over time giving more precise and detailed guidance to the state. The government increased budgetary resources by orders of magnitude over a few years, and created a much more coherent bureaucratic response. Initially, the state did not even have a set of statistical indicators to track the problem, but one based largely on proposals from the Monitoring Commission was adopted under Court order. Progress on actual enjoyment of rights—as opposed to bureaucratic capacity—was, of course, more difficult. But even here, much progress was achieved along many

[25] Decision SU-559 of 1997 (Eduardo Cifuentes Munoz, J.).

[26] Decision T-153 of 1998 (Eduardo Cifuentes Munoz, J.).

[27] Cesar Rodriguez-Garavito, "Beyond the Courtroom: The Impact of Judicial Activism on Social Rights in Latin America" (2011) 89 Tex. L. Rev. 1669; Landau, "Reality of Social Rights" (n 15).

[28] Cesar Rodriguez-Garavito and Diana Rodriguez-Franco, *Radical Deprivation on Trial: The Impact of Judicial Activism on Social Rights in the Global South* (CUP 2015).

dimensions, such as emergency aid, housing assistance, job and educational help, and other immediate needs of IDPs. Progress was, however, uneven nationally (as is typical of Colombia), since the bureaucratic response was far better in Bogotá and other major cities than in remote (and conflict-ridden) areas of the country. Progress also lagged badly on more politically-fraught or structural aspects of the problem, such as restitution of land—many displacements had economic motives at the behest of major landowners—and prevention of future displacements.

Still, the achievements of the Court in ameliorating an extraordinarily sweeping and polycentric problem deserve to be highlighted. As well, one of the major effects of the decision was to focus more public and political attention on a problem that was easily one of Colombia's most serious, but which had largely been overlooked. The Court's framing of the problem as one of mass violations of the rights of victims of Colombia's internal armed conflict gained traction over time. In 2011, the Congress passed the Victim's Law, which legislatively adopted many of the rights developed by the Court, and also created new mechanisms (such as special land restitution courts) to advance enjoyment of rights.[29] Compliance with the Victim's Law has had its own problems, and in 2020 the Court ordered the law extended for ten more years rather than expiring, finding that many of the problems leading to passage of the law were still in place.[30] But the passage and implementation of the law also show the profound impact that the Court's jurisprudence on IDPs has had on Colombian politics and society.

The Colombian IDP case sparked a period of remedial creativity on the Court. In a second decision, T-760 of 2008, the Court declined to issue a "state of unconstitutional affairs" but nonetheless developed a remedy that was similar in key respects in a case involving pervasive failures in the healthcare system, which had caused a cascade of individual *tutelas* seeking treatments or medicines. The Court in T-760 opened with the ringing statement that "health is a fundamental right to which all individuals are entitled," and then proceeded to conduct a thorough analysis of deficiencies in the existing healthcare system, before issuing structural orders to remedy the most significant problems.[31]

In T-760 as well, the Court maintained jurisdiction, deputized a standing panel of justices, created a fulltime bureaucracy, recognized civil society

[29] Law 1448 of 2011, Diario Oficial 48.096.

[30] Decision C-588 of 2019 (Jose Fernando Reyes Cuartas, J.).

[31] Decision T-760 of 2008 (Manuel Jose Cepeda Espinosa, J.), translated in Cepeda Espinosa and Landau, *Colombian Constitutional Law* (n 17) 172.

commissions, held public audiences, and issued periodic follow-up orders. Over time, the Court achieved substantial compliance with many of the orders in that case as well.[32] Since T-760, the Court has not used such a full-fledged monitoring model in any subsequent case; commentators often note that the sheer scale and cost of the remedy made it prohibitive to employ repeatedly, even for major social problems.[33] But it has experimented with variants of such a model in a more contained and economical way, for example by delegating more power to a committee made up of state actors (in a new case involving prisons)[34] and by delegating work to a lower-level court (in a case involving children's living conditions in one region of the country).[35]

T-025 of 2004 has been influential among scholars and courts in the rest of the region. A key moment of influence came in 2015, when the Brazilian Supreme Federal Tribunal adopted the Colombian "state of unconstitutional affairs" label for a major case involving prison conditions.[36] The Peruvian Constitutional Court also adopted the label in a series of cases.[37] What remains to be seen is whether the deeper remedial creativity and patient drive to shape bureaucratic, structural reforms is replicable elsewhere. Structural orders in the region are still not particularly common, although they are not unheard of. Many judges in the region remain wedded to a vision of the separation of powers that makes structural enforcement an overreach, although attitudes are changing. And where structural remedies have been used, as in a major Argentine case involving river pollution, their record is mixed.[38]

Making structural remedies work is difficult, but they surely offer great promise in combatting large-scale deprivation of socioeconomic rights. The constellation of Colombian cases around T-025 of 2004 offers a harder-edged, more aggressive equivalent to the "weak-form" review made famous in *Grootboom* and then transformed in a series of subsequent decisions.[39] In that

[32] Aquiles Ignacio Arrieta-Gomez, "Realizing the Fundamental Right to Health Through Litigation: The Colombian Case" (2018) 20 Health and Hum. Rts. J. 133, 143 tbl. 1.

[33] Natalia Angel-Cabo and Domingo Lovera Parmo, "Latin American Social Constitutionalism: Courts and Participation" in Helena Alviar-Garcia et al. (eds.), *Social and Economic Rights in Theory and Practice: Critical Inquiries* (Routledge 2015) 85, 95.

[34] Decision T-762 of 2015 (Jose Fernando Reyes Cuartas, J.).

[35] Decision T-302 of 2017 (Aquiles Arrieta Gomez, J.).

[36] Vanice Regina Lirio do Valle, "An Unconstitutional State of Affairs in the Brazilian Prison System," ICON Blog (September 25, 2015), at http://www.iconnectblog.com/2015/09/an-unconstitutional-state-of-affairs-in-the-brazilian-prison-system/.

[37] For a list of these orders, see https://www.tc.gob.pe/jurisprudencia/estado-de-cosas-inconstitucional/.

[38] Martin Sigal, Julieta Rossi, and Diego Morales, "Argentina: Implementation of Collective Cases" in Malcolm Langford, Cesar Rodriguez-Garavito, and Julieta Rossi (eds.), *Social Rights Judgments and the Politics of Compliance: Making it Stick* (CUP 2017) 140, 155.

[39] Young Chapter 21 in this volume; Brian Ray, *Engaging with Social Rights: Procedure, Participation, and Democracy in South Africa's Second Wave* (CUP 2016).

sense, the deeper value of T-025 is as an invitation to make social rights not just justiciable, but effective, via experimentation and a more flexible conception of the separation of powers.

III. An Emerging Anticanon? The *Gonçalvez Cordeiro* Case (1997) and Individual Enforcement of the Right to Health in Brazil

As courts across Latin America struggle to enforce social rights, the most commonplace approach is not the structural approach of T-025 but is instead the issuance—en masse—of individual orders. The impact of these cases, by definition, is best seen through their overall impact on enjoyment of rights and state budgets. But some of these cases do have a substantial effect on state policy and academic debates. One case along these lines that has been the subject of scholarly commentary is the 1997 decision involving João Batista Gonçalvez Cordeiro, a 12-year-old child who brought an action to the Brazilian judiciary because he was suffering from a rare and fatal disease called Duchenne's muscular dystrophy. The disease was not treatable in Brazil or elsewhere in Latin America, but there was a single clinic in the United States that offered the promise of treatment—indeed of an experimental cure via cell transplantation—for $63,806, which was about twenty times Brazil's nominal GDP per capita at the time.[40]

Despite prevailing jurisprudence holdings that social rights were primarily programmatic in nature and thus sharply limiting judicial enforcement, the lower courts ruled in favor of the petitioner. The case was eventually appealed to the Brazilian Supreme Federal Tribunal (STF), with the state raising concerns about resource constraints and the effects of similar rulings on the healthcare system. Nonetheless, the Court ruled in favor of the petitioner, issuing a preliminary ruling requiring that the treatment be issued. In the process, the Court set an important precedent that would be used in enormous numbers of subsequent cases.

In the core passage of the brief opinion, Justice Celso de Mello held as follows:

> Between protecting the inviolability of the right to life, which qualifies as an inalienable subjective right guaranteed by the Constitution of the Republic

[40] Pet 1246 SC, Medida Cautelar Na Peticao, January 31, 1997 (Celso de Mello, J.) (STF).

> itself …, or making a financial and secondary interest of the State prevail against this fundamental prerogative, I understand … that ethical-legal reasons impose on the judge one and only possible option: the undeniable respect for life. For this reason, I reject the request made by the State of Santa Catarina, since the decision handed down by the Judiciary of Santa Catarina—far from characterizing a threat to local public and administrative order, as the State Government intends—translates, in the case under analysis, as a gesture worthy of reverent and solidary appreciation for the life of a minor, who, belonging to a poor family, does not have the means to defray the expenses of the only medical treatment capable of saving him from inevitable death.[41]

Thus, the justice viewed the case as a simple weighing of the rights to health and life as against financial considerations raised by the state. So viewed, it held that it must grant the petition and enforce the right at issue, ordering the treatment to be granted.

According to Motta Ferraz, the case was decided on the cusp of a new era of Brazilian jurisprudence on the right to health and was followed by a massive increase in the number of claims brought by individual petitioners. Many of the subsequent cases used similar or identical language to that quoted above, giving automatic priority to the right to health over all other considerations.[42] Petitioners thus won the overwhelming majority of the claims they brought, with courts ordering them to be provided particular treatments or medicines.[43] The reason petitioners generally win their claims is because, as the *Gonçalvez Cordeiro* case noted, their rights to health and life are inevitably given priority, with resource constraints relegated to a "secondary" consideration. Many of the cases ordered the provision of treatments that were made unavailable in the Brazilian healthcare system because of high cost; the best-known became ones (like *Gonçalvez Cordeiro*) that ordered provision of treatments unavailable anywhere in Brazil.[44]

Notice that the Brazilian Court's ruling in the *Gonçalvez Cordeiro* case (and its progeny) is the opposite from the one made by the South African Constitutional Court in the *Soobramoney* case, in somewhat similar

[41] ibid.

[42] Octavio Luiz Motta Ferraz, "Harming the Poor Through Social Rights Litigation: Lessons from Brazil" (2011) 89 Tex. L. Rev. 1643, 1656.

[43] Florian F. Hoffmann and Fernando R. N. M. Bentes, "Accountability for Social and Economic Rights in Brazil" in Varun Gauri and Daniel M. Brinks (eds.), *Courting Social Rights* (CUP 2008) 100.

[44] Motta Ferraz, "Harming the Poor" (n 42) 1661.

fact-situations. In *Soobramoney*, the South African Court refused to grant relief to a man who suffered from a chronic kidney disease, whose life could be prolonged by dialysis.[45] It held that the state's broader policy of prioritizing scarce dialysis machines for those who could be cured was reasonable, and moreover that it lacked the resources to cover everyone in a similar situation as the petitioner.[46]

Soobramoney is sometimes viewed as anticanonical because it seems to deny justiciability or enforceability to socioeconomic rights, even in a situation where life is at stake. It is ironic, then, that the opposite approach has been very widely criticized in Latin America. In the region (and perhaps more broadly), the *Soobramoney* approach is the outlier, and the approach demonstrated in *Gonçalvez Cordeiro* is extremely common. Indeed, it probably reflects the most common approach to social rights enforcement in Latin America, especially of the right to health. Aside from Brazil, courts in other countries such as Colombia, Costa Rica, and Uruguay also have developed individualized enforcement of the right to health, with similar characteristics.[47]

What could possibly make the issuance of this kind of order—which after all *grants* priority to socioeconomic rights—potentially anticanonical? The critiques against this kind of enforcement stem from several factors. The first is the opposite problem from that in *Soobramoney*: the Court's refusal to consider the broader or systemic impact of its decision. Absent from the Court's reasoning is any consideration of why the treatment had been denied or whether that denial, looked at within the healthcare system as a whole, was reasonable. The Court acted as though it was only deciding one case, for one petitioner, in isolation. Of course, a large number of cases followed, with large effects on the national budget. Similarly, the Court failed to look deeply at the underlying science.[48] In its brief decision, it accepted as fact the argument that the treatment would save the life of the child at issue. But, as noted, the treatment was offered by a single U.S. clinic and was viewed as deeply experimental.

[45] *Soobramoney v Minister of Health, KwaZulu-Natal*, 1998 (1) SA 765 (CC).

[46] ibid.

[47] Landau, "Reality of Social Rights Enforcement" (n 15) 209; Bruce M. Wilson and Olman A. Rodriguez, "Costa Rica: Understanding Variations in Compliance" in Langford, Rodriguez-Garavito, and Rossi (n 38) 111, 114–115; Lucía Berro Pizzarossa, Katrina Perehudoff, and José Castela Forte, "How the Uruguayan Judiciary Shapes Access to High-Priced Medicines: A Critique through the Right to Health Lens" (2018) 20 Health and Hum. Rts. J. 93.

[48] Motta Ferraz, "Harming the Poor" (n 42); Berro Pizzarossa, Katrina Perehudoff, and José Castela Forte, "How the Uruguayan Judiciary Shapes Access" (n 47) (arguing that Uruguayan decisions on medicines are similarly poorly tied to international legal and scientific standards).

Tragically, more than twenty years later there is still no cure for Duchenne's muscular dystrophy, although new treatments continue to be developed.[49]

Related to this critique are concerns about equity. The direct benefit of these kinds of decisions accrue only to those who actually bring the lawsuit. The relevant Brazilian legal mechanisms are complex and costly. While the evidence is contested, some work finds that plaintiffs tend to be relatively affluent, rather than the most marginalized, because those kinds of petitioners have the resources and knowledge needed to navigate the system.[50] Similar evidence exists in Colombia.[51] Thus, Motta Ferraz argues that the Brazilian model of social rights enforcement has actually "harmed the poor" by funneling resources away from the system as a whole and towards higher-income plaintiffs.[52]

The direct distributive effects of litigation might be ameliorated if this model of litigation, over time, had a beneficial impact on the healthcare system. But it may not do so. Instead, it may reduce pressures for reform by offering a shortcut to benefits for a relatively privileged group of litigants. Rather than reforming practices more generally, state or private healthcare providers may find it more economical to continue unconstitutional practices, granting relief only in the relatively unusual cases where they face litigation. The result may be the construction of a two-tiered system of social provision—one tier for those willing and able to sue, and another, poorly-functioning tier for everybody else. In this way, litigation may become part of the cause, rather than the solution, for state failure within systems already plagued by it.[53]

Thus, *Gonçalvez Cordeiro* and its progeny have come to represent, for some scholars, a model of social rights enforcement that although very common in Latin America, is normatively undesirable. It suggests that robust or active, but uncreative, enforcement of social rights can coexist with an absence of social transformation, and may even reinforce social inequality.

But is this positioning of *Gonçalvez Cordeiro* as a potentially anticanonical case convincing? That depends on an empirical picture that is in many ways

[49] Eleanor Bird, "Potential Treatment Strategy Found for Muscular Dystrophy," Medical News Today (September 17, 2020), at https://www.medicalnewstoday.com/articles/potential-treatment-strategy-found-for-muscular-dystrophy.

[50] Motta Ferraz, "Harming the Poor" (n 42); Octavio Luiz Motta Ferraz, "The Right to Health in the Courts of Brazil: Worsening Health Inequities?" (2009) 11 Health and Hum. Rts. J. 33; Virgilio Alfonso da Silva and Fernando Vargas Terrazas, "Claiming the Right to Health in Brazilian Courts: The Exclusion of the Already Excluded?" (2011) 36 L. & Soc. Inq. 825.

[51] Landau, "Reality of Social Rights Enforcement" (n 15).

[52] Motta Ferraz, "Harming the Poor" (n 42).

[53] The Colombian Constitutional Court raised exactly these kinds of equity concerns when it decided to issue a structural remedy for the right to health, in Decision T-760 of 2008. Alicia Ely Yamin and Oscar Parra-Vera, "Judicial Protection of the Right to Health in Colombia: From Social Demands to Individual Claims to Public Debates" (2010) 33 Hastings Int'l. & Comp. L. Rev. 431.

still incomplete. There is now a robust academic literature on the distributive impact of individual lawsuits on the right to health, reaching divergent conclusions.[54]

Perhaps an even more difficult issue to study is the effect of right to health litigation on the welfare system.[55] Everyone agrees that there are some cases where individual judicial decisions helped to spark changes in bureaucratic practices. In Brazil, a notable example was HIV medication, which the state started covering following judicial decisions requiring provision.[56] More recently, some revisionist scholarship has pushed back on the simple story that litigation of the right to health in Brazil has led to mere "queue-jumping" without any impact on the broader system. Danielle da Costa Leite Borges found, for example, that over time (albeit a long time), both judicial and administrative actors developed new mechanisms to ameliorate some of the distortions caused by the pattern of extraordinary judicialization of the right to health in Brazil. These included a new working group formed by the National Council of Justice on coordinating best practices, the creation of a new scientific body to make transparent decisions about the inclusion and exclusion of medicines and treatments from the healthcare system, and the growth of mediation mechanisms before lawsuits were filed.[57]

These kinds of changes suggest that although mass individualized enforcement of social rights may raise serious problems, courts and other actors are not helpless in finding ways to turn this jurisprudence in more productive directions. Rather than merely accepting unfounded claims about the effectiveness of costly, experimental treatments, as occurred in *Gonçalvez Cordeiro*, courts and administrators can over time help to develop a more rational, scientific inquiry into the parameters of the right to health. Judicial pressure may thus in some cases improve, rather than undermine, already dysfunctional systems of social provision.

One further reason calls for caution before one labels the large-scale Latin American judicialization of the right to health a failure. Judicializing healthcare in large part for the middle-class, rather than the poorest, may

[54] For a good summary, see Tatiana S. Andia and Everaldo Lamprea, "Is the Judicialization of Health Care Bad for Equity? A Scoping Review" (2019) 18 Int'l. J. Equity in Health 61.

[55] Daniel M. Brinks and Varun Gauri, "The Law's Majestic Equality? The Distributive Impact of Litigating Social and Economic Rights" (2014) 12 Perspectives on Pol. 375.

[56] Danielle da Costa Leite Borges, "Individual Health Care Litigation in Brazil Through a Different Lens: Strengthening Health Technology Assessment and New Models of Health Care Governance" (2018) 20 Health and Hum. Rts. J. 147, 149–150.

[57] ibid. Changes to judicial practices in Costa Rica suggest a similar story. Olman Rodríguez Loaiza et al., "Revisiting Health Rights Litigation and Access to Medications in Costa Rica: Preliminary Evidence from the Cochrane Collaboration Reform" (2018) 20 Health and Hum. Rts. J. 79.

seem undesirable. But judicial enforcement of social rights for relatively affluent groups may help to build up support for those rights over time.[58] This is particularly true given the often patchy, poorly functioning social welfare nets in the region, which experience widespread failure across a range of socioeconomic classes. There may be a risk, in other words, that judicial enforcement aimed only at the poorest may leave courts vulnerable to backlash, particularly if their interventions have significant effects on budgets. Broadening the base of social rights may help to protect judicial enforcement of these rights in much the same way that more universal welfare programs are generally found to be more durable than narrowly means-tested programs.[59]

All of this suggests that it would be foolhardy to brand the whole line of Brazilian jurisprudence on the right to health anticanonical; even less so the widespread Latin American approach of enforcing the right to health individually. What we might more confidently label anticanonical are the kinds of cases epitomized by *Gonçalvez Cordeiro* itself, where courts undertake a well-intentioned but blind effort of placing a particular conception of rights above all other considerations, and without engaging in the broader scientific and political context within which the case occurs. There is too much of this kind of jurisprudence in the region. But just as we saw the Colombian case T-025 as an influential but largely unfulfilled invitation for courts to engage in guided experimentation with structural remedies, we might see *Gonçalvez Cordeiro* as a challenge for courts and their interlocutors to find ways to challenge and improve, rather than distort, systems of social provision.

IV. Conclusion

Latin American courts have grappled for many years now with enforcing social rights. This brief chapter wields the concept of a canon to make sense of this enforcement. Perhaps above all, regional experience demonstrates the profound difficulties of social rights enforcement—there is a significant gap between

[58] Rosalind Dixon and David Landau, "Constitutional Non-Transformation? Socioeconomic Rights Beyond the Poor" in Katharine G. Young (ed.), *The Future of Social and Economic Rights* (OUP 2019) 110.

[59] Gøsta Esping-Andersen, *The Three Worlds of Welfare Capitalism* (Princeton UP 1990).

have courts enforce social rights, which nearly all countries in the region now do, and having courts enforce them effectively. In different ways, both the canonical case T-025 of 2004 (Colombia) and the potentially anticanonical case *Gonçalvez Cordeiro* (Brazil) illustrate the challenge. They invite us to think more deeply about the conditions under which courts can wield rights to catalyze social change, as well as the limits of a judge-centered strategy.[60]

[60] Katharine G. Young, *Constituting Economic and Social Rights* (OUP 2012).

23

The Due Process Canon

Tom Ginsburg[*]

I. Introduction

"Due process of law" is a term originating in the common law of England and forming a major component of American constitutional law. It is also a broader concept that is instantiated in virtually all administrative law systems, including the *droit administratif*; in the right to a fair trial as adjudicated by international human rights courts; and various standards of protection in international investment law. The term "global administrative law" gestures at the ubiquity of the concept: government should not act without providing some basic procedural guarantees.[1] And its location at the center of Franz Kafka's famous novel *Der Process* (known in English as *The Trial*) is testament to its powerful cultural attraction.[2]

Scholars locate the origin of the principle in chapter 39 of Magna Carta, prohibiting the king from penalizing men except "by the law of the land," though as with many features of that document it may precede it by a century. The actual phrase dates to a 1354 statute granting due process for any man "to be put out of land or tenement, taken, or imprisoned."[3] It was developed further by Edward Coke, the great seventeenth-century jurist who revived Magna Carta and drafted the Petition of Right against King Charles I in 1628. In the famous case of *Thomas Bonham v. College of Physicians* (1610), concerning a licensing statute, Coke asserted the supremacy of the common law and its principles of natural justice over a parliamentary scheme in which the College of Physicians was both judge and party in licensing.[4]

* University of Chicago Law School.

1 Benedict Kingsbury and Megan Donaldson, "Global Administrative Law" in *Max Planck Encyclopedia of Public International Law* (Oxford University Press, 2011).

2 Franz Kafka, *Der Process* (Verlag Die Schmiede, 1925).

3 28 Edw. III c. 3 (1354). Keith Jurow, "Untimely Thoughts: A Reconsideration of the Origins of Due Process of Law," American Journal of Legal History 19: 265 (1975).

4 Jerry Mashaw, *Creating the Administrative Constitution: The Lost 100 Years of American Administrative Law* (Yale University Press, 2012).

Tom Ginsburg, *The Due Process Canon* In: *Global Canons in an Age of Contestation.* Edited by: Sujit Choudhry, Michaela Hailbronner, and Mattias Kumm, Oxford University Press. © Tom Ginsburg 2024.
DOI: 10.1093/9780191956942.003.0023

Coke had a local political motive but sowed the seeds for many concepts of modern liberty. These seeds became more apparent with the 1689 Bill of Rights, instantiating many of the rights of Englishmen, including showing cause before punishment, the right to a jury trial, protection against excessive bail, and cruel and unusual punishments. Blackstone consolidated these sources in the eighteenth century, and his distinctive concern was to reconcile the doctrine of parliamentary sovereignty with the ideas of political liberty that had been so important during the seventeenth century.[5] Procedural justice was the central way of accomplishing this reconciliation.

Both Blackstone's and Coke's accounts were enormously influential on American state colonial law and early state constitutions. Indeed, by the time of the drafting of the U.S. Constitution in 1787, the phrase could be found in the constitutional bills of rights of nine of the eleven states with such documents.[6] It was thus a rather short step to include it in the national Bill of Rights, and it is located in the Fifth Amendment to the U.S. Constitution.

Though the precise phrase is of common law origin, variations can be found in the jurisprudence of civil law jurisdictions. In the continental tradition, some scholars trace its origins back to the fourteenth century, although it is more conventional to treat the French Revolution as a starting point.[7] The Declaration of the Rights of Man and of the Citizen provides for legality in imprisonment and prevents arbitrariness (though this obviously did not prevent the Terror.) And, of course, the notion has spread to many constitutional orders in the last two centuries.[8]

In this chapter, I consider three canonical cases, and one anticanonical case. Because procedural guarantees are inherent in any system of law, I will range broadly, including examples from national, supranational, and international jurisdictions. This range is useful for illustrating just how central due process-type ideas are to legal thinking, especially when an individual's interests are to be limited by governmental power. Since governmental power is now exercised on multiple legal planes, it is not surprising that due process has canonical applications on all of them.

[5] Howard L. Lubert, "Sovereignty and Liberty in William Blackstone's 'Commentaries on the Laws of England,'" The Review of Politics 72(2): 271–297 (2010).

[6] Georgia and New Jersey being the exceptions.

[7] Katia Weidenfeld, *Histoire du Droit Administratif* (2010), as discussed in Marcos Dominguez, *International Administrative Due Process* (JSD Dissertation, University of Chicago, 2019).

[8] See, e.g., Const. India (1947), Art. 21 ("No person shall be deprived of his life or personal liberty except according to a procedure established by law"). Felix Frankfurter famously advised B. N. Rau to avoid using the term due process in the Constitution, as it might become a fountainhead of judicial activism.

We start with an American case, *Mathews v. Eldridge*, which sits at the border of constitutional law and administrative law. By placing the case in conversation with proportionality doctrine, on the one hand, and with earlier due process cases, on the other, we can illuminate how these ideas have evolved in the United States in a direction similar to those of other advanced legal systems. Next, we will move to the level of international law, in elaborating the *Kadi* cases at the European Court of Justice. And, finally, we examine the standard of investment protection preventing what is called denial of justice, sourcing it in the *Neer* case before the US–Mexican Claims Commission. Due process ideas weave throughout these cases, each advancing the principle in its own sphere.

II. Substance or Process?

At its core, due process requires procedural steps before a deprivation of certain core rights. The question then becomes how much process is due for any particular deprivation. To answer this question, one must consider the stakes of the deprivation. The level of process that should be applied for a parking ticket is obviously different from the level to be applied for the death penalty.

For many years, the United States had a distinct approach to interpreting its due process clause, which is found in the Fifth Amendment to the U.S. Constitution, providing that no one could be deprived of life, liberty, or property without due process of law. With the passage of the Fourteenth Amendment in 1868, seeking to extend citizenship and equal treatment to formerly enslaved Black people, the requirement of due process was extended to the states. One might have thought that this new constitutional clause would be used to limit state abuses. But, of course, in 1879, "Reconstruction" of the South ended, and the period of so-called Redemption began. This was followed by immediate restrictions on the franchise, and the passage of a whole set of "Jim Crow" laws intended to institute apartheid in the American South.

The due process clause was of no help to those who sought to challenge these developments. Instead, the clause became an instrument of large businesses seeking to fight the rising demands for regulation.[9] The central case is called *Lochner v. New York*, which has the status of an anticanonical case in the

[9] It was also an issue with regard to the taxing power, though courts were more amenable here. *Londoner v. Denver*, 210 U.S. 373 (1908) and *Bimetallic v. State Board of Equalization*, 239 U.S. 441 (1914) are a pair of cases that deal with the taxing power under the due process clause. The first held that there was an individual right to be heard individually while the second limited hearing rights for the imposition of a general tax, in situations in which all interests were more or less similar.

United States.[10] Interestingly, it developed this anticanonical status relatively late in life, replacing other cases such as *Allgeyer v. Louisiana*[11] and *Coppage v. Kansas*.[12] All these cases were decided on "substantive" due process grounds, but *Lochner* was the one that gave its name to an entire era, the period from roughly 1900 to 1937 when the Supreme Court was hostile to regulation. The case concerned a New York statute that limited bakers' hours to ten hours a day and sixty hours a week, a significant reduction compared to the norm. The Supreme Court struck the law as an infringement of the freedom of contract.[13]

The role of the due process clause in this analysis was odd. The Constitution contains no explicit right to freedom of contract, but the due process clause applies to deprivations of life, liberty, or property. Finding that the freedom of contract was a liberty interest, the Supreme Court found that legislation could not infringe it, except in the limited exercise of "police powers of the state."[14] Presumably this meant that a court could interfere with a baker's freedom of contract in the course of a specific dispute, but that the legislature was not free to pass general regulations restricting many individuals' freedom at the same time, without giving them "process." As Cohen-Eliya and Porat note, this decision was both formalistic, in the sense that it proceeded by logical deduction without considering the social interests at stake, and ideological, grounded in a libertarian conception of natural rights.[15]

The incorporation of substantive elements into the due process clause is not uniquely American. In the 1985 case of *Re BC Motor Vehicle Act*, the Supreme Court of Canada did the same in interpreting the due process clause of the Charter of Rights and Freedoms.[16] In that case, the Court struck down a law creating strict liability for driving without a license, with imprisonment for seven days. The Court found that this was inconsistent with a principle of fundamental justice that the innocent should not be punished. This idea of fundamental justice has been used in several other cases in Canada. Still, the vast majority of courts adjudicating the issue focus on the procedural aspects, and the United States now does so.

[10] *Lochner v. New York*, 198 U.S. 45 (1905). See Jamal Greene, "The Anticanon," Harv. L. Rev. 125: 379–475, 446 (2011).

[11] 165 U.S. 578 (1897).

[12] 236 U.S. 1 (1915). See Greene (n 10) at 448.

[13] *Lochner* (n 10) .

[14] ibid at 53.

[15] Moshe Cohen-Eliya and Iddo Porat, "American Balancing and German Proportionality: The Historical Origins," ICON 8(2): 263–286 (2010).

[16] *Re BC Motor Vehicle Act* [1985] 2 SCR 486. See Frank Iacobucci, "Some Reflections on *Re BC Motor Vehicle Act*," Ottawa L. Rev. 42(3): XX (2011); Victor Ramraj, "Four Models of Due Process," ICON 2: 492–524 (2004).

III. *Mathews v. Eldridge* and the Problem of Proportionality

Americans like to think about due process problems in cost–benefit terms, and in this regard the canonical treatment is the U.S. Supreme Court case of *Mathews v. Eldridge* (1976).[17] The case is a mainstay of administrative law courses, but actually concerns the due process clause of the Fifth Amendment, which prohibits the national government from depriving someone of life, liberty, or property without due process of law. (A similar clause is incorporated into the Fourteenth Amendment, which extends the prohibition to states.)

Mathews concerned the national social security scheme, which provides for welfare benefits for the aged and disabled. George Eldridge was a recipient of disability benefits who received a letter from the Social Security Administration informing him that his status was ending, so that his benefits would be terminated. The relevant procedures provided for an evidentiary hearing before a final determination was made, but the benefits were cut off before the hearing.

The case is often paired with an earlier case, *Goldberg v. Kelly* (1970), which concerned twenty individuals who were denied public assistance benefits because of suspicion of fraud. [18] The City of New York withheld the benefits but allowed the recipients to petition for reinstatement. The case held that a welfare recipient was entitled to a pre-termination hearing before her benefits were denied. The question in *Mathews* was then whether the welfare and disability contexts were similar or different in terms of whether a pre-deprivation hearing was required. In denying Eldridge the right to a pre-termination hearing, the Court articulated a famous threefold test. To determine how much process is "due" in any particular context, one must weigh: "(1) the private interest that will be affected by the official action; (2) the risk of an erroneous deprivation of such interest through the procedures used, and probable value, if any, of additional procedural safeguards; and (3) the Government's interest, including the fiscal and administrative burdens that the additional or substitute procedures would entail."[19]

The case is a classic for pedagogy because it challenges students to think through whether there is in fact a difference between welfare benefits and disability benefits. Most students have trouble articulating the distinction. But regardless of the factual ambivalence, the legal test has great power. What the *Mathews* test does in effect is to say that government should adopt procedures

[17] 424 U.S. 319 (1976).
[18] 397 U.S. 254 (1970).
[19] 424 U.S. 319 (1976), at.

up to the point where the marginal cost is equal to the marginal benefit. Because cost–benefit analysis and the balancing of interests is so critical to the conceptualization of administrative decision making, *Mathews* has become canonical in the United States. It embodies and crystalizes a whole way of thinking about process: process should be proportional to the interest at stake.

In this, of course, it has a good deal in common with the proportionality doctrine which has spread around the world as a means of adjudicating decisions about rights. As has been well documented, this test began with German administrative law in the nineteenth century.[20] In that context, it was thought of as a logical principle that embodied the idea of the *Rechtstaat*, a state governed by law.

Cohen-Eliya and Porat argue that the balancing approach to constitutional rights emerged in the United States in reaction to *Lochner* and its ilk. Justice Oliver Wendell Holmes wrote a brutal dissent in the *Lochner* case, attacking it as formalism, and arguing that the Court was simply preferring one set of social interests, business, over another, labor. Responding to *Lochner*, progressives laid out a theory of balancing in which the various interests would be considered against each other, and rights weighed against the public interest. It was this approach that came to define American constitutional jurisprudence on rights for much of the twentieth century.

Balancing is not proportionality. One distinction is that balancing was introduced to limit the overprotection of rights associated with the *Lochner* era, whereas proportionality was initiated to ensure the state did not overreach.[21] Proportionality, particularly as developed by the German Constitutional Court and then exported around the world as a general principle of constitutional law, is not concerned only with procedure, and it requires more than a weighing of interests. Instead, it requires ensuring that the challenged action poses the least infringement on the right as possible.[22] But it is here, in evaluating procedure at the margin, that the *Mathews* test has something in common with proportionality. By essentially demanding that the state adopt at least enough process so as to protect the relevant private interests, the *Mathews* court set up a rigorous framework for distinguishing various cases. It thus reflects the evolution of the due process clause from a narrow substantive conception of formalistic rights protection into a tool of rigorous procedural evaluation. While it is rare for the Supreme Court to actually require a proportionality inquiry under

[20] Cohen-Eliya and Porat (n 15).
[21] ibid.
[22] Vicki Jackson, "Constitutional Law in an Age of Proportionality," Yale L.J. 124: 3094 (2015).

the due process clause (punitive damages in civil cases is an exception),[23] the adjudicative approach often gets to the same place as the more widely used proportionality framework.

The fact that a court undertakes an evaluation does not mean that it will always restrain the government. In some cases both inside and outside the U.S., courts have been highly deferential. In the U.K. case of *Liversidge v. Anderson*, the judges deferred to an order to detain someone without providing any reason.[24] This case is often held up as an example of extreme deference during wartime, which of course leads to the possibility that government will abuse the national security justification. Yet it is also the case that in ordinary administrative law contexts, the due process principle has been deeply instantiated, and read into the law even when not explicitly articulated.[25]

IV. International Due Process: The Security Council and the European Court of Justice

The principles of due process have spread around the world, being embodied in national constitutions and procedural law. The list of countries with such a constitutional guarantee is diverse, including several Latin American countries, common law countries like Ghana and Tuvalu, and civil law countries such as Albania and Tunisia. One mechanism for such diffusion has been the instantiation in international human rights instruments, such as the International Covenant on Civil and Political Rights. Article 14 of that document contains a number of procedural guarantees for criminal defendants, such as a fair and public trial, right to representation, and presumption of innocence. Regional human rights instruments like the American Convention of Human Rights do the same.

Whether such guarantees apply to international institutions themselves has been the subject of some debate. In particular, the United Nations Charter does not provide for judicial review of actions by the U.N. Security Council, which has authority under Chapter VII to make decisions that bind all member states on matters of peace and security. This means that whether or not a particular decision is compliant with the Charter is a matter for the Security Council itself

[23] *State Farm Mut. Auto. Ins. Co. v. Campbell*, 538 U.S. 408, 426 (2003) (punitive damages must be "both reasonable and proportionate to the amount of harm to the plaintiff and to the general damages recovered").

[24] [1941] UKHL 1. See also *R. v Halliday* [1917] UKHL 1.

[25] *Cooper v. Board of Works for the Wandsworth District* (1863) 143 ER 414.

to decide. Like the College of Physicians in *Bonham's Case*, it is both judge and party in the same case.

For much of the postwar period, this was of little consequence as Chapter VII was rarely invoked. But as the Cold War ended, the Security Council was reinvigorated and began to take decisions that directly touch individuals. This was especially true in the counter-terrorism context.

The *Kadi* case concerned the United Nations Security Council Resolution 1373, which established the Counter-Terrorism Committee of the Security Council in the immediate aftermath of the 9/11 terrorist attacks.[26] Adopted at a meeting that was five minutes long, the resolution required states to set up mechanisms for intelligence sharing, domestic criminalization of terrorist acts, and monitoring of asylum seekers. The Counter-Terrorism Committee was created to monitor implementation, and a Sanctions Committee that had originated in earlier U.N. resolutions targeting Al Qaeda was expanded. This committee created a list of organizations and individuals who were subject to sanctions, including travel bans and asset freezes. Specifically, it was empowered to place people on the list of sanctioned individuals or organizations.

Yassin Kadi was a Saudi businessman who had met Osama Bin Laden at one point, and given funds to a charity that in turn supported Hamas. At the instigation of the U.S. Office of Foreign Assets Control (OFAC), he was put on the list of persons whose assets were to be frozen after September 11. While he had some rights to appeal this determination as a matter of American administrative law, there was no comparable process at the level of the Counter Terrorism Committee or Sanctions Committee, on whose list he was placed without notice or hearing, or even the possibility of judicial review.

The European Union implemented the asset freeze within its jurisdiction, relying on a regulation which transposed the asset freeze obligation into EU law, and Kadi sought delisting. Kadi challenged the regulation, but lost the case before the EU Court of First Instance (later renamed the General Court) on the grounds that the U.N. Security Council had primacy over EU law with its procedural guarantees. Kadi then appealed this decision to the European Court of Justice (ECJ).

In a stunning decision in 2008, the ECJ ruled in Kadi's favor (*Kadi I*), on the grounds that the individual EU nations that had frozen his assets had not provided Kadi with a meaningful opportunity for judicial review of the decision.[27]

[26] Joined Cases C-402/05 P and C-415/05 P *Kadi and Al Barakaat International Foundation v. Council and Commission* [2008] ECR I-6351.

[27] ibid. See discussion in Juliane Kokott and Christoph Sobotta, "The *Kadi* Case—Constitutional Core Values and International Law—Finding the Balance?," European Journal of International Law 23(4): 1015–1024 (2012).

Following the lead of Advocate General Miguel Poiares Maduro, the Court grounded the decision in "constitutional principles" agreed to in the treaty establishing the European Community.[28] It specifically denied the primacy of the U.N. Charter over these principles. Since the European Community was based on the rule of law, the Court wrote, "neither its Member States nor its institutions can avoid review of the question whether their acts are in conformity with the basic constitutional charter, the EC Treaty, which established a complete system of legal remedies and procedures designed to enable the Court of Justice to review the legality of acts of the institutions."[29] The principle of legality requires full review by a court, to which an individual had access.[30] The decision stands for a kind of insistence by judges, coordinating at both the national and international level, that procedures be subject to judicial scrutiny.[31]

In response to this decision, the EU Commission provided a summary of the basis for the decision to list Kadi, giving him an opportunity for comment. It then renewed the asset freeze, shortly thereafter. This led to a new round of litigation. (Meanwhile, in a less well-known proceeding, Kadi sued OFAC in the United States on due process grounds, and also challenged the freeze before U.K. courts.)[32]

In 2009, the Security Council revised its procedure to provide for delisting requests to be monitored by an Ombudsman.[33] The Sanctions Committee also provided additional information to the European Commission as to the basis of naming Kadi. In 2010, the EU General Court struck down the revised listing, saying the scheme still did not address Kadi's rights to defend himself and receive effective judicial protection.[34] Noting that the *Kadi I* case had made clear that the EU legal order was autonomous and that its fundamental rights guarantees were not displaced by Security Council decisions, the Court evaluated the revised U.N. scheme. "In essence," it noted, "the Security Council has still not deemed it appropriate to establish an independent and impartial body responsible for hearing and determining, as regards matters of law and fact, actions against individual decisions taken by the Sanctions Committee."[35] The

[28] *Kadi* (n 26) paras. 5, 285.
[29] ibid 81.
[30] ibid paras. 326–327, 336.
[31] Eyal Benvenisti, "United We Stand: National Courts Reviewing Counterterrorism Measures" in *Democracy, Separations of Powers and the Fights Against Terrorism* (Andrea Bianchi, Alexis Keller, eds., Cambridge University Press, 2007).
[32] *Kadi v. Paulson et al.* (Court Filing), D.D.C., No. 1:09-cv-00108 (Docket 56), March 20, 2012.
[33] U.N. Sec. Council Res. 1904.
[34] Case T-85/09 *Kadi v. Commission* [2010] ECR II-5177.
[35] ibid para 128.

decision was ultimately confirmed by the ECJ in *Kadi II*. Finally, in October 2012, the U.N. Security Council delisted Kadi; OFAC followed in 2014.

While the decision is often debated in terms of the commitment of the European legal orders to a kind of dualist approach to international law, it is in fact the leading judgment on due process limits of the Security Council's Resolution 1373 sanctions regime. And while that regime still does not meet minimal standards of due process that would be acceptable within a constitutional democracy, the pushback from the European Union's top court, as well as several important national courts, led to revisions in the procedural protections it did provide. By suggesting that even the U.N. Security Council is subjected to a due process framework, the *Kadi* cases did what the drafters of the U.N. Charter failed to do: it extended rule-of-law values to the Security Council itself.

V. The Minimum Standard of Treatment in Investment Law: *Neer* and Beyond

A third canonical case in the law of due process comes from the field of international investment. This system is still in the relatively early stages of development, but draws on an older body of law concerning the customary international law regarding the treatment of foreigners. Concern about the targeting of the foreigner, one might say, can be found even in the Bible, with its injunction to be kind and inclusive toward the "stranger in your midst." As commerce expanded in the nineteenth century, newly independent countries would frequently target foreign nationals, leading to much international conflict. One response was to demand "national treatment," by which foreigners could not be subjected to more onerous rules than locals. This basic principle of fairness became a core feature of international economic law.

Soon, however, it became clear that this principle was not sufficient. With the communist revolution of 1917, the new Soviet government confiscated *all* property. This left foreigners with no recourse: after all, they had been treated identically with domestic property owners in the mass expropriation, and so could not argue that there was unfairness. (Indeed, because they were not subject to murderous purges, they may have been treated better than the local citizenry.) But foreign nations did not accept the argument that no compensation was due, and eventually negotiated claims settlements with the USSR to provide foreign citizens with some redress.

This was not the only such conflict of the era. The Mexican Revolution of 1910–1920 overthrew the dictator Porfirio Diaz, and initiated a program of land reform that took some decades to complete. It resulted in much conflict with the United States, and led to the creation of a body called the Mexican–US Claims Commission, to deal with claims by each country's nationals against the other's government. A Special Claims Commission had specific jurisdiction over events that occurred between 1910 and 1920. This became a model of mixed claims commissions, in which a "neutral" third party arbitrator joined nationals from each state party to adjudicate claims against governments. This was an important step in the evolution of international law.

Paul Neer was an American citizen living in Mexico, working as a mine supervisor near Durango. Riding on horseback with his wife one day, he was shot and killed by a group of Mexican bandits. [36] The U.S. espoused a claim on behalf of his widow and daughter for $100,000. While there was no assertion that the killers were agents of the Mexican government, the U.S. alleged "an unwarrantable lack of diligence or an unwarrantable lack of intelligent investigation in prosecuting the culprits."[37] Evidence showed that the authorities waited three days to investigate the crime scene, and never offered a reward. Mexico countered that it had undertaken an investigation, and that in any case, its internal administration of justice was a sovereign concern. This meant that "[o]ther nations ought to respect this right ... as the administration of justice necessarily requires that every definitive sentence, regularly pronounced, be esteemed just, and executed as such—when once a cause in which foreigners are interested has been decided in form, the sovereign of the defendants, can not hear their complaints."[38] In short, the two parties disputed whether one country's allegedly deficient administration of justice could even give rise to an international claim.

The US–Mexico Claims Commission took the opportunity to define denial of justice, an older idea in international law. In particular, denial of justice is about a minimum standard of treatment owed to foreigners, without regard to how local actors are treated. As the Commission famously said, "the treatment of an alien, in order to constitute an international delinquency, should amount to an outrage, to bad faith, to willful neglect of duty, or to an insufficiency of governmental action so far short of international standards that every reasonable and impartial man would readily recognize its insufficiency."[39]

[36] *Fay H. Neer and Pauline Neer (USA) v. United Mexican States*, US–Mexico Claims Commission, IV Reports International Awards 60 (1926).

[37] ibid.

[38] ibid at 64.

[39] ibid at 61–62.

Finding that the evidence indicated some effort by Mexico to investigate, the Commission disallowed the claim, since Neer's treatment did not fall below the minimum standard. In doing so, it first noted that "[i]t is not for an international tribunal such as this Commission to decide, whether another course of procedure taken by the local authorities at Guanacevi might have been more effective."[40] So doing would turn the international adjudicator into a kind of court of appeal for all domestic adjudication involving foreigners. Instead, the Commission set a high bar to finding a violation by a state in the administration of justice.

While Neer's decedents lost the claim, his namesake case was foundational for the development of the entire body of law that we now call investment protection. Denial of justice is a claim that sounds in customary international law, but has also been embodied in thousands of bilateral investment treaties. Sometimes it is named directly, but it is also assumed to be embodied in the notion of fair and equitable treatment, an umbrella concept.[41] The standard of non-arbitrariness also draws on and overlaps with denial of justice. The precise categorization of the branches of the tree look different to different scholars. But at bottom, the right to fair process, including protection of core interests, is at the heart of the field of investment protection. And denial of justice has been the basis for many successful claims against governments.[42]

Again, it is important to emphasize that it is an objective standard of behavior, not one that requires evaluation relative to a national of the offending party. Even if a regime expropriates and tortures its own citizens, and denies them access to courts, it cannot do so when foreigners are involved, or the government will open itself up to international liability.

Denial of justice binds not only the judicial system and law enforcement authorities, but can also extend to acts of an executive or legislature. For example, in one unpublished arbitral decision, the principle was used to find that Lesotho had violated the standard by participating in the closing of the South African Development Community Tribunal.[43] That body had provoked the ire of Zimbabwean demagogue Robert Mugabe after deciding that his government had denied its white citizens justice by expropriating farmland without compensation.

[40] ibid at 62.

[41] Roger P. Alford, "Ancillary Discovery to Prove Denial of Justice," Va. J. Int'l. L. 53: 127 (2012).

[42] See, e.g., *Dan Cake v. Hungary*, ICSID Case no. ARB/12/9 (August 24, 2015).

[43] *Swissbourgh Diamond Mines (Pty) Ltd., Josias Van Zyl, The Josias Van Zyl Family Trust and others v. The Kingdom of Lesotho*, PCA Case No. 2013-29, April 18, 2016, Partial Final Award on Jurisdiction and Merits.

To be sure, the vagueness of the standard means that claims under it are not always successful. For example, the claim was raised in the famous *Loewen* case under the North American Free Trade Agreement.[44] This case concerned a Canadian funeral home company, against which a Mississippi jury awarded punitive damages of over one billion dollars. Mississippi procedure required a bond of 90% of the damages in order to launch an appeal, and this in turn drove Loewen into bankruptcy. The Tribunal then dismissed the case because there was no continuous Canadian nationality after the reorganization, and also because the company had failed to exhaust its remedies. These cases show that while due process is an important idea in the field of international investment law, tribunals tend to give a good deal of leeway to national authorities in determining how much process is due.

VI. Conclusion

From its origins in the common law, due process has become a major tool of limiting government actors. It is safe to say that it now enjoys the status of a "general principle of law" that can be used to fill in gaps in existing international rules.[45] It is by its nature vague in terms of what any particular context requires. This leaves a good deal of work to courts to figure out how much process is due in response to a particular deprivation. But precisely because of this imprecision, due process is an area in which canonical cases become extremely important as touchstones of judicially developed law.

[44] See William S. Dodge, "*Loewen Group, Inc. v. United States*. ICSID Case No. ARB(AF) /98/3.42ILM 811 (2003)," AJIL 98(1): 155–163 (2004).

[45] Charles T. Kotuby and Luke A. Sobota, *General Principles of Law and International Due Process: Principles and Norms Applicable in Transnational Disputes* (Oxford University Press, 2017).

24

Drawing Their Own Boundaries

Constitutional Interpretation and the Constitutional Role of Courts

Catherine O'Regan

I. Introduction

One of the canonical texts in comparative constitutional law is the decision of the US Supreme Court in *Marbury v. Madison*,[1] in which the US Supreme Court held that it had the power to declare laws in conflict with the Constitution to be invalid. 'Certainly,' held Chief Justice Marshall, 'all those who have framed written constitutions contemplated them as forming the fundamental and paramount law of the nation, and consequently the theory of every such government must be, that an act of the legislature repugnant to the Constitution is void.'[2] *Marbury* thus authoritatively determined the Court's power of judicial review, a power that at the time was unusual, but which has since become commonplace. And so *Marbury* can be read as having enunciated the principle upon which the jurisdiction of courts in constitutional democracies all over the world is now based. In addition, *Marbury* also provides an illustration of how courts play a determinative role in drawing the boundaries of their own jurisdiction, when they interpret the relevant constitutional provisions. This chapter identifies several seminal cases in which courts have through a process of constitutional interpretation drawn the boundaries of their own jurisdiction.

Jeffrey Goldsworthy has argued that judicial 'interpretive methodology constitutes [judges'] response to the tension between fidelity to the terms of the constitution, including its amending procedure, and the need to act creatively to resolve indeterminacies in its meaning or (perhaps) even to modify that meaning to deal with other pressing difficulties'.[3] Given that *Marbury* requires

[1] 5 US (1 Cranch) 137 (1803).
[2] ibid para. 138.
[3] See Jeffrey Goldsworthy, 'Constitutional Interpretation' in M. Rosenfeld and A. Sajó (eds), *The Oxford Handbook of Comparative Constitutional Law* (OUP, 2012), 690.

Catherine O'Regan, *Drawing Their Own Boundaries* In: *Global Canons in an Age of Contestation*. Edited by: Sujit Choudhry, Michaela Hailbronner, and Mattias Kumm, Oxford University Press. © Catherine O'Regan 2024.
DOI: 10.1093/9780191956942.003.0024

no further canonization, this chapter seeks to identify three other canonical texts that illustrate how this tension has been managed in three constitutional democracies—Australia, India, and South Africa. These cases all concern the interpretation of constitutional provisions that affect the courts' constitutional jurisdiction and so all undertook a task similar to that in *Marbury*. They are all examples of courts adopting innovative constitutional interpretations concerning the powers of courts within a constitutional framework. Like *Marbury*, they demonstrate how interpretations by courts may become durable over time, where that durability is evidenced by the acceptance and application of those interpretations by subsequent courts and by other branches of government. These three cases suggest that courts in very different constitutional jurisdictions continue to face questions similar to those raised in *Marbury* and that it is often courts that, through a process of constitutional interpretation, draw the boundaries of their own jurisdiction and in so doing bring some certainty to the law.

The chapter commences with a brief discussion of constitutional interpretation and why it matters. It then turns to a brief consideration of some of the key literature relating to constitutional interpretation and then the main part of the chapter identifies and analyses the three leading constitutional cases that are the three canonical texts presented by this chapter.

II. Constitutional Interpretation

Modern written constitutions[4] are authoritative legal documents, most of which perform two key functions: they establish and regulate the key institutions of government and they provide a catalogue of fundamental rights that primarily regulates the relationship between the state and its citizens. Constitutions are therefore of central political and institutional importance in modern societies and how they are interpreted matters.

Yet the meaning and application of constitutions is often a contested exercise for at least three reasons. First, even in cases where constitutions seek to regulate the institutions of government carefully, circumstances arise that the text does not explicitly regulate. When legal disputes come before courts in such circumstances, courts have, by and large, a duty to resolve the disputes, unless they develop a prudential technique to avoid deciding the case.[5] In the absence

[4] The vast majority of modern states have written constitutions.

[5] See in this regard, e.g., Mark Tushnet's discussion of Madison's view that separation of powers disputes between the executive and the legislature should be resolved politically, M. Tushnet, 'The United

of a technique of avoidance, courts must fill the gaps or indeterminacies in the text, and they must do so through the process of interpretation.

Secondly, amendment of a written constitution is often more difficult than amendment of legislation and, in some cases, it is very difficult if not impossible. The interpretation of constitutions by courts is therefore an important way in which the meaning of a constitution may change over time. As political and social circumstances change, courts may adopt innovative constitutional interpretations to address those changing circumstances.

Finally, constitutional provisions are often expressed in broad, open-ended language which does not fully determine the meaning of the provisions. When courts then interpret those provisions of the constitution, their interpretation often becomes authoritative. Moreover, as time passes, and some constitutions are long-lived, the original meaning of the words in the constitution may be rendered archaic by changing circumstances and practice, which once again may result in courts adopting different interpretations of provisions to those previously considered authoritative.

Constitutional interpretation is thus of crucial importance to the practice of constitutionalism. It is accordingly not surprising that constitutional interpretation by courts has generated a substantial literature. Much of the literature has focused on the question of the legitimate techniques that judges may employ to interpret the constitution. In Germany, for example, it has been long accepted that the classical quartet of reasoning methods identified by Von Savigny in the mid-nineteenth century—grammatical, systematic, teleological, and historical—are those that may be employed by courts in interpreting the constitution. [6]

In the United States, Philip Bobbitt has identified a sixfold typology of arguments evidenced in the practice of constitutional interpretation and argued that constitutional arguments could be historical, textual, structural, prudential (self-conscious of the situation of the reviewing institution, as for example in the political question doctrine), doctrinal, or ethical. [7] Bobbitt's typology,

States: Eclecticism in the Service of Pragmatism' in J. Goldsworthy (ed.), *Interpreting Constitutions: A Comparative Study* (OUP, 2007), 21–22.

[6] See Winfried Brugger, 'Legal Interpretation, School of Jurisprudence, and Anthropology: Some Remarks from a German Point of View' (1994) 42 *Am J Comp Law* 395, 396. For English-language accounts of the approach to constitutional interpretation in Germany, see Donald P. Kommers and Russell A. Miller, *The Constitutional Jurisprudence of the Federal Republic of Germany* 3rd edn (Duke University Press, 2012), ch. 2, 'The Basic Law and its Interpretation'; Donald P. Kommers, 'Germany: Balancing Rights and Duties' in Goldsworthy (n 5).

[7] See Philip Bobbitt, *Constitutional Fate: Theory of the Constitution* (OUP, 1982). For a similar account, see Tushnet (n 5), 27–43.

however, belies the deep political disagreement in the United States as to how courts should interpret the constitution. The debate concerns the centrality of the intentions of the framers of the constitution to the task of interpretation. Many politicians, judges, and scholars argue that what is called 'the original intent' of the framers should be paramount to the interpretive task.[8] But others have argued that there are profound epistemic challenges for this theory (how can we decide who the framers are, and how can we determine their intent)[9] as well as normative challenges (even if we could determine the intent of the framers, why should it determine a contemporary interpretive exercise?).[10] The contours of the debate are beyond the scope of this chapter but its intensity signals the importance of the study of constitutional interpretation for the field of comparative constitutional studies.

Scholars, too, have developed general typologies of interpretive argument. Neil MacCormick, for example, identified three categories of interpretative argument: linguistic, systemic (which includes arguments from contextual harmonization, from precedent, from history, and from general principles of law, amongst others), and substantive argumentation (including teleological and deontological).[11]

These typologies share common features, and they could perhaps be harmonized, although it should be noted that nearly all of them overlook contemporary modes of reasoning in constitutional interpretation, such as reliance on international law norms, or citation of jurisprudence from other jurisdictions. But what is often absent in these typologies is how courts should (and do) employ these arguments, whether there should be (or is) a clear hierarchy amongst them, and how courts should (and do) reason when different types of argument in a particular case may lead to a different outcome.

Although these typologies are helpful in classifying the types of arguments that courts may employ in the process of constitutional interpretation, they are thus not particularly helpful in predicting how courts will reach decisions. This chapter argues that in cases where interpretation is contested, the contest is often best understood as whether courts should adopt the interpretation most consistent with text or precedent or whether they should develop the law in an equitable interpretation of it on the other. This is the tension mentioned in the

[8] See, e.g., Robert Bork, *The Tempting of America: The Political Seduction of the Law* (Collier-Macmillan, 1990) and Antonin Scalia, *A Matter of Interpretation* (Princeton UP, 1997).

[9] See the useful analysis by Aileen Kavanagh, 'Original Intention, Enacted Text and Constitutional Interpretation' (2002) 47 *Am J Juris* 255, 255–256.

[10] ibid.

[11] Neil MacCormick, 'Argumentation and Interpretation in Law' (1993) 6 *Ratio Juris* 16–29.

Goldsworthy quote in the opening paragraph to this chapter and it echoes in some respects the work of Joseph Raz, who identified and analysed this tension as one central to the task of interpretation.[12] Raz argued that the tension arises because interpretation seeks to serve different and, at times, conflicting values. So respecting text and precedent in interpretation serves the values of authority and consistency. Yet there are other values that interpretation serves too, according to Raz: the values of legal development and equity. Given these different values, legal interpretation is often 'Janus-faced', looking both forward and backward. Interpretation that serves the values of authority and consistency look backward and are, in Raz's phrase, 'conserving interpretations' while interpretations that serve legal development or equity look forward and are 'innovative interpretations'. The competing values that inform the task of interpretation lead Raz to conclude that there may be more than one good interpretation of a legal text.

The three cases that are identified in this chapter all concern the interpretation of specific constitutional provisions, and each case involves a powerful dissenting opinion in which the disagreement between the majority and minority turns to a large extent on different interpretations of the constitutional text. In this respect, the cases diverge from *Marbury*, which was a unanimous decision. It is not the purpose of this chapter to assess the relative merits or demerits of the three decisions, rather its purpose is to seek to analyse the different interpretive approaches that result in the disagreement evident in the cases. In all three cases, the majority arguably adopts an 'innovative' interpretation whereas the minority adopts a 'conserving' one. And in each case, the courts developed their own jurisdiction in a manner that was not fully determined by the language of the text or by existing precedent. Yet, in each of the three cases, subsequent jurisprudence has followed the innovative interpretations adopted in the three cases, demonstrating that these innovative interpretations have proved durable. The innovative decisions have thus served the role of what natural lawyers have long called *determinationes*,[13] the process of giving more determinate meaning to rules and principles. Whatever the merits of the reasoning provided to support the innovative interpretations, their

[12] J. Raz, *Between Authority and Interpretation: On the Theory of Law and Practical Reason* (OUP, 2009), 237–240.

[13] See Jeremy Waldron, 'Torture, Suicide and *Determinatio*' (2010) *Am J Juris* 1–30; John Finnis, *Natural Law and Natural Rights* 2nd edn (OUP, 2010), 284–290; Neil MacCormick, 'Reconstruction after Deconstruction: A Response to CLS' (1990) 10 *OJLS* 539–558, 548. For a related concept, see Hans Kelsen's conception of the 'concretisation' of norms, discussed by Waldron, cited in this note, 1, and MacCormick, cited in this note, 548.

durability, the chapter argues, is a mark of their jurisprudential success,[14] but not of their doctrinal cogency or even plausibility.

III. Selection of Canonical Materials

The three cases come from three different constitutional democracies: Australia, India, and South Africa. All are former British colonies, currently members of the Commonwealth in which the dominant language of constitutional adjudication is English. All three democracies have written constitutions and in all three, courts have the power to interpret and apply those constitutions. The constitutions, however, are from three different eras: the Australian Constitution is one of the oldest surviving constitutions in the Commonwealth having come into force in 1901, the Indian Constitution came into force in January 1950, and the South African Constitution in February 1997.

The three constitutions differ significantly: Australia and India are federal states, whereas South Africa is largely unitary, with some federal aspects. The Indian and South African Constitutions both contain extensive bills of rights which are interpreted and applied by the courts, the Australian Constitution does not. There are also differences in the approach to constitutional interpretation in each of the jurisdictions. In a country-based comparative study of constitutional interpretation that included Australia, India, and South Africa, its editor, Jeffrey Goldsworthy, concluded that of these three jurisdictions, Australia had the most 'legalist' or 'positivist' legal culture, where judges express 'aversion to changing the Constitution through creative interpretation'.[15] India, on the other hand, was found to be the most 'normativist' or creative court interpretively, while the approach to constitutional interpretation in South Africa, was seen as being somewhere between the approaches in India and Australia.[16]

All three cases selected were decided by the highest courts in each jurisdiction and all are considered important or even seminal in their jurisdiction. Accordingly, they have all been extensively cited, applied, and developed in the subsequent jurisprudence. All three establish key principles of the separation of powers that relate either directly or indirectly to the role courts play in each of the three democracies. Each is based on the interpretation of the relevant

[14] See J. Goldsworthy, 'Raz on Constitutional Interpretation' (2003) 11 *Law and Philosophy I* 167–193, 170.
[15] See J. Goldsworthy, 'Conclusion' in Goldsworthy (n 3)
[16] ibid.

constitutional provisions and each decision contains an engagement with judicial decisions in other jurisdictions.

Perhaps most interestingly, each involved a powerful dissent that was both doctrinally and constitutionally plausible. The existence of plausible dissents in each case provides a frame to analyse and assess the reasoning in the majority decision. Each of the three cases in some significant way established a precedent that has had a material impact on how the separation of powers works going forward in that constitutional order, yet in each case the decision was constitutionally contingent, as is evident from the powerful dissenting judgments.

I will discuss the three in chronological order. The first, *R v. Kirby; ex parte Boilermakers' Society of Australia* ('*Boilermakers*')[17] was decided nearly seventy years ago; the second, *Kesavananda Bharati v. State of Kerala* ('*Kesavananda*')[18] over fifty years ago, and the third, *Doctors for Life International v. Speaker of the National Assembly and Others* ('*Doctors for Life*')[19] just twenty years ago.

IV. *Boilermakers*

Building on earlier decisions of the High Court,[20] *Boilermakers* established two core principles of Australian constitutional law: that only judicial bodies established under chapter III of the Australian Constitution[21] may exercise the judicial power of the Commonwealth; and that such judicial bodies may exercise no power that is not Commonwealth judicial power. It is a seminal case and has been described as being 'synonymous with the separation of powers in Australia'[22] and as having 'had a significant impact on the nature and content of power exercisable by the respective branches of government'.[23]

First, a little background. As Fiona Wheeler has described, *Boilermakers* was a 'battle in a protracted war between employers and unions' over the enforcement of industrial awards.[24] It arose from an industrial dispute between an

[17] [1956] HCA 10; (1956) 94 CLR 254 (HCA).
[18] (1973) 4 SCC 225 (SCI).
[19] (2006) 6 SA 416 (CC).
[20] *New South Wales v. The Commonwealth* (the *Wheat case*) (1915) 20 CLR 54; *Waterside Workers' Federation of Australia v. JW Alexander Ltd* (1918) 25 CLR 434; and *Victorian Stevedoring & General Contracting Co Pty Ltd & Meakes v. Dignan* (1931) 46 CLR 73.
[21] Commonwealth of Australia Constitution Act 1900, ch. III.
[22] Fiona Wheeler, 'The *Boilermakers'* Case' in H. P. Lee and G. Winterton (eds), *Australian Constitutional Landmarks* (CUP, 2003), 160.
[23] See M. Foster 'The Separation of Judicial Power' in C. Saunders and A. Stone (eds), *The Oxford Handbook of the Australian Constitution* (OUP, 2018), 672.
[24] ibid 161.

ironworkers' union and Mort's Dock & Engineering Company, a Sydney shipyard, over the rates paid to riggers. The Boilermakers' Society imposed bans in support of the ironworkers' strike that the employers' association, the Metal Trades Employers' Association, considered to be in breach of the Metal Trades Award and so they took the Boilermakers' Society to court to compel compliance with the award. The Arbitration Court ordered the Boilermakers' Society to comply with the award, but some of the members of the Boilermakers' Society then contributed to a fund to support the Ironworkers' Union, which led the Arbitration Court to impose a fine for contempt on the Boilermakers' Society. The Boilermakers' Society challenged both the order to comply and the imposition of the fine in the High Court on the basis that the conferral of these powers on the Arbitration Court was in breach of the Constitution. The Arbitration Court's award was not exceptional: it was one of many contempt orders issued against unions to compel compliance with industrial awards at the time, which had given rise to deep union dissatisfaction with the Arbitration Court's use of its contempt powers.[25] Bert Evatt, the leader of the Australian Labour Party in opposition at the time, is reported to have said that '[t]he trade unions have had to suffer penalties quite out of proportion to the occasion'.[26]

The key constitutional issue in the case stemmed from the fact that the Arbitration Court performed arbitral functions as well as enforcement functions in the field of industrial law. The Boilermakers' Society argued that arbitral functions were not judicial functions within the meaning of the Constitution and that the Constitution did not permit it to exercise both judicial and non-judicial functions.

The High Court divided 4:3. The majority judgment by Dixon CJ with McTiernan, Fullagar, and Kitto JJ, made only bare reference to the bitter industrial-relations disputes that underlay the challenge, and focused instead on the text and structure of the Constitution. The majority judgment has been described as 'an example of the "strict and complete legalism" that Chief Justice Dixon believed should mark the Court's reasoning'.[27]

The majority held that, properly construed, chapter III of the Australian Constitution meant not only that federal judicial power could only be exercised by chapter III courts, but that chapter III courts could perform no other function. The majority implied this latter principle from the structure of the

[25] See the full account in Wheeler (n 22), 164–166.

[26] See *Sydney Morning Herald*, 3 March 1956, cited in Wheeler, ibid 165.

[27] See Wheeler, ibid, 166; and see A, Stone, 'Constitutional Orthodoxy in the UK and Australia: The Deepening Divide', review of Aileen Kavanagh, *Constitutional Review under the UK Human Rights Act* (CUP, 2009) (2014) 38 *Melbourne LR* 836–857, 856.

Constitution, and its establishment and regulation of the three branches of the Commonwealth government (executive, legislative, and judicial) into three separate chapters. Central to the decision was the majority conclusion that the arbitral powers conferred upon the Arbitration Court were not judicial. It also observed that chapter III of the Constitution provides a catalogue of judicial powers but fails to mention any non-judicial powers a court may exercise. Finally, the importance of the judiciary within the federal structure was noted, which the majority held meant 'that the powers of the federal judicature must therefore be at once paramount and limited'.[28] Accordingly, the judgment concluded that it would be 'entirely incongruous' to conclude that powers could be conferred upon a chapter III court that were non-judicial in nature.[29]

The majority judgment acknowledged that a range of earlier cases of the High Court had taken a different view.[30] In weighing this authority, the court reasoned that:

> [s]uch matters as judicial dicta, common assumptions tacitly being made and acted upon, and the fact that the legislation has passed unchallenged for a considerable period of time, may be regarded as raising a presumption which should prevail until the judicial mind reaches a clear conviction that consistently with the Constitution, the validity of the provisions impugned cannot be sustained. But they cannot be regarded as doing more.[31]

The three dissenting judgments[32] accepted the first leg of the majority position, that only chapter III courts may exercise Commonwealth judicial power, which was what the text of the Constitution explicitly stated. But they did not accept the second leg of the argument, that chapter III courts were barred from exercising non-judicial powers, given that the text did not explicitly contain such a bar. According to Williams J, 'If there is a prohibition against their doing so, it must rest on some implication in the Constitution arising from the vague concept of the separation of powers'.[33] Williams J then indicated that the implications of the Constitution seemed to go the other way. In addition, Williams J disagreed that there was anything inconsistent in a judge conducting arbitral proceedings, which on his view 'are proceedings which should be conducted

[28] *Boilermakers*, majority judgment, para. 3.
[29] ibid para. 8 of majority decision.
[30] ibid para. 27 of majority decision.
[31] ibid para. 28.
[32] ibid by Williams, Webb, and Taylor JJ.
[33] ibid para. 8 of decision of Williams J.

with that fairness and impartiality which should characterise proceedings in courts of justice'.[34]

The High Court decision was unsuccessfully appealed to the Privy Council. But the government did not wait for the outcome of the appeal and in 1956 introduced an amendment to the Conciliation and Arbitration Act to give effect to the majority judgment by establishing two separate institutions—the Commonwealth Conciliation and Arbitration Commission, which was tasked with the prevention and settlement of industrial disputes, and the Industrial Court to enforce industrial awards.

It is clear on a reading of the majority decision that this constituted a sharp departure from existing High Court jurisprudence in favour of its interpretation of the constitutional text based on an implication, which was strongly disputed by the minority decision. The majority decision can thus be described as an 'innovative one' while the minority decision was 'conserving', cleaving to the existing understanding of chapter III. It is also noteworthy that the effect of this innovative decision was to limit the role that the federal judiciary could perform under the Australian Constitution, not to extend it. By narrowly construing the concept of judicial function, and by holding that the Constitution implied that federal chapter III courts could only perform judicial functions, the role of the federal courts was constrained.

It is perhaps not surprising, given its innovative character, that the majority judgment in *Boilermakers* was the subject of strong criticism. For example, the next Chief Justice, Barwick CJ, complained that the decision 'leads to excessive subtlety and technicality in the operation of the Constitution without, in my opinion, any compensating benefit'.[35] Despite the criticism, the majority decision has been durable and it is clear that both limbs of its reasoning are firmly entrenched as principles of Australian constitutional law,[36] although the Australian courts have reduced the inflexibility of the second limb, for example by recognizing the principle that a judge may in his or her personal capacity undertake non-judicial functions, such as chairing non-judicial tribunals or commissions of inquiry.[37]

Despite that flexibility, the long-term implication of *Boilermakers* is the strong version of separation of powers it adopted in relation to the

[34] ibid para. 11 of decision of Williams J.

[35] See *R v. Joske: Ex parte Australian Building Construction Employees and Builders' Labourers' Federation* (1974) 130 CLR 87, 90.

[36] See Foster (n 23), 682–683.

[37] See *Hilton v. Wells* (1985) 157 CLR 57; *Grollo v. Palmer* (1995) 184 CLR 348; and see discussion in Wheeler (n 22).

Commonwealth judiciary. Fiona Wheeler suggests that '[i]f the case had not been decided, or if the dissenting judgment of Williams J had prevailed, it is hard to imagine that the separation of judicial power—including the first limb of that doctrine—would have the vigour it has today'.[38]

Boilermakers can thus be seen as an innovative decision in relation to the development of the doctrine of the separation of powers in Australia that limited the role the federal judiciary could perform. The principles it established have largely endured. Subsequent cases applying the *Boilermakers* principles have largely been 'conserving' in their approach to interpretation, so illustrating the reciprocal relationship between innovative and conserving approaches to interpretation in constitutional jurisprudence.

V. *Kesavananda*

The decision of the Indian Supreme Court in *Kesavananda* established the principle that the power to amend the Indian Constitution provided in Article 368 did not authorize Parliament to amend 'the basic structure' or 'essential features' of the Constitution. Like *Boilermakers*, *Kesavananda* is a seminal case, described variously as 'arguably the most monumental decision' in the history of the Indian Supreme Court,[39] 'the bedrock of constitutional interpretation in India',[40] and as having saved 'the soul of the Constitution and the liberty of citizens against the might of a majoritarian state'.[41]

Again some background. The Indian Constitution is—at least on a reading of its text—more amendable than either the American or Australian Constitutions. Article 368 provides that a two-thirds majority of those present and voting in both Houses of Parliament is all that is required, save in circumstances where federal structures or relationships are affected or the powers of the judiciary or President are to be amended, in which case the amendment will require, in addition, ratification by the legislatures of half of the states. And, again, unlike the American and Indian Constitutions, the Indian Constitution has been frequently amended, indeed there have been more than 100 amendments since 1950.

38 Wheeler, ibid 174.

39 See Zia Mody, *Ten Judgments that Changed India* (Penguin, 2013), ch. 1.

40 Granville Williams, *Working a Democratic Constitution: A History of the Indian Experience* (OUP, 1999), 258.

41 N. R. Madhava Menon, 'Book Review: TR Andhyarujina *The Kesavananda Bharati Case: The Untold Story of Struggle for Supremacy by Supreme Court and Parliament*' (2011) 53 *Journal of India Law Institute* 678–671, 678.

Yet the scope of Parliament's power to amend the Constitution has been under scrutiny in the courts since the first amendment of the Constitution. In an early case, *Shankari Prasad*, the question was whether a constitutional amendment fell within the ambit of Article 13, which provides that laws that breach the rights in the Bill of Rights are invalid. The case concerned reforms introduced in the states of Bihar, Uttar Pradesh, and Madhya Pradesh to end the zamindari system, a form of feudal tenure.[42] The Court rejected the challenge holding that constitutional amendments are not laws within the meaning of Article 13 and so do not have to be consistent with the Bill of Rights.[43] Nearly fifteen years later, the decision in *Shankari Prasad* was confirmed in *Sajjan Singh v. State of Rajasthan* although not unanimously.[44]

But this approach to constitutional amendments was reversed a few years later in *Golak Nath*, another challenge to land reform legislation this time enacted by the states of Punjab and Mysore, where it was held that the source of the constitutional amendment power did not lie in Article 368, but derived from Articles 245, 246, and 248, and that constitutional amendments were within the scope of Article 13.[45] All these early decisions on the constitutional amendment power had concerned the right to property and challenges to legislation which in one way or another affected existing property rights. The great biographer of the Indian Constitution, Granville Austin wrote that 'the Golak Nath case began the great war, as distinct from earlier skirmishes, over parliamentary versus judicial supremacy. It gave fresh life to the issue of property and the Constitution, which had run, and would continue to run, insistently through decades of Indian politics.'[46]

It was not long before Prime Minister Indira Gandhi and the Congress Party sought to reverse *Golak Nath* by introducing three constitutional amendments. The Twenty-Fourth Amendment amended Article 13 to make clear that constitutional amendments did not fall within its ambit and so would not be required to be consistent with the Bill of Rights[47] and also amended Article 368 to state the Parliament may 'amend by way of addition, variation or repeal

[42] See V. R. Jayadevan, 'Interpretation of the Amending Clause: The Brawl between the Spirit of Natural Law and the Ghost of Analytical Positivism' (2010) 33 *Hamline LR* 260–261.

[43] See *Shankari Prasad Singh Deo v. Union of India* 1951 SC 458 and see the discussion in M. Khosla, 'Constituting Democracy, Constitutional Amendment' in S. Choudhry, M. Khosla, and P. B. Mehta, *The Oxford Companion to the Indian Constitution* (OUP, 2016), 236; and Jayadevan (n 42), 243.

[44] See *Sajjan Singh v. State of Rajasthan* AIR 1965 SC 845. The court divided 3:2. Again, see the fuller discussion in Khosla (n 43), 236–238.

[45] See *Golak Nath v. State of Punjab* AIR 1967 SC 1643.

[46] Granville Williams, *Working a Democratic Constitution: A History of the Indian Experience* (OUP, 1999), 198.

[47] By inserting a new sub-article (4) into the provision to read: 'Nothing in this article shall apply to any amendment of the Constitution made under Article 368.'

any provision of this Constitution'.[48] The Twenty-Fifth Amendment replaced the previous requirement that when property is expropriated, compensation would be paid with a provision that 'an amount' would be paid;[49] and inserted a new clause in the Constitution stating that legislation enacted in order to give effect to certain of the Directive Principles of State Policy could not be challenged on the basis of their inconsistency with certain of the fundamental rights and that no law stating that it was for such a purpose 'shall be called in question in any court'.[50] The Twenty-Ninth Amendment added two pieces of Kerala land reform legislation to the Ninth Schedule to the Constitution, with the effect that they could not be rendered void on the ground that they infringed the fundamental rights in the Constitution.[51]

All three amendments were challenged in *Kesavananda*. The case was brought to the Supreme Court by Swami Kesavananda Bharati Sripadagalvaru, the hereditary leader of the Edneer Mutt (a Hindu monastic institution) in the southern province of Kerala, who challenged the two land reform Acts introduced by the Kerala government that imposed restrictions on the management of religious property and which were the subject of the Twenty-Ninth Amendment. Thirteen judges were enrolled to hear the case and the hearings began on 31 October 1972 and lasted till mid-March 1973. Tensions around the case were very high. At least some of the judges felt under intense pressure and sensed that finding against the government might harm the judiciary.[52]

If one assumes that canonical cases should be read by most comparative constitutional lawyers, then perhaps *Kesavananda* is not a good candidate for a canon because the judgment runs to nearly 800 pages of the law reports. Eleven judgments were written, each covering in exhaustive detail the arguments that the Court had heard in the many days of hearing. Much of the many hundreds of pages of reasoning engages with the jurisprudence of a range of jurisdictions including the United States, Australia, Sri Lanka, and the United Kingdom. For all its erudition, it is not clear how influential the comparative jurisprudence was to the interpretation of Article 368, for as Hegde and Mukherjea JJ observed in their judgment:

[48] A portion of the newly inserted sub-article (2). The amendment also changed the marginal heading to read 'Power of Parliament to amend the Constitution and procedure therefor.'

[49] Art. 31(2) of the Constitution was thus substituted by the new provision which provided in relevant part that: 'No property shall be compulsorily acquired or requisitioned save for a public purpose and save by authority of a law ... for an amount which may be fixed by such law ...'

[50] The new provision was Art. 31C.

[51] Art. 31B, which was inserted by the First Amendment in 1951.

[52] See Williams (n 46), 270ff.

> The scheme of no two Constitutions is similar. Their provisions are not similar. The language employed in the amending clauses differs from Constitution to Constitution. The objectives lying behind them are also bound to differ. Each country has its own needs, its own philosophy, its own way of life and above all its own problems. Hence in our opinion, we will be clouding the issues, if we allow ourselves to be burdened either by the writings of the various writers on other Constitutions or by the decisions rendered on the basis of the provisions of other Constitutions, though Counsel on either side spared no efforts to place before us various opinions . . .[53]

The judgments address the cases raised in the arguments at great length, but at least according to the dicta in the judgments, the comparative jurisprudence seems to have had little influence in the key decisions in the case. However, we should not be too quick to criticize, at least one of the roles of a judgment is to explain why arguments made before the court have not been persuasive.

Unusually, nine of the thirteen judges issued a short statement that was appended to the judgment, titled 'The view by the majority', apparently to clarify the findings of the majority.[54] This statement makes clear that the judgment in *Golak Nath* was overruled (on my reading, unanimously), that the Twenty-Fourth and Twenty-Ninth Amendments were valid (again, on my reading unanimously), and that the Twenty-Fifth Amendment was valid, save for the second part of the proposed new Article 31C which stated that 'and no law containing a declaration that it is for giving effect to such policy shall be called in question in any court on the ground that it does not give effect to such policy' (this, on my reading, by a majority of 7:6). The most important element of the summary is its statement that the majority concludes that 'Article 368 does not enable Parliament to alter the basic structure or framework of the Constitution' (again, this by a majority of 7:6).[55]

The majority was formed by Sikri CJ, Shelat and Grover JJ (in a joint judgment), Hegde and Mukherjea JJ (in a joint judgment), Jaganmohan Reddy J and Khanna J, all of whom declared the second portion of the Twenty-Fifth Amendment to be invalid and all of whom supported the basic structure doctrine. The 'view of the majority' was signed by these seven judges as well as by Palekar and Chandrachud JJ. The remaining four judges Ray, Beg, Mathews,

[53] *Kesavananda Bharati v. Kerala* 1973 (4) SCC 225 at para. 659. See for similar remarks, e.g., the judgment of Sikri CJ at para. 347, and that of Ray J at para. 981 ('Our Constitution does not breathe through conventions and principles of other countries').

[54] *Kesavananda Bharati v. Kerala*, p. 1007. And see the discussion in Williams (n 46), 265ff.

[55] *Kesavananda v. Kerala*, para. (2) of the view by the majority.

and Dwivedi JJ did not sign it. They together with Palekar and Chandrachud JJ upheld all three constitutional amendments without exception.

There was no explicit language in Article 368 that curtailed the scope of the amendment power. Accordingly, the approach adopted by the minority is grounded in the text. The minority view was captured by Ray J as follows, '[t]he theory of implied and inherent limitations cannot be allowed to act as a *boa constrictor* to the clear and unambiguous power of amendment'.[56] Whatever one's view on the reasoning in the case, as in *Boilermakers*, it cannot be said that the view of the minority was implausible.

As Madhav Khosla has argued, a court holding that a constitutional amendment is inconsistent with the Constitution is quite different from a court holding that a legislative provision is in conflict with the Constitution. For a constitution and the amendment of it, according to standard constitutional theory, is an exercise of sovereign power. When a court reviews legislation for constitutional compliance, it is doing so at the behest of the sovereign, but when it judges constitutional amendments that are validly made, it is arguably judging the sovereign.[57] In circumstances where amendment is achieved not by direct recourse to the people, as for example in a referendum, but by the legislature, the defence of a substantive limitation on the amending power may be better understood as a challenge to the legislature's role in representing the sovereign.[58] These questions are engaged in the majority and minority judgments in *Kesavananda*. Hegde and Mukherjea JJ, for example, reasoned that, '[w]hen a power to amend the Constitution is given to the people, its contents may be construed to be larger than when that power is given to a body constituted under that Constitution. Two-thirds of the members of the two Houses of Parliament need not necessarily represent even the majority of the people ...'[59] Ray J put the contrary position asserting that a constitution can only be amended 'in accordance with the process laid down in the Constitution' and '[o]nce the Constitution has vested the power to amend in the bodies mentioned therein that is the only body for amending the Constitution. The people who gave the Constitution have expressed how it is to be changed.'[60]

The disagreement between the majority and minority judgments was profound. There can be little doubt that the approach adopted by the majority was startlingly 'innovative'. It overturned *Golak Nath*, and by implication found

[56] ibid para. 901.
[57] See Khosla (n 43), 233.
[58] ibid.
[59] *Kesavananda Bharati v. Kerala*, para. 653.
[60] ibid para. 796.

there to be a sharp limitation on the amendment power in Article 368 of the Constitution. Unlike in *Boilermakers*, which had also implied a provision into the Constitution, *Kesavananda* enhanced the role that courts play under the Indian Constitution and limited the power of the legislature. It is the courts that determine which principles of the Constitution form part of its 'basic structure' and those parts of the Constitution do not fall within the amending power conferred by Article 268.

It is noteworthy that in the decades since the basic structure doctrine as propounded by the majority has become deeply rooted in India's constitutional framework. The doctrine has been relied upon to challenge a wide array of constitutional amendments.[61] The full contours of the 'basic structure' of the Constitution remain unclear and perhaps always will. As Khosla has argued, 'whether the basic structure doctrine remains an integral and vibrant feature of Indian constitutionalism will depend neither on the technical distinction between sovereignty and government nor the rules for amending the Constitution, but quite simply on how persuasively the doctrine is applied'. [62]

VI. *Doctors for Life*

In *Doctors for Life*, a majority of the Constitutional Court of South Africa held that once a Bill had been signed into law by the President, the Court could consider whether Parliament had acted properly to facilitate public involvement in the law-making process and if it found that Parliament had failed to do so would render the relevant legislation invalid.[63] The case related to four pieces of legislation concerning health, one concerning traditional health practitioners, one regulating abortion, one regulating dental technicians, and one sterilization. The Court held that two of the pieces of legislation were invalid on the basis that Parliament had failed to facilitate public involvement. The Court suspended both orders of invalidity for a period of eighteen months to permit Parliament to re-enact the statutes in a manner consistent with the Constitution.

As to background, the applicant, Doctors for Life International, is a not-for-profit company established in response to the need 'to protect the sanctity of life from fertilisation until natural death' and 'judeo-christian ethics within

[61] See for a full discussion, Khosla (n 43), 241ff.
[62] ibid 250.
[63] The author was a judge of the Constitutional Court at the time and a signatory of the majority judgment.

the medical profession'.[64] The case, however, was not politically contentious at the time. No *amicus curiae* applied to appear in the case which is common in contentious cases in South Africa. However, the case raised important constitutional questions that were raised again within a year in a more politically contentious case concerning the redrawing of provincial boundaries.[65]

The Court split 8:3 in *Doctors for Life*. Four judgments were written, the majority was written by Ngcobo J, there was a concurrence by Sachs J, and two dissenting judgments by Van Der Westhuizen and Yacoob JJ. The majority judgment noted that two of the four bills (the one regulating traditional health practitioners and the one regulating abortion) had generated public interest, and that the upper house of Parliament, the National Council of Provinces, had decided that public hearings should be held in each of the provinces on the bills. However, most of the provinces had not held hearings on the bills and nor had the National Council of Provinces itself. The majority judgment held that the failure of the upper house to facilitate public involvement in these two bills was unreasonable and in breach of its obligations in terms of section 72(1)(a) of the Constitution.[66] The majority also held that one of the bills (the one regulating dental practitioners) had not generated public interest and it was not unreasonable for the upper house not to have held public hearings on that bill.[67]

The majority also noted that it would be appropriate to establish a narrower approach to standing in cases where litigants argue that Parliament has failed to facilitate public involvement in law-making. It noted that the applicant in this case had made 'repeated and persistent' efforts to make representations to Parliament on the subject matter of the bills. The majority reasoned: 'this Court will only consider an application to declare legislation invalid on the grounds set out in this judgment where the applicant has sought and been denied an opportunity to be heard on the Bills and where the applicant has launched his or her application for relief ... as soon as practicable after the Bills have been promulgated'.[68] The majority justified this narrow approach to standing on the basis that it had to find a balance between 'avoiding improper intrusions into the domain of Parliament' and ensuring that Parliament's duty to facilitate public involvement in its processes 'is not rendered nugatory'.[69]

[64] See their website: https://www.doctorsforlife.co.za.

[65] See *Matatiele Municipality and Others v. President of the RSA and Others* [2006] ZACC 2.

[66] Section 72(1)(a) provides that: 'The National Council of Provinces must facilitate public involvement in the legislative and other processes of the Council and its committees.'

[67] The fourth bill had not been signed by the President and the Court held that it could not consider the constitutionality of the bill before that stage of the law making process (see *Doctors for Life*, [56]–[58]).

[68] ibid [216], per Ngcobo J.

[69] ibid [218], per Ngcobo J.

In his minority judgment, on the other hand, Yacoob J held that the requirement to facilitate public involvement did not constitute a prerequisite to valid legislation[70] and that to read the provision to impose such a prerequisite was 'to impermissibly undermine the legislature and the right to vote'.[71] And Van Der Westhuizen J stated, 'I am concerned about the separation of powers, which is crucial in any democracy and probably more so in a young one. … If the approach in the minority judgment is logically and constitutionally at least as defensible as the majority approach, the former must perhaps be preferred, out of respect for the separation of powers.'[72]

The majority judgment considered in great detail international human rights law on the right to political participation, including the International Covenant on Civil and Political Rights, the African Charter on Human and Peoples' Rights, and the Inter-American Convention on Human Rights, as well as comparative constitutional jurisprudence, including Tanzania, Portugal, and Colombia,[73] concluding that 'the general right to participate in the conduct of public affairs includes engaging in public debate and dialogue with elected representatives at public hearings'.[74]

The minority judgments did not draw on either international human rights law or comparative constitutional jurisprudence in reaching their conclusions. Neither of the minority judgments mentioned Article 9 of the UK's 1689 Bill of Rights, which as Stephen Gardbaum has pointed out, was perhaps the first constitutional principle to determine the relationship between Parliament and the courts and which has been very influential.[75] Article 9 rendered 'proceedings of Parliament immune from impeachment or questioning in any court'. Again as Gardbaum has noted, '[t]he autonomy of legislative proceedings from judicial oversight is the flip side of the independence of the judiciary from undue or inappropriate legislative interference'.[76]

The key difference between the majority and minority judgments in *Doctors for Life* hinges on what constitutes 'inappropriate' interference with legislative proceedings. As in both *Boilermakers* and *Kesavananda*, the dissenting judgments are plausible on the text of the Constitution. As in *Kesavananda*, the effect of the majority judgment is to confer a jurisdiction on the Constitutional

[70] ibid [319], per Yacoob J.
[71] ibid [339].
[72] ibid [244].
[73] ibid [90]–[105].
[74] ibid [105].
[75] See Stephen Gardbaum, 'Pushing the Boundaries: Judicial Review of Legislative Procedures in South Africa' (2019) 9 *Constitutional Court Review* 1, 3.
[76] ibid.

Court to ensure that Parliament facilitates public involvement in the legislative process. In this regard, the majority judgment is probably best understood as adopting an 'innovative' interpretive approach, while the minority judgments are 'conserving' in their approach.

The majority judgment has become rooted in South African constitutional practice. Indeed, as Stephen Gardbaum has pointed out, the Constitutional Court has developed a substantial jurisprudence relating to Parliament in the years since.[77] The principle that the Constitutional Court will at times consider and rule on the proceedings of Parliament is thus well established as a principle in South African constitutional law. In his interesting examination of this practice, Gardbaum locates it within the practice of parliamentary democracies over the last century and the weakening, largely as a result of the role played by political parties, of parliamentary oversight of the executive. He argues, 'in both two-party and multiparty competitive democracies, the relative loss of parliamentary independence in the face of party government and growing "executive supremacy" has meant that that the capacity of legislatures to subject the executive to meaning political accountability has been in secular decline everywhere'.[78] As with the basic structure doctrine in India, it is likely that the principles and practice of judicial review of parliamentary processes will continue to develop.

As in both *Boilermakers* and *Kesavananda*, the interpretive approach of the majority was clearly 'innovative' rather than conserving, which better describes the reasoning in the minority judgments in each of the three cases.

VII. Conclusion

Each of these three canonical cases resulted in the clarification of the constitutional role of the judiciary, in circumstances where the interpretation of the constitutional text can be described as innovative. In all three cases, the principle has endured and has, by and large, been accepted as a core constitutional principle. But the principles had differing effects. In *Boilermakers*, the decision narrowed the role that federal courts could perform, whereas both

[77] ibid. And see, e.g., *Matatiele Municipality v. President of the RSA* [2006] ZACC 12; *Oriani-Ambrosini MP v. Sisulu MP, Speaker of the National Assembly* [2012] ZACC 27 (on the question of private members' bills); *Mazibuko v. Sisulu and Another* [2013] ZACC 28 (on scheduling of motions of no confidence in the President); *EFF v. Speaker of the National Assembly* [2016] ZACC 11 (on Parliament's failure to hold the President to account); and *United Democratic Movement v. Speaker of the National Assembly* [2017] ZACC 21.

[78] Gartbaum (n 75), 15.

Kesavananda and *Doctors for Life* expanded the role of courts. The three cases, like *Marbury*, suggest the important role courts play in determining their own jurisdiction. Despite differences of history, text, and legal culture, these three courts issued innovative decisions that fundamentally altered the role of the courts in their constitutional settings, in a manner that has endured.

25

Techniques of Judicial Avoidance

Richard Albert[*]

I. Introduction: The Rise of Juristocracy

In what may have been the most deft and strategic exercise of judicial authority in the history of the United States, Chief Justice John Marshall asserted—but did not exercise—the extraordinary power to invalidate executive and legislative actions for running afoul of the Constitution.[1] Marshall seized the opportunity to declare the constitutional supremacy of the judiciary, exclaiming that "it is emphatically the province and duty of the Judicial Department to say what the law is."[2] He insisted that the boundaries of the Constitution are to be determined by the Supreme Court alone.[3]

Over two centuries later, many countries around the world have lived their own *Marbury* moments.[4] Constitutional review has become a significant source of judicial power, so much so that the idea of juristocracy now permeates studies of modern constitutionalism, the critique being that considerably more is decided today by courts than by the people and their elected representatives.[5] In every region of the world, we see evidence of the "judicialization of mega-politics,"[6] a reference to the most important matters of political significance that constitute, define, and divide polities—and that are now often adjudicated by high courts intervening into what some might regard as the political sphere. Courts have with increasing frequency resolved matters that were once seen as

* William Stamps Farish Professor in Law, Professor of Government, and Director of Constitutional Studies, The University of Texas at Austin. My sincere thanks to Michaela Hailbronner, Sujit Choudhry, and Mattias Kumm for including me in this innovative project, and to Jasmin Rauch for helping to coordinate the effort.

[1] *Marbury v. Madison*, 5 U.S. (1 Cranch) 137.

[2] ibid. at 177.

[3] ibid. at 178.

[4] Steven Arrigg Koh, "*Marbury* Moments" (2015) 54 *Columbia Journal of Transnational Law* 116.

[5] For the most influential exposition and use of this term, see Ran Hirschl, *Towards Juristocracy: The Origins and Consequences of the New Constitutionalism* (Harvard University Press, 2004).

[6] See Ran Hirschl, "The Judicialization of Mega-Politics and the Rise of Political Courts" (2008) 11 *Annual Review of Political Science* 93 at 94.

Richard Albert, *Techniques of Judicial Avoidance* In: *Global Canons in an Age of Contestation.* Edited by: Sujit Choudhry, Michaela Hailbronner, and Mattias Kumm, Oxford University Press.
DOI: 10.1093/9780191956942.003.0025

political, not at all legal: from banning political parties in Algeria and Turkey, to ruling on elections in Mexico, Russia, and the United States, to hearing disputes on fiscal policy and foreign affairs in Brazil and the United Kingdom, to judging the legitimacy of the governing regime in Fiji and South Korea, and to deciding whether and how a province can secede from Canada.[7] There is no doubt in the world today that courts are supreme in more than name alone.

II. Limitations on Judicial Power

Yet alongside these extraordinary judicial powers, there are equally meaningful limitations on its exercise. Constitutional designers have sometimes codified restrictions on the scope of judicial authority. For instance, the Indian Constitution signals the importance of "directive principles" of policy and governance but expressly limits the justiciability of these principles, specifying that they "shall not be enforceable by any court."[8] In Albania, the Constitution prohibits the Constitutional Court from reviewing the constitutionality of a constitutional amendment on any grounds but its procedural correctness.[9] And in the United Kingdom, courts may issue no more than a mere declaration of *incompatibility* of state action—not its outright legal *invalidity*—with the European Convention of Human Rights.[10] These codified constitutional rules reflect the range of limitations that constitution-makers have expressly imposed on the powers of courts.

In this chapter, my focus is not on these kinds of codified limitations on judicial power. I focus instead on peculiar forms of self-imposed limitations on judicial power, namely those applied by courts upon themselves to avoid certain disputes despite there being no constitutional requirement for them to do so.[11] Drawing from three different jurisdictions—Canada, France, and the United States—I highlight three distinguishable techniques of judicial avoidance: remedial judicial avoidance, jurisdictional judicial avoidance, and substantive judicial avoidance.[12]

[7] See ibid. at 100–106.
[8] Constitution of India, Part IV.
[9] Constitution of Albania, art. 132.
[10] Human Rights Act 1998, c. 42, s. 4 (U.K.).
[11] This chapter complements an important article examining judicial avoidance as it relates to interinstitutional dialogue. See Erin F. Delaney, "Analyzing Avoidance: Judicial Strategy in Comparative Perspective," 66 *Duke L.J.* 1 (2016).
[12] Note that the specific cases chosen for each jurisdiction are not intended to represent a single national approach. It could well be that courts in a single jurisdiction deploy all three techniques of judicial avoidance. These three specific cases are best understood as illustrations of judicial phenomena visible in high courts around the world.

We can understand these three techniques of judicial avoidance as a species of deference. Much as courts have developed forms and doctrines of deference to guide them in determining when and how to defer to other branches of government—for instance, standards of review, tiers of judicial scrutiny, the principle of proportionality, and the margin of appreciation—courts have likewise exercised techniques of judicial avoidance when they determine it is inappropriate to resolve a legal dispute or to implement a ruling.

Before discussing in detail the three major techniques of judicial avoidance, an introductory word on each is useful to map the landscape to be canvassed in this chapter. The first technique of judicial avoidance involves judges exercising restraint in their interaction with institutional counterparts. To illustrate with an example from Canada, judges sometimes respond to a constitutional violation with a delayed remedy. Imagine that the immediate invalidation of a statute would create a serious void in law or an interregnum in the legal order. Rather than forcing political actors into these legally and politically impracticable circumstances, courts in Canada have sometimes resorted to suspended declarations of invalidity in order to afford political actors time to revise a statute into conformity with the Constitution. The idea is simple but its effect is substantial: courts declare a statute invalid but delay the coming into force of the judgment for a specific duration of time in order to give political actors the opportunity to replace the invalid law.[13] This is a form of *remedial judicial avoidance*.

We find in France a second form of self-imposed judicial restraint: *jurisdictional judicial avoidance*. Like remedial judicial avoidance, jurisdictional judicial avoidance is a choice made by courts to constrain their own powers. But unlike remedial judicial avoidance, jurisdictional judicial avoidance is not rooted in the court's concern for the dangers of a legal void or an interregnum in law, nor does it derive from the nature of what is appropriate for a court to do. Jurisdictional judicial avoidance arises instead where a court rules that it lacks the jurisdictional authority to intervene even if the dispute does indeed involve a legal dispute.[14]

A third form of judicial avoidance is evident in innovative doctrines intended to check the power that judicial supremacy entails. In the United States, for example, federal courts have articulated a series of limitations on the types of cases they will hear. Courts are doctrinally committed to declining to rule on

[13] *Reference re Manitoba Language Rights*, [1985] 1 SCR 721 ("*Manitoba Language Rights*").

[14] Conseil constitutionnel (CC) (Constitutional Council) decision No. 62-20DC, November 6, 1962, Rec. 27.

nonjusticiable matters, including those assessed to be unripe or moot, or those requiring judges to issue an advisory opinion. An additional type of dispute that federal courts in the United States will ordinarily refuse to hear are those than can be said to raise "political questions," hence the "political question doctrine" that counsels federal courts to decline to exercise their power of constitutional review. This third form of judicial avoidance may be defined as a *substantive judicial avoidance*, insofar as it is driven by the court's own evaluation of the subject-matter of claims it may appropriately resolveIn the remainder of this chapter, I will discuss three separate high court cases, one each from Canada, France, and the United States. I will suggest that two should be treated as canonical for the concept of judicial avoidance, and one as anti-canonical. On remedial judicial avoidance, the Canadian case *Reference re Manitoba Language Rights* should be treated as canonical. On jurisdictional judicial avoidance, the French case on the direct election of the president should be treated also as canonical. And on substantive judicial avoidance, the American case *Bush v. Gore* should be treated as anticanonical.[15] I will also offer reflections on a pivotal lesson in the construction of judicial power: all three distinguishable techniques of judicial avoidance can sometimes be deployed strategically to preserve or increase judicial power, not to reduce it.

III. Remedial Judicial Avoidance: A Canadian Innovation

The first illustration of judicial avoidance answers a fascinating question: "how should a court exercise its power when it invalidates the entirety of a jurisdiction's laws?" These were the circumstances confronting the Supreme Court of Canada in *Manitoba Language Rights*,[16] a case in which the Court was asked to evaluate the legality of the body of statutes passed by the Manitoba legislature. Since 1890, virtually all of the legislature's laws had been enacted in the English language alone. These unilingual laws posed a serious problem in light of constitutional rules to the contrary. Those rules, codified in the Constitution Act, 1867, require that both English and French "shall be used in the respective Records and Journals" of legislatures and moreover that laws "shall be printed and published in both those languages."[17] And so, too, the Manitoba Act, 1870, requires that both English and French "shall be used in

[15] 531 U.S. 98 (2000).
[16] See n 13.
[17] Constitution Act, 1867 (U.K.), 30 & 31 Vict., c. 3, s. 133.

the ... Records and Journals" of the Manitoba legislature and that "the Acts of the Legislature shall be printed and published in both those languages."[18] The question, then, was both stark and solemn: what happens to the rule of law in the Province of Manitoba if the Court finds all of these unilingual laws constitutionally invalid ?

The Court indeed held all laws "invalid and of no force or effect,"[19] striking down the overwhelming majority of laws in force at the time in Manitoba. The Court explained that the legislature was bound by "the manner and form of enactment of its legislation."[20] The Court moreover explained the sociological context animating these manner and form requirements of bilingualism. They are not merely suggestions for good governance, insisted the Court. They are designed to protect "the substantive rights of all Manitobans to equal access to the law in either the French or the English language."[21] These manner and form requirements are therefore mandatory rules rooted in the fundamental promise made at Confederation that English and French Canadians would be governed under their own language. As the Court explained, "the importance of language rights is grounded in the essential role that language plays in human existence, development and dignity."[22] And the responsibility to protect the linguistic minorities falls to the Court: "The judiciary is the institution charged with the duty of ensuring that the government complies with the Constitution."[23]

There were serious consequences to the Court's judgment. Issuing its ruling, without more, would have eliminated much of the legal infrastructure in the province. In the Court's own words, "the difficulty with the fact that the unilingual Acts of the Legislature of Manitoba must be declared invalid and of no force or effect is that, without going further, a legal vacuum will be created with consequent legal chaos in the Province of Manitoba."[24] The Court explained the gravity of the situation in this way:

> [Thus, to find that the unilingual laws of Manitoba are invalid and of no force or effect would mean that only laws enacted in both French and English *before 1890*, would continue to be valid, and would still be in force even if the law had purportedly been repealed or amended by a post-1890 unilingual

[18] Manitoba Act, 1870, RSC 1970, App. II, s. 23.
[19] *Manitoba Language Rights* (n 13) at 747.
[20] ibid at 744.
[21] ibid.
[22] ibid.
[23] ibid at 745.
[24] ibid at 747.

statute; matters that were not regulated by laws enacted before 1890 would now be unregulated by law, unless a pre-confederation law or the common law provided a rule.[25]

Other troubling implications would follow from such a state of legal affairs. Any public body whose creation or authorization relied on an English-only law enacted since 1890—including courts, municipalities, school boards, professional accrediting societies—would be acting, as the Court observed, "without legal authority."[26] Moreover, no rights or duties arising since 1890 could be applied without some doubt, and one could even question the legality of the composition of the Manitoba legislature.[27] Seeing these circumstances, what was the Court to do? The Court resolved that the "only appropriate resolution" was to "declare all the unilingual Acts of the Legislature of Manitoba to be invalid and of no force and effect and then to take such steps as will ensure the rule of law in the Province of Manitoba." But how would the Court manage to do both?

In solving this legal puzzle, the Canadian Supreme Court was the first in the world to use a device now known as a suspended declaration of invalidity.[28] Recognizing that "it would be impossible for all the Acts of the Manitoba Legislature to be translated, re-enacted, printed and published overnight," the Court appreciated the reality that "there will necessarily be a period of time during which it would not be possible for the Manitoba Legislature to comply with its constitutional duty" to enact all laws in conformity with the bilingualism requirement. The Court ultimately turned to theory and practice to find a solution. It landed on the doctrine of necessity as applied in Pakistan, Turkey, and the United States, which as the Court understood it stands for the proposition that "courts will recognize unconstitutional enactments as valid where a failure to do so would lead to legal chaos and thus violate the constitutional requirement of the rule of law."[29]

The Court fashioned an innovative remedy to deal with these unusual circumstances. All laws that had failed to meet the bilingualism requirement would be declared invalid but the actual invalidity of those laws would not take effect until a subsequent date sufficiently delayed to allow the Manitoba legislature properly and lawfully to re-enact its otherwise valid laws. As a consequence

[25] ibid.
[26] ibid at 748.
[27] ibid.
[28] Kent Roach, "The Judicial, Legislative and Executive Roles in Enforcing the Constitution" in Richard Albert & David R. Cameron (eds.), *Canada in the World: Comparative Perspectives on the Canadian Constitution* (Cambridge University Press, 2017) 264 at 266.
[29] ibid at 766.

of this unique remedy, "all Acts of the Manitoba Legislature which would currently be valid and of force and effect, were it not for their constitutional defect, are deemed temporarily valid and effective from the date of this judgment to the expiry of the minimum period necessary for translation, re-enactment, printing and publishing."[30] The Court was clear about future laws, however, stressing that "the Constitution requires that, from the date of this judgment, all new Acts of the Manitoba Legislature be enacted, printed and published in both French and English." Any laws passed contrary to this rule "will be invalid and of no force or effect,"[31] and will not be shielded by the Court's innovative remedy fashioned to preserve the rule of law in Manitoba.

IV. Jurisdictional Judicial Avoidance: A French Concession

The second illustration of judicial avoidance comes from France. In one of the most politically charged constitutional cases in the Fifth French Republic, the Constitutional Council interpreted the Constitution as denying it jurisdiction, and the Council ultimately chose to impose limits on the exercise of its own power.[32]

The controversy was triggered by the design of the French Constitution. At its beginnings, in 1958, the Constitution did not authorize voters to elect the president in a direct vote. Instead, the Constitution created an electoral college to select the president in a mediated vote.[33] The electoral college was composed of roughly 80,000 persons, including parliamentarians, mayors, municipal councilors and other officials,[34] each of whom would cast a vote for president.

The president at the time, Charles de Gaulle, had been elected by the electoral college. But despite his victory in this representative election, he wanted to discard this mediated vote in favor of a direct election by the French people themselves. He therefore tried mightily to persuade the Parliament to introduce a constitutional amendment to replace the electoral college. But his campaign of persuasion failed. Parliament refused to agree to propose an amendment to create a directly elected presidency.

[30] ibid at 767.
[31] ibid at 768.
[32] Conseil constitutionnel (CC) (Constitutional Council) decision No. 62-20DC, November 6, 1962, Rec. 27.
[33] constitution of France, art. 6 (1958) (later amended in 1962).
[34] Stanley H. Hoffmann, "The French Constitution of 1958: I. The Final Text and Its Prospects," 53 *Am. Pol. Sci. Rev.* 332, 342 (1963).

Confronting resistance from an uncooperative Parliament, de Gaulle pressed ahead with an innovative plan—a plan that some argued was unconstitutional.[35] He went over the heads of parliamentarians, directly to the people in a referendum, to propose the creation of a directly elected presidency. This was an unusual act because the Constitution does not authorize constitutional amendment in this way. The Constitution permits an amendment only where the president or a member of Parliament initiates an amendment in Parliament,[36] after which both chambers of the Parliament must pass identical versions of the amendment bill within certain time limits before the proposal may proceed to ratification in a national referendum.[37]

President de Gaulle therefore skipped Parliament altogether and went straight to the voters. Although the Constitution's amendment rules did not authorize his irregular procedure for a constitutional amendment,[38] the Constitution did give the president the power to hold a referendum.[39] De Gaulle invoked this authority to hold a referendum, though he unilaterally transformed his referendum-proposal power into a referendum-amendment power, in the process departing from the Constitution's amendment rules and simultaneously undermining Parliament. Parliament was displeased with De Gaulle's irregular amendment maneuver for two reasons: first, Parliament would be shunned to the sidelines in the constitutional amendment process—a process that makes parliamentary approval a necessary condition of success;[40] and, second, were the referendum-amendment somehow to prove successful, Parliament would see the president win a direct mandate from the people, a powerful claim that the existing design of the electoral college had at the time denied to the president.[41]

The people ultimately approved de Gaulle's referendum amendment.[42] But the referendum vote did not end the story. The Senate President challenged the constitutionality of the referendum amendment at the Constitutional Council.[43] He contended that the law was neither properly a constitutional act

[35] See François Mitterrand, *Le coup d'état permanent* (Plon, 1964).
[36] Constitution of France, art. 89(1).
[37] ibid. There is only one expressly codified exception to this procedure: an amendment proposal need not be ratified by a national referendum where the president chooses to submit a government amendment bill to Parliament convened in Congress, in which case the proposal will become official if it is approved by a three-fifths vote of parliamentarians. ibid at art. 89(3).
[38] Constitution of France, art. 89(1).
[39] ibid at art. 11.
[40] ibid at art. 89(1).
[41] Henry W. Ehrmann, "Direct Democracy in France," 57 *Am. Pol. Sci. Rev.* 883, 883 (1963).
[42] Richard Albert, Malkhaz Nakashidze, & Tarik Olcay, "The Formalist Resistance to Unconstitutional Constitutional Amendments" (2019) 70 *Hastings L.J.* 639 at 661–665.
[43] Conseil constitutionnel (CC) (Constitutional Council) decision No. 62-20DC, November 6, 1962, Rec. 27.

nor an organic law, but rather just an ordinary law, which would mean that the Council could intervene to invalidate the referendum amendment.[44] The Senate President argued moreover that the law's enactment by referendum did not shield it from review by the Council.[45] A referendum, he argued, should in all cases respect the rules in the Constitution.[46] And, here, in his view, the referendum had been held in violation of the Constitution's amendment rules.

The Constitutional Council rejected the Senate President's challenge by a vote of six to four.[47] In its judgment, the Council evaluated its own jurisdictional authority. It explained that its power was circumscribed by the text of the Constitution and also by the organic law on the Constitutional Council.[48] In its short decision, the Council distinguished "direct expression[s] of national sovereignty" from "activities of public authorities."[49] The former, according to the Council, have a higher priority than the latter, and there is no basis for the Council to intervene when the people have spoken.[50] What mattered for the Council was not the content of the referendum but the very holding of the referendum. The Council declared that it had no jurisdiction to review a referendum result: neither the Constitution nor the organic law gave the Council the power to review the constitutionality of a "bill adopted by the French people by way of referendum."[51] The Council dismissed the constitutional challenge, holding that it did not have the jurisdiction to deny the expressed will of the people. The referendum result was therefore treated as valid. French presidents have been elected by direct popular vote ever since.

V. Substantive Judicial Avoidance: An American Peculiarity

A third form of judicial avoidance emerges from sensitive contexts where courts determine that they should refrain from getting involved because the disputes present what courts characterize as "political questions" inappropriate for judicial resolution. The best jurisdictional expositor of this form of substantive judicial avoidance is the United States. Federal courts are bound by precedent not to hear constitutional cases that raise what amounts to a "political

[44] ibid.
[45] ibid.
[46] ibid.
[47] John Bell, *French Constitutional Law* (Oxford University Press, 1992) 153.
[48] Conseil constitutionnel (CC) (Constitutional Council) decision No. 62-20DC, November 6, 1962, Rec. 27.
[49] ibid.
[50] ibid.
[51] ibid.

question." And yet the Supreme Court of the United States has ignored its own precedent and inserted itself into the most highly charged political question of all—the election of a president. The Court's violation of its own political question doctrine, in *Bush v. Gore*,[52] should be treated as an anticanonical case.

The Court explained forty years prior, in *Baker v. Carr*, why it should decline to intervene in constitutional disputes that raise a political question best resolved by non-judicial actors.[53] The reason, the Court wrote, is "primarily a function of the separation of powers."[54] The Court fashioned this doctrine in response to the concern that, were it to decide each and every dispute, it sometimes could risk intruding into the constitutionally delegated authority of a co-equal branch of government. But this concern can go only so far. After all, while it is true that other branches have their own powers, the Court has its own responsibilities, the most important being to ensure respect for the boundaries of the Constitution. That responsibility entails monitoring the conduct of other branches—a responsibility that may pull the Court into the sphere of politics.

In *Baker*, the Court made clear that choosing whether to resolve a dispute is "a delicate exercise in constitutional interpretation, and is a responsibility of this Court as ultimate interpreter of the Constitution."[55] The Court acknowledged the difficulty of the task but conceded that its mandate will inevitably intersect with politics in some form. The Court stressed an important distinction: the political question doctrine "is one of 'political questions,' not one of 'political cases.'"[56] After all, many constitutional cases that reach the docket of federal courts involve some form of politics, even narrowly defined. Surely courts cannot decline to hear these cases only because politics are somehow implicated, if only tangentially. As the Court has explained, even if a dispute involves politics, the duty of the Court is to ensure respect for the Constitution. In the Court's own words, "the courts cannot reject as 'no law suit' a *bona fide* controversy as to whether some action denominated 'political' exceeds constitutional authority."[57]

The question therefore presents itself: where is the line separating the Court's authority in law from its authority in politics? Put another way, what counts as a political question? According to the Court in *Baker*, there are six general

[52] 531 U.S. 98 (2000).
[53] *Baker v. Carr*, 369 U.S. 186 (1962).
[54] ibid at 210.
[55] ibid at 211.
[56] ibid at 217.
[57] ibid.

categories of cases that show how and when the political question doctrine applies—six kinds of disputes in which the Court should not intervene:

> Prominent on the surface of any case held to involve a political question is found a textually demonstrable constitutional commitment of the issue to a coordinate political department; or a lack of judicially discoverable and manageable standards for resolving it; or the impossibility of deciding without an initial policy determination of a kind clearly for non judicial discretion; or the impossibility of a court's undertaking independent resolution without expressing lack of the respect due coordinate branches of government; or an unusual need for unquestioning adherence to a political decision already made; or the potentiality of embarrassment from multifarious pronouncements by various departments on one question.[58]

These six categories are certainly not mutually exclusive. There is overlap among them. But collectively they convey the principal point of the political question doctrine: that courts should exercise prudence when faced with political matters best resolved by political actors themselves.

The Court disregarded this crucial precedent in a constroversy involving the election of the president of the United States—a dispute that, for many, raises a paradigm instance of a political question.[59] At bottom, the issue in *Bush v. Gore* involved whether and how to count ballots in the presidential election of 2000. In choosing to answer the question, the Court traveled onto terrain that it had itself described in *Baker* as a nonjusticiable "political question." Recall the first of six political question limitations on the Court's power: "Prominent on the surface of any case held to involve a political question is found a textually demonstrable constitutional commitment of the issue to a coordinate political department. …"[60] In this case, there was a relevant textual commitment of power to the Congress. Article II, Section I, Clause 3 enumerates each of the steps involved in how Congress is to tabulate the votes for president, and it moreover provides a mechanism to resolve disputes in the event of a disagreement. The text of the Constitution delegates to Congress the task of resolving electoral disputes like these, and yet the Court made the decision itself, in the process violating its own holding in *Baker* that federal courts should refrain from entering the political thicket where the constitutional text is clear that the

[58] ibid.
[59] 531 U.S. 98 (2000).
[60] *Baker* (n 53) at 217.

responsibility for resolving the dispute has been assigned to another branch of government.

The Court's decision to ignore its own political question doctrine was made even more problematic by the margin of decision as well as by the nature of its holding. First, although the Court's judgment was denominated "*per curiam*," meaning "by the Court," it was not in fact supported by the entire court. The remedy portion of the judgment won the support of only a bare majority of conservative justices. The optics could not have been worse: five conservative judges ruling in favor of the conservative candidate for president, while the four liberal judges ruled in favor of the liberal candidate for president. These circumstances are precisely the ones for which the political question doctrine was created. It could have been deployed here to protect the standing of the Court and to shield it from both the perception and reality of its politicization. Second, the Court ultimately held that its intervention in this case was warranted to evaluate the equal protection claim that disparate standards had been applied across electoral jurisdictions to otherwise similar facts. Yet in evaluating the equal protection claim, the Court seems expressly to have withheld precedential value to the holding, declaring that "our consideration is limited to the present circumstances, for the program of equal protection in election processes generally presents many complexities."[61] The holding, therefore, will have no application beyond these narrow facts. This irregularity in decision making should raise a red flag about the motivations behind this ruling.[62]

VI. Strategic Judicial Avoidance

Courts do not always choose to avoid exercising their own power out of a genuine concern for the proper judicial role. Courts often choose to engage in judicial avoidance in order to extricate themselves from a battle they are unlikely to win. Returning to *Marbury*, recall that Chief Justice Marshall asserts

[61] *Bush* (n 59) at 109.

[62] Some have defended the judgment in *Bush v. Gore*. Their defenses generally fall in one of three claims: the Court was more competent than the Congress to resolve the dispute, see Richard A. Posner, *Breaking the Deadlock: The 2000 Election, the Constitution, and the Court* (Princeton University Press, 2000); the Court was correct to intervene to save the country from chaos and perhaps even constitutional crisis, see, e.g., William Safire, "The Coming Together," *N.Y. Times*, December 14, 2000; and the Court was correct to honor the federalist framework of American elections, see, e.g., Richard A. Epstein, "'In such Manner as the Legislature Thereof May Direct': The Outcome in *Bush v. Gore* Defended," 67, *U. Chi. L. Rev.* 613 (2001). Each reflects a distinctly minority view that does not disturb the core of the claim that *Bush v. Gore* should be seen as an anticanonical case.

the power of the Court to say what the law is, even if that entails declaring that acts of the executive or legislative branches are unconstitutional. Yet even though Marshall concludes that Marbury has a right to his judicial commission, he does not order James Madison to deliver it, holding in the end that Marbury had improperly filed his case as an original action at the Supreme Court seeking an order compelling Madison to deliver the commission.

Imagine instead that Marshall had ordered Madison to deliver that commission. There was a serious risk that Madison would quite simply have refused to obey the order of the Court. And this would have been devastating for the young court—recently established a few years prior by the new constitution of 1787[63]—as it tried to establish itself as a co-equal government branch despite having "no influence over either the sword or the purse,"[64] in the words of Alexander Hamilton.

The same dynamics were at play in Canada and France, in 1985 and 1962, respectively. In Canada, the Charter was just three years old when the Court decided to fashion its innovative remedy to save the Manitoba legislative from seeing its vast body of law rendered void and inoperative at a moment's notice. Had the Court exercised the full measure of its authority to nullify the entirety of Manitoba's unconstitutional laws, there is a risk that Manitoba and the rest of the country would have reacted with incredulity at the Court's disconnection from the realities of governance. How could Manitoba continue to govern its jurisdiction, under the umbrella of the Constitution of Canada, with the overwhelming majority of its laws rendered unenforceable? Such an irresponsible ruling would have undermined the Court at a time when much of the country feared that the Charter had granted it extraordinary powers that it could not exercise responsibly.

In France, just four years after the coming into force of its 1958 Constitution, the Council bowed to the realities of the political context when it invoked the doctrine of jurisdictional judicial avoidance to refuse to rule on the constitutionality of De Gaulle's referendum. It is unclear what other option the Council had before it other than to declare that it had no jurisdiction to disturb the expressed will of the people. De Gaulle had already shown his willingness to challenge constitutional actors in France, having gone over the heads of parliamentarians even in the face of charges that he was acting unconstitutionally. Why would he not defy the Council, too? Recognizing that it would not win a

[63] Constitution of the United States, art. III.

[64] The Federalist no. 78 (Alexander Hamilton) in Jacob E. Cooke (ed.), *The Federalist* (Wesleyan University Press, 1961) at 523.

battle in the public forum against de Gaulle, the Council declared itself without jurisdiction to decide the matter, simultaneously shielding itself from the risk of de Gaulle's non-compliance with a potentially adverse order while also reinforcing the foundational principle of popular sovereignty in the French constitutional order.

VII. Conclusion: The Virtues of Judicial Avoidance

There is good reason for courts to avoid exercising their power when the circumstances warrant, even if there are no extenuating political circumstances as there quite clearly were in the Canadian and French cases—and especially where the public perception of judicial involvement could lead to the conclusion that naked politics have motivated the judicial decision, as could be argued in relation to *Bush v. Gore*.[65]

Alexander Bickel long ago called for courts to take a posture of modesty in the face of charged policy and political contexts.[66] Bickel feared that courts would exceed their authority and in turn "dwarf the political capacity of the people."[67] He therefore encouraged courts to deploy "passive virtues" [68]—for example, doctrines of ripeness and mootness, and denials of *certiorari*—ultimately to avoid intervening in matters of high public salience that straddle the boundary between law and politics.

There is much to commend an approach of judicial minimalism in judicial decision making. Judicial minimalism recognizes that, to borrow from Cass Sunstein, "sometimes the best decision is [for judges] to leave things undecided."[69] This theory of judicial minimalism counsels courts to "proceed[] in the away that is catalytic rather than preclusive, and that is closely attuned to the fact that courts are participants in an elaborate system of democratic deliberation."[70] As Sunstein has suggested, judging should where possible send the decision back to political actors and invite them to make "deliberative judgements by democratically accountability bodies"[71] in a way that "trigger[s] or

[65] N 59.

[66] Alexander M. Bickel, *The Least Dangerous Branch: The Supreme Court at the Bar of Politics* (2nd edn., Yale University Press, 1986).

[67] ibid at 169 (quoting J. B. Thayer, *John Marshall* (Houghton Mifflin, 1901)).

[68] ibid 111–198.

[69] Cass R. Sunstein, *One Case at a Time: Judicial Minimalism on the Supreme Court* (Harvard University Press, 1999) 263.

[70] ibid.

[71] ibid at 26.

improve[s] processes of democratic deliberation [by] provid[ing] spurs and prods to promote democratic deliberation itself."[72]

> A minimalist court settles the case before it, but it leaves many things undecided. It is alert to the existence of reasonable disagreement in a heterogeneous society. It knows that there is much that it does not know; it is intensely aware of its own limitations. It seeks to decide cases on narrow grounds. It avoids clear rules and final resolutions. Alert to the problem of unanticipated consequences, it sees itself as part of a system of democratic deliberation; it attempts to promote the democratic ideals of participation, deliberation, and responsiveness. It allows continued space for democratic reflection from Congress and the states.[73]

This modest approach to judicial power advances democratic constitutionalism by promoting popular choice, either directly by the people or indirectly through their elected representatives. It moreover advances "democratic goals, not simply by leaving things undecided but also by allowing opinion to coalesce over time and by spurring processes of democratic deliberation."[74] The larger goal of judicial minimalism is to prevent "excessive judicial intervention into political domains."[75]

Of course, some jurisdictions will require courts to exercise a prominent role that exceeds what is contemplated by a posture of judicial minimalism. Sometimes the constitution itself will require it, sometimes the political context will require it, and sometimes it will be understood that courts can and should exercise a more dominant place than is otherwise customary. Yet there should be a baseline expectation for how courts are to exercise their authority. Judges should be attentive both to the risks to their own power inherent in challenging the other branches of government, and also to the reality that they hold power in trust, delegated by the constitution, to act in the name of the makers of the higher law as its interpreters, not as its authors or amenders.

[72] ibid at 27.
[73] ibid at ix–x.
[74] ibid at 259.
[75] ibid at 28. For a discussion of judicial minimalism in the context of constitutional amendment, see Richard Albert, *Constitutional Amendments: Making, Breaking, and Changing Constitutions* (Oxford University Press, 2019).

PART IV

BEYOND THE STATE AND THE INDIVIDUAL

26

The City as an Anti-Canonical Concept in Constitutional Law (and Recent Attempts to Change That)

Ran Hirschl[*]

I. A State-Based Constitutional Canon

Urban agglomeration is one of the most significant demographic and geopolitical phenomena of our time. The figures are striking. In 1900, about 150 million people, representing fewer than 10% of the world population at that time, lived in cities. As at 2021, 4.5 billion people, or 57% of the world population, lived in cities. In other words, within the last century, the world's urban population has increased nearly thirtyfold. This trend is projected to continue. By 2050, 70% of the world's population will reside in cities. The majority of the growth is in the Global South; but the Global North has seen its fair share of change, also at accelerating rates. Projections suggest that megacities of 50 million or even 100 million inhabitants will emerge by the end of the century, mostly in the Global South, with cities such as Lagos, Kinshasa, Dar-es-Salaam, Mumbai, and Karachi leading the way. In light of this ever-accelerating urbanization, it is hard to think of a more glaring omission from the customary canon of constitutional thought than the city. In that conventional epistemological consensus, cities, home to the majority of mankind, ubiquitous and crucial to every aspect of twenty-first-century society, culture, economics, and politics, are virtually absent.

As I have shown elsewhere, the constitutional blind spot with respect to urbanization and the metropolis is baffling.[1] Pertinent legal discourse about cities

* David R. Cameron Distinguished Professor in Law and Politics, University of Toronto. Parts of this chapter draw on materials included in Ran Hirschl, *City, State: Constitutionalism and the Megacity* (Oxford University Press, 2020). The author thanks the volume editors for their helpful comments on an earlier draft, as well as the Alexander von Humboldt Foundation for the generous support enabling the research for this chapter.

[1] Ran Hirschl, *City, State: Constitutionalism and the Megacity* (Oxford University Press, 2020).

Ran Hirschl, *The City as an Anti-Canonical Concept in Constitutional Law (and Recent Attempts to Change That)* In: *Global Canons in an Age of Contestation.* Edited by: Sujit Choudhry, Michaela Hailbronner, and Mattias Kumm, Oxford University Press. © Ran Hirschl 2024. DOI: 10.1093/9780191956942.003.0026

occurs largely within the confines of administrative law or municipal law, with occasional excursions to so-called global law, but seldom in constitutional law.[2]

Even within scholarship or jurisprudence on federalism—presumably the most relevant aspect of constitutional law to city status—the oversight of cities is evident.[3] Respect for subsidiary levels of government, for local autonomy, and for place-based difference in general is perhaps the key feature of federalism as a theoretical concept and as a practical mode of political and constitutional government. Yet despite federalism's embedded predisposition towards subsidiarity and regionalism, cities are often excluded from the purview of contemporary federalism, both in theory and in practice.

As Heather Gerken writes of the American context: "Federalism scholars have typically confined themselves to states, the only subnational institutions that possess sovereignty."[4] A similar trend is evident elsewhere in federalism scholarship, where the Westphalian, state-centered framework continues to dominate the discussion, with its notion of sovereign territorial states whose boundaries took shape well before the current "urban era", and that are divided along ethnic, religious, and linguistic cleavages and reflecting conventional notions of nationhood, peoplehood, and/or historical patterns of conquest and settlement. In this conceptual universe, cities—home to the majority of mankind—are often overlooked.

Whereas a large number of constitutions recognize local government, cities are seldom construed as an equal partner or as an adequate order of government within the national constitutional scheme. In some countries, notably the United States, Canada, and Australia, cities remain a non-entity, constitutionally speaking, and are subject to near-complete subnational control. What is more, most constitutions that do recognize local government fail to distinguish between small settlements and megacities—all are often referred to generically as "municipalities." But size matters a great deal in this context. The

[2] A few examples of such global law accounts are: Yishai Blank, "Localism in the New Global Legal Order Symposium: Comparative Visions of Global Public Order (Part 2)," *Harvard International Law Journal* 47 (2006): 263–282; Gerald E. Frug and David J. Barron, "International Local Government Law," *The Urban Lawyer* 38 (2006): 1–62; Helmut P. Aust, "Shining Cities on the Hill? The Global City, Climate Change, and International Law," *European Journal of International Law* 26 (2015): 255–278; Janne Nijman, "The Urban Pushback: International Law as an Instrument of Cities," *Proceedings of the ASIL Annual Meeting* 113 (2019): 119–123.

[3] As with any generalization of this kind, there are notable exceptions. A few examples include Erika Arban ed., *Cities in Federal Constitutional Theory* (Oxford University Press, 2022); Daniel Weinstock, "Cities and Federalism," in James E. Fleming and Jacob T. Levy (eds.), *Federalism & Subsidiarity: NOMOS LV* (New York University Press, 2014), 259–290; Loren King, "Cities, Subsidiarity and Federalism," in James E. Fleming and Jacob T. Levy (eds.), *Federalism & Subsidiarity: NOMOS LV* (New York University Press, 2014), 291–331.

[4] Heather Gerken, "Foreword: Federalism All the Way Down," *Harvard Law Review* 124 (2010): 4–74, at 21.

challenges that face large metropolises regarding infrastructure and service provision, transportation, housing, immigration, education, public health, environmental protection, and the accommodation and management of the super-diversity that is typical of modern urban life, are markedly different than the governance challenges faced by small villages in the countryside. The lumping together of the village and the megacity reveals a lapse in constitutional thought about cities. More generally, this blind spot suggests that the spatial dimension of canonical constitutional thought is under-theorized and appears increasingly detached from the terrain-changing (pun intended) processes of urban agglomeration.

While geographers, sociologists, economists, and political theorists have devoted tremendous intellectual energy to cities and to the urban condition more generally, one would be hard-pressed to name more than a handful of contemporary constitutional treaties devoted to the city and its place in twenty-first-century government. The few constitutional accounts that do exist focus on single jurisdictions (often the U.S.) rather than on urbanization and cities as a universal phenomenon posing a general constitutional challenge.[5] Despite the tremendous renaissance of comparative constitutional law, very few (if any) comparative studies consider constitutional innovation and stalemate from the standpoint of city-state relations. In fact, the metropolis is virtually non-existent in comparative constitutional law, constitutional design, and constitutional thought, and is quietly accepted as something fully subsumed within existing federalism and "separation of powers" doctrinal schemes. *The Oxford Handbook of Comparative Constitutional Law*,[6] for example, is a major state-of-the-field collection that includes over fifty chapters spread over a thousand pages. Not a single chapter addresses the urban challenge—not even in passing, let alone in significant detail. A similar silence resounds in virtually all other definitive handbooks, companions, and textbooks on comparative constitutional law.[7]

Why the constitutional blind spot? The near-complete constitutional silence concerning cities—whether in constitutional texts, jurisprudence, or scholarship—can be attributed to a number of factors. First, historical

[5] See, e.g., Gerald Frug, "The City as a Legal Concept," *Harvard Law Review* 93 (1980):1057–1154; Richard C. Schragger, *City Power* (Oxford University Press, 2016).

[6] Michel Rosenfeld and András Sajó, eds., *The Oxford Handbook of Comparative Constitutional Law* (Oxford University Press, 2012).

[7] See, e.g., Mark Tushnet, Thoams Fleiner, and Cheryl Saunders, eds., *Routledge Handbook of Constitutional Law* (Routledge, 2013); Vicki Jackson and Mark Tushnet, *Comparative Constitutional Law*, 3rd edn. (Foundation Press, 2014); Roger Masterman and Robert Schütze, eds., *The Cambridge Companion to Comparative Constitutional Law* (Cambridge University Press, 2019).

inertia: for centuries, the state has been the predominant constitutional and sovereign unit. By 1800, the early-modern state and its overseas colonies had replaced the city-state as the dominant political unit in Europe. Subsequent political paths converged, with few exceptions, upon a single form of medium-sized, centralized state, with the later addition of federalism as a joint-governance pact between subnational administration and a national government. It was during this phase of the evolution of city-state relations that substantial urban communities lost much of their previous autonomy and status; states sought to establish their monopoly over the legitimate exercise of physical force and authority, enhance their influence on economic and social life, and, most importantly, control "who gets what, when and how" within their respective territories. They also laid stronger and stronger claims to be the focus of popular loyalty and collective identity. As state-centered bureaucracies and governance structures emerged, cities were increasingly perceived as mere components of nation-states and as cogs in national economies, however dominant their contribution.[8] As Gerald Frug showed, in his seminal 1980 *Harvard Law Review* article, the city came to be conceived as a powerless "creature of the state"—an entity authorized by the state to solve purely local problems. In that process, Frug argues, "it is not simply that cities have become totally subject to state control—although that itself demonstrates their powerlessness—but also that cities have lost the elements of association and economic strength that had formerly enabled them to play an important part in the development of Western society."[9] As the statist project of national constitutions (both centrist and federalist) achieved prominence, the effect on the constitutional imagination with respect to political geography and spatial autonomy was immediate and complete. This led to a dearth of creative thinking concerning city governance.

Second is what Ayelet Shachar and I have elsewhere termed "spatial statism"—the notion that public law, through its spatial ordering, helps to sustain a state-oriented locus and focus of sovereign control of its territory in the face of competing forces, real or perceived.[10] When it comes to constitutional control of cities, where the state remains the master of the domain, that claim certainly holds true. Specifically, as Nick Barber observes, "[C]onstitutionalism is a doctrine that is derived from, or at least tightly connected to, the state. It applies to those creating states and, also, to those who act within and upon the structures of the state."[11] By their very nature, national constitutions reflect

[8] Peter J. Taylor, *World City Network: A Global Urban Analysis* (Routledge, 2004), 15.

[9] See Frug (n 5) at 1119–1120.

[10] Ran Hirschl and Ayelet Shachar, "Spatial Statism," *International Journal of Constitutional Law* 17 (2019): 387–438.

[11] N. W. Barber, *The Principles of Constitutionalism* (Oxford University Press, 2018), 11.

an overwhelmingly statist outlook that often conceptualizes cities as "creatures of the state," fully submerged within a Westphalian constitutional outlook and framework, and assigned limited administrative local governance authority. Akin to its agnostic (at best) approach toward other non-statist territorial and jurisdictional claims for greater autonomy (e.g. by indigenous populations), the statist constitutional order is not keen on voluntarily granting cities extended authority.

Third, from a statist point of view, large cities can serve as nurseries for potentially unruly radicalization, which in turn may lead to an undermining of state power and possibly even to political revolution. Large cities are consistently more diverse and socially progressive than other parts of the country. By their very nature, such cities are densely populated and are home to critical masses of people. They facilitate close human interaction and feature public spaces where large crowds can easily congregate, allowing for the rapid spread of ideas that may be politically or socially destabilizing. Cities, in particular capital cities, are home to important government buildings, national monuments, and media outlets that provide concrete targets for protestors; the popular capture of these emblems of power has both practical and symbolic meaning. As street warfare in Hong Kong, mass demonstrations in Tahrir Square, widespread protests in the streets of Santiago de Chile, or the riots in American cities following the killing of George Floyd suggest, the city features a potentially explosive combination of people, ideas, and spatial conditions. The result is that, from a statist point of view, the city is best kept in check.

A fourth reason for the general constitutional silence on cities and urban agglomeration more generally is constitutional rigidity. By their very nature, constitutions are hard to change; they create a systemic state of path dependence. Constitutional jurisprudence and constitutional commentary often follow suit in reflecting the existing constitutional zeitgeist. Many constitutional orders in the so-called Global North were adopted before the current trend of urban agglomeration reached its zenith in the latter half of the twentieth century. What is more, by structuring political representation around national and subnational constituent units, and by making the costs of constitutional change significant, these established constitutional orders create considerable disincentives for incumbent power-holders to enhance cities' constitutional status.

There may be other reasons too. The stalemate may also reflect the fact that cities, unlike capital, are fixed in place; this anchoring spatial factor means that cities have no credible "exit" or "capital flight" options and are therefore limited in their bargaining power. Additionally, large cities tend to be culturally diverse, cosmopolitan, and socially progressive—these facts often put cities at odds with the worldviews and policy preferences of central governments or of voters in semi-urban and rural areas. As a result of these trends, cities—by far the most common form of modern life and home to the vast majority of humanity—are seldom featured in conventional constitutional thought or constitutional practice.

In the remainder of this chapter, I consider three notable attempts to break away from this blind spot by inserting the city, and the urban condition more generally, into mainstream constitutional discourse: (i) Henry Lefebvre's intriguing yet abstract "right to the city" and its difficult operationalization in so-called "human rights cities"; (ii) the constitutionalization of city status in South Africa's constitution (1996)—the most successful attempt to date to grant constitutional status to cities; and (iii) the constitutional transformation of Mexico City (2017) from a federal district to an autonomous state through a large-scale exercise of constitutional crowdsourcing. While novel experimentation in constitutionalizing city status has taken place in a few other settings and contexts, these three examples represent some of the most significant attempts to date to introduce cities into mainstream constitutional discourse. That these novel and daring changes remain largely overlooked by (and indeed mostly unknown to) mainstream constitutional thought attests to the intellectual path dependence and embedded statist outlook that characterizes much of that enterprise's unofficial canon.

II. Lefebvre's "Right to the City"

Arguably the most important conceptual innovation of the last half-century concerning the normative foundations of city and city dwellers' rights is the *right to the city*, introduced in the late 1960s by French philosopher Henri Lefebvre in his groundbreaking book *Le droit à la ville*.[12] Lefebvre's right to the city emphasizes the spatial and political uniqueness of the city; it emanates from the urban condition itself, not from the application of a general constitutional right to urban realities. Befitting its anticanonical status, this potentially transformative work was not translated into English until 1996, after which it quickly became a well-known work among urban theorists. However, with very few exceptions (one of which, the Constitution of Brazil 1988, I discuss

[12] Lefebvre's original work was published in 1968. It first appeared in English in 1996. See Henri Lefebvre, "The Right to the City," in Eleonore Kofman and Elizabeth Lebas, eds., *Writings on Cities* (Blackwell Publishers, 1996), 63–184.

later in the chapter), Lefebvre's right to the city has remained outside the purview of canonical constitutional discourse, and is seldom, if ever, invoked in constitutional theory, design, or jurisprudence.

Unlike classical Marxism, which saw urbanization as a byproduct of industrialization, Lefebvre conceptualized the urban space as a distinct political field and space of power. He argued that the tendency towards "complete urbanization of society" preceded industrialization, and that it has gone on "to impose itself throughout modernity," driving social change, class struggle, and reification of advanced capitalism differently than the exploitative labor relations in factories, mines, or chains of production described by Marx and Engels.[13]

Lefebvre did not only conceptualize urban space as a political field or sphere of power; he also offers normative grounds for restructuring the power relations that underlie urban space, and calls for a transfer of control from capital and the state to urban inhabitants.[14] Conceptually, he argues that the right to the city is the right to "urban life, to renewed centrality, to places of encounter and exchange, to life rhythms and time uses, enabling the full and complete usage of ... moments and places."[15] The context for Lefebvre's formulation was his vision—in the spirit of the neo-Marxist tradition of the late 1960s—of city inhabitants incrementally reclaiming space in the city through enhanced communal interface, so that a web of social interactions could form between people and ultimately trump the social atomism and alienation brought about by advanced capitalism. Yet Lefebvre never fully elaborated on the concrete meaning of the right to the city. Over the last half-century, philosophers and political theorists have been offering various interpretations of Lefebvre's abstract formulation. As Margaret Kohn astutely observes, that the exact meaning of the term remains hard to pin down is due in part to the broad interpretive literature itself, the evolution in Lefebvre's own formulation of the concept, and the tension between Lefebvre's historical-materialist critique of urban power relations and his utopian vision of urban renewal.[16] And so, its theoretical significance notwithstanding, Lefebvre's right to the city has remained without much concrete constitutional operationalization. It remains commonly overlooked by constitutional theorists, drafters. and jurists alike, many of whom are not

[13] Bianca Tavolari, "The Right to the City: Conceptual Transformations and Urban Struggles," *Revista Direito e Práxis* 11 (2020): 470–492.

[14] Mark Purcell, "Citizenship and the right to the global city: reimagining the capitalist world order," International Journal of Urban and Regional Research 27 (2003): 564–590.

[15] See Lefebvre (n 12) 178.

[16] Margaret Kohn, *The Death and Life of the Urban Commonwealth* (Oxford University Press, 2016), 177–178.

even aware of Lefebvre's work on the right to the city and its various meanings and interpretations.

In recent years, cities worldwide have started to look for creative ways to materialize the right to the city in alternative ways. While lacking formal standing in international law, international city and mayoral networks have formed around an array of common goals—from joining the U.N. Habitat program, to vowing to implement the Paris Agreement, to demanding representation at global and pan-European policymaking forums concerning the refugee crisis. Meanwhile, progressive cities and city leaders have assumed important roles in key policy areas, such as public housing, education, undocumented migration, and climate change. A number of cities, mainly in North America and Europe, have declared themselves "sanctuary cities," often in defiance of national anti-migrant policies, in order to provide city residents, including undocumented migrants, access to essential services.

Another intriguing path of urban self-empowerment along the lines of Henri Lefebvre's right to the city, is found in the concept of "urban citizenship," often given effect through city issuance of identification cards or residence certificates that allow their holders access to local public services. From a normative angle, political theorists such as Avner de-Shalit and Rainer Bauböck have advanced an intriguing notion of urban citizenship (or "city-zenship"), envisioned as an alternative or as a complement to extant models of state-based membership.[17] While such ideas remain largely theoretical, in practice, several American (e.g. New York, San Francisco, Philadelphia, and Chicago) and European cities (e.g. Paris, Amsterdam, Madrid) have introduced municipal identification card systems that provide cardholders, including undocumented migrants, with formal identification, as well as access to essential services such as public schooling, libraries, and public health facilities.

The issuance of such municipal identity cards, in theory and in practice, are certainly not an inconsequential development. At the very least, they plant the seeds for building a distinct urban identity, separate from the national equivalent. However, in the vast majority of instances, they affect neither the cardholders' nor the issuing cities' constitutional status or standing. In fact, the entire notion of a distinct "urban citizenship," either as an alternative to national citizenship or even as complementary to it, runs up against the very

[17] See, e.g., Avner de-Shalit, *Cities and Immigration: Political and Moral Dilemmas in the New Era of Migration* (Oxford University Press, 2018); Rainer Bauböck, "Reinventing Urban Citizenship," *Citizenship Studies* 7 (2003): 137–158. See also Murray Bookchin, *The Rise of Urbanization and the Decline of Citizenship* (Sierra Club Books, 1987).

conceptualization of modern statehood and the statist outlook of its constitutional order.

Arguably, the most significant of the self-empowerment efforts by cities is the so-called "human rights cities" trend, which sees cities promoting and implementing various human rights protections at the municipal level, mainly through close adherence to international human rights standards in city policies and municipal legislation.[18] This trend has been seen to reflect the proliferation of human rights discourse and human rights regimes beyond the state. Human rights city initiatives may be driven by principled motives such as city leaders' genuine commitment to human rights, or by cities' or mayors' interests in fostering their reputation, nationally or internationally, as inclusive and socially progressive polities. It may also simply reflect a question of scale: cities are perhaps better suited to enforce human rights commitments than the very large and often detached state apparatus. Either way, the hope driving the human rights cities trend is that cities can and will "deliver where nation states have failed,"[19] ideally leading to "a new urban utopia: a place where human rights strive to guide urban life."[20]

These developments, embryonic as they are, may have significant symbolic, educational, and at times practical, significance. They signal a city's genuine commitment to international human rights standards as well as to an inclusive, socially progressive public policy agenda. Such city charters may also have some self-determination effects by signaling the community's commitment to a shared set of values. Nevertheless, the real legal or constitutional effect of such human rights city charters is unclear at best. In most instances, city charters can't ground legal claims against states or central governments, and they seldom if ever replace or operate in lieu of polity-wide constitutional guarantees of pertinent rights and entitlements.[21] The compliance and enforcement

[18] On the scope, potential, and challenges of the "human rights cities" trend, see Barbara Oomen, Martha F. Davis, and Michele Grigolo, eds., *Global Urban Justice: The Rise of Human Rights Cities* (Cambridge University Press, 2016); Barbara Oomen, "Human Rights Cities: The Politics of Bringing Human Rights Home to the Local Level" in Jeff Handmaker and Karin Arts, eds., *Mobilising International Law for "Global Justice"* (Cambridge University Press, 2018), 208–232; Barbara Oomen and Moritz Baumgärtel, "Frontier Cities: The Rise of Local Authorities as an Opportunity for International Human Rights Law," *European Journal of International Law* 29 (2018): 607–630. Among the cities experimenting with human rights legislation that seminal collection discusses are Barcelona, Mexico City, Montréal, Utrecht, and San Francisco.

[19] Oomen, Davis, and Grigolo (n 18) at 2.

[20] Michelle Grigolo, *The Human Rights City: New York, San Francisco, Barcelona* (Routledge, 2019).

[21] Some scholars of human rights cities have suggested that at least in the United States the trend may have some concrete legal bite; interpretation of federal intervention in state affairs as "appropriate" may ensure that human rights protection does not fall below federal standards, thereby shielding cities from pre-emptive rights-curtailing legislation by states. See, e.g., Martha F. Davis, "Design Challenges for Human Rights Cities," *Columbia Human Rights Law Review* 49 (2011): 28–66; Martha Davis, "The

mechanisms created by such charters are limited. Even avid proponents of the human rights cities idea note that very few of the charters adopted to date create effective legal remedies that allow individuals or groups claiming human rights violations to seek any meaningful legal relief.[22] What is more, with a few exceptions where political incentives so warrant, national governments cannot be bound by such policy initiatives. Unlike, constitutional rights commitments at the national level, it is unclear what actual "duties" city rights create. In other words, human rights cities may promise various rights protections, but the actual duty to realize such rights is often well beyond cities' legal ambit. No support or resources are provided by the state, which remains the primary, and often the only, relevant agent and duty-bearer of human rights commitments vis-à-vis the international arena.[23] Consequently, meaningful as these attempts to realize the right to the city through self-emancipatory initiatives by cities may be at the practical or symbolic level, their concrete *constitutional* bite is seriously limited in a state-dominated constitutional universe. With few exceptions, these initiatives live beside the formal constitutional or international law frameworks that govern national jurisdictions, rather than existing as a part within (let alone as a viable alternative to) these prevalent legal frameworks. Moreover, attempts by progressive cities and city leaders to extend human rights city charters to include so-called "urban citizenship" as complementary to national citizenship may be seen directly "offensive" to the constitutional order, as such attempts challenge the state's exclusive monopoly in defining the status, rights, and duties of its members, as well as the boundaries of membership itself.

III. Constitutionalizing City Status in South Africa

The post-apartheid Constitution of South Africa, enacted in 1996, features what is arguably the most comprehensive and successful endeavor to date to grant cities constitutional status and standing. As part of its distinct democratizing break with the country's political and constitutional past, the new South African Constitution explicitly aimed to empower local government while

Upside of the Downside: Local Human Rights and the Federalism Clauses," *St. Louis University Law Journal* 62 (2018): 921–938.

[22] See, e.g., Cynthia Soohoo, "Human Rights Cities: Challenges and Possibilities," in Oomen, Davis, and Grigolo (n 18) 257–275.

[23] Johanna Kalb, "The State of the City and the Future of Human Rights: A Review of Global Urban Justice," *Columbia Human Rights Law Review* 75 (2017): 75–97, 88.

curbing provincial power. To that end, Article 40(1) holds that "government is constituted as national, provincial, and local spheres of government which are distinctive, interdependent and interrelated." Chapter 7 (Secs. 151–164) of the Constitution further marks a fundamental shift away from the pre-1996 order.[24] It builds upon and operationalizes Article 40(1) by giving municipalities the ability to legislate and administer regulations in a number of areas (e.g. municipal planning, health services, public transport, trade), and, most important, the ability to raise funds in these areas, subject to some oversight by provincial and national governments.

As the Constitutional Court (Justice Johann Kriegler) noted shortly after the new constitution came into effect:

> The constitutional status of a local government is thus materially different to what it was when Parliament was supreme, when not only the powers but the very existence of local government depended entirely on superior legislatures. The institution of elected local government could then have been terminated at any time and its functions entrusted to administrators appointed by the central or provincial governments. That is no longer the position. Local governments have a place in the constitutional order, have to be established by the competent authority, and are entitled to certain powers, including the power to make by-laws and impose rates.[25]

Chapter 7 of the Constitution sets out three categories of municipalities. A "category A municipality" refers to major urban centres, currently the metropolitan areas of Johannesburg (metropolitan population 10 million), Cape Town (4.5 million), and Durban (3.5 million), as well as the smaller urban areas of Bloemfontein and East London. The creation of these unified metropolitan governments and, by extension, integrated urban space, was a direct response to the apartheid policy of excluding certain neighborhoods (notably Soweto in Johannesburg) from city boundaries and administration, thereby depriving these neighborhoods from representation, services, or subsidies.

Chapter 7 further provides that a municipality has the "right to govern, on its own initiative" (Sec. 151(3)). Section 156 provides three avenues for municipalities to exercise their power: executive authority, the right to administer, and the authority to make and administer bylaws. In addition, Section

[24] Robert Cameron, "The Upliftment of South African Local Government?," *Local Government Studies* 27 (2001): 97–118, 102.

[25] *Fedsure Life Assurance Ltd. & Others v. Greater Johannesburg Transitional Metropolitan Council & Others* 1999 (1) SA 374 (CC), 1998 (12) BCLR 1458 (CC), para. 38.

156(5) enables municipalities to exercise any power incidental to the effective performance of their functions.[26] Municipalities' significant revenue-raising functions are entrenched in Section 229 of the Constitution, which confers the ability to impose rates on property and surcharges on fees for services as well as other taxes if authorized by national legislation. The Constitutional Court has referred to the municipal revenue-raising power as an "original power," clarifying that the imposition of rates and surcharges does not require enabling federal legislation.[27] Consequently, a decade after the adoption of the new constitution, South African municipalities were estimated to have raised more than three-quarters of their operating revenue through their own taxation functions. Additionally, municipal governments are entitled to an equitable share of the revenue raised by the national government, to enable them to provide basic services and perform the functions allocated to them.[28]

Until recently, the consensus among observers of municipal affairs in South Africa was that the constitutional recognition of local government has been effective in allowing cities to provide improved services to their residents. This seemed to hold true even when a major city (such as Cape Town) is governed by an opposition party (the Democratic Alliance).[29] This is not to say that the relations between major South African cities and the other orders of governments do not occasionally sour. Indeed, recent accounts suggest that since the late-2010s, the constitutionalization of city status in South Africa has not been as effective as in the first twenty years of its existence in providing sufficient protection for city autonomy and authority, and has fallen short of fully countering political and economic preassures on city stature.[30] However, unlike in India or Brazil, the constitutional order and the constitutional jurisprudence

[26] What is meant by "incidental" was elaborated by the Constitutional Court in *In re: DVB Behuising (Pty) Ltd. v. North West Provincial Government and Another* 2001 (1) SA 500 (CC), 2000 (4) BCLR 347 (CC). While this case dealt with provincial incidental powers, the Constitutional Court held that powers usually falling within the domain of the national government were *intra vires* the provincial government, as they were "inextricably linked to the other provisions of the Proclamation." The same standard would likely apply to municipal incidental powers.

[27] *City of Cape Town v. Robertson* 2005 (2) SA 323 (CC), 2005 (3) BCLR 199 (CC), para. 56.

[28] A municipality's claim to an equitable share of national revenue was found to be justiciable in *Uthukela District Municipality & Others v. President of the Republic of South Africa & Others* 2002 (5) BCLR 479.

[29] See, e.g., Robert Cameron, "Vertical Decentralisation and Urban Service Delivery in South Africa: Does Politics Matter?," *Development Policy Review* 32 (2014): 81–100.

[30] See, e.g., Marius Pieterse, "A Year of Living Dangeoursly? Urban Assertiveness, Cooperative Governance and the First Year of Three Coalition-Led Metropolitan Municipalities in South Africa," *South African Journal of Political Studies* 46 (2019): 51-70; Marius Pieterse, "Anatomy of a Crisis: Structural Factors Contributing to the Collapse of Urban Municipal Governance in Emfuleni, South Africa," *Urban Forum* 32 (2021): 1–15.

stemming from it have relatively successfully shielded cities from the *exclusive* grip of federal or provincial governments.

The constitutional protection provided to South African cities has been reinforced by several landmark rulings of the South African Constitutional Court pertaining to intergovernmental disputes under the 1996 Constitution.[31] In *City of Johannesburg Metropolitan Municipality v. Gauteng Development Tribunal* (2010), to pick one example, the Constitutional Court ruled that cities have exclusive authority over municipal planning, including zoning and land use management, and that national or provincial powers may not be used in ways that usurp or subvert municipal planning powers. In another important ruling two years later, the Constitutional Court ruled that while intergovernmental cooperation is to be favored, a national competence may be limited by the exercise of a municipal competence.[32] Specifically, the court held that the granting of mineral mining rights by the national government cannot circumvent municipal zoning decisions. In a 2020 ruling involving a state-owned communication service provider whose built structure contravened Cape Town's zoning laws, the court sided with the city authorities and affirmed the constitutional objective of establishing "wall-to-wall municipalities with powers to control and regulate land use within their areas of jurisdiction," separate and distinct from provincial and national planning.[33]

While large South African cities remain marred with problems that extend well beyond the constitutional realm, their protected constitutional autonomy has had a considerable effect on their ability to adopt socially progressive policies in land use and housing. The City of Johannesburg, for example, has drawn on its expansive, constitutionally assigned land use and planning powers to adopt legislation requiring that all future residential private development projects with twenty units or more to include 30% affordable homes, regardless of

[31] Johannesburg, e.g., was involved in major litigation against the Gauteng Development Tribunal, a provincial body that has equivalent and parallel authority to the municipality to regulate land use. In a judgment affirmed by the Constitutional Court, the Supreme Court of Appeal declared two chapters of the Development Facilitation Act 67 of 1995 unconstitutional, as they encroached on the authority of municipalities to engage in "municipal planning" as set out in Part B of Sch. 4 (see *City of Johannesburg v. Gauteng Development Tribunal* (335/08) 2009 ZASCA 106; confirmed by the Constitutional Court in *City of Johannesburg Metropolitan Municipality v. Gauteng Development Tribunal and Others* 2010 (6) SA 182 (CC). More recently, the city launched a legal challenge against the chairman of the National Building Review Board. In this case, the Constitutional Court confirmed the ruling of the High Court of South Africa, Gauteng Division that Sec. 9 of the National Building Regulations and Building Standards Act, which empowered the board to exercise appellate review powers over municipal decisions, was unconstitutional (see *City of Johannesburg Metropolitan Municipality v. Chairman of the National Building Review Board* 2018 (5) SA 1 (CC).

[32] *Maccsand (Pty) Ltd. v. City of Cape Town and Others* 2012 (4) SA 181 (CC).

[33] *Telkom SA SOC Ltd. v. City of Cape Town and Another* (CCT287/19) 2021 (1) SA 1 (CC).

the project's location. The stated goal of the policy is to address the substantial inequality and segregation that persist in South Africa's largest metropoles.[34]

In September 2019, Johannesburg won the Sustainable City and Human Settlements Award from the U.N. for its partnership with local developers to build South Hills—a development of nearly 6,000 housing units—in the south of the city. The U.N. recognized the city's "outstanding demonstration in promoting sustainable cities and human settlements, as well as the implementation of sustainable development goals." The project features a mix of fully subsidized homes, subsidized rental units, and open-market units, with more than 90% of the units within local legislation's definition of affordable housing. None of these new inclusionary policies would have been possible without the constitutional entrenchment of city powers in the post-apartheid Constitution of South Africa.

In other words, the constitutionalization of city status in South Africa reflects a genuine breaking with the past. While large South African cities still face daunting challenges, the constitutionally entrenched three-tier governance system allows urban centers a meaningful voice in addressing these issues. As such, the South African model represents what is arguably the most successful experiment to date in introducing more balanced city/state constitutional relations in an evermore urbanized world. As such, it provides a significant yet seldom-addressed example of a daring anticanonical constitutional innovation in action.

IV. The Constitutional Emancipation of Mexico City

A more recent illustration of groundbreaking constitutional empowerment of cities is the transformation of Mexico City from a federal district to a full-fledged state. The city's estimated population in 2020 was 22 million, and it has been listed among the ten most populous cities in the world for the last forty years. Under the 1917 Constitution, the capital city was set up as a creature of the national government. Until the recent change in its constitutional status, the city's official name was the Federal District (*Distrito Federal*), or as almost everyone called it, the "D. F."

The idea to return Mexico City to its residents by turning it into an independent state with constitutional status similar to that of all other subnational

[34] Justice Malala, "Why Are South African cities still so segregated 25 years after Apartheid?," *The Guardian* (October 21, 2019).

governments of the Mexican confederation was raised occasionally throughout the twentieth century, but never gained real traction until the mid-1980s. Calls for local autonomy in Mexico City began to gain momentum following a devastating earthquake in 1985 and citywide disappointment over slow and unorganized federal and state relief efforts.[35] In 1987, the federal government responded to growing demands by granting the city a locally elected governing body with a narrow scope of legislative authority. A subsequent reform in 1996 gave the citizens of Mexico City the ability to elect their own executive head of government, a mayoral position that had previously been filled by presidential appointment.[36] In 2000, Andrés Manuel López Obrador (who, as at early 2024, is President of Mexico) of the center-left party of the Democratic Revolution (Partido de la Revolución Democrática, PRD) was elected mayor of Mexico City. During his term in office, López Obrador gained national and international recognition as an activist, a visionary mayor, and a keen advocate for city emancipation as a necessary tool to enhance democratic representation and to effectively fight poverty. The federal government was less impressed with López Obrador's quest to emancipate Mexico City, and sought to retain budgetary control over the city as a federal district. López Obrador's increased national political prominence led to him being seen as a political threat to the right-wing populist administration led by Vicente Fox of the National Action Party (Partido Accíon Nacional, PAN). Consequently, López Obrador's call to free Mexico City from the federal government's grip failed to take off at the federal level.

López Obrador left the Mexico City mayoralty in late 2005 in order to run as the PRD candidate for the 2006 presidential elections. He lost that election, by a margin of less than 250,000 votes, to Felipe Calderón of the PAN. The ideological and political animosity continued between the PAN-led federal government under Calderón and the PRD-led Mexico City leadership of Mayor Marcelo Ebrard. In 2007, amid these tensions, Mayor Ebrard introduced legislation that decriminalized abortion in the district. Later, in 2009, he introduced another piece of progressive legislation that established gay marriage in the district. In a symbolic act of autonomy in 2007, Mexico City's municipal government supported a move by local activist groups to adopt a "Mexico City Charter for the Right to the City."[37] The Charter's drafting process included

[35] Diego Rabasa, "Mexico City Is 'Crowdsourcing' a New Constitution. But Will It Change Anything?," *The Guardian* (June 2, 2016).

[36] Viridiana Rios, "Mexico City Will Become a State," *Wilson Center: Mexico Institute* (June 3, 2016).

[37] For an account of the drafting process, see Ana María Sánchez Rodríguez, "The Right to the City in Mexico City" in Oomen, Davis, and Grigolo (n 18) 220–236.

mass public consultations held at the city's central plaza, the Zócalo, a symbolic locus of Mexican statehood. Mayor Ebrard continuously emphasized the strategic value of the drafting process, so that "the city we dream can become reality." The drafting process concluded in 2009, yielding one of the most socially progressive bills of rights ever drafted—in bold opposition to the national government's conservative, business-friendly worldview. In an attempt to create some international buzz around the city's quest for emancipation, the completed draft of the Mexico City Charter for the Right to the City, officially adopted in 2010, was presented at the Fifth World Urban Forum organized by the U.N. Habitat in Rio de Janeiro. The mayor of Mexico City was present. Mexico's federal government did not join the celebration.

A breakthrough at the national level came following the 2012 presidential elections, won by Enrique Peña Nieto of the centrist-statist PRI (Partido Revolucionario Institucional) —the dominant political party in Mexico throughout much of the twentieth century. In December 2012, President Enrique Peña Nieto struck a deal with the PRI's two main rival political parties, PAN and PRD, to endorse the so-called Pacto por México (pact for Mexico). This pact involved a comprehensive series of energy, education, fiscal, and telecommunication reforms aimed at giving a major boost to Mexico's stagnant and crisis-laden economy, and at overcoming the gridlock that had characterized Mexican politics since the Ernesto Zedillo presidency (1994–2000).[38] The mayor of Mexico City, Miguel Ángel Mancera of the PRD, was among the prominent politicians with whom Peña Nieto bargained. In exchange for the mayor's support for the pact, and the PRD's support for it more generally, Peña Nieto agreed to back amendments to the Mexican Constitution that would turn Mexico City into the thirty-second "federal entity"—basically on a par with a state. And so, approximately a century after the Mexican Revolution and the adoption of the 1917 Constitution, a national political pact that required Mexico City's support allowed the city to release itself from federal control and to control a considerably larger part of its municipal budget. As celebratory signs all over the city declared, "Adiós DF, Hola CDMX" (goodbye federal district (DF), welcome Mexico City, (*Ciudad de Mexico*, CDMX)).[39]

Two constitutional changes were required to realize this proposed new status: an amendment to the national constitution assigning full state status to Mexico City and the adoption of a state constitution. To address the first

[38] For an astute political analysis of the pact and its aims, see Andres Sada, "Explainer: What Is the Pacto por México?," *Americas Society/Council of the Americas* (March 11, 2013).

[39] See Gregory Scruggs, "The People Power behind Mexico City's New Constitution," *City Lab* (February 3, 2017).

requirement, Article 44 (originally designating Mexico City as a federal district) and Article 122 (defining the parameters of governance applicable to the federal district) of the national constitution were amended in 2016.[40] This officially allowed for a change in the status of Mexico City from a federal district to a state named Mexico City. The amended Article 122 states that Mexico City is an autonomous entity within the Mexican federation, with respect to "everything related to its domestic regime, and its political and administrative organization."[41] It further stipulates that "the government of Mexico City is responsible for its local powers, as established in the Mexico City Constitution," and defines the prerogatives of the newly established state's governing institutions in a way similarly to other Mexican states. Importantly, the amended Article 122 states that:

> Mexico City will adopt for its domestic regime a republican, representative, democratic, and laic form of governance. Mexico City public power shall be divided for its exercise into the legislative, executive, and judiciary. Two or more of these powers shall not be vested in a single person or corporation, nor the Legislative shall be vested in a single individual. Mexico City Constitution, according to its jurisdiction, shall establish norms and guarantees for the enjoyment and protection of human rights as provided by article 1 of this Constitution.[42]

President Peña Nieto announced the approval of these enabling amendments by saying, "[a] long-awaited wish has become a reality: Mexico City has been recognized as a state with genuine autonomy ... [T]he amendment marks the culmination of a debate that began with the discussion of the Constitution of 1824 and has been present for nearly two centuries. During this period, new states have been incorporated until today, when Mexico City was finally acknowledged as a federal state."[43]

With the amended provisions of the national constitution in place, the stage was set for the adoption of a new state constitution for Mexico City. Mere days after the constitutional reform gained assent at the federal level,

[40] On the history and process of amending the Mexican Constitution, see Mauro A. Rivera León, "Understanding Constitutional Amendments in Mexico: Perpetuum Mobile Constitution," *Mexican Law Review* 9 (2016): 3–27.

[41] The original text reads: "La Ciudad de México es una entidad federativa que goza de autonomía en todo lo concerniente a su régimen interior y a su organización política y administrativa."

[42] I am grateful to Luis Sanchez Soto for the translation of the original Spanish text into English.

[43] President Enrique Peña Nieto, "Mexico City's Political Reform is a triumph of dialogue, democracy and its inhabitants" (Official press release, January 29, 2016).

a unique, first-of-its-kind exercise of megacity constitution-writing began. There were three major steps. First, a committee of legal experts, academics, and activists selected by Mayor Mancera produced a draft state constitution. The draft was then published widely in print and online, and extensive citizen response was sought in an open "crowdsourcing" exercise. Finally, a 100-member constitutional assembly, comprising 60 members elected by city residents and 40 drawn from Congress (14), Senate (14), or appointed by the mayor (6) and the country's president (6), considered the popular input and negotiated the document's final version. The composition of the assembly was heavily criticized by left-leaning groups for the excessive inclusion of presidential appointees, and more generally for the overrepresentation of federal and party interests. Criticism notwithstanding, the constitution-making process marched on. In its year-long deliberations, commenced in September 2016, the assembly held 21 plenary sessions, considered 544 suggestions by assembly members and 978 proposals by citizens, with an estimated direct participation of over 10,000 people.[44] The outcome, symbolically dubbed the "CDMX Carta Magna," officially came into effect in September 2018, despite not having been put to an approval referendum as initially recommended.

The elaborate constitution-making process produced a socially progressive and inclusive document that boosts the city's autonomy within Mexico's federal system and gives the mayor more power, while devolving some decision making to neighborhood-level elected councils. The document also includes provisions protecting LGBTQ+ rights, cultural diversity, education, green spaces, as well as a general "right to the city" along the lines discussed earlier, with the hope of protecting vulnerable and marginalized populations from the forces of real estate speculation, police brutality, economic exclusion, and gentrification.[45] Alongside criticism of the drafting process as well as of the constitution falling short of committing to extensive social housing and collective property schemes, observers have noted that the process brought about unprecedented citizen engagement; city-based collective identity; and identification with core values of democracy, transparency, and self-government.

From a broader, constitutional theory standpoint, the transformation of Mexico City's constitutional status raises fascinating questions concerning the

[44] Alejandra Reyes, "The Evolution of Local Government in Mexico City: Pursuing Autonomy in a Growing Region," *IMFG Perspectives* 25/2019 (University of Toronto, Institute on Municipal Finance and Governance), 12.

[45] For a comprehensive elaboration of the constitution-making process and the content of the new Mexico City Constitution, see "Political Constitution of Mexico City: Background and Fundamental Advances," *CDMX, Unit for Political Reform of Mexico City*; online at: Constitucion_CDMX_antecedentes_En.pdf.

pertinent constituent unit in federalism theory in an age of widespread urbanization. It likewise highlights the potential of popular, city-based constitutional mobilization, akin to nation-wide "constitutional moments."

V. Conclusion

In an earlier work, I suggested that too much is made in comparative constitutional law of "a small number of overanalyzed, 'usual suspect' constitutional settings and court rulings."[46] The jurisprudential "unofficial canon," I argued, consists of roughly "[t]wo dozen judicial court rulings from South Africa, Germany, Canada, and the European Court of Human Rights alongside a more traditional set of landmark rulings from the United States and Britain and an occasional tribute to India or Australia."[47] Consequently, "the constitutional experiences of entire regions ... remain largely uncharted terrain, understudied and generally overlooked. The result is that purportedly universal insights are based on a handful of frequently studied and not always representative settings or cases."[48] But another apparent shortcoming of that unofficial canon is its tendency towards intellectual path dependence, and its preoccupation with traditional concepts and "classic" matters of constitutional law. This leads in turn to the field's scant attention to new frontiers of inquiry, some of which—climate change, migration, the spread of "big brother" technology, or rising economic inequality and the uncontrolled accumulation of wealth in the hands of the few—are commonly classified among the greatest challenges facing humanity in the twenty-first century.

Extensive urban agglomeration is one of these challenges—critical, yet often overlooked. Statist in its outlook and locked in a long-standing conceptualization of sovereignty, spatiality, and political geography more generally, mainstream constitutional thought pays no attention to the city—the most common form of human settlement. Though we live in the century of the city, we are still captives of constitutional structures and doctrines that were developed alongside the modern nation-state and which are the tied to the historical subjugation of the sovereign city to those states. Consequently, large cities, some of which are far more populous than most sovereign countries, are treated as creatures of the state, fully submerged within a Westphalian

[46] Ran Hirschl, *Comparative Matters: The Renaissance of Comparative Constitutional Law* (Oxford University Press, 2014), 4.
[47] ibid at 163.
[48] ibid at 4–5.

constitutional framework, and assigned limited administrative authority over local governance.

In this chapter, I explored three important attempts to break away from that reality: Henri Lefebvre's intriguing, yet fuzzy, "right to the city" and the attempts to implement it through self-emancipatory means such as urban citizenship or human rights cities operating alongside the established statist constitutional order; the relatively successful constitutionalization of city status in post-apartheid South Africa; and the constitutional transformation of Mexico City from a federal district to an autonomous state within the Mexican confederation. These three important experiments with city status have all taken a socially progressive direction, advancing values such as participatory democracy, accommodation of difference and social inclusion, and where applicable, redistributive land use, urban planning, and public housing policies. Taken together, they may be seen as an attempt, modest yet promising, to bridge the stark gap between ever-expanding urbanization worldwide and mainstream constitutional thought's persisting fixation with the state and its institutions as the gravitational centerpiece of the constitutional universe.

27

The Canon of Nature Rights

Alexandra Huneeus[*]

I. Introduction

In constitutional as in human rights law, rights seek to define the relationship of the individual to government and society. The canonic texts of both fields of law emphasize themes such as individual autonomy against incursions by government, how governments can ensure a life with dignity, and meaningful individual participation in the democratic process. Their focus, in other words, is on the relations of humans among themselves. Even the rights of fictional entities such as corporations and nation-states are ultimately rooted in claims of how humans can best conduct their relations with each other. The claim of rights of nature is a radical departure. It says that positive rights law can extend beyond relations among humans to encompass an entirely new domain of concern: human relations with those entities falling into the category of "nature," or the non-human world.

The 2008 Constitution of Ecuador was the first to recognize the rights of a non-human natural entity, Mother Earth.[1] In contrast to other constitutions that declare humans to have a right to environment, the Ecuadoran Constitution views nature as having intrinsic value, and as itself (herself) holding the right to exist and to be restored. Rights of nature laws have since been passed by a handful of countries including Bolivia, Panama, and New Zealand at the national level; Mexico at the level of state constitutions; Argentina, Brazil, and the United States at the level of city ordinances; and, within the U.S., tribal law by Native nations. Additionally, high courts in Colombia, India, and Bangladesh have recognized the rights of rivers through judicial interpretation in the absence of explicit provisions in positive law. Beyond the nation-state, the United

* University of Wisconsin. The author would like to acknowledge Arwen Bleksley for her research support and brilliant questions. (This chapter was originally written in 2020, during quarantine, but has been updated.)

[1] Constitución Política de la República del Ecuador arts. 56–60, available at http://pdba.georgetown.edu/Constitutions/Ecuador/ecuador08.html#mozTocId64283.

Alexandra Huneeus, *The Canon of Nature Rights* In: *Global Canons in an Age of Contestation.* Edited by: Sujit Choudhry, Michaela Hailbronner, and Mattias Kumm, Oxford University Press.
DOI: 10.1093/9780191956942.003.0027

Nation General Assembly initiated a dialogue with experts of "Earth jurisprudence"[2] in 2015, and in 2017 the Inter-American Court of Human Rights declared that rights protect nature "not only for its connection to human use ... but also for its importance to other living organisms with whom we share the planet, and who are worthy of protection in and of themselves."[3]

Taken together, this cluster of laws, judgments, and resolutions suggests that nature rights have quickly become part of the transnational lexicon of rights. Though a recent and still liminal trend, they have begun to inform approaches to environmental protection as well as to relations with indigenous peoples, and in particular to the connection between the two. This chapter explores three foundational texts in the rights of nature *corpus juris*: a 1972 dissent by Justice Douglas in *Sierra Club v. Morton* arguing that a valley of the Sierra Nevada should have standing to defend itself in court; the Ecuadoran Constitution of 2008; and the 2016 judgment in which the Colombian Constitutional Court (CCC) declared the Atrato River to be a rights-bearing body.[4] Anyone practicing or theorizing in the area of environmental rights is likely aware of these three texts. The reason for including them in this volume, however, is that they are also texts of which anyone theorizing in the area of comparative constitutional law or human rights law should be aware. This is not because they shape environmental practice on the ground. So far, such rights have done little to actually alter the way the rivers and forests that bear them are managed. Their power lies instead in what we often refer to as the "symbolic" realm: it challenges rights laws' focus on humans precisely at a time in which climate change has begun to make itself felt in daily life, pushing us to rethink how we engage with the environment. Further, most rights of nature claims are efforts to assert in national legal systems ideas and values advanced by indigenous peoples and other ethnically identified communities, and to rewrite their relationship with the state by altering how the state conceptualizes their lands. These texts also merit induction into the canon of rights and constitutional law, in other words, because they are among the few texts in the transnational lexicon of rights that can claim their origin in the worldviews of indigenous and Afro-descendent peoples of South America, the indigenous peoples of New Zealand, and other non-Western worldviews.

[2] General Assembly resolution 70/208, *Harmony with Nature*, A/RES/70/208 (December 22, 2015).

[3] The Environment and Human Rights, Advisory Opinion Oc-23/17, Inter-Am. Ct. H.R. (Ser. A), para. 62 (November 15, 2017) (author translation).

[4] Ecuador Constitution (n 1); Judgment T-622/16 (the *Atrato River Case*) 2016 (Constitutional Court of Colombia); *Sierra Club v. Morton* 405 U.S. 727 (1972).

A skeptic might object that rights of nature are simply a new way of talking about the perennial questions of distribution of natural resources among humans; that they are nothing but a legal fiction designed to tip the balance toward conservation, but doomed to redundancy and ineffectiveness.[5] Further, such claims are not harmless: they carry the risk of eroding the priority of human rights and individual dignity as understood at the close of the Cold War. Our skeptic might point out that rights of nature as a legal idea was forged in the smithy of the Bolivarian constituent assemblies of the 2000s, drawing on socialist, anti-development, anti-imperialist discourse alongside indigenous ideas in Ecuador and Bolivia. They could argue, in other words, that if these texts deserve serious study it is because they pose a threat to the global canon of rights-based constitutionalism and human rights that developed starting in the 1990s, and are perhaps yet another symptom of its decline.

The argument advanced here, however, is that while rights of nature have already become prominent in the lexicon of rights, it is too early to decide whether they will be viewed as an extension of or a threat to the project of constructing rights-based liberal democracies. Examination of the three texts reveals three distinct strands of argumentation for the importance and meaning of rights of nature. The first strand views the legal personhood of nature as a useful legal fiction that allows us to better assign value to natural areas in decisions about whether and how they should be developed, echoing what Craig Kauffman and Pamela Martin refer to as the legal personhood model of nature rights.[6] The second strand is more audacious: it views rights of nature as expressing and advancing an ontological shift in how we understand the relations between humans and the environment. Taken to its extreme, it is a view that destabilizes the line law draws between humans and other living entities and, just as disruptively, the line Western thought draws between living and nonliving entities.[7] The third strand views rights of nature as part of a practice of multicultural constitutionalism committed to acknowledging and giving legal weight to the worldviews of indigenous peoples and other non-Western ethnically identified groups. Those who advocate for rights of nature tend to draw on all three strands of justificatory argument at once without distinguishing

[5] For arguments against rights of nature, see, for example, Noah Sachs, "A Wrong Turn with the Rights of Nature Movement," (forthcoming) 36 Georgetown Environmental Law Journal.

[6] Craig M. Kauffman and Pamela L. Martin, *The Politics of Rights of Nature: Strategies for Building a More Sustainable Future* (MIT Press 2021) 14–17. (The three strands of argumentation resonate with the ideal models of rights of nature set out by Kauffman and Martin. However, they differ in that they refer to arguments used in justification, rather than to actual structures set up to safeguard nature rights.)

[7] Elizabeth Povinelli, *Geontologies: A Requiem to Late Liberalism* (Duke University Press 2016).

between them. Yet the three strands are analytically distinct and are positioned differently vis-à-vis traditional liberal democratic values. Ultimately, whether rights of nature will be viewed as participating in the liberal democratic canon or challenging it may turn on which strand predominates.

The chapter unfolds in four sections. The first three sections discuss each rights of nature text respectively, arguing for its significance and using it to examine a distinct strand of argumentation for rights of nature claims. The final section examines the analytical tensions between and political interdependence of these three strands of rights of nature arguments, as well as their shifting relationship to the traditional tenets of constitutional democracy.

II. A Modest Proposal: The Douglas Dissent

In 1969, the Sierra Club, an environmental non-governmental organization (NGO), sued to stop Walt Disney Enterprises from developing a large ski resort in the Mineral King Valley, in the Sierra Nevada of California. The case made its way to the Supreme Court, which held that the Sierra Club lacked standing as it had failed to show a direct interest in the case. A generalized concern for the underlying natural resource is not enough to qualify for standing. However, the Court indicated that the Sierra Club *could* claim standing by showing that at least one if its members was directly affected. In this case, that would mean that a member actually "uses" the valley and could thus credibly claim harm to "aesthetic, conservational and recreational values." [8] This came to be known as representational standing.

Justice Douglas's dissent attempts to broaden standing in a different direction from that argued later. He argued for legal standing for "the inanimate object about to be despoiled, defaced, or invaded."[9] Standing for the inanimate object would allow third parties acting as guardians to have a voice in the proceeding, much in the same way that third parties speak in cases involving children.[10] Douglas does not directly explain why standing for natural objects is preferable to representational standing as a way to facilitate third party involvement more generally. Either form of standing could achieve his objective, which is that the natural object could be defended in court by "existing beneficiaries" with an "intimate relation" to the area: "[t]hose who hike it fish it, camp in it,

[8] *Sierra Club v. Morton* (n 4) 738.
[9] ibid 741 (Douglas dissenting).
[10] ibid 742 and 750.

frequent it, or visit it merely to sit in solitude and wonderment."[11] However, his dissent gives prominent place to an article published that same year, "Should Trees Have Standing?" by Christopher Stone, which does make the argument for several procedural benefits. For example, the Supreme Court's more liberalized standing of the time was developed through interpretation of statutory law such as the Administrative Procedure Act. Standing for nature, by contrast, would be available even outside the context of federal administration action, Stone argues, and in cases where "public-lands and waters were not involved."[12] After arguing for several other advantages based on procedural matters, Stone adds that standing for trees "may encourage the institutions whose actions threaten the environment to *really think* about what it is doing"[13] and may also subtly shift the way judges reason, in response to argument over "injuries not presently cognizable" such as the death of "inedible crabs" and "commercially valueless birds."[14]

What stands out about the Douglas dissent, when juxtaposed to the Latin American rights of nature jurisprudence, is that he is not arguing that nature is a living entity or that it should have its own set of fundamental rights. Although the dissent closes with reference to Aldo Leopold's land ethic of humans as in community with "soils, waters, plants, and animals," the argumentative thrust is rather to advance a procedural mechanism that already exists in our legal system, and that better captures the value our society already assigns to preservation of natural areas.[15] The Douglas proposal is partly captured by what Craig Kauffman and Pamela Martin call the "legal personhood model" of nature rights, which draws on existing legal provisions to establish standing for a particular natural entity.[16] It is also important to note that the Douglas dissent views itself as rooted firmly in Western thought. Stone cites Western thinkers from Socrates to Darwin but mentions indigenous peoples only once (to briefly question the idea that Native Americans live in harmony with nature).[17] Further, the grant of legal personality in the Douglas dissent, as in the Stone article, is not concerned with protecting the ways indigenous peoples live on

[11] ibid 744–755.
[12] Christopher D. Stone, "Should Trees Have Standing? Toward Legal Rights for Natural Objects" (1972) 45 Southern California Law Review 450, 470.
[13] ibid 484.
[14] ibid 475.
[15] *Sierra Club v. Morton* (n 4) 752.
[16] Kauffman and Martin, *The Politics of Rights of Nature* (n 5) 14–17.
[17] Stone, "Should Trees Have Standing?" (n 11) 450.

their territory, but rather with the ways hikers, hunters, and other recreational users interact with the land.[18]

The Douglas dissent thus aligns easily with liberal constitutional traditions, more so than the other strands of argumentation for nature rights discussed later. But one might question whether it merits induction to the canon of comparative rights constitutionalism. Douglas was arguing for a particular mechanism, legal standing, rather than for any substantive fundamental right. Further, Douglas did not win the day, and no subsequent effort at establishing the standing of natural entities through judicial fiat has succeeded in the United States. Nor have rights of nature taken hold in the United States at the level of constitutional law or even national law, only through local ordinances that tend to lose when challenged in court, and tribal laws that have yet to be tested.[19] Beyond the United States, rights of nature that have been written into law or read into the constitution are most often linked to an expression of a distinct non-Western way of understanding the relation between humans and the natural world. Yet the Douglas dissent is routinely cited by scholarship on this theme. Perhaps its greatest impact has been to call attention to Stone's article, setting it on the path to become one of the most cited texts in the rights of nature movement. The Stone article was referred to by those advocating for rights of nature in Ecuador's constitutional assembly and in many subsequent processes, and the 1972 Douglas dissent and Stone article are often cast together as the point of origin of the rights of nature movement.

III. A Bold Turn: The Constitution of Ecuador

Like many Latin American constitutions, the Ecuadoran Constitution of 2008 contains a generous list of rights, emphasizing socioeconomic rights, and including the "right of the population to live in a healthy and ecologically balanced environment."[20] It also includes, for the first time in a constitutional text, a chapter focused on the Rights of Mother Earth (referred to in Kichwa as *Pacha Mama*). It declares:

[18] Indeed, Native Americans were removed from lands in order to create national wilderness areas. William Cronon, *Uncommon Ground: Rethinking the Human Place in Nature* (W. W. Norton & Co. 1996).

[19] Alexandra Huneeus, "The Struggle for Nature Rights in the United States" (2022) 21(2) Wisconsin Law Journal 133–162

[20] Constitución Política De La República Del Ecuador art. 14, available at http://pdba.georgetown.edu/Constitutions/Ecuador/ecuador08.html#mozTocId64283.

> Article 71. Nature, or Pacha Mama, where life is reproduced and occurs, has the right to integral respect for its existence and for the maintenance and regeneration of its life cycles, structure, functions and evolutionary processes. All persons, communities, peoples and nations can call upon public authorities to enforce the rights of nature. … [The State] will promote respect for all the elements that form an ecosystem.
>
> Article 72. Nature has the right to be restored. This restoration shall be apart from the obligation of the State and natural persons or legal entities to compensate individuals and communities that depend on affected natural systems …

These provisions of the Constitution became famous upon passage, inspiring efforts to pass similar laws in other countries throughout Latin America and beyond. They contain three features that characterize rights of nature codification. First, the provisions distinguish what is owed to nature from what is owed to humans, clearly stating that nature is an end in itself, and not only a means for human sustenance. Second, they articulate the substantive dimensions of the rights of nature, which are analogous to but different from human rights: respect for existence, regeneration of life cycles, and a right to be restored. Third, they create procedures for humans to speak for nature in court.[21]

Although the constitution alludes to the Kichwa concept of *Pacha Mama*, the inclusion of rights of nature was part of a national project to remake the constitutional order not just as it relates to indigenous peoples, but for everybody. María Akchurin writes that leading up to the constituent assembly of 2007, various political factions were able to find common ground through this concept. Environmental groups, drawing on Stone's article and other legal scholarship, first proposed to the constituent assembly the idea of granting a new legal status for nature as a path to more sustainable approaches to environmental governance.[22] For indigenous social movements, the idea proved attractive because it aligned with their priorities: it would give them more power to exclude extractivist projects from their territories even as it articulated respect for their cultural traditions and perspectives. Importantly, the idea also appealed to Leftist critics of the neoliberal economic model of development. With the backing of these various factions, the proposal eventually prevailed.

[21] This instrument goes further than others, seemingly allowing anyone in the world to call on the Ecuadoran government to promote and defend the rights of nature.

[22] Maria Akchurin, "Constructing the Rights of Nature: Constitutional Reform, Mobilization, and Environmental Protection in Ecuador" (2015) 40(4) Law and Social Inquiry 937–968.

The 2008 charter is a far more ambitious and far-reaching project than simply creating a procedural mechanism that better captures the value we assign to nature, as proposed by the Douglas dissent. Indeed, the Constitution's provisions on nature extend well beyond the rights provisions. Throughout, it upholds the government's duty to care for nature and preserve biodiversity, and the documents opens in the preamble by "celebrating nature ... of which we are a part and which is vital to our existence."[23] One reading of this constitutional text is that it introduces an ontological shift: it brings into constitutional law a new understanding of the relationship between humans and their environment in which natural entities are viewed as moral beings with whom we have social relations.[24] It forms part of a multifaceted political project that sought to unseat several traditional fundamentals of Western constitutionalism, including the very notion of the nation-state, by recognizing different groups within the state as nations. At the same time, the Constitution commits the national government to the provision of social and economic rights and would seem to require a strong central government able to raise significant revenue.[25]

The initial progressive political project conceived by President Correa (2007–2017) has since foundered, but the 2007 Constitution survives, and the legal figure of the rights of nature within Ecuadoran law is being slowly developed through administrative governance as well as through dozens of judgments. In a study of rights of nature court cases, Kauffman and Martin find that while rights of nature arguments often lose in high-profile politicized cases that come before Ecuadoran courts, lower-level judges have been steadily developing the concept through less publicized, lower-stakes cases. [26] At the same time, the concept has become a more widely recognized frame used to discuss development projects at the national level in the political realm. They conclude that, thus far, "Ecuador's constitutional RoN [rights of nature]

[23] Constitución Política De La República Del Ecuador arts. 56–60, available at http://pdba.georgetown.edu/Constitutions/Ecuador/ecuador08.html#mozTocId64283.

[24] Eduardo Viverios de Castro, "Exchanging Perspectives: The Transformation of Objects into Subjects" (2004) 10(3) Common Knowledge 43–484. See also Marisol de la Cadena, *Earth Beings: Ecologies of Practice across Andean Worlds* (Duke University Press 2015) and Martin Holbraad and Morten Pedersen, "Introduction: The Ontological Turn in Anthropology" in *The Ontological Turn: An Anthropological Exposition* (New Departures in Anthropology, 1–29) (Cambridge University Press 2017) 1–29.

[25] Rickard Lalander, "Entre El Ecocentrismo y El Pragmatismo Ambiental: Consideraciones Inductivas Sobre Desarrollo, Extractivismo y Los Derechos De La Naturaleza En Bolivia Y Ecuador" ("Between Ecocentrism and Environmental Pragmatism: Inductive Considerations on Development, Extractivism, and Environmental Rights in Bolivia and Ecuador") (January 1, 2015) 6(1) Revista Chilena de Derecho y Ciencia Política 109–152 Available at SSRN: https://ssrn.com/abstract=2604633.

[26] Craig M. Kauffman and Pamela L. Martin, "Can Rights of Nature Make Development More Sustainable? Why Some Ecuadorian Lawsuits Succeed and Others Fail" (2017) 92 World Development 130–142.

articles do matter in the sense that RoN activists are using them as tools to strengthen RoN jurisprudence and norms in a way that are having real impacts." The impacts they find are: (a) low-level wins in particular local disputes; (b) the ongoing development of the doctrine and familiarization of judges with it; and (c) that the concept of rights of nature is now a regular part of national discourse. More recently, however, the Constitutional Court declared a law allowing economic activities in mangrove ecosystems to be in violation of the mangrove ecosystem's constitutional rights.[27] This high-level victory suggests that the ongoing development of nature rights doctrines through low-level litigation is starting to bear fruit at the appellate level, as suggested by Kauffman and Martin.[28]

The Ecuadoran Constitution's rights of nature provisions have arguably had greater impact outside Ecuador. They were immediately celebrated both as an important idea in environmental law, and as a form of epistemic justice to rectify the past erasure or appropriation of indigenous ways of knowing. A stream of rights of nature laws followed. In 2010, Bolivia passed national rights of nature legislation.[29] Bolivian President Morales also promoted the idea at the level of the United Nations, which declared April 22 to be the day of Mother Earth.[30] New Zealand declared the Whanganui River and the Te Urewara forest to be rights-bearing persons in 2014 and 2017, respectively, as part of a treaty settlement process with Māori tribes. Three Mexican states have amended their constitutions to include rights of nature, and many local ordinances in the United States and Latin America also proclaim that natural entities hold rights. Perhaps the Ecuadoran Constitution's greatest impact has been in the way it provides a resource for civil society. Today, there is a network of local, national, and transnational NGOs focused on rights of nature in the Americas and beyond: all frequently cite the Ecuadoran experience. One NGO established a Tribunal of the Rights of Nature, which meets yearly to consider cases of extreme environmental degradation around the world.[31]

[27] *Corte Constitucional de Ecuador se pronuncial sobre los derechos de la naturaleza y de los manglares en relación con las actividades extractivas que lo amenazan*, Diario Constitucional.cl (October 23, 2021), https://www.diarioconstitucional.cl/2021/10/23/corte-constitucional-de-ecuador-se-pronuncia-sobre-los-derechos-de-la-naturaleza-y-de-los-manglares-en-relacion-con-las-actividades-extractivas-que-lo-amenazan/.

[28] ibid.

[29] La Ley 71 de 2010 (Ley de derechos de la Madre Tierra) y la Ley 300 de 2012 (Ley marco de la Madre Tierra y desarrollo integral para vivir bien).

[30] "General Assembly Proclaims 22 April 'International Mother Earth Day' Adopting by Consensus Bolivia-Led Resolution" (*United Nations*, 22 April 2009), https://www.un.org/press/en/2009/ga10823.doc.htm.

[31] See https://www.rightsofnaturetribunal.org/.

IV. A Multicultural Lens: The *Atrato River Case*

No state other than Ecuador has written nature rights provisions into its national constitution. Courts in neighboring Colombia, however, were the first to interpret their constitution to encompass rights of nature by implication. In a 2016 judgment finding that the government had failed in its duty to protect the Atrato River from the effects of illegal mining and deforestation, the Colombian Constitutional Court (CCC) declared that the river was a subject of rights which the government must protect, conserve, maintain, and restore. In reaching this conclusion, the CCC reasoned:

> … Nature [is] a cross-cutting element of the Colombian constitutional order. Its importance lies, of course, in attention to the human beings that inhabit it and the need to have a healthy environment to live a dignified life in decent conditions; but also in relation to the other living organisms with whom the planet is shared, which are understood to be worthy of protection in themselves. … This is a position that is particularly relevant in Colombian constitutionalism, given the principle of cultural and ethnic pluralism that supports it, as well as the knowledge, usages and ancestral customs bequeathed by indigenous and tribal peoples.[32]

Like the Ecuadoran Constitution, the Rio Atrato rights of nature doctrine is an amalgam that draws from multiple sources. A strong emphasis of the judgment, however, is on multicultural constitutionalism. The case was brought against the government by Black communities and indigenous peoples and the judgment opens by describing Chocó, the region through which the Atrato River flows, as having a population which is 87% black Colombian and 10% indigenous, and 96% of which is composed of collectively owned territories.[33] Throughout, it frequently grounds itself in the "ancestral knowledge and alternative currents of thinking" of Colombia's ethnically identified communities.[34] Further, it views the survival of Colombia's ethnically identified peoples as entwined with the protection of their lands from environmental harm,

[32] Judgment T-622/16 (the *Atrato River Case*) 2016 (Constitutional Court of Colombia) (author translation).

[33] Colombia's Law 70 of 1993, which recognizes the rights of black Colombians to collectively own and occupy their ancestral lands, uses the terms "*comunidades negras*" to refer to the different types of communities of African descent. It was promoted and drafted by multiple black social movement organizations from different ideological orientations and origins. Honoring the terms used by the activists who drafted this law, I use the term "Black communities."

[34] *Atrato River Case* (n 31) 28 IV. 5.9.

acknowledging "the profound and intrinsic connection that exists between nature, its resources and the culture of the ethnic and indigenous communities that inhabit it, which are interdependent and cannot be understood in isolation from each other."[35] The protection and preservation of biological diversity is essential to the conservation of cultural diversity, and vice versa.[36] Protection of biodiversity does not mean excluding human activity. The *Atrato River Case* acknowledges that biocultural rights include the right of Black communities to continue artisanal mining even as other types of mining are proscribed.[37] The rights of nature emphasized here are an aspect of the Colombian constitutional commitment to a multicultural society and to treating ethnically identified people with a "differential" lens.[38]

Such an understanding of rights of nature is more limited than the stronger ontological claim described in the prior section. In that claim, the rights of nature provisions sought to bring a different understanding of the relation between humans and nature into the law applicable to the entirety of Ecuadoran society, and arguably even beyond Ecuador into international relations. A main line of reasoning in the *Atrato River Case*, by contrast, roots the recognition of nature rights in the "special" relation that indigenous and other peoples have to their territory—in other words, it is a claim that attaches to them, and not to others within Colombian society. This grounding gives Black communities and indigenous peoples leverage to exert control over and protect their way of life and their collectively held lands against extractivist projects such as industrial mining.

This is not the only reading of the *Atrato River Case*, and subsequent cases have explicitly gone beyond protection of the territories of Black communities and indigenous peoples. In 2018, for example, the Supreme Court of Colombia issued a climate change ruling in which it declared the Amazon basin to be a subject of rights which the government had a duty to protect from illegal deforestation.[39] The case was partly modeled on the famous *Juliana v. United States* climate change cases brought by children in the U.S., but adding distinct legal arguments, including that of the Amazon basin as itself a rights-bearing body. The plaintiffs were not indigenous peoples claiming to have a special

[35] ibid 5.11.
[36] ibid arts. 51 and 52.
[37] ibid V (seventh court order).
[38] For an analysis of how black social movement organizations in Colombia stressed ethnic differences rather than claims to equality, see Tianna S. Paschel, "The Right to Difference: Explaining Colombia's Shift from Color Blindness to the Law of Black Communities" (2010) 116(3) American Journal of Sociology 729–769.
[39] Judgment STC4630-2018 (the *Amazonas Case*) 2018 (Supreme Court of Colombia).

relation to the Amazon, but rather, as in *Juliana*, a diverse group of individual children claiming a more general stake in a future free of the ravages of global warming in excess of the 1.5–2°C to which states, including Colombia, committed through the Paris Climate Change Accord. The Supreme Court found that the state had obligations to the children and to future generations. It also declared that the Amazon basin was a legal subject with rights. Other subsequent Colombia cases, by contrast, rest more heavily on the reasoning of differential treatment pursuant to multicultural constitutionalism. For example, the Special Jurisdiction for the Peace (JEP), which is a transitional justice mechanism created to attend to the crimes committed during the fifty-year armed conflict, has declared that certain territories are victims of the war alongside human victims.[40] However, it is only the territories of Black communities and indigenous peoples that have been recognized as victims of the violence. Other areas in the same regions do not have this status. Further, the JEP only grants this status pursuant to a petition from the local communities: it does not proactively impose this view of territory on the communities involved. The two strands of justification, one based on multiculturalism and one based on promoting an ontological shift for society more generally, thus coexist in Colombian constitutionalism.

On the ground, implementation of the Atrato River judgment has faced many setbacks. The judgment sets up a system of guardianship of the river under the supervision of the government and the groups that filed the lawsuit. However, the plaintiffs argue that the government has not prioritized the restoration of the river, and has not put adequate resources into the project.[41] While local communities use the judgment in their struggle to defend the river, they report having had mixed success in restoring the river through implementation of the judgment. If the measure of a judgment's impact is instead its influence on subsequent jurisprudence and on social movements, however, then it is an important case indeed. Today, at least eight Colombian rivers have the status of rights-bearing subjects, as do the Amazon forest and the Páramo de Pisba, a bleak plateau. Each of these received their status through judgments that grounded themselves in the *Atrato River Case*. The Special Jurisdiction for the Peace has also relied heavily on the case in declaring the territories of indigenous and black Colombian groups to be victims of the war. Beyond Colombia, the *Atrato River Case* can be seen as contributing to a distinct line

[40] Alexandra Huneeus and Pablo Rueda, "Territory as a Victim of Armed Conflict" (2021) 15(1) International Journal of Transitional Justice 210–229.

[41] See, e.g., "The Atrato River: A river with rights webinar" (*YouTube*, December 15, 2020), https://www.youtube.com/watch?v=Gi3qcibqObM&t=555s.

of rights of nature laws which endow rivers with legal personality and rights to protection and restoration.[42] Most prominently, high courts in India and Bangladesh also read rights for major rivers into their constitutions, in 2017 and 2019 respectively.[43] The *Atrato River Case* itself cites the New Zealand prior grant of legal personality to the Whanganui River, as do the Indian and Bangladeshi cases. Both the New Zealand and Atrato River cases have been seminal. A difference is that the New Zealand rights of nature laws were passed pursuant to two treaty settlements between the Australian government and Māori groups, whereas the *Atrato River Case* is a general interpretation of constitutional law.

V. Nature Rights between Canon and Anti-Canon

Each of the three texts has had impact on subsequent law-making, jurisprudence, and social movements and merits consideration as a significant contribution to the transnational conversation on constitutional law and human rights. It is less clear, however, whether these texts, alone or taken together, will become part of the canon of liberal constitutionalism, defined as [here refer to hailbronner et al intro here], or whether they might be considered instead as the anticanon [and here].

The Douglas opinion can be read as advocating for a different process for assessing the value of a natural entity as considered against other social interests, without fundamentally recasting the ways we conceive of that value. It does not on its own pose a challenge to the U.S. constitutional tradition or stand in tension with the liberal tradition. The Constitution of Ecuador, by contrast, seeks to take constitutionalism to new terrain. It announced a constitution that no longer views the environment as the stage on which social life unfolds, or only as an object to be developed, conserved, or redistributed, but also as a living subject whose well-being, like that of the human being, must be considered in and fostered by each decision and action that government takes. Constitutional law must actively pursue the well-being of nature and protect it from harm, just

[42] See, e.g., International Rivers, Earth Law Center and Cyrus R. Vance Center for International Justice, "Rights of Rivers: A Global Survey of the Rapidly Developing Rights of Nature Jurisprudence Pertaining to Rivers" (2019); Gabriel Eckstein et al., "Conferring Legal Personality on the World's Rivers: A Brief Intellectual Assessment" (2019) 44 Water International 804; Craig M. Kauffman and Pamela Martin, "How Courts Are Developing River Rights Jurisprudence: Comparing Guardianship in New Zealand, Colombia, and India" (2019) 20 Vermont Journal of International Law 261.

[43] *Mohd. Salim v. State of Uttarakhand*, 2017 PIL No. 126 of 2014 (High Court of Uttarakhand) 10–11; *Human Rights and Peace for Bangladesh v. Government of Bangladesh and others* [2016] HCD Writ Petition No. 13989 of 2016, judgment declared on February 3, 2019 (Supreme Court of Bangladesh).

as it protects humans and other legal persons. These ideas disrupt some of the most profound commitments of the rights-based constitutional tradition: the priority of the individual, and the idea that rights are rooted in our shared humanity. From the perspective of liberal constitutionalism, prioritization of rights that do not belong to individuals and might even come into conflict with human rights is inherently risky and illiberal. Thus far, the meaning of rights of nature has mostly been determined through disputes over development or use of particular protected areas. In these disputes, the rights of nature allow broader standing, and tips the balance toward protection of those resources, although there are cases in which rights of nature claimants lose out as well.[44]

Rights of nature in the Colombian *Atrato River Case*, if understood as a type of multicultural constitutionalism, also stand in tension with liberal constitutionalism. The judgment can be read to emphasize the idea that the state has a duty to treat ethnic groups with a differential lens, including them within Colombian society by respecting their different cultures, traditions, and worldview. Under this view, the rights of nature are a tool for structuring the relation of government to indigenous and other ethnic groups. By legally recognizing the river's rights, the state acknowledges the traditions of the peoples of Chocó, while granting them a greater level of autonomy within the nation-state. Arguably, however, this recognition also challenges the liberal state's neutrality between different belief systems. Further, insofar as rights of nature rest on the special relation of a people to their local environment, they tend toward the illiberal ideal of one people, one territory, precisely at the time that climate change threatens to render so many places uninhabitable.[45] Finally, it treats people as group members, rather than individuals, which inherently creates tensions with liberal individualist ideals.

These are tensions which liberal constitutionalism has come to embrace, however uneasily. Colombian constitutionalism in particular has struggled to balance the competing values of a neutral liberal state that nonetheless grants a differential regime of rights to certain minority groups.[46] The regional human rights bodies, the Inter-American Human Rights Commission and Court, have similarly developed a line of decisions that demands differential treatment of indigenous groups, acknowledging the special status of indigenous

[44] Kauffman and Martin, "Can Rights of Nature Make Development More Sustainable?" (n 25).

[45] This tension is captured in the Orange Country Florida Rights of Nature ordinance that limits standing to those who have legal residence in the United States, thereby excluding the many residents who do not have documented status. See Section 704.1—Right to Clean Water, Standing and Enforcement.

[46] Will Kymlicka, *Multicultural Citizenship: A Liberal Theory of Minority Rights* (Clarendon Press 2019).

peoples and others whose traditional ties to the land merit special protection even if this means, at times, that rights apply differently to certain groups.[47] While some worry about this posing a conceptual challenge to liberal politics, others worry it is all too easily subsumed by neoliberal politics. Charles Hale argues that by focusing political battles on the symbolic realm of cultural recognition, cultural rights weaken the push for actual structural changes. They thus "not only pose little challenge to the forward march of the neoliberal project but also induce the bearers of these rights to join in the march."[48] Hale was writing about cultural rights, not rights of nature claims, but rights of nature are an attractive idea that could similarly be used to mask the absence of structural change.

Although we have analyzed these different strands in rights of nature as analytically distinct, it is also the case that they are interlinked: each of the texts examined here draws on more than one justificatory strand in constructing its argument. The Douglas dissent alludes to expanding "the boundaries of the community to include ... the land."[49] The Ecuador Constitution also gives special consideration to the relation of indigenous people to their land and self-consciously understands rights of nature as rooted in Kichwa thought. The *Atrato River Case* at times steps outside the multicultural frame to announce that the Atrato River is a subject of rights under Colombian constitutionalism not because the people of Chocó thus view it, but because their views are true: nature has moral value as an end in itself, and the relations between humans and non-humans is a moral, social relation. Further, the concept of rights of nature implies reliance on a procedural base of standing for non-humans, consonant with the Douglas dissent. Thus, while each text relies primarily on one of the justificatory strands, each bolsters its argumentation by drawing from all three.

The rights of nature legal texts examined here began life as off-canon and even anticanon moves seeking to alter the status quo. In a very short time, however, they have come to be accepted, cited, and copied. As an idea, at least, they have gained traction in a brief period. Arguably, it is precisely by quietly shifting between the different strands of argumentation highlighted here that

[47] United Nations Declaration on the Rights of Indigenous Peoples (September 13, 2007); Indigenous and Tribal Peoples Convention (entered into force September 5, 1991) ILO Convention 169; Roberto Rojas Dávila, "Afro-descendants as subjects of rights in International Human Rights law" (*SUR 28*, 2018), https://sur.conectas.org/en/afro-descendants-as-subjects-of-rights-in-international-human-rights-law/, accessed December 8, 2020.

[48] Charles Hale, "Neoliberal Multiculturalism: The Remaking of Cultural Rights and Racial Dominance in Central America" (2005) 28 PoLAR: Political and Legal Anthropology Review 10–19, 13.

[49] *Sierra Club v. Morton* (n 4) 752.

the texts succeed. The legal concept of rights of nature connects indigenous social movements to different types of environmentalist movements and to critics of neoliberal economic development, while at the same time providing a legal idea that is palatable to lawyers and workable for judges. Further, it is an idea rooted in indigenous cultures and environmental activism, but also in U.S. Supreme Court jurisprudence and the legal academy. Despite the differences and even contradictions between them, the three justificatory strands work together to open a space for the legal figure of rights of nature within the canon of rights-based constitutionalism.

28

Canonizing the Corporation

Liberal, Social, and Transformative Varieties of Corporate Constitutionalism

Michael Riegner

I. Introduction: From Hidden Protagonist to Constitutional Canon

If the 'canon' of constitutional democracy comprises those texts which comparatists consider 'foundational' for their discipline,[1] the corporation does not seem to be part of it.[2] Canonical documents like the US federal constitution or the French Declaration of Human Rights do not explicitly mention the corporate form. None of the leading cases discussed in typical textbooks pertain to the corporation, and no current handbook on comparative constitutionalism includes a thematic chapter on corporate matters. The corporation is treated as a creature of private law, left to private comparatists and their respective disciplinary canon.[3]

This first impression, however, is misleading. The corporation has long played an important role in constitutional orders around the world—albeit a hidden one, overshadowed by other protagonists that populate the constitutional canon: individuals, states, peoples, etc. Historically, trading companies played a significant role in the evolution from colonial to constitutional government, canonized in revolutionary narratives like the Boston Tea Party.[4]

[1] Michaela Hailbronner, 'Constructing the Global Constitutional Canon: Between Authority and Criticism' (2019) 69(2) University of Toronto Law Journal 248.

[2] For the purposes of this chapter, 'corporation' is understood in minimalist terms as a legal entity with a separate legal personality and limited liability. The main focus is on for-profit business corporations, but their constitutional status is not always differentiated from non-profit entities. For a similar approach, see Teemu Ruskola, 'What is a Corporation?' (2014) 37 Seattle University Law Review 639.

[3] See, e.g., András Sajó and Michel Rosenfeld (eds), *The Oxford Handbook of Comparative Constitutional Law* (Oxford University Pres2012) (mentioning 'corporations' twice in passing at 384, 1037).

[4] Philip Stern, 'The Corporation in History' in Grietje Baars and André Spicer (eds), *The Corporation* (Cambridge University Press 2017); Adam Winkler, *We the Corporations* (Liveright Publishing 2018), ch. 1: 'In the beginning, America was a corporation.'

Michael Riegner, *Canonizing the Corporation* In: *Global Canons in an Age of Contestation.* Edited by: Sujit Choudhry, Michaela Hailbronner, and Mattias Kumm, Oxford University Press.
DOI: 10.1093/9780191956912.003.0028

Economically, the corporate form entrenched the move from feudalism to capitalism, from status via contract to organization.[5] Politically, corporations have long been sites, objects, and actors in power struggles between social classes and political parties, democrats and authoritarians, capital-importing and capital-exporting countries, North and South.[6] The corporate form thus embodies the tensions and complementarities between capitalist economy, fundamental rights, and democratic self-government that animate many contemporary contestations of constitutionalism.

These historical, economic, and political developments have left their mark not only in private corporate law, but also in constitutional law. While some canonical texts are silent on corporations, others explicitly address their formation, rights, or responsibilities. This is especially true for younger constitutions from the Global South, but also for some texts in the North that are often overlooked—such as the state constitutions of Delaware and New York.[7] In constitutional practice, corporations have been strategic litigants and repeat players, outnumbering and outperforming individual plaintiffs at critical moments of constitutional development, especially in the US.[8] In Europe, some of the most iconic leading cases bear the name of the companies that litigated them, beginning with *van Gend & Loos* in 1963.[9] Even in international human rights law, corporations have incrementally acquired many of the protections said to flow from the nature of 'human' beings, while the debate on business and human rights raises the question with renewed urgency whether corporations also have obligations under international law.[10] Despite these developments in domestic and international law, comparative constitutionalists have been slow to recognize the corporation as an important actor, and sometimes

[5] David Ciepley, 'Beyond Public and Private: Toward a Political Theory of the Corporation' (2013) 107(01) Am Pol Sci Rev 139, 140; Katharina Pistor, *Code of Capital* (Princeton University Press 2019), 48 et seq.

[6] Bastian van Apeldoorn and Naná d Graaf, 'The Corporation in Political Science' in Baars and Spicer (n 4).

[7] For a comparative overview with further references, see Jedidiah Kroncke and Michael Riegner, 'Corporation' [2020] *Max Planck Encyclopedia of Comparative Constitutional Law* https://oxcon.ouplaw.com/browse?prd=MPECCOL.

[8] Adam Winkler, 'The Long History of Corporate Rights' (2018) 98 Boston University Law Review Online 64, 67; John Coates, 'Corporate Speech & the First Amendment' (2015) 30(2) Constitutional Commentary 223.

[9] On corporate litigation before the ECJ, see Walter Mattli and Anne-Marie Slaughter, 'Revisiting the European Court of Justice' (1998) 52(1) International Organization 177, 188–189.

[10] Anna Grear, *Redirecting Human Rights* (Palgrave Macmillan 2010); Marius Emberland, *The Human Rights of Companies* (Oxford University Press 2006); Jochen v. Bernstorff, 'Business and Human Rights: On the Expansion of Human Rights Obligations to Abusive Corporate Practices' in Christina Binder et al. (eds), *Corporate Social Responsibility and Social Rights* (Nomos 2010).

even protagonist, in their own field. If they compare the corporation at all, they do so within a theoretically limited, rights-based framework.[11]

This chapter argues that uncovering the protagonist role of the corporation enables us to reappraise and broaden the canon of comparative constitutionalism, and to theorize its implicit assumptions about constitutional agency, economic organization, and political economy. These assumptions tend to be shaped by liberal constitutional theory, with its focus on the political system and civil and political rights. Its underlying epistemic framework is constituted by foundational dichotomies of state vs individual, public vs private, political vs economic, authority vs rights, sovereignty vs property, democracy vs markets, national vs international. In this binary framework, the corporation is typically attributed to the realm of the private and the economic, of rights, property, and markets.

In practice, this theoretical attribution is irritated by the empirical role of the corporation as an intermediary organization that often stands in between these dichotomous categories.[12] It also obscures alternative conceptions of the corporation in other varieties of constitutionalism. Extending the comparison beyond the liberal type enables comparatists to identify at least three types of corporate constitutionalism: a liberal, a social-democratic, and a transformative variety.[13] These varieties understand the corporation not only as a bearer of rights against the state, but also as a site of worker representation, and as an institution with constitutionalized relationships to other stakeholders, to the national economy, and to the environment.

To illustrate this argument, this chapter analyses three constitutional cases as canonical texts: the US Supreme Court's 2010 decision in *Citizens United* as part of the liberal (anti-)canon; the German Federal Constitutional Court's judgment in the 1979 co-determination case as an element of a social-democratic constitutional canon; and the 2018 decision by the Constitutional Court of Ecuador in the case against Chevron as an instance of transformative constitutionalism. These judgments typify three distinct ways of conceptualizing the constitutional role of the corporation. They originate from three different world regions and language communities, and from three constitutional orders that emerged from three distinct waves of constitution-making.

[11] Peter J. Oliver, *The Fundamental Rights of Companies* (Hart 2021); Mirjam Baldegger, *Menschenrechtsschutz für juristische Personen in Deutschland, der Schweiz und den Vereinigten Staaten* (Duncker & Humblot 2017). For a broader comparative framework, see Kroncke and Riegner (n 7).

[12] For empirical categorizations, see e.g. van Apeldoorn and Graaf (n 6); Gerald Davis and Suntae Kim, 'The Corporation in Sociology' in Baars and Spicer (n 4).

[13] Kroncke and Riegner (n 7), paras 10 et seq. On constitutional typologies, see Mark Tushnet, 'Editorial: Varieties of Constitutionalism' (2016) 14(1) ICON 1.

They are not only important leading cases within their respective jurisdictions but have also resonated internationally—either as a model to be emulated or as anti-model to be avoided. As such, they also reflect the global political economy of knowledge production that affects any attempt at canonizing comparative constitutional law.[14]

II. The Liberal (Anti-)Canon: *Citizens United* in the US Supreme Court (2010)

A. Context

It is rare for a sitting US president to directly attack the Supreme Court in a State of the Union address. Yet this is what president Barack Obama did in 2010, a week after the Court had decided *Citizens United v. Federal Election Commission.*[15] Based on the First Amendment's free speech clause, the Court had invalidated a federal law that prohibited corporations or labor unions from financing political advertising for or against specific candidates in federal elections with their general treasury funds. For Obama, this decision struck at US democracy itself: 'Last week the Supreme Court reversed a century of law that I believe will open the floodgates for special interests—including foreign corporations—to spend without limit in our elections.'[16]

Obama's criticism foreshadowed a decade of renewed debate about the role of corporations in US constitutional democracy, in which *Citizens United*, rightly or wrongly, became a focal point for critiques of corporate power in US politics.[17] This concern resonated in legal debates around the world: the Federal Supreme Court of Brazil, for instance, extensively discussed *Citizens United* in a 2015 decision, only to reach the opposite conclusion: corporate

[14] cf. Daniel Bonilla Maldonado, 'The Political Economy of Legal Knowledge' in Colin Crawford and Daniel Bonilla Maldonado (eds), *Constitutionalism in the Americas* (Elgar 2018); Christine Schwöbel-Patel, '(Global) Constitutionalism and the Geopolitics of Knowledge' in Philipp Dann, Michael Riegner, and Maxim Bönnemann (eds), *The Global South and Comparative Constitutional Law* (Oxford University Press 2020).

[15] 558 U.S. 310, judgment of 21 January 2010.

[16] See https://obamawhitehouse.archives.gov/the-press-office/remarks-president-state-union-address.

[17] See only Justin Levitt, 'Confronting the Impact of "Citizens United"' (2010) 29(1) Yale Law and Policy Review 217; Robert Post, *Citizens Divided* (Harvard University Press 2014); Winkler, *We the Corporations* (n 4).

campaign expenditures were not protected, but *prohibited* by the Brazilian Constitution.[18]

In global comparison, it is thus tempting to see *Citizens United* as a global outlier and a pathology of US free speech libertarianism—an element of the anti-canon, confirming the declining international influence of US constitutionalism.[19] On closer inspection, however, the decision presents a more complex picture. Beneath its anti-canonical cover lie many pages of the liberal constitutional canon, in which the corporation plays a protagonist role as a rights-bearing entity, embodying ideas of economic liberty and associational freedom. In that sense, *Citizens United* is also an opportunity to uncover the corporation as a hidden protagonist of liberal constitutionalism.

B. The Case: Facts and Decision

Citizens United, a private non-profit corporation, intended to publicize a movie criticizing Hillary Clinton, who was running in presidential primary elections at that time.[20] Federal election law prohibited corporations and labor unions from funding such political advertising from their general treasury. It allowed such financing only through separate legal entities, so-called political action committees, to which shareholders, employees, or union members contribute on a voluntary basis.[21] Such restrictions on corporate political spending, with roots dating back to the 1907 Tillman Act, sought to limit the influence of concentrated economic wealth in elections and to prevent corporate executives from misusing 'other people's money' for their personal political preferences.[22]

In a narrow 5–4 decision, the Supreme Court struck down the prohibition as a violation of the First Amendment's free speech clause. The majority opinion rests on three propositions, partly grounded in earlier case law, partly overruling earlier precedent: First, spending on political advertising is constitutionally protected speech, and such speech does not lose its protection

[18] Supreme Federal Tribunal, *Conselho Federal da Ordem dos Advogados do Brazil v. Presidente de la República et al.*, judgement of 17 September 2015, ADI 4650. On the broader responses, see Shannon O'Neil, 'Latin America v. Citizens United' [2015] Foreign Policy https://foreignpolicy.com/2015/10/07/brazil-citizens-united-supreme-court-elections/#.

[19] See generally Heinz Klug, 'Model and Anti-Model' [2000] Wisconsin Law Review 597; David Law and Mia Versteeg, 'The Declining Influence of the US Constitution' (2012) 87 New York University Law Review 762.

[20] *Citizens United v. FEC*, Opinion of the Court (Kennedy J) (2010) 08-205 558 US no. 310 1 (US Supreme Court), 2–4.

[21] 2 U.S.C. § 441b.

[22] Adam Winkler, '"Other People's Money"' (2004) 92 Georgetown Law Journal 871.

'simply because its source is a corporation'.[23] Second, prohibiting such spending amounts to a ban on 'corporate political speech',[24] even if political action committees remain permitted to speak.[25] Third, such a ban can only be justified by a compelling state interest, yet none of the three rationales advanced by government withstands such strict scrutiny: neither the safeguarding of political equality against distortions resulting from concentrated private wealth, nor preventing the corruption of candidates, nor the protection of dissenting shareholders against corporate speech they disagree with.[26]

To the majority, distortions of public opinion-formation by corporate money are irrelevant because the government has no legitimate interest 'in equalizing the relative ability of individuals and groups to influence the outcome of elections'.[27] Likewise, the fact that corporate election spending effectively purchases 'influence over or access to elected officials does not mean that these officials are corrupt'.[28] To the contrary, '[t]he fact that a corporation, or any other speaker, is willing to spend money to try to persuade voters presupposes that the people have the ultimate influence over elected officials'.[29]

The dissenting minority of justices harshly criticized this reasoning, which effectively ruled out distinctions between corporate and individual speech rights. The dissenters would have upheld the law in question because it did not 'ban speech' but only regulated the modalities of financing political speech, and because the legal characteristics of corporations differentiated them sufficiently from individuals to justify greater restrictions.[30] Based on earlier precedents, the dissenters would have accepted a compelling governmental interest in preventing 'the corrosive and distorting effects of immense aggregations of wealth that are accumulated with the help of the corporate form and that have little or no correlation to the public's support for the corporation's political ideas'.[31]

[23] *Citizens United v. FEC*, Opinion of the Court (Kennedy J) (n 20), 25.
[24] ibid 2, 40, 45, 46.
[25] ibid 21–23.
[26] ibid 33–46.
[27] ibid 34, citing *Buckley*, 424 U.S. at 48; and *Bellotti*, 435 U.S. at 791, fn. 30.
[28] ibid 43.
[29] ibid 44.
[30] *Citizens United v. FEC*, Dissenting Opinion (Stevens J), 1–2, 24, 27, 29–32.
[31] ibid 49.

C. Canonical and Anti-Canonical Elements: The Corporation as Bearer of Rights Against the State

The controversy surrounding *Citizens United* should not obscure the fact that the decision builds on widely shared premises concerning the status of the corporation in liberal constitutionalism.[32] As these premises emerged over time, they have given a relatively concrete and stable meaning to one important aspect of constitutional liberalism, which is otherwise a multilayered and contested ideal.[33] The first of these liberal premises is the idea that the corporation is a private 'association of citizens'[34] that aggregates individual liberty and property, not a public privilege conferred by the state. This conception reflects the nineteenth-century move from the concession theory of the corporation to a contractual understanding based on free incorporation.[35] The corporate form is thus conceived primarily as a creature of private law, and corporate governance as a result of private legal ordering.

From this first premise follows a second, namely that in terms of constitutional law, the corporation is conceived as a bearer of fundamental rights against the state. [36] Beginning in the nineteenth century, the US Supreme Court extended constitutional rights to the corporation, starting with economic rights like property and later including politically relevant rights like free speech.[37] For if 'the individual person's right to speak includes the right to speak *in association with other individual persons*',[38] then the association itself must also be protected against government interference. The first two premises implied, thirdly, a specific conception of political economy: they differentiated economic activity from the political process and located democracy in the sphere of the state—not in the sphere of corporate capitalism. The primary role

[32] On the liberal constitutional conception of the corporation, see already Kroncke and Riegner (n 7), paras 10–11; Ruskola (n 2).

[33] On 'liberalism' and 'liberal constitutionalism' as multivalent concepts, see only Michael Freeden, *Liberalism* (Oxford University Press 2015); Massimo Fichera, 'Liberalism' [2017] *Max Planck Encyclopedia of Comparative Constitutional Law* https://oxcon.ouplaw.com/home/MPECCOL.

[34] *Citizens United v. FEC*, Opinion of the Court (Kennedy J) (n 20), 38.

[35] James W. Hurst, *The Legitimacy of the Business Corporation in the Law of the United States, 1780–1970* (University of Virgina Press 1970), 13–57. Free incorporation has been constitutionalized in some state constitutions in the US to the extent that they prohibit special incorporation by statute, see e.g. Art. IX §1 Delaware State Constitution.

[36] *Citizens United v. FEC*, Opinion of the Court (Kennedy J) (n 20), 23.

[37] cf. *Bank of the United States v. Deveaux* (1809); *Dartmouth College v. Woodward* (1819); *Santa Clara County v. Southern Pacific Railroad Co.* (1886) (often cited as the first case extending the Fourteenth Amendment protection to corporations). But see for discussion, Winkler, *We the Corporations* (n 4), 35 et seq.; Naomi Lamoreaux and William Novak, 'Corporations and American Democracy' in Naomi Lamoreaux and William Novak (eds), *Corporations and American Democracy* (Harvard University Press 2017).

[38] *Citizens United v. FEC*, Concurring Opinion (Scalia J), 7–8, emphasis in original.

of the democratic state was to regulate negative externalities of corporate activity, and its regulatory reach was limited by doctrines regarding permissible restrictions of constitutional rights.[39]

These three premises are canonical in the sense that they are widely shared among liberal constitutional democracies. Free incorporation is the norm in capitalist market economies and constitutionally protected, to varying extents, by freedom of association rights.[40] Corporations are recognized as holders of constitutional rights in many jurisdictions, sometimes by explicit textual provisions like Article 19(3) of the German Basic Law, and more frequently by judicial interpretation.[41] There is basic agreement among liberal constitutionalists that state and corporation belong to separate spheres and are subject to different logics—public vs private, sovereignty vs property, democracy vs liberty etc.—and that public regulation of private corporate activity is limited by fundamental rights.[42]

Beneath each of these basic premises, however, lurk conceptual disagreements and doctrinal divergences between different varieties of liberalism and capitalism. The applicability of rights and the intensity of their protection vary considerably among liberal-democratic constitutional orders.[43] The variation within liberal democracies become particularly stark with respect to the regulation of corporate participation in public opinion-formation, campaign finance, and the law-making process. It is here that the *Citizens United* majority turns to an anti-canonical libertarianism that prioritizes corporate freedom of expression over competing values of political equality and democratic integrity.[44] Other theories of liberal-democratic constitutionalism in the US and abroad give more weight to these competing values and tend to conceive of the corporate form as a legitimate proxy for concentrated wealth that risks

[39] Herbert Hovenkamp, 'Capitalism' in Kermit L. Hall (ed.), *The Oxford Companion to the Supreme Court of the United States* (2nd edn, Oxford University Press 2005); Elizabeth Pollmann, 'Constitutionalizing Corporate Law' (2016) 69 Vanderbilt Law Review 639, 654–657; Kroncke and Riegner (n 7), 11.

[40] See only Ulrich Preuß, 'Associative Rights' in Sajó and Rosenfeld (n 3); John Armour et al., 'What is Corporate Law?' in Klaus Hopt et al. (eds), *The Anatomy of Corporate Law* (3rd edn, Oxford University Press 2017).

[41] Oliver (n 11); Baldegger (n 11); André Ramos Tavares, *Direito constitucional da empresa* (Grupo Gen/Editora Método 2013), 29; Emberland (n 10).

[42] Kroncke and Riegner (n 7), 11, 22; Ruskola (n 2), 642 et seq.; and generally Frank Michelman, 'Constitutions and the Public/Private Divide' in Sajó and Rosenfeld (n 3).

[43] Peter Oliver, 'Companies and Their Fundamental Rights' (2015) 64(3) ICLQ 661; Kroncke and Riegner (n 7), para. 22; Emberland (n 10), 155 et seq. It should be noted that the US Supreme Court does differentiate between corporate and individual rights in areas such as the Fourteenth Amendment, but recent case law has considerably expanded the reach of First Amendment rights.

[44] Kathleen Sullivan, 'Two Concepts of Free Speech' (2010) 124 Harvard Law Review 143; Post (n 17).

undermining them. Not all egalitarian-minded courts go so far as to constitutionally *prohibit* specific corporate political activities, as the Brazilian Supreme Court did, but many *permit* legislatures to limit or even ban corporations from engaging in campaign finance, electioneering, or political activity more generally.[45]

Even these jurisdictions, however, grapple with the limitations of a liberal corporate constitutionalism centered on rights, at the expense of questions concerning economic organization and democratic representation. The more corporate rights expand from the economic to the political realm, the more pressing becomes the question of who controls their exercise.[46] Who really speaks when the corporation speaks, and who determines what it has to say—shareholders, directors, or employees? In *Citizens United*, the majority dismissed concerns of representation because it saw 'little evidence of abuse that cannot be corrected by shareholders "through the procedures of corporate democracy" '.[47] The notion of 'corporate democracy' does more to obscure than to resolve the agency problems well known to corporate lawyers, but it does highlight their constitutional dimension.

III. The Social-Democratic Canon: Co-Determination in the German Constitutional Court (1979)

A. Context

When the Federal Constitutional Court announced its judgment in the co-determination case in March 1979,[48] a collective sigh of relief reverberated through the West German republic. The decision ended a decade-long

[45] Elin Falguera, Sam Jones, and Magnus Ohman (eds), *Funding of Political Parties and Election Campaigns* (International IDEA 2014), 22: 'Around one in five countries bans corporate donations'; Eugene D. Mazo and Timothy K. Kuhner (eds), *Democracy by the People* (Cambridge University Press 2018).

[46] Lucian Bebchuk and Robert Jackson, 'Corporate Political Speech: Who Decides?' (2010) 124 Harvard Law Review 83; Pollmann (n 39). In some jurisdictions, legislators have addressed these problems in corporate law, see e.g. ss. 366 et seq. UK Companies Act 2006.

[47] *Citizens United v. FEC*, Opinion of the Court (Kennedy J) (n 20), 46, citing *Bellotti*, 435 U.S. at 794; see id, at 794, fn. 34. On 'shareholder democracy', see Abraham Singer and Amit Ron, 'Models of Shareholder Democracy: A Transnational Approach' (2018) 7(3) Glob. Const. 422.

[48] *Mitbestimmung* (1979) 1 BvR 532, 533/77, 419/78, BvL 21/78 50 BVerfGE 290 (Federal Constitutional Court). An English translation of the summary prepared by the Court's press office is reprinted in Herbert Wiedemann, 'Codetermination by Workers in German Enterprises' (1980) 28(1) American Journal of Comparative Law 79.

stand-off between the Court and the reform-minded federal government, which had come to power in the wake of the 1968 movement.[49] When its leader Willy Brandt took office as the first social-democratic chancellor of the Federal Republic, he proclaimed nothing less than a constitutional moment, a profound democratization of a hierarchical state and society: 'We wish to dare more democracy … We want a democratic society, in which everyone contributes towards an expansion of co-responsibility and co-determination.'[50]

The Co-Determination Act of 1976, which expanded worker participation in corporate governance, was a signature project of this social-democratic reform agenda. It was hailed by labor unions and opposed by employer associations and major players in corporate Germany like Daimler-Benz, Bayer, and Bosch, which all filed a joint constitutional complaint. The original complaint was signed by industry leader Hanns Martin Schleyer, who was soon after kidnapped and murdered by the anti-capitalist 'Red Army Faction'.[51] Given the intensity of confrontation, 'the impression has arisen that the composition of the supervisory board in the large enterprises has become the life and death issue of the country'.[52]

In this atmosphere of crisis, the Constitutional Court handed down a unanimous judgment that unequivocally upheld the new co-determination law. Eventually accepted by all sides, the carefully crafted decision defused social tensions and muted institutional criticism of the Court. While it is tempting to compare the co-determination judgment to the US Supreme Court's decision in *West Coast Hotel v. Parish*, it has not gone down in history as a pragmatic surrender in the face of political pressure, but rather as 'a statesmanlike articulation of enduring principle'.[53] As such, it bears all the hallmarks of a foundational text in the social-democratic constitutional canon.

B. The Case: Facts and Decision

In the German system of corporate governance, a company is governed by two boards: a management board, which runs the day-to-day business, and

[49] Justin Collings, *Democracy's Guardians* (Oxford University Press 2015), 109 et seq.; Michaela Hailbronner, *Traditions and Transformations* (Oxford University Press 2015), 64, 86–87, 132.

[50] Willy Brandt (1969) 71 Verhandlungen des deutschen Bundestages Stenographische Berichte, 20, 28–29, author's translation. On the constitutional implications, see Collings (n 49), 110–113 ('Brandt proclaimed the Federal Republic's first authentic, popular constitutional moment', at 112).

[51] On the political context of the judgment, see Collings (n 49), 177–179; Wiedemann (n 48), 84.

[52] Wiedemann (n 48), 83.

[53] Collings (n 49), citing *West Coast Hotel v. Parish*, 300 U.S. 379 (1937).

the supervisory board, which elects and monitors the management board. As a rule, the supervisory board is elected by the shareholders. The 1976 Co-Determination Act changed this rule for corporations with more than 2,000 employees.[54] For those companies, the Act mandates equal representation of workers on the supervisory board: half of the board members are to be elected by employees, half by shareholders. In the event of a tied vote, the chairperson of the supervisory board casts an additional, decisive vote. The chairperson is elected by a two-thirds majority of board members in a first voting round, but if that super-majority fails to materialize, the shareholder representatives ultimately decide alone.[55]

'Co-determination' thus did not amount to full parity for workers: if united, shareholder representatives ultimately prevail, but only after going through procedures encouraging negotiation and compromise typical of the German 'social market economy'.[56] Corporate employers, however, worried that even near-parity would interfere with efficient management, and thus violated their constitutional rights to property (Art. 14 of the Basic Law), to freedom of association and collective bargaining (Art. 9), and to professional and entrepreneurial freedom (Art. 12), as well as the capitalist 'economic constitution' allegedly enshrined by the Basic Law.[57]

The Constitutional Court rejected these arguments one by one. First setting out the constitutional standards against which to measure the law, the Court emphasized that the Basic Law did not constitutionalize a specific economic order: it was 'neutral with regard to economic policy' and left economic ordering to the democratically legitimated legislature.[58] Co-determination legislation had to respect the specific individual rights enshrined in the constitutional text, but these rights did not amount to an abstract institutional guarantee of capitalist market economy.[59]

In a second move, the court developed a deferential standard of scrutiny with respect to the specific rights at issue. The rights to property, freedom of association, and professional freedom were applicable to legal persons by

[54] For an overview of the Act and its initial application, see Hans-Joachim Mertens and Erich Schanze, 'The German Co-Determination Act of 1976' (1979) 2 Journal of Comparative Corporate Law and Securities Regulation 75.

[55] §§ 1, 7, 27, 29, 31 Gesetz über die Mitbestimmung der Arbeitnehmer vom 4.5.1976 (BGBl. I S. 1153). An English translation of the legal text currently in force is reprinted in Federal Ministry of Labour and Social Affairs, *Co-Determination 2019* (2019). For an overview of the different kinds of worker involvement at that time, see Wiedemann (n 48), 79–83.

[56] On the coordinated variety of capitalism exemplified by the German social market economy, see Peter A. Hall and David W. Soskice (eds), *Varieties of Capitalism* (Oxford University Press 2001).

[57] Wiedemann (n 48), 84; *Mitbestimmung* (n 48), para. 65.

[58] *Mitbestimmung* (n 48), paras 140–141.

[59] Collings (n 49), 179.

virtue of Article 19 paragraph 3 of the Basic Law, but their limitation was subject to a lenient proportionality assessment. In the corporate context, the exercise of these rights was highly dependent on other rights holders, especially workers. Corporate property thus entailed particular social obligations, as enshrined in Article 14 paragraph 2, which the legislator was empowered to concretize.[60] Hence, the co-determination legislation was ultimately justified by legitimate interests: namely, 'alleviating the subordination of workers under management's authority', 'complementing the economic legitimacy of management with social legitimacy', and 'encouraging cooperation and integration' so as to 'politically secure the market economy'.[61] These interests outweighed potential inefficiencies in corporate management, although the legislator remained obliged to monitor the effects of the law in practice and to remedy any dysfunctions which might occur.[62]

C. Canonical Elements and Limitations: From Rights to Representation

In its constitutional reasoning, the judgment echoed long-standing tenets of a social-democratic constitutional thought. Contemporary social-democratic constitutionalism is often equated with a redistributive welfare state and social rights to health, education, and social security.[63] But in its original formulation, social democracy was as much about the extension of constitutional principles of equality and democracy from the realm of political organization to economic organization.[64] In this conception, the capitalist corporation is not understood as a voluntary contractual association, but as a hierarchical organization which sustains asymmetric power relations between workers and employers, to be equalized and democratized by law. Legally, the social-democratic corporation is thus conceived as a site of economic democracy and worker representation.[65] The constitutional paradigm thus shifts from rights to representation, from corporate personality to the internal organization of economic institutions.

[60] *Mitbestimmung* (n 48), paras 149–173.
[61] ibid para. 169, author's translation.
[62] ibid paras 131, 138, 228.
[63] See only Tushnet (n 13), 3.
[64] Ben Jackson, 'Social Democracy' in Michael Freeden, Lyman T. Sargent, and Marc Stears (eds), *The Oxford Handbook of Political Ideologies* (Oxford University Press 2015).
[65] Ruth Dukes, *The Labour Constitution* (Oxford University Press 2014), 13–20; Ewan McGaughey, 'The Codetermination Bargains' (2016) 23(1) Columbia Journal of European Law 135; Kroncke and Riegner (n 7), 12–14.

A prototypical expression of this approach can be found in the Weimar Constitution of 1919, which contained an entire chapter on the 'economic order' and constitutionalized worker participation in corporate governance in its Article 165.[66] This provision was only partially implemented in legislation and read down by the Weimar courts, but it continued to influence legislation and constitutional thinking in postwar Germany and abroad.[67] In light of this constitutional legacy, the 1976 Co-Determination Act was not just a piece of ordinary legislation, but part and parcel of Chancellor Brandt's constitutional movement, aiming to extend democratic principles to the economic and social spheres.[68]

While the Constitutional Court stopped short of constitutionalizing this vision explicitly, it adopted several of its core principles in its reasoning.[69] First, it accepted the premise that the corporation is a hierarchical organization that tends to subordinate workers: it was this 'heteronomous determination' (*Fremdbestimmung*) that justified co-determination (*Mitbestimmung*) in the first place.[70] Second, the Court embraced a theory of property rights that emphasized its social function based on Article 14 paragraph 2: the farther removed a property interest is from the personal sphere of individual human beings, and the more its enjoyment depends on cooperation with others, the more social obligations attach to it, and the more discretion and deference legislators enjoy in regulating it. In the context of large, impersonal corporations, property rights thus entail particular social obligations, reinforced and circumscribed by the workers' rights to professional freedom.[71] Thirdly, the Court recognized that co-determination gave workers a voice in defining 'the conditions under which employees exercise their fundamental right to professional freedom'.[72] Workers' rights thus justified restrictions on private property, or, in other words, they had some form of horizontal effect.[73]

Co-determination and its underlying ideals have resonated in legal orders around the world. Since the Weimar Constitution, worker participation

[66] K. D. Ewing, 'Economic Rights' in Sajó and Rosenfeld (n 3), 1039–1040.

[67] Dukes (n 65), 20–22, 33–42.

[68] This was certainly the view of social-democrats and the labor movement, but the law also reflected a broader political consensus across partisan lines, cf. Mertens and Schanze (n 54), 75.

[69] It is widely believed that the judgment was authored by Konrad Hesse, who was a student of Rudolf Smend and nominated to the Court by the Social Democratic Party, see Collings (n 49), 165, 180.

[70] *Mitbestimmung* (n 48), 169.

[71] ibid 148–167.

[72] ibid 169.

[73] While horizontal effect is an old idea, social democrats gave it a specific meaning in the context of twentieth-century corporate capitalism, closely linking it to collective labor rights and ideas of industrial democracy, cf. Gavin W. Anderson, 'Social Democracy and the Limits of Rights Constitutionalism' (2004) 17(1) Can. J. Law Jurisprud. 31; McGaughey (n 65).

in corporate management has found its way into constitutional texts, e.g. in Italy, Portugal, Brazil, and India, which tend to even mandate some form of co-determination.[74] Similarly, the social function of property has become a staple feature of many constitutions.[75] Finally, horizontal effect has been a global success story, although its ideological foundations have diversified together with its fields of application.[76]

In comparison with more ambitious versions of social-democratic constitutionalism, the co-determination judgment may even seem as a timid, and less canonical, variant. Yet, the judgment did achieve something that has remained elusive for social-democratic ideas in many other contexts: namely, practical effectiveness and broad societal consensus, which helped entrench co-determination politically, if not constitutionally. In a historical and comparative perspective, the co-determination case thus deserves its canonical status not for its innovating ideas of social-democratic constitutionalism, but for convincingly fleshing them out and giving them practical effect in a decisive area of economic organization.

The relative success of the German co-determination jurisprudence does not necessarily mean that it is a model to be emulated everywhere. Even if co-determination currently seems to be experiencing a timid revival, its proponents are well advised to empirically study the practical functioning and contextual determinants of different models.[77] In the context of a globalized economy, it remains to be seen whether co-determination will wither away in the face of transnational corporate mobility, or carry forward the social-democratic tradition in some form of transnational societal constitutionalism.[78]

[74] Luke Mason, 'Labour Rights' [2017] *Max Planck Encyclopedia of Comparative Constitutional Law*. See, e.g., the Constitution of Portugal (1976), Arts 54–57; Italy (1947), Arts 39, 43–46; Brazil (1988), Arts 7 para. 11, 173–177; India, Art. 43A.

[75] Sheila Forster and Daniel Bonilla Maldonado, 'The Social Function of Property: A Comparative Law Perspective' (2011) 80 Fordham Law Review 101.

[76] See only Manfred Stelzer and Colm O'Cinneidel, 'Horizontal Effect/State Action' in Mark V. Tushnet, Thomas Fleiner, and Cheryl Saunders (eds), *Routledge Handbook of Constitutional Law* (Routledge 2015); Mark Tushnet, 'The Issue of State Action/Horizontal Affect in Comparative Constitutional Law' (2003) 1(1) ICON 79.

[77] On the complexities of the German model in practice, see Katharina Pistor, 'Co-Determination in Germany' in Margaret Blair and Mark Roe (eds), *Employees and Corporate Governance* (Brookings Institute 1999).

[78] Sara L. Hernández and Zane Rasnača, 'Can Workers' Rights Ever Catch Up? The *Erzberger* Case and EU Cross-Border Reality' (2019) 48(1) Industrial Law Journal 98; Gunther Teubner, 'Transnational Economic Constitutionalism in the Varieties of Capitalism' (2015) 1(2) Italian Law Journal 219.

IV. Towards a Transformative Canon: *Chevron v Rights of Nature* in the Constitutional Court of Ecuador (2018)

A. Context

On 10 July 2018, the Constitutional Court of Ecuador handed down its decision in the *Chevron* case, upholding a US$9.5 billion civil judgment against the oil giant for massive environmental damage in the Amazon rainforest.[79] The decision concluded fifteen years of domestic litigation in the Ecuadorian courts, but it was not the last word in the epic legal battle between Chevron and 30,000 plaintiffs from five indigenous communities in the Amazon. What began in 1993 as Alien Tort Claims Act litigation in the US courts soon morphed into a worldwide web of proceedings and investigations—ranging from lawsuits and criminal prosecutions in Ecuador and New York to enforcement litigation in Argentina, Brazil, Canada, and Germany to investment arbitration before the Permanent Court of Arbitration in The Hague.[80]

The struggle of the indigenous 'David', embodied by laborer-turned-lawyer Pablo Fajardo, attracted global support from environmentalists, celebrities, and documentary filmmakers.[81] The corporate 'Goliath', in turn, mustered an army of lawyers in its defense and alleged that the trial judge and expert witnesses in the Ecuadorian first instance court of Lago Agrio had been bribed by the plaintiffs.[82] These allegations convinced the Permanent Court of Arbitration in The Hague to issue an unprecedented award in August 2018, ordering Ecuador 'to remove the status of enforceability from the Lago Agrio judgement' and 'to preclude any of the Lago Agrio Plaintiffs ... from enforcing any part of the Lago Agrio Judgment'.[83]

[79] *Chevron v. Ecuador* (2018) Sentencia 230-18-SEP-CC, Caso 0105-14-EP (Constitutional Court of Ecuador).

[80] Sarah Joseph, 'Protracted Lawfare: The Tale of Chevron Texaco in the Amazon' (2012) 3(1) Journal of Human Rights and the Environment 70; Judith Kimerling, 'Lessons from the Chevron Ecuador Litigation' (2013) 1 Stanford Journal of Complex Litigation 241; Antoni Pigrau, 'The Texaco-Chevron case in Ecuador: Law and Justice in the Age of Globalization' (2014) 5(1) RCDA 1.

[81] Patrick Keefe, 'Reversal of Fortune: The Lago Agrio Litigation' (2013) 1(3) Stanford Journal of Complex Litigation 199; Joe Berlinger et al., 'Crude: The Real Price of Oil', documentary film, 2009.

[82] Theodore Boutrous, 'Ten Lessons from the Chevron Litigation: The Defense Perspective' (2013) 1(2) Stanford Journal of Complex Litigation 219.

[83] Permanent Court of Arbitration, *Chevron Corp. and Texaco Petroleum Corp. v. The Republic of Ecuador*, UNCITRAL, PCA Case No. 2009-23, Track II Award of 30 August 2018, pp. X-3–4, at paras 10.13(i)–(viii).

If true, these allegations of procedural fraud would certainly be anti-canonical and antithetical to transformative constitutionalism, which holds a strong commitment to the rule of law and integrity of the judiciary. But irrespective of these allegations, the case remains significant for comparative constitutional law because it illustrates both the origins and effects of important 'transformative' elements of the 2008 Constitution of Ecuador.[84] This Constitution was the first to recognize nature as a bearer of rights, it enshrines socio-environmental and indigenous rights, and it has been hailed as an example of 'transformative constitutionalism' in Latin America.[85] The *Chevron* judgment illustrates that this type of transformative constitutionalism is not just 'constitutional poetry'[86] but has normative force and practical effects—with global repercussions even for powerful transnational corporations.[87]

B. The Case: Facts and Decision

In 1964, Ecuador granted a concession for oil exploration and production in the Amazon region to a local subsidiary of the US-American corporation Texaco, which later merged with Chevron. The Texaco subsidiary operated the oil wells, production facilities, and pipelines until 1992, when a state-owned enterprise took over. When Texaco left the country, it left behind environmental damage, the cause, extent, and consequences of which are disputed.[88] Victims claim that toxic wastewater pits, pipeline spills, and persistent water contamination are still causing significantly higher levels of cancer, spontaneous miscarriages, child malnutrition, and other illnesses in the local population.[89] Texaco claims that its operations were in line with the standards of the day, that only its local subsidiary was legally responsible, and that all liability claims were settled in an agreement with the government of Ecuador in 1995.[90]

[84] Andreas Gutmann, 'The Ecuadorian Chevron Judgement: Blueprint for a Neoconstitutional Environmental Law?' (19 June 2020). Juwiss Blog https://www.juwiss.de/92-2020/.

[85] Ramiro Ávila Santamaría, *El neoconstitucionalismo transformador* (Abya Yala 2011); Daniel Bonilla Maldonado, 'The Rights of Nature and a New Constitutional Environmental Law' in James R. May and Erin Daly (eds), *Human Rights and the Environment: Legality, Indivisibility, Dignity and ~Geography* (Elgar 2019).

[86] Uwe Kischel, *Rechtsvergleichung* (C. H. Beck 2015), 664. Sceptical also Wilton G. Mendoza, *Acciones jurídicas para establecer responsabilidades por daño ambiental en el Ecuador* (Fundación Regional de Asesoría en Derechos Humanos 2010), 129 et seq.

[87] cf. Keefe (n 81), 200 (citing the lawyer for the plaintiffs: 'This is the first time that a small developing country has had power over a multinational American company'), 201 (citing Chevron lobbyist: 'We can't let little countries screw around with big companies like this').

[88] Joseph (n 80), 71–72; Kimerling (n 80), 242–244; Pigrau (n 80), 6–7.

[89] Pigrau (n 80), 4–5.

[90] cf. Keefe (n 81), 200, 209; Pigrau (n 80), 12–13.

A first lawsuit by the Ecuadorian plaintiffs against the oil company, brought in the US courts under the Alien Tort Claims Act, was ultimately dismissed based on the *forum non conveniens* doctrine.[91] In 2003, the Amazon Defense Coalition, an NGO representing 30,000 victims, thus sued Chevron for damages in a first instance court in Ecuador. In 2011, the court finally handed down a multi-billion-dollar verdict against Chevron, based on the Ecuadorian Civil Code and the 1999 Environmental Management Act. The judgment was essentially upheld on appeal.[92]

Chevron then asked the Constitutional Court of Ecuador to overturn the civil judgments for violations of procedural guarantees and legal certainty, enshrined in Articles 76 and 82 of the Constitution, among others. Besides allegations of procedural irregularities, Chevron claimed that the civil judgments violated the *res iudicata* effect of the 1995 settlement agreement, that they retroactively applied the Environmental Management Act of 1999, and that the excessive assessment of damages went beyond even the plaintiffs' demands.

The Constitutional Court rejected Chevron's arguments in an extensively reasoned, 149-page decision. After dismissing allegations of procedural fraud on jurisdictional grounds,[93] the Court justified the liability imposed on Chevron with reference to the plaintiffs' environmental rights (Art. 14 Constitution of Ecuador), to the rights of nature (Arts 71–72, 395–396), and the close connection between human rights and the environment as recognized in the Inter-American human rights system and its case law.[94]

With regard to the 1995 settlement, the Court found that the agreement could only bind its parties, namely Chevron and the state of Ecuador, but not third parties such as the plaintiffs.[95] Besides, the victims' right to live in a healthy environment guaranteed in Article 14 precluded the government from disposing of such constitutionally protected liability claims in transactions with corporate investors.[96]

With respect to non-retroactivity, the Court found that this principle was not absolute but had to be balanced against other constitutional values, especially

[91] cf Joseph (n 80), 72–76; Kimerling (n 80), 245 et seq.

[92] The procedural history in the US and Ecuador is recounted with further references in Joseph (n 80), 72–80; Pigrau (n 80), 8–21; Kimerling (n 80), 245–261.

[93] *Chevron v. Ecuador* (n 79), 65–81. As in many jurisdictions with a specialized constitutional court, the Constitutional Court of Ecuador does not review the correct application of ordinary law or evidentiary rules, and it does not review civil judgments on the basis of factual allegations that have not been proven before the ordinary courts.

[94] ibid 92, 93, citing IACtHR, *Kawa Fernandez v. Honduras*, judgment of 3 April 2009, para. 148.

[95] ibid 86–91, 95–99.

[96] ibid 91–94, 98. Before the enactment of the 2008 Constitution, a similar right was contained in Art. 19 para. 2 of the Constitution of 1978, as amended in 1984, cf. ibid 92.

the rights of nature to integral respect and reparation (Arts 71–72). This conflict was to be resolved according to the principle of *in dubio pro natura*, established by Article 395 of the Constitution: in the case of doubt, environmental law had to be applied in the way that was most favorable to the environment—i.e. the more stringent law enacted in 1999.[97]

Finally, the Constitutional Court also upheld the assessment of the damages by the civil courts, which had included far-reaching systemic reparations, such as funding for a new regional drinking water system and a plan for the restoration of indigenous communities.[98] The Court found that while the plaintiffs had not individualized each and every environmental harm, the collective and systemic nature of the reparations was nevertheless justified by the constitutional right of nature to integral reparation (Arts 72, 397) and by the indigenous peoples' collective cultural and land rights (Arts 56–57, 60, 171, 257).[99]

C. Towards a Canon of Transformative Constitutionalism: The Corporation as Anti-Subordination Device

The *Chevron* case exemplifies a transformative conception that conceives the corporate form as an anti-subordination device that enables economic sovereignty, distributive justice, and societal change.[100] This normative conception originates, counterfactually, in the distinctive context of the Global South, marked by (post)colonial legacies, geopolitical asymmetries, and socio-economic disparities. In response, constitutions tend to be conceived not only as restraints on governmental power, but as vehicles of socio-economic change.[101] Today, this approach is associated with the concept of transformative constitutionalism,[102] but it had already been a feature of the developmental states of the decolonization era.[103] Thus, if social democracy had

[97] ibid 105–115.

[98] See also Pigrau (n 80), 11, 18.

[99] *Chevron v. Ecuador* (n 79), 115 et seq., esp. 119, 128, citing IACtHR, *Sawhoyamaxa v. Paraguay*, judgment of 29 March 2006, para. 118.

[100] Kroncke and Riegner (n 7), 17–18.

[101] Philipp Dann, Michael Riegner, and Maxim Bönnemann, 'Towards a Southern Turn in Comparative Constitutional Law: An Introduction' in Philipp Dann, Michael Riegner, and Maxim Bönnemann (eds), *The Global South and Comparative Constitutional Law* (Oxford University Press 2020).

[102] Karl Klare, 'Legal Culture and Transformative Constitutionalism' (1998) 14(1) South African Journal on Human Rights 146; Oscar V. Vieira, Upendra Baxi, and Frans Viljoen (eds), *Transformative Constitutionalism* (Pretoria University Law Press 2013).

[103] Luis Eslava, 'The Developmental State: Independence, Dependency, and History of the South' in Philipp Dann and Jochen V. Bernstorff (eds), *The Battle for International Law in the Decolonization Era* (Oxford University Press 2019); David Trubek and Marc Galanter, 'Scholars in Self-Estrangement: Some

shifted attention from corporate rights to worker representation, then transformative constitutionalism addresses the relationship of the corporate form to the national economy, to external stakeholders, and to the environment. The *Chevron* case illustrates these economic, social, and ecological dimensions of transformation.

First, the historical origins of the case hark back to economic constitutionalism of the decolonization era. As political independence of developmental states remained severely restricted by continued economic dependence, many constitutions in the Third World embraced public ownership of natural resources and the nationalization of key industries, and state-owned enterprises thus became a common feature during the decolonization era.[104] In this vein, the Ecuadorian Constitution of 1967, and all subsequent texts, stipulated public ownership of natural resources, especially petroleum.[105] When Ecuador formed its state-owned oil company, it first entered into a consortium with Texaco in 1973, then over the years acquired the majority shareholding, and eventually took over operations in 1992.[106] Per capita GDP doubled within a decade after oil production began, but the costs and benefits of extractivist development were distributed very unevenly.[107]

In response to persistent inequalities, the 2008 Constitution envisaged a second, social transformation, to be driven by an expansion of justiciable social and collective rights.[108] The *Chevron* case indicates that these rights not only aim at redistribution of public resources, but also constitutionalize relations between private parties.[109] The corporation thus becomes an addressee of collective rights claims by external stakeholders, such as affected local communities and indigenous peoples. This emphasis on *corporate* human rights responsibility seems to be characteristic of Southern jurisdictions.[110] In this context, horizontality also serves as an argument for piercing of the

Reflections on the Crisis in Law and Development Studies in the United States' [1974] Wisconsin Law Review 1062.

[104] Yash Ghai, 'Control and Management of the Economy: Research Perspectives on Public Enterprise' (1976) 9 VRÜ/WCL 157; Sundhya Pahuja and Anna Saunders, 'Rival Worlds and the Place of the Corporation in International Law' in Dann and Bernstorff (n 103).
[105] Arts 1, 317, 408 of the Constitution of 2008; Art. 46 (1978); Art. 55 (1967).
[106] Pigrau (n 80), 6.
[107] Keefe (n 81), 202.
[108] Arts 12 et seq.
[109] Gutmann (n 84).
[110] David Bilchitz, 'Corporate Law and the Constitution' (2008) 125(4) South African Law Journal 754; Upendra Baxi, 'Human Rights Responsibility of Multinational Corporations, Political Ecology of Injustice' (2016) 1(1) Business and Human Rights Journal 21; Michael Riegner, 'Regionalizing Business and Human Rights' (2020) 93(1–2) Journal of International Peace and Organization/Die Friedens-Warte 70–95.

transnational corporate veil: in the *Chevron* case, the civil courts not only assumed jurisdiction over the financially potent mother company domiciled in the US, but also pierced the corporate veil of the undercapitalized local subsidiary, arguing that maintaining the legal separation would 'imply a manifest injustice'.[111] Compared to liberal and social-democratic constitutionalism, transformative constitutionalism thus displays a greater willingness to disregard corporate personality to protect weaker parties.[112]

Third, the *Chevron* case is also a practical example of the ecological transformation of legal personality. In the case, rights of nature prevailed over more traditional corporate rights. If rights of nature indeed mean that 'nobody holds an acquired right to pollute the environment',[113] as the Constitutional Court argues, then they significantly restrict the property interests and legitimate expectations of those who hold mining concessions and industrial permits, which basically confer such acquired rights.[114] If taken seriously, this has the potential to transform the legal relationship of nature to corporate capitalism: from an subordinated object of exploitation to a subject of rights.

In sum, the *Chevron* litigation exemplifies broader trends in the constitutional orders of the Global South, which justify the inclusion of the case in an emerging canon of transformative constitutionalism. This inclusion widens the canonical focus on the redistribution of public resources through social rights and draws attention to economic institutions that determine the initial distribution, including the corporation. At the same time, the *Chevron* litigation also points to internal tensions and external limitations of transformative corporate constitutionalism. Internally, state-centered forms of economic constitutionalism inherited from extractivist, developmental states stand in tension with the rights of nature,[115] and such rights may have more in common with corporate constitutional rights than is often acknowledged—including problems of representation and agency.[116] Externally, transformation by means of state constitutions is nationally bounded—unlike corporate capitalism: at the time

[111] cf. Pigrau (n 80), 14; *Chevron v. Ecuador* (n 79), 61–64.

[112] See, generally, Mariana Pargendler, 'How Universal is the Corporate Form?' (2019) 58 Columbia Journal of Transnational Law 1.

[113] *Chevron v. Ecuador* (n 79), 112.

[114] Gutmann (n 84).

[115] For a discussion of the tensions, see Roger Merino, 'Reimagining the Nation-State: Indigenous Peoples and the Making of Plurinationalism in Latin America' (2018) 14 Leiden Journal of International Law 1.

[116] Kimerling (n 80), 261 et seq., points to problems of representation in the collective exercise of environmental rights that are familiar from other contexts, including the corporation.

of writing, the plaintiffs have been unable to enforce the judgment because Chevron does not have any assets in Ecuador and has successfully resisted enforcement in foreign jurisdictions with the help of an investment arbitration award from the Permanent Court of Arbitration.[117]

What remains are two competing truths, sanctioned by competing judicial procedures at the national and international levels. Each truth is associated with competing narratives about judiciaries and corporations in the Global South, which too often stereotype both as corrupt and lawless.[118] Contemporary comparatists are well advised to be wary of any such stereotypical narratives—in particular, when engaged in the delicate exercise of constructing a global canon of constitutionalism.

V. Conclusion

The three cases discussed in this chapter point to three distinct constitutional traditions—or canons—whose distinctive elements come into sharp focus when compared through the lens of the corporation as a constitutional protagonist. Each of these varieties of corporate constitutionalism emerged in a distinct historical and social context and thus have their distinct strengths and weaknesses. Taken together, they offer an analytical framework for further comparison that best treats varieties of corporate constitutionalism as analytical ideal types that rarely exist in a pure form in any one jurisdiction but evolve over time, take hybrid forms, and migrate across and coexist within jurisdictional boundaries.

For comparative constitutional law more broadly, treating the corporation as a constitutional protagonist offers an opportunity to further pluralize the epistemic foundations of the disciplinary canon. For one, it suggests that the move from a liberal epistemic framework to studying varieties of constitutionalism should be multidimensional, i.e. extend beyond the dimension of political government and include systems of political economy. Moreover, it

[117] Hannah Franzki and Johan Horst, 'On the Critical Potential of Law—and Its Limits: Double Fragmentation of Law in *Chevron vs. Ecuador*' in Kerstin Blome et al. (eds), *Contested Regime Collisions* (Cambridge University Press 2016); Lorenzo Pellegrini et al., 'International Investment Agreements, Human Rights, and Environmental Justice: The Texaco/Chevron Case From the Ecuadorian Amazon' (2020) 23(2) Journal of International Economic Law 455.

[118] See, e.g., Jorge Esquirol, 'The Geopolitics of Constitutionalism in Latin America' in Colin Crawford and Daniel Bonilla Maldonado (eds), *Constitutionalism in the Americas* (Elgar 2018).

shifts attention from rights to institutions and structure—not just with regard to the organization of the state and public power, but also to the economy and its institutions. Third, as a transnational subject and organizational form, the corporation transcends state-centric accounts of nationally bounded constitutions and citizens. If the future of constitutionalism is transnational, then it is also corporate—for better or worse.

29

Act of State and Diplomatic Protection in the Modern Constitution

Two Case Studies

*Phoebe Okowa**

I. Introduction

This chapter seeks to explain and elaborate on two national decisions that have a credible claim to canonical status in constitutional adjudication. The cases selected are *Kaunda v. Republic of South Africa*[1] and *Belhaj v. Straw*.[2] They are respectively concerned with *diplomatic protection* and *act of state*, two concepts that originated in the heyday of absolute sovereigns, but which have been radically reinterpreted in light of contemporary demands of the rule of law and the separation of powers.[3]

The cases, I argue, are of significance because they depart fundamentally from the older cases[4] and encapsulate a distinct rupture in the jurisprudence by subjecting both diplomatic protection and act of state to modern

* Professor of Public International Law, Queen Mary University of London; Member, United Nations International Law Commission. A draft version of this chapter was presented at the University of Maryland, Carey School of Law, Comparative Constitutional Law Colloquium and the Faculty, Legal Theory Workshop, in Spring 2022. I am grateful for the many insightful comments from the participants, especially Professor Peter Danchin. I have also benefited enormously from conversations with Professors Eirik Bjorge and Ewan Smith on the complexities of the UK cases on act of state. I am also thankful to Ms Olivia Flasch and Icarus Chan for their excellent research assistance.

[1] *Kaunda and Others v. President of the Republic of South Africa and Others*, Case CCT 23/04 [2004] ZACC 5 (Constitutional Court of South Africa).

[2] See also *Belhaj and another v. Straw and Others* [2017] UKSC 3, [2017] 2 WLR 456 [103]–[105] (Lord Sumption).

[3] On historical origins of act of state, see: *The Duke of Brunswick v. King of Hanover* [1848] 9 ER 993; *Buron v. Denman* (1948) 2 Exch 167; *Secretary of State for India v. Kamachee Boye Sahaba* (1859) 7 Moore Ind App 476, 529, 19 ER 388, 407; *Elphinstine v. Bedreechund* (1830) 1 Kn 316, 12 ER 340, cited in *Rahmatullah (No. 2) (Respondent) v. Ministry of Defence and Another (Appellants)* [2017] UKSC 1. See also *Belhaj and another (Respondents) v. Straw and Others* [2017] UKSC 3, [2017] 2 WLR 456 [103]–[105] (Lord Sumption).

[4] See *The Parlement Belge* (1880) 5 PD 197, 208, [1874–80] All ER Rep 104 (CA 1880), 109 (Brett LJ), cited in: Ewan Smith, 'Regal Indignity' (2022) 138 *Law Quarterly Review* 381.

Phoebe Okowa, *Act of State and Diplomatic Protection in the Modern Constitution* In: *Global Canons in an Age of Contestation*. Edited by: Sujit Choudhry, Michaela Hailbronner, and Mattias Kumm, Oxford University Press.
 DOI: 10.1093/9780191956942.003.0029

constitutional limitations and the demands of fundamental rights in a democracy. More generally, they reconstruct and delimit the impact of the separation of powers, human rights treaties, and constitutional guarantees in bills of rights on the interpretation of concepts that were formulated in a radically different historical period.[5] A central concern in the judgments is the extent to which their interpretation has been influenced by the increased public sensitivity to the importance of human rights norms, *jus cogens* principles, and the rule of law. Diplomatic protection and act of state were historically regarded as reflecting the prerogatives of states, and courts were generally expected to show judicial restraint in situations where they were operative. The cases illustrate how modern developments in international law have circumscribed their sphere of operation and that courts are increasingly wary of accepting judicial restraint where individual rights are at play or where such restraint is difficult to reconcile with access to justice as a constitutional imperative.

The two cases are decisions of the highest national courts in their respective countries and, in the context of this project, offer a roadmap for future courts that may be called upon to delineate their field of operation. By employing fundamental norms of international law as an operative yardstick, they also challenge the traditional dualist dogma that rules of international law can only operate or influence domestic decisions if they have been formally adopted through national legislative filters.[6] The canonical status of the decision in *Belhaj* is not in doubt; it has been followed and applied largely without qualification in material respects, in three subsequent decisions of superior courts including in a decision of the UK Supreme Court.[7] *Belhaj* has also ignited a lively discussion as to the parameters of judicial restraint where private rights and *jus cogens* norms are involved.[8] *Kaunda*, I argue, has a putative claim to canonical

[5] *Belhaj v. Straw* (n 2) [123] (Lord Neuberger), stating that domestic courts should not normally determine issues which are only appropriate for diplomatic or similar channels. See Ewan Smith, 'Acts of State in Belhaj and Rahmatullah' (2018)134 *Law Quarterly Review* 20.

[6] See, e.g., *In Re Mckerr (AP) (Respondent) (Northern Ireland)* [2004] UKHL 12 [52] (Lord Steyn); Paul Craig, 'Engagement and Disengagement with International Institutions: The U.K. Perspective' in Curtis A. Bradley (ed.), *The Oxford Handbook of Comparative Foreign Relations Law*, Oxford Handbooks (OUP 2019); Eirik Bjorge, 'Can Unincorporated Treaty Obligations be Part of English Law?' (2017) *Public Law* 571.

[7] See *His Highness Sheikh Mohammed Bin Rashid Al Maktoum v. Her Royal Highness Princess Haya Bint Al Hussein and Others* [2021] EWCA Civ 129 [30]; ruling that foreign act of state did not apply in a case of foreign espionage in the context of a dispute about guardianship of children and that, even if it did apply, the case would fall within the public policy exception as set out by the Supreme Court in *Belhaj v. Straw* (n 2). See also *Ukraine v. The Law Debenture Trust Corp. Plc* [2018] EWCA Civ 2026 holding that the public policy exception applied to the foreign act of state doctrine, with the result that Ukraine could rely on defences of duress in a case of breach of contractual obligations because the contract with Russia had been procured through illegal use of force and violations of *jus cogens* norms under Art. 2(4) of the UN Charter. These subsequent cases also outline how the foreign act of state may be implicated.

[8] *Belhaj v. Straw* (n 2) [97], [102] (Lord Mance).

status because it is the first case, to my knowledge, that offers a comprehensive assessment of how a discretionary right of diplomatic protection can be reconciled with fundamental guarantees in a bill of rights.[9]

II. *Kaunda v. Republic of South Africa* and Diplomatic Protection

A. Introduction

In *Kaunda and Others v. President of the Republic of South Africa and Others*, the Constitutional Court of South Africa was asked to consider whether the public international law doctrine of diplomatic protection, which entitles a state to make representations on behalf of a national who has suffered a wrong at the hands of another state, could, in the context of the South African Constitution, be regarded not as a discretionary right but a justiciable duty subject to judicial review. The Court was faced with the question of whether under Section 3 of that Constitution, this discretionary right under international law was a justiciable right of citizenship enforceable at the behest of individuals. The case also highlights the dilemma about which law should prevail when the constitutional order provides a higher standard of protection for the individual, which sits in tension with other core principles of public international law, such as due regard for the sovereign rights of third states in relation to matters occurring on their territory. Does constitutional entrenchment radically improve the position of the aggrieved individual or does it create no more than an expectation that the request for diplomatic protection will be seriously considered? How should conflicts between international and constitutional values be resolved when they arise? If international law required deference to matters within the sovereign jurisdiction of third states, can interference nonetheless be justified in order to give effect to individual rights under a national constitution?

The case was also concerned with how the concept of diplomatic protection should be interpreted in a situation where the constitution putatively demands more of a state above and beyond what is required by international law. Can an individual insist that he/she has a justiciable legal right to diplomatic protection even if international law only provided for a discretionary right? It also left

[9] *Kaunda and Others v. President of the Republic of South Africa and Others*, Case CCT 23/04 [2004] ZACC 5 (Constitutional Court of South Africa).

open the question whether the constitutional imperative is applicable where the constitution itself is silent on the question of citizenship rights. Finally, *Kaunda* also brought to the fore the question of whether the discretionary nature of the international law right was reconcilable with obligations in human rights treaties, which South Africa had ratified, and which were therefore a direct source of law under its Constitution.

In making the case for *Kaunda*'s putative canonical status, I note that *Kaunda* went further than the previous cases that had considered the question in affirming that the discretion of states in the field of diplomatic protection had to respect structural constitutional principles.[10] By confirming that diplomatic protection had to be interpreted in light of binding human rights treaties, it imbued the concept with vigour and impact that it had until then lacked. The majority, although affirming the discretionary nature of the right, accepted that it is subject to judicial supervision. In a compelling dissenting opinion, Justice O'Regan went as far as acknowledging that the constitutional right of citizenship and commitments in human rights treaties operated as positive constraints on state discretion by creating an enforceable right. It is suggested that, read as a whole, the *Kaunda* case represents a significant advance on the challenges to the dominant positivist narrative that the discretionary rights of states in foreign affairs are not subject to judicial review or other rule of law concerns in a modern democratic state.[11]

B. Diplomatic Protection: Regressive or Relevant?

It is important to preface the discussion of the decision of the Constitutional Court in *Kaunda* by giving a very brief overview of the trajectory of diplomatic protection. This is not the place to recount the imperial history of international law but it is impossible to appreciate the stagnation in the application of much of the law of diplomatic protection without an overt acknowledgement of its regressive origins.[12] It was designed primarily to protect the interests of capital-exporting countries of Europe and North America in their relationship with the so-called 'new world'. At its most basic, it required that foreign investors be subjected to an international minimum standard of treatment by host states,

[10] *R (Abbasi and another) v. Secretary of State for Foreign and Commonwealth Affairs and another* [2002] EWCA Civ 1598, [2003] UKHRR 76, 126.

[11] See generally Campbell McLachlan, *Foreign Relations Law* (CUP 2014), 347–374.

[12] See generally Mira L. Siegelberg, *Statelessness: A Modern History* (Harvard University Press 2020), 12–48, 193–227.

even if this contradicted local law.[13] Moreover, the investor could not opt out of state protection by subjecting all disputes to local law. The parent state retained the right to enforce these standards through the institutions of international law, including adjudication, and in doing so it was recognized that it was enforcing its own right and not that of the individual.[14] It therefore comes as no surprise that in the radically altered circumstances that accompanied decolonization, diplomatic protection gradually fell into disuse. Moreover, most states realized that the investments of their citizens could be better protected through bilateral treaties. Because the right belonged to the state and not the individual on whose behalf the state was acting, the state had absolute discretion in the matter. It alone was entitled to decide whether it should take the case and how far it would go in pursuit of its rights. The point was made with absolute clarity by the International Court of Justice in the *Barcelona Traction* case:

> ... within the limits prescribed by international law, a State may exercise diplomatic protection by whatever means and to whatever extent it thinks fit, for it is its own right that the State is asserting. Should the natural or legal person on whose behalf it is acting consider that their rights are not adequately protected, they have no remedy in international law. All they can do is resort to municipal law, if means are available, with a view to furthering their cause or obtaining redress. The municipal legislator may lay upon the State an obligation to protect its citizens abroad, and may also confer upon the national a right to demand the performance of that obligation, and clothe the right with corresponding sanctions. However, all these questions remain within the province of municipal law and do not affect the position internationally.
>
> The State must be viewed as the sole judge to decide whether its protection will be granted, to what extent it is granted, and when it will cease. It retains in this respect a discretionary power the exercise of which may be determined by considerations of a political or other nature, unrelated to the merits of the particular case. Since the claim of the State is not identical with that of

[13] Antony Anghie, *Imperialism, Sovereignty and the Making of International Law* (CUP 2005), 209, 224.

[14] 'By taking up the case of one of its subjects and resorting to diplomatic action or international judicial proceedings on his behalf, a State is in reality asserting its own right—its right to ensure, in the person of its subjects, respect for the rules of international law.' See *The Mavrommatis Palestine Concessions (Greece v. UK)* (Objection to the Jurisdiction of the Court) PCIJ Rep Series A No. 2, 112. The ILC Special Rapporteur on Diplomatic Protection had proposed *de lege ferenda* for an enforceable right of diplomatic protection but this was ultimately rejected by the Commission. See ILC, 'First Report of the Special Rapporteur on Diplomatic Protection' (7 March–20 April 2000) UN Doc. A/CN.4/506 and Add. 1, arts 3 and 4.

> the individual or corporate person whose cause is espoused, the State enjoys complete freedom of action.[15]

There were profound questions raised by international lawyers on whether an institution that was so outdated in outlook could survive in the wake of new commitments to the universality of human rights that developed in the aftermath of the Universal Declaration of Human Rights in 1948.[16] Moreover, by focusing on nationality as the basis of protection, it did not go unnoticed that diplomatic protection lacked a democratic spirit at its core, since those most in need of protection are usually stateless persons, resident aliens, and refugees.[17] In addition, nationality for the purposes of diplomatic protection was a highly formalized concept, restricted only to those having a real and effective link with the state.[18] Yet, in many cases, those most at risk and in need of protection may technically be aliens or those with putative claims to citizenship but who cannot themselves assert their claims because they are minors. The possible extension of the right to long-term residents has been mooted even in the absence of formal ties of citizenship, but so far unsuccessfully.[19] The risk of mass displacement and forced migration as a result of war has and will continue to render many people 'de facto stateless', increasing the need to devise new frameworks of protection under human rights norms and outside the formal structures of diplomatic protection.[20]

Much of its subsequent history of diplomatic protection involved the making of adjustments and realignment, a recognition that it was a relevant remedy not just in the context of the protection of foreign investment but regarding any breach of an obligation under international law which could give rise to a right of protection by the aggrieved state.[21] The International Court of Justice acknowledged as much in the *Diallo* case:

[15] *Case concerning the Barcelona Traction, Light and Power Company, Limited (Belgium v. Spain)* (Second Phase) [1970] ICJ Rep 3 [78]–[79].

[16] Francisco V. García-Amador, 'State Responsibility: Some New Problems' (1958) 94 *Recueil des Cours de l'Académie de Droit International* 421, 437–439; Hersch Lauterpacht, 'Diplomatic Protection and Criminal Jurisdiction over Aliens' (1947) 9(3) *Cambridge Law Journal* 330.

[17] First Report on Diplomatic Protection (n 14). Josef Kunz, 'The *Nottebohm* Judgment (Second Phase)' (1960) 54(3) *American Journal of International Law* 26.

[18] *Nottebohm Case (Lichtenstein v. Guatemala)* (Second Phase) [1955] ICJ Rep 4; Siegelberg (n 12) 216; Ian Brownlie, 'The Relations of Nationality in Public International Law' (1963) 39 *British Yearbook of International Law* 284.

[19] First Report on Diplomatic Protection (n 14).

[20] Siegelberg (n 12) 235.

[21] See Emanuela-Chiara Gillard, 'Reparation for Violations of International Humanitarian Law' (2003) 85 *International Review of the Red Cross* 529.

> Owing to the substantive developments of international law over recent decades in respect of the rights it accords to individuals, the scope *ratione materiae* of diplomatic protection, originally limited to alleged violations of the minimum standard of treatment of aliens has subsequently widened to include, *inter alia*, internationally guaranteed human rights.[22]

But there were arguments, too, that the institution had fallen into desuetude in the face of the proliferation of many institutions exercising oversight of human rights violations. These were, however, met with short shrift by the International Law Commission's Special Rapporteur on diplomatic protection, Professor John Dugard: the proliferation of human rights norms had not been marched with parallel institutions for their enforcement in many parts of the world, perhaps with the exception of Europe.[23] Moreover, access to human rights institutions remained largely optional, with the result that for most individuals, diplomatic protection provided the only meaningful avenue to a remedy. In justifying the decision by the International Law Commission to include the topic on its agenda, Dugard observed that:

> Contemporary international human rights accord to nationals and aliens the same protection, which far exceeds the international minimum standard of treatment for aliens set by western powers in an earlier era. It does not follow that these developments have rendered obsolete the traditional procedures recognized by customary international law for the treatment of aliens. Although individuals today enjoy more international remedies for the protection of their rights than ever before, diplomatic protection remains an important weapon in the arsenal of human rights protection. As long as the state remains the dominant actor in international relations, the espousal of claims by states for the violation of the rights of their nationals remains the most effective remedy for the promotion of human rights. Instead of seeking to weaken this remedy by dismissing it as an obsolete fiction that has outlived its usefulness, every effort should be made to strengthen the rules that comprise diplomatic protection.[24]

[22] *Case concerning Ahmadou Sadio Diallo* (*Guinea v. DRC*) (Preliminary Objections) [2007] ICJ Rep 582 [39].

[23] John Dugard, 'Diplomatic Protection and Human Rights: The Draft Articles of the International Law Commission' (2005) 24 *Australian Yearbook of International Law* 75.

[24] First Report on Diplomatic Protection (n 14) [32].

C. 9/11 and the Syrian Conflict: Renewed Interest in Diplomatic Protection

In a number of new constitutions,[25] there are objectively verifiable rights of citizenship, essentially a social contract between the state and the citizen, guaranteeing a minimum standard of protection in a number of key areas. Although these did not necessarily mention diplomatic protection, they generated a legitimate expectation that the rights would be enforceable rights against the state. The traditional discretionary nature of diplomatic protection thus sits uncomfortably within a constitutional order based on legality, fairness, and compliance with the bill of rights.

There has been a remarkable rise in the number of cases of nationals seeking diplomatic protection in the aftermath of 9/11. The threats posed by terrorists has led to a marked increase in extraterritorial state action, such as increased surveillance and interrogation techniques, much of it in disregard of the normal rule-of-law safeguards. Moreover, as the Guantanamo Bay cases[26] demonstrate, the interrogation techniques employed in these cases are almost always suspect but at the same time beyond the reach of institutions that would normally have oversight in national law. These are situations where there are usually no journalists, lawyers, or intergovernmental organizations such as the International Committee of the Red Cross. Related to this is the increasing number of legislative and executive policies in most states, designed to restrict immigration including for those with well-founded fears of persecution and a putative claim to refugee status. Many of these measures are carried out extraterritorially, again in circumstances where there is no oversight.

There is therefore a renewed interest in transgressions of governments outside their territories, and under circumstances where diplomatic protection may be the only credible avenue for obtaining a remedy. These cases present other unique challenges: unlike the merchants of the nineteenth century, the putative victims are particularly vulnerable; but they are also those who on account of their alleged activities are only of marginal interest to the states of their nationality. The case for a justiciable right of diplomatic protection thus becomes even more compelling in these circumstances.

[25] Examples include the constitutions of Albania, Belarus, Bosnia and Herzegovina, Bulgaria, Cambodia, China, Croatia, Estonia, Georgia, Guyana, Hungary, Italy, Kazakhstan, Latvia, and Poland. For a full list, see First Report on Diplomatic Protection (n 14) [80].

[26] *R (Abbasi) v. Secretary of State* (n 10); *Canada (Prime Minister) v. Khadr*, 2010 SCC 3, [2010] 1 SCR 44 (Federal Court of Appeal).

Moreover, given the state-centric world in which diplomatic protection evolved, it is unclear if it is available as a remedy in respect of wrongs by non-state groups or by states acting extraterritorially.. For all the progress made in the intervening years, the subject has remained very much tied to its imperial origins, a remedial instrument in inter-relations.

There have been appalling derogations from human rights standards carried out by non-state groups such as ISIS and Al-Shabab in areas under their control.[27] Specifically, since 2019 following the collapse of ISIS, many of these nationals, most of them women, have been held in inhumane and life-threatening conditions in camps under the control of non-state groups primarily in northern Syria. In many of these cases, the victims have made compelling arguments that the state of their nationality have an enforceable duty to repatriate them or in some way intercede on their behalf, especially when they are being held in total disregard of some of the most basic human rights standards.[28] The fact that diplomatic protection is a right available only to states in interstate relations has been used to decline extending diplomatic protection to individuals held by militia groups in Northern Syria. Asserting diplomatic protection in these situations, it is argued, may have the perverse effect of extending recognition to non-state entities. States have also repeatedly invoked national security concerns, maintaining that these concerns trump any putative rights under the law on diplomatic protection. In those cases where assistance has been given, it has been individualized and not justified within a broader normative framework.[29]

It was noted that the nineteenth-century doctrine of diplomatic protection was very much wedded to formal ties of nationality but, in some of the contested cases after 9/11, it was maintained by a number of the applicants that the right should extend to permanent residents or other persons who, although not nationals in a formal sense, could still be regarded as entitled to protection

[27] See Open Society Justice Initiative, 'European States' Obligations to Repatriate the Children Detained in Camps in North East Syria' (New York, Open Society Foundations, July 2021), https://www.justiceinitiative.org/uploads/d9762590-424c-4cb6-9112-5fedd0d959d1/european-states%E2%80%99-obligations-to-repatriate-the-children-detained-in-camps-in-northeast-syria-20210722.pdf, accessed 24 July 2023.

[28] See *Case of H. F. and Others v. France*, App. nos 24384/19 and 44234/20 (ECHR, 14 September 2022). The case concerned unsuccessful requests by the applicants for the repatriation by the French authorities of their respective daughters and grandchildren, who were being held in the al-Hol camp in north-eastern Syria run by the Syrian Democratic Forces. Their application was based on Art. 3 (prohibition of inhuman or degrading treatment). The applicants allege that the refusal to repatriate their respective daughters and grandchildren exposed them to inhuman and degrading treatment. See also Ordonnance, 19/129/C (Tribunal de première instance francophone de Bruxelles, Section civile) 30 October 2019; Arrêt, 2019/KR/60 (Cour d'appel Bruxelles, 18Fe chambre affaires civiles) 5 March 2020.

[29] Open Society (n 27) [24].

on the basis of informal ties of allegiance.[30] This category of persons, in the absence of a progressive and generous interpretation of citizenship, are largely left without a remedy. Moreover, a considerable body of empirical evidence illustrates the gross inequality in the capacity of states to protect their citizens and there is nothing in the structure of international law to mitigate those inequalities. The decision of the Constitutional Court in *Kaunda*, it is suggested, offers a pathway for a principled and transparent application of diplomatic protection that extends it beyond its historical roots.

D. The Decision of the Constitutional Court in *Kaunda*

1. The Facts

In *Kaunda*, South African mercenaries were arrested and detained in Zimbabwe amid allegations that they were involved in an attempted coup to overthrow the government in Equatorial Guinea.[31] The complaints, in respect of which they sought judicial review, related to the conditions of detention in Zimbabwe but also a concern that the Zimbabwean authorities had threatened to extradite them to Equatorial Guinea, where they would face an unfair trial in disregard of due process guarantees and a real risk of being subjected to capital punishment after an unfair trial. The applicants sought orders that would require the South African government to make representations to the government of Zimbabwe and Equatorial Guinea and obtain assurances that they would not be prosecuted or tried in circumstances where they were unlikely to get a fair trial and, if convicted, be subjected to capital punishment. They also wanted assurances that in the event of a trial, rights guaranteed to them under the South African Constitution, including the right to a fair trial, would be respected by the two governments. Ideally, their preference was for extradition to South Africa, where they would be certain that any trial would be in accordance with the due process guarantees in the South African Constitution.[32]

It is quite clear from the facts that the applicants were not model citizens and, understandably, the respondents did not want to expend much capital on their diplomatic protection. Moreover, the remedy sought—in effect a *mandamus* compelling South Africa to take steps to ensure that guarantees under the South African Constitution would be respected by foreign governments in

[30] *R (Al Rawi) v. Secretary of State for Foreign and Commonwealth Affairs* [2006] EWCA Civ 1279, [2007] 2 WLR 1219.

[31] *Kaunda v. The President of South Africa* (n 9).

[32] ibid [4] (Chaskalson CJ).

the context of a trial concerning wrongful acts on the territory of that state—would on any view be difficult to reconcile with the sovereignty of states over matters within their territorial jurisdiction. Thus, their claims for diplomatic protection were extravagant on even the most generous interpretation of the doctrine. Moreover, the alleged wrongs at the time judicial review was sought had probably not crystallized, and it was speculative whether any future trial in Zimbabwe or Equatorial Guinea would in fact be unfair. It was perhaps on the facts not an ideal case for exploring the ambit of diplomatic protection in modern constitutions.

2. The Majority Judgment in *Kaunda*

The majority judgment written by Chief Justice Chaskalson began with an analysis of the status of international law in the South African Constitution, noting that that Section 232 confirmed that customary law was part of the law of South Africa unless it was inconsistent with the Constitution or with an Act of Parliament. However, as the international law right was discretionary, it could not form the basis of a *mandamus* order against the respondents. It was the applicants' argument that the customary law rule of diplomatic protection should be extended to encompass a mandatory duty where the rights threatened were a grave breach of an internationally recognized wrong.[33] The Court declined the invitation to embrace an extended conception of diplomatic protection, noting that the discretionary nature of the right had been settled in a long line of cases. If further noted that the proposal to include an enforceable duty of diplomatic protection had received a cool reception when it was introduced in the International Law Commission.[34] The Court also noted that there was no treaty-mandated right of diplomatic protection, observing that neither the Universal Declaration of Human Rights, the 1966 International Covenant on Civil and Political Rights, nor the African Charter on Human and Peoples' Rights provided for a right of diplomatic protection. In addition, the obligations in these instruments were territorially circumscribed and South Africa could not police compliance outside its borders.

3. A Constitutionally Mandated Diplomatic Protection?

It was contended on behalf of the applicants that there was a constitutionally mandated right of diplomatic protection under Section 3 of the South African Constitution. The Section provides that:

[33] ibid [21].
[34] ibid [23], [29].

1. There is a common South African citizenship.
2. All citizens are

    a. equally entitled to the rights, privileges and benefits of citizenship; and
    b. equally subject to the duties and responsibilities of citizenship.

The judgment confirmed the centrality of citizenship rights in the South African Constitution, noting that South Africans were entitled to request from the government protection under international law against wrongful acts, and although such a request should not be unreasonably refused, the state was required to consider the request but not obliged to act.[35] Justice Ngcobo observed that:

> … the commitment of our government to promote and protect fundamental human rights; the obligation of the government, in general, to protect South Africans citizens here and abroad; the fact that citizenship is a constitutionally entrenched right; the fact that diplomatic protection is one of the tools available to protect human rights; and the fact that there is a growing trend within international law to grant diplomatic protection to nationals abroad, I am satisfied that diplomatic protection is one of the benefits, if not the right of citizenship.[36]

This is a significant advance on the absolute discretionary mantra that had characterized almost all previous considerations of diplomatic protection in national and international law.[37] The Court noted that a request for protection where the evidence is clear would be very difficult to refuse, especially if fundamental human rights were involved. Moreover, the content of diplomatic protection was buttressed substantially by obligations in human rights treaties and constitutional guarantees. An unreasonable refusal was therefore subject to judicial review.[38]

There was considerable discussion in the judgment as to how far the Court should go in reviewing the executive decision, with disagreement between the majority and the dissent of Justice O'Regan in that respect. However, both the majority and the dissent agreed that the Court could not interfere in matters of

[35] ibid [70].
[36] ibid [186] (Ngcobo J).
[37] *Rudolf Hess v. Federal Republic of Germany* (Case No. BvR 419/80) reprinted in (1980) 90 *ILR* 387; *R (Abbasi) v. Secretary of State* (n 10).
[38] *Kaunda v. The President of South Africa* (n 9) [193], [210] (Ngcobo J).

detail such as the form and manner of representations, the language in which they should be couched, or the sanctions, if any, which should be applied in the event that the representations were ignored.[39] In this respect, the Court noted that the diplomats were best placed to weigh the competing interests in such sensitive negotiations.

Significantly, the Court observed that the exercise of all public power under the South African Constitution was subject to judicial control. Thus, an irrational response to a request for diplomatic protection could be reviewed, or if the decision was taken in bad faith, but the Court could not substitute the substantive decision of the executive or direct that the review should take a particular form.[40] In other words, any action taken by the Court had to respect the constitutional framework of the separation of powers, and that even in the context of a rights-centric constitution the boundaries between law and politics must be maintained.

4. Limits of Diplomatic Protection: Deference to Third State Sovereignty Claims

Central to the applicants' request for judicial review was the contention that if tried in Zimbabwe or Equatorial Guinea they would not only receive an unfair trial but that they ran the real risk of being subjected to capital punishment, in violation of guarantees under the South African Constitution and international human rights treaties. The allegations were supported by reports by Amnesty International, the International Bar Association, and a Special Rapporteur of the United Nations Commission on Human Rights. The Court paid short shrift to both arguments; it noted that in both respects the applications were premature as the applicants had not been put on trial or subjected to capital punishment, and it was difficult to gauge in the abstract whether the threshold for acceptable boundaries had been crossed.[41] The majority went to great lengths to confirm that any acts taken by way of diplomatic protection had to respect the boundaries of state jurisdiction in international law.[42] The South African Constitution had no extraterritorial effect, and any attempt to insist that South African constitutional guarantees be observed in Zimbabwe or Equatorial Guinea undermined the territorial sovereignty of those states as a matter of international law. The Court further observed that it would be a breach of South Africa's duty to Equatorial Guinea and of its international

[39] ibid [77] (Chaskalson CJ), [175] (Ngcobo J), [244] (O'Regan J).
[40] ibid [79] (Chaskalson CJ).
[41] ibid [101], [105].
[42] ibid [122].

obligations, in particular to other African countries, to frustrate a criminal investigation simply because it did not conform to South African standards of justice.[43] Thus, although foreign judicial processes are not immune from scrutiny in deciding whether or not to proceed to judicial review, there is a need for qualified respect for the foreign legal order. In relation to the death penalty, the Court noted that although there was a strong abolitionist movement in international law, the death penalty was not illegal under the Universal Declaration of Human Rights, the International Covenant on Civil and Political Rights or the African Convention on Human and Peoples' Rights.[44] The fact that capital punishment was illegal under the South African Constitution was not a reason for insisting that it could not be applied extraterritorially in circumstances where its application would be lawful.

5. Dissenting Opinion of Justice O'Regan

In her separate opinion, Justice O'Regan took a different view on the potential reach of obligations under the South African Constitution. She argued that since the state had obligations to secure effective protection of human rights under international treaties, this placed it under a mandatory duty to act to prevent or repair egregious violations of human rights of its nationals even if committed extraterritorially. This was an independent duty of the state arising even in the absence of a request for diplomatic protection by an aggrieved national.[45] For her, diplomatic protection was an enforceable right and privilege of citizenship within the meaning of Section 3 of the South African Constitution.[46] O'Regan also took a different view on the ripeness of the application; the application was not premature in respect of the relief sought against Equatorial Guinea. The mere fact that Equatorial Guinea had sought their extradition was an indication that they faced an appreciable risk of being subjected to a trial that was not fair and, if convicted, subjected to the death penalty.[47]

Both the majority and the dissent were prepared to adopt an expansive concept of citizenship, which if adopted could substantially widen the ambit of those coming within the scope of diplomatic protection. The concept of citizenship was not confined to nationals, and although the majority of those coming

[43] ibid [44].
[44] ibid [98].
[45] ibid [212], [214] (O'Regan).
[46] ibid [236], [238].
[47] ibid [268].

within the ambit of constitutional protection would invariably be nationals, it left open the possibility of extending the right to non-nationals. Moreover, Justice O'Regan noted that a state had the responsibility as a matter of international law to ensure that the rights of those under its jurisdiction were respected and that could extend to foreign nationals. There are other problems in restricting the right of diplomatic protection to formal ties of nationality other than citizenship, since the international law concept of nationality is not necessarily synonymous with citizenship and may preclude a category of persons who ought to benefit from diplomatic protection.

E. Conclusion

Even though it will be overstating the case to see *Kaunda* as a radical judgment, it represents a significant advance on the 'discretionary' narrative that has characterized diplomatic protection. By linking diplomatic protection to the constitutional rights of citizenship and positive obligations in international human rights treaties, it will potentially expand the availability of the remedy at a time when states are showing a brazen disregard for fundamental human rights norms on considerations of national security. Moreover, a liberal concept of citizenship offers the possibility for refugees, resident aliens, and stateless persons to obtain a remedy especially in circumstances when other options are not available.

III. *Belhaj v. Straw* and the Act of State Doctrine

A. Introduction

The second case is *Belhaj v. Straw*.[48] *Belhaj* concerned the 'act of state doctrine', under which it is said that a domestic court (State A) lacks the competence to adjudicate on the executive acts of a foreign government (State B) occurring either abroad (State C) or on their territory (State B). It is a rule of restraint which requires the forum to decline jurisdiction that it might otherwise have, in certain instances, although the precise areas of application remain indeterminate

[48] *Belhaj v. Straw* (n 2). See also Andrew Sanger, 'Review of Executive Action Abroad: The UK Supreme Court in the International Legal Order' (2019) 68(1) *International and Comparative Law Quarterly* 35.

and contested.[49] *Belhaj* represents the most comprehensive attempt to delineate the parameters of this rule in the recent history of constitutional adjudication in the United Kingdom. In some instances, where the act of state relates to property, it is no more than a particular application of the private international law rule in favour of the *lex situs*. The second limb of the doctrine operates as a rule of non-justiciability calling for judicial restraint in those situations where it applies such as matters of high policy in relation to the making of peace and war, or the making of treaties, or the conduct of foreign relations, or more generally if the resolution of the matter is beyond judicial expertise. In *Belhaj*, the act of state doctrine was not available as a defence and the judgment is largely devoted to an examination of why on the facts of the case judicial restraint was not called for. Subsequent cases have tried to delineate the circumstances when it might be available but the law in this area, to quote Lord Mance, remains protean.[50]

In *Belhaj*, the Supreme Court was asked to consider whether act of state could be available as a defence in a case concerning executive accountability for abuse of power abroad. In the alternative, it was invited to consider whether, in the particular circumstances of the case, if the doctrine applied, it could be overridden by public policy considerations, especially in those instances where the application of the doctrine was in tension with fundamental human rights recognized in common law or under public international law.[51] It was the government's case that insofar as the application turned on the government's alleged complicity in acts of torture, detention, and ill-treatment by foreign-government officials abroad, those actions engaged the doctrine and were therefore non-justiciable; that at its most basic, the doctrine required a forum state to refrain from adjudicating on foreign governmental acts carried out on their territory or extraterritorially even where it amounted to a tort. The majority judgment and the separate opinions were alert to the incoherence and

[49] Frederick Alexander Mann, *Foreign Affairs in English Courts* (OUP 1986), 70; Lord Mance, 'Justiciability' (40th Annual F A Mann Lecture, London, 27 November 2017), https://www.supremecourt.uk/docs/speech-171127.pdf, accessed 24 July 2023, 10.

[50] See *Al Maktoum* (n 7): foreign act of state not applicable in relation to allegations of espionage made against the ruler of Dubai in the context of a wardship dispute involving two children. The Supreme Court was recently asked to define the contours of the doctrine in a case involving allegations of coercion in the procurement of a contract contrary to international norms prohibiting the use of force: see *Ukraine v. The Law Debenture Trust* (n 7) (judgment is pending at the time of writing). See also *Shergill v. Khaira* [2014] UKSC 33; Lord Mance, 'Justiciability' (n 49).

[51] There is no uniform consensus on the infinite variety of situations covered by the act of state doctrine, but the following definition by Lord Millett is a reasonably accurate description of the incidents contemplated: '... the act of state doctrine is a rule of domestic law which holds the national court incompetent to adjudicate upon the lawfulness of the sovereign acts of a foreign state'. See *R v. Bow Street Metropolitan Stipendiary Magistrate and Others, Ex parte Pinochet Ugarte (No. 3)* [2000] 1 AC 147 (HL), 269 (Lord Millett).

haphazardness that has characterized much of the doctrine's application in almost all legal systems.[52] The judgment's most important contribution is that it articulates for the first time the proper limits of act of state in a modern constitutional democracy and its relationship to peremptory norms of international law.[53] All the judges were in agreement that act of state did not apply, although the majority and separate opinions displayed different understandings of the ambit of the doctrine's application. Lower courts have taken the judgment of Lord Neuberger as a point of departure in delineating its parameters.[54] The majority and Lord Sumption, who was in the minority, disagreed on whether the act of state doctrine could extend to foreign executive acts performed within the territory of a state, but which were unlawful under the law of that state.[55] *Belhaj*'s great contribution in this context is to disaggregate and unpack different principles usually lumped together under foreign act of state. It also explains that some of these incidents are no more than the logical consequence of the application of the rules of private international law in the field. The case also clarifies the reach of public international law principles in constitutional adjudication.[56] *Belhaj*, it is suggested, is also a rebuttal of the predominant positivist dogma that international law cannot be applied domestically in the absence of dualist filters such as incorporation through legislation.[57] It supports the case for the direct application of international norms where these bolster individual rights even in the absence of an explicit domestic instrument endorsing their application.

1. The Facts

The applicants sought declarations of illegality and damages arising out of the UK government's alleged participation in the unlawful abduction,

[52] Frederick Alexander Mann, 'Judiciary and Executive in Foreign Affairs' (1943) 29 *Transactions of the Grotius Society* 143, reprinted in Frederick Alexander Mann, *Studies in International Law* (OUP 1972), ch. 11; Mann, *Foreign Affairs* (n 49) 164.

[53] *Belhaj v. Straw* (n 2) [175] (Lord Sumption).

[54] *The Law Debenture Trust Corp. Plc v. Ukraine* [2019] QB 1121.

[55] The two different approaches have now received extended consideration in the recent decision of the Supreme Court in *Maduro Board of the Central Bank of Venezuela (Respondents/cross Appellant) v. Guaidó Board of the Central Bank of Venezuela (Appellant/cross Respondent* [2021] UKSC 57, which treated as largely indefensible a rule unlawful under the law of the legislating state being given effect abroad when it would ordinarily be treated as a nullity in the state in which it originated.

[56] See Eirik Bjorge and Cameron Miles, 'Crown and Foreign Acts of State before British Courts: Rahmatullah, Belhaj, and the Separation of Powers' in Curtis A. Bradley (ed.), *The Oxford Handbook of Comparative Foreign Relations Law* (OUP 2019), 715–734.

[57] See, in particular, *Belhaj v. Straw* (n 2) [255] (Lord Sumption)—'... the municipal law of a state could be disregarded ... on the ground that it constituted a sufficiently serious violation of international law'—citing *Kuwait Airways Corp. v. Iraqi Airways Co. (Nos 4 and 5)* [2002] 2 AC 883, where the House of Lords disregarded an Iraqi decree because it was in serious violation of international law, and affirming the court's obligation to give effect to clearly established principles of international law.

detention and rendition of the applicants. It was alleged that the government had, pursuant to a policy of information sharing and cooperation, facilitated the applicant's rendition, and that Mr Straw, the British Home Secretary, was aware of and authorized the operation and/or took no steps to prevent it.

Mr Belhaj and his wife, Mrs Boudchar, were opponents of the Libyan leader Muammar Gaddafi. Mr Belhaj was the leader of the Libyan Islamic Fighting Group, an organization opposed to the government of Colonel Gaddafi and which, at the time of his arrest, had been designated a terrorist organization. Both applicants alleged that they were detained by the Malaysian authorities as they were trying to board a flight to London and were transferred to a CIA detention centre where they were tortured and interrogated by Thai authorities before being transferred to Libya where both were incarcerated and tortured for considerable periods. Mr Belhaj was detained for six years before being released in 2010. Mrs Boudchar was released in 2004, having been detained for more than three months.[58] They alleged that British intelligence officials passed information to the Libyan intelligence services and in other respects colluded in their detention and transfer, and in acts of torture, by sharing intelligence with the various detaining authorities (including Libya) in violation of international human rights obligations by which the United Kingdom was bound.

It was also alleged that British officials took advantage of the illegal detention of Mr Belhaj in Libya where they interrogated him twice. The applicants also argued that UK intelligence services knew that the US government operated a covert rendition programme and a network of 'black sites' at which detainees were held incommunicado and tortured. It was further alleged that they knew that if the applicants were abducted as part of the US rendition programme, there was a real risk that they would be held incommunicado and tortured.

The pleaded causes of action were in the nature of private law claims: false imprisonment, conspiracy to injure, trespass to the person, and conspiracy to use unlawful means. The government's central argument was that insofar as it was alleged that it was complicit in unlawful acts carried out by foreign officials, the 'act of state' doctrine was engaged with the result that the forum had no jurisdictional competence to hear the claim.

2. 'Act of State': Application of an Inherently Uncertain Concept

In general, when the act of state doctrine is operative, it has the effect of precluding the courts from adjudicating on the validity, legality, or lawfulness of executive conduct, even if this is in the context of purely private law claims.

58 *Belhaj v. Straw* (n 2) [3]–[4] (Lord Mance), [177] (Lord Sumption).

The English jurist and leading critic of the act of state doctrine, F. A. Mann, described it as 'one of the most difficult and most perplexing topics which, in the field of foreign affairs may face the municipal judge'.[59] He regarded it as an incoherent doctrine which should have no role where the jurisdiction of the forum is clearly established.[60] The complexity and confusion that surrounds the doctrine was also noted by Lord Reid in *Attorney-General v. Nissan*. He observed that:

> I think that a good deal of the trouble has been caused by using the loose phrase 'act of state' without making clear what is meant. Sometimes it seems to be used to denote any act of sovereign power or of high policy or any act done in the execution of a treaty. That is a possible definition, but then it must be observed that there are many such acts which can be the subject of an action in court if they infringe the rights of British subjects. Sometimes it seems to be used to denote acts which cannot be made the subject of inquiry in a British court. But that does not tell us how to distinguish such acts: it is only a name for a class which has still to be defined.[61]

In *Belhaj*, the Law Lords were very much alive to the confusion and incoherence that attends the act of state doctrine.[62] If the doctrine was to rest on a secure legal basis consistent with the rule of law, it was important to articulate comprehensively the legal principles on which it was based. It is significant that the Law Lords regarded act of state as a creature of the common law and not a mandatory requirement under public international law. It follows that it is the common law cases and principles that defines its parameters.[63]

Although they agreed that it did not apply on the specific facts of the case to bar any inquiry into liability on the basis of complicity in tort, they offered a bewildering array of reasons and principles that underpin the doctrine.[64] The court was invited to consider the limits of the act of state doctrine and whether it extended to governmental acts that were unlawful under the laws of the state where the acts took place.

[59] Mann (n 19) 164.
[60] ibid.
[61] *Attorney-General v. Nissan* [1970] AC 179, 211–212.
[62] *Belhaj v. Straw* (n 2) [198] (Lord Sumption), [118] (Lord Neuberger), [33] (Lord Mance).
[63] ibid [200] (Lord Sumption). In *Nevsun Resources Ltd v. Araya* [2020] SCC 5 (Supreme Court of Canada), a majority of the Supreme Court of Canada held that act of state was not part of Canadian law.
[64] See, e.g., *Belhaj v. Straw* (n 2) [35]–[36] (Lord Mance), [118] (Lord Neuberger), [199] (Lord Sumption).

The clarifications offered by the judges are of profound constitutional significance and the *ratio* has been applied in a recent decision of the Supreme Court concerning the validity of executive acts by competing claimants to the presidency in Venezuela.[65] It has also been followed by the Court of Appeal in *Re al-Maktoum*[66] and *Law Debenture Trust*.[67]

The Court of Appeal had accepted that the act of state doctrine was relevant to the claimants' allegations in *Belhaj*, and that it precluded the claim unless those allegations could be brought within recognized exceptions to the doctrine. The applicable exceptions included situations where the act of state claim was incidental and the resolution of the dispute did not turn on it, where the acts in question were done outside the territory of the foreign state or where the claimed act of state was contrary to public policy or violated fundamental norms of international law including human rights. Although finding that the act of state doctrine was engaged, the court disallowed its application on the grounds of public policy as the alleged acts violated fundamental norms of international law prohibiting torture.[68] The government appealed to the Supreme Court.

3. The Relevant 'State Interests' in Pleas of Immunity and Act of State

What is the precise governmental interest protected in a plea of act of state or immunity? There is a considerable body of literature and case law on questions of immunity but none of these directly considered the question of 'state interest' protected by immunity where a state is indirectly impleaded. It was the government's case that the existence of 'state interest' was decisive in all cases of indirect impleading in the context of immunity but also 'act of state'. The government argued that a finding of liability in tort would indirectly implead foreign governments since it was integral to a claim of complicity that the foreign states or officials had acted contrary to their own laws.

The court rejected the argument that the claims of complicity indirectly impleaded the foreign governments (specifically the United States, Malaysia, Thailand, and Libya). It noted that the alleged tortious conduct of the foreign officials would not be engaged in any legal sense by the proceedings for complicity and the court's decision would not bind them.[69] In their separate opinions,

[65] *Maduro v. Guaidó* (n 55).
[66] *Al Maktoum* (n 7).
[67] *Ukraine v. The Law Debenture Trust* (n 7).
[68] *Belhaj and Another v. Straw and Others* [2014] EWCA Civ 1394, [2015] 2 WLR 1105 [31].
[69] *Belhaj v. Straw* (n 2) [173] (Lord Neuberger), [12]–[31] (Lord Mance), [196]–[197] (Lord Sumption).

both Lords Mance and Sumption clarified that a state was not directly impleaded merely because the proceedings could affect some indeterminate interests; rather, that the interest capable of acting as a bar to proceedings must be concrete in the form of a stake in property, whether movable or immovable. The government had relied on the definition of interest in Article 6(2) of the UN Convention on the Jurisdictional Immunities of States and their Property, which provides:

> A proceeding before a court of a State shall be considered to have been instituted against another State if that other State:
>
> (a) is named as a party to that proceeding; or
> (b) is not named as a party to the proceeding but the proceeding in effect seeks to affect the property, rights, *interests* or activities of that other State.

Their Lordships clarified that the interests referred to in Article 6(2)(b) were clearly limited by the context. They contemplated only those consequences that were proximately related to property interests and did not extend to reputational or like disadvantages that could result from the proceedings.[70] The relief sought was a declaration and damages against the United Kingdom and these would have no effect against the rights of the foreign states mentioned. The commentary in the International Law Commission discussions on draft Article 6 of the Convention confirms that a narrow reading of 'interest' was intended.[71] This clarification significantly narrows the number of cases in which a claim of immunity or 'act of state' might be upheld and excludes judicial restraint merely because abstract or remote interests of states might be engaged.[72] In any case, Article 6 could not be treated as dispositive, since the Convention on Jurisdictional Immunities had not been ratified by the United Kingdom and was not in force.[73] The judgment also clarifies the different rationales of claims of immunity and act of state, the latter being a substantive bar to a claim, while immunity was a procedural bar to adjudication. It follows that claims of act of state were not *necessarily* inconsistent with human

[70] ibid [29] and [31] (Lord Mance). See also Roger O'Keeffe and Christian J. Tams (eds), *The United Nations Convention on Jurisdictional Immunities of States and Their Property: A Commentary* (OUP 2013), 109, 112.

[71] See UN General Assembly, 'Report of the Secretary-General on the Convention on Jurisdictional Immunities of States and Their Property' (1992) UN Doc. A/47/326.

[72] Hazel Fox CMG QC and Philippa Webb, *The Law of State Immunity* (3rd edn, OUP 2013), 307.

[73] *Belhaj v. Straw* (n 2) [25] (Lord Mance).

rights provisions guaranteeing access to the courts, since the question of access did not arise where the claim had no foothold in the domestic forum in the first place.

B. Consideration of 'Act of State' in the Supreme Court

1. The Legal Question

It was the government's case that insofar as the alleged torts were carried out by foreign officials acting under their territorial jurisdiction, English courts could not adjudicate on their legality by virtue of the act of state doctrine. Since this question was central to the appeal, it received extended consideration in both the majority judgment of Lord Neuberger and the extensive separate opinions of Lords Mance and Sumption. The judgment offers both an understanding of the discrete principles at play in any claim of act of state and clarifies the place and limits of the act of state doctrine as an overarching principle of non-justiciability in a modern constitutional democracy.

Taken as a whole, the judgment identifies the contours of the relationship between the act of state doctrine and domestic public policy considerations. It also identifies the tension inherent in a robust recognition of act of state claims and the increased public sensitivity to human rights values and how these developments, particularly the recognition of *jus cogens*, may have affected the content of the right. Although there is no uniformity in their approach to this question, the majority and individual judges, especially Lords Mance and Sumption, clarified the circumstances when the doctrine may be inapplicable on account of public policy considerations, including situations where upholding the doctrine would stand in marked tension with peremptory norms of international law.[74]

The Supreme Court also considered whether a finding of non-justiciability would be compatible with Article 6 of the European Convention on Human Rights. Under that provision, a victim of human rights violations has a right to a remedy before the courts. Having made the substantive finding that no act of state was engaged and the matter could proceed to trial, the court did not find it necessary to dwell on this point at length, noting in passing that as the act of

[74] ibid [153] (Lord Neuberger), [83] and [107] (Lord Mance), concluding that the conduct of the defendants was not covered by 'act of state' and there was therefore no need to consider the public policy exception. See also ibid [249]–[280] (Lord Sumption), who argues in favour of a public policy exception in relation to situations fundamentally at odds with English public policy or where the alleged conduct conflicts with peremptory norms of international law having the status of *jus cogens*.

state doctrine was a substantive bar to a claim, it precluded any consideration of Article 6 with regard to those cases that have no domestic foothold in the forum.[75]

All the judges agreed that that 'act of state' would be engaged if the activities in question could be classified as governmental as opposed to non-governmental. Drawing parallels with analogous issues in the law of immunity, the executive acts in question had to be *jure imperii* as opposed to *jure gestionis*.[76] Yet the distinction between governmental and non-governmental acts is in itself not free from controversy and rests on political assumptions as to the proper remit of state activity.[77] The International Law Commission was unable to reach a consensus on this issue in its consideration of the Jurisdictional Immunities of States and their Property, and the case law reveals that there is much disagreement on this issue, especially in legal systems that have not developed a clear distinction between public and private spheres of activity.[78] In this respect, *Belhaj* was a missed opportunity to provide guidance on a much contested formula.[79] In the subsequent case of *Al Maktoum*, both the High Court and the Court of Appeal regarded allegations of espionage and surveillance in the context of wardship proceedings as non-governmental and could not therefore attract judicial restraint on account of act of state.[80]

2. Meaning and Jurisdictional Reach of the Act of State Doctrine: Four Discrete Rules

The Supreme Court's decision in *Belhaj*'s great contribution is to clarify what is meant by 'act of state' and to delineate the consequences in those situations where the act is said to be operative. It is, as Lord Sumption notes in his separate opinion, 'an attempt to rectify the indiscriminate use of act of state to cover situations which are quite distinct and different in law'.[81] Their Lordships

[75] ibid [109]–[110] (Lord Mance).

[76] ibid [44] (Lord Mance), [147] (Lord Neuberger), [183] (Lord Sumption); confirmed in *Al Maktoum*, which concerned allegations of complicity in illegal surveillance in the context of wardship proceedings; espionage on an estranged spouse not governmental and therefore not act of state. That in any case foreign act of state did not apply to activities taking place in the United Kingdom. See *Al Maktoum* (n 7), [39]–[42].

[77] Ian Brownlie, *Principles of Public International Law* (6th edn, OUP 2003), 330–331.

[78] James Crawford, 'International Law and Foreign Sovereigns: Distinguishing Immune Transactions' (1983) 54(1) *British Yearbook of International Law* 74; 'The Draft Articles on Jurisdictional Immunities of States and Their Property, with commentaries' in ILC, 'Report of the International Law Commission on the Work of its 43rd session' (29 April–19 July 1991) UN Doc. A/46/10 [28].

[79] Writing extrajudicially, Lord Mance has given some indication of matters which may be regarded as governmental. They include; the conduct of armed operations overseas, whether by way of armed intervention or by way of self-defence against another state or against non-state actors targeted by Security Council operations. See Lord Mance, 'Justiciability' (n 49).

[80] *Al Maktoum* (n 7).

[81] *Belhaj v. Straw* (n 2) [227] (Lord Sumption).

also clarify that unlike state immunity, which is a legal imperative under public international law, 'act of state' is wholly a creature of the common law and is at best permitted but not mandated by international law.[82] It follows that states are entirely free to amend or depart from its application without incurring any sanctions as a matter of international law.

3. The Majority, the *Ratio* of Lord Neuberger

Four distinct rules can be distilled from the judgment of Lord Neuberger[83] as potentially forming part of the act of state doctrine. Each will now be considered in turn.

a) Rule 1

The first rule provides that English courts will not question the validity of foreign legislation or other laws in relation to any acts which take place or has effect within the territory of a foreign state.[84] For Lord Neuberger, the rule was a logical consequence of the territorial sovereignty of states in relation to acts taking place on their territory. However, Rule 1 is confined to acts that take place on the territory of the state concerned.[85] Like Lord Mance, he saw the rule as in part stemming from the choice of law or proper law rule of private international law under which the *lex situs* was always dispositive. In *Maduro*, the Supreme Court recently narrowed the scope of application of the rule, noting that judicial restraint is not called for if the legislation relied on has been rendered a nullity by a final court of the state in question.[86] Further, that there is nothing to stop the English courts from scrutinizing foreign judicial decisions and the effect of those decisions on local laws.

b) Rule 2

The second rule relates to foreign executive acts and, as in the case of legislation, the courts will recognize and will not question the effect of foreign executive acts which take place or are given effect within the territory of that state.[87] There has been some controversy whether effect should be given to acts that

[82] ibid [200] (Lord Sumption). See also *Nevsun Resources* (n 63).

[83] Lord Neuberger's judgment has been treated as containing the *ratio* of the case. Lord Wilson, Lady Hale, and Lord Clarke agreed with his judgment, therefore constituting a majority. See *Belhaj v. Straw* (n 2), [113]–[173] (Lord Neuberger) and [174] (Lady Hale and Lord Clarke). In *Maduro*, the Supreme Court again treated the judgment of Lord Neuberger as containing the *ratio* of the case. See *Maduro v. Guaidó* (n 55) [112].

[84] *Belhaj v. Straw* (n 2) [121].

[85] ibid [135] (Lord Neuberger).

[86] *Maduro v. Guaidó* (n 55) [176].

[87] ibid [122].

are unlawful by the law of the foreign state, based on the argument that the forum lacks institutional competence to pass judgement on any aspect of their validity. Lord Neuberger found this troubling as a matter of principle, since the foreign executive act would have a more far-reaching effect in the forum than it would at the place of acting. He was prepared to deny recognition to executive acts which are unlawful by the laws of the state concerned but considered that in the interest of certainty and clarity, effects should be given even to laws that are unlawful.[88] In any case, he would limit the second rule to property cases and it would have no relevance to non-property cases, such as causing physical or mental harm that is unlawful under the laws of that state.

It is in relation to the scope of Rules 1 and 2 that one finds a wide difference between the majority and Lord Sumption. Lord Mance, like Lord Neuberger, would not extend the doctrine to executive acts unlawful under the laws of the foreign state, except where they concern property under the foreign states' jurisdiction in times of civil disorder. He was categorical that the second rule should be confined to the property context and could not extended outside the property arena to cover personal wrongs.[89] Lord Sumption, by contrast, adopted a wide definition of 'act of state' which would subsume Rules 1 and 2 and which he referred to as the municipal law 'act of state'. On this conception of 'act of state', English courts will not adjudicate on the lawfulness or validity of a state's sovereign acts under its own law, and although the category he notes has traditionally been confined to property cases it need not be. Lord Sumption observes that:

> Once it is accepted that executive acts may be acts of state, there is no rational reason why the principle should be limited to executive seizures of property, as opposed to injury to other interests equally protected by the municipal law of the place where they occurred. I see no rational ground for distinguishing between the expropriation of property by executive act, and no sensible basis on which the former is to be treated as an act of state and the latter not. For the same reasons, I think that personal injury and other wrongs against the person inflicted by the agents of a foreign state are as much capable of being acts of state as destruction or detention of property.[90]

88 ibid [138].
89 ibid [74]–[78], [80].
90 ibid [231] (Lord Sumption).

In his view, the acts carried out by Malaysia in deporting Mr Belhaj and Mrs Boudchar, as well as their interrogation in Libya, were domestic exercises of governmental authority falling within the act of state doctrine. This is broadly in keeping with his particular view of the separation of powers, that courts should not generally stray into matters that are within the competence of the executive branches.[91]

In the most recent decision in *Maduro* before a differently constituted bench of the Supreme Court, without explicitly saying so, the court appears to have adopted Lord Sumption's wide reading of 'act of state' as finding support in practice. The *Maduro* judgment has also clarified that the rule:

> ... does not turn on a conventional application of choice of law rules in private international law, nor does it depend on the lawfulness of the conduct under the law of the state in question. On the contrary, it is an exclusionary rule, limiting the power of the Courts to decide certain issues as to the legality or validity of the conduct of foreign states within their proper jurisdiction. It operates not by reference to law but by reference to the sovereign character of the conduct which forms the subject matter of the proceedings. The fact that executive acts may lack any legal basis does not prevent the application of the rule. In my view we should now acknowledge the existence of the rule.[92]

In *Maduro*, the Supreme Court clarified that there was no support in the pre-*Belhaj* decision for restricting Rule 2 to property cases and therefore no reason why it should not extend to other acts even if unlawful by the law of the foreign state. Regrettably, the Supreme Court did not take advantage of the opportunity offered by *Law Debenture Trust*[93] to clarify the juridical basis of the second rule and whether it extends beyond property cases to include other acts including those that are otherwise unlawful. The rationale of extending 'act of state' to acts that are 'de facto' nullities by the law of the place of acting is not immediately obvious, and as Lord Neuberger rightly observed, it would give those acts greater effect than they would have in the foreign state, undermining the rationale for deference.

[91] Lord Sumption, 'The Limits of the Law' in N. W. Barber et al., *Lord Sumption and the Limits of the Law* (Hart Publishing 2016), 15–26.

[92] *Maduro v. Guaidó* (n 55) [135].

[93] *Ukraine v. Law Debenture Trust* (n 7); *The Law Debenture Trust Corporation PLC v. Ukraine* [2023] UKSC 11

c) Rule 3

The third rule essentially encompasses a broad doctrine of non-justiciability and has many components. All judges in the Supreme Court agreed on the substance of this third rule, although their terminology varied. Lord Sumption, for instance, refers to it as an 'international law act of State' to underscore the fact that it may cover situations where the domestic court is exercising judicial restraint other than for reasons of non-justiciability.[94] The judgment is particularly insightful in identifying the myriad contexts in which the 'international law act of state' is said to apply.[95]

The rule, it is said, 'involves issues which are inappropriate for the courts of the United Kingdom to resolve because they involve a challenge to the lawfulness of the act of a foreign state which is of such a nature that a municipal judge cannot or ought not rule on it'.[96] There are echoes here of a broad principle of deference on account of a lack of institutional competence. The courts will not under this rule interpret or question dealings between sovereign states, matters relating to the making of war and peace, making treaties with foreign sovereigns, and annexation and cession of territory. The courts will also not determine the legality of a foreign government in the conduct of foreign affairs. Since this is a rule of judicial restraint, in which the forum is declining jurisdictional competence which it would otherwise have, the Supreme Court was unanimous that the rule should be applied sparingly so as not to conflict with fundamental human rights including access to a remedy.[97] Lord Neuberger noted that an act of state should be something exceptional; an unusual situation, and strong evidence should be required for courts to decline jurisdiction.

This third limb of the rule, although not classified as such, is broadly identical in terms of its reach to what Lord Sumption refers to as an 'international law act of State'.[98] First, whether or not a particular issue or claim is justiciable will have to be resolved on a case-by-case basis.[99] In *Al Maktoum* and *Law Debenture Trust*, the Court of Appeal distilled a number of guiding principles in the application of this rule. Broadly speaking, courts will not exercise judicial restraint under the third rule where the claim has a domestic foothold, in the sense of a basis for legal analysis in English law; conversely it will decline jurisdiction in

[94] *Belhaj v. Straw* (n 2) [234].
[95] ibid [237].
[96] ibid [123].
[97] ibid [123] and [144] (Lord Neuberger).
[98] ibid [234]–[239] (Lord Sumption), [40]–[55] (Lord Mance).
[99] ibid, 11 (iv), 107 (iv) (Lord Mance), [147] (Lord Neuberger); *Al Maktoum* (n 7) [42]: 'It was not unfair or inappropriate to resolve the father's personal complicity in unlawful UK surveillance, and for that purpose it was not appropriate to prevent the mother relying on technical and other evidence as to how and by whom the hacking had been undertaken.'

claims lacking a domestic basis such as pure questions of public international law between sovereign states beyond the competence of the English courts to resolve.[100] Second, the courts will decline to adjudicate on those cases which, on a strict interpretation of the separation of powers doctrine, are beyond the constitutional competence of the courts.[101] Third, the courts will be inclined to assume jurisdiction if the claim of act of state arises in the context of a private law claim, such as a serious infringement of privacy in domestic wardship proceedings.[102] Moreover, the courts will be inclined to assume jurisdiction where fundamental rights such as rights of liberty, access to justice, and freedom from torture are manifestly engaged.[103] Equally relevant is whether the parties have voluntarily invoked or submitted to the jurisdiction of the forum and whether the contested acts occurred or affected persons in the United Kingdom.[104]

d) Rule 4

A possible fourth rule identified by Lord Neuberger, but which finds no support in the separate opinions of Lords Mance and Sumption, concerns those cases where the courts will not investigate acts of a foreign state where such an investigation would embarrass the government, for example in those situations where the executive has publicly committed itself to a particular policy. Lord Neuberger conceded that there was very little authority to support the rule in English law, but if it was to be regarded as part of the received law, it would require very exceptional circumstances for it to be invoked.[105] Lord Neuberger noted that there were many matters in which an executive certificate was always conclusive so far as the courts were concerned, for instance the recognition of a foreign state, the territorial limits of a foreign state, and whether a state of war exists. In these situations, it may be prudent for the courts not to contradict the executive position.

[100] *Belhaj v. Straw* (n 2) [44] (Lord Mance); *Buttes Gas & Oil Co. v. Hammer (No. 3)* [1982] AC 888; *Ukraine v. Law Debenture Trust* (n 7) [155], [225] (Lord Sumption).

[101] *Ukraine v. Law Debenture Trust* (n 7) [43] (Lord Mance), [227] (Lord Sumption).

[102] *Al Maktoum* (n 7) [33].

[103] *Belhaj v. Straw* (n 2) [144] (Lord Neuberger): 'it seems to me that there is force in the argument that, bearing in mind the importance which both the common law and Human Rights Convention attach to the right of access to the Courts, judges should not be enthusiastic in declining to determine a claim under the third rule ...'; 11 (iv) (Lord Mance).

[104] ibid [237] (Lord Sumption); *Law Debenture Trust v. Ukraine* (n 54) [175]–[178] (Sales LJ, Richards LJ, and Dame Elizabeth Gloster).

[105] *Law Debenture Trust v. Ukraine* (n 54) [132].

C. Public Policy and the *Jus Cogens* Conundrum

The majority accepted that the act of state doctrine, where applicable, was subject to a public policy exception, although Lord Neuberger was sceptical of adopting a largely international law-inspired conception of public policy, and preferred to ground it firmly within domestic law, specifically English law standards of public policy, of which the Nazi confiscatory law in *Oppenheimer* is given as an example.[106] The public policy exception would limit the application of act of state in relation to the four different situations in which an act of state may be deemed operative[107] and may in appropriate cases be applicable because the alleged act violates fundamental human rights norms.

It has already been noted that Lord Sumption adopts a wide view of the act of state doctrine and unlike the majority would extend it to cover executive acts on the territory of that state even if unlawful by the law of that state.[108] However, his wide reading of 'act of state' is curtailed by an expansive public policy exception. In addition to situations that would clearly contradict domestic public policy, he would disallow its application where the alleged conduct violates fundamental norms of international law having the status of *jus cogens*, such as acts of torture, unlawful detention, rendition, and enforced disappearance.[109] On the facts of *Belhaj*, he notes that:

> It would be contrary to the fundamental requirements of justice administered by an English Court to apply the foreign act of state doctrine to an allegation of civil liability for complicity in acts of torture by foreign states. Respect for the autonomy of foreign sovereigns, which is the rationale of the foreign act of state doctrine cannot extend to their involvement in torture, because each of them is bound *erga omnes* and along with the United Kingdom to renounce it as instrument of national or international policy and to participate in its suppression.[110]

Lord Sumption is alert to the danger that a wide exception to the rule may result in normative incoherence, but nevertheless succumbs to it.[111] In relation to norms having the status of *jus cogens*, his formulation of the public policy

[106] ibid [154] (Lord Neuberger); *Oppenheimer v. Cattermole (HM Inspector of Taxes)* [1976] AC 249.
[107] *Belhaj v. Straw* (n 2) [153]–[154] (Lord Neuberger).
[108] ibid [230]–[231] (Lord Sumption).
[109] ibid [278].
[110] ibid [262] (Lord Sumption).
[111] ibid [253] (Lord Sumption).

exception is both under-inclusive and over-inclusive in terms of the interests it purports to protect. It is under-inclusive, because under it the courts would not disallow an act of state claim in relation to allegations of mistreatment or unlawful detention not amounting to *jus cogens*; in other words, only the most egregious violations would defeat a plea of act of state. As Lord Mance points out, these forms of mistreatment may not meet the *jus cogens* threshold but the values underpinning them are equally deserving of protection as fundamental individual rights.[112] It is over-inclusive because it would entitle an English court to assume jurisdiction, for example, over the illegal annexation of territory, because on any view, egregious acts of use of force meet the *jus cogens* threshold. In this, Lord Sumption finds support in the *Kuwait Airways* case, where the House of Lords refused to uphold the validity of an Iraqi decree that divested Kuwait Airways of its property because the decree was a consequence of an illegal annexation contrary to Article 2(4).[113]

Lord Mance is alert to the danger of an over-expansive public policy exception rooted in international law. He notes that:

> If violation of a *jus cogens* were a primary test of whether a domestic court could adjudicate upon an issue which was otherwise non-justiciable and upon which it would otherwise have to abstain from adjudicating, central areas identified by Lord Sumption would become potentially amenable to adjudication. The prohibition on use of armed force and on aggression are core examples of *jus cogens*. Yet these are, rightly … be treated by Lord Sumption himself as giving rise to core examples of issues upon which domestic courts should refrain from adjudicating.[114]

Illegal use of force is precisely the kind of activity that would on any view be regarded as on the international plane and non-justiciable in a domestic forum. Moreover, if there is a presumption of justiciability in all cases where the alleged conduct violates a *jus cogens* norm, there is a real risk of normative indeterminacy since it is not clear whether the municipal court will have clear standards for distinguishing exceptional *jus cogens* situations not engaging 'act of state' and instances where judicial restraint is called for because 'act of state' is operative.

112 ibid [107].
113 *Kuwait Airways v. Iraqi Airways* (n 57). See also *Law Debenture Trust* (n 54) [174].
114 ibid [107] (Lord Mance).

D. Conclusion

Despite doubts about the continuing relevance of the two doctrines, both the South African Constitutional Court and the UK Supreme Court have confirmed diplomatic protection and 'act of state' as part of positive law. Both courts also unequivocally confirm that the doctrines must be interpreted in light of modern constitutional principles. They therefore lay to rest arguments that the doctrines have fallen into desuetude and are no longer relevant in modern constitutional democracies.

Both decisions, it is suggested, have made great strides in clarifying how fundamental values of international law may influence the content of domestic rules. Also, in relation to diplomatic protection, it is clear that domestic constitutional litigation offers the best hope for expanding its ambit of protection by anchoring it to rights of citizenship in a modern constitutional democracy. As the two cases illustrate, fundamental human rights treaties also give both doctrines a domestic foothold, by emphasizing the primacy of state obligations in these treaties, and the existence of a concomitant duty to enforce them. Thus, diplomatic protection may be a practical way of giving effect to human rights treaties, and traditional state discretion may be limited by the demands of binding human rights norms.

It is significant that both cases unequivocally confirm the presumption of justiciability; that access to the courts is essential in holding public power accountable and that it is only in the most exceptional of cases that access to the courts will be denied.[115] In *Belhaj*, the Court of Appeal and the Supreme Court both reaffirmed the justiciability of private law claims; if what is presented before them is in the nature of a private law claim, they will not deny access to the courts merely because it will cause embarrassment to the government. Deference to executive power on account of 'act of state' remains an exceptional remedy which must be interpreted in light of the demands of the rule of law.

Both cases involve a rebuttal of the prevailing dualist dogma that international law cannot be applied domestically in the absence of dualist filters, such as incorporation in a domestic statute. We see this especially in the judgment of Lord Sumption in *Belhaj*, who is prepared to curtail the outer limits of 'act of state' by referring to norms of international law, including Security

[115] Campbell McLachlan, 'The Foreign Relations Power in the Supreme Court' (2018) 134 *Law Quarterly Review* 1.

Council resolutions, even if these ordinarily have no domestic foothold unless given effect to in a statute.[116] Similarly, in *Kaunda*, there was an acceptance by all the judges that the content of diplomatic protection was to be determined by reference to human rights standards in treaties even if those treaties have not been formally domesticated.

[116] *Belhaj v. Straw* (n 2) [175]–[285] (Lord Sumption); see also *Ukraine v. Law Debenture Trust* (n 5).

30

The Hollow Canon of Transnational Constitutional Engagement

*Vlad Perju**

I. Introduction

At the turn of the century, an effervescence of cross-constitutional references in judicial decisions from new constitutional democracies in Hungary and South Africa to more established systems such as Canada, Italy, and the United States marked what, at the time, looked like a new constitutional era.[1] Complex processes of globalization seemed capable of infiltrating not only economics and public policy but also the realms of constitutional discourse and perhaps even doctrine, which in the past had been somewhat more insulated from transjurisdictional stimuli. In most constitutional systems, such transnational references were incorporated without much contestation. The fierce and deeply polarized debate that ensued in the United States around judicial practices of invoking foreign law that were significantly more sparse than in other jurisdictions,[2] seemed at first as yet another American constitutional oddity. And so it was, except that the American debate captured normative concerns that, while muted elsewhere, are undeniably relevant to modern constitutionalism.[3] For instance, it is not self-evident why foreign law has or should have normative weight in the process of interpreting and applying a democracy's charter of constitutional self-government. Nor is it apparent how such practices can be deployed in the principled fashion we expect

* Professor and Dean's Distinguished Scholar, Boston College Law School.

[1] See Vicki Jackson, *Constitutional Engagement in a Transnational Era* (Oxford University Press, 2013); Ran Hirschl, *Comparative Matters: The Revival of Comparative Constitutional Law* (Oxford University Press, 2014).

[2] An empirical study from 2013 found 63 citations to foreign law in 225 years. See Stephen Simon, "The Supreme Court's Use of Foreign Law in Constitutional Rights Cases: An Empirical Study," Journal of Law and Courts 1(2): 279–301 (2013).

[3] Jeremy Waldron, *Partly Laws Common to All Mankind: Foreign Law in American Courts* (Yale University Press, 2012).

Vlad Perju, *The Hollow Canon of Transnational Constitutional Engagement* In: *Global Canons in an Age of Contestation*. Edited by: Sujit Choudhry, Michaela Hailbronner, and Mattias Kumm, Oxford University Press.
DOI: 10.1093/9780191956942.003.0030

from courts of law. The canon of transnational constitutional engagement took shape around these questions.

This chapter turns to and on that canon. Its derisory sketch of alternative jurisprudential worldviews has failed to stabilize and support the practice of using foreign law in constitutional interpretation. Without support, transnational constitutional engagement of this type became victim to the vicissitudes of political and socioprofessional factors that had brought it about in the first place. It is not only in American constitutional law that engagement with foreign law has dried up over the past decade or so. Elsewhere, including in South Africa, such engagement has greatly diminished in extent and purpose. Nowhere, it seems, has transnational engagement delivered the doctrinal transformation that its proponents once saw as its promise.

I start by introducing the constitutional world of two death penalty cases as examples of transnational constitutional engagement: *Roper v. Simmons* (2005)[4] in the United States and *S v. Makwanyane* (1995)[5] in South Africa. Both cases attracted significant attention, yet their doctrinal and social legacies are complex. Section II explores those legacies through later cases involving life imprisonment without parole. Not only *Roper*'s detractors but also its own heirs undermined the promise of aligning American constitutionalism to norms of global constitutionalism as a mechanism for protecting children from cruel and disproportionate punishments. The next two sections connect the failures of constitutional engagement to the faulty theories offered in its support. The most common and weakest is pragmatism. A more promising but limited and ultimately unconvincing theory is Jeremy Waldron's conception of foreign law as the new *jus gentium*.

II. Death Penalty: The Constitutional World of *Roper* and *Makwanyane*

Roper v. Simmons was not the first or even the most visible case in which the U.S. Supreme Court used foreign law to interpret the U.S. Constitution, but it is the case that galvanized to an extent greater than most others what, in retrospect, is the canon of transnational constitutional engagement. *Roper* is part of a new chapter in the Supreme Court's protracted and non-linear jurisprudence on what the Eighth Amendment to the U.S. Constitution requires of states as far as capital punishment is concerned.[6] Central to this new doctrinal

[4] 543 U.S. 551 (2005).

[5] *S v. Makwanyane and Another* (CCT3/94) [1995] ZACC 3.

[6] U.S. Constitution, Eighth Amendment: "Excessive bail shall not be required, nor excessive fines imposed, nor cruel and unusual punishments inflicted."

chapter is a shift away from the crime or the method of execution and toward the offender.[7] In *Atkins v. Virginia* (2002),[8] the Supreme Court held that death is an inherently disproportional punishment as applied to mentally disabled offenders. The question in *Roper* was whether the Eighth Amendment allows a state to sentence to death a person under the age of 18 at the time of the offense.

The Court held that it does not. The insufficiently well-formed character of juveniles, their lack of maturity and underdeveloped sense of responsibility, as well as their susceptibility to negative influences and outside pressures all pointed to their diminished culpability. These traits lessened the penological justifications —retribution or deterrence — and made death a punishment always disproportionate, and therefore cruel and unusual, when applied to a minor. *Roper* drew "essential instruction"[9] from developments at the sub-federal level ranging from infrequent application of the death penalty to juveniles to the rejection of this type of punishment or a consistent trend towards abolition in the majority of U.S. states. But state law is only part of the framework of reference. The "evolving standards of decency that mark the progress of a maturing society"[10] open up the constitutional analysis of what constitutes a cruel and unusual punishment. But the breadth of the new framework it is a matter of interpretation. One narrow interpretation confines the constitutional analysis to the national realm, whereas a broader approach searches for such standards within the tradition of the common law, or of the legal cultures of the West, or, conceivably, at the global level. The majority in *Roper* proceeded in concentric circles, with different degrees of engagement at each level of analysis. Starting from the largest and presumably the most eclectic global perspective, the Court's survey concluded that the "US is the only country in the world that continues to give official sanction to the juvenile death penalty."[11] Moving inward towards its own common law tradition increased the Court's level of comfort with more robust engagement with foreign jurisdictions. Justice Kennedy, writing for the Court, reviewed the reasons behind

[7] For a comprehensive account, see Carol S. Steiker and Jordan M. Steiker, *Courting Death: The Supreme Court and Capital Punishment* (Harvard University Press, 2016)

[8] 536 U.S. 304 (2002).

[9] *Roper*, at 564.

[10] *Trop v. Dulles*, 356 U.S. 86, 100–101 (1958).

[11] This may sound stark but it is not, considering that Art. 37 (a) of the U.N. Convention on the Rights of the Child, to which all countries except the U.S. are signatory, reads: "No child shall be subjected to torture or other cruel, inhuman or degrading treatment or punishment. Neither capital punishment nor life imprisonment without possibility of release shall be imposed for offences committed by persons below eighteen years of age." Nevertheless, the issue of what constitutes parole has become a matter of dispute. U.N. bodies, such as the U.N. Human Rights Committee, have stepped in to identify when the possibility of parole is so remote that a sentence is de facto life without parole. See Dirk van Zyl Smit and Catherine Appleton, *Life Imprisonment: A Global Analysis* (Harvard University Press, 2019), at 105–108.

the elimination of the death penalty for juveniles in the United Kingdom, and deemed those reasons similar to *Roper*'s majority.[12]

Roper's use of foreign law placed it in a larger constitutional age of transnational engagement. In *S v. Makwanyane*, the newly established Constitutional Court of South Africa considered whether the death penalty violated the country's new Constitution. In a remarkably erudite and thoughtful opinion, President Chaskalson mentioned a plethora of foreign judgments, from India to Canada and from the U.S. to Tanzania to the European Court of Human Rights. Interpreting them through the theoretical lens of theories of punishment, he used these foreign judgments as dicta to strike down death as a form of punishment permissible under the South Africa's constitutional protection of rights to life and dignity. *Makwanyane* showed the world what constitutional engagement with foreign and international law could look like.[13] To be sure, *Makwanyane* was to some extent the result of special circumstances.[14] Building a new constitutional order on the legacy of apartheid left judges in need of traditions to serve as anchors and points of reference. References to foreign law could supply some of the missing traditions. Reputational considerations also must have played a role for a legal and political system seeking the recognition of more consolidated constitutional democracies. Finally, and of particular importance, South Africa's Constitution explicitly allows references to foreign law in constitutional interpretation.[15]

The lack of comparable textual foundations might explain some of the *Roper* Court's defensiveness in regard to cross-jurisdiction references. Arguing, vaguely, that what other countries "do" is "instructive," the majority in *Roper* wrote that "the opinion of the world community, while not controlling our outcome, does provide respected and significant confirmation for our own

[12] It is proper that we acknowledge the overwhelming weight of international opinion against the juvenile death penalty, resting in large part on the understanding that the instability and emotional imbalance of young people may often be a factor in the crime. See Brief for Human Rights Committee of the Bar of England and Wales et al. as *Amici Curiae*, 10–11.

[13] As befits an institutional innovator, the *Makwanyane* Court mentioned that, "[i]n dealing with comparative law, … [it is] required to construe the South African Constitution, and not an international instrument or the constitution of some foreign country" and, therefore, it can "derive assistance from public international law and foreign case law, but we are in no way bound to follow it.". *Makwanyane*, para 39 (footnote omitted). The historical record notes the existence of earlier and equally impressive, in range and depth, instances of transnational engagement, such as Decision No. 23/1990 (X.31.) AB (Hungarian Constitutional Court).

[14] Special, not unique. For comparison, see Frank Michelman, "Reasonable Umbrage: Race and Constitutional Antidiscrimination Law in the United. States and South Africa," 117 Harvard Law Review 1378 (2004).

[15] Constitution of South Africa, Art. 39, 1: "When interpreting the Bill of Rights, a court, tribunal or forum—b) must consider international law; and c) may consider foreign law."

conclusions"[16]—conclusions that, presumably, the Court had reached independently of foreign law. Seeking to deflate criticism that interpreting a political community charter of constitutional self-government must be confined strictly to sources originating in that community,[17] Justice Kennedy opined that "[i]t does not lessen our fidelity to the Constitution or our pride in its origins to acknowledge that the express affirmation of certain fundamental rights by other nations and peoples simply underscores the centrality of those same rights within our own heritage of freedom."[18]

The reference to the heritage of freedom echoes another, much-discussed case of the U.S. Supreme Court, *Lawrence v. Texas*,[19] that struck down a statute criminalizing homosexual sodomy. Holding that the statute deprived gay and lesbian Americans of their liberty under the Due Process Clause of the Fourteenth Amendment, the Court, again per Justice Kennedy, referenced foreign law to show that the liberty interest whose protection the claimants sought in that case "has been accepted as an integral part of human freedom in many other countries."[20] The Court drew that conclusion from the legal cultures of the West, as reflected in the cases of the European Court of Human Rights, as well as from developments in English law. The jurisprudence that supports this approach seems to be one where constitutions instill the normative commitments to abstract values such as liberty or equality of a political community but contingencies of time and place shape the meanings of those commitments in ways that may obscure some of their dimensions.[21] Courts may seek to overcome those contingencies by reaching out to foreign law in order to bring to light "components of liberty in its manifold possibilities" and thus properly come to "appreciate the extent of the liberty at stake."[22] The claimant's case may ultimately turn on the ability of courts to reveal and understand these new possibilities. By contrast to *Roper*, the goal in this subset of cases is not to draw on a unitary world legal practice or a near universal norm but rather to carve out a shared, trans-jurisdictional normative space in which constitutional rights can be interpreted.

What about the risk that such transnational spaces harbour nominalist and self-serving beliefs that impermissibly undermine the promise of democratic self-government? Constitutional contingency is, for some, tantamount to

[16] *Roper*, at 578.
[17] That reaction originates in *Thompson v. Oklahoma*, 487 U.S. 815 (1988) (Scalia, J., dissenting).
[18] *Roper*, at 578.
[19] 539 U.S. 558 (2003).
[20] *Lawrence*, at 577.
[21] See Vlad Perju, "Cosmopolitanism and Constitutional Self-Government," 8 ICON 326 (2010).
[22] *Lawrence*, at 567.

political identity. I consider these arguments later. Noteworthy for now is that the weight of this objection is greater when, as in *Lawrence*, the constitutional decision-maker selects and often has to construct a particular legal tradition as opposed to situations such as *Roper* when the legal traditions of the world seem to overlap. By this standard, it seems that the anchor of *Roper*'s usage of foreign law runs considerably deeper. How deep, though, is what subsequent cases would reveal.

III. Life Imprisonment without Parole: *Makwanyane*'s and *Roper*'s Complex Legacies

The canon of transnational engagement treats *Makwanyane* and *Roper* as defining moments in setting the normative interface between constitutional legal orders. Yet, cases downstream reveal their legacies as more tentative and, in *Roper*'s case, considerably frailer than the canonists had assumed or hoped.

Makwanyane ordered that offenders already sentenced to death be subject to other "appropriate and lawful punishments."[23] In most cases, that meant life imprisonment. The number of "lifers," or offenders sentenced to life imprisonment, at least theoretically with the possibility of parole after serving the non-parole part of the sentence, increased dramatically a few years later when legislative reforms imposed mandatory minimum sentences for a significant number of crimes, including premediated murder and some forms of aggravated rape but also for crimes such as trafficking and some terrorism-related offences.[24] The Constitutional Court upheld the facial constitutionality of the Act on separation of powers grounds, with a rich apparatus of references to both foreign constitutional law and theory.[25] But a more narrowly calibrated challenge subsequently struck down mandatory minimum sentences when the offender was a child between the ages of 16 and 18 at the time when they committed the crime.[26] Relying, in part, on a constitutional provision that children "are not to be detained except as a measure of last resort" and "only for the shortest appropriate period of time"[27] and, in part, on international law, especially the U.N. Convention on the Rights of the Child, as well as on foreign

[23] *Makwanyane*, para 150.
[24] Criminal Law Amendment Act of 1997.
[25] *S v Dodo* (CCT 1/01) [2001] ZACC 16, paras 27–41.
[26] *Centre for Child Law v. Minister of Justice and Constitutional Development* (CCT98/08) [2009] ZACC 18.
[27] Art. 28, 1, (g).

cases, the South African judges interpreted the principle of proportionality of punishment to require that children be imprisoned only as a measure of last resort and for the shortest period of time.[28] The attempt to protect children from this extreme form of punishment must be understood in the context where, as former Justice Cameron argued, South African prisons "are clogged within an inordinate number of lifers." [29] Studies show that, in 2019, life imprisonment sentences represented 12% of the total prison population, an increase of more than forty-three times compared to the early 1990s. Between 2000 and 2014, the population of South Africa's lifer population grew by 818%. Meanwhile, "violent crime still plagues" South Africa.[30] Since even among convicts who qualify for parole hearings, the possibility of being granted parole is sometimes purely theoretical given its uneven application, it seems fair to wonder if the life imprisonment regime in effect complies with *Makwanyane*'s broad interpretation of the constitutional dignity guarantees.

In the United States, where the death penalty remains constitutional, about one in seven people in prison are serving life sentences. Indeed, studies show that more people are serving life sentences today than there were people in prison serving any sentence in 1970.[31] The number of offenders who serve sentences to life imprisonment without parole has increased steadily over the past decades, to include in the most recent study more than a quarter of all sentences to life imprisonment.[32] The Supreme Court has interpreted the U.S. Constitution to permit such sanctioning regimes.[33] The only exception involves children.

In view of *Roper*'s reliance on the profile of offenders, it was only a matter of time before the legality of the next harshest available form of punishment for juveniles, life in prison without the possibility of parole, would also be put to a constitutional test. Five years after *Roper*, the Supreme Court ruled in *Graham v. Florida* (2010)[34] that life without parole violates the Eight Amendment as applied to a juvenile convicted of a nonhomicidal offense. *Graham*, like *Roper*,

[28] Ann Skelton, "Balancing Autonomy and Protection of Children's Rights: A South African Account," 88 Temple Law Review 887 (2016).

[29] Edwin Cameron, "South Africa's prisons are crowded with 'lifers,' at great cost to our economy and even human rights," in *The Daily Maverick* (10 November 2021) (available at https://www.dailymaverick.co.za/article/2021-11-10-south-africas-faulty-approach-to-life-sentences-is-catching-up-with-us/).

[30] ibid.

[31] The total number in 2021 was 200,000. See https://www.sentencingproject.org/publications/no-end-in-sight-americas-enduring-reliance-on-life-imprisonment/.

[32] https://www.statista.com/statistics/818006/number-of-people-serving-life-sentences-without-parole-in-the-us/.

[33] *Harmelin v. Michigan*, 501 U.S. 957 (1991).

[34] 560 U.S. 48 (2010).

cited research on the differences between children and adults in terms of their "lack of maturity" and "underdeveloped sense of responsibility."[35] Justice Kennedy, writing for the Court, duly noted "the overwhelming weight of international opinion against"[36] life without parole for nonhomicide offenses committed by juveniles. He qualified this statement with the reminder that international opinion played only a confirmatory role, albeit "respected and significant,"[37] for the Court's own conclusions.

Graham was important as a statement of principle but it affected only a little over 100 inmates held in state courts, mostly in the state of Florida. A far greater number of convicts—around 2,500—had been sentenced to life without the possibility of parole for homicide. Since both *Roper* and *Graham* spoke about children's vulnerability in general terms, it seemed certain that those sentences would eventually be challenged under the *Roper/Graham* rationale. In *Miller v. Alabama* (2012),[38] the U.S. Supreme Court considered whether a sentencing scheme that mandates life in prison without the possibility of parole for juveniles convicted of committing homicides is consistent with the Eight Amendment's prohibition of cruel and unusual punishment. Justice Kagan, writing for the Court, answered the question in the negative. Since the reasoning in *Graham* and *Roper* was not crime-specific, it follows that the grounds why special punishments had to be carved out for children apply irrespective of the severity of the crime.

Yet, *Miller* made no mention of foreign law. The discontinuity with the *Atkins–Roper—Graham* line of interpretation was noteworthy since, here as in those earlier cases, foreign law reflected the consensus of the world legal systems. Amici had shown that "virtually every other country in the world either has never engaged in or has rejected"[39] sentencing juveniles to life without possibility of parole regardless of their crime. *Miller*'s failure to cite foreign law might at first seem inconsequential. Having already mentioned as dicta the

[35] *Graham*, at 68.
[36] ibid at 81.
[37] ibid (citing *Roper*).
[38] 567 U.S. 460 (2012).
[39] Brief of Amnesty International et al. in Support of Petitioners, 3 (available at https://eji.org/cases/miller-v-alabama/pleadings/). In Germany, the Federal Constitutional Court held that life without parole violates human dignity in *Life Imprisonment* 45 BVerfGE 187 (21 June 1977). The Supreme Court of Canada struck down life without parole in *R v Bissonnette*, [2022] SCC 23. The European Court of Human Rights first held that life imprisonment without parole violates Article 3 of the European Convention of Human Rights in *Vinter v. United Kingdom*, 66069/09, 130/10, & 3896/10 (ECtHR, 2012), although that holding was later qualified in *Hutchinson v United Kingdom* 57592/08 (ECtHR, 2017). For a comparative analysis of these constitutional developments, see Mugambi Jouet, "The Abolition and Retention of Life Without Parole in Europe: A Comparative and Historical Perspective", The European Convention on Human Rights Law Review 4 (2023): 306-354.

weight of foreign opinion in *Graham* in support of the constitutional principle against life without parole, perhaps it seemed unnecessary to restate it in *Miller*. Or, perhaps an anticipation of the chorus of protest, both from within the court and from outside, might have dissuaded the Court from explicit transnational engagement. Only two years into her Supreme Court justiceship, Justice Kagan was perhaps unwilling to recant on her testimony during the Senate confirmation hearings about the irrelevance of foreign law in constitutional interpretation.[40] Support from foreign law seemed, moreover, optional. Here was a judgment that extended protection to vulnerable rights holders against state policies that indiscriminately inflicted cruel and unusual punishments. True, unlike prior decisions, this one did not explicitly rely on foreign law in interpreting the Eighth Amendment. But, again, why care? Wasn't it enough that *Miller* was a victory for criminal defendants?

It certainly seemed that way for a while. When deciding if *Miller*'s holding applied retroactively to over 2,000 juveniles then serving life sentences in state penitentiaries, the Court held, in *Montgomery v. Louisiana* (2016), that it did. The effect was to make those prisoners eligible for resentencing hearings. Such hearings, however, could still result in sentences to life without parole. Since *Miller* had only held that mandatory sentences violated the Eighth Amendment, it remained possible that courts could resentence juvenile offenders to life without parole so long as those sentences were discretionary, that is, so long as sentencing judges had discretion to impose a lesser sentence than life. Under *Miller*, life without parole can satisfy the proportionality requirement of the Eighth Amendment but only for juvenile criminals that courts deemed permanently incorrigible. Hence, the dispositive question became what constitutional requirements govern a judicial finding of permanent incorrigibility. If the constitutional mandates are stringent, for instance by requiring a separate factual finding by virtue of the reduced culpability of juvenile offenders, then *Miller*'s legacy will be of one kind. But if those mandates are lax, for instance if the Constitution requires only a discretionary sentencing procedure where judges take into consideration a defendant's youth, however they see fit, then an incorrigibility finding might not pose much of an obstacle to state courts bent on sentencing juveniles to life without parole with comparable frequency as they had before *Miller*.

[40] One can surmise why Justice Kennedy, still on the Court at the time *Miller* was decided, joined his junior colleague's majority opinion without writing separately. Perhaps Justice Kennedy decided against writing separately for considerations of collegiality and also because a failure to reference foreign law was not sufficiently significant, in this context.

The answer to that question would reveal *Miller*'s fragility. In *Jones v Mississippi* (2021),[41] a new Supreme Court majority held that the Eighth Amendment required no separate factual finding of permanent incorrigibility at a sentencing hearing, or an on-the-record sentencing explanation of an implicit finding of permanent incorrigibility or any other formality to that effect. Sentencing judges comply with *Miller* whenever they have discretion to impose a sentence other than life without parole. But since, post-*Miller*, sentencing courts always have such discretion, *Jones*'s validation of implicit incorrigibility determinations makes at least understandable its dissenters' charge that *Jones* overrules *Miller sub silentio*. That much is clear, although it is worth noting that this claim relies on a broad interpretation of *Miller*'s holding. But that is not how the dissenters in that case, who became the majority in *Jones*, interpreted *Miller*'s holding. For them, at least as recounted retrospectively, *Miller* was not a sentencing overhaul or a big step to protect vulnerable defendants from a particularly cruel form of punishment. They saw it, rather, as a purely procedural rule that imposed a categorical ban on sentences mandatory under state law. It is an open question whether the narrow or the broad interpretation of this holding is correct. And that is precisely the point. *Miller*'s meaning thus seems adrift, subject to whatever constitutional winds will blow its way.

It is probably naïve to believe that a reference to foreign law in *Miller* would have prevented *Jones*'s turn. So determined is the current Supreme Court majority to undo protections for criminal defenders that little can stop it, much less a reference to foreign or international law of the kind jurists of this ilk have long opposed. Nevertheless, a reference to foreign law would have anchored *Miller*'s meaning. And, in so doing, it would have exposed the extent of *Jones*'s departure from the line of precedent running from *Roper* to *Miller* to *Montgomery*. If *Miller* had sought to align American law with the near universal ban on sentencing persons under 18 to life without parole, then *Jones*'s dissenters would have been more convincing when arguing that the majority in *Jones* guts the "essential holding" of *Miller*.[42] *Miller*'s disconnect from the transnational engagement of its own doctrinal lineage is not shallow, as if references to foreign law are a gratuitous adornment. To the contrary, that discontinuity impacts *Miller*'s—and *Montgomery*'s—essential holding. Detached from foreign law, what *Miller* (might have) meant as the exception became, at the hands of the future *Jones* majority, the rule. Seen retrospectively, *Miller*

[41] 593 U.S. __ (2021).

[42] *Jones*, Sotomayor, J. (dissenting), slip op. 1. On the domestic front, as of early 2023, more than half of the U.S. states have banned juvenile life without parole. See https://www.sentencingproject.org/policy-brief/juvenile-life-without-parole-an-overview/ (last accessed September 2023).

aimed (merely) to invalidate mandatory sentences but left open the possibility of discretionary sentences of juvenile to life without parole. That could only happen if the alignment of transnational constitutionalism was not within *Miller's* scope.

From this perspective, most surprising about these recent Eighth Amendment cases is neither the hollowing out of recent precedent nor the Constitution's permissive approach to a cruel and racialized criminal justice system. Surprising, rather, is the deafening silence that surrounds the Court's failure to engage with foreign and international law in its development of core Eighth Amendment doctrine. Neither the majority in *Miller* and *Montgomery*, nor the dissent in *Jones*, mentioned foreign law despite its doctrinal ramifications. Amici briefs that pressed the point—"[t]he community of nations rejects sentencing any juvenile offender to die in prison, whatever the offense," read the Amnesty International brief[43]—fell on deaf ears. Most striking, however, is that the silence on foreign law went beyond the Supreme Court. An otherwise active commentariat did not pick up the omission or express much concern on that score neither contemporaneously with *Miller* nor retrospectively after *Miller* was gutted.[44] The community of jurists, many of whom righty lamented the Court's decision in *Jones*, did not seem to believe that alignment with foreign law could have made a difference to the meaning of the Eighth Amendment. References to foreign law, and reliance on foreign law as a frame of reference, had simply vanished from this area of constitutional doctrine and from constitutional discourse.

IV. Constitutional Paths Not Taken

It might be tempting to explain the demise of engagement with foreign law in the United States Supreme Court by reference to obstacles that its defenders tried but failed to overcome. Why, asked the critics, should courts in well-established constitutional systems ever reach beyond the authoritative legal materials of their political community in interpreting that community's constitutional charter of self-governing? How should normative commonality

[43] See n 39, p. 5.

[44] An exception is the ever-vigilant Heritage Foundation, which saw in the "mysterious disappearance" of international law arguments a "welcome shift in the Court's jurisprudence." Charles Stimson and Jonathan Levy, "The Mysterious Disappearance of International Law Arguments from Juvenile Sentencing in *Miller v. Alabama*" (available at https://www.heritage.org/report/the-mysterious-disappearance-international-law-arguments-juvenile-sentencing-miller-v) (last accessed September 2023).

be conceptualized and operationalized for judicial use, especially in a legal system that conditions legality on pedigree?[45] Importantly, what elements of a judge's commission authorize the use of extraneous references in a constitution that, unlike South Africa's, is entirely silent on this matter? How could judges ever defensibly navigate real difficulties of understanding the meaning and cultural valence of foreign legal norms, especially given the limits of their knowledge, time, and resources? These are difficult questions. If answers fail to convince, little wonder that the practice of using foreign law itself would crumble. To be sure, given its proximity to power, constitutional theory is not always, or perhaps even often, convincing for reasons intrinsic to its theoretical worth.[46] Its appeal is a combination of anticipated usage, perceived through a political or ideological lens, as well as normative attractiveness, timeliness, discursive compatibilities, ease of use, and so on. It is how constitutional ideas and methods fit within a political and jurisprudential worldview, and how that worldview stands to benefit from the additions to its constitutional capabilities, that explain constitutional success or failure. The dominance of an isolationist conception that sought to defend its vision of American constitutional exceptionalism against an alternative jurisprudential worldview open to foreign law would, thus, explain transnational constitutional disengagement.

This line of reasoning explains disengagement as part of a wider, and presumably irresistible, set of cultural forces or even of redoubtable challenges aimed directly at undermining constitutional reliance on foreign law. That may be true, to some extent. But transnational engagement has also come undone under the weak defenses of its supporters. Judges perhaps are bound to invoke the strictures of their role morality to deny foreign law any precedential force. But what about other jurists? The orthodox assumption that foreign law can have at most persuasive, but never precedential, authority is ripe for questioning but rarely questioned. So is the oft-repeated claim that the use of foreign law is inescapably random and subjective. It seems hardly sufficient to offer, in response to the challenge that a commitment to democratic self-government restricted the array of sources that constitutional decision-makers can legitimately access, to the exclusion foreign law, an answer that foreign law could nevertheless sometimes be instructive or useful as a heuristic device.

Critics of foreign law took it more seriously than its defenders. The former understood and rightly feared the effect on their jurisprudential worldview of

[45] *Erie Railroad Co. v. Tompkins*, 304 U.S. 64 (1938).

[46] Originalism's rise to dominance in American constitutionalism serves as Exhibit A. See Edward A. Purcell, Jr., *Antonin Scalia and American Constitutionalism: The Historical Significance of a Judicial Icon* (Oxford University Press, 2020).

an expansive engagement with the experiences in self-government of other political communities. Despite reassurances about the confirmatory role of foreign law, such references carried more than a tad of normativity. Recall that *Atkins*, *Lawrence*, and *Roper* relied on foreign law to overrule precedent.[47] Significantly, the precedents they overruled were not old decisions that had fallen into desuetude but, rather, they were recent cases dating back just about a decade—a blink of an eye, in constitutional time. The description of the role of foreign law as purely confirmatory, as if judges first reach their decisions using traditional sources and only then turn to foreign law for confirmation, is not self-evident. As the South African cases reveal, albeit without sufficient conceptualization, there seems to be more reliance on foreign law than the confirmatory paradigm suggests. One amicus brief in *Miller* describes the prohibition against life without parole for juvenile offenders as "one of the most widely accepted international human rights norms."[48] That is no sleight of hand. It implies a robust normative view of foreign law.[49]

Perhaps the critics' most significant concerns involve how references to foreign law alter the nature of constitutional discourse. A robust judicial practice of incorporating such references invites lawyers to present arguments about foreign law and thus opens new dimensions of constitutional analysis. Similarly to how originalism brought a particular kind of history to the heart of constitutional discourse, so transnational engagement could make foreign law central to constitutional argument. In the view of critics, such a development would undermine the integrity of American constitutional discourse.[50] As modern legal positivism teaches, since public officials identify norms they recognize as law,[51] changes to the categories of legal discourse can impact at a deeper level the inner workings of the legal order. The concern is that if foreign law enters the discursive stage, it may, in time and under propitious circumstances, harden into legal doctrine and even reshape its rule of recognition in the U.S. legal system.

While critics respond to this prospect with concern, one might expect defenders of transnational engagement to see the ascendency of foreign law as

[47] *Atkins* overruled *Penry v. Lynaugh*, 492 U.S. 302 (1989); *Roper* overruled *Sanford v. Kentucky*, 492 U.S. 361 (1989); *Lawrence* overruled *Bowers v. Hardwick*, 478 U.S. 186 (1986).

[48] See n 39, p. 2.

[49] I sketch out such an account in Vlad Perju, "Elements of a Doctrine of Transnational Constitutional Norms," 22 ICON (forthcoming 2024).

[50] Charles Fried, "Scholars and Judges: Reason and Power," 23 Harvard Journal of Law and Public Policy 807 (2000).

[51] Legal positivists see that recognition as what makes law in a modern state. For a discussion in the case of foreign law, see Jeremy Waldron (n 3), at 54–56. The underlying jurisprudential theory is presented in H. L. A. Hart, *The Concept of Law* (2nd edn., Oxford University Press, 1994).

an opportunity for renewal of a constitutional system that has been showing its diminished capacities for responsiveness, whose mechanisms of self-correction are in disrepair, and whose claim to impartiality has been torn apart by ideological polarization. Progressives have despaired about the trajectory of American constitutionalism at least since the Rehnquist court and with ever greater urgency over the past two decades. Among their concerns have been the rise of the unitary executive, the crumbling of the wall that once separated religion and state, the erosion of remedial racial classifications, the undoing of the right to privacy and especially reproductive freedom, the failure to afford education and other social entitlements and so on. Foreign law may not be the *deus ex machina* of constitutional adjudication, but, at least so long as courts continue to review the validity of political acts, many if not all of these doctrinal areas would benefit from recasting within a broader global constitutionalist framework. On the methodological front, foreign law might have countered, as much as anything could, the growing dominance of originalism and the turn inwards in American constitutionalism that has accompanied it. The point, again, is not that foreign law is a panacea for all constitutional ills. Foreign law can be abusive and abused.[52] But the paucity of alternative sources of renewal is such that foreign law arguably has sufficient potential to destabilize constitutional doctrines, challenge the exceptionalist nationalist vision that underpins them, and hopefully replenish to some extent the capabilities of American constitutionalism. But such an effect depends on the availability of conceptions that justify its legitimacy and its principled deployment.

V. Pragmatist Detours

Pragmatism fits the bill, though its valiantly "anti-theoretical" stance prevents it from casting itself that way.[53] Pragmatism's first move is to displace the debate from a territory of abstract theory and into one about reality, facts, and the-world-as-it-is. "It is not the cosmopolitanism of some jurists," Justice Breyer writes extrajudicially, that justifies transnational constitutional engagement,

[52] An early contribution that drew attention to this phenomenon is Kim Lane Scheppele, "Aspirational and Aversive Constitutionalism: The Case for Studying Cross-Constitutional Influence Through Negative Models," ICON 1(2): 296–324 (2003). A recent study is Rosalind Dixon and David Landau, *Abusive Constitutional Borrowing* (Oxford University Press, 2021).

[53] Dworkin adds to anti-theoretical also the charge of populism, in Ronald Dworkin, "Darwin's New Bulldog," 111 Harvard Law Review 1718, 1718–1719 (1998) ("Posner's arguments are in the service of a populist anti-theoretical movement that is now powerful in American intellectual life"). That label might apply to Richard Posner's version of pragmatism, which was the context in which Dworkin made the charge, but it does not apply to Justice Breyer's.

"but the nature of the world itself that demands it."[54] The world demands it because its economic, technological, and political interconnectedness brings to courts cases with significant transnational dimensions. There are, however, important distinctions between engagement through international treaties, reliance on customary law, enforcement of extraterritorial norms, adjudication of multijurisdictional commercial agreements, and so on. In this landscape, reliance on foreign law in constitutional interpretation is in a category of its own. What of the objections about the inherent malleability and illegitimacy of this particular form of transnational engagement? They are "important in the abstract," Breyer concedes, but do not represent reality. That is, they "do not reflect the reality of today's federal dockets, including the Supreme Court's." Since there is "no direct relation between the underlying fears they express and corresponding changes in American jurisprudence," he writes, the critics "overstate their concerns" and are "beside the point." [55]

The point, as Justice Breyer sees it, is that law matters in the world and that high theory only feeds the kind of conceptualism or formalism that pragmatists have long dismissed as transcendental nonsense. Foreign law is comparative law in action, a method of constitutional problem-solving. Judges use it when they deem it useful; otherwise, they discard it. Foreign law can, for instance, reveal the consequences of alternative legal ordering in matters such as the federal control of state subunits,[56] the role of the executive during states of emergency,[57] the effect of racial quotas,[58] or the impact of constitutionalizing a right to physician-assisted suicide.[59] There are, of course, limits to these comparisons, given differences in social, political, and economic structures wherein different constitutional norms are embedded and shape the social effect of these norms and thus limit the usefulness of trans-jurisdictional comparisons. Be that as it may, pragmatists trust the decision-maker to control for such differences. They trust, for instance, that if these differences are too great, judges will sidestep foreign law. Disagreements among judges about the usefulness of foreign law are to be expected. But so long as judges justify their conclusions, disagreement is no more concerning in this context than in any other.

Note that, from this perspective, foreign law is at most useful but not controlling. In fact, according to pragmatism, no source or method of interpreting

[54] Stephen Breyer, *The Court and the World: American Law and the New Global Realities* (Vintage, 2016), at 245.

[55] ibid at 245.

[56] *Printz v. United States*, 521 U.S. 898 (1997).

[57] *Youngstown Sheet & Tube Co. v. Sawyer*, 343 U.S. 579 (1952).

[58] *Grutter v. Bollinger*, 539 U.S. 306 (2003).

[59] *Washington v. Glucksberg*, 521 U.S. 702 (1997).

the meaning of the Constitution is *a priori* controlling. Each can be relevant, depending on its practical effect in specific contexts. Thus, legal authority can never be abstracted from context. Much turns on the assessment of practical effect. For instance, should practical effect be understood as the distributive effect of legal norms or as the most efficient allocation of entitlements? If practical effect is understood consistently along the lines of one or the other or some third conception, that consistency must be supported by background justification that likely conflicts with pragmatism's adamant rejection of abstract theory. If, by contrast, the legal interpreter lacks any background consistency, then pragmatism opens itself up to a critique that its usage of foreign law is inherently strategic and unprincipled.

This latter possibility leaves pragmatism exposed to the methodological challenges that the use of foreign law is inherently unprincipled. It is, as critics like to say, like going to a party and chatting only with your friends. Even within the same legal tradition, there will almost always be some jurisdictions that will support one's side, for instance regarding the demands of constitutional equality and liberty on practices such as abortion, same-sex marriage, or physician-assisted suicide, just as there will be others that support the opposite conclusion. How, then, can one assess if foreign law is used in a principled manner?[60] This difficulty is compounded by challenges in handling references to foreign law. There is a worry that such references cannot lead to a result disfavored by the interpreter because their inherent manipulability makes it always possible to avoid any such result. Left addressed, these difficulties may end up contributing to the public's growing distrust in judicial decisionmaking. Now, it is true that courts sometimes must dedicate resources to the elucidation of the meaning of foreign norms.[61] But the use of foreign law in constitutional interpretation is not such a situation. The inherent difficulties of handling foreign law references with accuracy thus seem eminently avoidable.

Note, however, that not all situations involving the use of foreign law afford a high level of discretion. References to foreign law in the *Atkins*, *Roper*, *Graham*, *Miller* line of cases do not select affiliation from an array of available options. In matters regarding the death penalty or life without parole for juvenile offenders, almost all of the legal systems of the world are in agreement that these forms of punishment are disproportionate. The challenge of malleability is pointless. Nor does utility capture the weight of foreign law in such cases.

[60] Eric Posner, "A Review," 126 Yale Law Journal 504 (2016) ("The key problem is that while the Court does 'engage' with the world (as Breyer puts it), Breyer gives no reason for thinking that the Court engages with the world *well*," at 504).

[61] *Animal Science Products, Inc. v. Hebei Welcome Pharmaceutical Co. Ltd.*, 138 S. Ct. 1865 (2018).

VI. Waldron's New *Jus Gentium*

Jeremy Waldron presents his original and multifaceted, if somewhat serpentine, account of foreign law as the new *jus gentium* as a jurisprudence for cases such as *Roper*. These cases have in common the existence of a near consensus of the legal systems of the world. Excluded from this account are individualized or "ad hoc" comparisons where there are profound divisions among legal systems. In those situations, foreign law is "sometimes sensible, oftentimes helpful and in rare cases indispensable."[62] That may be good enough for a pragmatist perspective but not for Waldron, who seeks to establish the normative authority of foreign law.

This framing allows Waldron to bracket institutional considerations regarding the judiciary and focus instead on the nature of the foreign law norms. These are norms that encapsulate global legal consensus, or areas of commonality among the legal systems of the world. Borrowing a concept that originated in Roman law, Waldron calls them norms of *jus gentium*. It means, in his interpretation, not "the law of any particular country, but the law of the world."[63] These norms result from the "convergent currents of foreign statutes, foreign constitutional provisions, and foreign precedents (that) sometimes add up to a body of law that has its own claim on us: the law of nations, or *jus gentium*, which applies to us simply as law, not as the law of any particular jurisdiction."[64] Courts that use foreign law in these situations are in fact applying the law of nations. The prohibition against the death penalty for crimes committed by minors, at issue in *Roper*, is Waldron's central example. The prohibition against life without the possibility of parole fits his model equally well.

Waldron insists that these norms are to be identified inductively by identifying areas of overlap among the legal systems of the world. His concern is that a deductive method, which proceeds top-down from first principles, might blur the distinction between *jus gentium* and natural law and thus undermine the view of *jus gentium* as positive law. Yet herein lies one tension at the heart of this model. On the one hand, the dual insistence on the positive nature of *jus gentium* norms and the inductive method suggests a relatively small subset of norms. On the other hand, the model itself generates pressure to expand that subset. [65] Waldron aims for a jurisprudential solution. He warns

[62] Waldron (n 3), at 7.

[63] ibid at 4.

[64] ibid at 3.

[65] It seems, rather, that Waldron expects *jus gentium* to overlap more or less with some narrow conception of the rule of law. Waldron does not provide a comprehensive list but does mention that "the body of *jus gentium* includes quotidian norms that secure the routine functioning of the legal system,

against confusing commonality or overlap in the positive laws of various legal systems with the norms of *jus gentium* themselves. Commonality is a feature that confers legal authority to the norms, but the process of identifying the norms on which that authority is conferred is a different matter. That process is interpretative, not statistical, in nature. Norms of *jus gentium* are principles, not rules. Waldron's conception at this point is Dworkinian through and through: "*jus gentium* consists of a body of principles, discerned interpretatively from the commonalities that exist among the positive laws of various countries, by a legal sensibility that is both lawyerly and moralized."[66] Thus, it seems, the starting point is the overlap in the positive laws of different legal systems. The process identifies what we might call areas of surface commonality. Once such commonalities have been identified, the jurist must dig deeper through a process of interpretation that will reveal the background, supporting principles. These background principles are the norms of *jus gentium*. These are not a garden variety of disjointed principles but combine into a system of law. Waldron writes about:

> taking seriously the possibility that deep, background principles, legal principles, may be inferred not just from a single existing body of positive law … but also from multiple legal systems taken together. Indeed, principles whose presence might not be so apparent in one legal system may come more clearly into view when we look at a whole array of legal systems. And if that is the case, then their presence as legal principles will be a characteristic of law in the world—laws common to all mankind—rather than just the property of the individual systems in which they figure one by one.[67]

This seems like a model for revealing "components of liberty" of the kind that *Lawrence v. Texas* sought to unveil through the use of foreign law. Dimensions of the principle of liberty, on which the petitioners in that case ground their claim, come more clearly into view by looking at other legal systems. Obstacles to the recognition of those claims, and implicitly of the claimant's dignity,[68]

such as the fundamental principles of contract and commercial law, as well as constitutional norms: the prohibition to execute people for crimes they committed as minors, rudiments of procedural due process, principles of the protection of free speech and religious freedom, probation against arbitrary arrest, the proportionality guarantee in criminal and constitutional law, guarantees of fair trial, basic elements of what we call 'rule of law', the law of self-defense," in Waldron (n 3), at 6 and 32.

[66] ibid at 35.

[67] ibid at 67.

[68] Joel Feinberg, *Rights, Justice and the Bounds of Justice* (Princeton University Press, 1980) ("What is called human dignity may simply be the recognizable capacity to assert claims").

appear as contingencies to overcome rather than aspects of liberty that must be entrenched further at the expense of the claimant's liberty interests. This direction of inquiry certainly seems productive. The problem is that this is precisely the individualized or selective type of comparison that Waldron does not wish to explore. For this reason, Waldron's immediate move in the above passage is to further specify that these should be laws common to all mankind. Identifying positivity and commonality across legal systems as defining features of universal norms of *jus gentium*, with the corollary that these norms are rooted in "social fact"—specifically the fact of "a consensus, characterizing the positive law of various countries in the world"[69]—aims to restore the distinction between selective and (near) consensus comparisons. But it also limits the use of the theory. For there is no good reason why the obscured dimension of liberty are, or should be expected to be, identifiable in all legal systems as a matter of positive law. Even when they are not, partial foreign law can reveal dimensions of a legal claim that decision-makers must identify and treat with due consideration.

One may speculate about Waldron's reasons for limiting so drastically his account to situations of near consensus. Institutional considerations likely played a role. A critic of judicial review,[70] Waldron might have thought that, were foreign law to radiate normativity beyond situations of near consensus, this might end up granting the judiciary powers beyond what he believes appropriate. Narrowness is the price to pay for depth. But if such concerns shaped the substance of the argument, then Waldron's account can hardly be said to bracket institutional considerations. If anything, these considerations, rather than the normativity of transnational norms, determine the shape of this theory.

A further difficulty concerns the conceptualization of *jus gentium*. True to its historical origins, Waldron's model sees these norms as addressing a gap in the legal system. Since *jus civile* norms applied exclusively to citizens, the question became what rules would apply to non-citizens, who were not the subject of enacted laws. One option might have been to derive these rules from *fas*, or moral principles. But the Romans opted for a different and, in retrospect, superior method of deriving this body of rules from the legal systems of the world. Note, however, that the norms of *jus gentium* were essentially meant to supplant a gap. As such, they were eminently of a different orientation than modern *jus gentium*/foreign law norms, where the problem is no so much the existence of a gap in the legal materials as the meaning or interpretation of

[69] ibid at 59.
[70] Jeremy Waldron, "The Core of the Case against Judicial Review," 115 Yale Law Journal 1346 (2006).

an existing norm. Put differently, the point of using foreign law in *Roper* or *Makwanyane* is not how to fill in the gap of a norm regarding the death penalty or a particular sanction; rather, it is the interpretation of an existing constitutional norms.[71] Rather than an account of gap-filling *jus gentium*, a defense of foreign law should theorize a transnational *jus civile*.

Finally, there is the question of democratic self-government. To his credit, Waldron's takes on the critique that granting normative weight to foreign law undermines democracy. In the specific context of American law, this critique extrapolates from settled doctrines regarding the absence of a federal common law. Waldron shows convincingly the limits of analogizing from *Erie* to reach conclusions about foreign law, as well the limitations of *Erie*'s own conception of law and legal authority. Rather than law as the command of the legislator, modern jurisprudence after Hart conceives of law as the recognition of legal officials. In this account, legality depends not on pedigree but on practice and recognition of officials. Still, it helps to recall that Hart's analytical account sets out to illuminate the concept of law, that is, law anywhere in the world. It seems necessary that, when that is a constitutional law setting the terms by which a political community of free and equals is to govern itself, the point that practice makes law and pedigree is not determinant is more a problem than an insight.

VII. Conclusion

I have argued in this chapter that the canon of transnational engagement has more often evaded rather than met the burden of justifying the use of foreign law in constitutional interpretation. At least in part as a result of that failure, such usage has declined and, in some legal systems, has come to a halt altogether. It is nevertheless the case, as this volume shows, that debates about foreign law have contributed to a broader interest in comparative constitutionalism. That interest has proven capable of sustaining itself without a direct lifeline to the practice of constitutional adjudication. That is probably fine, except insofar as the disconnect has undermined the normative ambitions of comparative constitutionalism. As far as the use of foreign law for interpretative purposes is concerned, it remains important to reflect on what it meant, what it could have been, and why it failed. "Thinking completes the act," Hannah

[71] This might well create interesting questions of "judicial redundancy" resulting from the "duplication of subject matter" between the foreign and domestic norms. Jeremy Waldron, "Constitutional Norms," in Seyla Benhabib et al., *Another Cosmopolitanism* (Oxford University Press, 2008), 85.

Arendt wrote, and added that "without the articulation accomplished by remembrance, there simple [is] no story left that could be told."[72] Telling the story for the purpose of remembrance may have its place, yet it is hardly gripping. But thinking—seriously and creatively—about foreign law for the purpose of preparing the next act is a project on whose success depends not just the future of comparative constitutionalism but that of constitutionalism itself.

[72] Hannah Arendt, Between Past and Future (Penguin Books, 2006), 6.

Index

For the benefit of digital users, indexed terms that span two pages (e.g., 52–53) may, on occasion, appear on only one of those pages.